D1604512

Florida's Minority Trailblazers

Florida Government and Politics

UNIVERSITY PRESS OF FLORIDA

Florida A&M University, Tallahassee
Florida Atlantic University, Boca Raton
Florida Gulf Coast University, Ft. Myers
Florida International University, Miami
Florida State University, Tallahassee
New College of Florida, Sarasota
University of Central Florida, Orlando
University of Florida, Gainesville
University of North Florida, Jacksonville
University of South Florida, Tampa
University of West Florida, Pensacola

FLORIDA'S MINORITY TRAILBLAZERS

The Men and Women Who Changed the Face of Florida Government

SUSAN A. MACMANUS

with Barbara A. Langham, Lauren K. Gilmore, and Tyler B. Myers

Foreword by David R. Colburn

University Press of Florida

Gainesville · Tallahassee · Tampa · Boca Raton

Pensacola · Orlando · Miami · Jacksonville · Ft. Myers · Sarasota

Printed in the United States of America on acid-free paper

This book may be available in an electronic edition.

22 21 20 19 18 17 6 5 4 3 2 1

Library of Congress Cataloging-in-Publication Data

Names: MacManus, Susan A., author. | Langham, Barbara, contributor. | Myers, Tyler, contributor. | Gilmore, Lauren, contributor. | Colburn, David R., author of foreword.
Title: Florida's minority trailblazers : the men and women who changed the face of Florida government / Susan A. MacManus with Barbara A. Langham, Lauren K. Gilmore, and Tyler B. Myers ; foreword by David R. Colburn.
Description: Gainesville : University Press of Florida, 2017. | Includes bibliographical references and index.
Identifiers: LCCN 2016027497 | ISBN 9780813062938 (cloth)
Subjects: LCSH: Florida—Politics and government. | Minorities—Political activity—Florida. | Civil rights—Florida—History. | Legislators—Florida—History. | Judges—Florida—History.
Classification: LCC JK4416 .C65 1999 | DDC 328.759092/2—dc23
LC record available at https://lccn.loc.gov/2016027497

The University Press of Florida is the scholarly publishing agency for the State University System of Florida, comprising Florida A&M University, Florida Atlantic University, Florida Gulf Coast University, Florida International University, Florida State University, New College of Florida, University of Central Florida, University of Florida, University of North Florida, University of South Florida, and University of West Florida.

University Press of Florida
15 Northwest 15th Street
Gainesville, FL 32611-2079
http://www.upf.com

To the trailblazers for sharing their experiences
and the USF student researchers who put their minds, hearts,
and souls into saving this piece of Florida's political history

CONTENTS

FIGURES

TABLES

FOREWORD

Florida has held a unique place in the American mind for seven decades. For many retirees, its environment has been like a healthy elixir that allowed them to live longer and more vigorous lives; for other residents, Florida is a place of renewal and new possibilities; for immigrants, it is a place of political freedom and opportunity. Historian Gary Mormino describes the state as a "powerful symbol of renewal and regeneration."

During World War II, Americans from all walks of life discovered Florida through military service, and it opened their eyes to the postwar possibilities. The beauty of the landscape and the beaches and the exotic climate and environment led many veterans to describe it to loved ones back home as a paradise. With the end of the war in August 1945, veterans initially returned home, but thoughts of Florida and the opportunities there remained at the forefront of their ambitions. Within months, many were back in the state and they were soon joined by hundreds and then thousands of Americans who embraced a new life in the Sunshine State. In the 70 years between 1945 and 2015, millions moved into the state, increasing the population by more than 18.5 million people, so that the state exceeded 20 million residents by 2015.

Florida's population growth, the settlement patterns of new residents, and their diversity had a profound effect on the state's place in the nation as well as the image Floridians had of themselves. Prior to 1940, Florida was the smallest state in the South and one of the poorest in the nation. Its society and economy were predominantly rural, agricultural, biracial, and segregated. Most residents lived within 40 miles of the Georgia border. These demographics and the state's history shaped the public's racial and cultural mindset and its politics. Florida was essentially a one-party state, controlled by the Democratic Party since the end of Reconstruction in 1876.

All that changed dramatically in the 70 years following World War II. Florida rose from being one of the poorest, most isolated states in the nation, with the smallest population in the South, to the most dynamic state on the east coast and, alongside California, the most diverse state in the nation. Most Floridians now reside closer to the Caribbean than they do to Georgia, and, for most of them, their image of themselves and their state has been significantly influenced by this new geographic orientation. At the onset of the twenty-first century, demographers viewed Florida as a microcosm of the nation, because of its size and population complexity. Others saw it as a benchmark by which to measure the nation's future.

As Florida changed, so too did its politics. Voters threw out the Constitution of 1885 in favor of a new document in 1968 which spoke to the needs of a new state. They then gradually abandoned the racial heritage of the past and the Democratic Party in favor of a dynamic two-party system. By the 1990s, Republicans used their expanding constituency and control of the districting process following the 1990 Census to take control of the state legislature and the congressional delegation. These were remarkable developments that reflected the dramatic changes taking place in the state's population. By 2008, Republicans dominated all state offices which were districted, as Democrats had prior to 1960. The Democratic Party, however, still remained viable in statewide races for Governor, U.S. Senator, and elected Cabinet positions, as well as in presidential contests that were not affected by districting. Democrats frequently won these races, and they continued to hold a lead of more than 400,000 registered voters over Republicans (4.577 million to 4.172 million), although an increasing number of voters identified themselves as having no party affiliation.

Such a politically and demographically complex and diverse population has made Florida today something other than a unified whole. The political maxim that "All politics is local" is truer of Florida than most other states. For example, those who reside in north Florida share little in common with those living in central or south Florida and vice versa. While those in southeast Florida see themselves as part of the "new America," those in north Florida view Miami as a foreign country. Ask a resident what it means to be a Floridian and few, if any, can answer the question. Ask a Floridian about the state's history, and even fewer can tell you that it has been governed under five different flags, or that its colonial history is much older than that of New England or Virginia. Perhaps one in ten or twenty residents can tell you who LeRoy Collins was, despite Republican Jeb Bush's recognition of this Democratic Governor as the model for all others who followed. It is literally a state unknown and indefinable to its people. Such historical ignorance and regional division become major obstacles when state leaders seek to find consensus among voters and solutions that address the needs of all citizens.

An essential purpose of this series is to put Floridians in touch with their rich political history and to enhance their understanding of the political developments that have reshaped the state, region, and nation. This series focuses on the Sunshine State's unique and dynamic political history since 1900 and on public policy issues that have influenced the state and the nation. As part of this series, the University Press of Florida also welcomes book manuscripts on the region that examine critical political and policy developments that impacted Florida.

There is perhaps no recent book that reminds readers of the state's rich political and diverse culture more than *Florida's Minority Trailblazers* by Susan MacManus. Her book covers a half century of trailblazers up through the last election, and it covers Congress as well as state government. She emphasizes that the story of Florida is more than just about new beginnings, population growth, and economic opportunity; it is also about the struggle for civil rights, equal justice, opportunity for all Floridians, and political background. Each individual she has chosen in this book "is a first—by virtue of race/ethnicity in combination with gender and, if applicable, political party to attain a legislative, judicial, or executive post at the state level or in Congress."

MacManus highlights those who overcame widespread discrimination in Florida because of their race, ethnicity, gender, or political identification, and became political and judicial leaders. She has gathered together the stories of each of these "trailblazers," who led the struggle for equality and who, in the process, redefined state politics by giving voice to the needs and concerns of Florida's citizens in the post–Civil Rights era. Equally important, they paved the way for others to follow in their footsteps.

MacManus preserves for writers, journalists, historians, teachers, and the general public this important story of Florida and the individuals who made it so. It was a story that was in danger of being lost, if she had not done so. To bring this story to life, she has combed through news accounts, legislative and judicial research materials, and completed lengthy personal interviews with the living trailblazers. Assisting her throughout this process were several of her students to whom she gives great credit. MacManus has often used her students in her research and writing in order to enhance their educational experience and to ensure that many of them will understand why this work has value beyond the classroom.

The stories told in this volume are manifold and compelling. MacManus highlights both the personal and professional struggles these individuals faced during their lives. Gwendolyn "Gwen" Sawyer Cherry, for example, participated in the Tallahassee Bus Boycott in May 1956 to desegregate the local bus lines. In the 1960s she also worked with demonstrators at Florida A&M to integrate lunch counters and retail stores in Tallahassee. She did not stop there. Following the passage of the Civil Rights Act of 1964 and the Voting Rights Act of 1965, she led the fight for women's rights in Florida and was state president of the National Organization for Women (NOW), founded in 1966 before being elected to the state legislature in 1970. She used her position of leadership to open doors for minorities and women in state politics.

Maurice A. Ferré's life took a dramatically different course from Cherry's. He came from a family with a rich history in politics. His paternal grandfather, who was born in Cuba, was the son of a French engineer who had joined Ferdinand de Lesseps to build the French Panama Canal. His grandfather's maternal family were Cuban independence patriots. But other family members were Puerto Rican. Ferré, a Democrat, was born in Puerto Rico. He ran initially for the Florida Senate in 1966 and lost, but then successfully ran for the Florida House in 1967 following a court-ordered special election. His victory made him Florida's first Puerto Rican–born House member. He served only a few months before being elected to an open seat on the City of Miami Commission. In 1973, Ferré was elected Mayor of Miami—a position he held for 12 years. His success was instrumental in inspiring other Hispanics and minorities to run for office. He had no special advice to prospective minority candidates, but he advised them "to concentrate on public service and good public policy."

As noted above, the book is more than a list of trailblazers and a collection of their personal biographies. MacManus offers historical context for the roles the trailblazers played, key insights into their lives and times, an understanding of how Florida politics evolved over time, maps of the state showing where various ethnic and minority groups were located, extensive photographs, and detailed information on the transition in state politics from Democrat to Republican in the last quarter of the twentieth century. It is a volume rich in detail and personal stories.

Readers learn how these trailblazers overcame obstacles in life and about the importance of the Civil Rights Act of 1964, the Voting Rights Act of 1965, the new state Constitution of 1968, the women's movement of the 1970s, and equitable apportionment opening doors and propelling people to run for public office.

MacManus describes the purpose of her work in both personal and scholarly terms, explaining why she defined "trailblazer" in the way she did, and the selection criteria she used in identifying them. Her book covers those trailblazers who were selected for the state house and senate, the state supreme court, and the U.S. Congress and the Senate. She also includes minority trailblazers in the executive branch—Governor, Lieutenant Governor, Cabinet—and a black female whom Governor Reubin Askew appointed to his "Little Cabinet," which was not officially part of state government but whom he consulted as part of his executive team.

MacManus's book is a fascinating read, full of intriguing stories of state leaders and their lives. These brief biographical portraits may seem daunting at first, but they are so well done and informative that one quickly realizes how valuable they are in telling the story of modern Florida. Perhaps more compelling, it is a book that will serve as a resource for teachers, students, and other Floridians for years to come.

David R. Colburn
Series Editor

PREFACE

This book is intended to provide Floridians with a more in-depth look at Florida's racial/ethnic history through the personal stories of minority trailblazers in modern-day Florida politics, beginning with the Civil Rights Movement of the 1960s and the historic U.S. Supreme Court cases ordering legislative and congressional districts to be drawn using the "one-person, one-vote" standard.

The Civil Rights Movement coincided with Florida's rapid population explosion that yielded the state more representatives in Congress with each successive U.S. census and ultimately changed the faces of state government officeholders in Tallahassee as well—a process that is ongoing. Looking back, one can clearly see that throughout most of the high-growth period, political science scholars in the state were heavily engaged in research using statistical models to explain the transitioning of Florida from a "yellow dog Democrat" state to a competitive two-party state. There was very little qualitative-oriented research gathering the rich personal stories of those whose faces made Florida's politics much more diverse and led to Florida's reputation as an "immigrant magnet" state.

My academic interest in racial/ethnic and gender politics was formed at an early age. I am the granddaughter of a German immigrant, G. Michael Riegler, who came to America in 1911 (Florida) with nothing but dreams and ended up a pioneer in the citrus industry in Pasco County. He often traveled to Tampa's historic Ybor City to sell his oranges and grapefruit to the area's large Cuban community. His son (my uncle) married a woman whose father was born in Cuba and immigrated to Florida. My aunt's father used to mesmerize us with his dialect and stories of his native Cuba. My fascination with the Spanish language continued into my college years as an exchange student in Valencia, Spain. In the late 1980s, a Fulbright fellowship to Yonsei University in Seoul, Korea to research the nation's evolving economic and political systems, introduced me to Asia. But it was my mother, Elizabeth Riegler MacManus, a local historian and author, who taught me the importance and joy of conducting personal interviews of a historical nature.

My collegiate and early academic experiences enabled me to experience the evolution of the civil rights and women's movements. The year I entered college at Florida State University, the Civil Rights Act of 1964 was passed. Graduate studies at the University of Michigan in the late 1960s allowed me to observe organized protest politics. After receiving my Ph.D. from FSU in August 1975, I began my career as a university professor at the University of Houston at a time when women were just being recruited into academia and when that Texas city had an active women's movement. Being in that booming and increasingly diverse metropolitan area also gave me the opportunity to observe the formation and operation of multiracial/ethnic political coalitions and their successes and failures at electing minorities to public office. It also introduced me to reapportionment and redistricting battles at the federal and state levels and the evolving interpretations of minority representation under the federal Voting Rights Act.

Historically, roadblocks to winning state and national offices have been particularly steep for persons of color, often serving as deterrents to their even contemplating a run for or seeking an appointment to higher office. So what has pushed some to try, successfully, while others have just stood by? Studying successes of pioneers can give us a keener sense of (1) the role of culture, kinships, friendships, and mentoring; (2) the importance of education, college and community organizations, and churches as socialization agents; (3) the impact of discrimination and legal roadblocks on candidacy and appointment rates; and (4) the importance of coalition building in settings where racial/ethnic minorities make up less than a majority of the voting public.

This book is a study of ambition and risk-taking by Floridians of color. It also traces change in the state's demographics and politics for more than half a century. The trailblazers selected for inclusion are combinations of race/ethnic group, gender, and political party. Their personal stories were gathered primarily via personal interviews conducted by the author, lasting nearly an hour on average. Other sources of first-person accounts were gathered from interviews done by others and available in public sources, speeches given and letters written by the trailblazers, as well as direct quotes reported by newspapers, blogs or electronic media.

In advance of the interview, each trailblazer interviewed by the author received the same set of questions:

1. *What* and *who* motivated you to run?
2. Was it the first time you ran for this office? Had you held previous political offices before you ran for this one?
3. Did the thought of being the "first" factor into your decision to run?
4. What was the most difficult part of running? Did anyone try to discourage you from running? Who and why?

5. [For women candidates] Was race or gender the bigger barrier for you?
6. What was the political environment like at the time you ran?
7. Where and how did you campaign? Who helped you on the campaign trail?
8. What endorsements did you receive? How much did they help you win?
9. How big a part did racial issues play in the campaign? Did you ever experience racial discrimination on the campaign trail, and if so, how did you handle it?
10. What was the most rewarding part of running and winning? When did the gravity of what you accomplished first set in?
11. Looking back, what advice would you give to other young minorities contemplating a run for public office today?

Not unexpectedly, there was considerable variation in which questions resonated most with the individual risk-takers. In some instances, the responses were in line with conventional wisdom. But there were plenty of surprises as well.

All trailblazers were given an opportunity to review and correct their stories, and the manuscript was scrupulously reviewed for factual errors before publication. Some readers may disagree with details or interpretations as a trailblazer recounted them. Despite that possibility, this study sought to preserve the trailblazers' experiences—in their own words and with respect for their perspectives.

Thanks Are Due to So Many

Overall, the interviews were one of the most enjoyable and enlightening research endeavors of my long academic career. I am extremely indebted to each of the trailblazers who so willingly shared of their time with candor, along with their spouses and staffers who rummaged through old photos and clippings to share with me.

Since my return to my native state to teach at the University of South Florida (USF), I have wanted to write this book. It has taken me over a decade to complete it, with the help of some terrific students with diverse backgrounds. I simply could not have begun this project without the initial research by two Honors College students for their honors theses—Tyler Myers (African American) and Lauren Gilmore (Hispanic). And I could not have brought the project to closure without the help of three student research assistants—Ashleigh Powers, Victoria Pearce, and Anthony Cilluffo—and graphics by David Bonanza. But each and every one of the students listed on the contributors page has made major contributions to the completion of this project. They have reinforced my love of teaching and learning from bright young college students.

The project gradually became more urgent as I began authoring books and articles on Florida government and politics. The final push was made possible by a 2014 grant from the Women in Leadership and Philanthropy group at USF, for which I am deeply grateful. The grant allowed me to complete the extensive travel needed to complete face-to-face interviews with the trailblazers and to have them transcribed by two wonderful women—Sharon Ostermann and Shari Allen.

Four academic colleagues were ready sources of historical facts and *inspiration*—historians extraordinaire Dr. David Colburn, University of Florida; Dr. Gary Mormino, USF, St. Petersburg Campus; and political scientists Dr. Steve Tauber and Dr. Lawrence Morehouse, my colleagues at USF, Tampa Campus.

Helping me retrieve historical documents were tremendously knowledgeable librarians at the State Archives of Florida in Tallahassee (part of the Florida Department of State's Division of Library and Information Services), Dr. Elizabeth Murell Dawson, curator and archivist at The Carrie Meek-James N. Eaton, Sr. Southeastern Regional Black Archives Research Center and Museum at Florida Agricultural & Mechanical University (FAMU) in Tallahassee, and Allen D. Stucks, Jr., *Capitol Outlook*—a black newspaper published in Tallahassee. In addition, The Florida Memory Project of the State Archives provided online access to a great selection of digitized historical records and photographs. Oral history collections at the University of Florida (the Samuel Proctor Oral History Program) and the University of North Carolina (Southern Oral History Program) have been terrific sources of interviews of early trailblazers. The scholars who conducted the interviews several decades ago are to be applauded. Craig Waters, public information director for the Florida Supreme Court, Erik Robinson, archivist at the Florida Supreme Court, and Martha Walters Barnett, retired senior partner with Holland & Knight, assisted in gathering information about the justices.

Getting a comprehensive and accurate list of black and Hispanic members who have served in the Florida House of Representatives, along with biographic materials from old publications and The Clerk's Manual(s), was made possible by Speaker of the House Will Weatherford enlisting help from House Clerk, Bob Ward, and premier researcher Kerry Laird. I am eternally indebted for their time on this monumental task that was crucial to the accuracy of information reported in the book. I greatly appreciate their help in verifying timelines and court cases for the many redistricting efforts during the 1960s.

I also want to thank Tampa friends: former Rep. Elvin Martinez, Laurie Stryker, former Deputy Commissioner of Education, Rep. Janet Cruz, Sen. Arthenia Joyner, Patrick Manteiga, publisher of *La Gaceta*—the state's only trilingual newspaper, Betty Castor, former state Senator and Commissioner of Education, Peter Rudy Wallace, former Speaker of the Florida House, Dr. Doris Weatherford, author of books on Florida women's political history, Dr. Liana Fox, former president of the Hillsborough League of Women Voters, and Sandra Graves, Pasco Republican State Committeewoman, for their unfailing willingness over the years to help me identify and contact key trailblazers. Invaluable assistance was provided by trailblazers Jennifer Carroll, former state Representative and Lieutenant Governor, and Annie Betancourt, former state Representative, in locating other trailblazers.

Most of all, I am blessed to have wonderfully understanding family members and friends who have been extremely supportive of all the time spent on travel, research, and writing and for my longtime friend and professional editor, Barbara Langham, who has always made my work better. It was she who winnowed down the long interviews, capturing the uniqueness of the hurdles each trailblazer had to jump to make history and the feelings they had after their historical achievement. Barbara, an author herself who works in the education field, brought to the project an in-depth understanding of the evolution of multiracial/ethnic politics in Texas' metropolitan areas.

CONTRIBUTORS

Susan A. MacManus is Distinguished University Professor in the Department of Government & International Affairs at the University of South Florida. She is the author of *Young v. Old: Generational Combat in the 21st Century?* and *Targeting Senior Voters*. She is the coauthor of *Florida's Politics* (4th ed.), with Aubrey Jewett, Thomas R. Dye, and David J. Bonanza; *Florida's Politics: Ten Media Markets, One Powerful State*, with Kevin Hill and Dario Moreno; and two local history books with her mother, Elizabeth Riegler MacManus—*Citrus, Sawmills, Critters, and Crackers: Life in Early Lutz and Central Pasco County* and *Going, Going, Almost Gone: Lutz-Land O' Lakes Pioneers Share Their Precious Memories*. MacManus has also edited two books on redistricting and reapportionment in Florida and been a political analyst for WFLA-TV (Tampa's NBC affiliate) for 20 years.

Barbara A. Langham is a professional writer and editor, specializing in public relations writing and corporate communications in Austin, Texas. Her clients include 3M Company and the University of Texas at Austin, where she is communications consultant for Explore UT, an annual statewide open house for K-12 students. For many years, she has been an editor of *Texas Child Care*, a quarterly journal for early childhood educators published by the Texas Workforce Commission. She has also published a children's book on the Texas state tree (pecan). She has a B.A. in English and an M.A. in communications from University of Texas at Austin.

USF Student Assistants and Researchers

All of these terrific student researchers are lifetime members of USF's Zeta Pi Chapter of Pi Sigma Alpha—the National Political Science Honor Society, with the exception of Lauren Gilmore, who was a member of the Phi Theta Kappa honor society.

Lauren K. Gilmore was a student in the Honors College at USF. She graduated magna cum laude with a B.A. in interdisciplinary social science (concentrations in religious studies and sociology) and a minor in history. She received an M.A. in sociology from the University of Central Florida and now teaches World History at Lake Wales High School in Florida.

Tyler B. Myers was a student in the Honors College at USF. He graduated cum laude with a B.A. in sociology and Africana studies. He is a Juris Doctor candidate at the Washington University School of Law in St. Louis, Missouri, and is staff editor for the *Washington University Jurisprudence Review.*

Amanda Chew Bappert graduated from USF with a B.A. in political science and a minor in women's studies. She completed her law degree at Florida A&M University College of Law where she was *Law Review* Senior Editor. She is now a Program Attorney II for the Manatee County Clerk of the Circuit Court and Comptroller. She lives in Bradenton, Florida.

Andrew Felipe Quecan, an Honors College student, graduated magna cum laude from USF with a B.S. in finance, a B.S. in electrical engineering, and an M.S. in electrical engineering. He later received an M.S. in electrical engineering from Stanford University, where he was a National Science Foundation Graduate Research Fellow. After completing his J.D. at the University of Texas School of Law, he became a registered patent attorney and resides in Washington State.

Kristine Zooberg Rodriguez, an Honors College student, received a B.A. in political science, with a minor in German, and an M.A. in political science, certificate in political campaigning cum laude, from the University of Florida. She is a consultant for the U.S. Chamber of Commerce's Corporate Relations and Development and lives in North Carolina.

Tifini LaFaye Hill received both a B.A. in political science and an M.P.A. from USF, where she served as president of Pi Sigma Alpha. She is currently a Budget Systems Administrator for the Hillsborough County Board of County Commissioners (Tampa).

Sandra Waldron graduated summa cum laude from the University of Miami with a B.S. in elementary education and psychology. At UM she was a Distinguished Student of Teaching and Learning. Waldron received an M.P.A. from USF and was a member of Pi Alpha Alpha—public administration honor society. She is currently a middle school geography teacher at Shorecrest Preparatory School in St. Petersburg, Florida.

David J. Bonanza, a National Merit Scholar, graduated from the USF with a B.S. summa cum laude in business economics. He is the coauthor of *Politics in Florida*, 4th ed., chapters in Larry Sabato's *Pendulum Swing* (2011) and *The Year of Obama* (2009), and numerous featured columns posted on *Sayfie Review*. His professional experience includes analytical roles with Fortune 100 companies in the banking and telecommunications industries. He is currently a high school math teacher in Melbourne.

Ashleigh E. Powers received a B.A. in telecommunications (news) from USF. She is an editor at Sayfie Media New York and the Digital Marketing/Production Crew Manager for SBI—a New York firm specializing in large-scale event production and planning. She resides in New York City.

Victoria M. Pearce graduated magna cum laude from USF with a B.A. in political science. She worked as a research associate for Dr. Susan A. MacManus before entering law school and is a Juris Doctor candidate (2018) at the Florida State University College of Law.

Anthony A. Cilluffo is an undergraduate in the Honors College at USF double majoring in political science and economics. He spent his junior year at the London School of Economics and plans to go to graduate school after he completes his undergraduate degrees.

1

Florida

Population Magnet, Microcosm of America, Trailblazer Incubator

> Florida is not a single entity but rather a composite of many diverse parts, each with its own unique identity. The huge influx of persons from other states and abroad over the past 50 years has given Florida cultural diversity and a melting-pot ambiance.
>
> Throughout the history of the United States, multiple racial and ethnic minority outsider groups have struggled to overcome stigmatization, discrimination, and exclusion in order to become equal insiders in the country's political, social, and economic spheres.

Trailblazers, as the word is used here, refers to those individuals in minority groups who have braved the tangled jungle of government in the past half century and carved out a trail for others like them to follow. Hundreds of individuals in minority groups in Florida have followed the blazed trail of their predecessors and continue to serve today. (See Appendixes B–E for comprehensive lists.)

The trailblazers in this book are from the past half century only. They were preceded by a large number of Hispanics who served in the territorial and state legislatures in the 1800s, and several blacks who were elected during Reconstruction. The focus on minorities since the 1960s reflects the increased opportunities for minorities to serve in public office made possible by laws, constitutional amendments, and court decisions that expanded civil rights.

Each individual in this book is a *first*—by virtue of race/ethnicity in combination with gender and, if applicable, political party to attain a legislative, judicial, or executive post at the state level or in Congress. Thus we have, for example, Joe Lang Kershaw, the first African American who was male and a Democrat elected to the Florida House, as well as Gwen Cherry, also African American and a Democrat elected to the House but who was female. Some individuals were trailblazers at more than one post. One is Ileana Ros-Lehtinen, the first Cuban-American female Republican elected to the Florida House, the Florida Senate, and then the U.S. Congress.

This book assumes that trail blazing at the state level represents a cumulative process, in which each person's achievements were built upon those of others at the city or county level, for example, or drew upon the growing strength of organizations like the NAACP and networks like the Bay of Pigs veterans. The "first" person in history to be elected or appointed to a given state office thus benefitted from earlier trail blazing that occurred in laws and regulations as well as in public attitudes and perceptions.

Acknowledging the cumulative process does not diminish the importance of the trailblazers in this book. All faced challenges, some more serious than others, that required a measure of courage, intelligence, and self-confidence, and all needed family and community support.

In some cases, however, the "first" came about as a matter of circumstance or apparent subterfuge. One state legislator of Korean heritage, for example, ran for office at the request of a state legislator seeking higher office and for whom she served as campaign manager. In another example, the "first" was a candidate who purposely hid his racial identity to take advantage of a name he shared with a well-known white official.

Nonetheless, as individuals and as a group, the people in this book introduced diversity into the state's politics and government. Having laid new paths in old territory, they are important to study.

First of all, they serve as role models. To minority professionals working quietly and steadily, yet heretofore ignored and overlooked for public office; to students mulling futures and careers; to housewives, laborers, and community activists struggling to overcome problems in their communities, the trailblazers offer a beacon of hope and inspiration.

Once elected or selected, trailblazers stand to make a difference, defying the business-as-usual policies and practices of the bodies in which they serve. Legislative agendas, for example, are more likely to contain proposals to improve education, jobs, and living conditions for minority populations. Hiring practices change in order to recruit a wider diversity of candidates.

Finally, and no less important, the election or appointment of trailblazers can improve the white community's racial attitudes and tolerance. Many who might have doubted the competence of minority officeholders gradually shift their perceptions. Young people, who have grown up with racial/ethnic and gender diversity in government, are more likely to accept diversity as a fact of life. They expect to see it among those who seek political office—from both major political parties.

Such significant effects raise questions. How did these trailblazers emerge? What triggered their embarkation on new paths? Why Florida? Are there lessons here from which officeholders, current and potential, in other states can learn? And what advice do these path-breakers have for young minorities contemplating running for office or dreaming of being appointed to top-level executive and judicial posts?

We can begin to answer these questions by looking first at the state's minority population growth and how it has changed the political landscape at the state and local levels.

Florida: Population Magnet, Microcosm of America

Trailblazers have emerged as Florida's population has grown over the past half century. The state has experienced an influx of retirees fleeing cold winters; Cubans fleeing Castro; Haitians fleeing poverty; Colombians, Venezuelans, Nicaraguans, and others from Latin America seeking economic opportunity or escaping political unrest.[1]

Florida has become a real "melting pot" of cultures. Once one of the least appealing, most racially polarized, and poorest states, Florida is now one of the most desirable and most diverse. The transition has altered the faces and politics of those chosen to govern the state. The transition largely began during the tumultuous 1960s, with the Civil Rights Movement and court-ordered changes that gave rise to more

Figure 1.1. State Rep. Gwen Cherry (*second from left in front row*) marches in a parade with fellow women legislators Gwen Margolis and Elaine Gordon. An ardent advocate for women's rights, Cherry served as state President of the National Organization for Women and headed the Florida branch of the National Women's Political Caucus. She introduced a bill for Florida to ratify the Equal Rights Amendment, which the House did twice, but each time it failed in the Senate. State Archives of Florida, *Florida Memory*, https://www.floridamemory.com/items/show/2697, n.d.

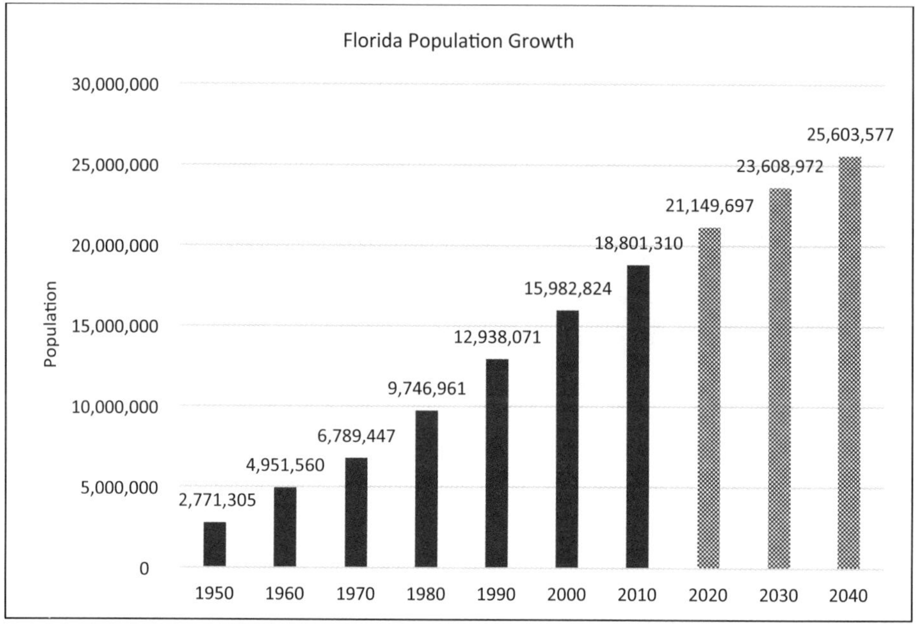

Figure 1.2. Florida's booming population. Sources: U.S. Census 1950–2010; Florida Demographic Estimating Conference, 2014; University of Florida Bureau of Business and Economic Research, Florida Population Studies, Bulletin 169, June 2014; http://edr.state.fl.us/Content/population-demographics/data/Pop_Census_Day.pdf.

representation for urban areas (the one-person, one-vote principle).[2] The push for gender equality began in the 1970s with the women's movement—out of which came Florida's first minority female legislator.

The paths followed by minority trailblazers have varied by their race/ethnicity, gender, political party, and geographical location. The tendency of immigrants to move to population centers with enclaves of other immigrants who share their heritage or country of origin explains why so many trailblazers in state and congressional offices have come from Florida's large metropolitan areas—Miami, Tampa, Orlando, and Jacksonville.

Florida, which became the nation's third largest state in 2014, has grown significantly in every decade since the 1950s (see figure 1.2). It has been transformed from a Confederate state to one best described as "a microcosm of America." More than two-thirds of its residents were not born in Florida—a pattern extending back to 1960 when the U.S. Census Bureau first began collecting this information. At the same time, the state has become the nation's premier swing state—evolving from a one-party ("yellow dog Democrat") state to a deeply divided purple state within a half century (see figure 1.3).[3]

Racial and ethnic conflict—Seminole Indian wars, slavery and emancipation, Reconstruction followed by segregation, the communist revolution in Cuba, and the

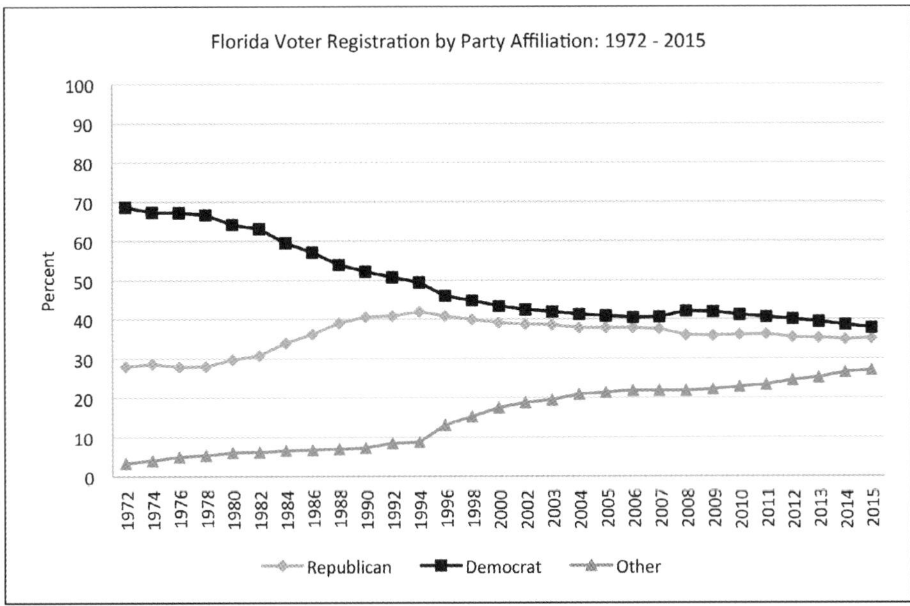

Figure 1.3. Florida voter party registration percentages: 1972–2015. Source: Compiled from data from the Florida Division of Elections.

Hispanic and Haitian migration to the state—has long driven Florida's political history. Racial and ethnic politics continues to shape public affairs in Florida and may grow even more important in the next century as the state's population continues to diversify.

The state's racial/ethnic makeup now mirrors the nation at large, more so than any other swing state (see table 1.1). However, broad racial/ethnic groupings widely cited by the media mask the fact that Florida's black and Hispanic populations have become considerably more diverse, driven by in-migration from Latin America (Caribbean—55 percent, Central America—22 percent, and South America—23 percent).[4] Nearly one-fifth of its residents are foreign born[5] (see figure 1.4), and three-fourths of those residents are from Latin America (see figure 1.5). Ethnic solidarity tends to be strongest among foreign-born residents.[6]

As immigrants have flocked to Florida, especially to the largest metropolitan areas (Miami, Tampa, and Orlando), the state has seen the rise of *country-of-origin*, or *identity*, politics.[7] But parlaying ethnic pride into racial/ethnic political representation requires naturalization. According to the U.S. Census Bureau, higher naturalization rates have occurred among immigrants from the Caribbean (54 percent) than from South (44 percent) or Central (32 percent) American countries. The highest rates among immigrants from Latin American countries are Jamaica (61 percent) and Cuba (56 percent).[8]

Do minorities register to vote? By the mid-2010s, nearly one-third of Florida's registered voters were minorities—Hispanics (15 percent), blacks (14 percent), Asians/

Table 1.1. Florida's racial and ethnic composition closely mirrors the nation

	Percentage of population			
	2000		2015	
Race/ethnicity	Florida (%)	U.S. (%)	Florida (%)	U.S. (%)
White	78.0	75.1	78.1	77.7
Non-Hispanic White	65.4	69.1	56.4	62.6
Hispanic/Latino	16.8	12.5	23.6	17.1
African American	14.6	12.3	16.7	13.2
Asian	1.7	3.6	2.7	5.3
Native American	0.3	0.9	0.5	1.2
Pacific Islander	0.1	0.1	0.1	0.2
Some other race	3.0	5.5	3.6	6.2
Two or more races	2.4	2.4	1.9	2.4

Source: U.S. Census Bureau.

Pacific Islanders (2 percent), and Native Americans/Alaskans (0.3 percent) (see figure 1.6). By far, the most solidly cohesive from a *party registration* perspective were blacks (see figure 1.17). Hispanics were more divided, with a sizable portion registering as independents (No Party Affiliation, or NPA). Asians were the most likely to register as NPAs—a pattern observed nationally as well.[9]

Partisan differences in the *voting patterns within* each broadly labeled racial/ethnic group (black, Hispanic, Asian, Native-American) are often explained by the country of origin of a candidate or candidate's family (for example, Cuba, Puerto Rico, Haiti,

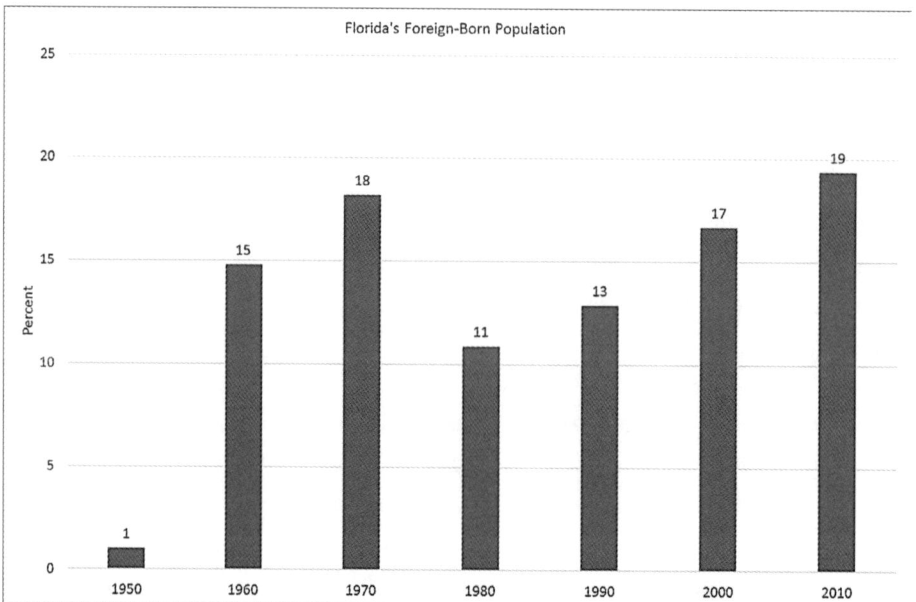

Figure 1.4. Florida's foreign-born population diversifies the state's population. Source: U.S. Census Bureau.

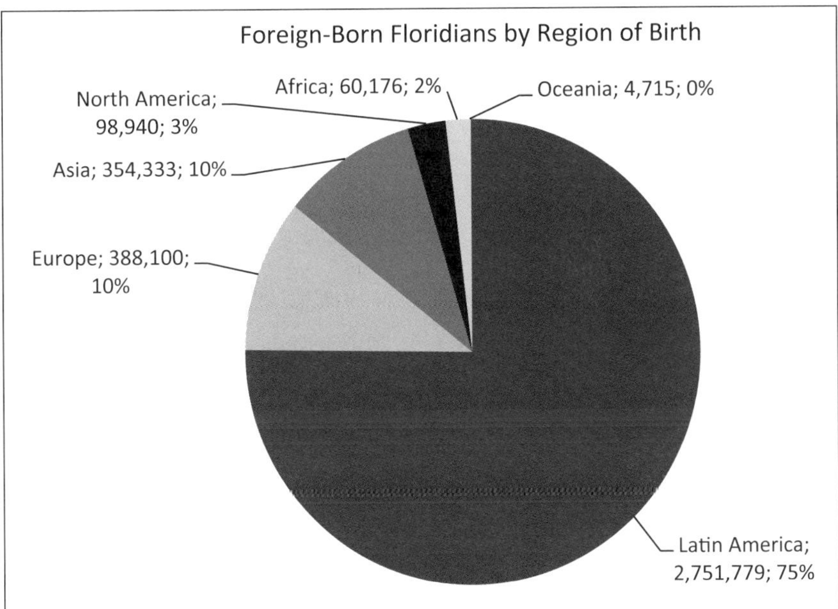

Figure 1.5. Foreign-born Floridians (2010) by region of birth. Source: U.S. Census Bureau, American Community Survey, 2010.

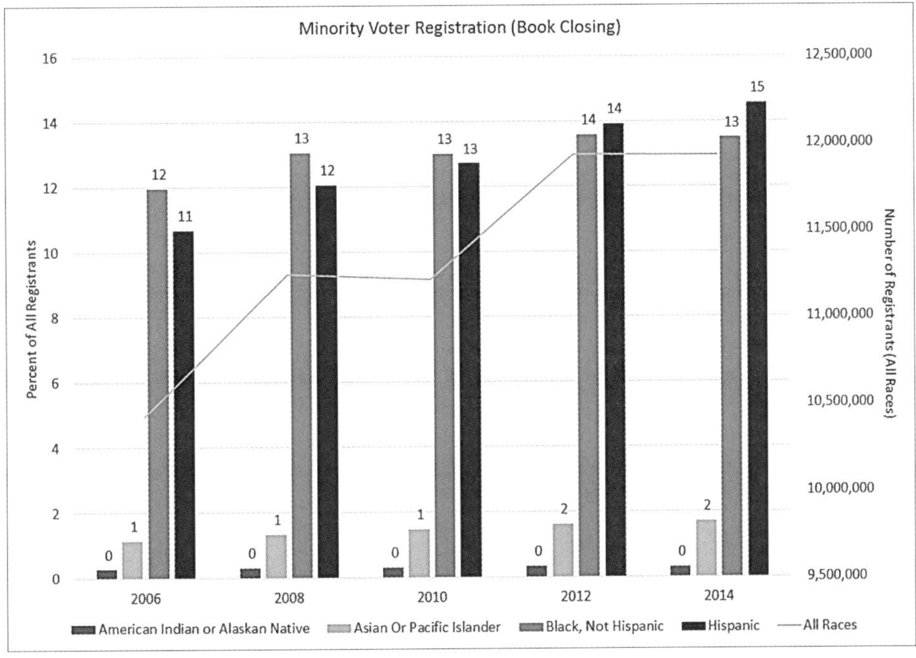

Figure 1.6. Political party registration by race/ethnicity (2014). Source: Florida Division of Elections.

Jamaica, Korea, China). Indeed, racial/ethnic heritage (identity politics) can trump party affiliation in voting decisions. Generational differences—length of residency in the United States and age—can also account for lower partisan cohesion levels among voters with a common heritage.

Minority Population Growth, More Political Clout

Traditionally, in Florida as in the United States as a whole, African Americans were the largest minority group. However, the Hispanic population has been growing sharply for the past half century, while the African-American population has grown more slowly (see figure 1.7). From 2000 to 2010, the state's Asian population grew the fastest (more than 70 percent), followed by the Hispanic (more than 57 percent), black (more than 26 percent), and Native-American (more than 20 percent) populations.[10] Hispanics surpassed blacks as the state's largest minority group in the late 1990s. Overall, Florida has become one of the most diverse states in the nation, ranking 3rd in Hispanic population, 11th in African-American population, and 23rd in Asian population.

To see how the state became more diverse, one can look at census maps comparing changes over the last decade in each minority group's population makeup of all 67 counties (see figures 1.8–1.11). Blacks form a larger share of North Florida counties (the old Cotton Belt area) and Broward County in South Florida. Hispanics are more concentrated in Central and South Florida counties, while Asians have settled

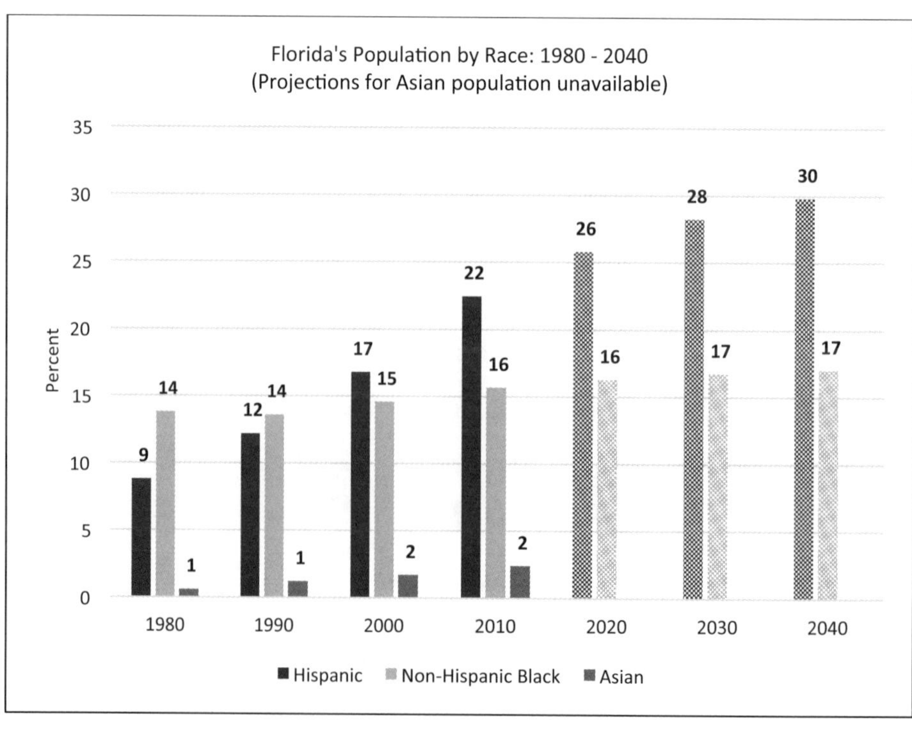

Figure 1.7. Racial and ethnic change in Florida: 1980–2040. Source: U.S. Census Bureau. Projections from Bureau of Economic and Business Research, University of Florida, June 2014.

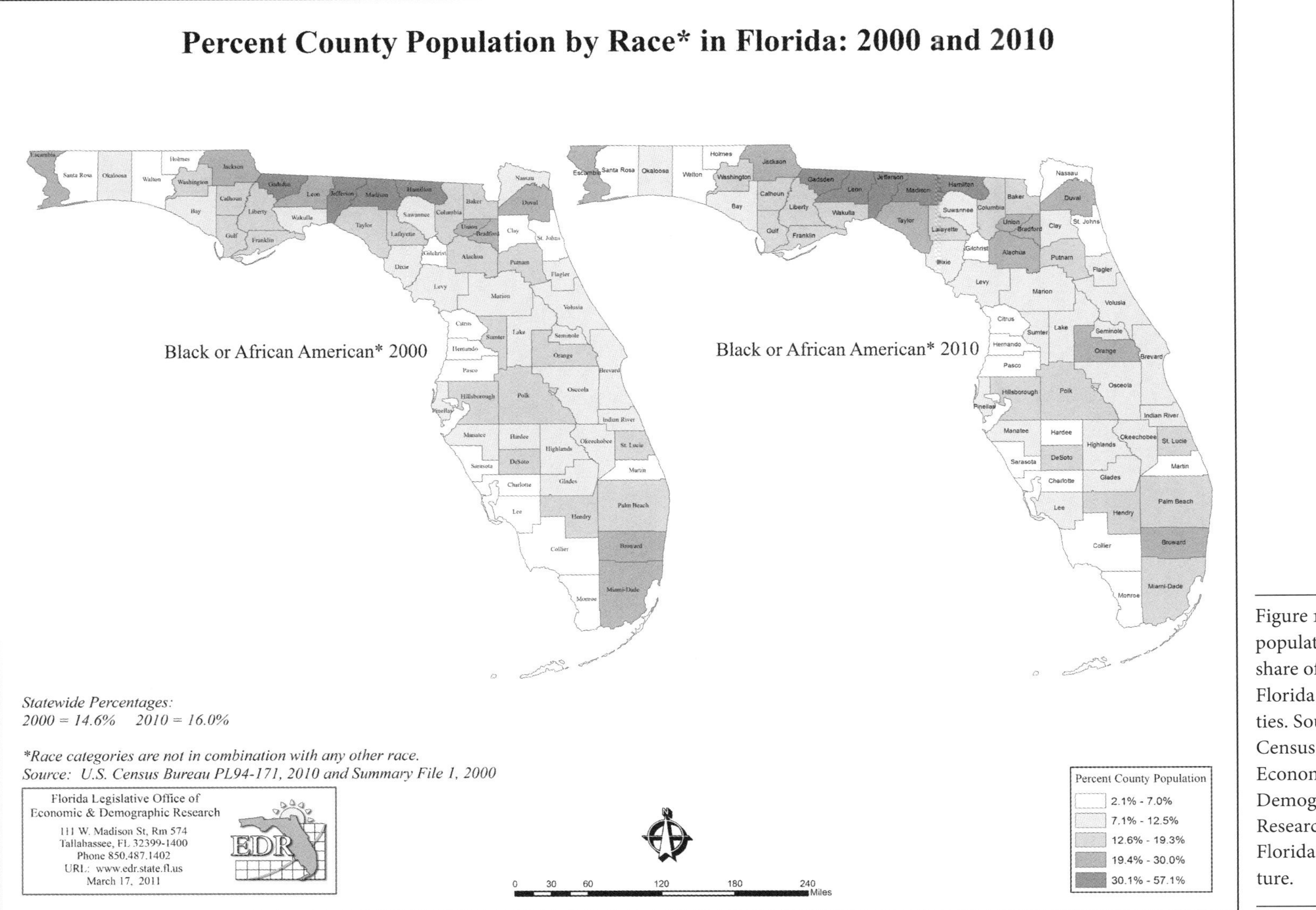

Figure 1.8. Black population larger share of North Florida counties. Source: U.S. Census data; Economic and Demographic Research, The Florida Legislature.

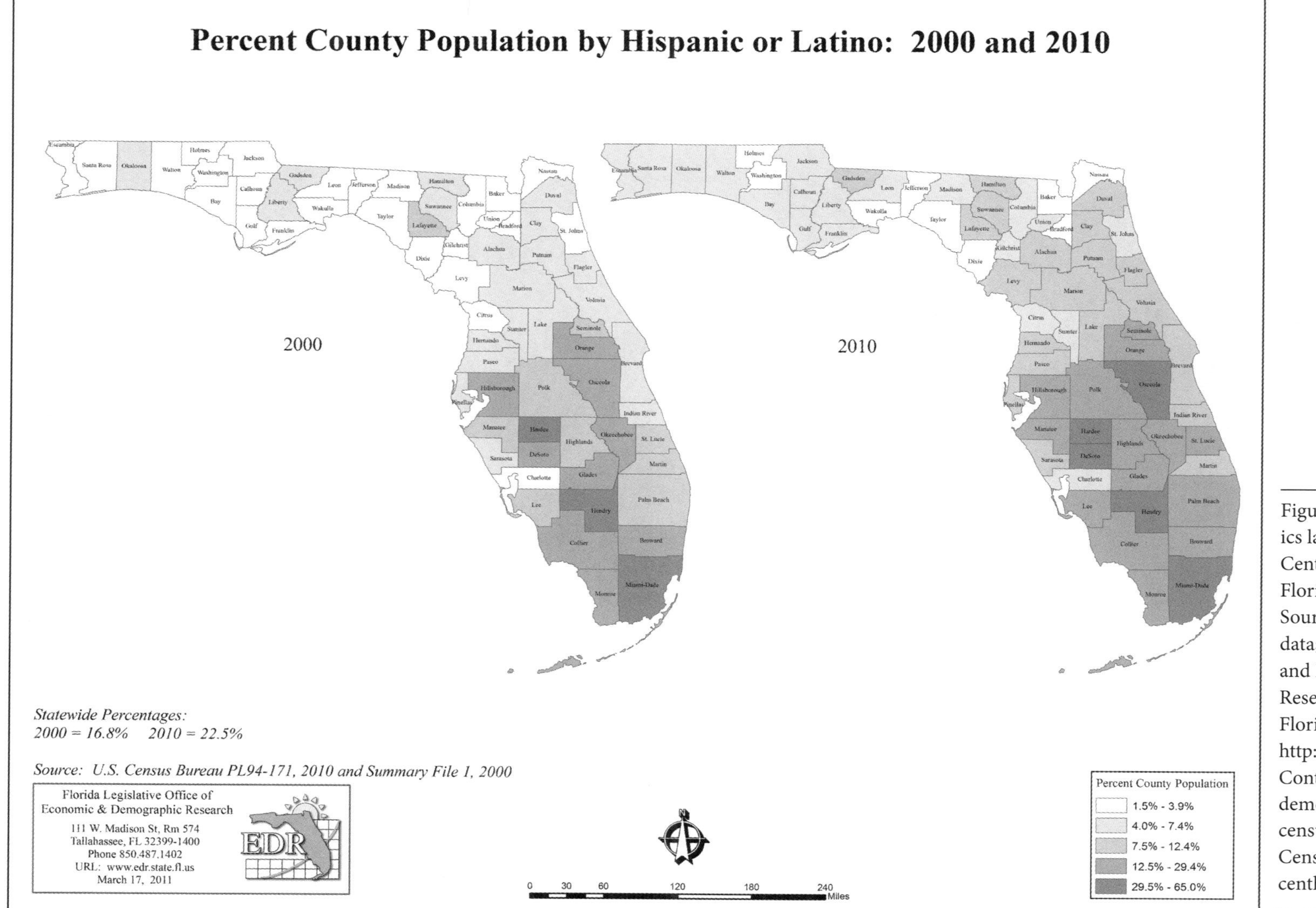

Figure 1.9. Hispanics larger share of Central and South Florida counties. Source: U.S. Census data; Economic and Demographic Research, The Florida Legislature. http://edr.state.fl.us/Content/population-demographics/2010-census/maps/Census_2010_percenthispanic.pdf.

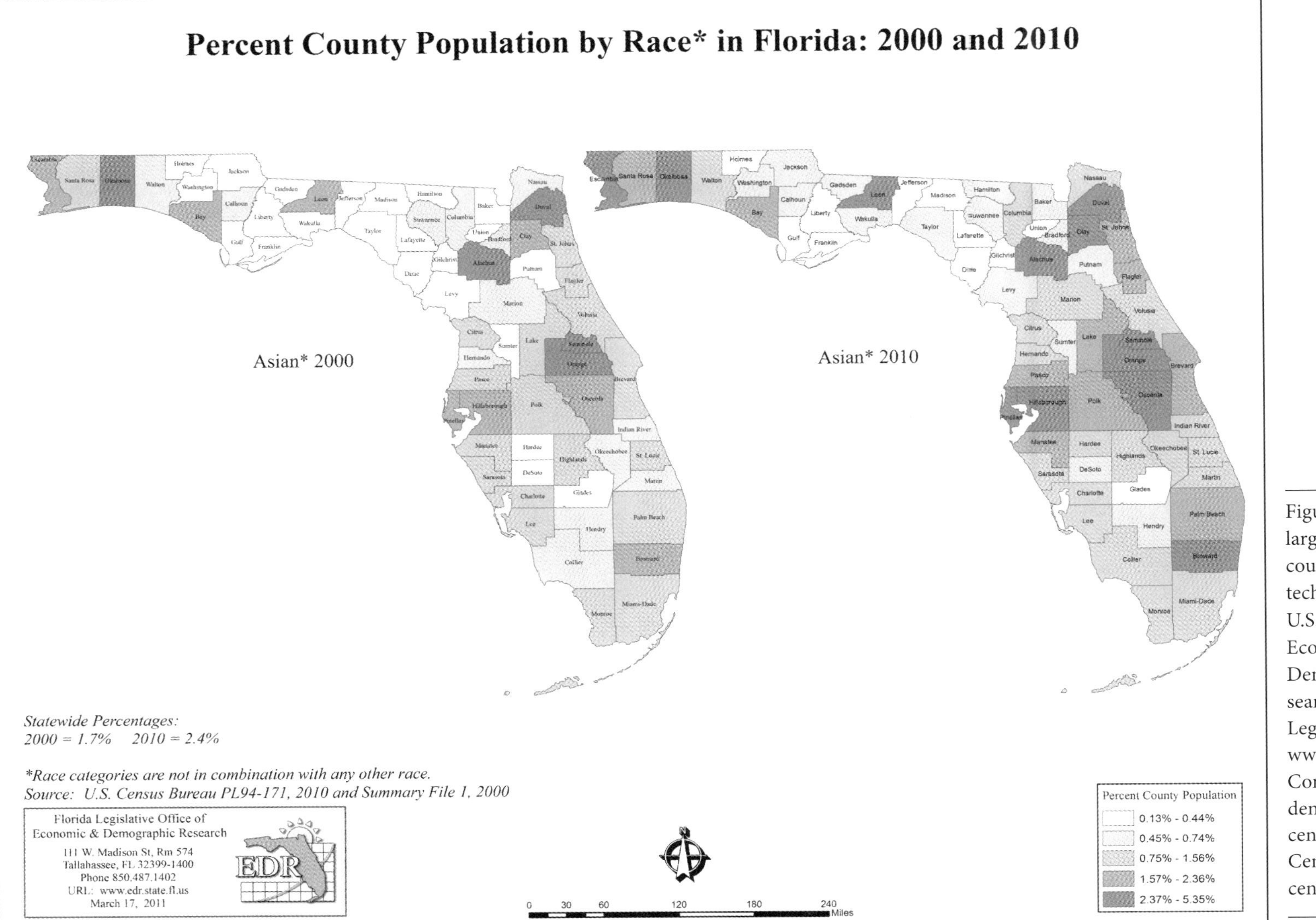

Figure 1.10. Asians larger share in counties with high-tech jobs. Source: U.S. Census data; Economic and Demographic Research, The Florida Legislature. http://www.edr.state.fl.us/Content/population-demographics/2010-census/maps/Census_2010_percentrace_alone.pdf.

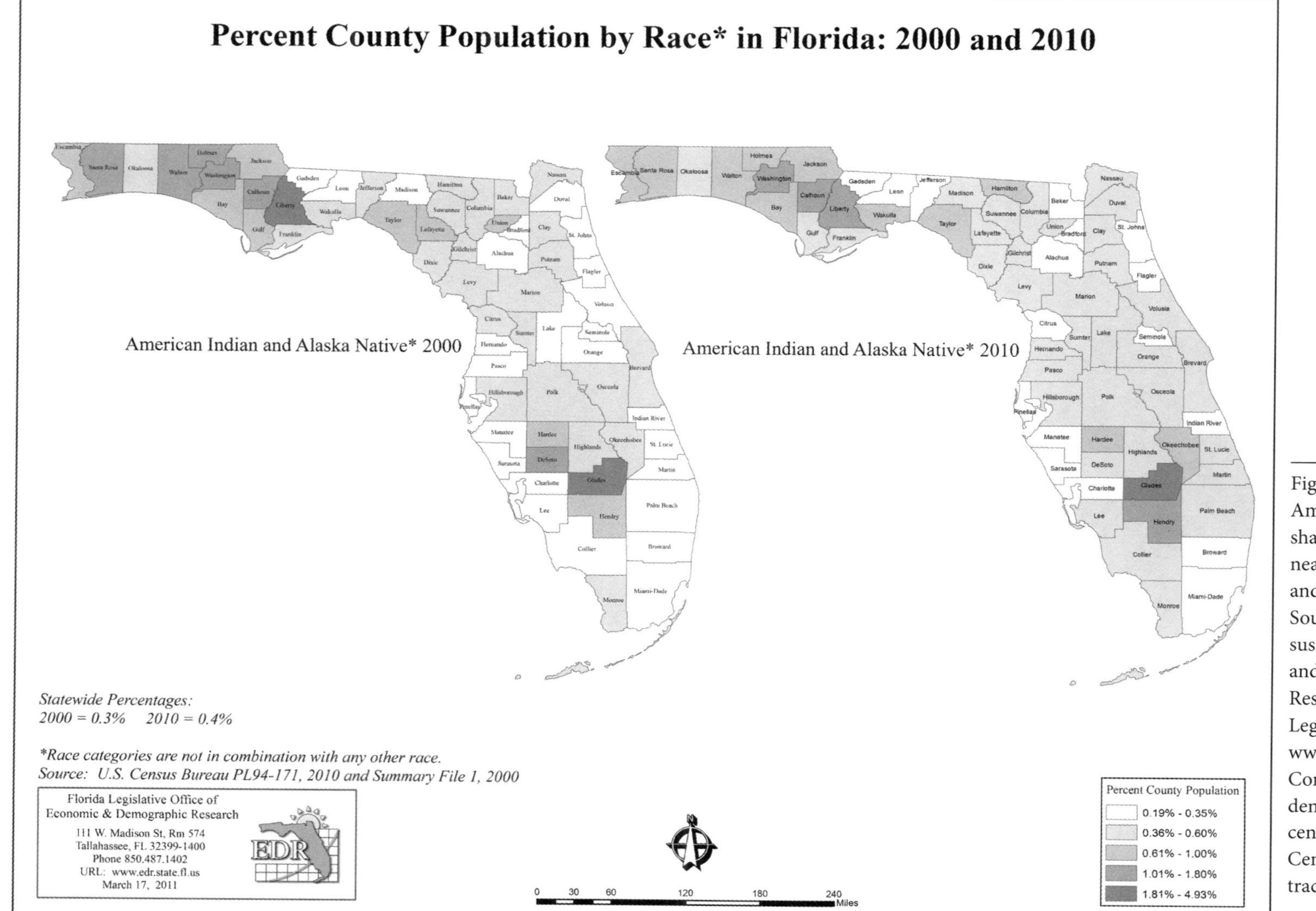

Figure 1.11. Native Americans larger share of counties near Everglades and Reservations. Source: U.S. Census data; Economic and Demographic Research, The Florida Legislature. http://www.edr.state.fl.us/Content/population-demographics/2010-census/maps/Census_2010_percentrace_alone.pdf.

in the high-growth I-4 corridor, North Florida counties with large military installations, and the heavily populated Broward and Palm Beach counties in South Florida. The largest Native-American populations are those in counties proximate to the Everglades, Lake Okeechobee, and the Big Cypress Reservation (Seminoles). Some of these residential patterns have taken a long time to evolve; others are more recent; all have altered the state's political landscape.

Florida's Black Population

As late as 1900, nearly half of Florida's population (44 percent) was African American. Yet blacks in Florida and elsewhere in the South were socially and economically deprived and politically repressed.[11] Many blacks left the region seeking better opportunity in the North. During Reconstruction, immediately after the Civil War, blacks actively participated in the political life of the state. Virtually all black voters and officeholders of this era were Republicans.[12] But by 1900, white Democrats had recaptured all the important offices. Democratic primaries became the only meaningful elections, and blacks were officially excluded by a rule requiring all primary voters to be white. Not until the U.S. Supreme Court outlawed the white primary in *Smith v. Allwright* (1944) were any blacks registered as Democrats in Florida.[13]

The Florida Legislature eliminated the poll tax in 1937, well before the 24th Amendment (1964) to the U.S. Constitution barred it throughout the nation. Black voting began to increase after World War II, especially in the state's larger cities. By the early 1950s about one-third of the state's eligible blacks were registered to vote. But in many rural counties, threats, intimidation, and extralegal means still prevented blacks from registering or voting. Led by civil rights activists Harry T. Moore, C. K. Steele, and others, black voting rose in the early 1960s. After the federal Voting Rights Act of 1965, black registration and voting increased dramatically[14] as the threat of federal intervention eliminated the last official obstacles at the local level.

Since the 1980s, blacks who have moved to the state generally fall into four groups: (1) middle-class persons drawn to the booming New South economies; (2) working-class persons who were turned away from manufacturing restructuring in the North; (3) retirees; and (4) Caribbean blacks fleeing from political unrest and/or economic crises (see figure 1.12). Some blacks who left Florida during the days of racial segregation have returned (reverse migration).

In recent years, the growing number of blacks immigrating to Florida from Caribbean countries has resulted in an increase in their political power, especially in multiracial South Florida. The Miami-Fort Lauderdale area is where the majority of black Caribbean immigrants in the United States reside. Three countries send the most of these immigrants to the United States—Haiti, Jamaica, and Trinidad and Tobago.[15]

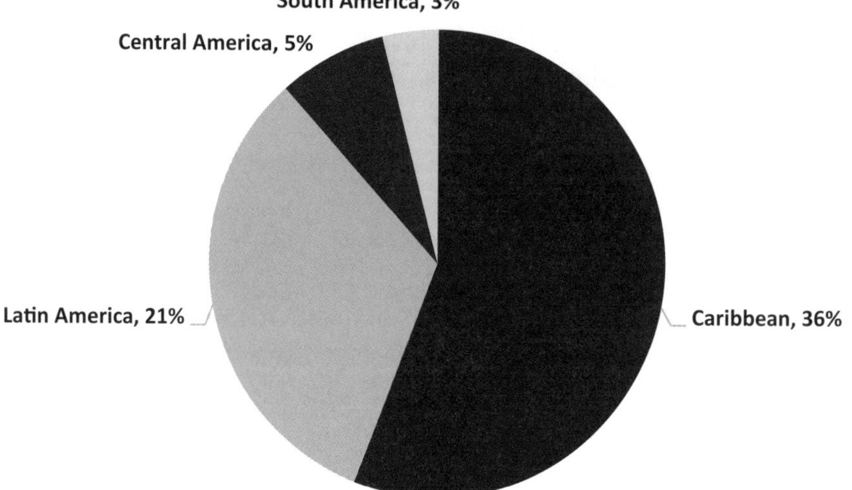

Figure 1.12. Regional origin of Florida's foreign-born black population. Source: U.S. Census Bureau, 2010 data.

Haitians are more dominant in Miami-Dade County, Jamaicans in Broward County.[16] The growing presence of Caribbean blacks has occasionally put them at odds with U.S.-born black Floridians.[17] "Residential as well as political strategies at the local level reveal that West Indians (Caribbean blacks) do not always match the black American pattern."[18] It has prompted many to demand that the media refer to them as Caribbean Americans or Caribbean blacks rather than African Americans, although some scholars have labeled them Afro-Caribbeans.[19]

The number of Haitians immigrating to Florida has exceeded that of all other foreign immigrants. Most have fled the abject poverty of their native land. The U.S. federal government considers most Haitian immigrants as economic rather than political refugees and, hence, not automatically entitled to political asylum. But efforts to turn back the tide of small rickety boats from Haiti have been generally unsuccessful. In recent years, large numbers of Haitian immigrants have moved north from their original "Little Haiti" inner-city residential area of Miami along the I-95 corridor into low-income housing in Broward and Palm Beach counties. More have become citizens: "We strongly want to be part of the American political process and not make the mistakes our parents made 20 years ago. They never became U.S. citizens. They never took part in the political system. They died here thinking they were going back to Haiti but never made it back. Let's face it. Most of us aren't going back," said one Haitian community activist from Fort Lauderdale.[20]

Bahamians[21]—another sizable group of black immigrants—have longer, deeper roots in South Florida. Initially, many regularly came to Key West for temporary work in fishing-oriented industries but then returned to the islands. Between the 1890s and 1940s, as Miami developed, thousands migrated from the Bahamas, drawn there by opportunities for permanent, better-paying agricultural, construction, and tourism-related service jobs—a "livelihood migration."[22] Coconut Grove and Overtown—two black neighborhoods in Miami—still have many residents with ties to the Bahamas.

By the mid-2010s, the largest concentrations of blacks were in the Panhandle and in the heavily urbanized Miami-Fort Lauderdale metropolitan area. These areas have elected the most African Americans and Afro-Caribbeans to state-level positions and Congress.

Florida's Hispanic Population

The label *Hispanic* refers to persons from many different countries with varying cultural, religious, and political backgrounds. As of 2010, Cubans were still the largest group in Florida, followed by Puerto Ricans, Mexicans, and Colombians (see figure 1.13). Spaniards, Florida's first Hispanic settlers, made up less than 2 percent.

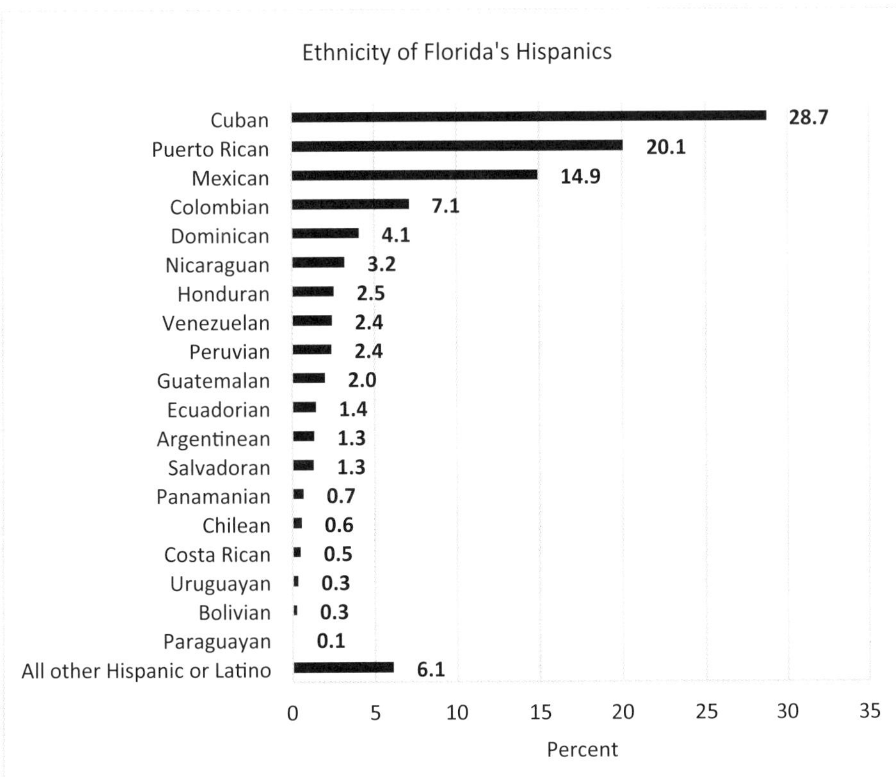

Figure 1.13. Ethnicity of Florida's Hispanics. Source: U.S. Census, 2010. The category of "All other Hispanic or Latino" includes the following census categories: Spaniard, Spanish, Spanish American, Other Central American, Other South American, and All other Hispanic or Latino.

The Spanish were the first Europeans to colonize Florida, and parts of the state have historically reflected a Latin culture. Shortly after the Civil War, Cuban and Spanish cigar makers established a thriving community in Key West. Later a Spanish industrialist, Martinez Ybor, expanded cigar production near Tampa in a community known as Ybor City. Tampa quickly became the nation's leading center for cigar making.

Cuba achieved independence from Spain in 1898, the same year that the city of Miami was incorporated. Miami soon became closely linked to neighboring Havana across the narrow Florida Straits. Refugees from unstable politics in Cuba arrived in Miami throughout the 1940s and 1950s. Even before Fidel Castro's revolution in 1959, the Little Havana neighborhood of Miami had developed.[23]

But it was Castro's revolutionary embrace of communism after 1959 that permanently changed Florida. Over the next four decades, nearly one million Cubans fled their homeland for the United States and most of them settled in the Miami area.

The earliest Cuban exiles were primarily business and professional people and their families whose assets and homes were seized by the Castro government. They were joined a short time later by others who had initially supported Castro but were quickly disillusioned by his abandonment of democracy and embrace of communism and the Soviet Union. These early Cuban exiles quickly revitalized the economy of Miami, which had deteriorated into a seedy retirement and tourist town. Some of them then moved into the political arena.

In the Cuban Adjustment Act of 1966, the U.S. government recognized Cuban exiles as political refugees and allowed them to enter without quotas and with permanent resident alien status. The 1980 Mariel boatlift brought an additional 125,000 Cuban exiles to Florida, some of whom were expelled from prisons by the Castro regime.

The Cubans fleeing Castro initially identified themselves with the perceived strong anti-communist position of the national Republican Party. Their business, professional, and financial backgrounds reinforced their Republicanism. The established Cuban-American leadership remains Republican today. But the influence of older anti-communist Cuban exile leaders[24] is waning due to generational replacement. Younger Cuban Americans ascending into community leadership positions are more concerned about domestic issues than foreign policy and lean more Democratic. Consequently, the Cuban vote in the mid-2010s is far less cohesive than in the past.[25] It is also now smaller than the non-Cuban Hispanic electorate, although still slightly more Republican.[26]

In recent years, in-migrants from Puerto Rico and Central and South American countries such as Mexico, the Dominican Republic, Colombia, Venezuela, and Nicaragua have swelled the ranks of non-Cuban Hispanics in the state and made it considerably more diverse politically. Economic and political turmoil in those regions

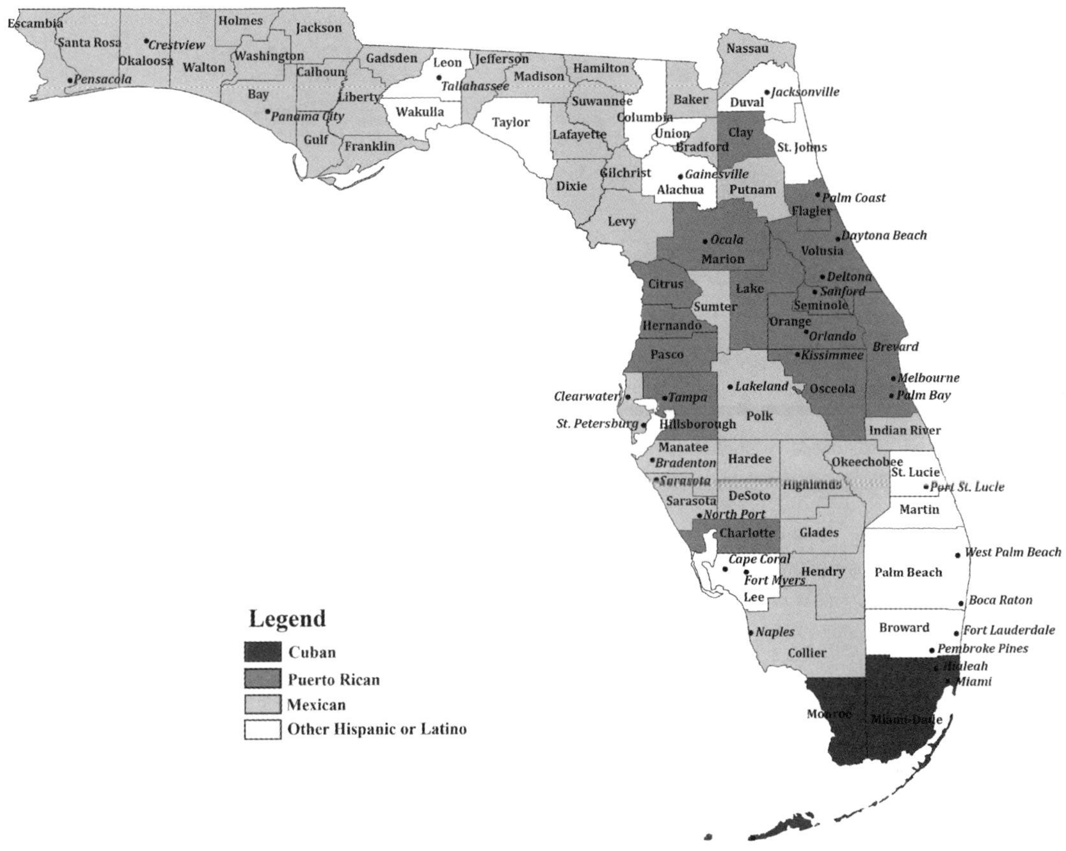

Figure 1.14. Hispanic ethnicity residential patterns across counties. Graphic represents largest Hispanic group in each county (2010 U.S. Census Data). Source: Office of Economic and Demographic Research, Florida Legislature.

has been a major impetus for Hispanics—and blacks—to leave those areas. (See Appendix A.)

While Hispanics of all origins are dispersed throughout Florida (see figure 1.14), Cubans are still the largest group in the Miami metropolitan area, followed by Nicaraguans and Colombians. A slightly different pattern characterizes Hispanics in Fort Lauderdale—Cuban, Puerto Rican, and Colombian. In Orlando, the largest groups (in order) are Puerto Rican, Mexican, and Cuban, while in Tampa, they are Puerto Rican, Cuban, and Mexican.[27]

Historically Cubans, Nicaraguans, and Colombians tended to vote Republican, while Puerto Ricans and Mexicans leaned Democratic. That pattern has changed significantly since the Republicans began taking a stronger stance on immigration reform—one that many Hispanics regard as too punitive. One exit poll of Florida Hispanics who voted in the 2012 presidential contest found that with the exception

Figure 1.15. Cuban Republican Mel Martinez (*center*) had been elected mayor of Orange County (Orlando) well before running for the U.S. Senate. He was quite aware of the growing diversity of the Hispanic vote in Florida and the need to campaign differently in Central than South Florida. In the Orlando area, "it was not about Castro" because more Hispanics were from Puerto Rico, Mexico, and other parts of Latin America. Crossing party lines, he voted to confirm the appointment of Judge Sonia Sotomayor, of Puerto Rican heritage, to become the first Hispanic on the U.S. Supreme Court. Photograph courtesy of Mel Martinez, 2004.

of Cubans, every Hispanic group surveyed voted heavily Democrat.[28] Among Cubans, the vote was split along place-of-birth lines. Those born in Cuba (80 percent of Cubans who voted) supported Republican Romney, while those born in the United States (20 percent of Cuban voters) narrowly supported Obama. While many have challenged the specific numbers reported in polls taken of small Hispanic subgroups (for example, Dominicans, Hondurans, and Peruvians), the direction of their partisan leanings has rarely been challenged. However, new waves of immigrants at a different point in time can reignite questions of a group's party preference. This has happened with Puerto Ricans.

The Puerto Rican population has grown rapidly, especially in the Orlando (Orange, Osceola, and Seminole counties) and Tampa Bay (Hillsborough County) media markets. In Orange County alone, the Puerto Rican population increased from 86,583 to nearly 150,000 over the past decade.[29] These two media markets combined form the I-4 corridor, reach nearly 45 percent of the state's registered voters, and are considered to be the swing part of the state. Puerto Ricans, while leaning Democratic, are considered to be "up for grabs," especially the newcomers who are more affluent and educated and are fleeing the island because of its poor economy.[30] Puerto Ricans who have lived for long periods in the United States and often move to Florida from New York and New Jersey tend to register as Democrats, but those who have come directly from the island recently are likely to register as independents—and are highly sought after by both Democrats and Republicans. As one Republican strategist put it: "The Hispanic vote has diversified" with the surge of Puerto Ricans in the Orlando area. For candidates running statewide, "it means coming down to Miami and having a Cuban coffee is still a must, but now there's got to be more to it than that."[31]

A majority of the state's Hispanic elected officials—Cuban and non-Cuban—have been from South Florida (Miami-Dade, Broward, and Palm Beach counties) or Central Florida (Orange, Osceola, and Hillsborough counties). Most of the non-Cuban Hispanic trailblazers whose stories are told in this book have been elected since 2000.

Florida's Asian Population

The Asian-American population in Florida has grown faster than any other major minority group in recent years,[32] a reflection of its small percentage (2.5 percent) of the population as a whole. Asian Americans, like Hispanics, are not monolithic. The census category "Asian" includes Chinese, Japanese, Koreans, Filipinos, Vietnamese,

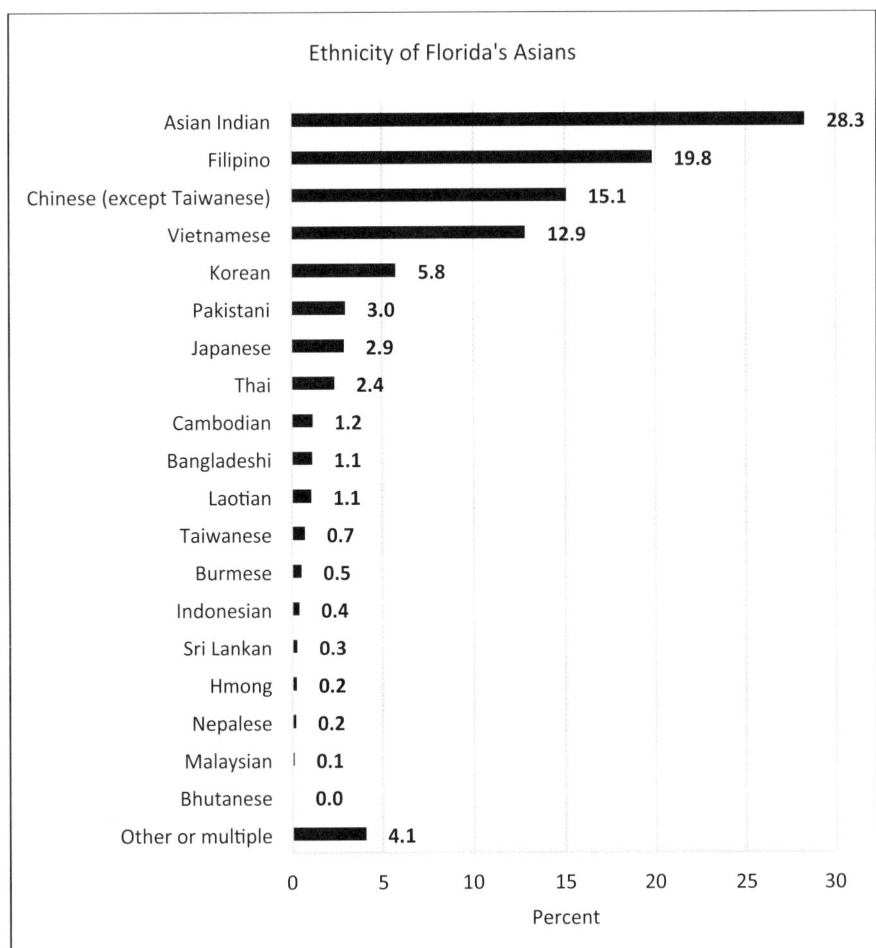

Figure 1.16. Breakdown of Florida's Asian population (2010) by country identity. Source: U.S. Census Bureau, 2010 figures. Includes all Asians, not just foreign born.

Asian Indians, Laotians, and Thais. In Florida the Asian-Indian population is the largest, followed by Filipinos, Chinese, Vietnamese, and Koreans (see figure 1.16).

Asian Americans are the best-educated, highest-income earning racial group in the United States, which helps explain their above-average concentrations in Gainesville (Alachua County), Orlando (Orange County), Jacksonville (Duval County), and the Crestview area (Okaloosa and Fort Walton counties) (see figure 1.10). Places where the economy is more knowledge based or STEM oriented—science, technology, engineering, and math—attract Asian Americans.[33] There is a high concentration of STEM jobs in Gainesville (University of Florida) and Orlando (aviation and aerospace, modeling, simulation, and training). Jacksonville and the Crestview area both have large military bases that issue high-tech-oriented contracts to firms employing highly educated Asians.

Asians from different countries vary considerably in their languages, religions, and cultural norms. Politically, they are a little more likely than Latinos or African Americans to register as independents (see figure 1.17), although that is changing as more are voting Democratic. As with Hispanics, there are differences in the voting patterns of different Asian-American ethnic groups. The only multilingual exit poll of subgroups of Asian Americans that voted in the 2012 presidential contest found the greatest support for Democrats among Bangladeshis and Pakistanis (more than 90 percent), followed by (in order) Indian Americans, Chinese, Koreans, and Filipinos. Vietnamese Americans were the only group to vote Republican.[34] The same survey by the Asian American Legal Defense and Education Fund found marked

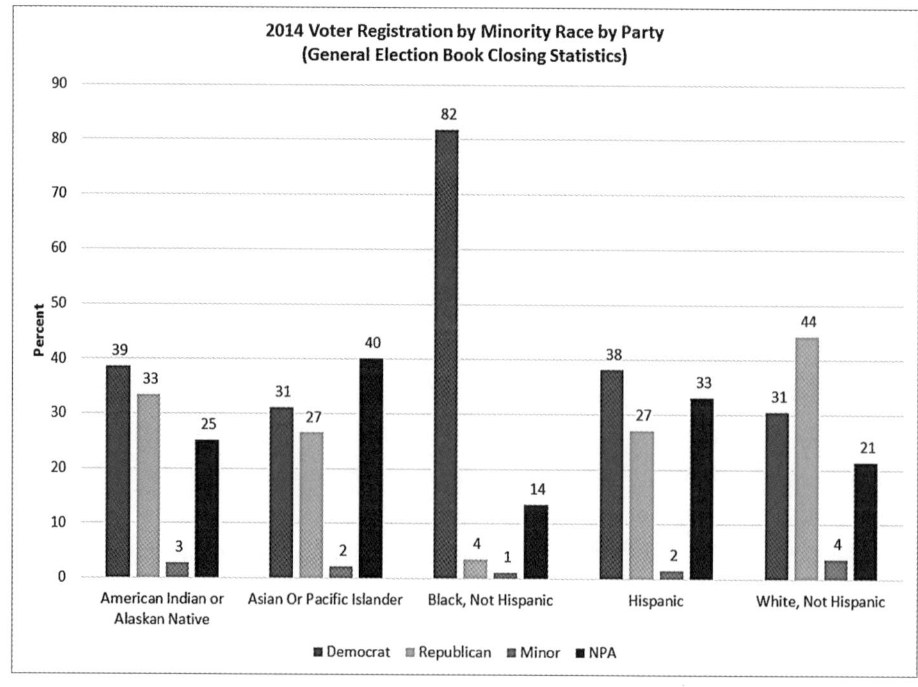

Figure 1.17. Blacks most closely aligned with a single political party (Democratic). Source: Florida Division of Elections.

generational differences, just as among Hispanics, with younger, liberal Asians voting more Democratic.

Fewer Asians have been elected to state offices than blacks or Hispanics, but they have had their greatest successes in South Florida. The first two Asians elected to the Florida Legislature were from Miami-Dade (Chinese) and Palm Beach (Korean) counties.

Florida's Native-American Population (American-Indian and Alaskan-Native)

As a minority category, Native Americans are often overlooked. They deserve inclusion here because Florida is one of 10 states with the largest American-Indian and Alaska-Native population. Florida's Native-American population grew 38 percent between 2000 and 2010—from 118,000 to almost 163,000.[35] Native Americans are not politically cohesive. In fact, they are fairly evenly divided in their political party preference, leaning slightly Democrat, with one-fourth registering as independents.

The Seminoles and Miccosukees are Florida's federally recognized tribes—Seminoles in 1957, Miccosukees in 1962.[36] Each tribe has its own governance structure.

The Seminole Tribe's Constitution (Aug. 21, 1957) was created and ratified through a long, difficult process prompted by threats of tribal termination by the Bureau of Indian Affairs to save money. The Seminoles were often at odds with the Miccosukees, who did not want to become part of the tribe in spite of efforts by Gov. LeRoy Collins to get them to join together. Seminole tribe historian Patsy West described the vote:

> All people over 21 were eligible to vote, and at least 30 percent of the 448-person Seminole population (and any Miccosukees who wished to) were required to vote in this election. The vote was 241 for and 5 against. Thus the Seminole Tribal Council replaced the traditional council of elders associated with the Corn Dance [Trail Indian] groups. The corporate charter of the Seminole Tribe of Florida, Inc. was also approved, by a vote of 223 for and 5 against. In this way, the members of the Seminole Tribe of Florida became the authors of their own destiny and the protectors of their inherent sovereignty.[37]

Today, the Seminole Tribe of Florida, Inc., is a federal corporation governed by a board of directors. Each tribal member shares equally in the ownership of the tribal corporation. The first elected chairman of the board was Billy Osceola. The first female chairperson, Betty Mae Tiger Jumper, was elected in 1967—making her the first female to head any Indian tribe in the United States. She chaired the Tribal Council from 1967 to 1971. Both Osceola and Jumper were among those who met under the Council Oak in Hollywood, voted to create the Seminole Tribe's constitutional government, and helped gain federal recognition of the tribe.

The Miccosukee Indians were originally part of the Creek Nation that moved to

Figure 1.18. Billy Osceola was the first elected chairman of the Seminole Tribe of Florida. State Archives of Florida, *Florida Memory*, https://www.floridamemory.com/items/show/82147. Photograph taken 1965.

Figure 1.19. Betty Mae Tiger Jumper was the first woman chairperson of the Seminole Tribe of Florida (elected 1967) and the first woman to head any Native-American tribe in the United States. State Archives of Florida, *Florida Memory*, https://www.floridamemory.com/items/show/4263, n.d.

Florida before it was even a state. The Miccosukee Tribe of Florida is smaller than the Seminole Tribe. Its operations and population are located on their Tamiami Trail Reservation. According to the Miccosukee Constitution, "the governing body of the Tribe is the Miccosukee General Council, which is composed of adult members 18 years of age or older. The officers of the General Council consist of the Chairman, Assistant Chairman, Treasurer, Secretary and Lawmaker. The officers are elected and seated during November and hold office for a term of four years."[38]

No member of either tribe has been elected to any state office in modern history. The tribes, particularly the Seminoles, have increased their influence over state politics, primarily on issues related to gambling. The tribes have been contributing large sums of money to candidates for state offices and state political parties for a number of years. It is just a matter of time before they push one of their own tribal members to seek a political office or position.

Why Study Florida's Minority Political Trailblazers?

Florida's role in national politics is well established. Part of the explanation for its growing muscle in national politics has been its extraordinary growth rate over the past several decades and its racial and ethnic diversity. This "melting-pot" state has produced some of the *nation's* minority path-breakers—the first of their race/ethnicity to hold national-level elected offices, such as Mel Martinez (R-Orlando), first Cuban to be elected to the U.S. Senate, and Ileana Ros-Lehtinen (R-Miami), first Cuban and the first Latina to be elected to the U.S. House of Representatives. In addition, Kendrick Meek and Carrie Meek are the first instance in national history of a son following his mother in the U.S. Congress.

The Sunshine State's minority populations are sizable, growing, and increasingly diverse. Its multiplicity of races, ethnicities, and countries of origin make it an ideal laboratory in which to study the commonalities and unique attributes of those we label *trailblazers*. Among the trailblazers included in this book, 41 percent were born outside the United States,[39] 12 percent had one or more parent born abroad, and 16 percent had one or more grandparent born outside the United States.

Within this rapidly growing state, minorities have forever changed the faces of the men and women from both political parties who govern at the state level (legislative, executive, and judicial branches) and represent Florida in the U.S. Congress.

To date, most studies of minority political successes in Florida have been time bound, focused on a specific race/ethnicity, and limited to specific offices. In contrast, this book uses a more evolutionary and holistic approach. Much of the historical data come from newspapers, government documents, and bibliographical sources. *But the richest data are the personal stories of the trailblazers themselves told in their own words.* It is these stories that form the heart of this book.

2

The Risk-Takers

Beating All Odds, Blazing the Trail for Others

Strategic candidates consider the past. Have other Latino, black, Asian candidates run for and won this office? Research has confirmed that **the initial hurdle is indeed the highest**.

Historically, roadblocks to winning state and national offices have been particularly steep for persons of color, often serving as deterrents to their even contemplating a run for higher office or acceptance of a path-breaking appointment. So what pushes some to be bold, while others just stand by?

Push Factors

Post-Reconstruction minority risk-takers in Florida were driven for a number of reasons—historical, demographic, structural/legal, political, and biographical. The last factor is oft-ignored but a trailblazer's personal attributes—gender, age, race/ethnicity, cultural identity, education, income, occupation, leadership experience—and networks, personal and professional, can help explain success at breaking down barriers. The time period also matters.

This chapter details the different push factors traditionally found in studies of who runs for office and why.

Historical

Historical Times

It has often been said that "timing is everything" in politics. Using that benchmark, one would expect minority path-breakers to have made their biggest gains on the heels of the Civil Rights Movement in the 1960s (African Americans), the feminist movement in the 1970s (minority women), and the large in-migration of Hispanics and Asians in the 1980s and 1990s.[1]

Issues of Injustice and Discrimination

For some, simply sitting on the sidelines while persons of their race/ethnicity were being subjected to severe discrimination became intolerable. Being part of the fight for civil rights became an integral part of their persona and forced them into action.[2]

Demographic

Changing Demographics; The Growing Clout of Racial/Ethnic Groups

The predominant theory is that the size of a minority group in a constituency is critical to minority candidate electoral success.[3] As Florida's population has swelled, minority shares of the population have grown, especially in the state's heavily urbanized areas, making it easier to carve out state legislative districts with sizable minority electorates. Initially, the federal courts' interpretation of the Voting Rights Act was that majority-minority districts had to be drawn wherever possible to enhance minorities' chances of being elected. But the U.S. Supreme Court changed its interpretation of the Act in the *Shaw v. Reno* (1993) ruling, which prohibits the use of race or ethnicity as the *primary* basis for drawing district lines. But there is clear evidence that redistricting at the state and local levels has increased minority representation in Florida.[4]

The growing size and clout of minority ethnic groups has also made it highly beneficial from a political perspective for Governors to appoint minorities to judicial posts at the highest level and at the trial court level when vacancies occur.[5] The Governor initially appoints the Justice of the Florida Supreme Court; voters later decide whether to retain the appointee for a full term. State court diversity—racial and gender—is carefully monitored by the National Center for State Courts.[6]

Structural/Legal

Multi-Member vs. Single-Member Districts

For many years, most legislators at the state level were elected from multi-member districts (MMDs).[7] In Florida, legislators ran for a specific seat within a larger geographical area (county or city) but were elected by all voters within the larger area. The gradual shift to single-member districts (SMDs) was largely driven by federal court rulings and laws judging MMDs to have a discriminatory impact on the election of minorities—much like at-large elections in general.[8] In 1982, with passage of the federal Voting Rights Act of 1982, Florida switched to SMDs to elect its state legislators.[9]

Redistricting (Open Seats)

A body of literature suggests that the creation of majority-minority districts either via redistricting or by court order enhances the chances a minority will be elected.[10]

In either situation, more open seats are created, which entices more first-time candidates to run. But there is no clear pattern of the impact of majority-minority seats, especially on Hispanic candidates.[11] Up for debate, even among minorities, is whether the creation of majority-minority districts may initially open up a seat but limit increases in the number of minority-held seats in the long term. Proponents of minority access or influence districts—minorities make up a sizable portion but not a majority of the district—make this argument.[12]

Term Limits (Open Seats)

Proponents of term limits argue that by creating open seats, they create more opportunities for minorities to win elective office.[13] Minorities, like Anglos, are more encouraged to run when there is no incumbent in the race. Indeed, there is evidence that in states with term limits, first-time candidates wait to run until there is an open seat.[14] At the same time, research has found a growing incidence of officials who are term limited out of one position seeking another.[15] So technically, even if it is an open seat, the presence of an experienced politico with high name recognition may have the same effect as having an incumbent in the race. This helps explain why some studies have found only moderate relationships between term limits and the election of minority candidates.[16]

Type of Position Sought

Theories along this line posit that minorities have a better shot at capturing legislative seats than executive or judicial posts and district-based positions more than statewide posts.[17] Within the executive branch, research shows women and minorities have better shots at the less-desirable offices and process-oriented jobs (agency heads) than at top-level positions (Governor, Lieutenant Governor, Cabinet).[18]

Vacancies Yielding Appointments and Special Elections (Open Seats)

Most research shows a higher incidence of election among those who have been appointed to fill vacancies, then sought election. In Florida, legislative vacancies must be filled by a special election. Many Florida trailblazers won their history-making office that way. Other research has concluded that minorities do better via appointments than elections. In Florida, the appointment-then-election pattern has more often been the case for minorities appointed to fill judicial[19] vacancies than vacant Cabinet posts.

Political

Party Competition (Bragging Rights)

In Florida, at least, there is some evidence that both major political parties have aggressively sought minority and female candidates and keep a score card on the number of each their party has in office.[20] Historically, Democrats have done better at recruiting blacks and Republicans at recruiting Hispanics, although each party has made inroads in recruiting candidates from each racial/ethnic group.

Volume and Tone of Media Political Coverage of Minority Candidacies

The role of the media in publicizing minority candidacies is up for debate. Some studies find the media is harmful in casting candidates narrowly as minority candidates and thereby limiting their potential crossover appeal. However, other studies find the media very helpful in promoting the idea of the path-breaker nature of a candidacy: "There is considerable debate about media coverage of minority candidates, especially about whether minority candidates receive less coverage than White candidates and whether minority candidates receive less favorable coverage than White candidates . . . [but] media coverage is *always* more extensive for the newer candidate."[21] There is a similar debate in the literature on women candidates.[22] Latinas often receive less frequent, more negative media coverage than their African-American counterparts.[23]

Discontent with Policies and Issues of the Day

Some entering the political fray are issue driven. This has become more of a candidacy driver in recent years as minorities have become more splintered in their political party and ideological leanings. They are upset that an issue of importance to them is either being handled poorly or receiving no attention at all. Issues such as immigration, vote suppression, capital punishment, education equity, homelessness, poverty, and health care have pushed some trailblazers to run. For many, their animosity was directed at the inattention to the issues by those in office at the time of their candidacy decision.

Racial/Ethnic Pride and Bloc Voting (Group Cohesion)

Minorities have a better chance of winning—especially in multicandidate races—because they bloc vote, often on the basis of the race/ethnicity of the candidate.[24] Victorious minority candidates frequently reflect ideological dispositions that are unique to their racial/ethnic background—a group consciousness and sense of linked fate.[25] Turnout and cohesiveness tend to be higher when a potential barrier breaker is running or if a minority candidate is under attack by Anglos. In general, this argument is more powerful for African-American than Hispanic or Asian candidates. Hispanics and Asians are more splintered politically than blacks[26] because those census group labels cover many ethnically and culturally divergent populations. However, in Florida, even the black population is becoming less cohesive as that population itself has become more diverse, often creating tensions between African Americans and Caribbean blacks (especially Haitians and Dominicans).[27] Other studies have also found that women tend to vote for women more than men for men regardless of party or race.[28]

Multiracial/Ethnic Coalitions

The smaller the minority population and the less cohesive, the more important white crossover votes become,[29] although minority women generate more white crossover votes than minority male candidates regardless of minority population size.[30] Asian-American candidates are more likely to depend on crossover votes than black or Hispanic groups.[31] In some instances, the major coalition is between the minority candidate and liberal whites (usually Democratic candidates), although in the case of Republican minority candidates it may be with conservative Anglos. However, in some tri-ethnic areas, the winning coalition might well be formed by two minority groups joining together against a white candidate.[32]

Biographical

Candidate Qualities: Gender, Age, Race/Ethnicity, Cultural Identity, Education, Income, Occupation, Leadership Experience

As with white candidates, successful minority candidates are better educated, wealthier, and more likely to have held leadership posts in civic or nonprofit groups than the bulk of their constituents and to come from the legal profession. For some minority trailblazers, their place of birth and family's cultural heritage reflect the strong country-of-origin (geo-based identity) sentiments among their constituents.

Gender and Race

The intersection of gender and race is often viewed as a "double negative," especially for women of color seeking political office—two hurdles to jump rather than one—"a struggle within a struggle." Historically, the common belief has been that it is a more difficult challenge to meet for Hispanic and Asian females because of their more patriarchal family structures than for black female candidates. But for black women seeking office, they, too, have confronted racism, classism, and sexism—and not always just from males.[33] By the mid-2010s, black and Hispanic women were running for and winning office at higher rates than men.[34] And research was showing that "minorities express greater support for female candidates than whites . . . attributable to the close correspondence between the political interests of blacks, Hispanics, and women."[35]

Candidate Networks

Kinship, friendships, and mentoring, often within the candidate's own minority community, can play a vital role. For blacks, networks developed through attending a

Figure 2.1. "*Because he showed us it could be done, we now have 12 where there was one.*" Members of the Legislative Black Caucus honored Joe Kershaw (*center, with plaque*) "for his pioneering spirt in becoming the first black to be elected to the Florida Legislature since Reconstruction." *Front row (L-R)*: Sen. Carrie Meek, Kershaw, and Sen. Arnett Girardeau. *Back row (L-R)*: Rep. Al Lawson, Rep. James Hargrett, Rep. Corrine Brown, Rep. Jefferson Reaves, Rep. James Burke, Rep. Doug Jamerson, and Rep. Alzo Reddick. *Not shown*: Reps. John Thomas and William A. "Bill" Clark. Photograph courtesy of and by Allen D. Stucks, Sr., April 1983, in the *Capitol Outlook*—a black newspaper published in Tallahassee.

historically black college or university, belonging to minority sororities and fraternities,[36] and membership in key black churches[37] have proven to be vital. For Hispanics and Asians, especially immigrants, religious and social organizations have historically provided valuable networks.[38]

A photo of 12 black legislators that appeared in the *Capitol Outlook*, a black newspaper published in Tallahassee, acknowledged the importance of alliances: "It is good to know that these 12 black legislators, like their national counterparts, the Congressional Black Caucus, recognize that while they may represent a specific constituency in the district from which they were elected, they also represent the hopes, dreams, needs and aspirations of all blacks in the state of Florida."

Understanding Trailblazers: What They Can Teach Us about Taking Risks for the Public Good

Studying the successes of pioneers can give us a keener sense of (1) the role of culture, kinships, friendships, and mentoring; (2) the importance of education, college

Figure 2.2. *Left to right*: State Reps. Luis Morse (R-Miami), Alex Villalobos (R-Miami), Elvin Martinez (D-Tampa), Miguel De Grandy (R-Miami), and Carlos A. Manrique (R-Miami) display a replica of the flag used by the Cuban exile group, Brigade 2506, that landed at the Bay of Pigs, Cuba, in 1961. Several legislators, including Morse, have ties to the Bay of Pigs, and the issue has been a unifying element for subsequent legislators. (Morse became the first Hispanic Republican Speaker pro tempore.) State Archives of Florida, *Florida Memory*, https://www.floridamemory.com/items/show/10262. Photograph by Donn Dughi (Donald Gregory), n.d.

and community organizations, and churches as socialization agents; (3) the impact of discrimination on candidacy rates; and (4) the importance of coalition building in settings where racial/ethnic minorities make up less than a majority of the voting public.

In the remainder of this volume, the trailblazers themselves detail what drove them to run (or accept an appointment), how they were successful, and, in the process, made political history. Their advice to young minorities considering a political career reflects their experiences along the way.

These personal accounts show that among Florida's successful risk-takers, individual push factors were clearly stronger motivators for some than others. But for all, effectively representing their constituents' needs was their primary goal once elected or appointed. Righting injustices and giving louder, more effective voices to Florida's underrepresented citizens were common threads binding them together over the past half century.

3

Trailblazers

The Florida Legislature—House and Senate

Minority successes in capturing legislative positions occurred in the House in the 1960s and in the Senate in the 1980s (see figures 3.2 and 3.3). In the early 1960s, U.S. Supreme Court rulings establishing the one-person, one-vote principle (*Baker v. Carr*, 1962; *Reynolds v. Sims*, 1964) forced major changes in the structure and geographical bases of state legislatures. Urban counties gained seats; rural areas lost some. The struggle for power between the old-time power brokers in the rural Panhandle of the state (labeled the "Pork Chop Gang") and the urbanites was fierce. Ultimately, the federal courts settled the battle.

Figure 3.1. Joint session of the Florida Legislature, 1979. State Archives of Florida, *Florida Memory*, https://www.floridamemory.com/items/show/20055.

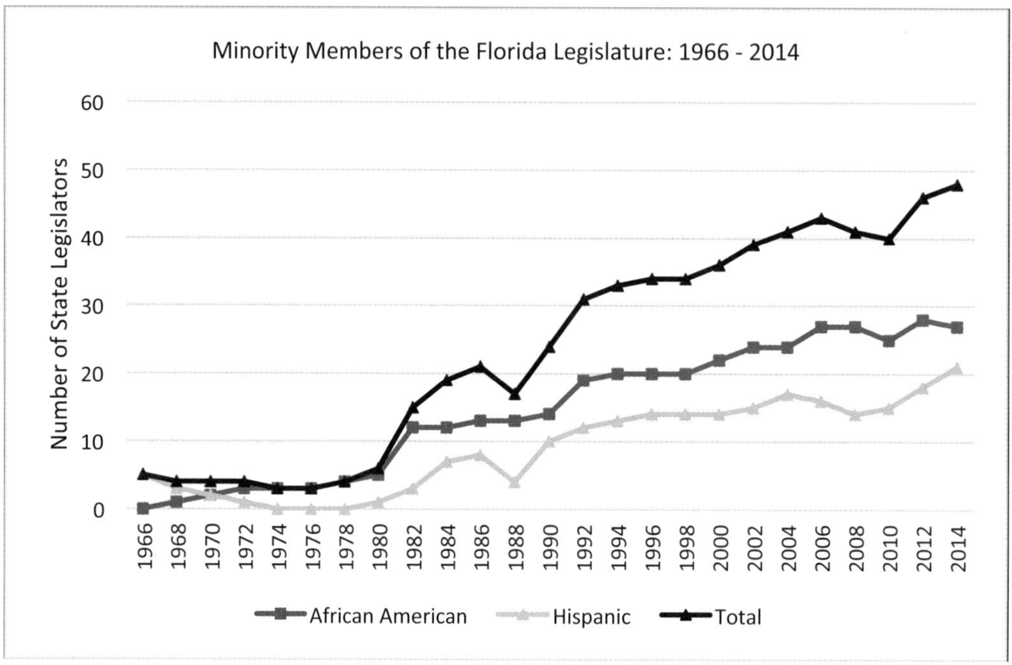

Figure 3.2. Minority members of the Florida Legislature, 1966–2014. Dates denoted are the beginning of the legislative term. Source: Compiled from Florida House and Senate Records. Excludes the two Asian Americans elected during this time period. (See Appendixes B, C.)

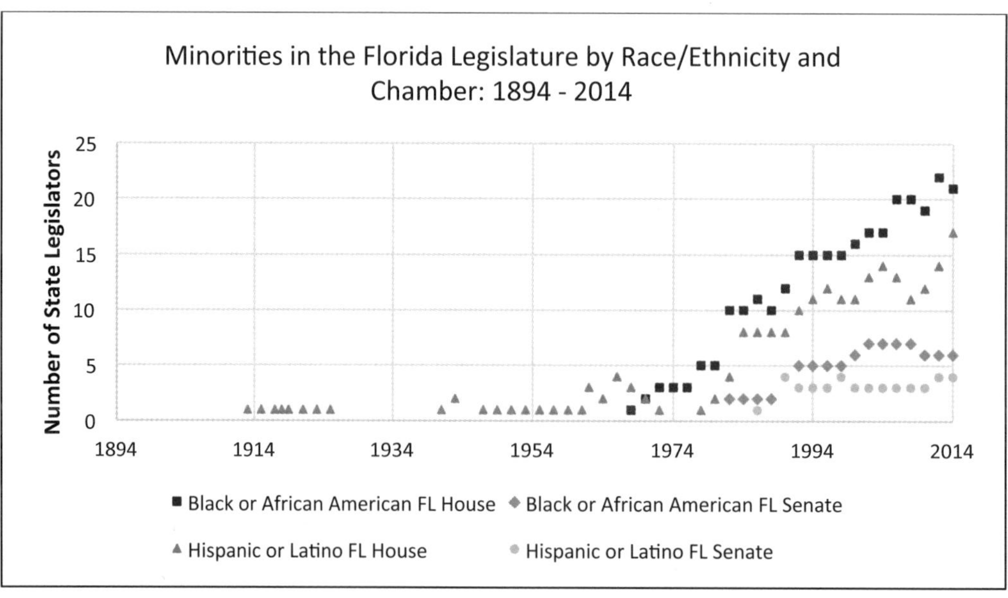

Figure 3.3. Minorities in Florida Legislature by race/ethnicity and chamber, 1894–2014. Dates denoted are the beginning of the legislative term. Source: Compiled from Florida House and Senate Records. (See Appendixes B, C.) Excludes the two Asian Americans elected during this time period.

Table 3.1. Changing size of the Florida House, 1962–1972 (two-year terms)

Election date/year	Number of members	Event
Mar. 26, 1962		*Baker v. Carr* (one-person, one-vote) ruling by the U.S. Supreme Court
Nov. 6, 1962	95	General election
Mar. 26, 1963	32	Special election to fill 30 additional seats following court-ordered reapportionment, plus two vacant seats due to resignations
Total	**127**	
Feb. 17, 1964		*Reynolds vs Sims*; U.S. Supreme Court rules that the one-person, one-vote principle was to apply to both houses of the Legislature
Nov. 3, 1964	112	General election
Nov. 8, 1966	117	General election; increase by court-ordered reapportionment
Jan. 9, 1967		*Swann v. Adams*; U.S. Supreme Court orders Florida to reapportion Legislature on one-person, one-vote basis
Mar. 28, 1967	119	Special election following court-ordered reapportionment
Nov. 5, 1968	119	Adoption of 1968 Constitution setting maximum size of House at 120; general election
Nov. 3, 1970	119	General election
Nov. 7, 1972	120	Legislature had approved maximum number during regular session reapportionment

Source: Personal communication with the Office of the Clerk of the House of Representatives, updated July 11, 2013.

Note: For details regarding the reapportionment controversies, see Skene, "Reapportionment in Florida."

The initial Florida reapportionment fight did not end until 1967, when a special federal court rejected a legislatively drawn plan and ordered a court-adopted plan into effect seven days before the regular session was to begin. Prior to that, multiple court-ordered reapportionments following various legislative attempts to redistrict each chamber produced several rounds of elections in different-sized chambers. (See table 3.1 for fluctuations in House size; table 3.2 for changes in Senate size.)

Other major structural changes occurred in the early 1980s and 1990s. In 1982, single-member districts replaced the old multi-member districts,[1] prompting more minorities to run for legislative posts. In 1992, Florida voters overwhelmingly (76 percent) approved Amendment 9 creating legislative term limits—two four-year terms for Senators, four two-year terms for Representatives. Minorities strongly believed that term limits would create more open seats and enhance the election of people of color.

Redistricting decisions made in 1992[2] and 2002, calling for drawing majority-minority or minority-influence districts where possible, also played key roles in ex-

Table 3.2. Changing size of the Florida Senate, 1962–1972 (four-year terms)

Election date/year	Number of members	Event
Mar. 26, 1962		*Baker v. Carr* (one-person, one-vote) ruling by the U.S. Supreme Court
Nov. 6, 1962	38	General election
Jan. 29, 1963	43	Special session; passed law to comply with order of U.S. District Court of Appeal
Mar. 26, 1963	43 (45)	Special election; two Senators carried over under law allowing them to complete full term
Feb. 17, 1964		*Reynolds v. Sims*; U.S. Supreme Court rules that the one-person, one-vote principle was to apply to both houses of the Legislature
Apr. 6, 1965	43 (44)	Regular session; one Senator elected in November 1962 carried over
Nov. 8, 1966	48	General election; size was increased by Legislature during regular session
Jan. 9, 1967		*Swann v. Adams*; U.S. Supreme Court orders Florida to reapportion Legislature on one-person, one-vote basis
Mar. 28, 1967	48	Special election; state was redistricted; all 48 who won election in 1966 had to run again under terms of the reapportionment order of the U.S. District Court of Appeal
Nov. 5, 1968	48	All 48 were elected for four-year terms
Nov. 5, 1968		Voter approval of 1968 Constitution setting maximum size of Senate at 40
Nov. 7, 1972	40	Legislature had approved maximum number during regular session reapportionment; set up staggered terms; initially four-year terms for Senators elected from odd-numbered districts, two-year terms for those from even-numbered districts

Source: Personal communication with the Office of the Clerk of the House of Representatives, updated July 11, 2013.

Note: For details regarding the reapportionment controversies, see Skene, "Reapportionment in Florida."

panding minority representation in both houses of the Florida Legislature (see figures 3.2 and 3.3).

It was in the 2000s that minority legislative trailblazers with family roots in Latin America began to get elected, reflecting several decades of significant in-migration from those countries . . . and not just from Cuba. The most recent trailblazers have roots in other Spanish-speaking countries and in Creole-speaking Caribbean countries like Haiti.

A Closer Look at Reapportionment Battles in the 1960s

Beginning in the mid-1950s, a decade before the 1967 court-adopted plan was put in place, Gov. LeRoy Collins (D) had begun pushing the legislators to develop a plan that would "allocate seats as nearly equal in population as 'practicable.'" At the time, 18 percent of the voters could elect a majority in the Senate and 17.6 percent a majority in the House.[3] Scholars like V. O. Key described Florida's Legislature as the most unrepresentative in the nation for its gross underrepresentation of the state's rapidly growing urban areas.[4]

During Gov. Collins's tenure, he called the Legislature into several special sessions, but they failed to produce any reapportionment plans. In 1962, Gov. Farris Bryant (D) convened the Legislature in a special session after a three-judge panel of the U.S. District Court in Tallahassee found Florida's existing constitutional and statutory provisions relating to apportionment to be "prospectively null, void, and inoperative." The Legislature submitted a proposed constitutional amendment to the voters to increase the number of Senate districts from 38 to 46 and the House seats from 95 to 135. The voters rejected it.

Gov. Bryant proceeded to call the Legislature into two more special sessions (November 1962, January 1963). During the second session, on February 1, 1963, the Legislature produced a 43-Senator, 112-Representative plan, which the three-judge special federal court allowed to stand through the 1963 session. However, in the 1963 session, there were still 45 Senators and 125 Representatives. Senators and Representatives elected in 1962, but whose offices would be abolished under the new apportionment, were grandfathered in.

The 43-Senator, 112-Representative plan was subsequently rejected by the U.S. Supreme Court and by the voters (who again decided against the legislative expansion). In January 1965, the three-judge panel of the U.S. District Court in Tallahassee ordered the Legislature to reapportion *both* houses on a population basis by July 1, 1965. The Legislature then adopted a reapportionment plan calling for 109 House members and 58 Senators. Again the three-judge federal court approved it, only to be reversed by the U.S. Supreme Court, which cited invidious discrimination against urban citizens.

Newly elected Gov. Haydon Burns (D) called the Legislature into special session in March 1966, and it passed a plan calling for 48 Senators and 117 House members[5] that stood until January 1967. The U.S. Supreme Court in *Swann v. Adams*, ordered the three-judge panel to reexamine the plan, and it did. It then rejected the plan along with an alternative 48-Senator, 120-House member plan. Both plans had population variances that the court determined were too high to meet the one-person, one-vote requirement. Ultimately, the three-judge court approved a 48-Senator, 119-House member plan submitted by Manning Dauer, a University of Florida political science professor, as an *amicus curiae* brief. His plan had only a 5 percent maximum population variance, compared to the 16 percent variance of the rejected alternative plan.

Within months a new Legislature was formed that oversaw the modernization of state government, the abandonment of segregation, and the rise of the Republican Party.[6] Although few white leaders would have acknowledged it in the '60s, federal officials had done Florida an enormous favor by removing racial extremism and rural domination from its politics.[7]

Some of the more intense redistricting controversies in recent years have featured conflicts between blacks and Hispanics, and between ethnic groups (identity or country-of-origin politics), especially in the heavily populated South Florida areas where residential segregation patterns are less evident than in years past.[8]

Beginning in 1982, each successive round of redistricting after a census has yielded major court battles challenging the fairness of the districting plans drawn by the Legislature. Even after voters approved a Fair Districts amendment mandating fairer drawing of districts (2010), litigation ensued after the 2012 redistricting, challenging the legislatively approved House, Senate, and congressional plans. As in the past, how well the newly drawn districts complied with the federal Voting Rights Act's requirements for minority districts was a key part of the litigation, as was the degree to which plans complied with the Fair Districts amendments. As of this writing, litigation is still ongoing with the plans for Senate and Congress.

African-American/Caribbean-Black Successes

The first black Floridians elected to the state House of Representatives during Reconstruction were Republicans (17 of 53 House members and 3 of 24 Senators). Many were delegates to the constitutional convention of 1868.[9]

One hundred years later (1968), Joe Lang Kershaw (D-Miami) made history as the first post-Reconstruction African American elected to the Florida Legislature. He was followed in 1970 by the first black female legislator, Gwen Cherry (D-Miami), an attorney and graduate of Florida A&M University. The first black state Senators since Reconstruction, both Democrats, were elected in 1982—Arnett E. Girardeau from Jacksonville and Carrie Meek from Miami.

The impact of several decades of blacks migrating to Florida from the Caribbean resulted in the election of several Caribbean black legislators from South Florida. Haitian American Phillip Brutus (D) was elected to the Florida House of Representatives in 2000. In 2002, he was joined by another Haitian state legislator, his ex-wife Yolly Roberson (D). Political party often matters less than national ancestry among Haitians when it comes to voting. In 2001, Joe Celestin, a Republican, was elected mayor of the City of North Miami, even though 87 percent of the Haitian voters were registered Democrats.

Figure 3.4. State Rep. Gwyndolen Clarke-Reed, D-Pompano Beach (*left*) joins colleagues *(L-R)* Hazelle Rogers (D-Lauderdale Lakes), James Bush III (D-Miami), and Maria Sachs (R-Delray Beach) in discussing a bill on the House floor, April 30, 2009. State Archives of Florida, *Florida Memory*, https://www.floridamemory.com/items/show/135428. Photograph by Meredith Hill Geddings.

South Florida is also home to the second largest Jamaican population outside Jamaica—heavily concentrated in Miami-Dade, Broward, and Palm Beach counties. Political turmoil in Jamaica in the 1970s prompted many to leave their country. As with Haitians, Jamaican-born blacks have successfully entered the political arena. Democrat Hazelle Rogers from Broward County was the first Jamaican elected to the state House in 2008. In 2011, Democrat Oscar Braynon II was the first of Jamaican (and Bahamian) heritage to be elected to the Senate.

In 2003, former naval officer and head of the Florida Department of Veterans Affairs under Republican Gov. Jeb Bush, Jennifer Carroll (R-Jacksonville), born in Trinidad, became the first black from that Caribbean country to be elected to the House of Representatives. She was also the first black Republican female to serve in the House.

A number of black trailblazers have strong family ties to the Bahamas—Edward Bullard (D-Miami) was the first person born there (Nassau) to serve in the House. Frederica Wilson (D-Miami)—House and Senate—has maternal grandparents and many cousins who still live there.

The connection of black legislators with strong Bahamian roots to those with Caribbean roots, especially Jamaican, was evident in the friendship between Bahamian Gwyndolen Clarke-Reed (D-Deerfield Beach),[10] whose grandparents came from the Bahamas, and Hazelle Rogers, who was born in Jamaica. Bahamians Perry Thurston (D-Fort Lauderdale), Oscar Braynon II (D-Miami Gardens), and Dwight Bullard (D-Miami) along with Haitians Ronald Brisé (D-North Miami), Yolly Roberson (D-North Miami Beach), Phillip Brutus (D-North Miami), and Daphne D. Campbell (D-Miami Shores) as well as Trinidad/Tobago-born Jennifer Carroll (R-Jacksonville) were part of the Caribbean Caucus—an informal group that routinely holds

"Caribbean Day" at the Capitol during April—Caribbean-American Heritage Month. Whether focusing on the Caribbean community or the entire state, Clarke-Reed, like many other legislators, has found her experience in the Capitol "humbling"—"just to try to get people to understand that we're all human beings and we all have needs and try to meet those needs."

In addition to Carroll, there have been only a handful of black Republican legislators since Reconstruction. In 1980, a black Republican named John "Gus" Plummer was elected to the Florida House from Miami. Interestingly, few knew he was black. His campaign strategy was to stay out of the public eye and to take advantage of the name of a prominent white family in the Miami area. His campaign slogan was "The family name Plummer speaks for itself." Gus was a one-term House member. The nature of his candidacy has led some to regard conservative Mike Hill of Pensacola, elected in 2013, as the first modern-day black Republican male legislator. Hill, along with Carroll, had a military background and both won special elections to fill vacancies.

Hispanic Successes

Even before Florida became a state in 1845, Hispanics had been involved in governing the people who lived there (see Appendix C). In the Usina family, who were Minorcan/Spanish and had settled near St. Augustine (port of entry for Ponce de Leon) in the 1500s, former Confederate soldier Domingo Benito Usina was elected to the House in 1891, setting a precedent for his grandson, Frederick Charles Usina, a trailblazer in this book.

Over the decades, Hispanic political influence in the state Legislature has increased. Those elected during the chaotic days of reapportionment in the early 1960s—all men and mostly Democrats—represented different countries of origin (Spain, Cuba, Puerto Rico). Maurice Ferré (Puerto Rican) and Elvin Martinez (Spaniard/Cuban) were elected from South Florida and Tampa, respectively—areas with long-established Hispanic populations. Several others (Frederick Charles Usina, Louis de la Parte) had families who in-migrated from Spain.

The next group of Hispanics elected to the House came in the early 1980s. Republican Roberto Casas became the first Cuban-American legislator in the Florida House in 57 years when he won a special election in 1982, just ahead of Humberto Cortina. Casas, Cortina, and Ileana Ros were the first class of Cubans to serve together in the House. Ros (later Ros-Lehtinen), who immigrated from Havana to Miami in 1960 at the age of eight, became the first Cuban woman elected to the state House of Representatives in 1982, then to the state Senate in 1986. In 1988, Casas and Javier Souto were the first Cuban males to be elected to the Florida Senate. When the legendary Democratic Congressman Claude Pepper died in 1989, Ros-Lehtinen won the special election for his vacant seat. The replacement of the aged liberal Democrat with a youthful Republican woman marked a historic shift in Miami and Florida politics.

In the 1990s, Miami's Annie Betancourt became the first female Cuban Democrat elected to the Florida House. Democrat Susan Bucher, of Mexican descent, also from South Florida (Broward County) followed in 2004. On a broader note, it was in the 1970s that female representation in the Legislature began an upward trend, reflecting the impact of the women's rights movement.

For years, Cuban Americans were actually overrepresented relative to their proportional makeup of Florida's population, while non-Cuban Hispanics were underrepresented. But that has been changing. The state's first Puerto Rican legislator was Maurice A. Ferré (D-Miami), elected to serve in the 1967 1968 session. In 2002, John Quiñones became the first Puerto Rican Republican to be elected to the House, while Democrat Darren Soto was the first Puerto Rican elected to the Florida Senate. Both were from the Orlando area where the Puerto Rican population was growing rapidly. The state's first legislator from Colombia was Juan C. Zapata (R-Miami), 2002; of Ecuadorian heritage, Ricardo Rangel (D-Kissimmee), 2012; and from Nicaragua, Ana Rivas Logan, a Republican (at the time) from Miami.

Asian Successes

Because Asian Americans make up a small portion of the voting public in most parts of the state, they must attract crossover votes from whites, blacks, and Hispanics to win. Asian-American candidates must also court other racial/ethnic groups because 30 percent of Asian adults are not citizens.[11] To date, multiracial coalitions have been a bit more successful in South Florida than elsewhere in the state.

The first Asian member of the Florida Legislature, Edmond "Eddie" Gong (D) from Miami-Dade County, was elected to the House in 1962, then to the Senate in

Figure 3.5. Freshman legislators Edmond Gong and Mary Ann MacKenzie, both Democrats from Dade County, enjoy meeting Rep. Lawton Chiles, D-Polk County (*left*) and House Speaker Mallory Horne, D-Leon County (*right*), the day before the 1963 session began. State Archives of Florida, *Florida Memory*, https://www.floridamemory.com/items/show/33541. Photograph taken April 1, 1963.

1966, becoming the first American of Chinese ancestry to serve in the Florida Legislature. He graduated from the large multiracial Miami High School, Harvard, and later the University of Miami School of Law.

The first Asian-American woman serving in the state House was Mimi McAndrews (D) from Palm Beach County, elected in 1992. McAndrews is Korean. Formerly the legislative aide to Democratic State Rep. Lois Frankel, McAndrews successfully ran for her boss's old seat in a special election. (Frankel had resigned to run for Governor.) Frankel gave McAndrews her blessing and enlisted party support for the candidate. But Frankel lost her bid for Governor and successfully wrestled her old seat back from McAndrews at the next election. Like Gong, McAndrews is a lawyer.

There have been no Republican legislators of Asian descent.

Leadership Posts: President of the Senate and Speaker of the House

Legislative leadership posts in each chamber are powerful positions. In addition to presiding over sessions of the full membership, the Speaker of the House and the President of the Senate have:

- The exclusive right to appoint the members of all committees and to remove committee members.
- The exclusive right to choose the chair of all committees.
- The exclusive right to refer bills to committees.
- The ability to influence, through the chair of the Committee on Rules and Calendar, the placing of bills on the Special Order Calendar.
- The authority to appoint members of their chambers and other citizens to councils and commissions that operate outside the Legislature, such as the Constitution Revision Commission and the Commission on Ethics.[12]
- The authority to determine all administrative actions including member parking, office space, staff hires, salaries, purchases, contracts, etc.

Both the Senate President and the House Speaker are elected by the members of their respective chambers, after having been nominated by the members of their own party in caucus. Their terms last two years, running from one organization session to the next. Politically, these positions have been viewed as launch pads for those aspiring to run for statewide or congressional offices.

Only two minorities, both Hispanics, have held the top legislative leadership posts in the Senate and the House. In July 1974, Louis de la Parte (D-Tampa), whose family is from Spain, stepped up from his Senate President Pro Tempore position to become President of the Senate after his predecessor Mallory Horne (D-Tallahassee) resigned to run for the Democratic nomination to the U.S. Senate.[13] De la Parte served as President only until the November Organization Session (after the general election) when Sen. Dempsey Barron (D-Panama City) took over. (As was/is the custom, Barron had already been selected before Horne stepped down.)

During Sen. de la Parte's long service in the Senate (1966–1974) and House (1962–1966), he focused on programs to help less fortunate and mentally disabled Floridians and was instrumental in building the Department of Health and Rehabilitative Services. His legacy lives on. In 1996, the Florida Mental Health Institute at the University of South Florida was named after him. He was personally touched by the gesture. By that time, he had already experienced the early onset of Alzheimer's. The impact of minority trailblazers on others was reflected in the comments of former State Rep. Bob Henriquez, a younger cousin of the Senator: "He was an idol of mine growing up. He was the icon of the family and represented everything that is good about public service and government service and really inspired me in ways that I don't think he ever knew."[14]

Marco Rubio, a Cuban Republican from Miami, was the first minority Speaker of the House, who served in the post from 2006[15] to 2008. On the day he was selected by his House colleagues to be Speaker-designate, Rubio referenced his heritage: "I want to send a special welcome to those who are listening to this ceremony on the island of Cuba via Radio Martí. One day, very soon, you too will be able to choose the men and women who represent you in government."[16] Prior to becoming Speaker, Rubio had served as Majority Whip, then Majority Leader. Rubio started his tenure as Speaker in a rather unusual way—by compiling a book titled *100 Innovative Ideas for Florida's Future* that he gave to each legislator. Rubio generated these ideas from traveling around the state prior to becoming Speaker.[17]

As Speaker, Rubio received a great deal of media attention that undoubtedly raised his name recognition among Florida voters. That, along with his fiscal conservatism appeal to Tea Party activists, helped him win a seat in the U.S. Senate in 2010—at the height of Tea Party successes at capturing offices across the nation.

Postscript: Lawsuits, Structural Changes, and Immigrant In-Migration Increase Diversity

The faces of Florida's legislators are now much more diverse than in the 1960s when civil rights leaders said, "Exclude us no more." The biggest breakthrough in minority representation occurred as a consequence of a series of U.S. Supreme Court decisions that pushed Florida away from a county-based to a population-based representational system, then ordered redistricting plans to be drawn in compliance with the federal Voting Rights Act. Blacks and Hispanics began capturing more seats in the 1960s, most noticeably in the House, when more legislators were elected from urban areas with the largest concentrations of minority residents.

The adoption of single-member districts in 1982 and the imposition of term limits in 1992 further opened up the system by creating more open seats. Waves of immigrants from Latin American countries under political duress and economic strife, along with the return of African Americans from northern states, grew minority populations in South and Central Florida and ultimately diversified each party's legislative candidate pool. The women's movement in the 1970s and the educational advancement of women served to bring more minority women into office as well.

The Florida House of Representatives

Figure 3.6. The House is in session. An interior view of the Florida House of Representatives. State Archives of Florida, *Florida Memory*, https://www.floridamemory.com/items/show/17753. Photograph by Donn Dughi (Donald Gregory), n.d.

Florida Minority Trailblazers—Florida House of Representatives: 1960s–2010s

Florida Representatives appear in chronological order. Those elected the same year are listed alphabetically.

Time frame	Male	Female	Male Speaker	Female Speaker
1960s	1942–1944, 1946–1966 Frederick Charles Usina, Jr.—D Spain—St. Augustine			
	1963–1966[a] Edmond J. Gong—D China—Miami			
	1966–1974, 1978–1997 Elvin Martinez—D Cuba, Spain—Tampa			
	1967–1968 Maurice A. Ferré—D Puerto Rico—Miami			
	1967–1970 Joseph M. Martinez, Jr.—R Spain—Hollywood			
	1968–1982 Joe Lang Kershaw—D African American—Miami			
1970s		1970–1979 Gwendolyn "Gwen" Sawyer Cherry—D African American—Miami		
1980s	1980–1982 John "Gus" Plummer—R[b] African American—Miami			
		1982–1986 Ileana Ros-Lehtinen—R Cuba—Miami		
	1982–1988 Roberto Casas—R Cuba—Hialeah			
	1982–1984 Humberto Cortina—R Cuba—Miami			
1990s		1992–1994 Mimi K. McAndrews—D Korea—Palm Beach County		
		1994–2002 Annie Betancourt—D Cuba—Miami 1998–2002 Frederica S. Wilson—D Bahamas—Miami		

Time frame	Male	Female	Male Speaker	Female Speaker
2000s	2000–2006 Phillip J. Brutus—D Haiti—Miami Shores	2000–2008 Susan Bucher—D Mexico—Palm Beach County		
	2000–2008 Edward B. Bullard—D Bahamas—Miami			
	2002–2007 John "Q" Quiñones—R Puerto Rico—Orlando Area	2002–2010 Yolly Roberson—D Haiti—Miami		
	2002–2010 Juan C. Zapata—R Colombia—Miami	2003–2010 Jennifer S. Carroll—R Trinidad—Jacksonville		
			2006–2008 Marco Rubio—R Cuba—Miami	
		2008–Present Hazelle P. "Hazel" Rogers—D Jamaica—Broward County		
2010s		2010–2012 Ana Rivas Logan—R Nicaragua/ Cuba—Miami-Dade		
	2012–2014 Ricardo Rangel—D Ecuador—Kissimmee Area			
	2013–Present Walter Bryan "Mike" Hill—R[c] African American—Pensacola Area			

Note: Consult Appendixes B and C for a full listing of minority officeholders in Florida.

[a]Minorities elected in 1962 were from a smaller House of Representatives that were elected before the federal courts found Florida's legislature to be in violation of the one-person, one-vote principle.

[b]Technically, John "Gus" Plummer was the first black Republican male elected since Reconstruction, but no one knew he was black. His advertising built off the name of a white Plummer who was already in the Legislature. Thus, Mike Hill (elected in 2013) became the first "openly black" male Republican. He defeated a white labor leader.

[c]See note b.

Frederick Charles Usina, Jr. (D)

First Spanish-American man to be elected to the Florida House of Representatives in the mid-1960s (the beginning time point for this book—the one-person, one-vote era; Usina actually served prior to that)

Personal: Born June 13, 1903, St. Augustine, Florida; married with three children. Died May 31, 1966.

Education: Graduated from eighth grade, no high school

Occupation: Alligator Farm Operator/Owner of Charlesdale's Clothing Store, which was later a bar

Trailblazer Elections:

- House of Representatives, 11 terms (1942–1944, 1946–1966)
- House of Representatives, St. Johns County, *Dem Primary* 1964
  - Frederick Charles Usina, Jr.—*Unopposed*
- House of Representatives, St. Johns County, *General Election 1964*
  - Frederick Charles Usina, Jr.—*Unopposed*

Figure 3.7. State Rep. Frederick Charles Usina served St. Augustine and St. Johns County for 22 years. His Minorcan family roots can be traced back more than 200 years to New Smyrna, then St. Augustine. In memorializing him, Democratic colleagues described him as "the conscience of the House of Representatives." Photograph courtesy of his children, Malinda Usina Jones and Gary Usina.

THE FREDERICK CHARLES USINA, JR., STORY

Although Frederick Charles "Charlie" Usina, Jr.,[18] served in the Florida House of Representatives for 22 years, he viewed his political career as more of a public service pastime. A highly successful businessman, he represented St. Augustine and St. Johns County through the post–World War II era and into the social and political upheavals of the Sixties.

"Going to Tallahassee was just a high for him to be involved," said his son Gary Usina. Politics "wasn't his sole source of support and income. I think he just enjoyed the process. It was not as acrimonious as it is today."

It was a different era and he was a different politician. "To the best of my knowledge, he never accepted any political contributions, and I don't think he ever made a dime off of whatever influence he might have had or didn't have," Gary continued. On one occasion, "there was a bill to increase the legislators' per diem, and he offered an amendment to reduce it."

Charlie was a Democrat at a time when Democrats dominated the state, serving through a succession of eight Democratic Governors. Because of the area he represented, he was a "pork chopper," the name given to rural legislators elected by a small proportion of voters but having big power in the Legislature. He enjoyed his position, not because he could wield power but rather because he knew what it was like to be powerless.

His roots were deeply implanted in colonial Florida. On his mother's side (Oliveros), ancestors were in St. Augustine in the late 1500s. On his father's side, one of his earliest ancestors, Antoni Alsina (as the name was spelled then), came to Florida's eastern coast two and a half centuries ago, before the American colonies declared their independence. Antoni had left his birthplace on the island of Minorca in the Mediterranean Sea when he was 19. His ancestors had lived in the Balearic Islands off the eastern coast of Spain since the 13th century.

Antoni came as part of a colony organized by a Britisher, Dr. Andrew Turnbull, after Britain had gained control of Minorca (1713) as well as Spanish Florida (1763). Turnbull gathered settlers at Minorca for the sea voyage, and because of recent crop failures on the island, many Minorcans, including Antoni, joined the group. Arriving at New Smyrna, which Turnbull had named after his wife's birthplace, Antoni and other settlers began clearing trees, draining swamps, and planting crops such as indigo. The harsh conditions plus disease and scarce food caused many to die, including Antoni's young wife. By 1777, things had gotten so bad that the settlers evacuated to St. Augustine, 70 miles away. They settled around Fort Mose, which later became a sanctuary for slaves escaping from the American colonies.

A few years later, in 1783, Spain recovered Florida as part of the Treaty of Paris, which ended the American Revolutionary War. Spain, in its turn, began offering land grants to settlers to strengthen its hold on the colony. With the influx of Americans plus the hostility between settlers and Indians, the U.S. military began expeditions into Florida. Andrew Jackson battled the Seminoles in what became known as the First Seminole War in 1817–1818.

In 1821 Spain ceded Florida to the United States, and in the 1830s, U.S. troops fought the Indians in the Second Seminole War, forcing them to move to what is now Oklahoma. A small band of Seminoles eventually found refuge in the Everglades, and the U.S. military gave up trying to capture them.

As a U.S. territory, Florida attracted settlers from the plantation country of Virginia, the Carolinas, and Georgia. By 1850, five years after Florida had become a state, nearly half its population consisted of African-American slaves.[19] The Usinas, who were small farmers and shopkeepers like most Floridians, populated St. Augustine and New Smyrna in growing numbers.

In January 1861, the Governor called a special state convention to consider Florida's secession from the Union. The delegates, most of whom were slave owners, voted to secede. Within a few weeks, Florida and other Southern states formed the Confederacy. In May 1861, Domingo Benito Usina (Charlie's grandfather) enlisted in the Third Florida Volunteers in the Confederate Army. He was only 16. In the summer of 1862 he fought in at least two battles in Kentucky and was honorably discharged after suffering a wound in the right arm. Earlier that year, federal troops had occupied St. Augustine. When Domingo tried to return home, he was imprisoned.

After the war, Domingo operated a dairy and dry goods store. In 1891 he represented St. Johns County in the Florida House of Representatives, unknowingly setting a precedent for his future grandson. He was one of the "Original 52" who supported U.S. Sen. Wilkinson Call (1879–1897) in holding his Senate seat against a challenger.[20] Domingo then served for six years as St. Augustine's postmaster (1892–1895) and six years as city treasurer (circa 1907–1910).

During this time Domingo and his wife reared six children, one of whom was Frederick Charles "Freddie" Usina, Sr. They were among the citizens of St. Augustine who bid farewell to the soldiers heading to Cuba in 1898 during the War with Spain. Domingo's residence displayed a banner, "God Bless Our Boys."

Around the turn of the century, Freddie Usina and a business partner operated a cigar factory that covered a whole block on Cordova Street and employed 200 workers. After the partner absconded with the money, Freddie made cigars in back of a garage on Saragossa Street where the family lived. He called the business La Usina Cigar Company. "He made this low-end cigar that everybody liked," said Gary. "Then he tried to go high-end and went broke." Cigar factories in St. Augustine shut down as machines were invented to roll tobacco.[21]

Charlie, who was born in 1903, attended Catholic schools in St. Augustine but never went beyond the eighth grade. As a teen, he worked odd jobs, one of which was selling clothing in a retail shop. On one occasion, he encountered Herbert E. Wolfe, probably the richest man in town. When Charlie complimented the tycoon's suit, Wolfe said, "Well, why don't you get you one, Charlie?" That remark, probably made in full knowledge that he couldn't afford one, served to motivate the young man.

He and longtime friend W. I. Drysdale, also a descendant of a colonial settler, opened a men's clothing store, Charlesdale's, when they were in their early 20s. "They did everything together," Gary said. "As young boys, they raised goats together." With ready access to first-class menswear—and perhaps still feeling the sting of Wolfe's comment—Charlie made it a habit to dress well. "He was the snappiest dresser you ever saw—and was known for that in the Legislature," said daughter Malinda Usina Jones.

In the early 1920s, as part of the Great Florida Land Boom, thousands of people swarmed into St. Augustine by train and automobile to buy land or spend the winter. Boom soon turned into bust, however, as the nation slid into the Great Depression. Perhaps anticipating better times and confident of their own business acumen,

Figure 3.8. Usina (*right*) and longtime friend and business partner W. I. Drysdale (another descendant of a colonial settler) purchased the famed Alligator Farm in 1937 during the depths of the Depression. Under their ownership, the Alligator Farm flourished and helped establish the state's tourist industry. In 1992 the attraction was listed on the National Register of Historic Places. Photograph courtesy of the Usina family (daughter Malinda Usina Jones and son Gary Usina), 1947.

Charlie and Drysdale decided to buy the Alligator Farm, which had been operating for 40 years on Anastasia Island.[22]

But getting the funding proved difficult. Gary remembered a story his dad told about going to talk to his Uncle Leonard, a Miami banker. While Charlie was inside trying to get a loan, Drysdale stayed outside. When Charlie and his uncle emerged, saying the bank had taken the loan under advisement, Drysdale said, "Some guy just tried to panhandle me for a quarter." Seizing the moment, Charlie said, "Where is he? Where is he? I've got to find him."

"They got the loan and bought the farm at possibly the worst possible time you could ever buy something," Gary said. It was 1937, when the nation was still in the grip of the Depression and the prelude to war was rumbling in Europe. At that time, the Alligator Farm consisted of a wood frame building, a gift shop, pens that contained numerous reptiles, animal and bird displays, and several acres of undeveloped land.

Within months of their purchase, fire destroyed the main building. Others might have given up, but not this pair. In rebuilding, they turned the new structure to face Anastasia Boulevard to attract more tourists. They chose a Mission Style design, inspired by Spanish American architecture. They began an aggressive promotional campaign, both locally and nationally. For example, they had a football made out of alligator skin to present to the winner of the Gator Bowl game every year. Later they hired the Bacon, Hartman, and Vollbrecht public relations firm in Jacksonville, which set up publicity events in New York and other cities. They formed the Florida Attractions Association, along with Silver Springs, Parrot Jungle, Monkey Jungle, the McKee Botanical Garden and the Serpentarium—all before Disney World came to Orlando.

"They were successful," Gary said. In his father's case, in particular, "I think his success was attributed to his love of people, all kinds of people."

In addition to running the Alligator Farm, Charlie began buying and selling real estate with another partner. They agreed to the partnership on a handshake. "His partner was a wonderful man," said Gary. After his father's death, as executor of the estate, Gary sat down with the partner to divide up 24 holdings. "Over two nights we just discussed like this: 'We'll take this one, you take that one.' It was very amicable, it went very smoothly."

Charlie bought at least one piece of property without a partner. "He bought this horrible house on Water Street in St. Augustine," said Gary. "I asked him why. He said, 'Because my father couldn't.'" Charlie had tried to buy a house on Water Street some time earlier, when the houses were owned by doctors and friends of Herbert Wolfe, and probably had deed restrictions. They sold to railway executives and other well-to-do families but not to Charlie. That practice implied discrimination against certain groups of people, such as those of Minorcan heritage. Over time, said Gary, "some of those deed restrictions in Florida have mysteriously disappeared."

When the Japanese attacked Pearl Harbor in December 1941, the United States entered World War II. In June 1942 four German saboteurs from a submarine came ashore at Ponte Vedra, just a few miles north of St. Augustine, carrying explosives and American money. They were captured before they could do any harm, but the incident terrified Floridians. Coast Guard units began patrolling the beaches.

Much of St. Augustine became involved in the war effort. The old Ponce de Leon Hotel, which had been built in 1888 by Standard Oil cofounder Henry Flagler, became a training academy for the Coast Guard. Camp Blanding, 70 miles to the west, had a sub-post in St. Augustine for training military police. Although the Civic Center provided recreational activities for soldiers, many chose to use their weekend passes at the Alligator Farm. With more soldiers in town, Charlie and Drysdale converted their clothing store into a bar.

By the time the war started, Charlie was in his late 30s and had decided to enter politics. Gary and Malinda never heard him say why, but they believe it was his desire to serve. His first term in the Florida House lasted from 1942 to 1944. After that, he took on "the political power structure of St. Augustine," said Gary. He ran for a Senate seat against former Mayor Walter B. Fraser, who was closely aligned with Herbert Wolfe. Charlie lost, but he ran for the House again in 1946 and served for the next 20 years.

Charlie enjoyed campaigning. Gary, who sometimes accompanied his father on the campaign trail, remembered driving along Highway 13: "He walked into every business establishment" with three-by-five cards printed with his photograph. "He would hand one to everybody he could find and visit with and talk with them. And I mean, he literally had it made. He didn't have opposition a lot of times. But when he did, he worked very hard on a one-to-one basis." Gary remembered only one opponent, a Republican from Ponte Vedra, when that party began attracting more members.

"He'd speak at any rally," Gary continued. "Herbert Wolfe used to give a big rally out on his farm. They parked a flatbed truck out there in the middle of the field where the speakers would get up and they'd have a little amplifier and a microphone. But the real reason everybody was there was a huge barbeque [with] pork and Brunswick stew, and it was free." "I remember him standing up there one night and thanking everybody for being there, thanking the people that had voted for him in the past and sent him to Tallahassee, that he enjoyed—this is almost verbatim—that he enjoyed representing them, and 'I want the opportunity to go back and represent you again because I really like it.'"

Malinda remembered that her father would also campaign at civic clubs, such as Kiwanis, in which he was very active. In addition, he would give push cards to "50 of us kids, and they'd ask you to go and stick them in the clips that were on the old-fashioned mailboxes." Toward the latter part of his campaigning, her father bought ads in the newspaper, on radio, and programs for high school sporting events. "It was a good time for high schoolers to sell ads in their football programs."

"I remember campaign managers," Malinda continued, "but it wasn't about money. It was just about arranging things for you to do, come speak to this group or that group."

"He'd never spend a lot of money to get reelected," Gary said, "therefore, he didn't need to raise it."

Of his time in the Legislature, Charlie was perhaps best known for his advocacy on behalf of people with disabilities. As chairman of the House Mental Health Committee (1958–1966), he worked to expand the State School for the Deaf and Blind, which had been located in St. Augustine since 1884. He served on the school's first Board of Trustees in 1963 and stayed on the Board until his death in 1966. It was said that he "really began to understand the needs and problems" of the school when he brought the girls' basketball team from St. Joseph's Academy, where he was the volunteer coach, to play the girls' team at the school.[23] The Legislature honored his contribution by naming the school's athletic stadium after him in 1967.

Before he died, he had been working on a bill prohibiting the involuntary placement of individuals in state institutions. It didn't pass in his last session of the Legislature, Gary said, but Maxine Baker, who succeeded Charlie as chairman of the Mental Health Committee, got it through in 1971. It became known as the Baker Act.

"I think he was interested in the way people were treated. He saw a segment of the population that just wasn't being treated well," Gary said.

Growing up in St. Augustine in an era of widespread prejudice may also have influenced his desire to help those isolated from the mainstream: "I believe being discriminated against for just being Minorcan or Spanish or poor made him a way more sensitive person to racial problems," Malinda said. Her father also took the larger view. As one family member recalled, Charlie used to say, "Everybody has a problem. What's yours?"

In 1959, Charlie played an important legislative role in creating the Historic St. Augustine Restoration and Preservation Commission. This state-sponsored agency sought to preserve the city's colonial and territorial heritage. At the local level, his friend and Alligator Farm partner headed up the 400th anniversary celebration of the city's founding and its legacy as America's earliest enduring European settlement. In 1992, the Alligator Farm was listed on the National Register of Historic Places as a historic district.

Near the end of his legislative career, Charlie fought to keep State Road 16 in its existing location. He "left a sick bed several months ago to attend a public hearing and express concern over attempts to move SR16 out of the Santa Rosa business area onto adjacent land."[24] Before his death, the County Commission voted unanimously to name the highway after him.

While in the Florida House, Charlie served on other important committees, including the Public Health Committee (of which he was vice chairman), the Finance and Taxation Committee, and the Advisory Committee for the Speaker of the House.

"He had lots of friends in the Legislature," Gary said. "I can't think of him ever being in a legislative conflict. Some of the young guys that were coming in he would not see eye-to-eye with, but I think that he liked them. I don't think there was much he didn't like about the [legislative] process. He told me, 'I will step aside when there's a good young man that comes along that can do the job for the county.' But they were never young enough or good enough."

Although Charlie was easygoing, he could get riled. "I witnessed first-hand in Garcia's Restaurant [now the Cypress] in Tallahassee a lobbyist trying to put the strong arm on him," Gary said. "This guy was a young lawyer in Tallahassee and he was pressing Dad on some point. At some time in the conversation the lobbyist asked, 'What do you know about such and such?' And Dad looked him in the eye and he said, 'I don't know anything you don't know. You know everything.'"

"He did it aggressively and he just kind of lashed out at him with it, and that was not his style at all. Oh, he was not a confrontational type of person but he wouldn't move off his ground." He recognized that lobbyists played a role in the legislative process, but experience taught him to remain firm to his principles. To a son-in-law applying for a job as a lobbyist, he advised: "Don't ever lie."

As an established politician and successful businessman, Charlie enjoyed important connections in the community. "My father had a back door into Ed Ball's office, which I don't know that he ever used," Gary said. Ball, financial advisor to the DuPont family and a key figure in the Pork Chop Gang, had hired Charlie's uncle, Leonard Usina, during the Depression to make sure taxes were collected to pay off bonds. The uncle later was promoted to president of the Florida National Bank of Miami.

"St. Augustine was small enough and Daddy was important enough in that orbit that we got exposed to people and events and places that the ordinary person will never experience," Malinda said. "We were around movers and shakers all the time." And it didn't hurt that both Charlie's wife and Drysdale's wife were reporters for the *St. Augustine Record*.

Aside from parties, business, and politics, Charlie delighted in sports. He regularly rode the fan bus to University of Florida football games but became a big Seminole fan when Malinda went to Florida State University. When he got older, he liked to play golf. "He belonged to a group called the Thieves," Malinda said. "He liked to be with people. He would go on hunting trips. I never knew him to get anything. He just would go. They'd have their bottles with their paper bags and their plastic and he'd have on those boots and those plaid shirts and vests. He'd be sitting there and them just telling stories and having a blast."

When Malinda was young, "we'd go down at the beach and throw a mullet net." They would put the fish into a charcoal pot and smoke them. "He was a fun-loving person."

"He had a laugh that resonated," Gary said. "It didn't matter whether you were 12 people at a cocktail party or in the middle of 300 at a convention center, you'd hear him when he laughed."

After Charlie's death, constituents came forward to say thanks for his help with solving problems. He helped extended family members too—paying off the mortgage of a grandmother whose husband left her in debt and providing a wedding for a cousin who had no money at the end of World War II, for example.

Colleagues held him in high regard. When St. Johns County got reapportioned from two seats to one, it looked like a big battle might be shaping up between Charlie and the other state Representative, Gus Craig (1958–1964 and 1966–1980). Craig came to Charlie, out of respect, and said he would never run against him. In January 1966 when Charlie learned he had cancer, he told Craig he would delay announcing his decision not to run for office again to give Craig time to file and run unopposed. Craig did that and won.

In February, Charlie announced that he would not seek another term because of poor health. He died May 31, 1966, at age 63. Gov. Farris Bryant (1961–1965) spoke at his funeral.

State Sen. Verle Pope (1948–1972) of Jacksonville, who had served with Charlie for many years, said, "Rep. Usina was a man respected throughout our state for integrity and a wonderful disposition. He has made many great contributions to Florida and was undoubtedly the most loved member of the Legislature."[25]

In June 1966 the Democratic Caucus of the Florida State Senate memorialized him as the "conscience of the House of Representatives" and "a man of unquestioned integrity and devotion to his family and church, a good companion to his friends and fellow members of the Legislature . . . and an inspiration to those who follow in his footsteps."[26]

Information about the late Frederick Charles Usina, Jr., was gathered from a telephone interview with his son Gary Usina (Nov. 12, 2014), and in-person interviews with daughter Malinda Usina Jones and her husband Bobby (Oct. 24, 2014) and B. K. Murphy, historian with the Museum of the Florida State School for the Deaf and Blind (Sept. 12, 2014), the family's genealogy, and various publications about his life and work.

Edmond J. Gong (D)

First man of Chinese ancestry elected to the Florida House of Representatives, 1963, and the Florida Senate, 1966

Personal: Born October 7, 1930, Miami, Florida; married with five children. Died May 19, 2015.

Education:

- Harvard College, A.B. (1952)
- Harvard Law School (1954–1955)
- University of Miami School of Law, LL.B. (1960)

Occupation: Lawyer

Trailblazer Elections:

- House of Representatives Dade Group 9 *Dem Primary Runoff Special Election* 1963
  - Edmond J. Gong (55%), John B. Orr (45%)
- House of Representatives Dade Group 9 *General-Special Election* March 26, 1963
  - Edmond J. Gong-D (68%), Bob Rosasco-R (32%)
- Senate District 40 (Dade County) *Dem Primary* 1966
  - Edmond J. Gong (74.6%), F. A. "Tony" Benedetto (25.4%)

VOTE
for
EDMOND J.
GONG
BEST QUALIFIED BY FAR
Group 9 • Lever 15A

Figure 3.9. Edmond J. Gong successfully ran for the Florida House in 1963, when legislators were still elected from multi-member districts. His response to his victory was "It's hard for someone from another country to understand that we in America come from different countries but now give our allegiance to one." Campaign literature courtesy of Edmond J. Gong.

- Senate District 40 (Dade County) *General Election* 1966
    - Edmond J. Gong-D (69.7%), Edythe R. Miller-R (30.3%)

For the full Edmond Gong story, see the Senate section, page 205.

Elvin L. Martinez (D)

First Cuban/Spanish man elected to the Florida House of Representatives, 1966
Personal: Born August 8, 1934, Tampa, Florida; married with five children.
Education:
- University of Tampa
- Stetson University College of Law, LL.B. (1962)

Occupation: Attorney
Trailblazer Elections:
- House of Representatives Hillsborough Group 4 *Dem Primary* 1966
    - Elvin L. Martinez (32.0%), Thomas K. McMullen (29.9%), Velma Pate Thomas (26.8%), Donald W. Crews (11.2%)
- House of Representatives Hillsborough Group 4 *Dem Runoff* 1966
    - Elvin Martinez (51.6%), Thomas K. McMullen (48.4%)
- House of Representatives Hillsborough Group 4 *General Election* 1966
    - Elvin Martinez-D (63.1%), William N. Hamilton-R (36.9%)

THE ELVIN MARTINEZ STORY

"Some people think if you're Hispanic you have to be an Aztec or an Inca, and you have to be brown-skinned," said Elvin Martinez. But all his ancestors came from Galicia in the northwest corner of Spain, and Spain is "the mother of Hispanics," he

Figure 3.10. State Rep. Elvin Martinez always had a close connection to Tampa's Cuban population even though both sets of his grandparents were from Spain (Galicia), the exception being his paternal grandmother, who was born in Cuba. His grandfather moved to Tampa in 1886, working as an executive in Tampa's burgeoning cigar industry. His father worked in the Tampa cigar industry as a selector for 50 years. So it was fitting that Rep. Martinez lit up a Bances Cuban Cigar with the assistance of Cuban princesses on Ybor City Day at the Capitol. State Archives of Florida, *Florida Memory*, https://www.floridamemory.com/items/show/103051. Photograph by Donn Dughi (Donald Gregory), April 30, 1987.

said, and because of that European heritage, his skin is white.[27] For Martinez and others like him, the *Hispanic* label said nothing of his ambition, his intelligence, and his will to do good.

On his mother's side, his Galician grandparents came straight from Spain to Florida. His grandfather, an executive in the cigar industry, settled in Tampa in 1886.

His father's family also originated in Galicia but at some point ended up in Cuba. (His paternal grandmother, who was born in Cuba, was of Basque heritage.) His father's parents married in Cuba and lived there until the grandfather's death. "Then my father took his widowed mother and brought her to the United States in 1910." Elvin's parents were married in 1917; they had nine children. As the youngest, "I always brag that I'm the smartest one because I simply learned from all eight of my brothers and sisters," Martinez said.

His father worked in the Tampa cigar industry for 50 years. "He was a selector, which is the artisan of thc cigar world. They're the last ones to touch the cigar." Selectors graded the cigars from light to dark, and put the best ones on top. He also collected dues for Centro Español, a Spanish mutual aid society that provided free medical care and other services to its members. Its medical facilities included a hospital on Bayshore Boulevard and clinics in West Tampa and Ybor City.

As a child, Martinez would accompany his father in collecting money on weekends. "We knew everybody on his route, of course, because that was kind of a personal thing," he said. His father trained his clients to leave the money in a designated hidden place if they were going to be gone on Saturday. "You got to learn, if you went to this house and nobody answered, you go under the flower pot, the third flower pot on the right. And if the other one wasn't at home, you don't look under the flower pot, you look under the seat there, that kind of thing."

Until 1939, Tampa had two public high schools: one in Plant, which served West Tampa and Ybor City, and the other in Hillsborough, which served the Seminole Heights areas. Tampa had grown so much by the late 1930s that a third high school was created. "No one will say it, but when they decided that they didn't want any more Latins—Italians, Cubans and Spanish—going to Plant and Hillsborough, they then created Jefferson High School," Martinez said. West Tampa, Ybor City, and the Latin community of Tampa went to Jefferson.

"There was a lot of prejudice, a lot of prejudice," he said. "We couldn't go to Sulphur Springs without getting into a fight unless we took our mother and father. You couldn't date anyone, except in your own community. You couldn't get a job anywhere. You couldn't work for Tampa Electric and expect to become anything, unless you wanted to climb poles—you couldn't be a supervisor." Consequently, "our parents decided what you need to do is get your education and preferably open a business or become a professional where you don't have to work for anyone."

Other families encouraged their children to do the same, and many Jefferson High alumni became prominent doctors, surgeons, lawyers, musicians, and scientists.

Some families in the Latin community chose to send their children to a small Jesuit high school in Tampa. "That was for two types of people, the rich and the incorrigibles, because Jesuits don't play around. I had a brother who gave my father fits, and my father sent him to the Jesuit school for one year and he straightened up."

After high school, Martinez served in the U.S. Army in the Korean War. When he left the Army in 1954, he married a young woman from Ybor City, worked odd jobs, and started college under the GI Bill at the University of Tampa, majoring in political science and history. Before finishing a degree, he enrolled in law school. "Stetson University Law School allowed veterans who had a B average or better to skip their senior year and be accepted into law school. I took advantage of that because I had two children and I needed to get on with my career. And I had always wanted to be a lawyer anyway," he said. At Stetson, he was elected vice president of the Student Bar, not because of any fraternity affiliations, but rather because "I had so many friends," many of whom were from Tampa.

The summer before he started law school, he took a job at the post office. "I started as a clerk, and they wanted to change my hours from the night shift to the day shift, and that meant I would've had to leave law school. So I declined." As fate would have it, an assistant postmaster named Morehouse heard about his resignation and called Martinez to his upstairs office. "He told me he found a spot for me that no one would bother. It was a special delivery." It turned out that Morehouse had been the mail carrier on his family's rural route years earlier. "He knew all about our family and my brothers who had been in the service and where they lived and all those things. He reached down and saved me, and I'll be forever grateful because of that."

After finishing law school in 1962, Martinez started working for a lawyer at the old Arcade Building in Sulphur Springs. "I got to know everybody there in Sulphur Springs. My sister and brother-in-law owned an appliance store there for 60 years, Star Appliance. Then the politics started."

At election time, one of his law school and army friends, Ray Tamargo, asked for help in running the campaign for his partner, State Rep. Tom Whitaker, Jr., (1958–1962). Martinez responded to others' calls for help, including the John E. "Jack" Mathews, Jr., campaign for Governor. "We made signs—silkscreen signs. We built the old wooden structure to lift the sign. We loaded cars and planted signs everywhere and held meetings," he said.

After a couple of years, fellow campaign workers and friends approached Martinez about running for a House seat. "They said, 'Look, you're always helping everybody, you're running around, why don't you run yourself?'" Before long he filed, and others started helping him.

Figure 3.11. Elvin Martinez's brother, Andrew, a florist, came up with the idea of using a four-leaf clover to help voters remember that he was a *Group 4* candidate. (At the time, representatives ran from a district-based group but were elected countywide—the old multi-member district elections system). The brothers bought bucketloads of four-leaf clovers from a friend who knew how to grow them and stapled them to every campaign card they passed out. Said Martinez, "No one got rid of the four-leaf clover or the card. We won." Button courtesy of Elvin Martinez. Photograph by Susan A. MacManus, July 12, 2013.

At that time, Florida was going through a series of reapportionments in response to the U.S. Supreme Court's establishment of the one-person, one-vote principle. As urban areas gained new seats in the Legislature, many people decided to run for them, including Martinez's friend Louis de la Parte, who had served in the House (1962–1966) and was running for the Senate. With so many candidates running, "the most popular was going to get the most votes, that was it," Martinez said. That's when his eldest brother Andrew came up with an idea.

"One of the biggest influences that I had getting into politics was my brother Andrew. He was 17 years older than I was, and he was just brilliant. He started the Mensa Society in the west coast of Florida. His IQ was 180 or more I guess, brilliant, brilliant, brilliant." He was also a highly creative person who ran a florist shop and directed plays.

"Andrew said we need to identify you as in Group 4 (candidates were listed by districts and groups). It so happened that he had a friend, Albert Greenberg, who was in the tropical fish business and he had mastered—get this—growing four-leaf clovers." That widely held symbol of good luck became the campaign theme. Cards, buttons, and other materials were printed with a four-leaf clover and the words *Group 4*. "We had buckets of them," Martinez said. When giving out his political cards, "we'd staple the four-leaf clover to them. Everywhere we went, we had that, and no one got rid of the four-leaf clover or the card."

"Another thing that we did that made it so much fun when we first ran, I had a cousin-in-law who had a trailer, a little flat-bed trailer, and he built a triangular stand with my big signs, 6-by-8 signs, and put them on there. He put a couple of loudspeakers on the truck, and played two recorded songs: 'I'm Looking Over a Four-Leaf Clover,' and 'Happy Days Are Here Again'" (the campaign song of Franklin Delano Roosevelt).

"We didn't have any consultants or anything. We did our own ads. Andrew and I would sit after a long day of campaigning and go over the next ad that we had to do." Early on, they recognized that the Martinez name would do well in West Tampa and Ybor City, but not in other parts of the county, "and, of course, we were running countywide." His supporters urged: "You need to get out to Plant City, go to Ruskin, go to Lutz. Stay out of West Tampa, you don't need any help in West Tampa. And we did that," he said. In Sulphur Springs his sister and brother-in-law campaigned for him through their appliance business.

An opportunity to expand his campaign presented itself in a young man named Carl Carpenter, who was running for the school board from Plant City. "Carl didn't know anyone in West Tampa, and I knew two or three people in Plant City." After one campaign appearance, while waiting for rides home, they began talking and decided that they would help each other. "That became such a good relationship," Martinez said. When Carpenter came to West Tampa, they would load his car with Martinez's signs, and when Martinez went to Plant City, he would load up with Carpenter's signs. "Wherever my sign was, one of Carl's signs was there too."

Sign placement was anything but random. "The most expensive and the larger ones, you want to put at a good place. All of my real estate friends would give me a list of places to put signs. They had all these listings and they were constantly in contact with the owners, and they'd give me a list. You can put a sign here, sign there. For example, I wouldn't put a little 3-by-5 yard sign at the corner of Hillsborough and Armenia." Having signs in supporters' yards was important "because no one's going to put a yard sign for somebody they're not going to vote for." In addition, "the more signs you see, the more you think, 'Well, this guy's strong. Look at all the people he's got.'" But you don't want too many in one place either: "I can't understand these people who just have money to burn. When you see 12 signs in a row in the same place, that means you had too many signs, you couldn't get rid of them, you put them all in one place."

"I was kind of aggressive, too," Martinez admitted. "If I saw someone out plowing a field, I'd run to the fence and wave him down and introduce myself. 'My name is Elvin and I'm running for the state Legislature. I'm glad to see a working man, and I'd love to have a working man's vote.'"

"I remember one time somebody told me, 'Hey, they're having a big community meeting in Keysville and you have to get out there because there's going to be a lot of people there.' I asked, 'What's the meeting about?' He said, 'I don't know, something about a school district or something.'" In Keysville, Martinez encountered a deputy sheriff that he happened to know: "Elvin, what are you doing here?" Martinez replied, "Well, they told me there was going to be a meeting with a lot of people." "Yeah," the deputy said, "it's a Ku Klux Klan meeting" to which Elvin replied, "Ooooohhh, shoot." He and the friend who had driven him to the event jumped back in the car and sped off.

"The black community was always friendlier toward the Latin community because they knew we were in the same boat," he said. He remembered a black family named Doby that lived near his neighborhood, for example, whose children walked to a segregated school. During campaigns, he occasionally spoke to black groups. "I got invited one time to a black church, and they sat me up there in the podium right in front of the choir." In addition, "they had put their collection basket in the front of the altar, and everybody in church walked by and dropped something in there. I only had a $10 bill on me, so the first time I went by, I dropped my $10 in the basket. I didn't realize they had two collections. Then I was flat broke. I told my friend Joe Cruz that I was broke and he understood me, and when I got out and walked around, he slipped me a five."

His family acted as censors. In one election, he had planned to run a series of ads saying "No more black box politics," insinuating that his opponent had been involved in secretive contracts with the government. "It looked sinister, and I wanted it to look sinister," Martinez said. "Well, the first morning that thing came out, my brothers and sisters, except for Andrew, organized and paid us a visit, saying we would have to stop that. Even my mother said: 'That's not the way you're going to run. That's dirty. Don't do it.'" That was Saturday, and they had to get the ad out of Sunday's paper. Fortunately, Andrew, who was a florist and knew everybody, contacted the man in charge of the advertising in the *Tampa Tribune*, and he pulled the ad. "Sunday it didn't appear. It appeared one time and, boy, did my family get upset." Aside from avoiding dirty politics, they learned a lesson that they used throughout every subsequent campaign: "Never spend your money or your time mentioning your opponent." They decided the old saying "It doesn't matter what you say about me, good or bad, just as long as you spell my name right" was not for them.

When it came to getting endorsements, they had little luck with the *Tampa Tribune*. "Maybe out of the 14 times that I ran for office, the *Tribune* may have endorsed me twice. One was by default because none of us were opposed," he said. "The *Tribune* was the epitome of prejudice. You couldn't rely on them, the editorial board anyway. The *Tampa Times* was a little different because it was smaller and it didn't mean as much, and *La Gaceta*, they've always helped me."

"It was just tireless. I was young and I had the drive to show people that I could speak English without an accent, that I could converse, and that I was someone other than the one who serves the Cuban bread in a restaurant. That's the perception they all had: 'Oh, you go to the Columbia Restaurant? Oh yeah? What's your father do? He's a server?'"

"It was all Democrats back then, and the Republicans were starting to run." He fought through two Democratic runoffs, winning the second by one vote. Significantly that year, Florida elected its first Republican Governor since Reconstruction, Claude Kirk (1967–1971).[28]

After the election, Gov. Kirk called the Legislature into special session to rewrite the Constitution. "While we were up there, the Supreme Court threw out our election. Those of us in the delegation ended up representing an area larger than the state of Delaware: Hillsborough, Pasco, Hernando and Citrus counties. We ran all the way up to Inverness. We had to run again in '67. It was a short time. They only gave six weeks to qualify and run. Since we had all just been elected and sworn in, it was kind of an easy thing." The delegation also increased the number of its Representatives to 11. They included Democrats John Culbreath from Brooksville and Tommy Stevens of Pasco County.

"Then we were a force to reckon with, and at one time we were all chairmen. Terrell Sessums (elected 1963), Guy Spicola (elected 1966), and John Ryals (elected 1966) from Plant City. We became a fraternity, a brotherhood," Martinez said, and they campaigned together. All drew Republican opponents. On one occasion, they appeared at a rally at the Inverness airport on Highway 41. The stage was a flatbed trailer with jury-rigged microphones. "We were sitting around, waiting for our time to talk. A microphone wire was running right in front of John Ryals, and by accident he stepped on a certain place on the wire and it cut off the microphone. He'd take his foot off, and the microphone would work again. So, needless to say, we didn't hear much from our opponents."

When Martinez took his seat in the Legislature, "The first roll call that we had, the clerk called my name Elvin Martin-ez. In Spanish the accent is on the next-to-the-last syllable, Mar-TIN-ez. That irritated the hell out of me, and I stood up and said, 'It's Mar-TIN-ez, and don't forget it.' He never called me Martin-ez again, no one did."

Interestingly, around the same time, a Northerner named Joe Martinez from Fort Lauderdale was elected. "He wanted to be called Martin-ez and they wouldn't do it. They would call him Joe Mar-TIN-ez. He didn't know how to speak Spanish either."

As a freshman legislator, Elvin took his brother Andrew with him to Tallahassee as an aide. At that time, a wave of Cubans fleeing Castro had settled in Florida, and they were starting to write letters to government officials. "The Secretary of State would send someone out with a stack of letters for Andrew to translate for them. They had no one that even spoke Spanish, much less able to interpret. So when Andrew and I got there, a whole world opened up as a new category of resource."

Martinez left the House in 1974 to run for the Senate seat vacated by Louis de la Parte. In that race, he faced his friend Guy Spicola, who had left the House in 1970 and had run unsuccessfully for the Senate. The race presented a difficult choice for Democrats. The *St. Petersburg Times*, considering the two veteran legislators, chose Martinez over Spicola "by a hair."[29] But Spicola won and served in the Senate until 1979.

Martinez ran again for the House in 1978, initially with some reluctance. "I had just come back from Spain with my wife, my sister and brother-in-law on a Friday night," he said. The next morning friends confronted him: "Elvin, you've got to run for the Legislature." Martinez said, "No, I'm through with it." They persisted: "You don't understand. It's a walk-in." They explained that Pat Collier Frank, who had held a House seat for two years, was leaving to run for the Senate. Martinez called his brother Andrew, and he said, "Do it!" He also said not to worry about the qualifying deadline only about four days away. "First thing we do," Andrew said, "we'll call all the Spanish restaurants and tell the waiters that you're running, and by morning everybody that ate there will know that you're running." And sure enough, the word spread quickly.

During his second go-round in the House, he served as Majority Leader (1980–1982) and chaired the Criminal Justice Committee (1982–1986) as well as the Appropriations Conference Committee (1991). His colleagues included Helen Gordon Davis (D-Tampa, 1974–1988), civil rights activist for women and minorities who would later be elected to the Senate (1989–1993).

"When I went back in '78, there were some new people there that I hadn't known before." One was a tall fellow from down south who had been there two or three years. After a while, when they got to know each other better, the man said, "When you first came up here, I thought to myself, 'There's another F'n Cuban. But now I realize you're a bilingual legislator.'"

Martinez retired from the Legislature in 1997 to become Hillsborough County Judge, as appointed by Gov. Chiles (D). His term ended in 2005.

What did he like most about serving in the Legislature? "Helping people," he said. "Oh, it was a lot of fun and getting things accomplished and being able to walk into the Governor's office and, you know, feel comfortable. At one point, every member of the Cabinet had served in the Legislature with me at one time: Bob Graham (1966–1968), Jerry Lewis (1966–1968), George Firestone (1966–1972), Richard Stone (Senator 1967–1970), and Bill Gunter (Senator 1966–1972)."

While hobnobbing with other legislators was fun, what really made it rewarding was "when you're able to help people who had no way around government, and they get stuck most of the time—not most of the time, a lot of the time." He gave a typical example: "We had to commit our daughter and they've got her up in Jacksonville. We can't go to Jacksonville every weekend, we have to get a motel, and it gets so expensive. Can you get her closer?"

The same was true of people wanting to visit a relative in prison. "You get someone in the Panhandle that tips over an outhouse, he gets four years in prison. You get a guy in Tampa or Miami who steals a car, he gets probation. So they're all up there (in Century near Pensacola), of course. The outhouse tipper, his family's all around there, but these people in Tampa and Miami they have to travel across the state, 500 miles, to see their children." It's impossible to know how many people in similar circumstances that he helped.

If advising a young person of Hispanic heritage about going into politics, he would say: "Just be ready to accept that everything has to be politically correct. Be wary of the press. Do not think that they're your friends. If you learn that lesson, just give them press releases and answer very short yes or no questions. It's like the old saying that we use when we instruct our witnesses on cross examination. 'Don't try and explain anything. I will give you the opportunity to explain, but do not try and explain on cross examination.' Then I have to explain: 'I will question you, they will question you, and then I'll have a chance to come back and question you again. If I think there's something that needs to be explained a little further, I will ask you.' That's how you should treat the press, and be ready."

While encouraging people to run for office, he warned: "Don't do it unless your family is in on it. Don't go it alone. Don't go it alone because two things: you'll make a horrible politician and you won't have a happy life. And you'll get divorced. So, unless you have a commitment from those you love around you that they're ready for it, don't do it." His wife Sylvia, although she didn't like politics, "was with me all the time partly because of the pride in knowing that we were going to do something that had been very difficult for a lot of people." His five children, while never bragging about the experience, remember growing up in a household "where you get a call from the Governor or the Senator, the Representative, the Congressman, and you're able to socialize with them." Because he was practicing law at the same time, it was a busy life. "Every time we had an opportunity, we'd do things in the family."

Another piece of advice to young people: "If you're lazy and you want to sit back, just don't even try it because it takes a hell of a lot of leg work. Although it's all changed with all the electronic and cyber things that are going on, that personal contact goes on." He remembered one time, after putting in a full day from 6 a.m. to 11 p.m., he told his brother Andrew he was going to bed. "No, you're not," Andrew said. "Bowling alleys are open all night. There are people that work all day who have leagues that bowl at 12:30 or 1:00 a.m." By going to a late-night venue, "you get to meet people, and people say, 'This guy's really serious about this stuff. He's out here when everybody else is asleep, he's out here getting votes.'" When he was on the east side of the county, near the phosphate plant at Gibsonton, "I'd be there at the change of the shift, see them coming in, going out."

Such outings provided learning experiences. His friend Ernesto "Ernie" Fonseca, a business manager for several unions including the waiters and the Cuban bread bakers, "hooked me up with going to see the bakers at Holsum Bakery at 2 a.m. It was early April, and spring had just started, and I'm shaking hands. Someone comes in and says, 'Hey it's raining.' All the Cubans went out in the rain and got soaking wet. I learned from that that in parts of Cuba, it's a tradition that if you get showered on by the first rain in spring, it will bring you good luck. That's what they believed. They all went out and came in soaking wet and proud of it, too. Steam would come out of their shirts. They were happier than hell."

In those experiences, "you get to see people the way they really are." On one occasion, accompanied by his daughter, "I was talking to a mechanic, and he had grease on his hands. After we finished talking, I extended my hand to shake his hand. He said, 'No, no, my hands are dirty.' My daughter remembers me responding, saying a working man's hands are always dirty. I shook his hand, yeah."

Elvin Martinez was interviewed in person by the author July 12, 2013.

Maurice A. Ferré (D)

First Puerto Rican elected to the Florida House of Representatives, 1967
First Puerto Rican mayor in the United States, 1973
Personal: Born June 23, 1935, Ponce, Puerto Rico; married with six children.
Education:

- Lawrence School, New Jersey (1953)
- University of Miami, B.S. in architectural engineering (1957)
- University of Miami, M.B.A. (1958)

Occupation: Business Consultant
Trailblazer Elections:

- House of Representatives District 91 (Dade County) *Dem Primary* 1967
  - Maurice A. Ferré (54%), Ronald R. Young (18%), Nicki Englander (17%), John H. Bomar (11%)
- House of Representatives District 91 (Dade County) *General-Special Election* 1967
  - Maurice A. Ferré-D (56.0%), Ronald A. Wedel-R (44.0%)
- Miami Interim Mayor, 1973
- Miami Mayor, 1973

Figure 3.12. In March 1967, Maurice Ferré (*center*) won a special election, becoming the first Puerto Rican Democrat elected to the state House. He was sworn into office on April 4, 1967, by Chief Justice Campbell Thornal. Ferré soon left state politics for local office. Gov. Claude Kirk (R) appointed him to a vacant seat on the Miami City Commission. He then made an unsuccessful run for mayor in 1970 (campaign featured in photograph), but later won that post in 1973. Photograph by Albert Coya, ca. 1966–1970, from Florida State University Digital Library.

THE MAURICE A. FERRÉ STORY

Maurice A. Ferré enjoyed three firsts in Florida politics:

- First Puerto Rican–born person to serve in the Florida Legislature,
- First Hispanic Mayor of Miami, and thus the first Hispanic to serve as mayor of a major U.S. city,[30] and
- First and only Puerto Rican elected to the Board of Commissioners of Miami-Dade County.

Ferré came from a family with a rich history in politics. His paternal grandfather, the son of a French engineer who had gone with Ferdinand de Lesseps to build the French Panama Canal, was born in Cuba. The grandfather's maternal family were Cuban independence patriots. The grandfather's cousin, Gen. Alberto Nodarse, "was a one-star general at age 23 and aide-de-camp to Cuban independence hero Gen. Antonio Maceo. Cousins Orencio and Alberto Nodarse were active in the Republic of Cuba's new government in 1903, one as Mayor of Havana and the other as Minister of the Interior."

An uncle, Luis A. Ferré, was active in Puerto Rican politics for more than 30 years. He served in the Constitutional Assembly in the early 1950s, Governor of Puerto Rico in the late 1960s, and President of the Senate in the 1970s. He also founded the PNP (Puerto Rico's Statehood Party) and was president of the Puerto Rican Republican Party (U.S.A.). "So I grew up listening at the dinner table to both Puerto Rican and American politics," he said.

His father, José, was a successful entrepreneur who expanded his business to Miami in the 1920s. That wealth made possible major contributions in the 1950s and 1960s to the Democratic campaigns of U.S. candidates—John F. Kennedy, Lyndon B. Johnson, Hubert Humphrey, and Tip O'Neill—as well as to Florida Gov. LeRoy Collins.

Miami would become a mecca for son Maurice, who had been born and grew up in Ponce, Puerto Rico. He not only chose to attend college at the University of Miami but also got married in Miami.

"Saturated by the enthusiasm of the times, I decided to run for the Florida Senate in 1966," he said. This was the year of reapportionment struggles and the creation of new seats that attracted many aspiring candidates. He lost to Lee Weissenborn (D-Miami), who had served in the Florida House since 1963. Among other Senate winners—and trailblazers—were Louis de la Parte from Tampa and Eddie Gong from Miami.

Undaunted, Ferré ran the following year for the Florida House in a special election and won. "I served during a golden state Legislature, with the speakership of Fred Shultz (1968–1970)," he said. Discovering a Democratic colleague with a Hispanic

Figure 3.13. Maurice Ferré speaks at the unveiling of the Ponce de Leon statue in front of the Miami Public Library while serving as Mayor of Miami. In 1973, he made history as the nation's first Hispanic Mayor of a major American city and Miami's first Hispanic Mayor. State Archives of Florida, *Florida Memory*, https://www.floridamemory.com/items/show/34938. Photographed in October 1977.

name, Jacksonville Rep. Ted Alvarez, Ferré introduced himself and said a few words in Spanish. Alvarez replied: "Why are you talking to me in Spanish? I'm as much of a redneck Florida cracker as you will ever meet. I don't like Catholics, I don't like Spanish people, so don't talk to me in Spanish again." They ended up being friends.

"I was honored when Sen. Reubin Askew asked me to run as his Lieutenant Governor, but I had set my mind on local politics," Ferré said. He saw an opening on the City of Miami Commission when Mayor Robert King High (1957–1967) died and was replaced by Stephen Clark. Ferré accepted a nomination to the Commission and was elected on his own three months later in November 1967.

In 1973, Miami Mayor David Kennedy (1970–1973) resigned, and Ferré replaced him. He ran on his own in November and "beat seven rivals by a fraction of one percent over 50 percent." He served as Mayor for 12 years, longer than any other Miami mayor to date, having been elected six times (1973–1985). (Now there are eight-year term limits.)

A few years later, he was elected to the Dade County Board of Commissioners, serving until 1996, including a position as vice chairman. He tried again twice for public office—for mayor in 2001 and for U.S. Senate in 2010—but was unsuccessful. He remained active in business and public affairs, notably transportation in South Florida and the political status of Puerto Rico. In 2012, he received an honorary degree, Doctor of Public Service, from Florida International University.

His motivation for entering politics came from family, especially his father, uncle, and aunt. His uncle, Luis, former Governor of Puerto Rico, and his aunt (sister to Luis), Isolina Ferré, a Catholic nun and missionary, each received the Presidential Medal of Freedom. He received it from President George H. W. Bush in 1991, and she, from President Bill Clinton in 1999.

Ferré was also influenced by his political contemporaries: Reubin Askew (House and Senate 1958–1970), Lawton Chiles (state Senator 1967–1970), Bob Graham (House and Senate 1966–1978), Sandy D'Alemberte (state Representative 1966–1972), Gerald Lewis (state Representative 1966–1970), Bill Gunther (state Senator 1966–1972), and George Firestone (House and Senate 1966–1978). Ferré counted among his political mentors Claude Pepper, longtime Florida congressman; Athalie Range, Miami civil rights activist and first woman to head a state agency in Florida; and Col. Mitchell Wolfson, first Jewish Mayor of Miami Beach (1943).

"Being first was never a factor in my political quests," Ferré said. "The most difficult part of running was separating the candidate from the political management of the campaign. Fortunately, I had exceptional political managers and helpers: Marie Petit, my Chief of Staff at the City of Miami for 10 years; her husband Don Petit, Chief of Staff for Claude Pepper for many years; Steve Ross, the most astute political operative of the time; along with Phil Hammersmith, Rick Sisser and later at County Hall, Manny Alfonso."

Because Miami and Florida were in transition in the 1960s, 1970s, and 1980s, he ran under constantly changing conditions. "In 1973, only 5 percent of the electorate in Miami was Hispanic. The Greek, Polish, and Lebanese communities were important in the '60s, but not in the '80s. The importance of the Cuban, Hispanic, African-American and Haitian vote varied in different campaigns. In 1979, I would not have beaten my main challenger, Commissioner Rose Gordon, without the Cuban-American vote," he explained. "In 1981, I only got 24 percent of the Cuban-American vote against Commissioner Manolo Reboso. That year I could not have won without the 64 percent black voter turnout [a record] and my getting 95 percent of that black vote. In 1993, I was in a runoff election for County Commissioner and won because of the strong Hispanic voter support I received," he said.

"Endorsements were never very important to me. On my first run, in 1966, I got the endorsement of all the major political figures of Miami Dade County and lost to Lee Weissenborn. In other campaigns, sometimes when I had the *Miami Herald* endorsement, I would lose, and when my opponents had that newspaper's endorsements, often I would win."

"Racial issues were never a conscious part of my political life. I was a child of privilege. I felt comfortable at the Surf Club, the Bath Club, the Miami Club, of which my father and I were members, but felt just as comfortable in Spanish, in European surroundings, and amongst African Americans and Haitians." But, he added, unfortunately, in the Miami and Florida of those years, one could not get away from racial and ethnic politics. "They affected me greatly. I never felt the sting of racial or ethnic discrimination personally because I always related to all of Miami's diverse communities, including the Southern, pioneer Miami of the '50s and '60s."

"Since I have never considered myself disadvantaged, discriminated against, or a minority, I think I got more done as an American," he said. He had no special advice to prospective minority candidates, but he would advise any candidate "to concentrate on public service and good public policy."

"The most rewarding part of my 30 years of public service was seeing the results of my visions and endeavors, and in the effective partnerships established. In politics you get more done with collegial relationships, but adversarial roles are sometimes essential." In Miami, in particular, "politics was like riding a surfboard: as the wave progresses and changes, you must distribute your weight differently, or be wiped out. As Miami changed demographically, political success became a factor of balance responding to changing dynamics."

"In the long run, in our American, republican democracy, elected positions are a balance between doing what the majority of your constituents wish and personal leadership to meet the 'better angels of our nature' that signify enlightenment and modernity, which translates into vision."

Maurice A. Ferré was interviewed via telephone by the author July 22, 2013, and provided written responses to the questions posed.

Joseph M. Martinez, Jr. (R)

First Spanish Republican man to serve in the Florida House of Representatives, 1967

Personal: Born June 3, 1928, Miami, Florida; five children. Died December 2, 2009, Pembroke Pines, Florida.

Education:

- Florida State University
- University of Miami, B.A. (1956)

Figure 3.14. At the time Joseph "Joe" Martinez, Jr., ran for the House, he was an executive for Southern Bell Telephone Company. He was particularly interested in doing something about crime and making sure Broward County got its fair share of road funds. State Archives of Florida, *Florida Memory*, https://www.floridamemory.com/items/show/16193, January 1970.

Occupation:
- Southern Bell Telephone and Telegraph Company, Manager
- Local Realtor

Trailblazer Elections:
- House of Representatives District 88 (Part of Broward County) *Rep Primary Special Election* 1967
    - Joseph M. Martinez, Jr. (57.1%), James A. Cabler, Jr. (42.9%)
- House of Representatives District 88 (Part of Broward County) *Special Election* March 1967
    - Joseph M. Martinez, Jr.-R (63.0%), Ed Haddad-D (37.0%)

THE JOSEPH M. "JOE" MARTINEZ, JR., STORY

Joseph "Joe" Menendez Martinez, Jr., the first Republican man of Spanish heritage to serve in the Florida House of Representatives, owes his place in history to Gov. Claude Kirk, the first Republican Governor of Florida since Reconstruction, as well as to the then-growing tide of support for the GOP across the state and nation.

A native of Miami, Martinez was the son of Joe Martinez, Sr., originally from Spain, and Ethel Colee of St. Augustine.[31] He graduated from St. Peter and Paul Catholic High School and served in the U.S. Army and the U.S. Marine Corps from 1946 to 1952, in the interval between World War II and the Korean War. He went on to Florida State University and graduated from University of Miami.

In the early 1960s, Democrats still wielded much of the political power in Florida and the South. Claude Kirk, who had made his fortune in insurance and investments and had headed the Florida for Nixon campaign, won an upset victory over his Democratic rival to become Governor in January 1967.

Martinez, a 36-year-old executive for Southern Bell Telephone Company where he had worked for 12 years, filed to run in the special election for state Representative in early 1967. From the outset, he was one of 10 men on a slate of Senate and House candidates put forward by Kirk's Citizens Committee.

He squared off in the Republican primary against five other candidates, each of whom cited different legislative objectives. For his part, according to the *Fort Lauderdale News and Sun-Sentinel*,[32] he pledged "100 percent support of Gov. Kirk's war on crime." A second major objective was to "do everything possible to improve the road conditions in Broward County," and ensure that the county would get "its fair share of road funds."

The newspaper endorsed James Cabler, a Fort Lauderdale attorney, who advocated for a fairer distribution of gasoline and raceway revenue to help fund growth in highly populated areas as well as increased control over bidding and auditing of state and county projects.

Candidate Edward Johns, a former Fort Lauderdale Mayor, also supported Kirk's war on crime but only as a third priority behind a revision of the tax structure and more money for roads. James Mackey, a Deerfield Beach insurance man, ran on a platform of ending government waste and raising school standards. William McConaghey, a construction firm executive, proposed a unicameral legislature and a state lottery. (He would end up with the least votes in the primary.) A fifth opponent was William T. Fox, whose information was unavailable to the newspaper on the day of publication.

Martinez won with 5,598 votes compared to the next top vote getter, Cabler with 3,909.[33] More Republicans on Kirk's exclusive slate won their primaries, but other factors had also come into play, as explained on the newspaper's editorial page. Voters had turned out in low numbers, reflecting their "discontent over reapportionment and the elections forced upon the state by a federal district court in Miami."[34] In addition, candidates had had only 18 days to campaign and educate voters about their qualifications and the issues.

Nonetheless, "Republicans will be interpreting the results in their favor and looking forward to enhancing the GOP strength in the election," the newspaper continued. Some winning candidates "were strictly newcomers to politics, making the impact of the Kirk organization more surprising."

Before and after the election, Kirk's Citizen Committee drew criticism from within the Republican Party. The GOP county executive committee chairman decried it as a "splinter group,"[35] and defeated candidate and former State Rep. Bernard Klassen called the victory a "hoax" perpetrated by a "small clique of manipulators."[36]

For the runoff two weeks later, the *Fort Lauderdale News* declined to endorse either Martinez or Cabler.

Before that election, Cabler espoused his legal skill in examining and arguing different aspects of Florida laws and, further, "I am not bound to any group of persons or corporation in any manner."[37]

Martinez explained his position this way: "The coming legislative session, faced with constitutional revision, has the opportunity to lay the guidelines for the future of Florida. At the same time, there are problems that require immediate answers. The mushrooming spread of crime is a disgrace. In the fields of education, transportation, and air and water pollution, Florida cannot wait for answers. I am committed to solving these problems without raising new taxes. I fully support Gov. Kirk and will continue to support him in the Legislature. Politics is far too important to leave to politicians."

Again Martinez won, garnering 8,204 votes to Cabler's 6,160.[38] As one political writer described it: "Every successful Republican vote getter is happily riding along on the tail wind that is assisting Gov. Claude Kirk's jet as it streaks hither and yon."[39]

The "tail wind" blowing in Kirk's favor had arisen in the previous general election in November. "Last fall the shift to the Republicans was attributed in part to the dissatisfaction with the Johnson Administration, inflation, the progress of the war in Vietnam, a division within the Democratic ranks in the state and other factors."[40]

As the general election approached, county Republicans came together. Gov. and Mrs. Kirk appeared as guests of honor at a reception in Fort Lauderdale that raised $10,000. The county chairman said he would use $1,500 for newspaper advertising for local candidates.[41] Martinez was part of a multicandidate ad.

In the general election, Martinez faced Democrat Ed Haddad, a Fort Lauderdale businessman. In campaigning, Martinez repeated his full support for Gov. Kirk. On the day before voters went to the polls, the *Fort Lauderdale News* gave him its endorsement.

Haddad, on the other hand, proposed consolidating local, state, and national elections on the same day, indicated tax relief support for property owners, suggested a mass transportation system for the Gold Coast area, and called for free public kindergarten.[42]

The victory was decisive. "Martinez comes into office after a Cinderella appearance as a candidate," according to the *Fort Lauderdale News*. "Avowedly put up as a token Republican candidate and with no prior experience, Martinez pummeled Ed Haddad in the 88th District with 46,527 to Haddad's 27,432."[43]

When interviewed by the newspaper, Martinez proposed "sweeping changes" that would benefit South Broward County. First, he said, "South Broward will have a voice in Tallahassee." Next, he would not condone annexations as recently happened with Pembroke Park and Hallandale.

He would continue to support Gov. Kirk's war on crime, including the use of the private Wackenhut detective agency to head the effort.[44] "Something has to be done about the chaotic crime situation," Martinez said.

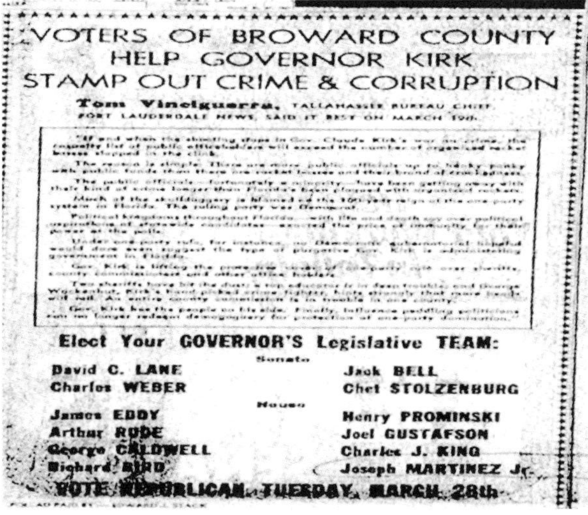

Figure 3.15. An ad for Gov. Kirk's Citizens Committee slate, including Joseph Martinez, Jr., ran in the *Fort Lauderdale News*, 1967.

In addition, he would back constitutional revision because the current one was in complete disorder, he would change the tax structure to give a larger portion of gas tax dollars back to counties that collect the most money, and would stick to campaign promises for highway improvement but no tax increases.

He criticized special tax districts such as Port Everglades and the South Broward County Hospital District. "They have excesses which should be channeled back to the state treasury," he said. He also favored a "limited form of home rule in which counties are allowed to make their own decisions."

Local Republican Party officials celebrated the shift from a one-party to a two-party county. The GOP made other gains in scattered parts of the state, but it "was by no means statewide as yet." Even so, "the vote makes it quite evident that the people want [Gov. Kirk] to have a chance to work things out in Florida's interests."[45]

The colorful and controversial Governor got his chance, but voters turned him out after only one term. Kirk lost his bid for reelection to Democrat Reubin Askew, a popular Governor who served from 1971 to 1979.

Martinez, too, served only one term. He became a local realtor along with his wife Helen until he retired in 1999. Together they reared five children: Joe III, Emmett, Eve, Diana, and Mary. Apart from business and legislative affairs, Martinez loved sports, fishing, camping, and flying. He died in 2009 at age 81.

Information about Joseph Martinez came from news clippings, primarily the *Fort Lauderdale News and Sun-Sentinel.*

Joe Lang Kershaw (D)

First African-American man elected to the Florida House of Representatives since Reconstruction, 1968

Personal: Born June 27, 1911, Live Oak, Florida; married with one child. Died November 7, 1999, of heart failure, Miami, Florida.

Education:

- Florida A&M University, A.B. (1935)
- Florida A&M University, M.Ed. (1955)

Occupation: Teacher, Consultant, Cultural Advisor, Public Relations

Trailblazer Elections:

- House of Representatives District 99 (Part of Dade County) *Dem Primary* 1968
    - Stephen H. Butter (34.5%), Joe Lang Kershaw (34.4%), Franklin J. Evans (31.0%)
- House of Representatives District 99 (Part of Dade County) *Dem Primary Runoff* 1968
    - Joe Lang Kershaw (53.5%), Stephen H. Butter (46.5%)
- House of Representatives District 99 (Part of Dade County) *General Election* 1968
    - Joe Lang Kershaw-D (63.6%), Roger Gunderson-R (36.4%)

Figure 3.16. State Rep. Joe Lang Kershaw, Florida's first black legislator since Reconstruction, ran for the House in 1968 at age 56. He was a fiery orator on issues he was passionate about—like continually fighting to exempt cane poles from the fishing license tax on equipment, with his rallying cry, "Axe the cane pole tax." It was a fight he eventually won for poor people around the state who fished for food and for whom fishing provided affordable recreation. State Archives of Florida, *Florida Memory*, https://www.floridamemory.com/items/show/21424. Photograph by Donn Dughi (Donald Gregory), 1971.

THE JOE LANG KERSHAW STORY

"I've always been an advocator to my family, been in politics ever since I was knee high to a duck," said Joe Lang Kershaw. When he was elected to the Florida House of Representatives in 1968, he became the first African American in the Legislature since Reconstruction. A man of humble beginnings, he had swept the floors there as a youngster.

Born in 1911 and educated during the Depression, he first registered to vote in 1936, at age 24, while Franklin Delano Roosevelt was in office (1933–1945). The son of a physician and a schoolteacher by profession, he went to register in the small town of Century (in Escambia County in the Panhandle) where he was teaching. The clerk automatically registered him as a Democrat. Later when he moved to Polk County, he was told he couldn't register. He showed them his previous registration and was allowed to register as a Democrat. "There were two city elections, I think, on bond issues. I couldn't participate because at that time there was a ruling that only freeholders—I think that was the expression that was used—could vote on bond issues."

When he moved to Miami, "blacks there were either registering with independents or Republicans. When I go to register as a Democrat—well, I don't know if it was because of the urban people are more fluent—they told me I couldn't register as a Democrat. Of course, I was proud that I had these two previous registration cards. I showed them and they said, 'No.' So I registered as an independent, recalling that at the time I'd have to wait for the general elections and there were very few independents."

In those days, the Democratic Party consisted largely of Southern conservatives and operated white-only primaries. In 1944, the U.S. Supreme Court in *Smith v.*

Allwright ruled against the white-only primary, and the Democratic Party in Florida opened registration to blacks. "Everything just cleared away," he said.

In the 1950s, civil rights activities began gathering steam across the nation. In 1954, for example, the U.S. Supreme Court ruled that segregation in public schools was unconstitutional (*Brown v. Board of Education*). During this time Kershaw taught and coached at black schools. "Joe was always one to tell the truth as he most perceived it, and he'd tell it at the appropriate time," said Robert Simms, University of Miami history professor who taught with Kershaw.[46]

Not content with the pace of progress in civil rights in general, black leaders organized sit-ins, freedom rides, and other demonstrations. In August 1963, 200,000 people participated in a march in the nation's capital, where Dr. Martin Luther King, Jr., gave his "I Have a Dream" speech.

Florida had its share of protests, particularly in Tallahassee and St. Augustine. In March 1964, for example, 1,500 people marched in Tallahassee in favor of a new civil rights bill pending in Congress. The bill, which became known as the Civil Rights Act of 1964, was signed into law by President Lyndon Johnson in July.

Kershaw had been interested in civil rights during the 1960s, "making contributions and sitting down and trying to map out programs and strategy. I just can't see how any black was not active in that." After passage of the Civil Rights Act, numerous groups conducted registration drives.

He decided on his own to run for the House of Representatives in 1968, at age 56. He ran in a multi-member district, in which each of five legislators represented 57,000 to 58,000 people.

After filing, he received threatening phone calls. Not to be cowed, he told one caller: "Every time you see me, I'm packing a .38, so it will be you or me." He also kept a whistle by all his telephones. He recalled: "You get these individuals who are kooks. You just reach over and get that whistle and blow it. You're not going to have any trouble from that guy anymore."

"They've taken to writing. One guy in particular, from the St. Petersburg-Tampa area, he would write these letters up there, and I ignored them. I assumed that this was a person that had a mental problem. Those kind of things, you just save them and don't say anything. The person doesn't know whether or not you got it." With no response, the person might wonder whether you're tracing the letter and investigating, and won't attempt it again.

On one occasion while campaigning, "I ran into some freak in Hialeah," he said. "The only thing I was advised to do was when you come into Hialeah, just come by the police department, let them know." People warned him that he would have trouble. "I think sometimes this intimidation is used with the hope of getting results, but when they find out you're bullheaded, and I had a reputation of being hard-nosed," that's the end of it. "In many cases, if a fellow came and looked in my car, he'd see my pistol laying there on the seat. I've got to protect myself. If I'm going to get elected, I want to be able to be sworn in. That kind of stuff puts the fear of God in them."

Later, as a member of the House, he saw nothing that prevented blacks from registering or voting in his district. "For instance, I don't see any economic dependency on whites, not important." No complicated registration forms either.

"Pure physical violence, not whatsoever," he continued. "In a certain area of my county some years ago, some intimidation was exerted. All of a sudden, the people from the Department of Justice were on the scene."

Perhaps because his district included a low-income area with roughly 40 percent blacks, his campaigns always lacked funding. "I think the highest money I ever raised was $8,000." But one thing helped: "I've had a tremendous amount of individuals who gave service, different clubs would go out and work for you. I've always run on the party ticket," and the party worked for a slate, he said.

"Some individuals say that running from a district would be cheaper. To me, it's not. When I buy radio time, I buy for the entire county because they don't restrict the services just for a particular area. When I buy advertisements in the major newspapers, newspapers circulate throughout South Florida. You've got to get TV time wherever they be. Then you also must go and get that local weekly because these boys feel slighted if you go into the major newspapers, pay that high rate for advertisement."

During campaigns, different political groups conducted phone banks and get-out-the-vote drives, offering transportation and babysitters. "It's the same old grassroots procedure," he said. Those methods were not restricted to blacks. "We just take a list of telephone numbers. For instance, they were bringing some girls to work with the communication workers, and they threw them into the battery of 50 to 75 telephones on an eight-hour shift, or four-hour shift, whatever they can work. They keep hammering like this. You just call a number and there's no way that they can indicate, or is indicated by that number, whether you're black or white." Likewise, "A black cab driver may pull up to get a white family" to go to the polls, or the reverse.

At one point in his first campaign, he was scheduled to appear at a Democratic countywide meet-the-candidate gathering just four days after Dr. King was assassinated. "I decided that this was the thing to hit and hit hard." Speaking at the event, "I told them that recent happenings in the last 96 hours tells me that we need to sit at the table and not in the street. I got a tremendous ovation," he said. "But the strangest thing, I received money that night and I don't know from whom I got it. Individuals just walked in and said, 'We want to help you.' There's five dollars here, 10 dollars here, there were a couple of 20-dollar bills. I got cards, 'Call me up. I want to work for your campaign. I think you're right.' Then they began to refer to me as a human relations candidate." (Once in office, he sponsored legislation that would lead to the creation of the Florida Human Rights Commission.)

He distinguished himself from opponents in another way. One candidate, a former city councilman, had approached Kershaw about a common practice of the "low man" helping the "high man" after the first primary. Before appearing at a public forum, Kershaw went by the clerk's office and picked up a tally of absentee votes, which showed that he was the high man by 50 votes. Once on stage, he was surprised to hear another candidate, a young man, say that he was leading the race. At Kershaw's turn to speak, he announced: "I want to set the record straight." Holding up the tally that showed he was ahead, he pointed to his opponent: "There's a man wants to go to Tallahassee to represent you and will not take the time enough to go across the bay to get it. This man attempts before he is ever elected to mislead you. Now right here with all these facilities available to him, he's not availing of himself of the opportunity to prove to be factual. What is he going to do in Tallahassee when you're not there to watch him? I'll at least work." Afterward, Kershaw said his opponent told him, "You hit me low." Kershaw responded: "There was no other place to hit you."

In his first primary, he failed to obtain the endorsement of the *Miami Times*, a weekly newspaper and powerful voice in the black community, and lost by only 61 votes to attorney Steve Butter for the Democratic nomination. With the support of Dr. Franklin Evans, who ran a close third in the race, Kershaw defeated Butter in the second primary. For the general election, having earned the endorsement of the *Times* as well as the *Miami Herald*, the South Florida AFL-CIO, and various professional groups, he beat Republican Dr. Roger Gunderson by a comfortable margin, 156,108 votes to 87,435.[47] He was reelected in successive elections, serving seven terms total ending in 1982.

Throughout his legislative career, he saw his responsibility as serving the public. "I can't do anything to help blacks without helping whites. I want to help people. I'm elected in Dade County, but I also work for the state of Florida. Now in many cases I can do things, and I feel that I have done things to straighten out some inequities that might have existed over the state of Florida. For instance, I tried to get more money for Dade County. If more money goes into Dade County, it doesn't just go for whites in Dade County, it goes for blacks in Dade County."

Early in his legislative career, he advocated for food stamps, which later came under a federal program. "Because of the way Dade County is constructed, the food stamp station is serving both blacks and whites. I didn't like the idea, the structure of it, not so far as the people doing the work. I thought the place was rather small, and I worked with colleagues of mine since we've been here. This is not a job that's done by myself. It was a cooperation of the people in my district. We have been fortunate enough to provide another food stamp area," which serves more blacks. But "I did it for individuals, for my district. Blacks are in my district, so blacks reap the benefits. By the same token, whites do also."

He worked on providing a number of public services for Dade County: more police officers on patrol to reduce crime, improved roads, housing, parks, and welfare.

Upon investigating complaints about welfare, for example, he found "that it was not the welfare department per se, it was the caseworker. This is a matter of personality sometimes with a client," he said. "I think on the whole, I haven't been able to ascertain yet that supervisors are willing to do a good job." Sometimes they "are so busy," they never get to it.

At one point, a special committee was looking at nursing homes. "I have talked with individuals on committees and made reports about conditions that exist in certain homes. I don't think it is right for me to overstep another person. If you were on the committee of health and welfare and I call it to your attention, then if I don't get any results," a telephone call would be in order.

Another time, Dade County firefighters "were not advocating that they get more money. They wanted more equipment and more men to be assigned on them. I supported their petition and I talked with the president of one of their locals. He said, 'We're working it out. As soon as the money's available, we're going to get it. But we are getting more consideration. Thanks for your services.'"

In 1971, he sponsored legislation that led to the creation of the Black Archives at Florida A&M University, his alma mater. In recognition of his efforts, a room on the first floor of the Carnegie Library was named in his honor.[48]

He was appointed by Democratic House Speaker Don Tucker (1978) to chair the important Elections Committee from 1974 to 1976, during the initial transition from Democratic control to a strong Republican presence in the Capitol.

Among his colleagues, he was known as "Cane Pole" because he continually offered an amendment to tax bills to exempt cane poles from the fishing-license tax on equipment. His rallying cry was "Axe the cane pole tax." He eventually succeeded in getting the exemption, thus helping poor people and blacks, for whom cane pole fishing provided food and recreation.[49]

He also conducted "my personal affirmative action program. I checked with personnel to find out what jobs are open, see if I can find a person that's capable as it appears to me and make them aware that this job is open, try to get it. There are certain times when individuals, because of the positions that they hold, think that they have divine rights to do things. In many cases blacks may be reluctant to go because of information that this person is hard-boiled, this person is a redneck, this person is prejudiced. I pick up the telephone and call: 'This is your state Representative Joe Kershaw calling. What about so and so? What does the law say about it? Who's your boss, who's your immediate supervisor?' I've gone into cases and called the immediate supervisor, I said, 'Now, don't give me that John Brown stuff. The law says this here, and you've got to be positive. The money is here and you're in position. I want to know why. It's not a job that requires a person to take an examination in this way.' I think that way I've helped."

In addition, he invited principals to bring students to the Capitol on field trips to understand how government operates. He spoke at schools, serving as a powerful role model simply by his presence.

As a House member, the only difficulties he encountered had to do with his being from Dade County and being a Democrat. "I get a tremendous amount of cooperation from my colleagues, from the Speaker's office, and from the administration," he said. As for "the pigmentation of my skin, I haven't run into that yet. Oh, maybe I'm so stupid I haven't realized it. They tell you quick, I'm a bull that will raise hell in a china closet, and they know me."

In addition, "the way this House is run, if you're in doubt about something, you pick up the telephone and get on the WATS (Wide Area Telephone Service) line. They really offer services, and they'll go out and try to find it for you."

He received cooperation from blacks as well as whites. "When I first came, I told them there were two buttons up here, a red one and a green one, and I know how to push either one of them—one didn't have any more value than the other."

On legislation that someone might want: "If you want it done, you got to come see me. You can do all the talking you want, but you don't introduce no bills and you don't vote on it. I'm up there. I've been up there seven years. I know the boys, and some fellows owe me some favors. It's just that plain. In this game, you've just got to come right to the point and meet them."

"We have a nice relationship here in the House. Democrats and Republicans going to see a fellow there, it's a matter of respect for your colleagues, and I think that I have the respect of all of them," he said. "If I've ever had any success in politics, it's been this: 'I'll hear you and I won't lie to you. When I give my word, that's my record.'"

Robert McKnight, former state Representative (1974–1978) and state Senator (1978–1982), said: "I found him to be a mentor of sorts—he would often sit with me and analyze members while they were debating on the floor. He was particularly astute at seeing through legislators and their real intent. He highlighted legislators who were hiding relevant facts during their debate—sort of strategic lying." Kershaw "represented his district and the state of Florida with great distinction and honor."[50]

Kershaw gave Democratic Gov. Reubin Askew (1971–1979) high marks. "As I look back over the Governors of the state of Florida, he is about as honest, as straight and dedicated to Florida government as you'd want a person to be. I don't agree with his program all the way, and he's not a politician in my book. I look upon him more as a statesman. The man wants to do the thing based on the knowledge he receives. I think he's been fair."

Overall, he felt that holding office in Florida was worth the effort. "As I told a fellow, I get into some bathrooms I didn't know existed," he said. "It gets back to that red and that green button. I've seen three or four votes go down in that Legislature that my vote or any one vote was a determining factor. I saw a vote tie there one time, and

I was on the other side. They came to me, and I said, 'I'm committed.' So you look back over, you want to be selfish, you can think and say, 'Well, I had the determining factor.' There have been situations that come up over amendments. They say, 'You better check with Kershaw.' So it gives a fellow personal pride."

In addition, he appreciated the firsthand education in government that he received as well as knowledge about a wide range of subjects. When he was placed on the pari-mutuel betting (wagering not against the house but against other bettors) committee, for example, he learned "what's involved from the standpoint of management or ownership on down to the training or to the fellow who works around the barn." A lobbyist who appeared before the committee praised him and State Rep. Jack Pope for their knowledge of the industry and admonished the other committee members: "What you need to do is study it like these people."

Despite such triumphs, political office was hard on family life, he said. It meant giving up time with family and living on a reduced income. (He started out on a salary of $1,200 a year and later earned up to $12,000 a year.) The job is supposed to be part-time, but it's full-time, he said. "It makes it so hard, especially if you come from a small family that's close-knit." The wife plans menus for the week, and a luncheon comes up, for example, which knocks things out of kilter.

The federal Voting Rights Act had a tremendously positive impact on helping blacks take part in Florida politics, he said. Individuals being what they are, they would not have granted voting rights without a law. They realized that if "Big Brother's going to watch us, then we'd better straighten up and fly right. Then, too, because of the amount of publicity that the Voting Rights Act received, because it was more of a national thing, individual papers began to carry it. Many states or many editors didn't like the idea of Big Brother coming and telling us what to do, but the fact that I've got Big Brother on my back now made individuals conscious. Then I think too the reaction from blacks was this—that if the federal government's going to do it, then I've got the federal government behind me, and so this is the thing that's helping me."

Nonetheless, voter registration had declined by the mid-1970s. One reason was "the purging of the books," he said. "They knocked off so many blacks and upped the whites." Another reason: "The people get tired," he said. "As I talked with the election committee and people, I think this is a philosophy from all poor people, all denied people, either black or white. They just feel that the federal government has the power, they can send the troops. So what I want to do is to get the person up there that I feel will send the troops, and that's the reason why you have a big turnout for a presidential election rather than a nonpartisan election electing local officials."

Kershaw witnessed much progress in civil rights during his career, but the struggle continued on different fronts, particularly in incidents alleging police brutality. Florida was not immune. In May 1980, for example, after Miami police officers were

Figure 3.17. State Rep. Joe Kershaw teared up when he received a stuffed rattler, the mascot of his alma mater Florida A&M University, from House colleagues. A teacher all his life, he earned both bachelor's and master's degrees at FAMU and routinely invited school principals to bring students to the Capitol to learn how government operates, spoke at many schools, and mentored many educators. State Archives of Florida, *Florida Memory*, https://www.floridamemory.com/items/show/102890. Photograph by Mark T. Foley, May 8, 1981.

acquitted in the beating death of insurance agent Arthur McDuffie, riots broke out in Miami and the black neighborhood of Overtown.[51] During debate on the House floor, Kershaw declared in his booming voice, "My district is under siege."[52]

After Kershaw's death in 1999, his son, Joe Lang Kershaw, Jr., a Miami attorney, said his father could not attend law school because so few schools accepted blacks in the 1930s. "I remember once he said to me, 'If they won't let me study law, at least I'm going to see if I can make some laws.'"[53]

Most of the information for this story was drawn from an interview with Joe Lang Kershaw, Feb. 10, 1976, as part of the Dr. James Button oral history project, University of Florida. The interview is available at http://ufdc.ufl.edu/UF00005813/00001.

Gwendolyn "Gwen" Sawyer Cherry (D)

First African-American woman elected to the Florida House of Representatives, 1970

Personal: Born August 27, 1923, Miami, Florida. Died February 7, 1979, from a car accident.

Education:

- Florida A&M University, B.S. (1946)
- New York University, M.S. (1950)
- Florida A&M University, J.D. (1965)

Occupation: Teacher/Lawyer

Trailblazer Elections:

- House of Representatives District 96 (Dade County) *Dem Primary* 1970
  - Gwendolyn S. Cherry (31.7%), Harvey Ruvin (24.4%), Elizabeth Jeanne Bettner (22.1%), Stephen H. Butler (21.9%)
- House of Representatives District 96 (Dade County) *Dem Primary Runoff* 1970
  - Gwendolyn S. Cherry (51.9%), Harvey Ruvin (48.1%)
- House of Representatives, District 96 (Dade County) *General Election* 1970
  - Gwendolyn S. Cherry—*Unopposed*

Figure 3.18. State Rep. Gwen Cherry takes the oath of office as the first African-American woman in the Legislature. Born in Miami in 1923, she was a lawyer, teacher, and author (*Portraits in Color*). She received her law degree, cum laude, from Florida A&M University in 1965. As she entered the Florida House, she informed her male colleagues: "You'd better listen to me. Mine is a voice you've never heard here before—that of a black woman." At left is State Rep. Dick Clark (D-Coral Gables). State Archives of Florida, *Florida Memory*, https://www.floridamemory.com/items/show/21280. Photograph taken November 17, 1970.

THE GWEN CHERRY STORY

A teacher for 20 years, Gwen Cherry could have retired in her early 40s. Instead she went to law school late in her career, earning a law degree in 1965. She became the first black woman to practice law in Dade County, and, in 1970, the first black woman to serve as a legislator in the state of Florida and only the tenth woman to serve in the Florida House of Representatives. Upon arrival, she informed her colleagues: "You'd better listen to me. Mine is a voice you've never heard here before—that of a black woman."[54]

She was born and raised in Miami, in the same area that would become the legislative district she would represent. Her father was a physician, and her mother ran a boarding house and hotel. "My father built the first hospital in the South—south of Tennessee—for blacks. He worked closely with the University of Miami, hoping to establish a black medical school," she said.

She had registered to vote in 1946, shortly after graduating from Florida A&M University (FAMU), a public historically black college in Tallahassee. She registered without incident but recalled that her father had encountered trouble, not with registering but with voting.

In the 1950s, she joined other protestors at the FAMU campus in the early struggles for civil rights. She participated in the Tallahassee Bus Boycott in May 1956, patterned after the Montgomery Bus Boycott (which eventually led to the U.S. Supreme Court's *Browder v. Gayle,* an opinion that found that segregated seating on public buses was unconstitutional). In the 1960s, she also worked with demonstrators at FAMU to integrate lunch counters and retail stores in Tallahassee.

By 1965, civil rights leaders, including Dr. Martin Luther King, Jr., had begun to speak out against the war in Vietnam. Unrest spread on college campuses from coast to coast, and in 1969 a march on Washington drew half a million antiwar demonstrators. It was during this turbulent year that Cherry gained her first public office, a federal appointment as an attorney for the Seventh U.S. Coast Guard District.

Because of her work on political campaigns plus her membership in organizations such as the National Association for the Advancement of Colored People (NAACP), the Urban League, and the American Civil Liberties Union (ACLU), people in the community urged her to run for a House seat in 1969. "They guessed it was time that someone made the effort toward breaking down the barrier," she said.

During the same period, women began to demand equal rights. Cherry was state president of the National Organization for Women (NOW), founded in 1966, and headed the Florida branch of the National Women's Political Caucus, founded in 1971. "The women's rights movement in the South was in the forefront, and I led that movement," she said. Activists in Florida took down the Male Only signs, "and we did it by quiet, peaceful persuasion." "We didn't have to file the suits, but [the barriers] were removed one by one."

Cherry's first campaign encountered an obstacle that faced many women—and minority—candidates at the time. "I think any woman candidate, and any minority candidate, any black candidate, is going to have a money problem," she said. "We're not going to have accessible to us the kind of wealth that the others or the majority of the people will have." In her initial campaign, for example, two candidates were millionaires. "They were both lawyers, young, handsome, one a classmate, the other a mayor. And they had all of the financial wealth." Also in the field of four candidates was another woman, a young PTA president.

"But I think you sort of underestimate the voter, if you think that he'll be fooled by all of that. I think he can very well see behind the façade and select whom it is he wants to represent him," Cherry said. What a penniless candidate has to work with is "actually getting the one-to-one, hand-shaking—what do they say, look them in the eyes, get at least contact. It's the only way you can overcome TV time and radio time and that sort of thing." That approach brought her victory in her first and subsequent races. She did obtain one- and two-dollar donations as well as labor union contributions, which were solicited by her campaign manager. She never got money from the Democratic Party, however. "I've never known what it is like to have the party's support."

Cherry, who could remember the Ku Klux Klan days, said racist politicking still existed, but "it's covert, it's hidden now. You have to be of a certain amount of sophistication to know what is happening," she said. "So many of our people are so easily fooled by what people say, rather than what they do. Politicians really know how to make hay with that. For instance, it is very difficult for me to tell people what I think of their Representatives, that their Representatives are really shafting them, because they won't even believe it. The fellows have it down so well. So I have to learn to fight just a little bit better than they do and just a little bit more sophisticated than they can." Instead of overt racism, politicians use code words and phrases such as *busing*, *welfare*, and *crime in the streets*, she said.

She was able to campaign freely as a black woman, encountering only innuendoes and veiled threats—"the type of thing that says, 'Well, you know where your place is.'" She was philosophical: "I think you sort of get accustomed to that." In addition, "Many people will think that you're presuming—presuming quite a bit—when you take it upon yourself to decide that you're qualified to run for it, for the first time ever."

In subsequent primary elections, she defeated Democratic opponents, one of whom was a black man, the Rev. Temperance Wright, and another was a white former mayor. She never had Republican opposition in the general election. The municipalities she represented were predominantly white, and she won a plurality of the vote.

Once she had taken her seat in the Capitol, she observed discomfort among the male legislators: "When I first came, they were very formal—and a little leery—until they found out that you're really not too different from them." To some, she was "a curiosity," but "they were friendly enough." Some would say things like, "What's a nice lady like you doing up here? Wouldn't you rather be home with the kids?"

Eventually, colleagues became accustomed to her. "I guess we come out more similar on a whole lot of things the more we get to know one another. They may not be particularly concerned with poor people or human priorities. I've got to be concerned with them because I see them all the time. And I've been up around them and within them, and these kind of priorities are going to come first with me. They may not come first with my colleagues," whose concerns may be business and roads.

"Everybody is the sum total of their total environment, right? The things I'm saying are the things I'm accustomed to. They've never seen that side of it. So, in many instances, I have a job of educating them up to my point of view," she said. "They don't know what I'm talking about when I talk about the welfare mother with 10 children that may want to work and how she gets caught in this cycle and can't get out of it and how all of these things take place."

"I have my priorities in order, and my black priorities come first and women second," she said. Case in point: One of the first bills she filed was intended to enable the state to levy taxes against the Florida Federation of Women's Clubs, a group of 20,000 women whose bylaws allowed only white women as members. "I couldn't get any action on it because they were a very powerful group throughout the state," she said. "But after I launched the bill, I was able to file suit against them on behalf of two clients who wanted admittance into that organization, and they did drop this from their bylaws."

Later Cherry introduced a bill in the House to ratify the federal Equal Rights Amendment (ERA), which had passed both houses of Congress by 1972. The Florida

House passed it twice, but the Senate turned it down. It could have passed, she said, if Democratic Gov. Reubin Askew (1971–1979) had gone out and campaigned for it all over the state, just as he had done to win support for a corporate tax.

In addition, Paula Hawkins, a Republican National Committeewoman who had been elected to the Florida Public Service Commission, "could have made a big difference with her Republican delegation when the ERA was up, to come before their committee, or to make any sort of attempt, and she did not," Cherry said. Other than consumer advocacy, Hawkins "hasn't related as a woman's candidate." (The national ERA ratification effort would fizzle out in 1982, the congressionally imposed deadline, when 35 states, including Florida, had not approved the amendment.[55])

A big legislative issue for Cherry was child care. As she explained, blacks needed child care to hold jobs and get job training. Mothers needed to feel comfortable that care was up to standard for children's safety, and that care was affordable and accessible. Among her accomplishments in office were an increase in child care facilities, testing for sickle cell anemia (a hereditary blood disorder), and an increase in aid paid to poor families with dependent children.

As a rule, she fought for human rights—and endured some hard losses. She fought hard against the reinstatement of capital punishment, for example, but was trumped by "community pressure" and an upcoming election. She deplored the Haitian refugee crisis. "We've got about three or four hundred people that have come to these shores," but they were sent to Miami jails, and some were committing suicide. That was ironic, she said, in a country where the Statue of Liberty says, "Give me your tired, your poor, your huddled masses yearning to breathe free."

Unafraid to take on substantial issues, she grew annoyed with House leadership that pigeonholed women legislators on committees like Education and Health, instead of Transportation or Energy. "I have been trying to get the fellows to see that we are tired of doing the housekeeping tasks. We do them all the time. I'm on Judiciary. That's still one of those, too, that they let women go on. But I have told the leadership, 'I'm moving up. I want decision making. I want a chairmanship, or I want [to be] a minority whip. I don't want this any longer, I want to move up. I'm tired of being stereotyped into this,'" she said. They refused.

She was active in increasing police protection in her district and worked on housing and welfare issues. "I'm on the Housing Committee and we haven't been able to get a housing bill out of here since I've been up here," she said. "I think everybody ought to be entitled to be adequately housed."

Election to the House shoved her into the state spotlight, both as a black and as a woman. "When you're voted in, you become like a legislator at large for the state of Florida. So therefore your duties and responsibilities are monumental." Colleagues regarded her as the spokesperson for blacks: "I speak on behalf of these people whose voices have not been heard, and who could do it better than I could? Others can sympathize, but they certainly can't empathize. They can't put themselves in black people's places."

In some ways, race worked in her favor. "Having been black, I know discrimination keenly," she said. So with other types of discrimination, "I can readily see them and understand them." Having this sensitivity, for example, she was able to talk to male colleagues about such things as giving rape victims access to female—not male—officers and attorneys.

Gov. Askew, whom she believed was a "sincere" and "well-intentioned" man, had not done enough for blacks and women. "He hasn't spoken out as strongly as I feel he should," she said. Neither his Human Relations Commission nor his Commission on the Status of Women had done anything. If the Human Relations Commission had been functioning, the state would have had an affirmative action program and it would have been doing meaningful things, she said.

On the other hand, his stand on busing was "a bold move" that had won the support of blacks. He had also made a number of black appointments, including Athalie Range as Secretary of the Department of Community Affairs, Jesse McCrary, Jr., as Secretary of State, and Joseph Hatchett to the Florida Supreme Court. "We still have further down the road to go," she said.

Where the Governor had made a mistake, in Cherry's view, were the handful of aides from out of state. One example was Dr. Claud Anderson, State Coordinator for Education, who was from Michigan. "I don't think that you bring a man in from Michigan to tell you what to do with education in Florida when you've got all these people here that are highly trained, that have been working in the educational system, that came up through it, were trained in it, and then you pick somebody like this. It's sort of a slap in the face." The aides may be good men, "but it's as though you didn't have anything available, the local talent didn't come up to par."

On the whole, however, she would rather deal with Southerners than Northerners. "Maybe it's because I'm more accustomed to it" or maybe Southerners are "more sincere" and "not as vicious" as Yankees. "I can even take [Alabama Gov. George] Wallace a lot better than I can a whole lot of Northerners that come down and ask for my vote. And you'll find more and more of that." Black people were turning to Wallace, a segregationist, because he was a known quantity. Furthermore, she believed that black and white Southerners, notwithstanding a troubled history, could work out their problems together. "We, black and white, can sit down better with one another than any other group of people," she said.

Working with other state officials, she experienced both racial and gender discrimination. "It's very embarrassing to me to be a part of the state, and the state is discriminating so blatantly on the face of it—blatantly! And when you call officials

Figure 3.19. State Rep. Gwendolyn Cherry (*left*), Florida's first black female legislator (1970), meets with Congresswoman Shirley Chisholm (*right*), the first black female elected to Congress (1968) and the first black female presidential candidate (1972), at the Democratic National Convention in Miami Beach in 1972. State Archives of Florida, *Florida Memory*, https://www.floridamemory.com/items/show/36455. Photograph ca. 1972.

in to tell them about cases where one may come to you, state employees will come and say I was laid off because of this or this happened, and you don't get the full cooperation of the state official in charge." She found the same was true of universities: "The women are screaming because nobody is doing anything, and they're forced to go back to the universities and they say discrimination is still blatant—all over." She lamented having to use the courts to enforce equal treatment for women and minorities. "The courts are effective I think only because they stop the monies, or they're punitive."

At the same time, she believed that blacks weren't as organized as they should have been. "I have been all over the state to try to interest blacks in running, because I really believe that this is where the action is and where we have to go to make the changes we want. We're trying to get together the black elected officials [about 50] in the state of Florida, but like I said, we're way behind." However, she believed one young black lawyer, Alcee Hastings, had a bright future. He had run unsuccessfully for the U.S. Senate in 1970 as a Democrat in a largely Republican district. Fundraising might be an obstacle for him, she thought, "but he is the nearest thing that we have to [national civil rights leader] Julian Bond down here." (Hastings would win a seat in Congress in 1992.)

With the influx of Cubans in Miami, she hoped for a political coalition between Cubans and blacks. "They are beginning to talk about it," she said. "Miami is becoming one-third black, one-third Spanish speaking, and one-third white." The city already had a Spanish-speaking mayor, Maurice A. Ferré, and a Dade County Commissioner. She believed that more Spanish-speaking people would run for office in the future.

Black women could more easily get elected than black men: "The door will open a little bit quicker for us," she said. "We have been playing a role of compromise ever since I can remember, between blacks and whites, in family situations, in home situations, in service situations, and everything."

In speeches to schools and groups around the state, she encouraged high school students to learn about politics and state government and urged them, especially girls, to consider running for office.

Getting organized was also necessary to register black voters. After the passage of the Voting Rights Act, labor unions, the Voter Education Project, the A. Philip Randolph Institute,[56] and other groups conducted voter registration drives in "block plans" where blacks lived. But they were only mildly successful because people didn't want to lose pay by taking time off from jobs to register. "Economic dependence on whites was an important factor."

She acknowledged that purging names from rolls could be a problem if people had not voted in a while. Registration forms were complicated and many blacks may not have been able to understand them, even with help. Moreover, registration hours were difficult and transportation was sometimes lacking, although deputized registrars had begun coming to neighborhoods. "The big problem is indifference—a feeling that their vote won't make a difference. They need living examples of how it can."

Black constituents also had little understanding of a legislator's duties. In some ways, they regarded her as a token. "They can't see anything you're doing, and it seems like they do not understand the job. They have not been exposed to it, so they come to criticize it. And it comes right back to that indifference that you get or apathy about even wanting to run for the jobs." She expressed frustration: "You're not really effectuating the kinds of changes that you might be able to do if you were not black or female."

Although it might have been hard to organize blacks, the same could not be said of women. "I think women are ready to place a woman in Congress. They have been waiting a long time," she said. "They are ready for a woman Lieutenant Governor, if Askew had sense enough to pick one." (Her predictions would prove correct: Paula Hawkins (R) would win election to the U.S. Senate in 1980, becoming Florida's first woman to that post, and Jennifer Carroll (R) would become the first black woman Lieutenant Governor in 2011.) One woman who had told Cherry that she planned to run for a statewide office was Roxcy Bolton,[57] a women's rights activist perhaps best known for stopping the practice of using only women's names for hurricanes.

Overall, Cherry found it challenging to hold office: "It's been lonely, it's been hard work, it's been demanding physically and financially. It's been a sacrifice, and I guess that's true whether you're black, white, male or female."

Despite the challenge, she had given some thought to running for higher office, possibly Congress. She never got the chance. She died in a car accident in 1979 before the end of her fourth term. She left behind a legacy not just for blacks and women but for all people facing oppression. "When you are talking about people's rights, if you are going to fight for one set of rights, you've got to fight for the other," she said. "It doesn't make sense if you don't."

Information for this story was drawn from two interviews with Gwen Cherry: (1) May 21, 1974, from the Southern Oral History Program, #4007A-47 in the Southern Historical Collection, University of North Carolina Library, Chapel Hill, and (2) Nov. 7, 1975, as part of the Dr. James Button oral history project, University of Florida, which is available at http://ufdc.ufl.edu/UF00005808/00001.

John "Gus" Plummer (R)

First Republican African-American man elected to the Florida House of Representatives, 1980

Personal: Born March 12, 1944, Miami, Florida. Died September 5, 1985.

Education:

- Florida International University

Occupation: School Bus Driver

Trailblazer Elections:

- House of Representatives District 114 (Dade County) *Rep Primary* 1980
  - John Plummer (50.7%), Ceferino C. Rodriguez (49.3%)
- House of Representatives District 114 (Dade County) *General Election* 1980
  - John Plummer-R (53.0%), Alan Rosenthal-D (47.0%)

Figure 3.20. John "Gus" Plummer (*second from left*) was the first black Republican man elected to the Florida House of Representatives in 1980, although few knew of his party affiliation—an intentional campaign strategy. He visited the Governor's Mansion with others, including minority trailblazers Carrie Meek (*center*) and Dr. Arnett Girardeau (*far right*). State Archives of Florida, *Florida Memory*, https://www.floridamemory.com/items/show/21419. Photograph ca. 1980–1982.

THE JOHN "GUS" PLUMMER STORY

John "Gus" Plummer was the first black Republican since Reconstruction to win election to the Florida House, but that distinction is sometimes withheld because of his elusive campaigning. As the *Miami Herald* reported when Plummer died in 1985, "It was widely speculated that Mr. Plummer was capitalizing on the last name he shared with one of Dade County's prominent white political families."[58]

A school bus driver with no previous political experience, he upset a favored Democratic rival, both running for an open seat in 1980. Many observers considered his campaign strategy deceitful, while others called him shrewd.

What is the real story?

Plummer, age 36 at the time of the election, had been a bus driver for the Dade County School District for five years, but he had also worked as a day laborer, delivered newspapers, done lawn maintenance, and run side businesses, such as selling art objects. "He was a smart person who just didn't have a college degree," said Mamie Pinder, his political advisor and a family friend. Described as a shy and gentle man, he was polite, especially to women, and helped neighbors by putting up awnings and painting houses, for example, all for nothing.

The son of Cassie and Morris Plummer, Gus had seven brothers and sisters. His mother worked and, interestingly, "raised Janet Reno from a little girl."[59] (Reno would become U.S. Attorney General under President Bill Clinton.) John's siblings grew up to assume various occupations: One was a firefighter, others included a nurse and teacher, and still another worked in sales for the *Miami Herald*. They "were good friends of all the blacks in South Miami for the most part. They were pioneers," Pinder said.

Pinder, whose family had come from the Bahamas, had been best friends in school with Plummer's older sister and brother. "As a kid in high school, there were about five or six of us from the Grove, and when we were learning to drive, our destination was to the Plummer family. His mother would have the collard greens and cornbread waiting for us every Sunday. So I halfway grew up in the Plummer family." Other neighbors would come to their home to watch movies. There was no theater in the neighborhood, said Pinder, so "the Plummer family bought a big screen and they would get movies and show them, and people would come over there."

As young adults in the 1960s, Plummer and Pinder witnessed the desegregation of Miami-Dade County public schools. Actually, Pinder was the first black teacher hired by the system and taught at several schools in a career lasting 26 years. They also lived through the implementation of President Lyndon Johnson's policy initiatives in such areas as civil rights, poverty reduction, health care (Medicare), environmental quality, and federal aid to education.

In 1973, evidently disgusted with the Democrats, Pinder switched to the Republican Party. At first she was content to stuff envelopes and work the phone, but after a few years she decided to form a club. She ran into trouble finding black Republicans: "So, I talked to God and I said, 'God, I am lonely. As you made a world, I want to make me some black Republicans.'" With the help of fellow party members, like Ted Lyons[60] (who was black) and Mary Collins and Angel Bradley (who were white), she succeeded in forming the All-American Republican Council of Dade County. Among the council members was Gus Plummer.

During a council meeting at Plummer's house, Pinder proposed that the group put up two candidates in upcoming elections as a way to get the club moving. "John came to me and said, 'I'll be one of your candidates. I would like to run for a legislator.' So I said, 'Oh, that's wonderful, John!'" (The other candidate was a 25-year-old businessman, Scott McPherson.)

Pinder quickly began offering advice: "I said, 'John, let's get started. You have a good political last name.'" She was referring to two white Democrats: J. L. Plummer, a longtime Miami Commissioner, and his brother Larry, state Representative. Their family owned a funeral business. Subsequently, she submitted an article to a friend who was editor of a local community newspaper. The article said that "'to many South Miamians, the name Plummer is a new name, but to the majority, it's an old established name because it's a name that's been around in the South.' What I was saying about the black Plummer was also true about the white Plummer because the white Plummer owned the funeral homes."

Pinder further advised: "'John, you're not going to take any pictures. You're going to leave the name out there to do the work. And when you get these invitations to go to these meetings to debate and all that, don't show up because we don't want to do nothing to hurt the name.' It's a good name right there because they just had to be Democrats to get that support they need to get elected."

"The cute part was John got called to come to the meetings because they were going to endorse and give money," Pinder said. "So he would go and wear his badge that said, 'Nothing But Mr. Plummer.' Not the first name, but his name. All the Democrats thought it was a Democrat. My God, he was black."

The campaign used the slogan "The family name Plummer speaks for itself" and distributed signs, door hangers, and other literature printed by one of Gus's best friends. Supporters met for campaign parties at Gus's house. "Reno was over there for the parties because this is all of South Miami," Pinder said.

In the September Republican primary, Gus defeated Ceferino Rodriguez with 50.7 percent[61] of the vote in the district. He won the right to run in the November general election, where he would square off against Democrat Alan Rosenthal, 28, a Coconut Grove lawyer running a second time for an office that he had almost won in the previous election.

Gus's clandestine campaign style did not escape the notice of the *Miami Herald*. In an Oct. 16 article,[62] the newspaper described the name confusion and noted that Gus "has denied several requests for an interview, failed to return phone calls, and refused to sit for a photograph."

Democrats, who outnumbered Republicans three to one in the district, acknowledged they had to take the contest seriously. Larry Plummer, the state Representative, said, "Even the colors on his signs are the same as mine, blue and gold." Furthermore, Rosenthal had raised nearly $29,000 to Gus's $1,642.

The newspaper was careful to solicit the view of the Republican side: "John Plummer has the full support of his party's regulars, according to Mary Collins, the Republican committeewoman coordinating campaigns in the county this year. Plummer, too, is a member of the party's county executive committee. 'When he ran for the county committee, he worked hard,' Collins says of Plummer. 'He's a hardworking guy. He's not an aristocrat. . . . He's out of the working force—that type. He's not afraid to get his hands dirty.'"

Gus must not have remained completely hidden because Rosenthal admitted to the newspaper that he had met Gus at a candidate forum of the Dade County League of Women Voters—and liked him. Furthermore, both men voiced support for single-member districts and the Equal Rights Amendment for women.

"The myth was that he basically stayed home during the campaign—that's just not true," said McPherson, who had campaigned and had been elected at the same time. "He would go out on the campaign trail. He would make speeches." McPherson remembered one countywide candidate forum organized by the Association for Retarded Citizens. "Candidates were allowed to stand up and give speeches and answer questions if there were any. This happened to be up in North Miami Beach somewhere off of 163rd Street. I was scheduled to speak and was waiting my turn in the back of the room. It was an evening event, fairly well attended, and Gus was talking. I was standing next to Alan Rosenthal."

"When Gus started speaking," McPherson continued, "Alan smiled and clapped his hand on the shoulder of his—we'll call him a consultant—and they smiled and proceeded to walk out of the room. I got the impression that may have been the first time Rosenthal actually saw Gus on the trail. But Gus did events such as that. He obviously spent a lot of time campaigning in Republican areas and at Republican meetings, but he did branch out and did campaign in the community and did campaign at political events which were designed by interest groups to get their people to see who their candidates were."

Rosenthal tried to overcome the name confusion by buying large ads. One in the *Miami Herald* had the headline "Alan Rosenthal's problem: He's endorsed by J. L. and Larry Plummer—but his opponent is named John Plummer!!"[63] The ads weren't enough.

Plummer defeated Rosenthal 38,147 to 33,995. "Family Name Is Plummer's No. 1 Helper," read the headline in the *Miami Herald*[64] two days later.

"John G. Plummer was the mystery man of the 1980 election. The nobody who outsmarted everybody. The political unknown whose odd strategy was to shun the media, avoid the usual forums, and spend less than $1,700 on advertising," the article began.

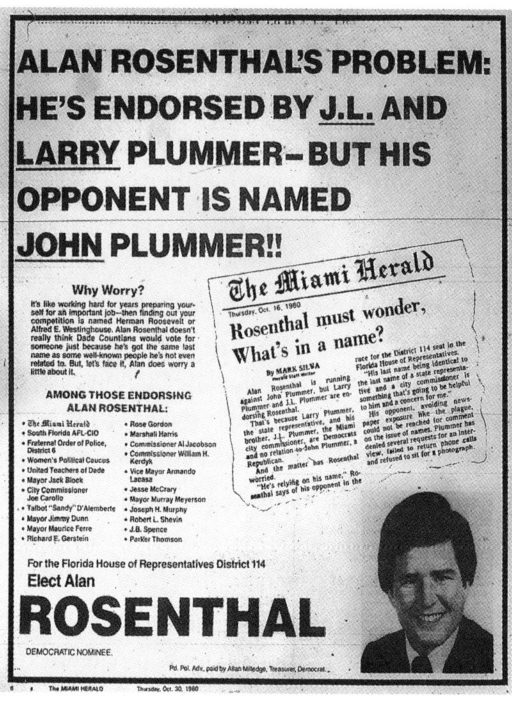

Figure 3.21. Running in a largely Democratic district, John "Gus" Plummer, a black school bus driver, capitalized on his last name when campaigning. At the time, there were already two prominent Plummers in office—white Democrats Larry (State Representative) and his brother J. L. (Miami City Commissioner). Alan Rosenthal, a white downtown lawyer, realized the effectiveness of Gus Plummer's tactic a little too late and was upset despite outspending the black Republican 30 to 1. Advertisement from the *Miami Herald*, October 30, 1980.

"He's an unpolished speaker. He wouldn't wear a three-piece suit. His usual method of campaigning was to walk around shopping centers giving out literature with a yellow cardboard elephant pinned to his T-shirt."

He won by gaining the votes of both Republicans and blacks, Pinder said. She readily admitted her role in framing the Plummer name: "I'm the one who started the name game." Others suggested that Gus, and other Republican winners that year, may have ridden the coattails of Ronald Reagan, who captured the presidency.

Gus insisted, however: "I didn't win because of my name." He told the *Herald* reporter how his seven brothers and sisters and numerous cousins had helped with the campaign. "It's my family name. Why shouldn't my family get credit just like any other politician's?" He explained his avoidance of the media as not wanting to be shaped by them. "I wanted to be independent. I was trying hard to prove a point."

Furthermore, he didn't want to be called a "black leader" but rather representative of "all the people." As part of that goal, "He wants to bring 'real' jobs to South Florida, not temporary government employment programs. 'I know what it is to work for nothing.'" He said he would quit his bus driver job and devote his full time to the legislative job, glad to exchange the $5,000-a-year salary with one of $12,000.

Once Gus was elected, Pinder advised him further: "I said, 'John, when you go up there, don't say anything for a while, just sit and for a few months, a few weeks, and learn the system and what's going on.' And that's pretty much what he did. He was there for almost a year and when he said something, they were shocked, everybody, you know."

Gus was more astute than that, McPherson said. "We used to marvel at how he would understand whose button to push. Obviously he was there on the caucus votes, and he was there on a lot of the philosophical votes, but he would almost instinctively know when he needed to follow, say, Carrie Meek's button [black Democrat] and when he needed to follow Tom Gallagher's button [white Republican]."

Sometimes freshmen were a little slow in voting. "Some of these procedural votes can be kind of dicey, and you're trying to parse out exactly where you're supposed to go," McPherson said. "Gus was never encumbered like that. I mean, boom, his vote was up on the board."

Pinder's say-nothing strategy may not have served him well. "In a June 1981 straw ballot," reported the *Miami Herald*, "the Tallahassee press corps voted him among the state's least effective legislators."[65] He sponsored three bills, one of which was designed to cut bureaucratic delays in hospital emergency rooms. When that bill passed, his fellow legislators gave him an ovation.

When Gus ran for reelection in 1982, he lost 2 to 1 in the primary to Theresa Ashkar, a real estate salesperson backed by Republican power broker Carlos Salman. "I think Plummer tried to capitalize on his name again," Ashkar said. "You have to give voters credit. It slipped by them last time, but they didn't let it happen again."[66]

"The redesigned District 114 was one of the few seats that was considered to be relatively safe for a Republican," McPherson said. "Definitely the numbers were better in that seat than they were in some of the other seats. So I guess it was just kind of inevitable that he would draw a primary opponent, and it would also be inevitable that the Democrats would find a good opponent," who turned out to be the eventual winner, Betty Metcalf (1982–1988).

"I think he wanted to be a part of something that was bigger," McPherson said. "He was blazing a trail down there in District 114, which was basically Coconut Grove, Coral Gables, South Miami, a part of South Miami. I think he obviously achieved that goal. It was regrettable that he wound up losing in a primary, but everybody I think was targeting that seat in 1982."

The defeat hit Gus hard, Pinder recalled. She blamed his demise on the controlling influence of a House Democrat, who was also black. "She got John up there and started working on him. Because he would tell me what she would tell him to do, and I would tell him to stick with the Republicans. That's the reason why they did not reelect him. They didn't reelect him because they felt like he was too much under her control."

He might have won, Pinder said, "if he had stuck with the Republicans and included them." She believed that he had the personality, counted whites among his friends, and got along well with people.

Gus died in 1985 at age 41. The family asked McPherson to speak at the funeral. "I was happy to do it because I felt that he was maligned." Gus was not the most skilled orator in politics, but "nonetheless, I thought by virtue of what he did and some of the bills that he filed, and the work he did in committee, and especially the way he was able to parse out 'Am I going with my party on this, or am I going with my color on this?'"

"His ability to move between the Black Caucus and the Republican Caucus I thought was outstanding," McPherson said. "I think he deserved an appropriate and respectful eulogy praising his political skill, acknowledging some of the flaws in his speech making. But I think that should not be the determiner of skill. Skillful oration is not, and should never be, the lone factor on which we judge our candidates or our politicians. It's their ability to grasp issues and their ability to stand firm and their ability to not be swayed if they believe that they are right. Those are all things that I think Gus stood for."

Another speaker at the funeral was, ironically, Larry Plummer, the white legislator. He spoke "because he and John would kid each other behind the scene that they were brothers," Pinder said.

As it turned out, then, the low-profile campaign strategy Gus used was not his own doing. It was the work of a party operative who seized upon the notoriety of a shared name. He may have been elusive to the media and to Democrats, but not to the Republicans and blacks who knew him.

Most of the information for this story came from interviews between the author and two people who knew John Plummer well: Mamie Pinder, on Aug. 14, 2014, and Scott McPherson (state Representative 1980–1982), on Sept. 11, 2014. Both Pinder, who was black, and McPherson, who was white, served with Plummer on Pinder's All-American Republican Council of Dade County.

Ileana Ros (R)

First Cuban woman to serve in the Florida House of Representatives, 1982
First Cuban to serve in the Florida Senate, 1986
First Cuban American and first Hispanic woman to serve in the U.S. House of Representatives, 1989

Personal: Born July 15, 1952, Havana, Cuba; married with one child, two stepchildren.

Education:

- Miami-Dade Community College, A.A. (1972)
- Florida International University, B.A. in education (1975)
- Florida International University, M.A. in educational leadership (1986)
- University of Miami, Ph.D. in higher education (2004)

Occupation: Teacher

Trailblazer Elections:

- House of Representatives District 110 (Part of Dade County) *Rep Primary* 1982
    - Ileana Ros (48.3%), Raul Pozo (40.2%), S.J. Rand (11.5%)

- House of Representatives District 110 (Part of Dade County) *Rep Runoff* 1982
  - Ileana Ros (55.6%), Raul Pozo (44.4%)
- House of Representatives District 110 (Part of Dade County) *General Election* 1982
  - Ileana Ros-R (58.5%), William (Bill) Oliver-D (41.5%)
- Senate District 34 (Part of Dade County) *Rep Primary* 1986
  - Ileana Ros-Lehtinen (88.0%), Bettina Rod-Inclan (12.0%)
- Senate District 34 (Part of Dade County) *General Election* 1986
  - Ileana Ros-Lehtinen-R (58.2%), Steve Zack-D (41.8%)
- U.S. House of Representatives District 18 (Part of Dade County) *Rep Primary Special Election* 1989
  - Ileana Ros-Lehtinen (82.8%), Carlos Perez (11.05%), David M. Fleischer (3.39%), John M. Stembridge (2.76%)
- U.S. House of Representatives District 18 (Part of Dade County) *General Special Election* August 29, 1989
  - Ileana Ros-Lehtinen-R (53.25%), Gerald F. Richman-D (46.75%)

For the full Ileana Ros-Lehtinen story, see the Congress section, page 415.

Figure 3.22. Ileana Ros-Lehtinen (*center*), a Cuban Republican, was the first Hispanic woman to serve in both the Florida House and Senate. In her time in the Florida House, she said she really enjoyed working with the Republican delegation from South Florida—as Cuban Republicans were just beginning to flex their political muscle. Shown *(L-R)*: Luis Morse of Miami, Roberto Casas of Hialeah, Ros-Lehtinen, Tom Gallagher of Miami, and Arnhilda Gonzalez-Quevedo of Coral Gables. State Archives of Florida, *Florida Memory*, https://www.floridamemory.com/items/show/21742. Photograph by Donn Dughi (Donald Gregory), May 19, 1986.

Roberto Casas (R)

First Republican Cuban man elected to the Florida House of Representatives, 1982

First Cuban Republican man elected to the Florida Senate (a first shared with Javier Souto), 1988

Personal: Born April 25, 1931, Havana, Cuba

Education: Havana Business University, B.A. (1954)

Occupation: Real Estate Broker/Investor

Trailblazer Elections:

- House of Representatives District 107 (Part of Dade County) *Rep Primary Special Election* 1982
  - Roberto Casas—*Unopposed*

- House of Representatives District 107 (Part of Dade County) *Special General Election* 1982
  - Roberto Casas-R (53.7%), Ed Cardounel-D (46.2%)
- Senate District 33 (Part of Dade County) *Rep Primary* 1988
  - Roberto Casas (52.5%), Rudolfo "Rudy" Garcia, Jr. (47.5%)
- Senate District 33 (Part of Dade County) *General Election* 1988
  - Roberto Casas—*Unopposed*

For the full Roberto Casas story, see the Senate section, page 226.

Figure 3.23. Roberto Casas, the first Cuban Republican elected to the Florida House of Representatives, was elected in a special election in January 1982. Once a Democrat, he along with many other Cubans of his era switched to the Republican Party because of the Bay of Pigs fiasco. State Archives of Florida, *Florida Memory*, https://www.floridamemory.com/items/show/21938. Photograph ca. 1982–1995.

Figure 3.24. State Rep. Roberto Casas served three terms in the Florida House before being elected to the Florida Senate in 1988. Bumper sticker courtesy of Roberto Casas.

Humberto J. Cortina, Jr. (R)

First class of Cubans in the Florida House of Representatives, along with Ileana Ros and Roberto Casas, 1982

Personal: Born August 7, 1941, Havana, Cuba; fled to the United States in 1960.

Education:

University of Florida, B.A. in international affairs (1968)

Occupation: President and Founder of HJC Consultants, Inc. Radio talk show host: Univision Communications Radio Mambí 710 AM

Trailblazer Elections:

- House of Representatives District 113 (Part of Dade County) *Rep Primary* 1982
  - Humberto Cortina (58.6%), Evaristo L. Marina (33.4%), Ceferino C. Rodriguez (8.0%)

- House of Representatives District 113 (Part of Dade County) *General Election* 1982
  - Humberto Cortina-R (53.1%), Lincoln Diaz-Balart-D (46.9%)

Figure 3.25. Cuban-born Humberto J. Cortina (*right*) is engaged in deep conversation with Elvin Martinez, D-Tampa (*left*). Cortina, a veteran of the Bay of Pigs invasion force Brigade 2506, was elected to the Florida House of Representatives in 1982 following adoption of single-member districts. The 1982 session saw three Cuban-born Republicans from Miami serving together in the House—Cortina, Roberto Casas, and Ileana Ros. Photograph courtesy of the Florida House of Representatives, 1984.

THE HUMBERTO J. CORTINA, JR., STORY

Humberto J. Cortina was born in Havana, Cuba, in 1941 into a prominent political family. A grandfather, Dr. José Manuel Cortina, a renowned lawyer, writer, and politician, served in Cuba as a Senator, Secretary of State, and the Cuban delegate to the League of Nations. His father, Humberto J. Cortina, Sr., and an uncle, Dr. Nestor Carbonell, served in the Cuba Legislature and were involved in Cuba's political history.

His family fled to Miami in 1960 after Fidel Castro came to power in 1959. The thinking within the family at that time was that the so-called revolution would last a short time. Many prominent Cuban families fled, most of them professionals, and survived economically by doing whatever jobs were available in Florida.

Within a month of his arrival, Cortina and several of his friends joined what became Assault Brigade 2506—the expeditionary force that landed at the Bay of Pigs, Cuba. He had realized what kind of revolution the Castro brothers had brought into Cuba from the high number of firing squads and killing of individuals without going through any kind of judicial process. One well-known assassin, in particular, was Che Guevara.

"That is what prompted me to join the training camps in Guatemala that eventually landed and is known as the Bay of Pigs invasion, in Cuba on the 17th of April in 1961," Cortina said.

"During the invasion, I was wounded in both legs and taken prisoner. I would like to point out that the members of Brigade 2506 were young Cubans of all aspects of Cuban society, from the wealthiest to the poorest, from all corners of the island, without a doubt, a cross-section of the Cuban people. They were honest and hard workers with one goal in mind—to liberate Cuba from Castro's Communist regime."

Cortina was head of communications of the Second Battalion that landed in Playa Larga at the Bay of Pigs. The battalion landed under heavy air attack, and his ship, the *Houston*, was sunk. "After three days of fighting and running out of ammunition, we were captured and imprisoned," he said.

In Florida, the Cuban Families Committee was created to negotiate the release of the prisoners. Castro asked for $53 million in food and medicine as donations for their release. After being freed, Cortina and other officers of the brigade were appointed lieutenants in the U.S. Army by President John F. Kennedy (D.).

After his U.S. Army service, he and a group of other officers decided to attend the University of Florida at Gainesville. The thinking was that it was close enough to Miami to take part in another attempt to overthrow the Castro regime should that have happened.

After graduation in 1968 with a bachelor's degree, and uncertain about his future plans of whether to get a master's degree or a law degree, "I received a call from an organization called The Council of the Americas [COA]. The chairman at that time was David Rockefeller. After a series of interviews, I received an offer to become the Council's director in Peru. After one year, I became regional director covering the Andean Common Market countries including Bolivia, Chile, Paraguay and Uruguay."

"After five years, the Council decided to promote me to New York. But instead I decided to return to Miami. I helped create and fund, with the support of the COA, the International Center [now the World Trade Center], of which I was the executive director. My time with the Council allowed me to interact with presidents in Latin America and top businessmen, from the United States and Central and South America. It allowed me to understand both the message of the United States and the interpretation of our message in Latin America."

"While at the International Center, I was offered the position of assistant city manager in the City of Miami—the first Hispanic and Cuban American to hold that position. Those were difficult times. There was no upward mobility in the city, perhaps resentment of the Cuban community, but with time my message prevailed."

"In 1982, I decided to run for office and was elected to the Florida House of Representatives. The ability to get elected at that time was enhanced by the Legislature deciding to change from a multi-member district to a single-member district. This reapportionment presented a great opportunity to run for the Florida House. I selected District 113, the heart of Little Havana."

Two other Cuban Americans were elected that year: Roberto Casas, from Hialeah, and Ileana Ros from West Dade County. Cortina believed they were taking a message to the state House: "I always explained to my colleagues that I was not the Cuban-American Representative; rather I was a Representative of Cuban-American descent. I always wanted to explain why the Cubans were in exile, what was our cause, and what happened at the Bay of Pigs," he said.

Figure 3.26. Four prisoners (*front row in t-shirts*), captured by Cuban forces in the Bay of Pigs invasion and released provisionally by Fidel Castro, take part in a news conference at Columbia University School of Journalism in New York. Shown *(L-R)*: Rolando Toll, Alvare Sanchez, Jr. (*in suit*), Enrique Ruiz Williams, Humberto Cortina, and Jose Smith. Sanchez was chairman of the Cuban Families Committee for Liberation of Prisoners of War, guiding efforts to raise ransom for men still held in Cuba. Photograph by Jacob Harris, Associated Press, May 14, 1962, published in an article by Joaquin Estrada-Montalvan, "On the 50th Anniversary of the Bay of Pigs" (Playa Girón)—http://www.ellugareno.com/2011/04/en-el-50-aniversario-de-bay-of-pigs.html?m=1. © 1962 Associated Press.

Although jobs and education continue to be major issues in the Hispanic community, in Miami, the Cuban issue continues to dominate any campaign. "Thirty-five years after my election, it stills dominates the radio waves in Miami, and that includes local, state, and federal elections," he said.

He remembered his feelings upon being sworn into office as "a tremendous honor." He continued: "It brings out the best in you because you realize that you are now serving, that I am here to serve the people."

"In addition," he said, "you start to understand what I call the American system. This amalgamation of so many people, so many languages, and inclusion in American society."

"It is also interesting," he commented, "when people have asked me if I thought that I was discriminated [against] in the United States, I have always said, 'Never. I have never felt that way.'"

During a session in the House of Representatives, while debating another colleague, he was defending the issue of continuing to offer a course covering Americanism versus Communism in the school system. As a follow-up, Ted Koppel invited Cortina and his fellow Representative to be on ABC's *Nightline,* and continue this debate. During the program, Cortina's colleague said, "That course doesn't mean anything." Cortina responded: "I think you're wrong. You must know your enemy. You must understand how they think. You must give the student an opportunity to understand what they are and what we are, what they represent and what we represent, what kind of economics they're looking at and which one we're looking at."

That interchange "opened my eyes a lot to how the state of Florida thought at one time," Cortina said: "I consider developing relationships in both parties a top priority. You first identify what you have in common. I realized that there are no permanent friends or enemies, only permanent interests."

"Information is power, knowledge is power, but how to use it is the factor that determines success. The art of governing is the art [of compromising] by developing relationships through good communications which are independent of your ideological differences. If you create that, you will succeed."

After leaving office, Cortina formed a successful business consulting company. Today, he hosts a radio talk show in Spanish, "Al Ritmo de Miami," Univision Communications Radio Mambí 710 AM. His topics cover local, national, and international issues. Guests include politicians, professors and entrepreneurs, and a variety of high-profile individuals. He does crossover interviews in English and in Spanish.

"I am often in a position of framing the image of Cubans and Hispanics, which includes U.S. Sen. Marco Rubio, Lt. Gov. Carlos López-Cantera, and Congresswoman Ileana Ros-Lehtinen. They are all close friends and colleagues," he said.

"My biggest strength is access. Access means that I can call all the politicians, business leaders, and they answer my call. When you have that access, it allows you to project not only your concern but the concern of the community on any particular issue; and it also allows you to explain your position."

Throughout his career, Cortina has fought for Cuba, talked about Cuba, and thought about Cuba. "Fifty-five years is a long time," he said. "Attitudes have evolved. Right now, there is only 8 or 9 percent of my generation still alive." During that time, he has witnessed three phases of the Cuban exile: (1) military during the 1960s and early 1970s; (2) economic from the early 1970s to the early 1980s; and (3) political at the local, state, and federal levels from the early 1980s to the present.

President Obama's move in December of 2014 to reestablish diplomatic relations with Cuba caused Cortina to think about his homeland even more. "Why is he doing it? A legacy? Belief that the Castros will give up power? It's hard to tell. But the reality is that no military dictator gives up power. You do not give power away. They don't say, 'Hey, you are right. I am going to change now.' It's all about economics. This possible reestablishment of diplomatic ties marks a new milestone in U.S.-Cuba relations. Will it also translate into the fourth phase in the evolution of the Cuban community in South Florida? It's too soon to say."

Whatever the outcome, Cortina has fond feelings for his adopted state and nation. "I think that the United States is the greatest country in the world. It is a warm and caring country, and I feel very proud to be part of it."

Humberto Cortina was interviewed in person by the author Dec. 17, 2014.

Mimi K. McAndrews (D)

First woman of Asian ancestry elected to the Florida House of Representatives, 1992

Personal: Born October 28, 1956, St. Joseph, Missouri; moved to Florida in 1974, married at 17, divorced with two children.

Education:

- Florida Atlantic University, B.A. in communications (1988)
- Georgetown University Law Center, J.D. (1992)

Occupation: Lawyer/Law Clerk/Former aide to State Rep. Lois Frankel

Trailblazer Elections:

- House of Representatives District 85 (Part of Palm Beach County) *Dem Primary* 1992
    - Mimi K. McAndrews (50.6%), Mark Hayes (49.4%)
- House of Representatives District 85 (Part of Palm Beach County) *General Election* 1992
    - Mimi K. McAndrews-D (56.2%), Remzey L. Samarrai-R (36.9%), J.D. Self-POP (Populist Party) (6.9%)

Figure 3.27. Mimi K. McAndrews, a Korean American, was the first Asian female elected to the Florida House of Representatives in 1992. Adopted by an American family, she did not fully realize the impact her election would have on Asian Americans across the state until afterward, when she received invitations from many Asian groups all over the state to speak to them. State Archives of Florida, *Florida Memory*, https://www.floridamemory.com/items/show/22584. Photograph ca. 1982–1984.

THE MIMI MCANDREWS STORY

"I was a Connie Chung wannabe. I really wanted to go into the media," said Mimi McAndrews. "I just thought it was great that this Asian woman is on TV on the major news network and how could I be like her." Then one day McAndrews encountered a local Asian reporter at a meeting of Women in Communications, a professional association. "Tell me what it's like being a reporter because I really think I want to do this," McAndrews said to her. "She sat me down and shattered all my illusions about what it's like to be in the news industry. I decided to go to law school instead."

The year she graduated from Georgetown University Law Center in Washington, D.C., she was elected the first Asian-American woman to the Florida Legislature.

Born in the United States of Korean descent, "I was adopted by an American family, so I didn't have the traditional upbringing that a lot of minority candidates had. I was raised by a German-Irish family in the Midwest, very union-oriented," she said.

She moved to Florida in the early 1970s. "I didn't have the traditional go to school, go to college, you know, I had lives in between." By the 1980s, she was attending Florida Atlantic University in Boca Raton, majoring in communications.

She got into politics through "a combination of things all happening at the same time," she said. In her senior year at FAU, while taking a class in American government, she met a local activist who always got involved with students. "The best I can recall, we started the Young Democrats at FAU." They gathered a few like-minded students together and attended a meeting of the local Democratic Party. It so happened that the members were electing delegates to the state party convention. "Apparently they could elect so many from their county or something. So I got up and made this little speech, not knowing anybody there, and I won." Furthermore, she had overheard the members saying they needed a student to balance the number of senior delegates. "Quite to the shock of everybody, I got elected as one of the delegates to go to the state convention."

"In that same government class, one of my friends was Lois Frankel's aide at that time. My friend told me that Lois was looking for a campaign manager for her reelection. So I applied. It was an easy campaign because no one filed to run against her. I then went on to become her legislative aide because he moved on to other things. I'm not even sure I really appreciated what a state legislator was because you don't learn a lot about the levels of government through school or even in college." But "I was able to pick up fairly quickly and learn from other people." The job proved to be "a real learning experience."

With Frankel's blessing, and a recommendation for law school, McAndrews left the job after graduating from FAU in 1989. "I would've been happy going to the University of Miami where it's nice and warm all year round, but when you get accepted to a place like Georgetown, and the price to go wasn't much different," the choice was plain, she said. Except for serving as the president of the Asian Pacific American Law Students Association for a year, she didn't get involved in politics. "Lois came up one year when she was campaigning for Congress," McAndrews said, "and I went around with her, but other than that, that was all."

While in law school, her future seemed straightforward. "I always thought I'll go to law school, I'll have my career and I'll come back and I'll run and be just like Lois, but it didn't happen that way," she said. After graduating in 1992, "I came back and was studying for the Bar. I was working at a law firm clerking, and I got a call from Lois about seven in the morning. That's the year she had planned to run against Alcee Hastings [for Congress], and a friend of hers was going to run in her House seat. Well, her friend, for whatever reason, backed out."

"She asked me if I would run," McAndrews said. "I'm tired and it's like, 'OK, Lois,' not really thinking about it." But the decision was made. "Having worked for Lois and seeing how successful she was, especially with the AIDS bill, I mean, that was just incredible," said McAndrews. As she understood the situation, "Nobody wanted to take on that issue. They gave it to [Lois] as kind of a newbie legislator (I think this was her second term) and she just took it on and ran with it. You really could see how one person could make a difference. That's the way I viewed her and I thought, 'Wow! What a privilege, what an honor, what an opportunity.'"

Thus, in addition to working full time and studying for the Bar, she began campaigning for office. Local protocol at that time required calling the presidents of all the Democratic clubs, some of whom she knew. "Nobody was rude to me on the phone, but come to find out later, there were a few people who didn't appreciate that, for whatever reason."

In the primary, she faced political consultant Mark Hayes. "I didn't know him either. Apparently a president of one of the local Democratic clubs in that district supported him, but I had the larger condo support."

McAndrews won by a narrow margin, perhaps 80 votes. "There was a recount and, of course, I was on pins and needles waiting for the election workers to finish counting. I mean, the condo commandos, they vote, but nobody else voted."

In the general election, she ran against two opponents: Republican Remzey Samarrai, and third-party candidate J. D. Self. The Samarrai name and her Korean heritage provided an opportunity for humor in the campaign. "I fondly remember being at one of the union meetings talking about this," she said. Her dad, a former business agent for the IBEW (International Brotherhood of Electrical Workers), "was a big help on my side, so I could stand up there and joke about who my opponent was."

But nobody really made an issue of her heritage, probably because she spoke perfect English and she had grown up in a union family. "I could relate to the union people, and they could relate to me, and they went all out. In fact, my dad came down for that election and to work with them and thank them for helping me," she said.

That is not to say that everyone was enthusiastic. Some in the agriculture community "hated Lois with a passion. These are your good ol' boys—really good ol' boy people—who immediately were put off by me just because of Lois, you know, guilt by association," she said. "Initially it was kind of a cold reception. I'm sure there were some people looking at me like, 'Who is she and what is she doing here?'"

The *Palm Beach Post* endorsed her in the primary but supported Samarrai in the general election. "I think they probably felt that he had a better business background, even though I had a business background, too. But I had just come back from college. I'd been out of the state for a few years, so I was not really well versed, especially on local issues, so I think they just kind of felt that he was more a part of the community." Other papers in her favor were the *Miami Herald* and the *Sun Sentinel*.

The Democratic clubs played a key role in her victory. "I had developed a strong relationship with the president of Golden Lakes, which was the strongest Jewish Democratic club in my district," she said. "I mean, there's really nothing that they wouldn't do for me if I needed it."

An officer of the county Democratic Party, Patty Brick, worked as her campaign manager. "She had been very involved in politics, much more than myself," and had campaigned for Harry Johnston, who had been elected to Congress in 1989. Brick, who was an educator, arranged for a group of high school government students who took on her campaign as a project. "We probably had about 6 to 12 kids, and they would come out and walk with me and help do the mailing. This was kind of their introduction into politics." After the election, the students went to Tallahassee and were recognized by the House. "It was great. I mean, looking at it in hindsight, I appreciate it even more now than I probably did at the time."

The support of Democratic clubs, unions, and area newspapers in Palm Beach County—"that was pretty much it," she said. "Maybe I raised $20,000 in the general election." She had also hired a political consultant to advise her about literature and strategy. "I definitely had somebody helping me. I couldn't do that on my own."

Surprisingly, neither she nor the Asian community knew about each other. "I knew there were some Koreans in West Palm Beach, and that's about all I knew," she said. Consequently, she didn't seek their help, and they didn't offer support. It was only after she was elected that they found out about her heritage. "Somebody must have read it in the paper, and I started getting contacted by various people," such as the Asian American Federation, which has groups all over the state, the Korean Dry Cleaners Association, and Korean martial arts groups. "I mean, it's like, 'Wow!'" she said. "They treated me like royalty." Few of them lived in her district, however, so they were actually more helpful in her reelection campaign, especially in raising money.

At a meeting of the Asian Bar Association in South Florida, she observed that the Asian community was starting to understand the need to get out the vote, run for office, and get people appointed to the judiciary. "When I ran, there were probably less than 1 percent in the entire district that was Asian," and when she knocked on doors, she didn't see a single Asian.

At that time, many Asians tended to not to join the two major political parties. "I'm not sure that the Asians, or any of the immigrants for that matter, really appreciate the history of the parties. That's part of why I could never be a Republican, even though maybe I shouldn't think that way because I'm clearly not as liberal as my predecessor."

Among the areas where she knocked on doors were the unincorporated parts of the county. There she saw Confederate flags hung on houses, pickup trucks parked in the yard, and big dogs barking behind fences with Bad Dog signs, straight out of a Jeff Foxworthy commercial, she said. But it turned out to be fine. "I can remember a few guys coming out and crossing their arms and this is the guy with the Confederate flag on his truck. Once I was able to talk to them, one on one, I think they appreciated that. You know, how many times do you have somebody come to your door that's running for office? Not very often. . . . I think that when it came down to it, they really wanted somebody that cared about their issues and who was at least going to try to do something for them."

"I love campaigning," she said. That was the best part of running for office. "I was just lucky enough to have that experience as a legislative aide. The problem is, there aren't enough opportunities for everybody to do that. Unless you're involved with the local party or just keenly, keenly on top of what's happening in politics, it makes it a little more difficult to go out there and try to run for that kind of an office because you just don't know the issues."

The year she ran (1992), Arkansas Gov. Bill Clinton was running for President, and the big issue was health care. In Palm Beach County, it was education. She ran on both issues, plus "taking care of the seniors because those were the voters," she said. "It's very hard to run a really intelligent campaign if you just don't understand what the issues are." She managed, with some help, "to make it short and sweet so people could understand and make it look like I knew what I was talking about when I really just slightly had a clue."

Watching the returns on election night, "as soon as I realized it was final, I felt like the whole world just fell on my shoulders," she said. "Oh, my God, now what am I supposed to do?" she thought. "It was a little scary. Overwhelming."

A Fighting Democrat For *Change*

"As a former legislative aide to Rep. Lois Frankel, I'm running to pick up where she left off. We must fight to make government work for the people."

Mimi K. McAndrews, 35, Democrat, was born and raised in the Midwest. She has been a resident of Florida for 15 years and has lived in Palm Beach County for ten.

LEGISLATIVE EXPERIENCE
Former aide to Rep. Lois Frankel

BUSINESS EXPERIENCE
Owned/managed successful small business.

LEGAL EXPERIENCE
Law degree from Georgetown University Law Center. Recently joined the firm of Weiss & Handler, P.A.

"I'm supporting Mimi to continue my fight for health care reform and to protect our children."
- Rep. Lois Frankel

Figure 3.28. McAndrews did not have a lot of time to plan a campaign. Rep. Lois Frankel called to ask Mimi to run for the House seat that Frankel was vacating to run for Congress after another Democrat chose not to seek the post at the last minute. Rep. Frankel's powerful endorsement was placed on McAndrews's campaign literature. Photographs of button and campaign literature courtesy of Mimi McAndrews.

Once in Tallahassee, "I knew from my legislative aide days that there's always a little hazing of the legislative freshmen and the first one to have a bill up," she said. Determined to "outsmart these guys, I filed an amendment that gave all the freshmen legislators the best parking spaces, the best seats in the chambers, [their choice of] committees, I mean, just stuff like that. It was designed to fail of course. Well, guess what? It passed the House." Instantly, cheers went up all around, and "the lobbyists were going crazy. [House Speaker] Bo Johnson's going, 'What the hell just happened?'" As it turned out, many senior Democrats supported it simply because it was a Democratic bill. "I think George Crady [D-Nassau County] and Fred Lippman [D-Hollywood] maybe knew because they kind of kidded me on the way out about the bill I had coming up. But the other ones didn't know."

"The delegation of the black legislators, at least some of them, assumed that I was naturally going to side with their issues. While I welcomed the fact that they wanted to kind of take me in, I also didn't necessarily appreciate that they just assumed that I would be like-minded," she said. "I like to think that I could think for myself, and that what I look like was not necessarily going to make a difference." As an example, she voted against a bill that would compensate descendants of the 1923 Rosewood Massacre. Her vote "really had more to do with the principle. It wasn't a racial thing. I agree [the massacre] should not have happened. I just don't know that I agreed with the way they wanted the state to make amends for it."

While in the Legislature, she was instrumental in passing a bill that helped deter unwarranted lawsuits against the state's vegetable farmers, legislation related to Sudden Infant Death Syndrome, as well as legislation clarifying the tax exemption for stadiums and other venues owned by cities.

At the end of her first term, she was astonished to find that her former boss filed to run against her. Frankel wanted her old seat back, having lost in her bid for Congress in 1992. "It was such an anomaly," McAndrews said. "I was everything that Lois represented. I mean, I was literally everything that she represented. To have her decide to run against me, especially after she had said that she wasn't going to, was a shock." McAndrews, though hurt and angry, said to herself: "Come on, you got to stay in there. You can't just give up, you got to fight."

It turned out to be a bitter, divisive campaign with negative press statements and ads. Frankel won handily. "She still had a very strong image among, I would say, non-local party people—people who were not involved in local politics. They still had a pretty good image of her, even though they didn't like her coming out against me the way she did." Frankel won the general election in 1994 and won three more terms thereafter before being elected Mayor of West Pam Beach in 2003 and to Congress in 2012.

"I got recruited very heavily from the Republican Party after that primary with her. I was on their e-mail list and their mail list for probably a couple of years after that. But I would have a hard time just being a Republican, even though some of my ideals might be there."

Through all her campaigns, "Nobody really ever made an issue about my ethnicity." She added, "I hate to say this because it sounds kind of snobbish, but it's because I wasn't acting different. I was just acting like somebody who cared." A candidate who asks, "What can I do to help you because I've got the same health problems that you do, I've got the same educational issues?" can reach voters more effectively. "That's what they want to hear about."

Nor did she promote her Asian heritage. Voters seeing her in person could assume she was Asian, although their guess would probably have been Chinese and not Korean. She neglected to put her photograph on one of her first campaign mailers, probably because of the rush to get it printed. Supporters chided her for the omission. "I thought it was actually kind of a good experiment because it was only the ones that really knew me that said why isn't your picture on there." When she went door-to-door, nobody mentioned her ethnicity.

Her childhood in Missouri in the late 1950s and early 1960s may have been a different matter. "Growing up as I did in an American household, in a city where there was only one or two other people that looked like me, I probably was discriminated against and didn't know it."

In Tallahassee, her ethnicity and gender garnered some attention. When she arrived to take her House seat, even though she had been an aide only a few years earlier, "people were looking at me like, you know, doing like a double take and they don't even know who I am or what I do or what I'm in there for. Now clearly they were people who had never seen an Asian before," except in Chinese restaurants.

She also remembered a committee meeting in which one legislator said there were "different faces at the table now." When she heard a comment like that, "I went out of my way to try to get to know them. Not only was I a female Asian but I had the 'Lois thing,' you know, all over me wherever I went." McAndrews felt she had to get people to "see me for who I am and get out of [Frankel's] shadow as well because she was such a strong personality."

She has received requests for help in running for office, but none from people of Asian descent. Her advice centers on a central theme: "You have to get there to be effective. You can stand on all your principles and all your morals and all your ethics, but if you can't get there, it doesn't matter."

Women, in particular, have had a hard time understanding this concept. "I would tell them, if you want to get something done, you might have to give a little wink, you might have to give a little hug, you might have to give a handshake to somebody that you don't want to be anywhere near. You have to have some alliances. You have to have support from people you'd rather not have to have it from, and that's just the fact of the matter. Maybe that sounds a little sexist to some extent, but that's what you've got to do if that's what it means to get somebody's vote, whether it's in the House or whether it's the guy next door, you've got to have votes. Some of them had a real problem with that."

Despite the reelection loss and the bitterness that erupted during the campaign, "I would still tell people to run, even if you lose. Even if you run twice and lose or run three times and lose. Again, just that experience of getting out there, meeting people. If you run, you obviously have some idealism or interest, I would hope, in thinking that you can make a difference. And it's just a great experience. How many people go out and run for office, you know?"

"I had a friend that would say, 'You need to be prepared to hang all your dirty laundry out in public,' because that's exactly what happens. That's pretty true."

Looking back on the legislative experience, she said, "It was just an honor to be one of 120 legislators," making decisions for millions of people in the state. It was "something I've never forgotten, just the ability to be involved in decisions that are going to affect the rest of the state, maybe forever."

Mimi McAndrews was interviewed in person by the author Oct. 7, 2013.

Annie Betancourt (D)

First Cuban Democratic woman elected to the Florida House of Representatives, 1994

Personal: Born March 3, 1947, Havana, Cuba; moved to Florida in 1960, widowed with one child and one stepchild.

Figure 3.29. Cuban-born Annie Betancourt was President of the Dade County League of Women Voters before running for the Florida House of Representatives in 1994. A League member had initially registered her to vote. Long after she left office, she was taking League members on educational tours of Cuba before the full normalization of relations with the United States had come to fruition. Photograph courtesy of Annie Betancourt.

Education:

- Miami-Dade Community College, A.A. in psychology (1972)
- University of Miami, B.A. in psychology (1974)

Occupation: Administrator, Miami-Dade County Public Schools; Board of Directors of the League of Women Voters of Florida

Trailblazer Elections:

- House of Representatives District 116 (Part of Dade County) *Dem Primary* 1994
    - Annie Betancourt (64.6 %), John Svadbik (17.9%), Ed Blanco (17.5%)
- House of Representatives District 116 (Part of Dade County) *General Election* 1994
    - Annie Betancourt-D (57.2%), Peter J. Gonzalez-R (42.8%)

THE ANNIE BETANCOURT STORY

Annie Betancourt's "defining moment" for entering politics occurred Oct. 21, 1960, the evening of the last of four televised debates between John F. Kennedy and Richard Nixon. "What a novel idea—an election," she thought. "You can literally pick your leader. Where I had come from, it was taken by force."

At the time, she was 13 years old. Her family was staying at a hotel in Miami Beach, waiting to see what would happen in Cuba after revolutionaries had overrun the island. Watching the historic debate, "I was amazed that here you elect people by the vote. In other words, the power is on the ballot box, not on the gun. That's what democracy is about—the transition." As a result, "I was hooked," she said. "I was sucked into the concept of public policy."

Betancourt came from a long line of professionals—not politicians. Her father and grandfather were engineers and members of the faculty at the University of Havana. Her great-grandfather was a dentist who had gone to dental school in Philadelphia in the mid-1860s when Cuba was fighting for independence from Spain. At that time, affluent Cubans would send their children to school in the United States. Her father's grandmother and her sisters went to an all-girls Catholic school in Baltimore. "I come from a family who values education and are career oriented, never political," she said.

The career part of that philosophy applied only to men, however. "It was a saying in my family that ladies should appear in the newspaper only three or four times in their lives—when they're born, when they have their *quinceañera* [celebration of 15th birthday], when they get married, and when they die," she said. "I think I broke the mold of being in the newspaper more than once."

In Cuba, Betancourt went to an all-girls Catholic school in Havana. The eldest of three daughters in her family, Betancourt "was raised with the mentality that I had to be good and behave because I had to give the example to my two younger sisters."

During her childhood years, the Cuban government was growing increasingly chaotic. Gen. Fulgencio Batista had seized power, and guerrillas led by Fidel Castro were battling against the regime. Her father, besides being a professor, worked as an electrical engineer and contractor. In the 1950s, having business in New York and Brooklyn, he opened a bank account in Miami. "He had a little money outside of the country so he never had to wait on tables or do dishes or anything," she said. Her family was "blessed that he had the vision of being prepared financially for the family."

When Batista fled the island and Castro began nationalizing farm land and commercial property, her family realized it was time to go. "We left Cuba in 1960 with a tourist visa. We were not part of that Pedro Pan[67] exodus of children," she added. That fall, while living in a hotel, she was enrolled in the eighth grade in a parochial Catholic school in Miami Beach.

She clearly remembered watching the last Kennedy-Nixon debate that October. "The moderator was Walter Cronkite and there were questions being asked by John Chancellor," she said. On the topic of communism and foreign relations, "Kennedy kept saying that the covert operations [were under way] and the enemy was 90 miles away," she said. "Of course, he had already been briefed by Allen Dulles, who was the Director of the CIA, and during the Eisenhower administration, there were already some mechanisms in place to figure out a way of getting rid of Castro."

That debate "was the beginning of a curiosity," she said, which led to learning the Preamble to the Constitution, the Bill of Rights, and the principles of American democracy. She was also intrigued by the centennial of the U.S. Civil War, which she was studying as part of the eighth-grade curriculum. "I developed a curiosity for government and how countries are run."

On April 16, 1961, a counterrevolutionary force of Cuban nationals, trained and funded by the CIA, landed at the Bay of Pigs to recapture their homeland. But within four days, they were forced to surrender. "Dad said, 'Well, it's time to get to work.'" They left Miami and relocated to Puerto Rico, where Spanish was spoken and the economy was growing. Her father resumed his engineering career, working for Cornell University, which was building a radar telescope in the northern coast city of Arecibo.

"My mother was not adapting well. My dad said, 'Well, give me five years. Let's see if I can get back on my feet.'" When the family moved back to Miami, Betancourt had finished high school and started attending classes at Miami-Dade Community College.

In July 1972, she became a naturalized citizen. The woman who registered her to vote in Coral Gables, where the family lived, was a member of the League of Women Voters. She explained that Betancourt would not be able to vote in the primary. "I stayed a No Party Affiliation for a year or two until I kind of figured out where things were going and where my center of gravity would fall."

That year was significant in two other respects: First, New York Mayor John Lindsay and Congresswoman Shirley Chisholm, both of whom were running for the Democratic nomination for President, visited Miami-Dade Community College where Betancourt was a student. Second, both Democratic and Republican national conventions were held that summer in Miami. South Dakota Sen. George McGovern won the Democratic nomination, and incumbent President Richard Nixon was renominated as the Republican candidate.

"The point is the excitement of seeing how democracy works and the participation concept—and getting people excited about knowing what's going on in your community. I think I had it in my genes or something. It excited me. I think that's why it's so important that during campaign time, the candidates visit colleges and universities. Because it sparks the mind of the activity and what you do obviously is also part of it."

After graduating from the University of Miami in 1974, she applied for jobs at city, county, state and federal government levels because she knew she wanted to work in public service. She ended up working for Dade County, where she gained a first-hand understanding of how county government worked and where different layers of funding came from. She also got married and gave birth to a daughter.

When her husband died in 1984, after a long illness, "I took refuge in my work, building a reputation, becoming a professional woman," she said. By then, she was working at Jackson Memorial Hospital, running the Affirmative Action/Equal Opportunity Program. Along the way, she had joined Hispanic women's organizations as well as the League of Women Voters, in which she would serve as president (1989–1991).

In the mid-1980s she started working for Roberta Fox (Democratic state Representative 1976–1982) and the Dade County legislative delegation, which included State Reps. Ileana Ros and Dexter Lehtinen. Democratic Gov. Bob Graham was serving his last term before running for U.S. Senate. "It simply didn't take me long to look around and see who were the kind of people who were getting elected. I started connecting the dots."

In addition, "We felt there was a void for a path of leadership, particularly for Hispanic women," Betancourt said. To help fill this gap, she began participating in leadership training programs. One was for Hispanic women at Harvard's Kennedy School of Government, and another was at the Center for Creative Leadership in Greensboro, N.C. After being tested at one session, the professor told her, "You know, sometimes there are errors that happen in this IQ testing because you came out very high." Did the professor doubt her score because of her gender, or was it her ethnicity, or both? It's hard to know.

Her leadership ability did not go unnoticed by her mentors, all of whom were Anglo men. They included community activist John Edward Smith, then-U.S. Sen. Lawton Chiles (1971–1989), and Miami-Dade Mayor Steve Clark (1974–1993).

In the early 1990s, while at a training program in San Juan Capistrano, Calif., she received a message saying that newly elected Gov. Lawton Chiles was calling. As it turned out, the message was from Joe Pena, a long-time aide to Chiles. "The Governor and the Lieutenant Governor are seriously considering you for an appointment," he said. She asked what kind of appointment—perhaps the Cosmetology Board? "We're not at liberty to tell you," he said. The next week, when she returned to Tallahassee, she had an interview with Lt. Gov. [Kenneth H.] Buddy MacKay, Jr., and his staff director Loranne Ausley (who would later be elected state Representative 2000–2008), and then with Gov. Chiles. He asked her to serve on the board of the South Florida Water Management District.

That job meant "a big learning curve for me—not being an environmentalist or a hydrologist, but simply a lay person who happened to care about my community," she said. Betancourt realized the job would not be easy. "We were in the middle of the Everglades litigation. I mean, it was big."

The appointment represented the trust people had developed in her abilities over time. "It gave me assurances that I could take risks. It was a gradual thing," she said. She had already been visible in the community as an activist and, through her jobs, had been exposed to a range of social issues such as women's rights, needs of the elderly, health care, and employment. Her work had "prepared me to learn and read and talk about policy." The water management appointment simply presented another opportunity to learn.

She would cross another threshold two years later, in 1993, when Democrat Bill Clinton started his first term as President. At a women's conference in Washington, a woman reporter asked who she was. "I had the audacity and the guts to say I'm running for office in Miami." The quote was picked up by the *Miami Herald*, and rumors started to fly. She insisted that her decision was not as random as it might appear. "I had a strong name recognition in Miami," she said, "and if you put together the dates, you can see that it was a gradual path, not out of the blue."

When word got out that Betancourt was ready to run, Joe Geller, chair of the Democratic Executive Committee in Miami, "steered me to run in Kendall because this was a vacant seat and this was easier than defeating an incumbent." Democratic State Rep. Art Simon (1982–1994) had vacated the Kendall seat, and the Democrats wanted to keep it in their party for at least the next eight years. Geller and others, who were familiar with her credentials and local connections, called out State Rep. John Cosgrove (1986–2000) from off the floor of the House about her possible run. Cosgrove came into their office and said, "Oh, Annie, please do." He thought she would be sure to get the *Miami Herald's* endorsement, and she did.

In a visit to Tallahassee before the election, perhaps with the League of Women Voters, "I saw Art Simon walking down the hall." She knew him from having worked in the Dade legislative delegation. "He was wearing boots and I was in my high heels," she said. "I stopped and put my foot next to his. 'Do you think I can fill your shoes?'" she asked.

The Kendall district consisted of an unincorporated area in Miami-Dade County that had grown rapidly in the 1970s and 1980s, particularly with gated communities. With no mayor to bless her candidacy, Betancourt decided to run a completely grassroots campaign. Because the seat was vacant, it attracted a large number of candidates—three Democrats and three Republicans, all men except for her.

Colleagues at Miami-Dade Community College, where she worked, were astonished at her daring and spirit. "I mean, people were totally in [disbelief]: 'Annie's got to be crazy. She's running for office.' Even members of the faculty at the Kendall campus of Miami-Dade [asked], 'Do you think she could win?'"

A major issue, with Clinton as President, was that Democrats had no family values. But before opponents could define her that way, "I jumped into portraying myself as having family values," she said. People knew she was a widow and that her late husband was a Bay of Pigs veteran. "They wouldn't even touch me on that one," she said. Plus she was a breast cancer survivor. "So there was no way they could tarnish my image as a public servant."

Campaigning "was primarily direct mail, a lot of walking and door knocking." Betancourt talked with constituents about her experiences in working with the poor and the elderly in her early days in the county government and in the community with the college. That gave her ways of communicating with the people in the district, especially those who were less educated.

"I ran that campaign like clockwork," she said. Her daughter, age 18 at the time, campaigned, saying, "Vote for my mom. She's the best man for the job."

"I beat them all," Betancourt said. In the primary, "I won by a big margin"—so much so that Gov. Chiles's campaign manager, Jim Krog, kidded her about being "Landslide Annie."

In Tallahassee, legislative staffers knew her well from her work with the League of Women Voters and the Dade delegation. In an orientation meeting, she ignored a suggestion that she would be appointed to women-oriented committees, such as health and human services. "I wanted to get on the Finance and Tax Committee," she said, and with the help of Democratic Rep. Peter Rudy Wallace (1985–1997), she got it. "That's what I did for the entire eight years I was in the House," she said. "I didn't have to listen to them."

She ran for reelection for the next three terms, and won each time. Republicans recognized she was a formidable target and made her a target in subsequent elections. What's more, they tried to persuade her to join them, hoping to build their strength in the House, as had already happened in the Senate with its even 20-20 split between the two parties. At one point, she attended the superconservative American Legislative Exchange Council (ALEC) conference in San Diego with Republican State

Rep. Debbie Sanderson (1982–2002) from Fort Lauderdale. "She was very gracious, very pleasant and all that, simply trying to sway me to change. But I didn't."

The state's shift from Democratic to Republican was already well underway in the 1990s. Betancourt traced the turning point to the Census of 1980, which coincided with the Mariel boatlift. On April 20 of that year Castro had announced that any Cubans wanting to leave could board boats in the port of Mariel and be taken to the United States. Betancourt, who was in Washington at a national convention of the League of Women Voters, remembered President Jimmy Carter giving a speech to the group. In the question-and-answer period that followed, Merle Frank, the Miami League's president, asked: "Mr. President, we are currently facing a situation in South Florida where all these people are coming. Where is the federal government?" Carter answered, "As long as they're running from communism, we will welcome them with open arms."

The next day, the President's welcoming words were splashed across the *Washington Post*. "The Cubans in Miami were furious," Betancourt sad. "He didn't do his homework. The President had not been briefed by his staff because many people who were arriving had criminal records or mental illness." Over the next few months, 125,000 Cubans crowded into 1,700 boats before the two countries agreed to halt the mass exodus.

After Mariel, for many Cubans, "it was 'We ain't going back, we're staying,'" she said. "There was a wake-up call then by Univision with a big voter registration drive called *Vota para que te respeten* [Vote so that they would respect you]." Carter's public relations failure, coming 20 years after the Bay of Pigs disaster, clinched the switch to the Republican Party. The Cuban community's response: "We're going to register to vote, we're going to participate. Oh, and by the way, we're going to register Republican," she said. "And you also had Richard Nixon, who had a second home in Key Biscayne, who got closer to the Cuban community."

Betancourt sensed the change in the political air again in 1993 while in a workshop in Washington, D.C. She and the other 20 women from across the United States were given the opportunity to visit with members of Congress as well as the Republican National Committee. During the RNC visit, as the women introduced themselves around the conference table, a man perked up at her turn. "'Oh, Florida. That's our next battleground state,' he said. So clearly this has been a methodical, deliberate, well-orchestrated plan to capture Florida. There's no doubt in my mind," she said.

Each time Betancourt ran for reelection, the Republican Party ran a woman against her, a strategy gleaned from analytical studies, or "data mining," as these studies are now called. "Twice they've moved women from another district to the Kendall area to run against me because they figured she'll beat the boys so we'll have to run a woman," she said. The first opponent was Dulce Cuetara, who had worked as a political aide in Tallahassee. In 2000, it was Alina Garcia, who had been a TV newsperson at Univision in Washington.

The 2000 election became a political landmark because of the ballot irregularities in the presidential race between George W. Bush and Al Gore. "I'll never forget it," Betancourt said. "My daughter was celebrating her 25th birthday. She was born Nov. 7, so we were at my victory party that night, and the results were not coming. I'm dancing tango, we're having all this music, and my father says, 'Annie, the results are coming in, and you're losing.' And my friend says, 'Don't worry, it's only the absentee ballots that are tabulated first.'"

That's when an alarm went off in her head. She remembered a woman who had come to her campaign some time earlier, offering services as a ballot broker. "She was telling me how she worked the absentee ballots. Well, my very dear friend Maribel, who's now the president of the League here, was standing behind her and she was shaking her head like saying 'Don't even think of hiring this woman because it doesn't sound right.' The broker said, 'I guarantee victory because I know how to do it and we have won so and so in Hialeah.' I listened because she was very persistent, she wanted to set an appointment to see me. Finally I said, 'We work all the ballots alike.'" The broker responded, "Sweetie, you don't know what you're talking about" and walked away. Betancourt learned later that her opponent had hired the woman.

On Election Day, "I was going precinct by precinct, and I ran into Republican Jorge Rodriguez-Chomat [state Representative 1994–1998]. He said, 'Well, this campaign is very tough. If Gore wins, you win, but if Bush wins, Alina wins.'" Afterward, "when we looked at the election results, Alina won in three precincts—the absentee ballots, but not the other ballots, not the ballots of the people who voted on Election Day." Betancourt concluded, "So these people [brokers] are bad."

When controversy arose in the presidential race, Betancourt was named to a committee to look into the balloting. She argued in favor of a recount: "I clearly said that 10,000 votes were not counted here in Dade County. Ten thousand votes disappeared. And I was very passionate. I also said that when I first became a naturalized American, I had never missed an election. That statement got me on national TV." She appeared on shows hosted by Sean Hannity and Andy Cohen with Republican State Rep. Mike Fasano (1994–2002, later elected state Senator 2002–2012, returned to the House in 2012, resigned in 2013 to become Pasco County Tax Collector). The controversy led to litigation and ultimately a U.S. Supreme Court decision in favor of Bush.

In 2002, Betancourt ran for Congress in the 25th District, a large geographical area that included her Miami-Dade turf but leaned conservative. She lost to Republican Mario Diaz-Balart, whose brother Lincoln had represented Florida's 21st District in Congress since 1993.

For her own elections, Betancourt proved to be a skillful and creative campaigner. In 1996, she raised $250,000 for her first reelection effort. Politicos, looking at that quarter-million-dollar war chest, were impressed: "Wow! She can raise money." Betancourt considered fundraising "an arm of campaigning" that required organizational skills and planning. "I have a lot of contacts and business friends through my family, through friends of a friend of a friend, and through my community," she said. "We put together a group called Top 40—my top 40 people. I said if this T-40 can each raise $1,000, that would be $40,000 and get the ball rolling." She also reached across party lines and formed a Republicans for Annie group.

At one point, she consulted a financial manager. She described her plan and showed him her campaign binder. "He kind of looked at me and said, 'Annie, forget the list. I would do a luncheon for you and at the drop of a hat, I can raise you $10,000.'"

When she turned 50, "I had a 'fun raiser,'" that is, an F-U-N party. She asked that contributions start at $50 a head but learned to ask for more. "At that party, we all had a blast and raised more than $10,000."

She also knew how to craft fundraising events that would draw lots of people. In one event, for example, at which Democratic U.S. Sen. Bob Graham (and a former Governor) gave the keynote speech, she donated some of her excess money to a scholarship fund at Miami-Dade Community College Kendall Campus.

Each reelection campaign presented challenges. In 1994 the issue on everyone's mind was an increasing number of break-ins and crime in the Kendall area. "We did some pieces on crime with law enforcement, feel-good stuff with children, my neighbors, the police."

In the 1996 campaign, Betancourt believed she had to come up with a catchy slogan that would distinguish her from all the other races that year for school board, city, and state. To help educate voters that she was running for a state office, she borrowed what real estate agents say about "location, location, location" and hit upon the slogan, "Kendall's Voice in Tallahassee." She used it on literature, signs, and pencils that she gave to students in schools.

She chose the words for her materials with care: "I never said 'Elect,' I said 'Vote'—making it all about the message, the message, the message." She had materials printed by a man recommended by Democratic State Rep. Debbie Wasserman Schultz (elected 1992). She never printed literature in Spanish: "I didn't need to. I could switch to Spanish anytime. And that didn't rub people the wrong way," she said. "I expect every person who casts a vote to be able to understand at least English."

She gave radio interviews, which she was willing to do in Spanish at any time, and found them helpful. Her experience showed that newspaper endorsements sometimes help sway voters, but "it depends," she said. In addition to the *Miami Herald*,

Figure 3.30. Latina Annie Betancourt's political successes led to features about her life in various Spanish-language publications. She saw such publicity as a way to encourage other Hispanic women to get involved in their communities and to run for office. Photograph of framed article courtesy of Annie Betancourt. The article was published in *Exito* (a free weekly supplement of the *Sun Sentinel*), vol. 5, no. 11 (March 15, 1995).

she received support from the Herald's Spanish-language supplement, *El Nuevo Herald*.

Betancourt turned Kendall's dense population and traffic congestion to her advantage by advertising on bus benches. She identified the busiest traffic intersections and plastered benches with slogans like "Kendall's Voice in Tallahassee" and "Let's Keep Annie Betancourt." People stuck in traffic, sitting at every red light, would see the benches at eye level. "It was all a matter of branding, and the bus benches worked marvelously," she said.

Throughout her legislative career, Kendall remained a Hispanic area. "The growth there is No Party Affiliation," she said. "The fascinating thing I think Steve Schale [Democratic political strategist] wrote recently is that in Dade County the Cuban vote is being diluted. It's been that pattern ever since." With the arrival of Venezuelans, Argentinians, and people of other nationalities, Cubans are no longer so concentrated as a Republican bloc.

For her political career, Betancourt drew inspiration from the League of Women Voters as well as individual women such as State Rep. Roberta Fox (1976–1982) and Betty Castor, former state Senator (1976–1978, 1982–1986) and Commissioner of Education (1987–1994), then University of South Florida president (1994–1999), who was appointed by President Obama to head the Bureau of Educational and Cultural Affairs in the U.S. Department of State.

Coming of age as she did during the peak of the women's movement, Betancourt has developed an affinity for women's issues. "I'm a product of that generation. I think in terms of what can I do for future generations, for my daughter and now my granddaughter, it's for them to stand on their own. Also I think very, very important, is to have financial stability."

Her advice to a young person interested in politics, especially Hispanics and young women, would be: "Get involved in politics. Know the issues. Know the policies." Equally important, "you must present solutions to issues."

She cautioned that some candidates try to jump too far too fast, before having a solid community grassroots organization and network. She disagreed with the idea that the only way to get into politics is through being a lawyer, which is no longer true. "Also the other thing here in Miami, the mentality was that if you're Cuban, you have to be a Republican to run. I broke that myth."

Most important to anyone seeking public office is passion. "I would say that's the element that makes it," she said. "Because you've got to project your passion and your convictions. You cannot fake it." In reflecting back on her first run for office, she mused that she did not have any formal political coaching and admitted that even now "it's my gut or the little voice inside who tells me what to do."

Annie Betancourt was interviewed in person by the author July 16, 2013 and via telephone Aug. 15, 2014.

Frederica S. Wilson (D)

First woman of Bahamian descent to serve in the Florida House of Representatives, 1998

First woman of Bahamian descent to serve in the Florida Senate, 2002

First woman of Bahamian descent to serve in the U.S. House of Representatives, 2010

Personal: Born November 5, 1942, Miami, Florida; widowed with three children.

Education:

- Fisk University, B.S. (1963)
- University of Miami, M.S. (1972)

Occupation: Teacher

Trailblazer Elections:

- House of Representatives District 104 (Parts of Dade County) *Dem Primary* 1998
  - Frederica S. Wilson (50.7%), Shirley Gibson (22.3%), Jacques Despinsosse (19.1%), Bernard W. H. Jennings (3.6%), Kevin A. Fabiano (2.3%), Judith Goode (2%)
- House of Representatives District 104 (Parts of Dade County) *General Election* 1998
  - Frederica S. Wilson-D (85.2%), Clyde Pettaway-R (14.8%)
- Senate District 33 (Part of Miami-Dade County) *Dem Primary* 2002
  - Frederica S. Wilson (72.3%), M. Tina Dupree (17.6%), John D. Pace, Jr. (10.1%)
- Senate District 33 (Part of Miami-Dade County) *General Election* 2002
  - Frederica S. Wilson—*Unopposed*

- U.S. House of Representatives District 17 *Dem Primary* 2010
  - Frederica S. Wilson (34.5%), Rudolph "Rudy" Moise (16.1%), Shirley Gibson (11.9%), Yolly Roberson (10.3%), Phillip J. Brutus (8.4%), Marleine Bastien (6%), Scott Galvin (5.6%), James Bush III (5.4%), Andre L. Williams (1.7%)
- U.S. House of Representatives District 17 *General Election* 2010
  - Frederica S. Wilson-D (86.2%), Roderick D. Vereen-NPA (13.8%)

For the full Frederica Wilson story, see Congress section, page 497.

Figure 3.31. For Frederica Wilson, colorful hats and matching outfits have served as a symbol of her Bahamian heritage throughout her political career. An educator, she first entered politics by running for the school board. She attributed her victory to her church family, her black women's sorority, and her school community, which considered her a hero for having shut down a composting plant across from the school where she was principal. State Archives of Florida, *Florida Memory*, https://www.floridamemory.com/items/show/23927. Photograph by Darryl Jarmon, ca. 2002–2010.

Phillip J. Brutus (D)

First Haitian man elected to the Florida House of Representatives, 2000

Personal: Born November 26, 1957, Port-au-Prince, Haiti; divorced with four children.

Education:

- University of Massachusetts, B.S. (1982)
- Suffolk University Law School, J.D. (1985)

Occupation: Attorney

Figure 3.32. Democrat Phillip J. Brutus, a lawyer, addresses fellow House members on March 9, 2006. He was often exasperated at the lack of concern of his colleagues and Americans in general for the poor plight of the Haitian people. He also detested assumptions among some that Haitians were inferior and was committed to eroding stereotypes about his community. Photograph by Meredith Hill, 2006. http://www.myfloridahouse.gov/Sections/PhotoAlbums/photoAlbum.aspx?MemberId=4244.

Trailblazer Elections:

- House of Representatives District 108 (Part of Miami-Dade County) *Dem Primary* 2000
    - Phillip J. Brutus (63.3%), Daisy M. Black (36.7%)
- House of Representatives District 108 (Part of Miami-Dade County) *General Election* 2000
    - Phillip J. Brutus-D (81.7%), Reginald Thompson-R (16.3%), Jesus A. Camps-NPA (1.9%)

THE PHILLIP BRUTUS STORY

Phillip Brutus found his way to the Florida House through a fortuitous chain of events. First of all, he came to New York from Haiti at age 14 because his father, a dentist, wanted his son to have a good education and return to Haiti to practice the same profession. But Phillip knew he wouldn't do that because "I hate blood."

After attending a high school of the arts (Erasmus Hall) in Brooklyn and realizing that he would not go into the fine arts field, he enrolled in Manhattan Community College. The campus was near "the old seedy Times Square," he said. "Going to school and seeing all these different types of people—bankers, policemen, prostitutes—it kind of opened my mind and my life to like, 'Gee, there's a big world out there that I had no idea existed.'"

He transferred to Boston State College (now the University of Massachusetts at Boston) because he had an aunt and cousins living there. While earning a bachelor's degree, he worked part-time as a janitor at One Center Plaza across from the Kennedy Center. One day "I was pushing a big ol' pail and I'm picking up trash" in the office of a law firm, Hale & Dorr. "Beautiful mahogany desks and books and these lawyers sitting there with bow ties," he recalled. At one point, he overheard a lawyer ask a young woman, "Have you ever heard the term *Errare humanum est*?" She had not but Brutus had because he had taken two years of Latin as well as two years of Greek along with English and Spanish in Haiti. "Being a wide-eyed young guy," he said to them, "'I know what it means.' And they turned around and said, 'Excuse me?' I said, 'Yeah, it's Latin. That means humans commit errors.' The man responded, 'You know, you should be a lawyer.'" And from that day forward, Brutus knew the direction of his education and career.

Although he wanted to go to a law school like Harvard, Yale, or Columbia, he was accepted to Suffolk Law School in Boston. He was glad it worked out that way when he learned that Suffolk was created in 1906 by Harvard law professors as an affordable alternative for the children of the working class. Believing that his parents had no obligation to support him as an adult, he drove a cab four hours a day to earn a living.

While in Boston, he obtained U.S. citizenship. He clearly remembered swearing to the oath administered by Judge David S. Nelson, a black federal judge. During those early years, Brutus never had a problem with going to school or working "because the country was still at an innocent stage. We didn't worry about terrorists; we didn't worry about these mass murders in schools and theatres. So everybody was just, 'You want a job? OK.' If I didn't want that job, I quit, go down the next street, I get another job. It was that easy."

He chose not to take the Bar exam in Massachusetts because he planned to move to a warmer climate. He remembered the day he made the decision: "I had class at night and I had this big ol' blue navy coat and I'm standing there, my car was in the shop and I mean, the wind is blowing. I had all the accoutrements you could think of—muffs and everything. And a friend of mine recognized me, he was driving by, it was 10 p.m. He says, 'Hey, Phil. Come on, you want a ride?' And when I got to the car, I sat down like that and I could not open my mouth. My skin was almost in frostbite. Frozen. And it took me a good five minutes of heat to say, 'Oh, my God,' I said. 'You know what? This is not meant for me.' I couldn't bear it."

When he graduated in June 1985, he packed all his belongings and drove with his soon-to-be-wife to Miami where he had a cousin. The cousin referred Brutus to the Haitian Refugee Center, a sister organization of the National Council of Churches, founded in 1973 to ensure that Haitian immigrants seeking asylum would have their cases justly evaluated.[68] Haitians had been coming to the United States since the 1960s to escape the brutal rule of "Papa Doc" Duvalier. In 1971 his son, "Baby Doc," followed with a similar regime of corruption and repression. Haitians arriving in boats without documentation, unlike Cubans, typically were imprisoned and deported because of the U.S. government's conflicting laws and regulations about their status as refugees seeking asylum or as indigents seeking work.

At the Refugee Center, Brutus met the Rev. Gérard Jean-Juste. The meeting was not his first, nor would it be his last, with the priest. While still in Boston, Brutus had encountered Jean-Juste celebrating mass at a Catholic church. Newly arrived in Miami, Brutus asked the priest whether the city had any Haitian lawyers. The priest referred him to Anthony Gerea on 79th Street.

Gerea empathized with the young couple and agreed to hire them. "What I remember the most about him is that there were times he didn't make enough money to pay us. And he said, 'Look, Phil, I know you have a wife and I think your wife's pregnant. I can't pay your salary, but I have an American Express with unlimited [credit] so I can offer you groceries. Okay? We'll go shopping, buy anything you want and I'll pay for it.' And that never left me. That really touched me deeply . . . he basically borrowed money to help feed me and my wife while we were working."

The next year when "Baby Doc" Duvalier was ousted as president of Haiti by a popular uprising (1986), Gerea wanted to return to the island to become a Senator. Unfortunately, he was killed in a car accident. "Let me tell you," Brutus said, "I love my father dearly but when this man died, it's like I lost my father. I was uncontrollably devastated." He wept openly even when someone called him a sissy for crying in public.

Before taking the Bar exam, Brutus found work with the county police as a crime analyst, studying crime data and identifying trends. When he started looking for a lawyer position, which is what he really wanted, law firms responded politely but never called him back. "Of course all the big law firms did not have any space for me," Brutus recalled. They knew nothing about Suffolk Law School nor that its Bar passing rate was higher than the bigger, more prestigious schools.

Finally while working with the police, a break came. "An officer told me that it was around the Miami River cops area [associated with police corruption], a lot of drugs and prosecutions. And he said they were doing some joint patrol with the marshals and for the first time he heard this guy's being represented by the federal public defender." Brutus checked it out. Federal public defender Ted Sakowitz recognized that Brutus had not graduated at the top of his class but, like so many other young lawyers, was somewhere in the middle. At the same time, Sakowitz knew that roughly 30 percent of his clientele were African American and another 30 percent were Haitian Americans. "We don't have a Haitian lawyer. And when people come here we have to hire an interpreter," Sakowitz said. "Do you speak Creole?" Brutus replied, "Of course." Sakowitz said, "OK, you've got a job."

"He offered me $32,000 a year," Brutus said. "'Oh my God, all this money!' I had never made that kind of money in my life." The police job had paid only about two-thirds that amount. Brutus worked as a public defender from 1987 to 1989 and then went into private practice.

During this time, Brutus became disturbed by what he saw happening to his fellow blacks and Haitians. He recalled one incident in which a Coast Guard patrol encountered Cubans and Haitians approaching the shore. The Coast Guard rescued the Cubans but sent the Haitian boat back to the high seas. "Everybody wanted to be in America for a better life. I could've accepted that," Brutus said. And he could understand the repugnance of Americans to Castro's communism in Cuba. "But to so vividly take the Cubans from the same boat—had that boat not rescued them, they would have drowned—and then you turn that loose, send it back, I think went beyond the pale. We were so upset. So we had a hunger strike, demonstration and everything." The strike made the front page of the local news section of the *Miami Herald*, and included Brutus's photo, which helped make him more visible in the community.

In another incident in the early 1990s, a client, Abner Alezi, went to the 79th Street shopping center to have his pants hemmed. "We don't know what happened. Somehow he came out bloody. He said the Cuban called him a derogatory name. All we know was that he called the radio, said somebody just beat him up, he's bleeding, and he thinks he's going to die. Of course he was exaggerating, just scrapes and cuts." The Rev. Jean-Juste went to the scene. When the police declined to arrest the assailant, the priest called for a demonstration. At one point, a bus carrying deportees came out of the Krome detention center to the gate where people were demonstrating. "He laid in front of the bus. And he was a priest. And he started praying Hail Mary, Our Father, Ave Maria," Brutus remembered. "I'm like, My God! As much as I love to fight for justice, I don't think I would put myself in front of tires. Some commanding officer came out and I guess they said this has a potential of getting out of hand, so the bus backed up, turned around and went back in and they closed the gate."

"I guess they got tired after about two or three weeks," Brutus said. In the Caribbean tradition of a carnival atmosphere, the site "became a hangout with people playing drums and people selling their water. . . . So I guess the leaders are talking about justice and other people were just doing their thing. But there was so many of them. Jean-Juste could put 5,000 people on the street. Now we cannot put 500. But eventually the police and everybody said let me help put an end to this."

His connection with Jean-Juste and the Haitian Refugee Center put him among a group of lawyers recruited by the center's director, Ira Kurzban, a Jewish immigration attorney, to help make the case for Haitians in court. In addition, as associate general counsel for the NAACP, Brutus provided legal assistance to individuals whose civil rights were violated. In one instance, he observed a demonstration that turned into a riot. "It's like the police really enflamed them," he said. "It was brutal. [The police] basically got on their horses and just charged people with the horses. They're falling . . . and a broken hand, broken arm. And then the riot police moved in and some people were scattering about. Cars are screeching to avoid hitting people." Such incidents made him realize that "the Haitian community needs somebody at some table somewhere in some capacity to be heard seriously, to hear the issues that are strangling the community, from police brutality to the immigration issue . . . whether it be a City Commissioner, County Commissioner, state Rep, or a Congressman. Because we had nobody elected in any position."

His first entry into politics came in 1994, when "there was an invisible move to get all the black judges off the bench. Every black judge drew an opponent that year." Brutus decided "to run as a black lawyer, a Haitian lawyer. And I said, hopefully that'll give them some inspiration at least. I don't know if it's going to give me any money or any strength, but I filed."

His opponents for the county judgeship were Ed Newman, an attorney and former offensive guard for the Miami Dolphins, and Lenny Cooperman, a young attorney who was disqualified because he had not been a member of the Bar for the required five years. Brutus recalled: "I put $100 in my account. [Newman] put $100,000 in his account. So the handwriting was on the wall. But I gave him a run for his money."

Newman received 97,000 votes and Brutus 47,000 votes. In an aside, Brutus noted that Newman's vote count was the second highest number ever cast in the Dade County judicial district.

Brutus, who had expected only 5,000 votes in his favor, found the loss inspiring: "I said, 'Oh, 47,000 people voted for me. They must think I have something of value, something that I can help.' So that's really when my baptism of fire happened. Because I thought nobody would vote for me and the Haitians were not citizens, there were not enough Haitians at the time."

The same year (1994), incumbent Democratic Gov. Lawton Chiles won reelection by a narrow margin over Republican challenger Jeb Bush. The state Representative at the time was Beryl Roberts-Burke, a black Democrat who had been elected in 1992. Brutus began looking at her seat with interest. "First of all, I didn't think she was doing anything to address us at all," he said. "When Jeb Bush was walking into the Capitol, she was one of the people accompanying him because she had voted for school vouchers prior to that, so she had started to veer off to the right. And that didn't set well with us down here and the unions."

"In '98 she was very cozy with Bush, and that's one of the reasons why I decided to run to bring a real Democrat in," he continued. "In fact, I said I'm going to run on Democratic Party core principles. One of them is that I went to public schools in New York and I think they did a halfway decent job with me. And we have no business taking money from the public schools to put in the private schools, and then not require the private school teachers to be certified, requiring the public school teachers to be certified, and using state money."

He lost to Roberts-Burke in 1998, but "I think I won that race because the night before I was ahead. There's a place called Sewell Park on North Miami Avenue. They had lost a box of ballots. And the next day the police said they found it, it was open. So I lost. At that time it was 130-something votes, so I asked for a recount." During that process, he observed irregularities similar to those that would surface two years later in the George W. Bush and Al Gore presidential race. When he pointed out a disparity, he was told, "Sir, let us do our job." Brutus thought: "I don't want this to get ugly. Before you know it, they're going to handcuff me. So I decided I'm going to let it go. They basically bungled the count. Even with that, it went down to 51 votes. But I figured she would step down anyway in 2000 [because of term limits]."

He ran again in 2000, beating two black opponents: Councilwoman Daisy Black in the primary, and Republican Reggie Thompson in the general election. His November victory over Thompson was decisive: "I mean we swept it. I got 82 percent of the votes."

In his campaigns, "my primary mode of communication was radio." Print "carries a certain weight, but not everybody reads," he said. And radio is free. "There are some people who never turn their radio off. The radio is always on because they don't want

Figure 3.33. It's opening day of the Legislature and State Rep. Phillip J. Brutus, the first Haitian man elected to the Florida House (2000), gets a congratulatory phone call from a constituent. Brutus, like a number of other trailblazers, lost his first race for public office (a judicial post) but found the loss inspiring: "I said, 'Oh, 47,000 people voted for me. They must think I have something of value, something that I can help.' So that's really when my baptism of fire happened. Because I thought nobody would vote for me and the Haitians were not citizens, there were not enough Haitians at the time." Photograph provided by AliciaPatterson.org.

to miss anything." He cited Radio Mambí WAQI 710 AM, a Spanish station with a news/talk format that is a favorite with Haitians, Cubans, and other immigrants to get news about the Caribbean. He also relied on his own weekly radio program on WLQY 1320 AM, a show that combined politics and legal advice.

"Whatever you would hear on CNN, you would hear me analyze it the same way . . . or perhaps with a different take, a different opinion on it. But I said I want the community to know, to come up to par with the mainstream society" on local as well as international events. His show was broadcast from 11:00 to noon on Saturday morning "because everybody's home and doing something." (He has since changed the time to 10:30 to 11 a.m. on Sundays.) Actually, while he was a state Representative, he would call a radio station and put the phone next to the speaker on his desk to let listeners hear debates on issues in real time.

A less effective campaign tactic was canvassing. "But back then because technology was not so advanced, you could knock on three blocks of homes and nobody's a citizen," he said.

Mass mailing was also difficult for the same reason. Today campaigns have access to databases that screen out noncitizens, "but way back, especially when I was running in '98, it was hard."

To raise funds, Brutus used a device that he called "A Dollar for Democracy." As he explained, "in this country you need money to be elected," and he didn't have money. But he reasoned: "If there are 100,000 Haitians here, if each of you give me a dollar, I would win this race hands down." So he would go to soccer games and other public gatherings with a tape recorder (to document funding sources) and announce that he was running. "I know you don't have any money. All I'm asking is a dollar of each of you," he would say. "But nobody ever gave a dollar. The least they gave me is $5.The average is $20.The only dollar I got was a little kid who gave me four quarters. I guess his father said, 'Give him four quarters.'" When he would go to a Haitian nightclub, the same thing happened. "Especially if they're having fun—they're either drunk or they're trying to impress the girlfriend. This guy puts $50 in the [basket], and I said 'What's your name?' He said, 'Eh, don't worry about it.'"

One recent issue that affects not only politics but also population-based federal funding is race/ethnicity versus country of origin. The census questionnaire allows respondents to choose race/ethnic categories such as white, Hispanic, and black or African American, for example. A movement is afoot to change those categories to reflect that Africa is not the country of origin for all blacks. Some have suggested adding a category such as "Caribbean American," but that option overlooks the linguistic differences in that region. Creole is the official language of Haiti, but Spanish, French, and Dutch are the official languages of other Caribbean countries. The goal, Brutus said, is not division but rather recognition of the diverse groups. The ability to identify Haitians, for example, would allow candidates to assess voting strength and finely target communication. Even so, direct mail and robocalls in Creole are not as important as radio and, increasingly, television.

Taking the oath as the first Haitian American in the Florida Legislature was an emotional moment. But he considers himself a "buffer Haitian" in that he came at age 14: "I was in Brooklyn, running on roller skates, playing handball, getting . . . up and down the subway going to school." While proud of being the first Haitian American, he resolved that he was not in the Capitol to represent only Haitians. "I got elected for everybody. And if you didn't vote for me, I have an obligation to represent you because I represent where you live."

Being sworn in called to mind the times he didn't have any money, a job, or citizenship, and yet "Here I am, I'm an American elected official." At the same time, he felt an obligation. He likened it to the feeling he had in law school when, after driving a cab, he would come in unprepared if a professor called on him. On taking the oath, he said to himself: "You better say something. Don't say anything stupid. Sound like a statesman. Because you are the ambassador of this community. And not just the Haitian Americans but the African Americans who themselves are oppressed or didn't have opportunities. And even some Hispanics don't have an opportunity. So I saw myself there as somebody to basically make them look good, make good arguments."

Serving as a state Representative brought a mix of good and bad moments. "I was a Democrat in a Republican majority. The good thing we had back then, Lois Frankel was the Minority Leader, she was a firecracker. Lois Frankel would go toe-to-toe with that Speaker. I'm like, 'My God where does she get the energy?'"

The legislative experience disillusioned him about what he could do for constituents: "I felt democracy meant I'm elected, I'm going to be able to deliver something to my community. . . . And I realized it's not about democracy, it's about who controls. It's about who has more votes."

As an example, he explained that the principal of a private school in Opa-Locka had molested a child. Unknown to the community, he had a criminal record. Brutus filed a bill requiring all teachers of minors to be fingerprinted regardless of the type of school where they worked. The bill was assigned to three or four committees and disappeared. "The next chair would not have me even calendared." One day, [Republican] Rep. Mario Diaz-Balart offered to help, "Look, Phil, I'm a Cuban American, you're Haitian American. Our countries have the same situation, except that your country had a right-wing dictator, and we have a left-wing dictator." He steered the bill to the House floor. "That bill was posted on the floor on the session calendar I think every day," Brutus recalled. On the last day, the Speaker took up one bill after another, but not his. When the Speaker took a break, Brutus approached him: "Mr. Speaker, we talked about this. This is not for me, it's about children." He said, "Don't worry, I'll get to it, I'll get to it." But he didn't, and the House adjourned. "The following year I filed it again, and when I realized the same thing would happen, I amended it onto [Republican] Jerry Melvin's bill" on major school reform. It passed. "I took credit for it," Brutus said.

Similarly, when he learned that newly elected Miami-Dade School Board member Jacqueline Pepper had hired her husband, Donald Jones, as an aide at a $55,000 salary. Brutus thought: "What is that? I thought we had anti-nepotism laws. Then they told me that because of the Home Rule Charter, Miami-Dade didn't have to abide by that state requirement. So I proposed the bill. Even that bill they gave me a hard time because I was a Democrat." (That bill also eventually passed as part of the school reform measure.)

Another example: One day while listening to National Public Radio on his car radio, he heard a University of Arizona professor say that Florida and one other state, in their constitutions, banned Haitians and everyone from Southeast Asia from owning land. Nobody complied with the ban, but "your constitution is your *raison d'être*, so to speak, as a state or as a nation. So I filed a bill to remove it," Brutus said. "Do you know people still had the nerve to say, 'Who cares? It's not enforced anyway.' But it's still in the Constitution. People in Malaysia or in Germany can [call our Constitution] anachronistic, archaic, racist." They killed it. "This bill was finally passed by another Haitian-American Rep. Ronald Brisé [Democrat] after I left. I guess they finally realized: 'This is ridiculous.' So that was to me a letdown in a way because I didn't see what was so hard, but it was because they just did not want a Democrat to go home to say, 'I passed a bill.'"

So it was the horse trading, that marked his darkest moments, he said, referring to "the reprisals if you don't march in lockstep, then they kill your bill." One day, disgusted with what he saw happening, he confronted the presiding officer: "Mr. Speaker, you can kill all my bills, but you'll never kill my spirit. I'll file the same bills again, you can kill them again, but you're not Speaker forever. You're Speaker for two years."

His proudest moment occurred on a resolution celebrating the 1948 creation of Israel by the United Nations. Back then, the only black countries in the UN were Haiti, the Dominican Republic, and Ethiopia; the rest of Africa was under colonization. House members heaped praise on the Jewish state for, among other things, being the only democracy in the Middle East. Taking the floor during the discussion, Brutus pointed out that it was the Haitian Ambassador, Emile Saint-Lôt, who cast the tie-breaking vote that created Israel. Without that vote, Israel's nationhood would have had to wait for another day. Hearing this, the chamber applauded.

And that was not the end of it. One night, as Brutus was among the last ones leaving a dinner at the Legislature, a Jewish man in a wheelchair asked to be photographed with him. "I did not know that Haiti cast that vote to create Israel," the man said. "I have a picture at least with one Haitian, so I could show my children and my grandchildren."

A legislator's performance is measured not only by voters but also by the media. Case in point: "The *Miami Herald* used to rate you by stars; 5 stars you're a good legislator, 4 stars, 3 stars," Brutus recalled, depending on passage of bills. "But there was one year under [Speaker] Johnnie Byrd [Republican], we had seven or eight legislative special sessions. We spent a ton of money. The *Miami Herald* gave me half a star. The Democrats only 2, some had 3. And I wrote them a scathing letter. . . . I said, 'How could a major paper decry, denounce the machinations of the Republicans wasting our money and all these special sessions, doing all these things, killing good bills on partisan basis, how could you, knowing we're up against this big machine, give them 5 stars and turn around and give me half a star, because of something you denounced?' I said, 'Something is wrong with this.' And you know what—I don't know if I should take credit for it, but they have stopped using stars since."

What advice would he give young blacks aspiring to be legislators? "Whether we acknowledge it or not, there's a perception that you became whatever you became because of affirmative action, because somebody had to do a favor. . . . It's like they give you a pass. So you have a duty to make sure you educate yourself. You at least get a bachelor's degree—and read. Because you can be a brilliant surgeon, a brilliant lawyer, and an idiot because you're not an intellectual because you don't read, you don't know what's going on in the world."

"I've seen legislators when they come down here and they're in rallies, they don't talk," he continued. "An issue may come up, they don't know about it, they don't read the papers, they don't read books, they don't do anything, so they don't have any opinion. And I think that's so bad. So me, I didn't speak on every issue, but as many as I could. . . . I felt I was on a mission to let people know we are not what the media say we are. We are more than that. We are just like everybody else. You've heard that before. We bleed the same blood. And as they said, scientifically, to the tiniest microcosm of atoms, we are the same, except climate."

"Some folks still think I'm inferior. A Haitian person could come here and say to me, 'Oh Mr. Brutus, I need a Jewish lawyer because I was in an accident.' A Haitian would tell me that. And I'd say, 'Well, I could not be your Jewish lawyer, but I'm a lawyer, too.' 'Yeah, but the Jewish lawyers are very smart.' So that's a symptom of slavery, of making you feel like you're really nothing."

Brutus helped banish the stereotype in his own way. "There was this guy and I think he's from the Panhandle somewhere. Nice guy. He saw me in the hallway walking and we would talk: 'Hey, Brutus, saw you, what's going on?' And he said, 'I really feel for Haiti. It's so unfair the way these people are suffering. We need to do something. Like we in America we have all kind of perks. I went to prep school, I learned Latin, we lived in a great [country], and you know, these poor Haitians live in hell.' And I said [to myself], 'Okay, this is my opportunity to really show him something.' I said, 'Oh, you took Latin?' He said, 'Yes.' I said, 'In French it's called *declinaisons* [declensions in English], but you know how many conjunctions they have in Latin?' He said, 'Well. . . . ' I said, 'I don't know how to say it in English, it's like *nominative, vocative, dative, genitive, ablative*. Like, you know, when you say *rosa, rosaro, rosam.*' And he was like, 'Whoa!' And let me tell you, every time he sees me, he says, 'There goes a Latin scholar,' in a friendly way."

His final bit of advice: "You need to fit the part. It's one thing to ask for an opportunity, but it's another thing to do it. And if you get the opportunity, you've got to deliver. To those much is given, much is expected."

Phillip Brutus was interviewed in person by the author June 10, 2014.

Edward B. "Ed" Bullard (D)

First man from the Bahamas to serve in the Florida House of Representatives, 2000

Personal: Born November 28, 1943, Nassau, Bahamas; married with one child.

Figure 3.34. Rep. Edward Bullard, D-Miami, debates a measure on the House floor. A former teacher, social worker, and assistant principal at an alternative school, he developed deep roots in the community and a vast network that he, his wife, and son would use as a base for winning elections. "Everyone knew the Bullards. And that's just the way it was," Edward said. State Archives of Florida, *Florida Memory*, https://www.floridamemory.com/items/show/135252. Photograph by Meredith Hill Geddings, 2006.

Education:
- Florida A&M University, B.S. (1972)
- Florida A&M University, M.S. (1977)
- Nova University, M.S. (1978)

Occupation: Assistant Principal
Trailblazer Elections:
- House of Representatives District 118 (Part of Miami-Dade County) *Dem Primary* 2000
  - Edward B. Bullard (30.2%), Donald Jones (18.1%), Israel J. Andrews (17.8%), Angela Solomon Lane (17.6%), Joseph G. Sewell (8.3%)
- House of Representatives District 118 (Part of Miami-Dade County) *Dem Runoff* 2000
  - Edward B. Bullard (50.8%), Donald Jones (49.2%)
- House of Representatives District 118 (Part of Miami-Dade County) *General Election* 2000
  - Edward B. Bullard—*Unopposed*

THE EDWARD B. "ED" BULLARD STORY

For Edward Bullard, the first Bahamian man elected state Representative in Florida, politics was a family affair, beginning with the election of his wife to the House in 1992. The "Bullard seat" in the Florida House was passed from Larcenia to Edward to their son Dwight, and the "Bullard Senate seat," from mother to son.

"The Bullard family was on the board in the House of Representatives for 20 years," Edward said. "There was always a Bullard in there because [Larcenia] did eight years, and I came in and did eight years, and Dwight followed me, and he did four years. So inside the House on the roll sheet, there was always a Bullard up there."

Edward, the second of six children, was born in Nassau and raised in Savannah Sound, Eleuthera, in the Bahamas. His father was a chef in the Royal British Air Force during World War II. The family came to the United States in parts—first the father, who found work as a butler in New York, and after a time the mother, after he found work for her as a maid. The children stayed in the Bahamas—the three oldest with their grandmother and uncle, and the two youngest with an aunt in Nassau. The sixth child was born in Miami in 1957.

"Eventually after my parents got a foothold or a toehold in the system and were able to make some money, they moved to Miami," Edward said. His mother returned for the children about 1954 and brought them to Richmond Heights, an all-black Miami suburb. Edward was 10 years old at the time.

Richmond Heights was "a middle-class community designed for African-American war veterans who used their GI Bills to purchase homes in the area," Dwight explained. The homes were two- and three-bedroom, one-bath dwellings designed for servicemen starting a family.

In moving to Miami, the Bullard family joined a community with a strong Caribbean—and, indeed, Bahamian—influence. "When Miami was established as a city, half of the people on the original charter were Bahamian," said Dwight. Before Henry Flagler had built the Florida East Coast Railway down to Miami in the late 1800s, he had hired Bahamians from the islands to work in his hotels. The Bullard and Gibson family names have "longstanding ties to the community. So when you say Bullard from the Bahamas related to the Gibsons, you have cousins popping out the woodwork." He mentioned a number of well-known politicians with Bahamian roots, including Frederica Wilson, Oscar Braynon II, Athalie Range, Carrie Meek, Kendrick Meek, Perry Thurston, and Gwyndolen "Gwyn" Clarke-Reed.

As a child, Edward developed strong religious beliefs, serving as an acolyte in the Episcopal (Anglican) Church. He "grew up under the tutelage of someone who would end up becoming a civil rights icon, especially in South Florida: Father Theodore Gibson, who would eventually be the first black Commissioner for the city of Miami during his time, but also led to things like busing desegregation and school desegregation in Miami," Dwight said. Father Gibson was "the person who gave [Dad] his formal training. The reason I say 'formal training' is because neither of his parents got their high school diplomas. So he relied on folks like Father Gibson and cousins, Dr. David and Tessie White, who helped him finish high school and go to college."

Edward graduated in 1963 from Arthur and Polly Mays Senior High School, one of the five black high schools in Miami-Dade County at the time. The other black schools were Booker T. Washington, George Washington Carver, Northwestern, and North Dade Senior High School. He went to Miami-Dade College for a few years before being drafted into the Army in 1966. Although the Vietnam War was at its height, he was stationed in Panama.

After three years in the service, he enrolled at Florida A&M University. He earned a bachelor's degree in 1972 and a master's degree in education administration (for grades 7–12) in 1977, followed with a second master's in education administration (for K-12) from Nova Southeastern University in 1978. In 1973, he began working in middle and high schools in the Miami Dade County public school system, where he was named a Master Teacher, one of 53 such teachers in the state of Florida when the Master Teacher program was instituted in 1983 by Gov. Bob Graham. Bullard spent much of his time in alternative education, worked for eight years as a school social worker, and became an assistant principal.

He met Larcenia in 1980 when the young widow moved to Miami from Philadelphia with her two sons, Dwight and Vincent, to live with her mother. "It just so happened that her mother lived on the same street that I lived on. How nice! So the Lord set her right down next door to me [smile]. Of course, with a new lady in town, and I was a divorcee, that made it nice," he said. They married in 1983 and stayed married for 30 years until her death in 2013.

Larcenia, a native of South Carolina, "was the politically ambitious one in the family." She had done campaign work in Philadelphia and wanted to pursue her ambitions in Florida. Her first attempt at running for state Representative in 1984 fizzled out for lack of support, but more important, she had begun building a campaign base, using Edward's connections.

"Dad was a guy who just developed a number of friendships locally. And so really, the truth be told, my mom benefited from that greatly," Dwight said. Edward called his former classmates, former students, family, and others on his wife's behalf, and "before you know it, you have this coalition of folks. I think that was eye-opening for my mom because she didn't realize how big his network was. I mean, you spend 30 years in a community in that time and your network is huge. So that kind of represented the foundation of the political platform that we would ultimately use for years to come."

Larcenia ran again for state Representative in 1990 and came in second in a field of five, losing in a runoff to former Air Force Captain Daryl Jones.

"There was a changing political landscape because there had never been an African American representing that district before," Dwight said. "And so the idea that there were two African Americans out of the five people that were running, kind of proved it again. It showed [Dad's] ability to navigate those waters and, again, you cut your teeth doing it. So he was out there getting posters made up. He was nailing up signs to the wall. He was putting yard signs up for neighbors, asking friends and family to host house parties to introduce his wife who wanted to run for office."

My dad "was never one of the talkative types," Dwight continued. "My mom would refer to him as 'still waters,' in terms of 'still waters run deep.' He was never really overly temperamental. Never really saw him get angry. I think in my 37 years I've only seen the man raise his voice maybe three times."

Coming in second place might have dampened the ambitions of some candidates, but not Larcenia. When Jones ran for the Senate in 1992, she ran for his seat in the House. "So my mother again got bitten by the political bug. My dad said, 'Oh, well, we've already built the network, let's go ahead and give it a go.' So he helped her. She could not have done it without him," Dwight said. "He was the absolute linchpin in her being able to get into public office."

Larcenia became the first woman elected to her House district. She served eight years before term limits forced her out in 2000. The previous summer, Edward began looking for someone who might run for her seat. He even suggested that Dwight might run. "No, I just graduated college, man," Dwight told him. Then one day Edward looked in the mirror and realized he had found the candidate. "The campaigner now turned into the candidate," Dwight said.

"Like many of our first races, as Bullards have come to know, it was a nail biter," Dwight said. "He ended up winning, I think, by 34 votes his first go-round." The

Figure 3.35. Rep. Edward Bullard and wife, Sen. Larcenia Bullard, confer on legislation during the 2004 legislative session. They prayed together, campaigned together, and often, but not always, worked together on bills. State Archives of Florida, *Florida Memory*, https://www.floridamemory.com/items/show/135256. Photograph by Mark T. Foley, 2004.

losing opponent went to court over the votes. "Even though there were folks in there trying to call into question just the ethics of politics, there was no questioning the relationships that he had established. So when [his opponent] tried to say, 'Hey, listen, here's this person over here . . . ,' they were like, 'Nah, that's Eddie who delivered the newspapers when we were kids.' 'That's Eddie who taught my son and kept my son from going to prison.' 'That's Mr. Bullard who taught at all these different schools.' So that just entrenched him as a fixture in the community."

In 2002 when Edward ran for reelection, Larcenia ran for the Senate for the first time. Although she faced formidable foes, she emerged the winner by just 800 votes and stayed in the Senate until 2012. "They ran together as a couple," Dwight said. "Just seeing a couple out there campaigning together was very interesting and, of course, whether I wanted to or not, I was drafted into the campaign as well. It definitely solidifies you as a family."

As the first already-married couple in the Legislature (Ileana Ros and Dexter Lehtinen married after they were elected in the 1980s), the Bullards structured their lives to support each other. They started each morning and ended each evening with prayer, for example, and were careful not to vent their legislative frustrations to each other at home.

Having his wife in the Senate provided an advantage: "You always have a Senate sponsor," Edward said.

In 2003, Edward was having trouble getting a bill passed that would permit certain Miami streets to be named after local people who had made significant contributions to the area. When the bill came to the Senate, Larcenia stood up wearing a yellow hat and yellow raincoat and holding a large jar of honey. "This is going to be my Honey bill," she announced. "He calls me 'Honey' and I call him 'Honey.' Just the other day, I said, 'Representative,' and he didn't answer. And then I said, 'Honey,' and he responded." The bill passed.[69]

Sometimes they were on the same side of a bill, and sometimes they were on opposite sides. On one bill dealing with alimony, she opposed it and he favored it. "It was lovely to see it play out," Edward said. His side won by a few votes, "but we didn't divorce over that particular bill."

Figure 3.36. Dwight M. Bullard learned politics from campaigning for both parents—his mother Larcenia Bullard, House of Representatives, 1992–2000, and Senate, 2002–2012; and his father Edward B. Bullard, House of Representatives, 2000–2008. Dwight was elected to the House in 2008, then the Florida Senate in 2012. He has the same office and desk as his mother did when she was in the Florida Senate and served as Chair of the Florida Legislative Black Caucus, 2014–2015. Photograph by House Photographer, 2008, myfloridahouse.gov.

In 2008 Edward sponsored a bill that would allow drivers to buy a specialty license plate showing the image of a cross in front of a stained glass window with the phrase "I Believe" below. The Legislature rejected the bill, and a similar bill that passed in South Carolina the next year was ruled unconstitutional by a federal judge: "Such a law amounts to a state endorsement not only of religion in general, but of a specific sect in particular."[70] Edward did not see it that way: If people can buy plates showing their belief in their college or sports team, why not a plate showing belief in their faith, he reasoned.

Edward reached term limits in 2008, and Dwight ran for his House seat. "He surprised us. We didn't push him into it," Edward said. "He just said one day, 'Hey, I've decided to run for that particular seat.' And when he ran, no one gave him a chance." But Dwight came out on top. When he ran for reelection in 2010, pitted against Kionne McGhee, Dwight won by a thin margin of 400 votes. In 2012, when his mother retired because of term limits, he ran for her Senate seat, again facing a crowded primary. He won with 35 percent of the vote.

On Dwight's first day in the Senate, Edward and Larcenia were on the floor with him. In keeping with tradition, the roll was called. At the name "Bullard," and before Dwight could open his mouth, Larcenia chirped, "Here." Heads turned toward her. Senate President Mike Haridopolos said, "No, no, no, no, no, we're talking about the other Bullard." The other Senators roared. Remembering that incident, Edward said, "My wife was very outspoken and she just was out of the system and didn't realize she was out of the system."

At the beginning of the family's entry into politics, campaigning was basically "word of mouth," Edward said. "We campaigned on the streets. We would go to the parks where the Optimists would be playing football games, and you had all the communities there in the park." They also spoke in churches. "A lot of candidates would come in and do a cameo for about 10 minutes and then hit the road. But when we went to a church, we stayed the whole time. Campaigning in the church was not our big issue. The fact was, since we were from the community, everyone knew us, so that helped." Often churches would invite them to speak. "You tried to do that before the campaign season. You don't wait 'til time to vote to make the trips to the church. That's not the way that we operated. We went to the churches during the off-season."

In addition, they advertised through the black media, mainly the *Miami Times* and the *Gospel Truth* magazine (a monthly publication). "Later on, as we became entrenched, we did receive some monies that we were able to do newspapers, such as the *Miami Herald*, or we were able to buy television time through the cable companies. But that took a good while to come into operation," Edward said.

In the early days, "We used to get $5 checks and notes in the mail saying, 'We're praying for you and this is what we have.' And you'd get a $3 check." Gradually larger contributions came in. "We always remembered when we got the first check when we were in the campaign office and Norbert Seals, our campaign manager, said: 'Stop! Major announcement! Major announcement! We got a $25 check!' So we laugh about that today."

But always, their success as a family political dynasty rested on Edward's ties to the community. "I taught so many of those kids in the community. It was a sense of love, and some of those kids that I taught earlier now have grandkids. They would come by to ask, 'What do you need?' These are some of my students and these are some I taught in the alternative school. I always had the 'bad kids.' So I loved them and they loved me. And they would do anything for me, these kids. And they have their kids and then some of them would go out and say, 'Hey, look, I go to such-and-such church, I would like to carry out some materials.' So we had people who would run off materials for us and take it to their churches and they'll have their kids do the same thing." They would also pass out leaflets on street corners and put them on car windshields wherever there were large crowds.

"We had a good record, a good community involvement, and we were members of all of the organizations, be it the homeowners, be it the Crime Watch, be it members of the fraternity or the sorority, the NAACP, you name it. Everything that was there to promote change, we were sitting on the front row. So everyone knew you and we were into it," Edward said. "Everyone knew the Bullards. And that's just the way it was."

During Edward's first campaign, he plastered a campaign banner on a Winnebago that he called his "Office on Wheels," which he would park at different places throughout his district. When both he and Larcenia were running, they used the Winnebago as a joint office. "That Winnebago went to places like Key West with me at the helm," Dwight said. It was his first time to drive such a vehicle and luckily he had no mishaps, "but it was always interesting going down those narrow streets in a motor home down in Monroe County, to say the least."

Traveling with his dad on the campaign trail, he observed the impact his father had had on students. "When people saw he was running, they'd be like, 'Hey, you all, Mr. Bullard's running,'" Dwight said. "We're talking about guys who he may have saved from lives in prison by helping to turn their lives around."

That experience "led me to want to be a better teacher because at that time I was applying for teaching jobs," Dwight said. "That really was the inspiration for me as to why one teaches. Why do people get into the profession? It's the idea that a guy who's 40-something years old who's sitting in a gas station finds out your dad's now running for office and trying to change professions, and all he can do is think back to when he was 18 and first interacted with your father and say, 'Hey, yeah, if there's anybody that is going to get my vote, it's Ed Bullard.'"

"Yeah, we had some people who really believed in us, and it was a joy to work the process," Edward said. "The longer you stayed in the process, the more you respected it, the more you learned about it, and the more people would join you."

All three Bullards fought in tough election campaigns. Larcenia and Dwight in their Senate campaigns, in particular, "ran against heavy hitters and ran against a lot of money," Edward said. Current campaign reports show candidates "running with $100,000, $200,000 easily. But Dwight, he's lucky if he gets $60,000. And I know when Larcenia was running, she was lucky if she got $20,000." When it came to raising money, the Bullards were always at the bottom end.

"Our name and sincerity and commitment to the total community is what we ran off and that's how we did it," Edward said. "And that beat money out, it beat money the whole time."

Over the past 25 years, he has seen changes in elections and political campaigns. The demographics of the communities changed, and as a result, "the campaigning started to cost more money" to target different groups of voters, he said. As much as 75 percent of the campaign budget would go to media and print advertising.

People used to vote for the "black candidate" they knew from their churches and schools. "But that base has just died out," he explained, and more people are coming in from Latin America and the Caribbean. Especially in Richmond Heights, "you have maybe five families staying inside a lot of those homes." In addition, growth and urban renewal have forced many people to move into the area. "And all of 'em are registered, and it's a big thing that's making the swing."

Moreover, money has changed whose names appear on the ballot. "It's not that they have a desire, they are being placed [there] because they have financial backing. Someone would back them just to put them in there to split votes," which can affect a candidate's sincerity, Edward said. "When I started out, those who were representing the district were usually from the district," but that is not always true now. "A lot of good candidates were just knocked out because they didn't have the financial backing."

In taking the oath of office the first time, Edward felt proud, knowing "you came up on an island, you came up in a house with no running water, especially no lights, and no one expected you to go anywhere. Out of our immediate family, our family was the only one that made it to the States," he said. "We got to America and we capitalized, I guess, off of hard work. No one gave us anything, but it was a lot of hard work. And doing what you were told to do in terms of trying to be right. And of course they beat this good old religion in your head and that kind of stuck in there anyway, but it was just your bringing up. And you didn't go up to Tallahassee looking for greed or trying to put your hand in the till or anything. Just sit tight, do what you can to help. What you can do, you help, and if you can't, you can't." Being in the minority party, he was always outvoted on everything. "You had to play the hand that was dealt, and you do the best that you can and let the chips fall where they may."

The most rewarding thing about serving in the Legislature "was the people that you met, many of whom are in Congress in the U.S. House in Washington today," he said. He also benefitted from meeting "some good people in the political arena all over the country in terms of going to conferences here and there and listening to different views and to see that it takes time to change anything and you have to have support to change it."

He encountered disappointment as well. "There were issues that I believed in and they were always voted down because of party affiliations. That's the hurting part that sometimes some of the members of the majority party that just tell you this ain't going to work, that say we're not going to do it if you don't do that. And then you had to compromise." A member of the majority can do things, while the only chance for the minority is to know the rules. "It's just a tough situation."

The advice he would give someone interested in going into politics is "be honest and true." "Become involved in the community and your city. What have you done that'll help you to do more?" Membership in organizations is not enough. "It's more than just going to the church, but you go and join your church and do something and you help somebody. What have you done to help somebody? Have you helped anybody? Because in the position that you will be in, you will be helping a lot of people, so you've got to understand the process of helping," he said. "You can change a system by being a part of joining in rather than looking on the outside and complaining."

Edward Bullard was interviewed by telephone by the author Feb. 12, 2015. Preliminary information was supplied in a personal interview with his son, Sen. Dwight Bullard, Feb. 3, 2015.

Susan Bucher (D)

First Mexican-American woman elected to the Florida House of Representatives, 2000

Personal: Born October 27, 1958, Escondido, California; moved to Florida in 1985, married.

Education:

- Palomar Junior College (1976)
- Mira Costa College (1981–1984)

Figure 3.37. Susan Bucher, Democrat from West Palm Beach by way of California, was the first person of Mexican-American descent to serve in the Florida House (2000). When Floridians would ask her what country she was from, she was somewhat taken aback. In southern California, nearly 40 percent of the population "looked like me." State Archives of Florida, *Florida Memory*, https://www.floridamemory.com/items/show/135012. Photograph by Mark T. Foley, 2003.

Occupation: Supervisor of Elections, Palm Beach County
Trailblazer Elections:

- House of Representatives District 86 (Part of Palm Beach County) *Dem Primary Special Election* 2000
    - Susan Bucher (49.2%), Bonnie Weaver (36.1%), Allan Kalish (10.1%), William "Bill" Washington (4.6%)
- House of Representatives District 86 (Part of Palm Beach County) *Dem Runoff Special Election* 2000
    - Susan Bucher (62.4%), Bonnie Weaver (37.6%)
- House of Representatives District 86 (Part of Palm Beach County) *General—Special Election* April 25, 2000
    - Susan Bucher-D (74.1%), Robert J. Kanjian-R (25.9%)

THE SUSAN BUCHER STORY

When Susan Bucher served in the Florida Legislature from 2000 to 2008, she acquired a reputation as a serious legislator who read proposed bills from cover to cover. "Because I read the bills, I usually had a lot of questions," she said. Those questions and her tenacity in seeking answers never won her any popularity points.

Shortly after her election, she was surprised to discover that she had become the first Mexican American in the Florida Legislature. A third-generation Californian, "I really was raised very American. I don't speak Spanish fluently—I learned Spanish at school. We didn't speak Spanish at home," she said. "When I first got to Florida in 1985, people used to ask me what country I was from. I was taken aback because I was from Southern California where 40 percent of the population looked like me."

For a legislator, "it doesn't necessarily matter the culture if you're willing to work hard and demonstrate that you will do the right thing with some integrity," she said.

She moved to Florida with her husband, who was in the investment business and wanted to live near his family in his home state. "I really didn't want to leave my job because I enjoyed it," she said. She designed service line extensions for a gas and electric company, a position that had taken her six years to reach. When she couldn't find a similar job in Florida, she started working for Palm Beach County, first in the building department and then in zoning. Building on that experience, she took a job as a land use planner for the Village of Palm Springs, near West Palm Beach. Eventually she became an administrator for a community redevelopment agency (CRA) for Westgate-Belvedere Homes.

It was at that time that she met the person who would pave her way into public office. Democratic State Rep. Edward J. "Ed" Healey, who had created a health care district in the area, had filed legislation to take away part of the incremental tax funding from the CRA. "He didn't think it was fair for the health care district to contribute part of its tax base to the CRA," she said. She went to talk to him, explaining that "We have this very impoverished community, and you're taking money away while we're trying to lay down basic services, sewer and water." He was not persuaded, and his bill passed.

A couple of years later, when she was out of work, she discovered that Healey had an opening for a legislative assistant. "He remembered that I had been very tenacious when I had come to visit him. I said, 'I really would like to get into the field of affordable housing. If I go one session to Tallahassee, will you help me learn how the appropriation process happens?' I knew there were some programs that funneled down money to the county, but I wasn't really sure how that happened. He said, 'Sure, that'd be a great thing. I might retire soon. Why don't you come with me for one session?'"

Once they were in Tallahassee, Healey "took me under his wing," she said. At that time, bills were still distributed to legislative offices in paper copies. "I read them all and started getting way involved in all the issues."

After that session, he asked her to stay on his staff: "If you'll continue to be my aide, I'll run again." She thought, "Well, great! This is very interesting." She realized that the job offered a good opportunity to learn the policy-making process, so she agreed. She also recognized Healey's tremendous fortitude in running for office. "Two different times he had been beaten and he came back." His 22-year tenure was separated into three periods: 1974–1980, 1982–1984, and 1986–2000.

Meanwhile, "I had learned a lot about many, many issues," she said. She was so well versed that Healey, then 75 years old and nearing his term limit, asked if she would be interested in taking his seat. "I thought about it and met with my family and said I think so." They arrived in Tallahassee in early March, and 10 days into the session, he died of a cerebral hemorrhage.

"I packed up and went home to prepare a funeral. I was very close to him," she said. Gov. Jeb Bush called a special election a few days later. "I filed to run for election and won. It was kind of crazy because back then there was a primary and a runoff. I think we did three elections in about five, six, seven weeks. It was one of the fastest elections in state history."

"On the night of the general election, my car was packed. I had anticipated that we probably would win. The person I hired as my campaign assistant became my legislative aide. We drove to Tallahassee and got there at 3 in the morning. We went to my legislative aide's apartment—it happened to be a two-bedroom—thank God—and she and I parked it there. We got a couple hours sleep and I was sworn in at 9 in the morning."

"It was not the way that I had planned it, but we had been talking for about six months that maybe after the session I would resign and then start campaigning. I always envisioned Mr. Healey would be there. He was somebody who had a tremendous influence on my personality—and not very many people can do that—and he was going to help me."

Before his death Healey had said, "The other half of the business is learning how to get elected." With that in mind, in her off time, she had been learning how to campaign. In addition to attending national training sessions on the subject, she had learned about computer targeting and operating data files. "I actually had run a couple of national elections in Palm Beach County for my party."

She became her own campaign manager. "I was out knocking [on] doors, and in between knocking on the doors, I was calling the lobbyists to see if I could raise any money. Because I only had about three weeks, I think that I put in a little personal money and I got maybe $20,000."

Having worked with Healey for six and a half years, "I knew the people who got out the votes, I knew where the territories were, I knew where the population was that came out and voted, and so I knew where to concentrate," she said. "Because we had a very short time, we went after the Democratic base. Typically you run the data file and you see where the largest populations that vote are, and you go backward until you run out of time or money. That's exactly what it is. It's not rocket science. That's what we did, and we continue to do that today."

"It was elementary," she said. A friend who worked for Democratic Congressman Robert Wexler (1996–2010) helped her find a vendor to design a mail piece. "I talked to this person for about half an hour about my background and what I knew." They took pictures in her backyard. The piece was ready the next day. "I approved it and we shot it into the mail. I think I did only three pieces of mail because of the shortness of time."

She did not advertise on TV or radio but received endorsements from both the *Sun Sentinel* and the *Palm Beach Post*. Bucher devised a slogan, "I can hit the ground running," based on her work with Healey. "I knew which bills were popular, what was being heard, what the controversy was going to be. I could quote you all the bill numbers that were the hot topics. I could talk about what the impacts were. Some of my passions were health care and children and senior services and DCF (Department of Children and Families). I was extremely familiar with all of that."

Healey had chaired the Transportation Committee, and even when the Democrats lost control of the House, he continued to serve on certain committees. "Fortunately when I got to Tallahassee, I got to serve on some of the major committees that Mr. Healey served on. My job with Mr. Healey was to read the backup and provide a synopsis. He wouldn't always ask all of the questions that I would write, but I had a pretty good handle on the agendas and what the issues were. The few times that I came into contact with the other candidates, they would talk in a very generalized way—'I'll work hard'—but I could hit the issues. I think that became very apparent quickly. I was just very fortunate to have been integrated in the community that I worked in for a long time."

In taking the oath of office, she felt awed: "I had served with a man that had a long history. Everybody around him, they would allow me to sit in the corner and listen to all of the old guys, like Phil Lewis (a long-time Democratic Florida Senator and former Senate President). Some people had just been elected, and some had been staff. Just sitting listening to them and the history that they taught me provided me with a lot of understanding." In those meetings, she could identify every person discussed because she had read *Florida in the Sunshine* by Lance deHaven-Smith, a Florida State University professor. "I was so taken aback because I never had thought that I would run for office. It wasn't something I set up for, it wasn't something that as a young person I had an aspiration for, but I knew the weight and responsibility because I had watched some of those statesmen. It was just such a great honor."

Her Mexican heritage played almost no role in her campaign. "At that time, the Hispanic voting population was not engaged at all. It just happened that I was Hispanic, but the majority of my constituents were Jewish. After the election it came on the front page that I was the first Mexican American. I didn't realize that until the day after I got elected."

"I've engaged with a lot of organizations over the years to try and bring forward Hispanic candidates, Hispanic voters," she said. "At one time the Palm Beach County Hispanic Coalition represented 42 countries. We had a great group of people, but there's a hierarchy structure of the elites and then down to the not-so-elites, and that generally takes about three months. Then there's some disagreement and it's not very easy to keep a group like that going and together."

Cultural differences often produced conflict. "There's Cuban versus Puerto Rican versus Colombian. Now we have a very large population of South Americans who are becoming extremely active now, and then there's Mexicans and all these different cultures. The Guatemalans don't want to be Latinos, and they don't want to be Hispanics, but their heritage is Mayan. So you have to respect all those cultures. It's difficult to keep everybody in the same room and going in the same direction. We really haven't had anybody from our communities take my place."

Did she encounter discrimination? "Probably not as a Hispanic, but as a female," she said. That attitude "still is very predominant. I was a very strong-willed legislator and that wasn't really popular when I first came in. In fact, it was always a point of contention with the leadership on the Republican side. They didn't tend to have a lot of females at that time that ran committees or were chair people. They gave most of the women education and health care and the things that you expect from the old school. Well, I came in the door doing economic development and transportation and things that Mr. Healey did, and still health care and education. But I had some other things that I knew about, and that was not extremely popular."

As a female, she found that having lots of questions was not popular either: "I saw some of my male colleagues on both sides of the aisle. Very few [of them had] read the bills, but if they [engaged in] the same line of questioning, they were treated with a little more respect. I really did expect answers and was very tenacious about trying to get them. I think now there are more females in the House and the Senate and it's becoming somewhat better. But it's still a boy's club."

When Hispanics come to her for advice, "I always tell them that if you want to run for public office and you think that you're going to get a leg up because you're Hispanic, that's not the best bench to mark your race on. Our community, it's pretty diverse. I don't think that it matters very substantially whether you're Jewish or African American or Hispanic. I think that the educated voters really weigh who you are. At no time have I relied on the Hispanic community to get elected or thought that that was a tremendous advantage or a tremendous disadvantage. Everybody's been very fair. You know, it just happens that I'm Hispanic. So it's interesting because as a state Representative, you want to carry forward your heritage. I tended to go looking for organizations that might be able to organize in a manner to provide leadership and eventually have somebody like me take my place. That didn't happen. And it hasn't happened again. But I anticipate that as our community diversifies more that it will."

In addition, "I always tell people that if they want to get involved in the political atmosphere, they need to be involved in their community. People come and say, 'I want to run for office.' Well, I've been around for a really long time in Palm Beach County. If I don't know them, that means nobody else knows them. I always recommend that you go find what your passions are and then go participate. If you happen to do well at representing your passions in our community, then typically it is a testament to your future. People will then approach you and ask you to run for office or there will be an appropriate time."

It's not enough to want to run for office. Bucher described an instance when a bright young Hispanic woman came to her and said: "I'm going to be just like you. I'm going to run for your seat and take your place." "I participate widely with children's groups, seniors, all kinds of things, and I had never seen her before," Bucher said. She told the young woman that perhaps she would like to get involved in the community first. And she did, and she eventually decided not to run for office. "You really need to demonstrate that you're interested in the issues and that you're interested in providing some kind of service to the public. Generally that's demonstrated by your actions out in the community."

In 2008, Bucher ran for Supervisor of Elections, counting on the Democratic base she carried in previous House races. She faced two opponents, including the incumbent. "I thought I would win in the primary and I didn't. So I had to go to the general. But we won handily in the general. And then this last round, the same thing. I did win in the primary though. In a presidential year like [2012] I wanted to win in the primary because I just couldn't understand how I was going to operate the office and run for office."

In the transition from legislator to supervisor, "you really have to have a different mindset. You're going to serve the entire population, its voting, and you have to give the same ease and access to everybody. I have just completely shut down any political activities that I used to do. I still take part in discussions. If I'm the speaker, I go to Democratic groups. If it's a special function like an annual dinner, I go, but I do not attend regular meetings. I'm not a member of the Democratic Executive Committee. I'm not highly involved anymore."

What has changed most in running campaigns is money. "Unfortunately, the way that a lot of people get elected now is to raise hundreds of thousands of dollars," she said. "On countywide campaigns that I have to run now, my colleagues, some of them have spent half a million dollars. I think last year I spent maybe $80,000 and I thought that was a lot. I'm still a grassroots, on-the-ground, do-it-myself person. I have a couple of people who help me with data and things because I have a full-time job now."

When she was a member of the House, "my legislative responsibilities were my full-time job." Mixing with people is essential. "Mr. Healey taught me that people like to kick the tires before they buy a car. I always remembered that. You have to go meet people, they have to know who you are, and you really have to get on the ground and be available. If you get elected, then you have to be accessible," she said. "What I found out very quickly is those kinds of big contributions don't come without strings. I don't believe that I have any strings but to the people, to my voters. As a result, it has cost me some personal fortunes to provide some of the funding for my campaigns, but I would rather do it in that manner than have to rely on somebody that wants me to do a certain thing a certain way just for them."

Getting out and meeting the people was her favorite part of campaigning. "I still do door-to-door. It's a lot different from the first time that I ran when you could walk into Century Village [a huge Democratic-voting senior condo community in Pembroke Pines] and knock on every single door there. Now they don't let anybody in the door there. In certain communities they are kind of cautious." But the flip side is how some people, regardless of their party affiliation, answer the door. They might say: "You are the first person running for office that has ever knocked on my door." Meeting people face-to-face is part of a candidate's responsibility. "What I'm seeing now are these new generation politicians who think they're going to shoot 15 pieces of mail and do a robo-call and have a TV commercial, and they're going to win."

In her last election round, "my opponent had a television commercial. I was astounded. It's not a statewide race." By contrast, Bucher knocked on doors: "I got out there and sweated in a lot of heat. It's good for you to get out there and work. I met a lot of people that I didn't know. I don't believe that my opponent knocked on any doors. It's unfortunate that politics is getting further and further away from the people because of the large volumes of campaign cash that people need." Those huge sums of cash "tend to formulate what their agenda's going to be. And so we're finding more and more special interest authority. I think all of that came with term limits."

"If the atmosphere had continued to be what it was when I was there, I probably still would be in the Legislature," she said. "I loved the policy side, not so much the politics." She lamented the different atmosphere today. "You don't have those individuals with long-term knowledge." She remembered that as Healey's aide, she could ask long-time legislators about the bills they sponsored and how tweaking them now might affect the programs. "Many of the current members really have little knowledge and rely very heavily on the legislative staff and on lobbyists to give them information."

"Mr. Healey taught me that information was power," she said. She was thrilled to read every bill before he had to hear it, and she continued that practice as a legislator. In fact, colleagues teased her about coming in with a pile of papers with highlighting marks and tabs on many pages. In her last year, when Marco Rubio was Speaker, "many times he'd come back to my desk and ask me about certain bills. He knew that if there were a lot of tabs, those were my questions, so he would try and get business rolling and pass a lot of bills." Sometimes while standing at the roster, he would say, "OK, Bucher, hold up that bill," and she would hold it up for everyone to see. If it had too many tabs, he would say, "Go talk to the bill sponsor." Few people are reading the actual legislation or understanding it, she said, "and that's where I think some of the wheels have come off of some of the programs because they're getting steered in a particular direction for campaign contributions."

She and Rubio, who belonged to different parties, "were kind of a class all our own because he had gotten elected in a special election two months before I did. As he continued to rise, we remained very cordial." When he was Speaker, she would quietly give him information, such as how changing a state law could generate federal dollars and how funding antirejection drugs for the needy could keep them alive. He would say to her: "I'm the bigger picture, and you're the details." The two had some philosophical differences, but "we knew that good public policy was important. His door was actually always open to me, and I always appreciated that."

Figure 3.38. Rep. Susan Bucher (*far right*) had a reputation for reading bills from cover to cover. That might explain why fellow legislators like Rep. Shelley Vana, D-West Palm Beach (*left*), and Rep. Terry Fields, D-Jacksonville (*center*), would come to her to make sense out of a proposed bill. Photograph by Meredith Hill, 2006. http://www.myfloridahouse.gov/Sections/PhotoAlbums/photoAlbum.aspx?MemberId=4182.

Rubio's reliance on Bucher's information was widely known among legislators as well as the press. One year, in its annual show making fun of legislators, the Capitol Press Corps produced a skit showing Rubio in his office having a dream—"more like a nightmare," Bucher said. "When he woke up, I had the gavel and I was the Speaker." Legislators laughed uproariously.

The press also knew about Bucher's penchant for thoroughly reading bills. One year a skit showed House Speaker Allan Bense (2004–2006) getting a new car with a voice-activated navigational system. When Bense got in the car, the system—in Bucher's voice—said, "Good morning, Mr. Speaker. Since this is a brand new car, I'm going to start from page one and read the entire manual to you."

Another skit made fun of Bucher and her opposite in the House, Adam Hasner (2003–2011). At that time, an often-aired TV commercial for a presidential campaign featured an exchange between two national political strategists, Democrat James Carville and Republican Karl Rove. The two were sitting on the U.S. Capitol steps having a soft drink, discussing various issues, and then playing football as great buddies. At the end they were again sitting on the Capitol steps. Rove said, "We should do this again sometime," and Carville said, "Not a chance." For the skit, Bucher and Hasner assumed the roles of Carville and Rove. "We played football, we threw paper airplanes down on the House floor, and all these funny things. At the end we were sitting on the old Capitol steps and Hasner said, 'You know, Bucher, we should do this again sometime.' And I said something like, 'Nah, not a chance.'"

"They always knew that I wasn't personalizing what I was doing. They always included me in the press skit taping because it was just always funny. They used to say it proved that I had a sense of humor."

Susan Bucher was interviewed in person by the author Oct. 7, 2013.

John "Q" Quiñones (R)

First Republican Puerto Rican man elected to the Florida House of Representatives, 2002

Personal: Born April 26, 1965, Rio Piedras, Puerto Rico; married with two children.

Education:

- University of Central Florida, B.S. (1988)
- St. Thomas University, J.D. (1992)

Occupation: Lawyer

Trailblazer Elections:

- House of Representatives District 49 (Parts of Orange and Osceola counties) *Rep Primary* 2002
  - John "Q" Quiñones (56.4%), Joe Mantilla (43.6%)
- House of Representatives District 49 (Parts of Orange and Osceola counties) *General Election* 2002
  - John "Q" Quiñones-R (54.1%), Jose Fernandez-D (45.9%)

THE JOHN "Q" QUIÑONES STORY

Figure 3.39. John "Q" Quiñones, the first Republican Puerto Rican man elected to the Florida House (2002) emphasized conservative values in campaigning. Nicknamed "Q," he helped pass legislation that allowed students who had failed the FCAT to continue their higher education and another that permitted individuals trying to overturn convictions to get DNA testing. Photograph by Mark Foley, 2006. http://www.myfloridahouse.gov/Sections/PhotoAlbums/photoAlbum.aspx?MemberId=4273.

Taking the oath as a newly elected state Representative from Orlando, John Quiñones remembered feeling a sense of wonder and astonishment: "It was like 'I can't believe this is happening to me.' I had not even gone to Tallahassee, I'd not gone to the chambers, so it was all new to me. It was like 'pixie dust,' as they call it when you're a new employee at Disney World, and I worked at Disney so I remember that. It was a very surreal experience."

At the same time, he was thinking, "Wow! What an honor, what a great responsibility I'm having now to my constituents." Back then, in 2002, no local officials were Hispanic. As a result, "all the focus on federal, state and local issues, when it came to Hispanic, was on me. You know, the media, the Telemundo, the Univision—every time that there was any comment that had to do with federal, state or local, they would call me for a response." But now there are other Hispanic legislators as well as local officials whom the media can call. "So, there was an enormous feeling of responsibility at that time."

The path that culminated in that historic moment began in Bayamón, a suburb of San Juan, Puerto Rico, where he grew up. His family left the island when he was 14 and moved to Central Florida. He went to Lake Howell High School in Seminole County and then Valencia Community College. "We weren't well off, so I had to work at Disney and go to Valencia," he said. With the help of Pell grants, he finished at Valencia and went to the University of Central Florida, where he graduated with a bachelor's degree in business administration. He finished law school at St. Thomas University in 1992, moved to Kissimmee, and established a law practice as a sole practitioner. "I was like one of four Hispanic attorneys in Kissimmee. Now you have probably 200," he said.

He voted for the first time in 1984, when he was 19 and Ronald Reagan was President. "I certainly listened to what he said. I liked him, so my first vote was for Ronald Reagan. As I went to college and analyzed both sides, I tended to side more with the Republicans. I think at the end I don't agree with everything the Republicans do, but I agree more with what the Republicans do than with the Democrats."

He first ran for political office in 2000 in a race for County Judge. Although he "lost badly," the experience gave him a glimpse into the election process. Two years later, when a new redistricting occurred, he was approached by local Republican Party leaders to run for an open seat in the House. "They saw that I had run for judge, and they saw that I was known in the community as an attorney."

State politics had not been in his future plans: "It took about six months for me to really think about it and sink in that that's what I wanted to do, and really do for my family and the community," he said. "So all of a sudden my first session was like six months in Tallahassee [for seven special sessions] and I had to shut down my law practice for that time. That was my introduction to the Legislature."

In deciding to run, "I had met with the community leaders, people that I still keep friends with today. Justina Marti comes to mind, and a few others that understood the significance of that particular seat. Up to that point there was no Hispanic in the Legislature from Central Florida. So they understood how important that seat was, and they encouraged me throughout the process." One of the first to encourage him was Lewis Oliver from Orange County, an attorney who is now his law partner.

No one gave Quiñones much of a chance in winning the primary. His opponent was a friend, Joe Mantilla, a Colombian. "He was the front-runner," said Quiñones. Mantilla "had raised over $60,000 for the primary, and I had put in like $5,000 of my own money. When it was all over, I think I raised maybe $10,000."

When he began campaigning, "I had no idea what I was doing. I had the energy, I had the passion, but I didn't know what I was doing." His political consultant, John Dowless, advised walking neighborhoods and meeting people face-to-face. "I guess he says that to all his clients and a lot of them don't do it, or they say they do it here and there. But that was the one thing that I knew I could do. I enjoy meeting people. I enjoy knocking on doors."

With money so limited, "we did a lot of things that were kind of unconventional. The palm cards were one of our mail-out pieces. We were sending out handwritten notes to people. I was walking about 100 houses a day almost. I remember I lost 20 pounds." The intensity of his grassroots efforts "took my opponents by surprise because they didn't expect me to win, with the little money that I had." He acknowledged that the Legislature had seen other surprises: "I think John Tobia [Republican elected 2008] was an underdog and ended up winning."

In that first primary, turnout was about 10 percent. The community was made up of older voters in the upper middle class. "This was essentially a campaign that was won, in my opinion, really in non-Hispanic communities like Hunters Creek, Deer Run, Deerfield, those South Orange communities there. That's where I got most of my votes," he said.

In the general election, he faced Democrat Jose Fernandez, a Nicaraguan. "Again, he was the one that was getting all the support from most of the establishment. In my commercials I did point out my origins, where I was from, how I arrived here. I think it was very important for people to know that I wasn't born with a silver spoon. I came here, lived the American Dream. I had to work to go to college and those things. So we did tell that story."

Voter turnout was higher but still low because it was a gubernatorial and not a presidential election. Many voters came from the Buena Ventura Lakes and Meadow Woods communities, the airport, and State Road 436. "I would suspect we probably had about 25 or 30 percent Hispanics that turned out to vote in that election."

His victory marked the first time a Puerto Rican Republican had been elected to the House. The only other elected Puerto Ricans were Democrats—Maurice A. Ferré in 1996 and Tony Sanchez in 1998.

"In the primary we stressed conservative values, especially fiscal responsibility," he said. "In the general election we still emphasized the conservative values because we felt, and I still feel, that Hispanics that are here, that Republicans tend to be more family oriented, conservative, on issues of abortion, issues of right to life and things like that. The ones that are coming from the island tend to be more conservative. The Hispanics that may come from up north tend to be more liberal. But we were addressing really what we felt was the sense of the Hispanics in general," he said. His campaign also addressed taxes, quality of life, jobs, diversification of the economy, and education. "We talked about ESL {English as a Second Language] students because I had been one," he said.

Education was important not only as a campaign issue but also as an action item in his legislative agenda. In 2004, he successfully spearheaded reform on the FCAT

(Florida's Comprehensive Assessment Test). The legislation allowed students that could not pass the FCAT to earn a certificate of completion from a community college and then move on to a university.

In early 2007, Quiñones resigned his House seat to run for the Osceola County Board of Commissioners. He served as chairman in 2009 and 2012.

Looking back on his days as a legislator, he said the most rewarding thing was making changes. "For instance, that FCAT bill—that was just a tremendous experience." Another bill he sponsored raised the penalty, on second offense, for racing vehicles on the highway. As a penalty, the offender would have to forfeit the vehicle. That issue was important because "we, especially in the Hispanic community, are losing too many kids to racing," as evidenced by crosses alongside the roads.

One of his most rewarding experiences was passage of a bill that allowed the DNA testing for individuals attempting to overturn their convictions. That bill, which was already law but about to expire, came close to defeat because certain members in the House, especially a former prosecutor who later became a judge in Fort Myers, opposed it. Quiñones also found it especially rewarding to pay compensation to Wilton Dedge[71] for 22 years of wrongful imprisonment.

As a first-term legislator, Quiñones had the idea that passing a bill was easy. "Then it was explained to me [in Clyde's, a popular bar] by a Senator. I was arguing why can't this bill pass? It was the last week of session, and I'm like, 'This is such a simple thing.'" The Senator responded, "You mean you're complaining because your bill made it all the way to the end of the session? I mean, you should just be happy that you're in that game. And you're a freshman?" At that moment, "it dawned on me that it's not so easy to pass a bill. So that was rewarding from a professional standpoint."

In addition to working on legislation, his office handled federal, state, and local requests from people in Hispanic communities. "We were sort of an arm for a lot of the outreach." Many requests dealt with school issues, which required contacting a school board member or superintendent. Other requests involved county issues, and still others, state issues, such as denials of Medicaid assistance. Certainly some legislators had bilingual staff members, but often Hispanic citizens felt more comfortable going to Hispanic officials.

As one of a few legislators who could speak fluent Spanish, "I would see [Gov.] Jeb Bush walking toward the Capitol sometimes and I would join him on the walk. Normally, if he saw me, he liked to talk in Spanish. I think he either wanted to practice Spanish or he just felt comfortable talking in Spanish." Talking with the brother of the President (George W. Bush) and having that kind of a relationship was "pretty awesome."

Among the most disappointing experiences in the Legislature was that special interests could sometimes have negative effects. "I'm not saying all the time because sometimes they do provide education and they provide information, all that, but

Figure 3.40. State Rep. John Quiñones promoted Hispanic student activities at the Capitol—and was a showman on the floor, having worked at Disney World as a college student. There were no local Hispanic elected officials at that time in the Orlando area, so he ended up fielding calls from Spanish media—Telemundo and Univision—any time a Hispanic issue arose at the federal, state, or local level. Photograph by Mark T. Foley, 2005. http://www.myfloridahouse.gov/Sections/PhotoAlbums/photoAlbum.aspx?MemberId=4273.

sometimes they can bring negative results. Bills that you think are worthy and good die for unknown reasons, but later on you find out that maybe there was something out there that was stopping it," he said.

In addition, living in Tallahassee meant leaving home and family behind, at least temporarily. "Being away from family, being away from the people that you represent, that's difficult. But, you know, it's part of the process."

During his years in public office, Quiñones witnessed demographic changes that included an influx of Colombians, Venezuelans, and Dominicans. "Maybe they still don't have that political power because they're still in the immigration process, or maybe they're permanent residents and they're not citizens yet, but they will be. That's why you can't say, 'Well, I'm going to serve the Puerto Rican community or the Dominican or even the non-Hispanic.' If you're going to be successful as a public official, in my opinion, you can't pigeonhole and say, 'Oh, I'm only representing Puerto Ricans or I'm only representing this or that.'"

While Central Florida grows increasingly diverse, Puerto Ricans continue to come because of economic opportunities. In addition, Puerto Ricans leaving the island "are just sick of the politics because politics over there is really a full-contact sport. They come here and they unfortunately don't get as involved with politics," he said. "Over there they vote, 80 percent for just a referendum. Then they come here and they turn off that spigot, they don't vote. I think that they're kind of turned off by politics and they register Independent because they don't really know if they're Republicans or Democrats."

Another factor is Puerto Rico's political status: Will it remain a commonwealth of the United States? Will it become the 51st state? Will it ask for independence? "What's going to happen is that those favoring statehood tend to get out of the island. And then when the state-hooders are in power, the pro-commonwealth supporters get out of the island. So they just go back and forth."

His advice to young people considering public office: "We need good people to run for office and certainly I have had young folks that come here and they're all gung ho and everything. I try to tell them, make sure that's what you want to do, make sure you talk to your family, make sure you talk to your friends, but don't be afraid.

Because at the end of the day, you're trying a new experience and certainly even trying can be very rewarding because you get to meet a lot of people. So I don't try to discourage anyone. If a young person comes here, I just say, 'If that's what you feel, if that's your passion, go for it.'"

John Quiñones was interviewed in person by the author June 4, 2014.

Yolly Roberson (D)

First Haitian woman to be elected to the Florida House of Representatives, 2002

Personal: Born October 26, 1955, Mirebalais, Haiti; divorced with one child.

Education:

- University of Massachusetts/Boston, B.S.N. (1983)
- New England School of Law, J.D. (1988)

Occupation: Nurse/Attorney

Trailblazer Elections:

- House of Representatives District 104 (Part of Miami-Dade County) *Dem Primary* 2002
    - Yolly Roberson (29.8%), Jacqui Colyer (23.7%), Anthony Williams (18.7%), Ronald A. Brisé (14.6%), Bernard W. H. Jennings (13.1%)
- House of Representatives District 104 (Part of Miami-Dade County) *General Election* 2002
    - Yolly Roberson-D (84.7%), Arlington Sands, Jr.-R (15.3%)

Figure 3.41. Democratic State Rep. Yolly Roberson, the first Haitian woman elected to the Florida House (2002), came from a prominent political family in Haiti. She said the most rewarding part of her legislative career came when she proposed a resolution commending Haiti as the first black country to gain its freedom by its own might—and the whole House stood with her. Photograph by Mark Foley, April 22, 2004. http://www.myfloridahouse.gov/Sections/PhotoAlbums/photoAlbum.aspx?MemberId=4283.

THE YOLLY ROBERSON STORY

For Yolly Roberson, politics provided a way to pursue her passion for public service. Paradoxically, however, public service is "the most frustrating experience I've had in my lifetime and the best experience of my lifetime."

In Haiti, she grew up in a politically active family. Her grandfather served as a legislator, her grandmother who died in Boston, Massachusetts, at the age of 103, campaigned for him, and often hosted the Haitian President at their home. Her father also served as a mayor and a judge.

Roberson has been passionate about public service for as long as she can remember, but she never intended to run for public office. She recalled her first year in America, 1977, when, as a teenage girl, she could barely speak and read English. With the help of a French/English dictionary, she managed to make sense of a small article from the *Boston Globe*, which quoted portions of Martin Luther King's "I Have A Dream" speech. "I was so mesmerized by Dr. King's vision for America, I cut out that article from the newspaper and pasted it in my photo album where it remains today," said Roberson. Later, in 1984, the late Gov. Mario Cuomo's "Tale of Two Cities" speech introduced the Democratic Party to her as the conscience of America, the party of unity, the party that "speaks for the minorities who have not yet entered the mainstream . . . for ethnics who want to add their culture to the magnificent mosaic that is America" and in 1988, Rev. Jesse Jackson's historic presidential campaign inspired her to believe that she, too, had a place in the Democratic Party, she, too, could be part of the solution to America's problems.

After she immigrated to Boston, Roberson worked her way through school. She briefly attended Jeremiah Burke High School in Dorchester, but, dismayed by the school's lack of discipline, she left and successfully sat for GED certification. "After that I attended Roxbury Community College just to learn English," she said.

She worked full time at night as a lab technician while attending nursing school at the University of Massachusetts in Boston, where she met Dr. Anne Kibrick, "an incredibly dedicated public servant," who led the effort to create the first public baccalaureate-level nursing program in the state of Massachusetts. Roberson graduated with a bachelor's degree in nursing in 1983, the first in her family to graduate from a U.S. college. She began her public service career as a registered nurse at the largest public health facility in Massachusetts, Boston City Hospital. There, she volunteered a great deal of her time serving as a Creole and French translator and an advocate for patients afflicted with HIV/AIDS. "I always wanted to help make life better for people. I was just always in the forefront," she said.

By that time, the U.S. Surgeon General's scientific report naming cigarettes as a major health hazard had been around for nearly two decades. It would not be until 1986 that another report would emphasize the dangers of secondhand smoke. Yet, Roberson led a campaign at Boston City Hospital to stop her nursing colleagues from smoking while giving reports (communicating patients' status to the next shift) during shift change. One day, unable to stand the smoke-filled room any longer, she decided to act. "I looked at every nurse sitting at the conference table. I was the only black there, and the youngest member of the leadership team [at age 23]." She hesitated, asking herself: "Do you want to take all of these people on just because of an issue of smoking?" After a moment, she decided: "It is worth it. I have to do it." She told them: "Listen, I don't have to take lunch with you, I don't have to go out with you, I don't have to do anything with you, but I must take reports from you." Then she explained how offensive the smoke was to her and asked them to refrain from smoking at least when giving reports. "They stopped it immediately." She described the incident as an issue of fairness: "I have always been an advocate for fairness," she said, "and I will never stop."

Meanwhile, she had realized that whenever her older sister wanted to consult with an attorney about her U.S. residency, she had to get up at 4 a.m. to drive to New York. "This is insane. It doesn't make sense," Roberson recalled. "Then, we did not have one Haitian attorney in Massachusetts." That realization prompted her to enroll at the New England School of Law in Boston, which was founded in 1908 as a law school for women. She earned her law degree in 1988.

Being a Registered Nurse and a lawyer, it would have been easy and logical for her to gravitate toward the areas of personal injury or medical malpractice after her admission to the Massachusetts Bar. Instead, motivated by her passion to serve, she went to work as a public defender in Roxbury, a predominantly black community.

"I was totally green, I had absolutely no experience with the criminal system, I believed all my clients were innocent," she recalled. But she got a rude awakening when one day a client casually admitted the senseless details of his crime. "That's when the conflict within started," she continued. "Once you start getting too conflicted, you've got to get out."

At the end of her third year as a public defender, she learned in the news of the influx in to Florida of refugees who were fleeing Haiti because of fear of political persecution after the fall of President Jean-Bertrand Aristide in September 1991 as a result of an army coup. "As I watched the news and I saw all these people coming in, I knew I had to do something to help," she said. She immediately contacted her supervisor and, with his approval, took a leave of absence and went to volunteer at the Haitian Refugee Center in Miami.

As she began working in the community, she decided after about a year to stay in South Florida. She got married and had a daughter. Eventually she went to work for the Fort Lauderdale Office of the Attorney General, the Dependency Unit, as a senior assistant attorney general prosecuting child abuse and neglect cases. (Today as a private attorney, she continues in her commitment to serve by representing disadvantaged individuals regardless of their ability to pay.)

In 2002, she ran to be the first black woman elected to the Circuit Court bench in Miami-Dade County. "To date, some 12 years later, we still haven't elected one," she said. Midway through her judicial campaign, however, she came to the stark realization that the $25,000 she had loaned her judicial campaign could not compare with the vastly larger sums being raised by her opponents. At that point, her advisors suggested that she run for the state Representative seat being vacated by Frederica

Wilson (Democratic House member 1998–2002). As a devout Christian, Roberson also firmly believed that the events that led to the House vacancy "was a sign that God wanted her to run for that seat."

Either the judgeship or the Representative position would help champion diversity. Either position would entail risks. "In order for you to be a bridge, you have to be willing to be stepped on." Being a trailblazer is "not a walk in the park," she said. "Everybody's looking up to you to either fail or make it. It's that you have so much to prove. Some people are just waiting for you to fail, and an awful lot of people who are threatened because you're challenging the status quo get busy orchestrating your fall."

Although no elected African American supported her judicial campaign or her campaign for the Florida House during the primary, openly or behind the scenes, she did receive the encouragement of the Haitian community. The only problem was that they didn't know how to support her with financial contributions: "They think the way they support you is by saying '*Mét la,* I support you.' . . . 'I'm with you.' They have the misconception that once you're elected, you're rich. They would come to me expecting me to help pay for the funeral of their loved ones, their rent and to simply make a phone call and get them free medical care." Her grandmother, for example, prepared her will bequeathing gifts to all her grandchildren except Roberson because she believed that being elected to public office is just like winning some type of lottery.

Having grown up in Boston during the school busing period of 1978, she was familiar with racial tension but was never personally a victim. In Boston's black community, she was "just another black woman, just one of them." She was never made to feel "less than" because she happened to be born in Haiti.

She had a similar experience with most of the black American voters she met while walking the community and knocking on doors during her campaigns. She found them to be "very welcoming." With them, she was "just a black woman, one of their own." Most important, her face-to-face interactions with the black Americans she met on the campaign trail reaffirmed her belief that "regardless of where we were actually born, our struggles, goals and aspirations are the same. We all simply want to be safe, to have access to health care, good education, meaningful economic opportunities, and a chance to provide a better life for our family. After all, don't we have the same vision for the black community, and in fact all other communities?"

"My grandmother taught me that hard work always pays off. She told me that she raised my siblings and me in a way that we [could] walk through gates of hell and come out intact. The key is how you conduct yourself," she said. "I believed her."

That belief was sorely tested in the Florida House. "The establishment was already there," she said, and "most, if not all, were perfectly satisfied with the status quo. As one of only two black women in the Florida Legislature with a law degree, one would think that my arrival in the Legislature would have been welcomed by that legislator who was then a four-year veteran of the Florida House." Instead, that legislator "did not waste any time to put me on notice of her special standing as an African American who had marched and gone to jail during the Civil Rights Movement. She was the most feared member of the Democratic Black Caucus, and those who were aware of the situation did not dare get caught in the crossfire." Roberson reminded the legislator that instead of preventing her from claiming a seat under the "Big Tent," she could have celebrated the fact that her hard work during the civil rights era had paved the way for her to now work side by side to continue the fight for equality. The legislator defended her actions by saying: "I have nothing against Haitians. My legislative aide is Haitian."

Roberson said the conduct of that legislator is "a reflection of all that is wrong with the Democratic Party. True, they will stand up and fight for you, but only to a certain extent. You are only allowed to reach a certain level. You are never permitted to go so high as to become a challenge to those in leadership or who aspire to be in leadership." There is no more powerful weapon than being arbitrarily branded "an angry black woman," she said. When certain people wanted to hinder President Obama's campaign, they labeled his wife, Michelle Obama, as "an angry black woman." And "in spite of his public relations machine, Michelle Obama has since retreated from showing her strong side as an educated, independent woman."

During her time in the Legislature, Roberson realized that the stated principles of the Democratic Party are not in alignment with its reality. "While I was well prepared to serve, I had no experience, nor did I have any connection with anyone with political experience. My success as the first Haitian woman elected to the Florida Legislature, rested almost entirely on the willingness of the Democratic Caucus, the Black Caucus, and the Democratic Party, to make room for me under the 'Big Tent,' to stand by me and make available to me meaningful learning opportunities."

"After serving eight years in the Legislature, I have yet to receive a call from any member of the Democratic Caucus, or the party. And on the rare occasions when I attempt to reach out to one, I rarely get a response." She added, "In my entire career, I have never felt the impact of the glass ceiling as much as I have during my tenure in the Florida Legislature. The more educated and prepared you are, the more of a threat you pose, the fiercer your opposition." Somehow, the reality is different for male legislators. They always manage to support one another.

Roberson considers herself a black woman, first and foremost. While there is not a black issue she cannot identify with, she has had the added obligation to advocate for issues unique to the Haitian-American community that few other blacks can fully appreciate. For instance, she introduced the first Dream Act in the Florida Legislature. She fought for the right for undocumented Florida residents to have a driver's license.

One of the most rewarding experiences of her legislative career came when her resolution commending Haiti as the first black nation to ever gain its freedom by its own might passed the House unanimously. "The whole House stood with me and former Rep. Ronal Brisé [also Haitian American]. Many Senators came over to the House chamber to also stand with me." She credited that moment "to the God-given good in everyone. That spark is always inside of us, always. Sometimes it takes a little bit of something to ignite it."

Roberson was often criticized for working closely with Republicans. She noted that based on her interaction with the members of both parties, "good public servants are good public servants irrespective of party affiliation, and bigotry, bias and prejudice are equal-opportunity afflictions." In South Florida, at least, "being a Republican in the black community, that's tantamount to being a traitor." She cited fellow Caribbean black woman, former House member, and former Lieutenant Governor, Jennifer Carroll. "They chastised her for being a Republican, yet anything they needed in the Florida Legislature, they would go to Jennifer for help getting what they needed done—for instance, passing a budget item."

Using a pie as an analogy, Roberson said the Democratic Caucus is given but one pie to share with its members. While the size of that pie never changes, the composition and size of the Caucus's membership are ever increasing. In the distribution of that pie, the only factor at play is the value the Caucus or the party assigned to any given group of members. "They have a piece for this ethnic group, they have a piece for the Hispanics, a piece for this, a piece for that. They have a piece for the African Americans. However, the last group is also entrusted with the responsibility of deciding whether or how much of their share to pass on to the Haitian-American Caucus members. As long as every group's piece of the pie remains undisturbed, no one cares about what happens to anyone else. It's 'survival of the fittest.'"

Democrats have been a minority in the Legislature for a long time. "Every Democrat is fighting for survival. They are under constant pressure to find a way to bring something back to their districts." She learned from other legislators "to hide budget items from fellow Democrats, lest they disappear without a trace." The lack of support she experienced from the Democratic and the black caucuses had more to do with the fact that they were afraid to lose their usual share of the pie. "Fear makes us do things that we're not proud of," she said. "Before you take things personally, [you have to] step back and see why it's happening. Because when you're afraid, the first instinct is survival."

Republicans made much of what she was able to accomplish in the Legislature—they helped her behind the scenes. One Republican for whom she had high praise was Allan Bense (elected to the House 1998, Speaker 2004–2006). She called him a "true gentleman . . . a class act." Even though the two disagreed on issues, he "would

Figure 3.42. State Rep. Yolly Roberson (*second from left*) discusses the state budget with fellow House members Carl Domino, R-Juno Beach (*left*), Kelly Skidmore, D-Boca Raton, and Julio Robaina, R-Miami. Photograph by Meredith Geddings, April 28, 2010. http://www.myfloridahouse.gov/Sections/PhotoAlbums/photoAlbum.aspx?MemberId=4283.

not hold your belief against you." She remembered one occasion when she opposed a bill on the licensing of naturopathic medicine, which he supported. At the same time he promised that he would keep a small amount in the budget for one of her community issues. "During the budget meeting, the way he let me know that the money's still there, he [looked at me and] nodded. And I nodded. And we understood each other. That meant so much to me."

Roberson found a friend and mentor in Chris Smith, a black Democrat and House member (1998–2006). He understood her predicament in the Legislature, gave her advice, but, to protect himself, refrained from getting directly involved.

In the end, "You have to work with all of them," she said. "The funny thing is that in spite of what they say or do, we are one. We are one community. If one group's children are not educated, everyone suffers from the impact of illiteracy in a community."

Until and unless the Democratic Party and the Black Caucus step up and practice what they preach at least in Florida, the Republican domination will not end, and the political system will continue to suffer from the current imbalance.

"There is strength in numbers. When your people don't stand with you, others will take advantage of you, especially when they know that no one is watching. If I had not been well anchored before I arrived in the Florida House, my experience there would have destroyed me, totally."

As a sole practitioner and a single mother, she fully understood the risk she was taking when she decided to run for the Florida House. What she could never have imagined was how much her service in the Legislature as the first Haitian-American woman would eventually cost her, personally and professionally.

She is unusual among legislators in that part of her term in the House overlapped part of the term of her ex-husband, Phillip Brutus. Noting that "the Florida House is a cesspool for gossip," she was determined that their relationship would never become an issue in the Legislature. "The first time I was approached about something that Mr. Brutus allegedly did, I made it clear that Mr. Brutus is a Representative just like me, that he has a vote and I have a vote, and that if anyone wanted to know what he thinks, they should speak to him. As a result, that issue was put to rest once and for all."

Taking the oath of office reminded her that she was "part of this great American dream." America is by no means perfect, she said. "The higher your rank, the clearer you can see its imperfection. Conversely, the lower your rank, the blinder you are." Accepting America with all its faults is like accepting one's own children with their imperfections.

"To me, the Florida House is the best place and the worst place. It's the best place in the sense that they have the power to change the trajectory of the state, do great thing to make life better for Floridians. Yet, it is the place where the worst things can happen," she said, noting that certain elected officials while in office can do enough favors for a friend that when out of office they can go to the friend and start making millions of dollars a year.

Also, with the advent of term limits, the staff of the Florida House "really run the show. It is like a fraternity." Most of the House staff have been at the helm for more than 30 years. "No question that most are wonderful people. But there is always that out-of-touch individual who, on occasion, poisons the well with impunity. The complete lack of diversity of the House staff does not serve Florida's diverse population well. Yet, to date, that issue has gone unnoticed to even the most conscientious members of the press."

Her advice for a young Haitian interested in running for political office is be sure to "set your priorities, make sure that you are financially secure, that family always comes first. Try the best you can to make sure that your constituents understand your position and the importance of working together with you. Always do your absolute best to remain authentic, to stay connected with your community, to consistently represent your constituents with integrity, dignity and respect. Take the time to try to create personal relationships with others, regardless of party or religious affiliation, ethnicity, and cultural differences, without compromising your core values. Never forget who you are, how you got to office, where you come from, or why you ran for public office in the first place. Finally, remember that whatever happens to you in the process—good or bad—is rarely personal, and at the end of the day the things that sustain you and get you through all the challenges, are your faith and your family."

Yolly Roberson was interviewed in person by the author July 17, 2014.

Juan C. Zapata (R)

First Colombian-American man elected to the Florida House of Representatives, 2002

Personal: Born December 9, 1966, Lima, Peru; single.

Education:

- Miami-Dade Community College, A.A. (1990)
- Florida International University, B.S. (1994)

Occupation: Businessman/Consultant

Trailblazer Elections:

- House of Representatives District 119 (Part of Miami-Dade County) *Rep Primary* 2002
  - Juan C. Zapata (35.7%), Frank Artiles (31.6%), Tim Hyman (29.1%), Armando V. Pomar (3.6%)
- House of Representatives District 119 (Part of Miami-Dade County) *General Election* 2002
  - Juan C. Zapata-R (72.2%), Mark S. Eckert-LPF (Libertarian Party of Florida) (27.8%)

Figure 3.43. State Rep. Juan C. Zapata (R-Miami), the first Colombian American elected to the Florida House, celebrates approval of his proposed amendment to the education budget on the House floor. State Archives of Florida, *Florida Memory*, https://www.floridamemory.com/items/show/135650. Photograph by Mark T. Foley, April 16, 2009.

THE JUAN C. ZAPATA STORY

When Juan C. Zapata first ran for the Florida House in 2002, many observers doubted he had any chance of winning because his heritage was Colombian, not Cuban. But he won, and so did another non-Cuban Hispanic, Puerto Rican John Quiñones. "For the Republicans, to get a Puerto Rican and a Colombian elected the same year really changed the perception," Zapata said.

Prior to that time, Cubans had dominated Hispanic members of the House. They had included Elvin Martinez (D), Lincoln Diaz-Balart (R), Ileana Ros-Lehtinen (R), Roberto Casas (R), Humberto Cortina (R), Annie Betancourt (D), and Marco Rubio (R). After the 2002 election, it became clear that the Cuban Legislative Caucus would have to become the Hispanic Caucus.

Figure 3.44. In campaigning, Zapata, a Colombian, knew he had to appeal to Cubans as well as non-Cubans to win his legislative seat. His campaign literature in Spanish answered the question *¿Quién es?* (Who is he?) and stressed common experiences of Colombians and Cubans. Source: campaign literature courtesy of Juan C. Zapata.

The changing composition of the Florida Legislature reflected a "Hispanic melting pot" in the population. The Venezuelans came in the early '80s, then the Nicaraguans, he said. "Every time there was an economic crisis or a political crisis, there were these waves of Colombians. They'd come in, and little by little those communities have grown."

At first the communities were segregated, each with its own radio station, for example. "That doesn't exist anymore. I mean, there's still some of it, but it's a lot more integrated now. You go to a Colombian restaurant, and there'll be just as many non-Colombians in the restaurant as Colombians." During campaigns when he knocked on doors, Zapata would often hear a resident say, "Oh, you know, my grandson is getting married with a Colombian." Or someone in the family would have a connection with a person in another Latin American country. "It's not that monolithic kind of community, but you have a community that's now intertwined," he said.

Colombians, like Cubans, have had to deal with guerrillas and violence in their homelands. "I've always been able to relate to the Cubans and the suffering of Colombia," he said. In the 1950s, a civil war between liberal and conservative factions in Colombia created much bloodshed. "My grandfather was very concerned for my dad and one of my uncles, and he convinced them to study here. They both went to the University of Michigan for one semester, and froze. They loved Ann Arbor, but they hated the weather. My uncle transferred to Auburn, and my dad transferred to Georgia Tech," Zapata said.

After graduating, his father "did a lot of work in Latin America for U.S. companies. My mom was like six, seven months pregnant, and they sent him to do a job in Peru for six months, so he figured, 'I want to be around when my kid is born.'" Consequently, Zapata was born in Peru, and three or four months later the family moved back to Colombia.

The schooling in Georgia was "where my dad fell in love with this country. He saw how great it was. So he always wanted my younger sister and me to come here." In 1977, when he was 11 years old, the family came to Florida.

Zapata became a citizen in 1980, perhaps 20 years after his father did. "He was very much Colombian, but he was also very American. He was just incredibly grateful to this country for the opportunity he got," Zapata said. They had come from a rural area in Colombia, in a small town outside Medellín. "He saw what an open society it was, the opportunities that existed here. So he always wanted that for his kids. And that's one of the reasons I've always been an immigrant advocate."

Because his father was a citizen, Zapata had only a three-year, instead of five-year, residency requirement for naturalization. For the citizenship test, he studied U.S. government and history. "I really took it to heart and I was very excited. I remember the guy who interviewed me telling me how he noticed my enthusiasm and how engaged I was and I wanted more questions about the history."

He also remembered the day he took the oath of citizenship in the Miami-Dade County auditorium: "I was very proud to be an American, even though I didn't live here for the first 11 years of my life. It's funny how I felt very American," he said. "I had to learn all the 50 states and at some point I think I knew all the 50 state capitals. I had a little U.S. map and I would study it as a kid." After Zapata graduated from high school, his family moved back to Colombia. With his family gone, he attended college, first at Miami-Dade Community College and then at Florida International University, where he earned a degree in finance and international business.

He traced his interest in politics to the Richard Nixon administration. "I was a Republican since a very early age because my dad was a big fan of Nixon," he said. When Nixon resigned in 1974 because of the Watergate scandal, Zapata shed tears. His father couldn't understand how an eight-year-old could feel so sad about the whole affair. Then, in the 1980s, when he was a college student, a City Commissioner, Cuban-born Rosario Kennedy, appointed him to a board. His involvement led to a greater empathy with the Cuban community and their view of themselves as exiles.

Although Cubans had been welcomed officially as refugees, the attitude had by no means been pervasive. "My dad told me he came to Miami for spring break one year and he saw signs in the yards that said, 'No dogs' and 'No African Americans'—but they used the 'N' word—and 'No Cubans.' He would see those signs and for him to tell me that and then for me to come to Miami and see what the Cubans had been able to achieve, I think it's a very good story to share with folks about perseverance and hard work. What the Cubans have been able to do is really work together as a community."

In 1999, Zapata made his first run for public office, a seat on the County Commission. He lost. "Part of it was I didn't run a good campaign," he said. He had been preoccupied at the time with a large exodus of Colombians coming to Florida as well as a court fight to prevent the return to Cuba of a five-year-old boy, Elián González.

At least three different Cuban groups had put aside their differences and worked together to support the boy's staying with an uncle in Florida, but the courts decided that he should be released to his father in Cuba.[72] In politics you don't have to agree on everything, Zapata said, "but as long as you're all more or less working in the same direction, not working to counteract what the other's doing, but all pushing, you can be separate but walking in the same direction—those are things that help a community a great deal," he said.

"I think that whole experience really helped the Cuban community evolve and mature to a point that they realized that we need to look at it in a much broader picture. We've got to do a better job of kind of sharing our story. I think it was a very good healthy process, and it laid the groundwork for me to be able to run a couple of years later and people to have a much more open attitude about a non-Cuban."

His run for the Florida House came about in this way: "In 2001, I had sold the business that I'd been involved in for years," he said. In addition, the not-for-profit group that had claimed his volunteer time had grown from almost nothing to having an $800,000 budget and a paid executive director. "I literally had nothing to do toward the end of 2001. I remember Omar Franco, who is now a lobbyist up in D.C, was chief of staff to Mario Diaz-Balart and worked in the Legislature. He said, 'They're doing redistricting and there seems to be a new district right where you live and it's for a Hispanic Republican. You should take a look at it.' I said, 'Well, I've been to Tallahassee maybe once, I think [for a friend who was getting sworn in]. What am I going to do over there and what is that like?' I was very familiar with the local politics and I followed state politics, but it was from afar. I gave it a little bit of time and then at the beginning of the year, in 2002, I said, 'Let me seriously take a look at it, and I mean, it's 60 days part-time. Well, that's not so bad.' It wasn't part-time and it wasn't 60 days, but at least that was a perception."

When he looked at the candidates and the demographics of the district, he saw that it was true. "A Republican would have obviously an edge, it was for Hispanics, and it was an area that I knew well." He knew the Mayor of Sweetwater and the County Commissioner, both of whom could help him with voters. Because the other candidates were first-timers, Zapata figured he could probably outdo them in fundraising. He also thought he understood the campaigning process better, having been through it twice before, and gotten elected in 1996 to a community council position (like a zoning board). "I had everything lined up," he said.

At the same time, he knew the challenge would be "to get the political money that you need to run a campaign as well as the votes. It was one of the things that motivated me," he said. He also knew that a couple of non-Cuban Hispanics had run for office previously and lost. He attributed their defeats to poor campaigning: "It's not that they did anything bad. I mean, they barely even performed."

As it turned out, in that first House race—and in every subsequent election—90 percent of his funding came from Cubans. Yet, "I understood the importance of the diversity. I mean, you look at all great cities in the world and they have diversity. For that diversity to be truly sustainable, you also need the diversity in your political leadership. It was something that gnawed at me."

"I never planned on having a life of politics," he said. "I've always been a lot more about business." After losing the county race in 2000, he thought, "Good. I got that out of my system." But, "as funny as it seems, all these things that were keeping me occupied all of a sudden were no longer a factor. So then I decided to run." One day at lunch with two friends, one of them said, "Yeah, unfortunately they'll never elect a non-Cuban Hispanic here." That remark "always stuck in my head. And she didn't mean it in a bad way. She wasn't trying to be discouraging, she was trying to be realistic."

"The issues at the time were basically run-of-the-mill Republican issues—effective government, less government, lower taxes. I sold myself as somebody who had a lot of community experience and who'd been involved in the community a great deal," he said. He believed he could be "an effective voice since I had been for many years an advocate for immigrant issues." In addition, "a lot of the activists knew me, and countywide I had a good base of support."

"It was a tough race but for the most part it was fairly clean, focused on issues. We all worked hard, and I raised the most money." On election night, he saw that he was in third place and moving up. He could tell from the precincts that were not yet counted that he would win, because those northern precincts were his political base, from Sweetwater to Florida City. "Sure enough, I started leapfrogging everybody and I ended up winning [the four-candidate primary] by 300 votes."

In planning his campaign, he had recognized the district's uniqueness. It was mostly unincorporated and had no major institutions or groups that could get behind him. "I knew I needed to reach out to three cities: Florida City, Homestead, and Sweetwater," he said. In Sweetwater he had the support of the Mayor and City Council. "They had a little political machine there and that was the largest precinct, so I knew that I didn't have to worry about that, that they would fight that battle, which freed me up to work the rest of the district."

"I knew I wasn't going to do well in the southern part of the district. There was an Anglo candidate and I figured everything south of probably 120th Street down to the Redlands and those areas, he was going to dominate," he said.

Zapata chose a strategy of going after "the high performing Republican voters," which meant the Cuban community. He educated himself about the Cuban patriot,

Jose Martí, incorporated his quotes into mailers, and sent them to Hispanics. In studying Cuba's history and geography, he learned about the Zapata Peninsula and Operation Zapata (the CIA's name for the Bay of Pigs invasion), for example. "I use those little things, and people relate to that."

He also found support among Cuban leaders, like Osvaldo Soto who started SALAD, the Spanish-American League Against Discrimination, and from elected officials, like Republican Gaston Cantens (state Representative 1996–2004). "That gave me credibility," he said.

He micro-targeted the large Puerto Rican, Colombian, and Nicaraguan groups. He sent mailers celebrating each of their independence days. "I tried to tell them, 'Look, I could be the first guy who can really be a voice for you,'" he said. "There's always been a sentiment out here where if you're not Cuban, you feel like you're not really totally represented."

"With Colombians, I never said 'I'm Colombian so you have to vote for me because I'm Colombian.' I always was very conscious that if you do that kind of campaign with the Colombians, my opponents could do it in the Cuban community." His message was "What you have is that the best candidate happens to be Colombian, and this is a great opportunity to have some political representation."

Opponents attacked him as a Colombian who would represent only Colombians. "I responded with a Jose Martí quote. I can't tell you how much people appreciated that, like the elderly Cubans, which in a primary campaign, will either make you or break you," he said. "The good thing about older Cuban American voters is they talk all day to friends and they have great networks."

"I didn't use that much radio. Radio over time has lost the strength that it's had down here. But at the time it was still very popular but not out in this area," he said.

"What I focused on was doing door-to-door in a particular corridor. I knew that if I focused on that block heavily, did some walking there, that that would give me the base that I needed. So I started early and I started strong. The strategy was to always try to stay one step ahead of any other opponent. I hit that area first," he said.

In addition, he fared well with newspaper editorial boards. "Fortunately, I've always gotten the *Miami Herald* endorsements. I've always read the editorial pages. You get a sense of their thinking, of their logic, and where they're coming from. And you learn to talk in their lingo," he said. "I've always been a guy who reads the paper every day, who stays very up-to-date on what's going on in the community and on the issues both locally at the state level and federal level." He added, "They didn't make a big deal of the fact that I wasn't Cuban," as he had anticipated. "But the English paper here did, and in a way I'm glad they did it. They basically focused on who, in their opinion, was the best candidate for the position."

"*El Nuevo Herald* was familiar with me because of my activism in the Colombian issues and immigration issues. This whole Colombia thing actually became a national story. I mean, I can tell you what I was doing Sept. 10th of 2001.[73] I had ABC News preparing a week-long series on this Colombian exodus, and they had spent basically three or four days in the office of the not-for-profit group interviewing people, doing all kinds of things, so people got to know me. And I was quoted. I came out in the *Wall Street Journal*, the *New York Times*, the *Washington Post*. I mean, the *Economist* quoted me once."

He had developed a media presence. "The local papers and the Spanish TV, they were very familiar with me so they were very curious. But I think everybody always thought that, 'Yeah, he's good, but he's not going to make it because he's not Cuban. We've never elected somebody who is not Cuban, and why should he be the chosen one, right?'"

"I ran the campaign knowing that I could win. I thought: 'I know what I'm doing, I know I can put together a campaign.' You have to make your peace with that. At a certain point you have no control over how the voters are going to react. But I knew I had as good a chance as anybody, and if I did things right that I should win." And he did—handily.

Getting sworn in marked an anniversary. "It took 25 years and a day of arriving in the U.S. that I got sworn in to the Legislature," he said. "I came here November 18th and I got sworn in November 19th, 25 years later." That anniversary "was an incredibly proud moment. My dad was watching," he said. "I remember sitting in the back row with him, saying, 'Can you believe this?' I know where my dad was born, it's a town of 3,000 people, it's like 12 hours away from Medellín. And just thinking, I remember being there as a kid. I mean, I picked coffee there during the summers and just thinking that I owed it to my dad. He passed away the last year I was in the Legislature, but I'm glad he got to see that."

"It was great because in my class there were five guys from Miami-Dade County who were freshmen. We all got sworn in at the same time, and we were called 'the Freshmen Five.'" He named Republicans Marcelo Llorente, J. C. Planas, Julio Robaina, and David Rivera. "David and I, we were involved in the party. We joined the Republican Executive Committee here in the early '90s," he said. "It was a very proud moment. And you're just in awe. The chamber's a beautiful place. The guy who swore us in was the first Hispanic Supreme Court Justice," Raoul G. Cantero III.

A lot of his friends traveled to Tallahassee to see the swearing-in. Because he was greeting well-wishers outside, Zapata came inside a little late for the ceremony and missed the preliminaries. Speaker Tom Feeney, checking attendance, called, "Representative Zapata." Sitting in the back row mostly among Democrats, Zapata answered, "Here." Laughter burst out around him. Surprised, he wondered what was so funny. Finally, another legislator turned around and pointed to a panel on his desk: "You've got to hit the button." So he hit the button, amidst more laughter.

"I always tell folks you win the election not because you're the better candidate, it's because you have more friends. And if you ever want to take inventory of who your real friends are, run for office and you'll find out real quick because it takes a real friend to stand there next to you and campaign during the summer in Florida." Consequently, "I was proud for my friends, who I know had put in a lot of effort, and I was proud for the Colombian community that they could in a way feel they had something positive to look forward to." He strongly felt his responsibility was to do a good job "because I don't want some kid who's now in school who maybe wants to run for office, to hear from somebody, 'Oh, the Colombian that's in office is a bum.' Or 'he's corrupt.' Or 'he does a terrible job.' There's a certain responsibility," he said, because you don't know who might be looking up to you.

As a state Representative, he quickly got involved in Hispanic groups. In the former Cuban Caucus, renamed the Hispanic Caucus, Zapata helped it develop a formal structure, with entities designated as 501(c)(4) and a 501(c)(3)[74] under the IRS Code. The group also developed and hired an executive director. He started the Board of Hispanic Caucus Chairs as a way for all the caucuses around the country to communicate. In addition, he became Chairman of the Board of NALEO (National Association of Latino Elected Officials), the largest group of Hispanic elected officials.

"Whenever I go anywhere, people would always assume that I was Cuban: 'Oh, you're from Miami, you're Cuban.' Then when I would tell them, 'No, I'm Colombian,' they would look at me, and they'd always find that fascinating."

He enjoyed the privileges that go with public life. "When I first got elected, I remember that year I got invited to the White House Christmas party. That was pretty cool to go there and meet the President [Bill Clinton]," he said. "You walk in and there's the Marine Corps Band playing Christmas jingles, and you walk into the big room and they have a huge Christmas tree." That year the theme for the tree decoration was the state birds. "Florida had its mockingbird," he said. On a second visit a couple of years later, the theme was the national parks. Florida was represented by the Everglades. "I mean, you're looking out the window from the White House and there's snow and you can see the Washington Monument. That was amazing."

Being a legislator provided opportunities for meeting famous people, such as South African social rights activist Desmond Tutu and former U.S. Secretary of State Colin Powell. In particular, Zapata remembered when former President George H. W. Bush participated in the farewell for Florida Gov. Jeb Bush in 2007. "The man was standing five feet away from me and he breaks down in tears as he's talking about his son and his first campaign run for Governor. I mean, I'm sitting there and this is surreal to me. I've got a former President here in tears over his son's leaving office. A Secret Service agent was right next to me, and he didn't know what to do."

There were great moments in sports, such as holding the Super Bowl trophy when the Tampa Bay Bucs won in 2002 and the World Series trophy when the Florida Marlins won in 2003. He met 2007 Heisman Trophy winner and former University of Florida quarterback Tim Tebow. "I remember everybody being very impressed by him. Here's this 19-year-old with this incredible talent, and he's sitting there and he's so humble and he speaks so well: 'This talent is a God-given gift that I want to share with everybody.'"

In addition to meeting famous people, Zapata met unsung heroes, such as "principals who turned around an F school to an A school. You're just in awe of these people. I remember meeting these guys, and I can't believe these people were able to achieve that," he said, wondering "What's the secret?"

Along the way, he developed "an incredible love" of the state's "fascinating places." He remembered getting lost once and coming upon a nuclear power plant—the Crystal River Plant in Citrus County. "I'm looking at the place and it's just gorgeous. I mean, it's just a unique landscape and scenery. In the middle there's this nuclear power plant and then the whole concept of a nuclear power plant, which is so cold and so industrial looking, and then this beautiful green space." He took advantage of trips to Tallahassee to drive different routes. "I went up U.S. 27 one time, I went up the western coast, I took (State Road) A1A all the way up to Jacksonville and then crossed over. You get to see the state."

The Legislature itself provided memorable moments. One incident, for example, demonstrated "how social media became a big player in politics." It happened during the debate over Senate Bill 6 (teacher tenure, pay for performance) the first year it came up. House members were sitting in the chamber, it was midnight or 1 a.m., and the television cameras were rolling. "Everybody was following this Facebook group that had like 50,000 people and they were all commenting on the debate in real time. One of the people noticed the TV shot. They go, 'Wow! All these legislators are on Facebook.' It's funny because when that happened and people read it, you immediately saw everybody looking around. Everybody noticed that everybody was looking at their computers and everybody was following this Facebook thread," he said. "I mean, there was even one where some guy got up to debate and somebody made a funny comment about his shirt and tie combination. Everybody kind of chuckled, and you could tell everybody was reading the same thing, laughing about the same thing. It was a surreal moment. I mean, that had never happened."

Another time, legislators were relaxing with drinks and conversation when suddenly their cell phones started ringing. Over the next several minutes, it became clear that a controversy was brewing over the legality of prolonging life support for a severely brain-damaged woman, Terri Schiavo. Legislators realized this was not the right time for a happy hour. "Everybody had that uneasy feeling, just how that whole thing unfolded."

Another serious moment occurred right before spring break in 2005 with news about the deaths of three children, one of whom was nine-year-old Jessica Lunsford, who had been abducted and murdered. "It was a very painful time. If I'd never gotten elected, I would've seen it as a very distant kind of thing. But these things happen in other towns in Florida, and they became very personal, very painful for everybody." In other words, he said, serving in the Legislature provided a chance for "seeing the best of people and seeing the worst of people."

"There are a lot of great moments when you're proud to be there, and other times where you don't know why you're doing this. I mean, like man, this is such a sacrifice and so difficult and so frustrating, what am I doing here?"

One man Zapata had respected and admired from childhood was Republican State Rep. Allan Bense (House Speaker 2006). "I think Allan Bense was by far the best Speaker we had during my time there," he said. "He was just such an example of a gentleman and the way you exercise leadership. Here was a guy who was a Democrat and became a Republican, lost his parents at an early age, became a very successful businessman, was very involved in his local community, then decided to go and serve—the true spirit of serving. You know, a guy who didn't need to do it. Nonetheless he did it and he did it very well and he set an example for many to follow. Meeting a guy like him made my whole experience worthwhile."

During Zapata's last year, he lost a committee chairmanship for opposing the closure of a mental health hospital in Baker County. "Out of the blue in the budget process, we were shutting it down. I mean, we never had a discussion or debate, and I just felt that that was just not the way you did things. Again using Allan Bense as an example, it's the process. How you do things is sometimes as important, if not more important, than what you do." The hospital was the county's largest employer. It had been located there a half century earlier to make up for the economic loss incurred for local people to stop producing moonshine, an industry that had made Baker County known as the moonshine capital of the state. Zapata's committee opposed closing the hospital. "The Speaker wasn't happy and nobody was happy," he said. "It became a fight and we prevailed and we saved Baker County."

He added a postscript: "The fine folks of Baker County are not completely out of the business because, sure enough, at the end of the session I got two little pints of moonshine: one regular moonshine, the other one cinnamon-flavored," he said. Overall, however, "it was a battle worth fighting. You pay a price but it's something that when you look back, you're proud that you did it in your time in service, so that was good."

His lowest moments came in 2003 and 2004 with the failure of his bills that would have granted in-state tuition to undocumented immigrants. "I could not understand why people cannot see the value in helping children who have done nothing wrong, and just the kind of unfairness of the entire process," he said. "It was just a very tough time where I realized that Tallahassee wasn't as democratic as it should be. I was very much in awe how people would go through all this, the sacrifice that you make to be in public office. And that at the same time to get to a place, and then basically not be able to truly represent your constituents. That manifested itself in a lot of different ways, and a lot of different times."

Another bad moment occurred during the first four weeks in his first legislative session with a bill that would surrender state authority on lands reserved to the Miccosukee Tribe. "The more I looked into it, the more I got concerned: How does that work? How do we protect Floridians who happen to be in Indian land? The only thing that protects them is Indian law and federal law," he said. He knew that many crimes, such as rape, were not covered by federal jurisdiction and that people seeking justice would have to go to Indian court. When the bill had passed the Senate and had reached its final committee in the House, he decided he would try to derail it using an obscure rule he had learned about in a breakfast meeting hosted by the Rules Committee.

When it came to the final vote, he voted in favor of the bill (a prerequisite for invoking the rule). "Then I said, 'Mr. Chairman, I want to invoke Rule. . . .' I think it was 7 point something. 'I move to retain this vote in committee.' That motion hadn't been used in years. And it kind of blew up. Everybody was looking at the rule book to see what I was talking about," and "the lobbyists started running up, and it just became a chaotic scene." It reminded him of an instance in Colombia when he had put a match to a pile of chemicals from the pharmacy and "it burned off my eyebrows." The committee chairman and the bill's sponsor, who was from Miami-Dade County, sat in shock. He said, "Oh, you should've told me." Zapata replied, "Well, you can't really tip your hand for this to work." The press jumped on the action, and "a lot of lobbyists said, 'Well, this guy is a freshman and he obviously read the rules.' But it's one of those things where you think you're doing the right thing, but at the same time a lot of folks who are your friends and your colleagues definitely don't take it well and take it very personally."

To help work off the stress and frustration of the job, he bought a punching bag that he used in his garage. "It's tough," he said. "People there in their first few years end up getting very frustrated toward the end. But, as crazy as it may seem, the system works and it works well. I mean, I think overall things in Florida have been done well. We make mistakes, we come back, we try to fix them, and those fixes create other problems, and we address those. But overall, I think that the state has done a great job of governing."

Asked about advice he might give to young people thinking about running for office, he said, "You know that song 'Mammas, Don't Let Your Babies Grow Up to Be Cowboys?' Well, somebody should do one about don't let your babies grow up to get into politics." On a more serious note, he said, "I would tell him, 'Look, focus on your life and your career first.' A guy like Allan Bense really had no reason to run for office. He ran because he really wanted to serve. I think that's where you want to be in life in order to really be an effective public servant. A lot of folks run for office to make a name for themselves, to become somebody. I think I got elected maybe 10 years too young. You need to have some real life experience to be able to serve well."

To young people, he would say, "Get involved in your community, set yourself up financially because this is no financial windfall whatsoever. To the contrary, we all make less money. This never gets talked about because there are a few bad apples, but it's a financial sacrifice. So I'd say live your life, establish yourself. Establish yourself financially because you will take a financial hit. And learn about the world and about your community a lot better before you run for office."

"It's great to run, and it's great to have the title," he said. "But you're making a lot of decisions that really have tremendous impact on people's lives. Of course you see a lot more at the local level than at the state level, but it's still a big responsibility and your ability to contribute is directly related to your experiences in life." His own experiences included health care (as a child, he had thought about becoming a doctor) and the condominium business. Life experiences "help you contribute meaningfully in discussions and debates and in establishing policy," he said.

Too often young people get involved in politics because they think it's good for their future, he said. "Your willingness to really take a tough position gets diminished if you're thinking about your personal future when you're out of the Legislature." That idea bumps up against his opposition to term limits. "Term limits are harmful because your first four years you're learning, and then your last four years you're planning your exit strategy. So where does the governing part happen?"

"If you have family, your family needs to be 100 percent into it. I'm not a married guy, I'm a single guy and I have no kids. I don't know how married guys with kids did it." He remembered legislators missing their children and trying to balance family and legislative career. "You need to let your family get a little older before you run for office." Political life is "unstable," he said, "because your life really revolves around this political process, whether it's the session, the special sessions, the elections that happen every two years."

"Make sure you're doing it for the right reasons," he added. It was not hard to tell which legislators were looking out for themselves or their constituents. "There was a difference in the way they behaved, and the whole dynamics of the chamber, of the folks who just had a life of serving others." The people he admired the most had been the ones who had volunteered in the community and came to share their wisdom and experiences—"even though many times I disagreed with them."

Reflecting on his time in the Legislature, he was glad that the Hispanic Caucus had grown. But he was careful to point out that "Florida's history with Hispanics goes back to Revolutionary times."[75] Furthermore, Miami's geographic location "smack in that middle of the hemisphere" has always provided a good entry point for Hispanics. "Latins have always felt very much that you're in the U.S., but at the same time you have a lot of your culture there. So that's why it's such a big appeal to them."

He offered the idea of setting up a room devoted to the history of Florida's Hispanic politicians. "The first Hispanic was in 1822," he said, referring to Joseph Marion Hernández, who represented the Florida Territory in Congress.[76] "Maybe folks won't appreciate it now, but I'm sure 20, 30 years from now they'll look back and they'll like to see how the Legislature operated in the days of Ileana Ros-Lehtinen and Lincoln Diaz-Balart and Roberto Casas," he said. "They must all have great stories."

In his farewell speech in 2010, he spoke about coming to the United States as an immigrant and feeling indebted for the opportunities open to him. "In Colombia if you're not from a political family, you don't get elected to anything. What more proof that this is just an incredible country than, for a Colombian to come in here and run for office and be elected?"

Juan C. Zapata was interviewed in person by the author June 6, 2014.

Jennifer S. Carroll (R)

First black Republican woman elected to the Florida House of Representatives, 2003

First black person and woman to be elected Lieutenant Governor of Florida, 2010

Personal: Born August 27, 1959, Port of Spain, Trinidad, West Indies; married with three children.

Education:

- University of New Mexico, B.A. in political science (1985)
- St. Leo University, M.B.A. (2008)

Occupation: Retired U.S. Navy Lieutenant Commander, Business Owner

Figure 3.45. State Rep. Jennifer Carroll, R-Jacksonville, delivers remarks prior to giving the opening prayer on Military Day on the House floor. Carroll, a retired Navy Lieutenant Commander Aviation Maintenance Officer, attributed her political success to Admiral Kevin Delaney at the Jacksonville Naval Air Station. As his aide, he "had me very involved with decision making, with sharing ideas, and being a liaison to our elected officials for our needs for the base, and that got me involved in community issues." Photograph by Mark T. Foley, April 19, 2007. http://www.myfloridahouse.gov/FileStores/Web/Imaging/PhotoAlbums/HousePhotoOriginal1926.jpg.

Trailblazer Elections:

- House of Representatives District 13 (Parts of Clay and Duval counties) *Rep Primary Special Election* April 15, 2003
  - Jennifer Carroll (65.5%), Linda Sparks (34.5%)
- House of Representatives District 13 (Parts of Clay and Duval counties) *General Special Election* 2003
  - Jennifer Carroll—*Unopposed*
- Florida Governor/Lieutenant Governor *General Election* 2010
  - Scott/Carroll-R (48.9%), Sink/Smith-D (47.7%)

For the full Jennifer Carroll story, see the Executive section, page 299.

Hazelle P. "Hazel" Rogers (D)

First Jamaican woman elected to the Florida House of Representatives, 2008

Personal: Born September 28, 1952, Jamaica, West Indies; married.

Education:

- New York City Community College, A.A.S. (1973–1976)
- Pace University (1980)
- University of Phoenix, B.S. (2003)

Occupation: Real estate professional/consultant

Trailblazer Elections:

- House of Representatives District 94 (Part of Broward County) *Dem Primary* 2008
  - Hazelle Rogers (38.9%), Eric Hammond (27.1%), Ken Thurston (22.1%), Roshawn Banks (4.7%), Robert L. Lynch (4.7%), Rubin Young (2.6%)
- House of Representatives District 94 (Part of Broward County) *General Election* 2008
  - Hazelle Rogers—*Unopposed*

Figure 3.46. State Rep. Hazelle P. "Hazel" Rogers, the first Florida legislator from Jamaica, never expected she would get into politics: "Honestly, coming to America and thinking that you're going to run for office, I can assure you that was never something, as an immigrant, I thought of." She got her start in politics by attending homeowners association meetings. Photograph by the House Photographer, November 10, 2008. http://www.myfloridahouse.gov/Sections/PhotoAlbums/photoAlbum.aspx?MemberId=4434.

THE HAZELLE ROGERS STORY

For Hazelle Rogers, the path to politics started in community engagement, and actually in a confluence of her involvement in a homeowners association and a women's sport known as netball.

Originally from Jamaica, she came to United States in 1969. She finished high school in Brooklyn, married, and relocated to Florida in 1981. "It wasn't my choice," she said. "My husband is an auto mechanic, and the weather in New York was not like here." She left the house hunting to him: "Hon, you go, and if you find a comfortable place and you like it, then it doesn't matter to me."

After arriving in South Florida, Rogers started attending the homeowners association meetings because the group's president was her neighbor. "We started going around the county to the Urban League, the NAACP. . . . We just bonded and started doing things together." That neighbor, Willie Webb, Sr., "was my inspiration and the strong support outside of my family for my advocacy and the work that I do," she said. He "really had me doing things that I didn't even imagine was in me to do." Sadly, he died before she was elected to the House.

In addition, she helped organize a netball program, a sport popular in her native Jamaica and other Caribbean countries as well as the United Kingdom, Asia, Australia, and New Zealand. It's similar to basketball, except that the goal has no backboard and a team consists of seven women. By 1989, "we were hosting teams from across the Caribbean here in South Florida, what we call the Florida Invitational Open. So netball players would apply for visas to come to participate in our games, and oftentimes that was their first time traveling abroad. It grew so well that we took a group of women to enter the world championships in Birmingham, England, and then in 2005 we were hosting the junior games here at the convention center for 10 days. We were just finding our way as women enjoying that game."

Working with people in netball tournaments and homeowners activities, she and others realized that they could help immigrants obtain citizenship. "We would pick up the applications from our congressional office and help them to fill out these forms," she said. She helped them understand not only the process of applying for citizenship but also the need to vote. "We encouraged residents to become citizens and then started promoting voter registration and voter education in those early days."

Rogers herself did not become a citizen until 1982, after coming to Florida. Although she had lived in Brooklyn for many years, "the city government was so far removed from our communities," she said. By contrast, in Florida she found herself in a smaller community with an engaged homeowners association and a city hall within reach. "When I got [my citizenship], I felt everybody needed to get theirs."

In 1995, she threw her hat into the ring for a city office. "I lost by two votes," she said. The next week, while getting her hair and nails done in a salon, a friend asked: "When is the election again?" Rogers couldn't believe her ears. If this person and a couple of others had voted, it would have made a difference.

Equally disheartening was that many first-time voters didn't know how to operate the voting machines. Rogers compared it to what would happen in 2000 in the Bush-Gore race for President. "I know they just went in there and did it and thought that was fine," she said. When she asked election officials about examining the ballots "with the hanging and dimpled chads" to determine voters' intent, they refused.

In the next election, "We knew how to have people inside the precincts to watch what was going on. We covered all of our bases. We learned well from the first race. We had people on the inside, we had people on the outside, and I was making phone calls, going on radio. We had people doing what they needed to do." She won that election.

She attributes her success to involvement in the community and organizations such as the Negro College Fund. "Honestly, coming to America and thinking that you're going to run for office, I can assure you that was never something, as an immigrant, I thought of. You're here to go to school and do something with your life and take care of your family and your children. So running for office is just because of everyone else saying you can do it. By going to the meetings I felt that I could make a difference."

After winning her election, she joined the Broward Black Elected Officials group, which became a major resource for her, and went to conferences hosted by the national, state, and county League of Cities. "I just knew I had to learn because, oh boy, what am I doing? I went to other commission meetings and sat in the back of the room just to see how they handled their meetings." At one point she told her accountant, "'This book they gave me, this is a budget, buddy, let's talk.' And that was one of the first things I did. I have learned over the years to monitor and legislate by the budget. Even with a nonprofit organization that I am engaged with, everything they wanted, I would say, 'Where's the budget?' You have to know your revenue streams and when you're over."

Her work in local government and the League of Cities groomed her for higher office, but it wasn't enough. A House member friend and former City Commissioner told her, "You've got to come up here and see the process and advocate for the city." Her secretary booked a flight to Tallahassee. At the airport, Rogers didn't like the looks of the small plane, and she hated flying anyway. So she took a bus.

As a local official, she understood the flow of dollars coming into the community, and she also knew and encouraged many people to run for state office. "I was campaigning for someone else to run, and my Congressman's Chief of Staff was campaigning for someone else. He had his sign and I had my sign. When he was leaving, he said, 'You're the person. You should've run for that seat.' That's what he said to me.

Figure 3.47. State Rep. Hazelle Rogers, D-Lauderdale Lakes, debates the budget on the House floor. One of the first things she learned in public office was to start with the budget: "You have to know your revenue streams and when you're over," she said. Photograph by Mark Foley, April 20, 2010. http://www.myfloridahouse.gov/Sections/PhotoAlbums/photoAlbum.aspx?MemberId=4434.

But I was not ready, and I was petrified of this flying back and forth," she recalled. Someone suggested that she could take a pill and sleep during the flight. "So my friends in politics started talking and so I decided to run."

In the 2008 election, she ran for a seat vacated by Matthew Meadows, who was forced out by term limits. She defeated five candidates in the Democratic Primary with 39 percent of the vote and ran unopposed in the general election.

That year, her friend, Democratic Rep. Gwyndolen "Gwyn" Clarke-Reed, also won her race, so the two became travel partners. "At least I will have someone else up there that I know," she said. Indeed, the friend held her hand many times during the flight. On other flights, she talked to seatmates about her fear: "I just want to warn you, if anything happens up here, your arm is the first one that belongs to me." Her colleagues helped too. "If it started bumping, they would yell from the back, 'Hazelle, how you doing up there?'" They joked, but she agonized. Gradually, flying became less stressful, but it was never easy.

No one tried to discourage her from running, and the possibility that she would be the first Jamaican in the Florida House didn't enter her mind. Instead, "it was all about my city and how I could help."

She realized that as a state Representative she would need to represent all eight cities in her district, not just Lauderdale Lakes. Concerned about fairness to all, "I had to readjust my thinking." She started a mayors' roundtable to exchange information before and after going to Tallahassee. "So we learned from each other, and my cities would benefit from the conversation, the best practices amongst my cities, and I learned from that experience also." Then she formed a similar coalition with church pastors to share information about faith-based initiatives. Communicating with the two groups in such fashion was practical. It was easier than her going to 20 different places.

Complicating the outreach was the strong and active immigrant population and the different languages spoken by them. "My district is a strong black majority here in Broward County with a vibrant and growing Haitian and Jamaican group. And then you have the Hispanic, which is a mixture more of Puerto Rican, Colombian, and Nicaraguan." Add to those the English-speaking from Trinidad, Barbados, and the Bahamas. Rogers herself understands some Creole "because I'm around it a lot, and I have friends who will always translate for me." She understands Spanish more because she grew up in Brooklyn and took Spanish in high school. "You can't just win an election from one population. You want to be able to be that elected official that can reach everyone because your message should be that broad. Your service should reflect that you're representing everyone and reflecting your values."

During the campaign, she received endorsements from various community groups. Getting a union endorsement "was the tough one. I went fighting for that," she said. She received an endorsement from a medical association, and her service on the board and as a volunteer in a mobile medical project helped.

Friction between African Americans and Caribbean blacks was sometimes evident in the community and in the schools. During redistricting before she was elected, for example, Rogers attended a meeting at a community center hosted by the state legislators on the redistricting committee, where she heard this question: "Are you representing the entire black community?" "I knew exactly what they were alluding to at the time," Rogers said. She didn't want to see a division in the community "because our strength is in our collective numbers," but she knew she had to speak up. "I think I said some phrase like 'If I don't say anything and you just look at me, you wouldn't know the difference. We are black.'"

Nonetheless, she recognized issues specific to the Caribbean community. One is the push for self-identification on the census form, "so you can say you're Jamaican or Guianese or Trinidad or whatever. And it was not just to separate ourselves, but we know that you have to market to different communities. It's all about dollars and cents," she explained. "We know we are black and we respect and honor the struggles and experiences endured by our African-American brothers and sisters."

Health is another issue: "My gynecologist would say to me that women from the Caribbean have the largest fibroids. Now, if we are not documenting who is here, how do you provide health care services to that population?" Numbers and demographics clearly affect services: "There are things that we advocate for as minorities within minorities."

To give voice to the Caribbean community, Rogers and fellow trailblazer Jennifer Carroll, who was elected to the House in 2003 and later became the state's first woman from the Caribbean to be elected Lieutenant Governor, started the Caribbean Legislative Caucus. "I remember the first year we did it. I said, 'You are the Republican. It's your folks that are in leadership. You will tell him what we want and you make it happen.'" To dramatize their cause, they brought a steel drum band, fully costumed, onto the House floor. "I was impressed with what we did, Caribbean.'" Since then, a Caribbean Day activity takes place in the Capitol in April every year, and a proclamation is issued, declaring June as Caribbean Heritage Month in the House. "You have a lot of folks from the Caribbean region living here in the United States, and they have contributed greatly to the economy of the state and this country and to the work force," she said.

In Broward, the business community organized a Caribbean Chamber of Commerce and a nonprofit Caribbean Cultural Coalition. Among other things, these groups work to educate local government about the community's needs and Caribbean customs, such as staying out until 3 or 4 a.m. in restaurants and nightclubs. "You have to be flexible in your policies to make sure you understand some businesses represent the culture of their clients to stay in business," she said. "A lot of cities have adjusted their hours of operation to accommodate nightclubs, restaurants, and lounges."

While acknowledging conflicts within cultures, "we said just make the pie a little bit wider and include everyone. There's no waiting your turn. If the votes are here and the numbers are here, we're going to run. And we're going to advocate. When there's an issue on your side, rest assured that we understand the politics of this country enough to know when we have to stand up as one community, black community, here in this country."

Rogers also acknowledged barriers to women's advancement: "It's in everything that we do—in the pay, in expectations, even from within your families." She emphasized women's reproductive freedom. Addressing male legislators, in particular, she said, "Leave our bodies alone." She spoke further against dictating abortion policies: "It's a decision that we should make with our families and with our doctors." At the same time, she welcomed conversations with her male counterparts on other issues: "We're capable, we're strong, we are thinkers. We can do everything that you can do, and you know the numbers are showing we are doing some of the same jobs. We're just not getting the salaries that [you're] accustomed to getting. But we're getting there. We're driving automobiles, race cars. We're playing basketball. We're doing everything. I don't think we have any limitations."

In campaigning, radio was paramount. "We have a Caribbean radio station and it's called the Heartbeat of the Caribbean. That's where we go for everything." Her constituents also go to the Caribbean ethnic media, including small newspapers, for information. "That is what they trust. And we encourage them to trust the news coming from one of your own. You have to tell your own story. You have to write your own story, so it can't be twisted." Live interviews with DJs were also important.

As other trailblazers have attested, walking neighborhoods was integral to the campaign. "Although I was president of the Broward League of Cities, I had to walk. I was able to get those endorsements from elected officials because they knew me. But I knew I had to know the people. Because I recognize people just don't follow everything their elected officials do. It helps but you have to touch and talk." Moreover, she learned from the experience. "You have to talk to people and they have to ask you a question and they have to feel you, so I did a lot of that."

As a Representative, her greatest satisfaction comes from sending dollars back to the cities in her district. That seemed impossible when she entered the House during the 2007–2008 financial crisis. The budget contained standard items for education and other needs, including funding for communities that had previously been funded. "No one was willing to take away anything or see whether or not they were effective—they'd been there for 15 years." She didn't sign off on the budget because it had nothing for her communities. Recognizing a need in her district for training, she developed a partnership with Broward College with an eye toward obtaining grant funding for seaport training. She advocated for that training for four years without success. "But I haven't given up. I just know every time it gets in the budget, I just can't get the Governors to leave it in the budget. It's just they don't see the need for that. And that's frustrating as a policy maker and legislator, when you can say my community needs this and it will bring value to my community. It's always a little politics."

Her greatest disappointment occurs when House members "get personal on the floor during debate," she said. "So I try my best, best, best not to get personal. But it happens sometimes and it hurts."

Taking the oath of office felt awesome: "I wanted to shrink," she said, reflecting on the 120 legislators who would be making decisions for 18 million people in the state.

She took a local community advocate to Tallahassee as her legislative assistant. "We were going to struggle together, we were going to fail together, and failing was not an option. So we fought and we disagreed but it was all about our district," she said. "We recognized that we were the first, so a lot was expected of us and we had to teach our community how to be respectful of us. We were in a teaching mode."

If asked for advice by someone interested in running for political office, she would say: "First make sure your finances are in order because it's going to take you away from your business. Most people won't remember what you do in your professional life, so make sure you know what you're doing. Focus on your business. See how whatever you're going to do will impact your life."

She would warn potential candidates that they will give up a lot of personal time and that would impact their families. Family members "have to be there in support of you because when no one else will walk, your family does the walking. When you're not there to cook for family, some other family member is taking care of your family. So you have to look at every aspect of your life before you decide to run for office." It could be especially hard on the families of officials who go to Tallahassee or Washington, unless the family moves with you or fully supports you.

She would also relate her experiences and challenges as a woman and as a black person. "You can't let it stop you from doing what you have to do. You knew this going in. Please! It happens in businesses. So this is just a big business. The state is a business. It generates revenue and it has to pay bills, and we as legislators must ensure the process is fair. And so we have to watch the dollars."

"I would not exchange [my experience] for anything else. I think I've grown from it," she said. "And thanks for those that encouraged and supported me, especially my husband and my mother."

Hazelle Rogers was interviewed in person by the author June 10, 2014.

Ana Rivas Logan (R)

First woman from Nicaragua to be elected to the Florida House of Representatives, 2010

Personal: Born May 16, 1961, Nicaragua; divorced with three children.

Education:

- Florida International University, B.S. in computer science (1988)
- Nova Southeastern, M.S. in computer science (1997)

Occupation: Educator

Trailblazer Elections:

- House of Representatives District 114 (Part of Miami-Dade County) *Rep Primary* 2010
    - Ana Rivas Logan—*Unopposed*
- House of Representatives District 114 (Part of Miami-Dade County) *General Election* 2010
    - Ana Rivas Logan-R (63.2%), Millie Herrera-D (33.4%), Denny Wood-NPA (3.4%)

Figure 3.48. Rep. Ana Rivas Logan, R-Miami, was the first Nicaraguan member of the Florida Legislature. She said she encountered discrimination not only because of her ethnicity (being a non-Cuban) but because of her gender. "I am a single mother, and I have been married a few times. So they started the whisper campaign." But she won. Photograph source is a Rivas Logan television campaign ad (see https://www.youtube.com/watch?v=SjhJD3uEFdk). Photograph courtesy of Ana Rivas Logan.

THE ANA RIVAS LOGAN STORY

Ana Rivas Logan, the first Nicaraguan member of the Florida Legislature, found strong female role models within her own family. Her grandmother was "very progressive for her time," said Rivas Logan. "She always told me, 'You study.' She made my mother study, too. My mother is a pharmacist."

Her grandmother came from the northern part of Spain. "She's a *gallega*, you know, a real tough lady. She's only five feet tall, not even, but I respected that lady. She pushed us all to study and study hard," Rivas Logan said.

Her mother was Cuban, and because "my grandmother was adamant about my mother getting an education," her mother went to Loyola, a Jesuit university in New Orleans. There she met a Nicaraguan studying at Tulane. They married and moved to Cuba. "My mother's family owned a famous restaurant over there, Palacio de Cristal [Crystal Palace], and there was really nobody to inherit it and my grandfather was getting older. So it was natural for my parents to go there and help with the family business and take it over. But the 1960s came, Fidel came, and he took everything from my family. So my family moved to Nicaragua. My older sister was born in Cuba, but I always say I was made in Cuba, but born in Nicaragua." (Her mother was pregnant with Ana when she left Cuba.)

The family moved to Florida in 1968, when Rivas Logan was in the first or second grade. Although there was no English as a Second Language (ESL) program—"It was sink or swim"—she learned the new language within the first year. "Everything was in English. The cartoons were in English, and Lord knows I had to watch my Saturday morning cartoons, and *Gilligan's Island*, and all that was on television," she said.

At first she went to a public school in Miami. "At that time busing had just gotten started. I was at Comstock Elementary and we were being bused to Dunbar. So it was a shock for me coming from a small Catholic school in Nicaragua to a public elementary school that is just going through this tumultuous time," she said. Eventually she was moved to St. Timothy's, a private Catholic school. "I never quite understood the racial or the ethnic differences. We just weren't taught that in my family. As a matter of fact, my daughter said to me, 'Mom, I didn't realize I was white until I was in elementary school. I didn't realize there was a difference.'"

Her family was among only a few Nicaraguans living in Florida at the time, but they began coming in waves after a massive earthquake in 1972, the Sandinista revolution in 1978, and the Contra war in the 1980s.[77] Many Nicaraguans came to escape communism,[78] she said, "and then a lot of them went back when communism was lifted. Now I would say that there's communism there, but it's a bit moderate. I've gone over there and I don't see the communism. I think it's just self-interest of the government at this time. They were just lining their pockets. A lot of corruption."

"My parents wanted me to remember my roots, to remember my Spanish—I was forgetting it. So I went back to Nicaragua and I lived there for a year with my aunt and uncle, and I went to Catholic school. It was a great experience because I was able to get in touch with my roots again, and I was able to pick up my Spanish again," she said.

"I hated my Spanish teacher. Today I love her because she used to make us do the accents and just the proper everything. She was such a stickler. She would make us do it over and over and over again. I mean, I was American learning Spanish in high school when everybody there had had 10 years of formal Spanish, and I'm coming in learning formal Spanish."

Her true academic heart lay in mathematics and science. "I took the first course in computer science. It was new back then because it was in the late '70s. I just loved it." She began studying computer science at the University of Florida. "Then I got married, and then I got pregnant and came back to Miami to be with the family." She managed to balance family and college, earning degrees in computer science—a bachelor's at Florida International University and a master's at Nova Southeastern. "I worked as a software engineer for a while and then after my third child, I said this is not going to happen. I'm going to go to a career that is good for women with children, and so I went into teaching."

"I loved it," she said. "I was able to do something to impact children's future and at the same time spend time with my own children, spend the summers with them. My kids still say, 'Mom, we had the most wonderful summers.' Our house was always the house where all the neighborhood kids came to play. I'd pack them all up and we'd go to the beach or we'd go to the park. I was so young. When I think about it, I wasn't much older than they were." She had her first child at 19. By the time she was in her mid-20s, her children were six, seven, and eight.

In 2004, "Someone came to me and said, 'Ana, we really need people on the school board. We really need somebody versatile for the school board and people who have an educational background.' At the time there wasn't anybody who had been in the classroom recently. Marta Pérez [Miami-Dade School Board, elected 1998] had been in the classroom but it was like 20 years ago. It was just mired in controversy and corruption, and so I said, 'Oh please, why would I want to do that to my family?'" By that time her children were in their early 20s, and the opportunity seemed right, so she decided to run.

"I went to the [county] elections department, bought a CD, and with my computer science background, I created a walking list. I think the CD cost me 10–15 bucks. I spent a whole summer knocking on doors. The more doors I knocked on, the more encouraged I got. And then the money came. Once I was on the radar in the polls, the money came. I won my school board seat by a landslide against an incumbent. There was such a hunger for new leadership, and especially a mother, an educator, and my children had been in the public school system. I believe in the public school system. I still do. I'm a strong supporter of the public schools. I think they're the great equalizer."

Although she identified herself as a moderate, "I'm still a conservative in many ways, but I'm also kind of libertarian," she said. "I think Nicaraguans are pretty split on parties." Some are Republican because they experienced communism or agreed with Ronald Reagan's support of the Contras. "But [a] lot of the lower socioeconomic level are Democrats. They just don't see anything that the Republican Party can do for them. Mind you, I talked to a lot of my Nicaraguan friends who are Republican, and they all agree that the Republican Party has done very little for the poor, for the lower socioeconomic level. So they do agree with this, but I think their big stance is No. 1, Ronald Reagan, and No. 2, the abortion issue is very big for a lot of the poor and the Catholics."

She ran as a moderate Republican in a moderate district. Her opponent, Frank Cobo, attacked her as non-Cuban. "It really hurt me because I've never experienced racism in my life, firsthand like that," she said. "It was tough. It was a long race. And school boards are huge seats." But her door-to-door campaigning paid off, and she won.

After serving on the school board for six years, she saw an opening in the Legislature. This time fellow teachers encouraged her to run. They said, "Ana, we really need some educational leadership at the state House."

"My opposition dropped out in the Republican primary," she said. In the general election, she faced a well-known Democrat. "She had her own TV show and her own radio show. It was not an easy race either. But I won."

"Running campaigns is exhausting," she said. "Raising money—that's the worst part." That means "you've got to call people."

Campaigning was also physically exhausting. In the school board race, "I got so skinny. My children said, 'Mom you look scary. You look like an Ethiopian poster child.'" In the 2010 House campaign, she broke her ankle. "I was coming out of someone's house and I was looking at the list and they had a step that went down. So with my glasses, because I'm looking down, I couldn't really see the step and I fell and I broke my ankle. That was it. Campaigning was over."

Her children had no enthusiasm for the nitty-gritty of politics. "My kids hate campaigning. They would not knock on doors. On Election Day they would stand at a poll for me. They hate it. Oh yeah, it's a street fight."

In campaigning, she encountered discrimination not only because of her ethnicity but also her gender. "I am a single mother, and I have been married a few times. So they started the whisper campaign. Oh, they flat out told some people that I was a whore—and used that word. I'm like, 'Oh, so if I was a man and I had been married a few times, would they say that about me?' Mind you, you really don't know why I got divorced. You have no idea what I went through in my marriages. You're saying that

Figure 3.49. A negative mailer against Rivas Logan cast her in a negative light for being a Nicaraguan. The same piece attacked her decision as a school board member to support an author (Dr. Crew) who wrote a book about traveling to Cuba (*Vamos a Cuba*)—which the Cuban exile community vehemently opposed. Ad courtesy of Ana Rivas Logan.

I'm a whore because I've been married a few times? And because I have a boyfriend? I mean, I'm not allowed to have a romantic involvement?"

The rumors continued as voters went to the polls. According to witnesses, when voters indicated they intended to vote for her, an opponent's follower would say, "Do you know the state took her children away from her?" At that point, Rivas Logan had had it. "I got an attorney, and he filed a cease-and-desist order on them," she said, and it stopped. "I mean, how low can one go?"

"When you hire people, sometimes people are very competitive. They're going to do whatever they can to win. But when it comes to your attention that that's happening, you put a stop to it right away as a candidate," she said. She recalled one of her campaign workers in the 2010 general election saying that the opponent was a communist. "I pulled her aside and I said, 'Excuse me. I don't run those kinds of campaigns.'"

"I always had a consultant that would help me identify what we were going to do. But you have to do everything in Miami. You have to do radio, mailers, TV, robocalls, knocking on doors. I knocked on thousands of doors." She used Steve Ferraro in the first House race and Sasha Tirador in the race for reelection.

On taking the oath, she did not realize that she was making history as the first Nicaraguan in the Legislature. "I just thought I'm here to do a job, and I'm going to do the job to the best of my ability. I also said thank God I don't have a husband or small children. I don't know how women do this and have a spouse and small children because it's all consuming. I mean, you're getting bills late at night that you're having to read for committee at 7:00 a.m. And then you have the floor vote, and you take your own bills you're carrying."

In 2012, in the race for reelection, redistricting put her head-to-head with another Republican incumbent, Jose Felix Diaz, a Cuban who appealed to the largely "die-hard Cuban Republican district. So they picked the right thing to attack me on—she's not Cuban. And it resonated. That, and a million dollars they put against me. There were attacks coming from everywhere."

She could have moved to another district, but "I'm not going to uproot my family for a $30,000-a-year job." Her household includes her eldest daughter and granddaughter. "She goes to the little neighborhood school and she's got little friends. I'm not going to uproot a little girl who has to deal with her father being disabled and going through serious PTSD [post-traumatic stress disorder]" as a result of the Iraq War.

She lost the election but had few regrets. "Going back to a normal life has been wonderful," she said. For one thing, it allowed her to spend a month with a daughter who had just had a baby. When she went back to teaching college, she wondered why she ever left. Serving in the Legislature is "not about working for the community anymore. It's about working for special interests. It got worse the longer I was in politics. I don't know if it's just that it got more tainted and I just didn't realize it at first—I was kind of in la la land—or it really did get more tainted." She questioned a process in which enormous amounts of money could be poured into a campaign for a $30,000-a-year job. "My parents would look at me and say, 'What's wrong with you? You're putting up with all this crap for $30,000 a year?' Then my daughter says, 'Let me get this straight. You gave up a full-time job for two part-time jobs?' They're right."

Nonetheless, she indicated a willingness to return to politics, but "It's got to be the right seat and it's got to be the right time." Furthermore, "in three years I'll be fully retired and fully able to engage battle again. I think I'm almost stronger for it. I've been able to do a lot of soul searching. I've become more spiritual. I've been able to travel the world," she said, citing an upcoming trip to Europe and Russia. "If the state goes blue, then I will definitely go back into it."

What she liked best about her term in the House was carrying bills that impacted so many lives. "I was very proud to get bills to the finish line," she said. At first she thought that as a rookie, she would accomplish little. Then "I said, 'Excuse me, I'm here to work. I'm going to get something done.' And I did." She cited property tax reform, vaccine availability in pharmacies, and domestic violence. "I go to the pharmacy and they have the shingles and pneumonia vaccines. I'm thinking, 'Oh my God, that was my bill,'" she said. Another bill allowed hearsay evidence in court in domestic violence cases. "I mean, how many lives have I saved with that?" In addition, "they wanted to get rid of adult education, and I fought for it," she said. Now that she's in education again, "I see how many people that helps."

"I voted against the party line a few times," she said. One time, she challenged the Majority Leader, Carlos López-Cantera (elected 2004), on the House floor. "I took seven or eight Republicans with me, and do you know, he went to each one of those Republicans and asked them why they voted for me and changed their vote." She was one of four Republicans that voted against a "paycheck protection" bill, which banned local and state governments from deducting union dues from paychecks. She sided with unions because "I get deductions out of my paycheck for things that I believe in."

On pension reform "I was the one who put the COLA [cost of living adjustment] back in. My parents are retired teachers, and you're asking me to give up their pension? That's not right. You're changing the third quarter of their lives," she said. "If you want to change the retirement system, you need to change it for the people coming in so they understand they accept the job based on the facts they have before them, but you can't change the game midstream."

"The first year I was there, it was just one bad bill after another bad bill, after another bad bill. It just felt like there were a million and one bad bills coming out on the Republican side. It just went against everything I believed in. Sometimes I would support them, sometimes I'd just walk away, and sometimes I'd say, 'Let me make this bill better.'"

She noted with approval that the Legislature, after a decade of failed attempts, passed a bill in 2014 that allowed in-state tuition rates for undocumented students. The bill was widely seen as a move by the Republican Party to court Hispanic voters. "At least elections sometimes do push people in the right direction for whatever the reason," she said. She noted that actually Florida International University and Miami-Dade Community College had already started waiving the out-of-state tuition rate for qualifying students.

Now an assistant principal at Robert Morgan High School in Miami, she works with students from different backgrounds. Most are from low socioeconomic families. "My job there is to help the seniors get into colleges and get them the money that they need to study. Most of our students, if they don't have the money to study, they just will not go." She mentioned one young Nicaraguan man who would be the first generation in his family to go to college. "I saw his scores and I saw his GPA and I said, 'You can do this.' He said, 'Miss Logan, I can't. I'm so afraid to fail my family.' But he is now on a full ride to FIU, so we are so proud of him. He's going into the health care profession."

She cited a young woman student as a similar example: "Her mom cleans houses. She says, 'Ms. Logan, what we get paid today we use it to pay our bills. We live paycheck to paycheck.' It was so sad because she did not know that her parents were here illegally. She had no idea. She found out when she was applying for college. Her

Figure 3.50. Ana Rivas Logan, who started her career as a software engineer, started teaching because she wanted a career that was good for a mother with children. She found the legislative process very satisfying: "I love what I do because I'm able to change people's lives. Where else can you do something that just positively impacts the future for years and years to come?" While in the Legislature, she was a "moderate Republican," but has since switched to the Democratic Party. "I am a Ronald Reagan Republican, but Ronald Reagan would not win a primary today," she said. Photograph courtesy of Ana Rivas Logan.

parents finally told her. So here is a girl with like five-point-something GPA, brilliant, a leader in the school, and she can't go to college because she doesn't have the money."

Nicaraguans want to become citizens. "They just don't know how," she said. "Many of them come over on a tourist visa or just to visit, and they just don't want to return." Some women come during the last trimester of pregnancy so that their children are born American citizens. The ones that are here illegally are usually from the lower socioeconomic class. "They don't have the money to go see an attorney that is going to help them get there. You know, immigration attorneys are very expensive," she said. "They don't want to be a burden to this country. They work. They earn an income."

"I love what I do because I'm able to change people's lives," she said, and not just that young man or that young woman but all their children and their children's children. "Where else can you do something that just positively impacts the future for years and years to come?"

"I do believe that everything happens for a reason," she said. In 2014, when a group from Homestead wanted her to run for Commissioner, she talked to Democratic Party leaders about who they might run in that race. They challenged her membership in the GOP, making her recall how no one in the Republican leadership had stopped the campaign attacks on her ethnicity. "Obviously there's a lot of racism in the party," she said. In addition, she had opposed the Arizona-style immigration enforcement bill that party members had pushed in the House and Senate. As a community leader, she had worked to help Hispanics obtain citizenship, register to vote, and vote in elections. She had also served on the board of NALEO (National Association of Latino Elected and Appointed Officials), which is working to create a path to citizenship for immigrants.

"I hate to say this, but my party has lost its moral compass," she said. "The Republican Party is the party of family values. Yeah, right. It is the party of Christianity? Well, is it Christian to do some of the things that they were doing? I mean, Christ came here to the jails, to the poor, to the people who were the worst off. That's what Christianity means to me. It's not about punishing people. No, you don't reward somebody for bad deeds, but certainly it's not our place to punish them. And where I am still pro-life, it's not my place to tell someone else what to do with their body. That's between them and their God. That's a very personal decision you make. Do I agree with it? No. Do I think that perhaps we need more education in that area? Yes, and I think the sonogram bill was awesome because it allowed the woman to see what she was going to endure."

"I am a Ronald Reagan Republican, but Ronald Reagan would not win a primary today," she declared. In February 2014, Rivas Logan became a Democrat. "I think it's one of the best decisions I've ever made. Before the announcement came out, I called my mom, who's been a Republican all her life, and she said she doesn't blame me, that she understands 100 percent. She votes Democrat a lot. My father is a Democrat. I think that that's the difference between the Nicaraguan background and the Cuban background." A sister who had been a lifelong Republican switched parties and campaigned for Obama in 2012. "She's an educator. She says she cannot stand what the Republicans are doing to education." One of Rivas Logan's daughters "is a Republican because of the abortion issue, but she says she's really more of a conservative Democrat." The other daughter is an independent. "She just could not understand why I was a Republican to begin with."

If advising young people considering a run for public office, she would say: "Develop a very tough skin." Even if you don't have any ruinous events in your background, "they'll make it up or they'll twist it. I mean, to say that the state took away my children was such a flat-out lie." In the event of such charges, "stay focused on the goal and what you want to do."

"If you can't raise money, don't even bother. You don't have somebody that's going to help you raise money you can't raise yourself, you can't even run for office," she said. "You've got to have a huge war chest in Miami." In the race for reelection, "We did mailers, we did some robocalls. My money just went for what I could and then I was drowned out. I was drowned out because they had 10 times the money I had. They dropped a mailer, a hit piece, every single day the last three weeks. Some days two would arrive in my mailbox. It got to the point where I just didn't want to go to my mailbox anymore."

She urged young people to get an education. "You can still make a life for yourself and your children, and you'll be much stronger for it." She quoted a colleague in engineering who tells his students: "I want you all to get a great education because I want to retire." He also urges students to avoid having a relationship in college. "What a brilliant thing to say to children, especially coming from a man that male students respect." She agreed with his attitude: A relationship in college "will take away from your focus. After you have a college education, you will have a relationship and you will have a much better one and you'll be all the stronger for it." Her students "have not heard this in their homes. Their parents are struggling, perhaps working two or three jobs."

She had special advice for young women: "You cannot come off as an emotional female because that's how you will be portrayed and even the females will turn against you. Everyone wants a strong leader, someone that they can rely on, someone that they can look up to." An emotional person comes across as unstable. "In private she can kick, scream, cry, whatever she wants, but in public, especially in debates, they will try to goad her so that she will react. She must find a way to just calmly answer the issue at hand without emotions. It's unfortunate. If a man is emotional, he's strong. If a woman is emotional, she's weak. That's a big difference." Furthermore, "a man who's very strong is a leader. A woman who's very strong is a bitch."

"You got to be strong and not show any weakness because they will come at you." In the past women candidates could expect to be treated like a lady, but no more. "You can have high standards, but don't ever think your opponent will have high standards—especially if you're running against a guy. These guys are in it to win at all costs. Ethical races are gone. If you can't be the pit bull, get yourself a pit bull."

Ana Rivas Logan was interviewed in person by the author June 10, 2014.

Ricardo Rangel (D)

First man of Ecuadorian descent to be elected to the Florida House of Representatives, 2012

Personal: Born June 5, 1977, Bronx, New York; three children.

Education:

- Warner University, B.A. (2008)
- Warner University, M.A. (2011)

Occupation: Senior Marketing Manager, AT&T

Trailblazer Elections:

- House of Representatives District 43 (Part of Osceola County) *Dem Primary* 2012
  - Ricardo Rangel—*Unopposed*
- House of Representatives District 43 (Part of Osceola County) *General Election* 2012
  - Ricardo Rangel-D (67.7%), Art Otero-R (32.3%)

Figure 3.51. State Rep. Ricardo Rangel's grandparents emigrated from Ecuador to the United States when his father was 12. The possibility of becoming the first person of Ecuadorian heritage to serve in the Legislature never entered his mind. The trailblazing achievement began to sink in when he started getting congratulatory calls from friends and people from Ecuador. "That was pretty cool," he said. Photograph by Meredith Geddings, March 21, 2013. http://www.myfloridahouse.gov/Sections/PhotoAlbums/photoAlbum.aspx?MemberId=4547.

THE RICARDO RANGEL STORY

A college government teacher inspired Ricardo Rangel to get involved in politics when she pointed out the advantages of his name and observed his qualities for leadership.

"Your name is Rick," Dr. Amy Hendricks told him. "No, my name is Ricardo," he countered. "We argued in front of the class about what my name was, and she started laughing." Then she explained: "You have the perfect political name. If you want to appeal to the Anglo Americans, your name is Rick. If you want to appeal to your Hispanic culture, your name is Ricardo." His last name was good too, she said. "Many people from the state of Florida have migrated from the state of New York, and people know the name Charlie Rangel [a Democratic New York Congressman]."

What's more: "I've been watching you. You're a leader. People naturally want to hear what you have to say. Every time I see you in the hallway, you're always surrounded by people." "Yeah," he said, "because I like to make people laugh." Then she pointed out the seating in the theater-style classroom. "You're placed strategically in the center. You sat down first and then everybody else sat down around you. That is a huge sign of a leader."

"See me after class," she said. "We've got a lot to talk about." He did, and his life changed. He registered to vote and met Al Yorston, the young man who would later become his legislative aide.

"What I liked about Dr. Hendricks is she taught me about both parties, even though she was a staunch Democrat. She said it was my choice of which party is going to be best for me." He interned for both parties and eventually realized "that for me the Democratic Party fitted my values and needs most."

Although he's no relation to the long-serving congressman, they share New York origins. Charlie was born in Harlem, and Ricardo in the Bronx. Ricardo's Ecuadorian grandparents had immigrated to the United States when his father was 12. His father and mother met in New York as teenagers and later got married. Because his father served in the U.S. Army for 22 years, the family lived all over the United States. When people ask him now where he's from, he says, "I'm from the U.S." After high school, he also joined the Army. After serving for 12 years, in 1999, he moved to Central Florida.

He started going to school, had his fateful meeting with Dr. Hendricks, and became active in the Democratic Party. He and Yorston got involved in the Young Democrats, began volunteering in campaigns, and after a couple of years were hired in paid positions. Rangel ended up running campaigns and consulting for about 10 years before he decided to run.

The one that pushed him to run for the House was Lorena Chambers, a good friend and Latina strategist based in Washington, D.C., with whom he had just fin-

Figure 3.52. State Rep. Ricardo Rangel, D-Kissimmee, was one of numerous House members whose photos appeared in a slide show that honored their military service and was shown above the Speaker's rostrum during Military Day on the House floor, March 11, 2014. A 12-year Army veteran, he said his military service helped him get voters' attention and raise some money for his campaign. Photograph courtesy of Ricardo Rangel.

ished working on a U.S. Senate race in Arizona. "She just was fascinated how I worked and what decisions I would make," he said. "Obviously I was out there trying to help other people, trying to get people involved, and recruit other candidates. Many people looked at me and said, 'Well, why don't you run? You have the best opportunity, you're educated, you're former military, you have the campaign experience.'"

"The first thing I did before I did anything was call all my friends, all my family members, and told them what I wanted to do. I would say, 'What do you think I should do? If I do this, would you be willing to give me money?' As soon as I reached a goal that I had set, which was about $20,000, I said, 'Well, at that point I could say I can run.'" He filed the papers, called back his friends, and said, "OK, it's real now, so you have to really give me that money."

One day, while making fundraising calls, he telephoned Yorston, who had moved to New York a few years earlier to live with his girlfriend. Yorston laughed and said, "How about I do something better for you?" Rangel wondered what could be better than giving him money. "I'm actually moving back to Florida," Yorston said, "so how about I run your campaign?" Rangel said, "OK. Wow!" and thought, "God works in mysterious ways."

All was not rosy, however. Unfortunately in Hispanic communities sometimes, he said, people feel like you don't represent them unless you're the same ethnicity, which in the case of this district was Puerto Rican. It's not everyone in the district but rather "a select few were trying to discourage me." Even a lot of consultants and lobbyists asked if he was Puerto Rican. "That's the first question they would ever ask. And I would say, 'No, I'm Hispanic but I know I'm going to win.'"

He drew confidence from his experience in running campaigns. He knew how to break down the numbers of Democrats versus Republicans versus independents or nonpartisan, as well as the numbers of Hispanics, African Americans, and Anglos in the district. "Because I had been a political operative, I had a little bit different mentality." He also looked at officials on whose campaigns he had previously worked, all the way from President to city councils and school boards.

"One of the most important things when you're actually working in the field is that voter contact," he said. "You really have to get out there and communicate with the voters and have a very good message. That's one of the things that I noticed even in my campaign against my opponent at the time. I had a message saying something of substance," citing his background in military service and volunteer work in the community as well as his intention to focus on education, jobs, and the economy.

By contrast, all his opponent wanted to say was, "I'm the only Puerto Rican in the race." Rangel said, "I was outspent three to one, and people were writing me off saying, 'Yeah, it's a Democratic seat, but you're not Puerto Rican.'"

His non-Puerto Rican heritage aroused the only discrimination in the campaign. "It's kind of a funny dynamic here in Osceola County because it's basically always the same people running," he said. "They felt that I just came out of nowhere. They felt that I didn't represent the Puerto Rican, and that's why I shouldn't be their Representative. I mean, they tried everything against me—that I was anti–Puerto Rican. That was the unfortunate part. But other than that, I did not really face too much discrimination. It is a pretty big Hispanic community."

"Fortunately, one of the things that does help me is that my last name doesn't really sound Hispanic. A lot of people really didn't put 2 and 2 together," he said. "Even when I was doing interviews for endorsements, I didn't feel any kind of discrimination."

He received no newspaper endorsements. "Not even the party wanted to help me, which was a little bit upsetting. They were writing it off because they were like, 'We shouldn't have to play in that race. It's a Democratic seat, and it looks like you may win it anyway.' I said, 'Well, I've got to get past the primary, I've got to get past the general.' You would think they wanted to make sure that they had that seat covered."

He found it equally hard at first to raise money from lobbyists. He knocked on their doors in Tallahassee, told them he was a military veteran, and asked for money. "The first thing they would say is, 'What seat are you in?' 'District 43 in Osceola County.' They would look at their paperwork and say, 'We didn't even know there

Figure 3.53. Rangel, whose initial interest in politics was sparked by a teacher, believed in involving young people in his campaign. Photograph posted on Rangel's Twitter page, http://twtrland.com/profile/rangel
4florida.

was a seat in Osceola County.' That was the hardest part of the campaign—trying to boost Osceola County up because this was the first time that Osceola had its own Representative."

He started his campaign with block walks and phone banks, using a half dozen college student volunteers. "Believe it or not, these young kids with these new computer systems now—they have these predictive dialers so you no longer waste your time dialing. I mean, we were burning through like 3,000 calls per week," he said.

About the middle of the campaign, the money started coming in as polling showed he was about 10 points ahead. "All of a sudden everybody wanted to be my friend."

In the last three weeks of the campaign, he sent out mailers—two in Spanish and two in English. No money was left for TV or radio, but he did have a presence on social media.

He chose not to campaign at church festivals. "I don't like mixing church and state. I feel that a religious institution should be protected as a religious institution. I take it as a false hope in a way. It's one of the things that I criticize politicians about—the fact that they're going to go there only when it's election time, but after that they're not going to go back there," he said. "But I think it's important to get some of those members involved and let people know that there is something going on, that we need to be active."

One difficulty with running in 2012, a presidential election year, was dealing with anti-Obama sentiment. "Everybody wanted to talk about Obamacare," he said. He would explain: "I can't do that. I'm not in the federal government. I'm running for state office."

In the end, Rangel won with "68 percent of the vote, which was higher than any federal candidate on the ballot that year."

What did he feel on taking the oath? "Nerves. Yes, honestly. I mean, it was even difficult to repeat the oath, even when you're lined up with four or five other members and none of us were even repeating everything exactly alike because everybody was nervous. It's that realization that we made it happen. It's reality now."

The possibility of becoming the first person of Ecuadorian heritage to serve in the Legislature had never entered his mind. "My focus was just Hispanic-based, just letting people know it doesn't matter what I am. I'm here to serve you no matter what. I don't care what race you are. I don't care what ethnicity you are within the Hispanic race," he said. The trailblazing achievement began to sink in when he started getting congratulatory calls from friends and people from Ecuador. "I was like, Wow! OK, that was pretty cool."

The most satisfying thing about serving in the Legislature was "being able to speak up for the community. I had a whole different outlook," he said. "One of the reasons I did want to run was because I felt that people were forgetting about representation. Being a voter all these years now gave me the feeling of 'Well, if Representatives are not doing what we want them to do, why are we keeping them there?' That was the same mentality I took when I wanted to run. I was like 'Nobody's working for the people anymore.' Both parties have become so ideological, it's overwhelming. It's like 'Well, if you're not too far to the left, you're not the right person. And if you're not too far to the right, you're not the right person.'" He found it polarizing. "We need to refocus and get people back to the center and help people get elected that are in the right position."

His first real sense of accomplishment came from overcoming the negativity associated with being non-Puerto Rican. "After I got elected, the biggest feeling that I have of accomplishment was fighting for the community, making the bills that I filed based on my community, not based on businesses or industries, or Tallahassee special interests. I focused mostly on what I felt the community needed."

Among those community interests were bills he filed that would lower the SAT score needed to qualify for a college Bright Futures scholarship.[79] The problem: "We're eliminating 75 percent of African Americans and 60 percent of Hispanics from even being able to qualify. The feedback that I get is, 'Oh, well, it was a merit-based scholarship.' Yes, I understand. They're like, 'You're just trying to lower the standards.' No, I'm not. I'm actually being realistic. We can't raise the standard higher than the national average because I wish we could say that everybody in the state of Florida was smarter than the rest of the United States, but we don't have that luxury," he said.

"My argument was that we have many different factors at play." One is the language barrier, and another is low socioeconomic level. "Maybe a parent doesn't have the $700 or $1,200 to pay for a tutoring service to get their child the SAT prep that they need." Feedback he received from students illustrated the dilemma. One, for example, had a 4.2 GPA, 600 hours of volunteer service, and several hours of internships. But the SAT score might have been 1150, "which is not too shabby, but they needed an 1170 or a 1270 to qualify. I just felt that that was just uncalled for."

He sponsored a community schools bill that took "a holistic approach to education, where you're not only helping the child but you're helping the parents as well. What you're doing is you're giving the extra tutoring services to the child, you're making sure that they have mental health, dental services, health care services all within the school. Then the community around that school will also have access to that community care as well, and parents will be able to do adult education, they'd be able to do preparatories for job interviews, things like that. So, you're not only helping the child, but you're also helping the parents at the same time."

Because 75 percent of Osceola County's land is used for agriculture, he sponsored a bill that would give an 8 percent tax credit to agricultural employers if they hired someone at a livable wage, $10 an hour, for 12 consecutive months. "It was tiered so if they paid them between $11 to $12 an hour, they get a 10 percent credit, and if they paid them more than $15 an hour, they would get a 15 percent credit at the end of the year." As a result, farm workers would receive a livable wage, and the farmers would get the labor they needed.

What he found most difficult in the Legislature was the partisanship. "I understand that you've got a majority party, you've got a minority party, but I thought that there would be more conversations. I thought there would be more opportunities to deal with the other side of the aisle. Now individually, yes, but not from the Speaker down," he said. He lamented that almost no Democratic bills had been heard in committee, let alone on the floor. "I thought that was a little bit unfair." One of his bills, for example, would have given a discount at state and county parks for surviving spouses of military veterans, firefighters, and police. "We tend to forget that there was a wife, there was a husband, there were children involved that really had to suffer a lot more than we did. I wanted to be able to give something back. It went through two committees unanimously and then because of a certain vote that I took on the budget, they killed my bill. That was unfortunate because that didn't benefit me, that benefitted people, the community."

In the 15 years since he first came to Central Florida, he has seen changes in the composition of the Hispanic community. In addition to Puerto Ricans, people are coming from the Dominican Republic and the adjoining country of Haiti, from nations in Central America, as well as from South America, including Brazil. Many of these new residents speak only Spanish, making it important for public officials to be able to speak the language.

Rangel is not only bilingual but also knows a thing or two about running successful campaigns. "A lot of people have that false conception where you're just going to go and throw your name in the ring, and things will just kind of fall into place. But there's a whole strategic approach to everything." People who have come to him, asking how to do it, often find that he gives advice freely.

He takes a step-by-step approach. First, before deciding to run, "you need to know if you're a viable candidate." The way to do that is to make a list of 200 people you can call, including family and friends. "Don't think with your wallet. It doesn't matter how much you think they can give you," he advises.

Next, bring the list to him to review, and note where each person works or how much each person earns. "Then we can make a guestimate of how much we think we can ask them for," he said. "Once we do all of that, I know who's serious—the ones who actually come back to me with their list." The ones that don't usually say, "Well, I don't know that many people."

The third step is to call the people on the list and ask for pledges. "You don't need to raise $100,000. You need to make sure you can raise at least enough so that people notice you, and then other people will start donating to you. I always give everybody a certain goal, depending on the race." For City Council, the goal might be $5,000 in pledges; County Commission, $10,000. "You don't actually collect the money until you're officially a candidate."

Once you reach your goal in pledges, the next step is to file the paperwork. "Then you call them back and you say, 'I'm official. Where's my money?'"

Part of the strategy in running campaigns is recruiting volunteers. Rangel gave an example of how he did it: "Over in Brevard County, in 2010, I was working on a state House race, and I knew one person that was in the high school and his cousin." They had been watching him progress through different campaigns and were curious about how he worked. After a little training in phoning and canvassing, they volunteered for a few days. "Wow! This is fun," they said. "I like to make it energetic fun," said Rangel. "We go out, we hang out. We laugh, we joke. We buy pizza. So they loved it." Then he suggested that each of them bring two of their friends. Little by little, the group started growing, and "they just did some huge massive thing to their Facebook, they talked to all their friends in school, and I ended up with 30 kids."

After training them all, he monitored their activity. "When they would go door-to-door, I would walk behind them to make sure that they're doing their job," he said. "We ended up getting a contract that helped us get money," he added. After a block walk, he was careful to locate every one of them. "They would call me Mr. GPS because they couldn't understand how I knew where every single one of them was." He described how he would estimate their whereabouts on a given street. He also explained: "You guys are in high school and I've got to make sure not only are you doing your job, but also are you safe. They loved that about me, and the parents loved it. Even when we had to work really late at night, the parents would call me up and ask if their kids were with me. It was awesome because the parents had great trust in me."

A final word to those interested in running for office: "Stick with me. Not only have I been elected, but I have a history of wins in other elections." In that respect, he considered himself a teacher: "I'm not afraid of somebody coming and taking my position. I want somebody to come and take it. Not while I'm in office, but I want to be able to help train those certain individuals that come in as young people, especially young Hispanics."

It's sad, he continued, that "nobody comes in and says, 'Let me grab you by the hand, come over here, let me show you how to do this. You can have a great future.'" Dr. Hendricks did that for him: "That was for me a very impactful thing because if it wasn't for her I wouldn't even be here."

Ricardo Rangel was interviewed in person by the author June 4, 2014.

Walter Bryan "Mike" Hill (R)

First African-American Republican man, acknowledged by many modern-day observers, to serve in the Florida House of Representatives, 2013

Personal: Born June 2, 1958, Scott Air Base, Illinois; married with three children.

Education:

- United States Air Force Academy, B.S. (1980)
- University of West Florida, M.B.A. (1988)

Occupation: State Farm Insurance Agent

Trailblazer Elections:

- House of Representatives, District 2 (Parts of Escambia and Santa Rosa counties), *Rep Primary Special Election* May 2013
  - Mike Hill (42.2%), Ed Gray (33.5%), Mark Taylor (9.1%), Jack Nobles (8.1%), Scott Miller (4.7%), David Radcliffe (2.3%)
- House of Representatives, District 2 (Parts of Escambia and Santa Rosa counties) *General Special Election* June 11, 2013
  - Mike Hill-R (57.9%), Jeremy Lau-D (42.1%)

Figure 3.54. State Rep. Walter Bryan "Mike" Hill, R-Pensacola Beach, speaks to an issue during a hearing of the Energy & Utilities Subcommittee. The hardest part of being a legislator is the "politics in Tallahassee." He entered office wanting to "change that culture." He refused to join caucuses and groups that were narrow in their membership: "Even if I'm a Republican, I still have to represent the Democrats. Everyone." Photograph by Mark Foley, February 12, 2014. http://www.myfloridahouse.gov/Sections/PhotoAlbums/photoAlbum.aspx?MemberId=4595.

THE MIKE HILL STORY

After a decisive win in the 2013 general election, many people thought that Mike Hill had made history as the first black Republican man since Reconstruction to be elected to the Florida House. Actually, John "Gus" Plummer had achieved that distinction more than three decades earlier. But because Plummer's campaign strategy had been to promote the Plummer name (associated with two well-known white Democratic elected officials) and to downplay his Republican Party affiliation, some modern observers think the "first" black Republican male legislator designation should go to Hill, who proudly and openly ran as a Republican. And, while not the first black Republican since Reconstruction to be elected from the state, Hill was the first from conservative Northwest Florida.

In running for office, "I want to be able to help in some way bring more of a respect and decorum to being an elected official, because right now when you say the word *politician*, it's usually either in derision or in jest," he said. "If we want people to respect that position, we have to respect the position and respect each other."

Hill began learning about respect and decorum while growing up on U.S. Air Force bases where his father was stationed. The environment on bases such as MacDill in Tampa and Eglin in Fort Walton Beach "helped structure my childhood," he said. Department of Defense schools on those bases were "small and protected." Students said the Pledge of Allegiance and a prayer every day. When Hill was a teenager, his dad was sent to Aviano Air Base, Italy, where the family lived for almost five years.

After high school, he was selected by Republican President Gerald Ford to attend the Air Force Academy. Upon graduating in 1980, he went to pilot training at Columbus Air Force Base in Mississippi and then to his first duty station in Montgomery, Ala. While in Columbus, he married a young woman who was attending Mississippi University for Women. Coming back to the South for the first time since he had left Eglin Air Force Base as a nine-year-old was "a culture shock." In the early 1980s in Montgomery, discrimination "was still pretty blatant," he said. "We would go to a restaurant and not get served. You know, just silly stuff. And so we would leave and go to another one that would serve us." Although he didn't much like living in Montgomery, "I loved my Air Force job," he said. "We were replacing the mainframe computers that run military installations around the world."

After four years, he was sent to Eglin Air Force Base, where he served as a test director. When he was selected as the Company Grade Officer of the Year, "the general of the base grabbed me and pulled me onto his team," he said. At first, Hill didn't want the job, but he grew to like it as he gave briefings to VIP visitors, which "exposed me to the civilian population."

One day, after a briefing at the Walton County Chamber of Commerce, a man in the group asked whether he had ever thought about becoming an insurance agent. Hill's military career had reached the 10-year point, and he had to decide whether to stay another 10 years or leave. "I decided that I wanted to take that opportunity that State Farm offered simply because I wanted to know, could I actually do that? You know, be a part of what I would call the American Dream of starting a small business from scratch and being successful at it."

He did so well that five years later State Farm offered to buy his agency and hire him as a consultant. He accepted, moved to Pensacola, and worked with State Farm's field leadership from 1995 until 2000. When an agent in Pensacola retired in 2000, Hill took over his agency and has been operating it ever since.

As he advanced in school and career, his political philosophy took shape. As a child, he had read stories about U.S. patriots, such as George Washington, John Adams, Thomas Jefferson, and Patrick Henry, and pictured himself doing their heroic deeds. He especially admired Presidents Calvin Coolidge and Harry Truman. Although Hill didn't agree with all of Truman's policies, he liked the man's principles and his demeanor. Those men "became my compass on how I should behave, on how I should perform. That and, of course, the Bible. The Bible's the foundation for me."

He began considering political parties in a ninth-grade civics class in Aviano, Italy. His textbook showed a picture of industrial plants along with one paragraph that said, "The Republican Party is for big business," and another paragraph that said, "The Democratic Party is for the people." "I must be a Democrat because I'm for the people," he thought. "That's what our Constitution says—'by the people, for the people.'" When he first heard the terms *liberal* and *progressive*, "I thought that meant you wanted to progress with technology and make sure there's the new way of doing things. Don't get stuck in a rut. I said, 'Sure I'm a liberal. Yeah, I'm a progressive'—until I began to understand what those terms actually meant."

He kept thinking he was a Democrat until Republican Ronald Reagan's second term. "His first term I listened to a lot of the Democratic talking points and thought, 'Well, maybe he is a racist. Maybe this won't work, this trickle-down thing.'" But in Reagan's second term, while Hill was working on his MBA in night school, he gleaned from his economics study that Reagan was right. That's when "I firmly became a conservative Republican."

In 2008, when Democrat Barack Obama was elected President, "I thought, 'Oh, no!' I said, 'Either I can sit around and complain or I can do something.' So in 2010, on my own, didn't ask anyone's permission or advice, I just ran for office," he said. "Didn't know what I was doing but was very passionate about it." He didn't start small. He ran for the Florida Senate against Republican Greg Evers, who had served in the Florida House since 2001.

For the campaign, Hill raised $70,000, which came in modest donations of $25–$200. He received 30 percent of the vote and lost. "What I enjoyed about that campaign is I met so many people I never would have been exposed to before. And I was introduced to some really good friends in places where I wasn't expected to be supported, such as Jay and Wausau." In Wausau, known for its annual Possum Festival, he asked the elderly couple who had started the festival: "Why a Possum Festival?" They said, "It's really a testament to the possum because during the Depression that's what kept us alive." They invited him to try a bit of cooked possum, but he declined. Nonetheless, meeting people like that "really got me more involved in politics."

The same year he lost that election, he started the Northwest Florida Tea Party. He quickly learned that the Tea Party is not homogenous. Each group "has its own flavor, its own passion, but the basis of it all, I believe, is the spirit of America," he said. While the party's name comes from the tossing of tea into Boston Harbor in 1773, the spirit of protest actually started earlier. As Hill explained: "Whenever tyranny raises its head, then a 'tea party,' a spirit of America, will rise up to defeat it." That spirit rose

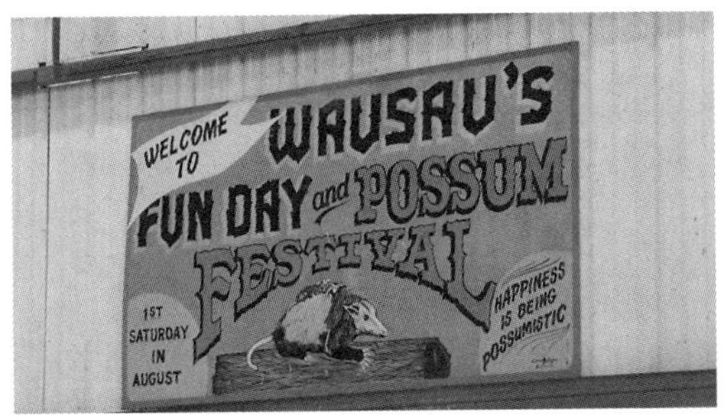

Figure 3.55. For North Florida candidates, attendance at the Wausau Possum Festival is a must-stop on the campaign trail. Photograph by Susan A. MacManus, August 2014.

up not only in the Revolutionary War but also in the abolitionist movement leading up to the Civil War and in the struggle for women's suffrage, he said. "I think it's a movement of people rising, saying that our government, almost at all levels, has become too big, too powerful, and too intrusive in our lives beyond the framework of how it was established, which is within the Constitution."

The group he started held a rally about every six months. Each rally was devoted to a single issue, and attendance varied from 300 to 400 people. The first rally, held at the University of West Florida, featured Republican Lt. Gov. Jennifer Carroll speaking on the nation's constitutional foundation. Another rally criticized the Transportation Security Administration (TSA), whose employees made headlines when they patted down an elderly lady wearing Depends®.

In March 2013, when Republican State Rep. Clay Ford passed away, a big lobbying group in Tallahassee asked Hill to run for the open seat in the special election. He said no. He mentioned the offer to his wife when he got home, and they both agreed that he would not run. The next day while they were eating lunch, she looked at him at one point and said, "You're thinking about this, aren't you?" Yes, he admitted. "It was kind of flattering that they would ask me and really it's kind of intriguing." Again, they agreed he wouldn't run. Over the next couple of days, he prayed about it. Then he said to his wife: "I've got to run for office." Ten weeks later he was elected.

Hill ran in a field of six candidates, including the local Republican Party favorite. "In the first poll, I understand I was dead last. Now, that's humbling. I said, 'How can I be last?'" Not discouraged by either the party favorite or the money he amassed, Hill stuck to a message of limited government, low taxes, personal freedom and individual responsibility. "It resonated so well with the people here, that and an anti-politician stand." People cheered, he said. "I think it had a lot to do with timing because so many folks were disillusioned with what they were seeing happening, primarily in Washington, D.C.," and to some degree in Tallahassee.

His campaign workers put in long hours for six weeks: "We would get up at 6:00 in the morning. Didn't start knocking on doors until about 9:30, wanted to make sure people were up. We would come back when it was dark, and that would be 8:00 to 8:30."

Hill felt "very comfortable" walking in white neighborhoods. "I think that's primarily because of my background. As I grew up, I was almost always the only black

Figure 3.56. Rep. Walter Bryan "Mike" Hill, R-Pensacola, won in a special election, after the death of State Rep. Clay Ford (R). Hill attributed his success to his message of limited government, low taxes, personal freedom and individual responsibility, and to the timing. "So many people were disillusioned with what they were seeing happening, primarily in Washington, D.C." and to some degree in Tallahassee. Campaign literature courtesy of Mike Hill.

person in the classroom." In the early 1960s, the Air Force had few minorities, the Army had more, and the Navy, hardly any, he said. "Now that's changed over time."[80]

In the primary, Hill detected one subtle incidence of racism in a radio ad run by the front-runner. "He used a female who had a black-sounding voice, saying why you should not vote for that Mike Hill because he doesn't represent us," Hill said. "It lasted about a week."

In the general election against Democrat Jeremy Lau, there was no racism. "I did have a number of black people campaign against me because they were Democrats. But it wasn't against me because of race at all. They were just Democrats."

Because he was a Republican, "the black community initially did not embrace me at all," he said, "and after I won, they still have not, to a big degree." He went to black churches and asked to meet with their pastors. "They haven't met with me yet." But he had pockets of black support, including some community leaders, who spread the word, albeit slowly.

The *Pensacola News Journal* endorsed him in the primary and the general elections. "Interestingly, that same paper endorsed me in 2010 when I ran against a Senator Evers." The reason a liberal paper endorsed him was "an opportunity to step beyond some boundaries," he said. "They also said that my conservative message is what resonates with the people in this area because this is a conservative area."

Hill tried to share with the Republican Party his successful campaign ideas about how to stop people who were leaving the party and becoming independents and how to appeal to more minority voters. During the primary, he pitched himself as a small business owner, a military veteran, and a minority with conservative values, thinking that was something the party would grab on to. "But they were hands off. Stayed out of it completely," he said. After the primary, when he was running out of funds, the party gave him money for some TV commercials. He also advertised on radio and used mailers.

He lamented the party's lack of enthusiasm for how to expand to other segments of society: "They don't see it," he said. "I've been asked by Reince Priebus [chairman of the Republican National Committee] to be a part of this national program to recruit minorities to be a part of the Republican Party. But they don't know how to go about doing it. They're really at a loss." Even when he tried to tell them that what worked for him was "to stay true to the conservative principles," they didn't understand. "Everyone wants the dignity of being able to work and have a job and to send their children to good schools, and to be able to keep their families together. Everybody wants that. And you're not conveying that message in a way that will resonate with them. You're simply saying, 'Government's too big.' Well, what does that mean? So you have to translate it into what will keep your families together. The family unit, the structure, is the foundation of any society."

The most rewarding part of being a Representative was passing legislation that "has touched everyone in the state of Florida." One bill he filed reduced the cost of renewing license plates and driver's licenses. "My name wasn't attached to it because it became a part of a larger tax package," he said. He worked on another bill with Agriculture and Consumer Services Commissioner Adam Putnam to ensure a new source of PECO (Public Education Capital Outlay) funding for schools that previously came from an energy consumption tax that only businesses pay. "We're able to divert just under 3 percent of that, instead of going into general revenue, to be dedicated directly to PECO."

Hill praised the Agriculture Commissioner as "a very smart guy." The Department of Agriculture and Consumer Services partners with the Florida Department of Corrections to collect, warehouse, pack and distribute fresh farm produce for the Farm Share Program that helps feed the hungry. Upon hearing that recent flooding had wiped out the Manna Food Bank, Hill arranged for Farm Share to divert two 18-wheelers to bring 29,000 pounds of food to flood victims in Brownsville and Gulf Breeze. "Because of my position, we were able to do that. That is what I find gratifying about being an elected official."

What he found hardest as a legislator was "the politics in Tallahassee," he said. "I don't want to be a part of that game, but you almost have to be to be effective. But at the same time I'm not going to immerse myself in it because I don't want to become a part of that culture. In fact, I want to, if I can in some way, change that culture of the politics that are there." Change requires respecting the position and each other. "For that reason and that reason only, I'm running for Speaker of the House," he said.

"I want to allow the Republican Party to be able to point to Florida and say 'that's how you do it.' We're inclusive. We balance our budget. We give money back to our constituents. We operate at a surplus. Not all states are doing that right now. Here we are, the third most populated state in the nation, pretty close with New York, and our budget is half of theirs. We're $77 billion, they're at $141 billion. The same number of people. If the Republican Party can point to Florida and say 'That's how it's done, that's what Republican conservatism does,' then perhaps that can mean something to the nation and this socialist slide that we're going on can be reversed."

Hill did not join the Legislative Black Caucus. "I didn't want to pigeonhole myself into any particular group or thought process." He told the Caucus they were "simply another wing of the Democratic Party. You vote lockstep with them. You don't break group with them at all. Even when you should, you don't. Even when it will help the black community, you won't." As an example, he cited school choice. Democrats are against vouchers and charter schools mainly because of the teachers' union, he said. "This is how the black schools are failing. We have to do something different. Why not give them a choice to either go to a charter school or a voucher to go to a school of their choice? Why would you keep them prisoned there?"

Hill declined to join other groups such as black Republicans, the John Birch Society, and the Military Officers Association of America. Furthermore, he pulled out of the Tea Party. "I'm no longer a member of the Northwest Florida Tea Party because I have to represent everyone," he said. "Even if I'm a Republican, I still have to represent the Democrats. Everyone."

Taking the oath of office was "an emotional moment," he said. A more emotional moment occurred during a visit to Tallahassee for committee week. As he strode toward the Capitol, "all of a sudden it dawned on me: I'm walking to my office in the Capitol, not going to see somebody in the Capitol." In the past he had gone there many times on behalf of organizations. He sat in his office and looked around: "I'm here," he said to himself. "I'm part of that history now of what is going to affect this state and thus our nation."

Asked for advice by young black Republicans on running for office, he has said: "Make sure you understand what your values are, what you're principles are. And don't veer from that. Don't leave those values and principles. Regardless of the temptation that will come that will pull you away from it. That temptation will come in the form of money, of course. It will come in the form of pressure from other groups wanting you to be a part of them, to think their way because they say they'll support you if you do, or they'll campaign against you if you don't. Don't go to the left or to the right, stay on the straight and narrow path. If you're successful, fantastic. If you're not, then you can still hold your head up and say, 'I didn't compromise to appease someone.'"

Mike Hill was interviewed in person by the author May 15, 2014.

The Florida Senate

Figure 3.57. Florida Senate in session, November 1978. State Archives of Florida, *Florida Memory*, https://www.floridamemory.com/items/show/271926.

Florida Minority Trailblazers—Florida Senate: 1960s–2010s

Florida Senators appear in chronological order. Those elected the same year are listed alphabetically.

Time frame	Male	Female	Male President	Female President
1960s	1966–1974 Louis A. de la Parte, Jr.—D Spain/Cuba—Tampa			
	1966–1972 Edmond J. Gong—D China—Miami			
1970s			1966–1974 Louis A. de la Parte, Jr.—D Spain/Cuba—Tampa	
1980s	1982–1992 Arnett E. Girardeau—D African American—Jacksonville	1982–1992 Carrie P. Meek—D African American—Miami		
		1986–1989 Ileana Ros-Lehtinen—R Cuba—Miami		
	1988–1992 Javier D. Souto—R Cuba—Miami			
	1988–2000 Roberto Casas—R Cuba—Miami			
1990s				
2000s		2002–2010 Frederica Wilson—D Bahamas—Miami		
2010s	2011–Present Oscar Braynon II—D Bahamas/Jamaica—Miami Area			
	2012–Present Darren Soto—D Puerto Rico—Orlando Area			

Note: Consult Appendixes B and C for a full listing of minority officeholders in Florida.

Louis de la Parte, Jr. (D)

First Spanish man elected to the Senate, 1966

First Hispanic President Pro Tempore of the Senate, 1972

First Spanish man to serve as President of the Senate, 1974

Personal: Born July 27, 1929, Ybor City (Tampa), Florida. Died September 28, 2008, Tampa, Florida.

Education:

- Emory University, B.A. (1950)
- University of Florida, LL.B. (1953)
- University of Florida, J.D. (1967)

Occupation: U.S. Air Force (1953–1956), Lawyer

Trailblazer Elections:

- Senate District 22 (Hillsborough County) *Dem Primary* 1966
  - Louis de la Parte (67.4%), R. M. "Dick" Ayers (20.3%), Jack Flynn (12.3%)
- Senate, District 22 (Hillsborough County) *General Election* 1966
  - Louis de la Parte—*Unopposed*
- Senate President, July-November 1974

For the full Louis de la Parte story, see the Senate Leadership section, page 268.

Figure 3.58. Sen. Louis de la Parte's paternal grandparents were from Spain (Asturias) and his maternal grandparents from Cuba. He credited them with having a strong work ethic and realizing the importance of a good education: "They struggled through a generation of getting on their feet, always remembering that the key was their children going to college, getting an education." De la Parte took it to heart. He worked hard to improve the state's mental health and education programs. In 1996, the Florida Mental Health Institute at the University of South Florida was named after him. State Archives of Florida, *Florida Memory*, https://www.floridamemory.com/items/show/20579. Photograph by Donn Dughi (Donald Gregory), March 14, 1972. Shown with de la Parte: Sen. Ken Myers (D-Miami).

Edmond J. Gong (D)

First man of Chinese ancestry elected to the Florida House of Representatives, 1963, and the Florida Senate, 1966

Personal: Born October 7, 1930, Miami, Florida; married with five children. Died May 19, 2015.

Education:

- Harvard College, A.B. (1952)
- Harvard Law School (1955)
- University of Miami School of Law, LL.B. (1960)

Occupation: Lawyer
Trailblazer Elections:

- House of Representatives Dade Group 9 *Dem Primary Runoff Special Election* 1963
  - Edmond J. Gong (55%), John B. Orr (45%)
- House of Representatives Dade Group 9 *General-Special Election* March 26, 1963
  - Edmond J. Gong-D (68%), Bob Rosasco-R (32%)
- Senate District 40 (Dade County) *Dem Primary* 1966
  - Edmond J. Gong (74.6%), F. A. "Tony" Benedetto (25.4%)
- Senate District 40 (Dade County) *General Election* 1966
  - Edmond J. Gong-D (69.7%), Edythe R. Miller-R (30.3%)

Figure 3.59. Democrat Gong was sworn in as Senator, along with four Republican colleagues from South Florida, by Justice Campbell Thornal on April 4, 1967, the opening day of the Senate's regular session. The redistricting of 1962 had greatly restructured districts in the Miami area and opened up seats there. Pictured *(L-R)* are Sens. Gong, Chester "Chet" Stolzenburg (R-Ft. Lauderdale), David C. Lane (R-Ft. Lauderdale), Charles H. Weber (R-Ft. Lauderdale), and John W. "Jack" Bell (R-Ft. Lauderdale). State Archives of Florida, *Florida Memory*, https://www.floridamemory.com/items/show/83038.

THE EDMOND J. GONG STORY

When Edmond Gong was thinking about running for office in the early 1960s, he was met with skepticism because Miami had so few people of Chinese descent and even fewer of those were eligible to vote. But he ran for office anyway. "To me, it proved the American dream," he said. "I think you've got to be willing to take a chance. That's the hardest part."

Gong's story of his election to the Florida House in 1963 and to the Senate in 1966 reads like the American dream.

His grandfather immigrated to Boston in the 1890s, planning to start a laundry. Finding too much competition, he went to Thomasville, Ga., where he had a friend. That town already had a Chinese laundry, but the town of Tifton didn't, so he started one there.

Gong's father, who was born in a farm village in China, left when he was 15 and went to Tifton to work in his father's laundry. "As Daddy used to say, the soil was getting pretty barren and not so productive, and they all wanted to come to the 'golden mountain' that was the name for America," Gong said. "Their goal was to come here and make a lot of money, then go back and build a big house and live like lords."

At that time, in the 1920s, men wore stiff collars that had to be starched and ironed. They were too much trouble for their wives, so they dropped off the collars at nearby laundries. While working, Gong's father taught himself English and, like his customers, spoke it with a Southern accent.

In 1925, his father returned to China to get married. As was customary at the time, the marriage had been prearranged, and the couple was not supposed to meet until their wedding. Gong's father, however, wanted at least a look at his bride beforehand. He found a go-between who sent him to a rice paddy where the path split to go to her village. "You can look at her, but you can't talk," he was instructed. As Gong's mother tells the story, she was coming from school and encountered a young man and woman on the path that caused her to lower her umbrella, and "he never got a good look." At the wedding, he must have liked what he saw because their marriage produced five children.

In 1926, Gong's father left his bride in China with her in-laws and came to Florida to take advantage of the land boom. He and an older brother started a laundry that became so successful they hired black women to do the ironing. He received daily letters from his bride, pleading with him to return for her. Her family were not peasants, but they made her carry the night soil (human waste)—two buckets full to the brim—out to the rice paddy every day. One night she was so late in coming back that they sent a search party to look for her. They found her in the rice paddy washing off the night soil that had spilled all over her when a bucket broke. "I never knew how bad it was until I lived in Hong Kong for a couple of years," Gong said.

His father kept writing back that he would come back after he had made a lot of money, and they would buy land, build a two- or three-story building, and live off the rentals. No, she said. Then one day she wrote a letter that had smudges at the bottom. "Those are my tears because I miss you so much," she wrote. When he saw that, it was all over. He went to China—the year was 1929—and brought her to Miami.

In time, big laundries forced out the hand laundries, and stiff collars went out of fashion. His father realized he had to go into a business that provided goods and services people needed and in a place where people lived. Miami, which was segregated at the time, had an unwritten rule that after sundown all the blacks had to be off Miami Beach, Gong said. "So they were really discriminated against." Sensing an opportunity, his father opened a mom-and-pop grocery store in Overtown, a black area, where whites were afraid to open businesses.

He called the store Joe's Market (an Americanized version of Chou because his name was actually Chou Fred Gong). Once, while in school, Gong was assigned to write about his ancestors for a history class. "They were part of the Zhou Dynasty

[Chou is also spelled Zhou in English]," his dad told him, and "they ruled China for nearly a thousand years." "A pretty good dynasty," Gong thought.

Once Joe's Market got off the ground, his father opened a meat market. One store followed another, and in 20 years, he had more than 20. "He would start them, get them going, then he would sell them to Chinese who wanted to come from New York" after selling their laundries there.

The timing was "brilliant," Gong said, because the large supermarkets like Publix had not yet formed. Black customers "were more comfortable buying their kind of food" at Joe's Markets. "We had pigs feet, pig tails, hog jowls, smoked hog jowls," as well as snuff and cigarettes. Always alert to opportunity, his father would break open a pack of cigarettes and sell five for a few cents, if the customer wanted.

"I think it was a service at that time for the blacks," Gong said. "Many of them came from Georgia, and they were pretty poor, but they'd start working" and earning money. "It was a heady time. I mean, the war was going on, and there was a lot of uncertainty. But I think that my father's economic timing was superb."

"He wasn't always successful, but he never got discouraged," Gong continued. "To his dying day he was an optimist, he never gave up."

In addition, he was loyal to friends. In one instance, he received a loan to build an office building with apartments and a grocery store in Liberty City, a black section of Miami. The lender had structured the loan as part of a corporation and charged him 20 percent interest, which was usury, as Gong later learned in law school. But his father never got mad at that lender. "He said, 'Well, he helped me when nobody else would.'"

Another time, his father overlooked his cash-and-carry policy and extended credit to a Bahamian man who had six or seven children. When Gong's mother found out that the credit amounted to more than a thousand dollars—a lot of money in those days—she gave her husband a hard time. The man said he couldn't pay that amount, but he had some land in the county that he would sell. Figuring that he would at least get something that way, his dad forgave the debt and bought the piece of land. When he went to find it, he discovered that it was a swamp, which was not uncommon in west Hialeah then. Instead of claiming he had been swindled, he held onto it. As it turned out, the swamp was later drained and he sold the property in 1966 for almost a million dollars.

Besides his entrepreneurial spirit, "Daddy was very politically conscious. He voted in every election. He was a Democrat. He loved Franklin Delano Roosevelt. He just loved politics. I mean, it was in his blood," Gong said. His father didn't proselytize, but he encouraged his children to run for office. In junior high, Gong was elected president of his class. His father helped make campaign signs at his store with pink butcher paper and a black ink pen. "You need a slogan that rhymes with Gong," his father said. “Bing, bang, bong, vote for Eddie Gong.” At Miami High School, Gong was elected president of the student body.

At that time there were almost no Asians in Miami. “The only Asians you had were cooks in the Chinese restaurants that came down for the winter season, and they would go back to New York or Chicago” in the spring. That would change by the 1990s, with the growth of Asian communities as well as their absorption into the populace. As an aside, Gong mentioned the existence of the Cuban Chinese as a group. “The largest Chinatown outside of San Francisco was in Havana, and there's some vestiges of it left.”

In 1947 Gong was selected to participate in Boys State, an educational program of the American Legion that provided an opportunity to learn about voting, elections, legislation, and other government operations. “They divide you into two parties, Nationalists and Federalists,” Gong said. For the Governor's race, he was nominated to run as a Federalist, and another boy, as a Nationalist. In an unusual move, a third-party candidate was also nominated, “someone they knew wouldn't win,” Gong said. “They figured he would split the vote” and deny Gong the victory, perhaps reflecting discrimination toward him. He won anyway. At the time, “it didn't bother me at all because, you know, I think kids at 15 and 16, they're pretty sharp.”

At Boys State, “I got the taste of [politics], and it was kind of heady,” he said. It was there that he met two fellow delegates: William D. “Wig” Barrow and Lawton Chiles, both of whom would be elected to the Senate with Gong in 1966 as Democrats.

Chiles would also represent Florida in the U.S. Senate (1970–1989) and serve as its Governor (1991–1998). “I could tell he had real charisma,” Gong said. “I mean, he was kind of like a god.” When Chiles ran for the U.S. Senate, Gong worked in his campaign. He remembered one incident when they were flying in a small private plane from Destin, Florida, to Tampa for a debate at the *St. Petersburg Times* with Bill Cramer, the Republican opponent. Flying over the Panhandle, they got caught in a thunderstorm, and the pilot seemed determined to go through the middle of it. Gong and Chiles, who were reviewing questions for the debate, noticed “the plane was kind of jumping.” Finally Chiles threw the papers down and yelled at the pilot to head in the direction recommended by the air traffic controller. “As soon as he turned away, it cleared up,” Gong said. “We never used that pilot again. They called him ‘Crash and Burn’ Evans.” In the debate, Chiles went in unflustered and performed well. “He was a tremendous, tremendous person,” Gong said. “He had hidden character, and he was a real, real Christian.”

In 1947, Gong was elected president of Boys Nation, the counterpart to Boys State but at the national level. At a big parade in New York, a reporter asked him about his background. “I remember saying without thinking, ‘I'm an American of Chinese ancestry.’ And the reporter really liked that.” Later when he went to Harvard, he would encounter other students of Chinese ancestry: some were from China and some from America.

"I really wanted to become a doctor and go to the University of Tennessee," but he was awarded a scholarship to Harvard by the Harvard Club of Miami. He changed his major to political science, graduated cum laude from Harvard in 1952, and earned a law degree from the University of Miami School of Law in 1960. In addition, all four of his sisters went to college: one was Phi Beta Kappa at Florida State University, and two went to medical school, all of which made his father proud. "He believed in education because he didn't have one."

By the 1960s, Gong was a seasoned campaigner and practicing attorney whose name was well known in Miami. When reapportionment created new seats in the Legislature, Gong, along with Louis de la Parte and others, filed to run for state Representative. One of Gong's opponents, John B. Orr, Jr., a former state Representative, was quoted as saying, "Gong is a nice young man, but I'm going to win, and when I win, I'm going to hire him as my attaché." Afterward, the *Miami Herald*, where Gong had worked for two years as a reporter, and the *Miami News* endorsed him. "I think that really helped," Gong said. Orr lost, but two years later he was elected mayor of Miami-Dade County. "It shows you that being the underdog sometimes ain't too bad," Gong said.

For that campaign, "We didn't have any money." He and friends passed out literature at supermarkets and community events, capitalizing on Miami's modest size: "It hadn't gotten really big yet in 1963," he said. "Everybody went to one of four high schools."

Unlike today, when Chinese parents pressure their children to make good grades and rank at the top of the class, his parents wanted him to be well rounded. "Not bookworms, but to be able to, like in my case, to run track, play intramural football—that was the challenge. I guess it's the Greek ideal," he said. "There's more to life than just books, and I think that was a great gift that they gave us." As part of that well-rounded development, his father had sent him to work in Joe's Market No. 2 in Overtown the summer he was 13. The reason, his father said, was that "I want you to learn our dialect, Chinese." So that summer Gong lived in Overtown, and while working at the store, he learned to converse with seven or eight men, all from the same village in China, and all "were making money to go back to it."

Having lived in Overtown and interfaced with the black community, Gong found that the blacks were more accepting of the Chinese than they were of the whites in the area, and that helped him politically. The *Miami Times*, a major newspaper in the community, was torn between Gong and Jack Orr "because he was very liberal and very helpful to the blacks," he said. "For my father and mother who didn't speak English too well, I think the blacks felt, not superior, but not inferior, if you know what I mean. You're not really American but you come here, you give us the opportunity to have good food and fresh food."

When he was elected to the House in 1963, "I felt it was a time of change, but the change was just starting," he said. The Civil Rights Movement was gaining momentum with Martin Luther King's "I Have a Dream" speech at the Lincoln Memorial. Betty Friedan had published *The Feminine Mystique*, reawakening the consciousness of women for equal rights with men. U.S. soldiers were advising the South Vietnamese Army, and Lyndon Johnson took over as President when John F. Kennedy was assassinated.

In Florida, a series of three redistricting measures changed geographical bases and shifted power from rural to urban areas. "We went from one Senator to two, and then two to seven," he said. That large field prompted him and others to run for the upper house. "Florida was still evolving and had a long ways to go."

As evidence, he recalled working with Lawton Chiles on a piece of legislation prohibiting conflict of interest among state employees. "We couldn't get it in the House or Senate because (some members) would say, 'I know what a conflict is, and I don't need these rules.'" The bill passed eventually.

Gong also recalled that legislators at one time could vote in committee with proxies. On one occasion when he had a bill in committee, a Representative from a small county told him, "That's a good bill, Mr. Gong, so I voted for it. But I have eight proxies to vote against it." So the bill was killed. "It was that type of thing you knew you couldn't do anything about," Gong said.

But change was coming to the Legislature and to government and politics in general. Chiles "was a bridge between that time and the modern era," Gong said. During Chiles's nearly four decades in public office, the state changed from mostly southern Democrats to an almost even split between Democrats and Republicans. As a U.S. Senator, Chiles fought for open meetings of regulatory agencies, federal paperwork reduction, and creation of Florida's Big Cypress National Preserve. As Governor, he successfully sought public funding for state office candidates and sued the tobacco industry to recover costs of treating smoking-related disease.[81] "It took someone like him from a county in Central Florida that understood the problems and that had problems itself," Gong said.

In Florida in the 1960s, "the House was an unruly bunch of men and women. We didn't have many women, unfortunately, then," he said. "The House is awfully big, there were over 100 people," he said. "It's hard to get focused unless you were part of the leadership," which meant committees like Rules and Appropriations, and positions like Speaker. "I never got into the Appropriations side like Marshall Harris, who had a mind for that type of thing. That didn't interest me but that's pretty important." Gong was also impressed with House Speaker Mallory Horne. "I thought he did a

The EDDIE GONG Record

State land for state people:

Thanks to a law written and fought through by Eddie Gong, more than 25,000 acres of land in South Dade has been saved to serve the recreation needs of Florida citizens, especially residents of Dade and Monroe Counties. It was about to be sold to Aerojet-General Corp. for development at a price of only $50 an acre, though it is now worth about $1000 an acre! But Eddie Gong's law, signed in 1965, requires the state to give Dade County first refusal at the same price offered by any other buyer, if the land will be used for public recreational purposes. And the Florida Supreme Court just decided that the Eddie Gong "Land Preservation Law" does apply. That means $25,313,000 worth of land at today's value saved for you, at a cost of only $1,265,650!

Ethics for legislators:

It took two sessions of the Legislature for Eddie Gong to get his "Honest Government" Bill passed, but in 1965 he did it. As a result, state officials have to disclose any financial interest they have in matters before them for decision. It seems like a simple, obvious precaution to avoid conflict of interest. But Eddie Gong had to battle for it. For you.

Easing your tax load:

For years, your taxes kept climbing while many big corporations made millions in Florida and didn't pay more than a few dollars. When the state needed more money, corporation lobbyists said "Raise the people's real estate taxes... raise the sales tax." It didn't seem right to Eddie Gong. And when Governor Askew came out fighting for a tax on corporate profits—to take some of the load off your shoulders—Senator Gong went right into battle beside him. The result: Florida is now in a sound financial condition again, with a $270 million surplus projected this fiscal year. And no new state taxes are being piled on you.

Against the gerrymander:

How do you like having a full vote in Tallahassee and in Washington? It wasn't always that way. The old-time politicians had carved up Florida's districts into weird gerrymandered shapes, to protect their own seats and concentrate political power in areas mostly full of cows, horses, palmetto and pine trees. Eddie Gong fought for fair redistricting—in the courts and in the Legislature. Now, we who live in downstate counties like Dade and Monroe enjoy full votepower.

Freedom of the press:

If a reporter can't protect his news sources, he isn't going to get much important news, especially the behind-the-scenes picture on how your government is working. And you need that picture to vote intelligently. That's why Senator Eddie Gong has sponsored legislation that would make a newsman's information source "privileged." It's important because, when the press loses its freedom, the people lose theirs.

Figure 3.60. Gong's campaign brochure for his Senate run emphasized his role in pushing for reform of the redistricting process. Literature provided by Edmond J. Gong.

great job. He understood the process." By contrast, the Senate was smaller and had less variety. "It was a challenge."

"I don't know if I could be in politics today because you get crossed up a lot and you get stabbed in the back a lot," he said. As an example, he described an incident that happened while he was in the House. He had a "going home" bill, which meant that he had to get it passed for the constituents back home. "Everybody had a going home bill," he said. "My going home bill was very simple: If the state owned property and they were going to sell it, they had to first offer it to the County Commission where the land was, for recreational purposes. I thought it was terrific." Jimmy Kynes, assistant to Gov. Farris Bryant, sent Gong a note, saying the Governor was going to sign it. "Well, I was happy," he said. But the Governor vetoed it, and Gong got "really mad" at both men. A short while later, when Kynes ran against Earl Faircloth for attorney general, an opportunity presented itself for retribution. Gong appeared on an hour-long program on the local ABC TV channel along with Faircloth and Dick Pettigrew, both fellow House members. "I told this story how Jimmy had stabbed me

Figure 3.61. Gong's campaign button was simple, no doubt thanks to the advice of his "politically conscious" father. When Gong ran for president of his high school student body, his father suggested a slogan that rhymed: "Bing, bang, bong, vote for Eddie Gong." Photograph courtesy of Edmond J. Gong.

in the back," Gong said. Kynes lost the election. "Jimmy wasn't a bad guy," Gong said, but he could have been more truthful.

"The thing I would say to anyone going into the Legislature, they should know the rules, backward and forward," he said. They should also know "all the precedents because every time you try to do something, if you didn't know the rules, you'd lose."

"One of the key things that I saw in the Legislature, if you were economically needy, you were vulnerable to influence," he said. "I think the struggle is between opportunity and having the shekels [money]." A young lawyer that graduated at age 30 and had three or four children wouldn't have much in savings, for example.

Besides financial stability, "I think you have to study government and I think you have to know something about government economics. Economics today is so important." Unemployment figures, for example, reflect the number of unemployed but do not take into account those that have quit looking for jobs. In addition, many jobs are more complicated than in the past, and the unemployed often need training to qualify for them.

A candidate in Miami needs to be bilingual, he said, because of the large Hispanic population. Another useful characteristic is the ability to "spot a phony pretty quick because you don't have much time" to develop relationships with colleagues. At the same time, "You have to be able to leave the door open for change because you could be wrong."

Candidates need to realize that public life can challenge family life. "If you have a spouse that loves public life, you're good," he said. "In my case, my [first] wife was a Jehovah's Witness, so she couldn't even vote for me." She gave him moral support but couldn't really help him. "I mean, you carry the baton as far as you can go."

All in all, his Chinese ancestry did not invite discrimination. "I thought being different was an advantage because people noticed you. When you're a minority if you're good, people think you're great. And if you're not good, they think you're really lousy," he said. "The majority doesn't expect you to excel. So if you excel, then you get more points than you deserve."

"That's what America does. I mean, here we had the grocery store in the black ghetto—that's what you would call it," he said. "It could only happen in America. My father, my grandfather, all had to come half way around the globe for us to have a chance because we wouldn't have had this chance. We'd have been working in the rice paddies in China."

Edmond J. Gong was interviewed in person by the author Mar. 22, 2014.

Arnett E. Girardeau (D)

First African-American man elected to the Florida Senate since Reconstruction, 1982

First African-American man elected Senate President Pro Tempore, 1989

Personal: Born July 15, 1929, Jacksonville, Florida; married with two children.

Education:

- Howard University, B.S. (1952)
- Howard University, D.D.S. (1962)
- Postgraduate work at Wayne State University
- Postgraduate work at Fisk University

Occupation: Dentist

Trailblazer Elections:

- Senate District 7 (Nassau and part of Duval County) *Dem Primary* 1982
  - Arnett E. Girardeau (44.6%), Andrew E. Johnson (34.3%), Eddie Mae Steward (12.8%) George Thomas Sessions (8.3%)
- Senate District 7 (Nassau and part of Duval County) *General Election* 1982
  - Arnett E. Girardeau—*Unopposed*
- Senate President Pro Tempore November 22, 1988
  - Arnett E. Girardeau—*Unanimous Vote of Colleagues*

Figure 3.62. Sen. Arnett Girardeau, a dentist, listens to Senate discussion while propping an injured foot on his desk drawer. (The injury happened when he tried to stop the fall of a heavy telephoto lens.) In reflecting on his early campaigns, he recalled that "the white community had tried to spread the idea of the Civil Rights Movement as being a black ragtag group of people doing sit-ins." But that did not work. State Archives of Florida, *Florida Memory*, https://www.floridamemory.com/items/show/102774. Photograph by Donn Dughi (Donald Gregory), February 2, 1988.

THE ARNETT GIRARDEAU STORY

Arnett Girardeau made his history-making debut in the Florida Senate in 1982 after serving three terms in the Florida House, beginning in 1976. Most of that time, he served in the forefront of the Civil Rights Movement in Florida.

"I had really never heard of the Civil Rights Movement while I was in college," Girardeau said. "But it turned out that I had been right there at Howard [University in Washington, D.C.] from 1947 to 1950, all the way until I went back to dental school in 1958. The Civil Rights Movement moved to Jacksonville in '60."

Before the 1960s, Jacksonville was like many segregated Southern towns under white political control. It had separate schools, churches, businesses, and residential neighborhoods. Girardeau's family was part of the black business community. His grandfather and three uncles ran barber shops on West Ashley Street, and another uncle, worked with a bail bonds company, American Dixie. Girardeau left his hometown for college in the late 1940s and served in the Army in the early 1950s.

On his first Army furlough in 1952, he returned home to find a Justice of the Peace election in progress. "Before that, elections were not that important. But what made this one different was for the Justice of the Peace, a black man was running for office, and that black male was Earnest Jackson." Girardeau later learned that Jackson had won the election, which would have been a first for African Americans. "But the white community quickly said the election was illegal," he said. "I never understood why. But because of that, they re-held the election and whites turned out in unusual numbers and defeated him."

Although African Americans had gained the right to vote in previously all-white primaries, as provided in *Smith v. Allwright* in 1944, they had little hope of winning election to public office. One reason was a lack of trust. "There were two Americas: a black America and a white America," Girardeau said. "Whites did not know blacks." He believed "that whites thought that if African Americans were elected to office, they would reverse the trend and treat them as badly as the whites had treated the blacks." As a result, "whites just did not vote for blacks, and blacks had a choice: vote for a white or no vote at all." Furthermore, he realized that "incumbents had the advantage of financing from people who knew them," and blacks had no incumbents.

As early as the 1940s, the black community in Jacksonville began confronting racism through NAACP activities. In 1960, the organization's youth members held sit-in demonstrations at lunch counters in downtown stores. Though students demonstrated peaceably, racial tensions escalated. On Aug. 27, 1960, Girardeau, who at 31 was older than the students, was selected captain for a sit-in at Grant's Department Store. As they were leaving the store, the demonstrators were attacked by a mob of white men armed with bats and ax handles. That day became known as Ax Handle Saturday.[82] "That's the movement that made me pursue civil rights," he said.

During the next several months, white and black leaders met for talks. Girardeau described one meeting in 1963 with the town's long-time Mayor Haydon Burns. Girardeau and an activist black teacher, Rutledge Pearson, wanted the Mayor to form a biracial committee. "We were ushered into the City Hall through the back entrance, carried up the back elevator" to a conference room on the 14th floor. "That was the first time that I'd seen someone, who later I understood was the Rev. [Dr.] Landon L. Williams, Sr., a preacher and the president of the Longshoremen's Association, a very powerful group." They talked, and "the Mayor said he'd see what he could do, but he never did anything. But that was the first time we really got a chance to talk to elected officials who could do something."

Burns left office in 1964 to run for Governor, and Louis "Lou" Ritter (D), who "was much less of a segregationist," was Mayor. He appointed Charles E. Simmons, Jr., who worked at the Afro-American Life Insurance Company and was "a very well-educated man," to the Civil Service Board to fill an unexpired term. Simmons later ran for reelection and won. In 1969, Wendell P. Holmes, Jr., was elected as the first black to the School Board. In fact, he was the first black elected to any Florida county school board.

Meanwhile, two teachers, Sallye B. Mathis and Mary L. Singleton, were elected to the City Council in 1967. "This pretty much told the community, which was approximately 44 percent black, that we had the ability to elect a mayor," Girardeau said. "So the white community began a strategy of how do we stop this?" Their solution was to consolidate the city and county governments. At that time Jacksonville had a mayor-city commission form of government. This meant that the Mayor appointed the police commissioner, the fire commissioner, and other officials. Those favoring consolidation argued that instead of the Mayor appointing city officials, the people would elect them, and that blacks would have more opportunity to be elected to the new council, which would consist of 19 members.

The issue split the black community. "The president of the NAACP and the Urban League and the black leadership in general were opposed to it," Girardeau said, because it would dilute the black vote. On the other side, Sallye Mathis believed that as more blacks had moved into the county, they would get city services—water, sewer, lights—and an opportunity to vote in city elections. "That's hard to argue against," Girardeau said. Mary Singleton and Earl Johnson also favored the measure as bringing more efficiency to local government.

Claude J. Yates, a retired general manager of Southern Bell Telephone, led the merger committee. Girardeau remembered Yates as a segregationist who once said there would never be any black ("and he didn't use the word 'black'; he used the N-word") telephone operators. With Yates in command, consolidation passed. "The slap in the face to me," said Girardeau, was that a local government building was named after Yates when it opened in 1989.

As he reflected on the issue today, Girardeau sounded a positive note: "In the final analysis, I think consolidation was the best thing to happen to the community, even though it destroyed our voting strength for 40 years." The first black Mayor, Alvin Brown, a Democrat, was not elected until 2011.

As consolidation got under way, Girardeau resolved that African Americans would run in every election that came along. In 1970, he saw the chance to run himself in an election that had no incumbents. At that time, candidates ran at-large in multi-member districts. Among his opponents were a young insurance executive and a former Representative, David Harrell, who seemed mostly interested in taxes. In the primary, the *Florida Times-Union* endorsed the insurance man as the best qualified and the one with new ideas. "I came in first or second," Girardeau remembered. In the runoff, the newspaper turned its support to the former state Representative because of all his experience. "So I lost," Girardeau said. Even so, the election showed that "African Americans had the power to elect someone if it's in a nearly fair fight." (Girardeau received the newspaper's endorsement in every subsequent campaign, for the House as well as the Senate.)

In that campaign, his treasurer was a young white attorney, fresh out of the University of Florida College of Law, Lyman Fletcher. An attorney in the same firm, William Sheppard, also white, "was one of the most aggressive lawyers in this area in defending the rights of minorities. When I lost, Fletcher said, 'They'll realize, as I did, that we just had not done enough campaigning.' We didn't have the money and we didn't have the expertise."

It was after that election that the NAACP focused its efforts on increasing black voter strength. "It was huge. That's the first time the black community ever had a voter registration of that type," Girardeau said. NAACP President Rutledge Pearson, asked Girardeau, a former high school classmate, to become his vice president. "We had already flexed our muscles and had elected two African Americans to the old city council," he said.

In 1970, Girardeau, now an established dentist, was elected president of the black Community Coalition, which consisted of five groups all working toward desegregation. As his visibility grew, Girardeau was selected for local and state political responsibilities. In 1971, Gov. Reubin Askew (D) appointed Girardeau and Lyman Fletcher to the state's first Human Relations Commission. Askew, who had beaten fellow Democrat Lawton Chiles in the '70 election, was from West Florida. People "didn't really know anything about his sentimentality toward race relations," Girardeau said.

"We began right away to try to develop a way of getting blacks into government." Realizing that they could get someone elected if districts were single-member instead of multi-member, they asked the Legislature to make that change in Duval County. "We were successful," he said. "The way that the districts were drawn, 85 percent of the African-American vote was in one district. That made it possible to elect an African American to office." Consequently, in 1972, Mary Singleton was elected to the Florida House. "Well, I sat back then and I was pretty satisfied that we had broken the code," he said.

In 1972, when George McGovern ran as the Democratic nominee for President against Richard Nixon, Girardeau was appointed a co-coordinator for McGovern's Duval County campaign. "McGovern was tagged as a liberal and as a result

[Republicans] made up a million-dollar bill with his face on it in order to show what a spendthrift he was," Girardeau said. "So that pretty much sunk his ship."

In the mid-1970s, Girardeau took his civil rights work to the national level. In 1974 he was the only black delegate to the Democratic miniconvention in Kansas City, Mo. He felt good about his election because other black delegates had been appointed by various groups "to help make up the deficit in black participation." One plank in the party platform, Article 10, said that blacks and other minorities must be sought out and not only invited but included in all the affairs of the Democratic Party at all levels. At that time, Florida had three blacks on its Democratic Executive Committee, a big advance over other Southern states. "The night before the vote, we agreed that we would ask Askew (Executive Governors Committee chairman) to commit to Article 10." If he did not get the Governors group to support Article 10, "all of the black delegates would walk out, and it would be an embarrassment to the Democratic Party. Not one or two—all."

The next morning, Askew asked Girardeau to come to his area for a talk. Democrat Charlie Bennett (Congressman from Jacksonville 1949–1993) "saw me going back to Askew and he wanted to be there as part of whatever happened. Ol' Charlie [who had contracted polio in New Guinea during World War II] took his braces and got his legs over those seats and crossed the aisles not going to the end of the aisle, and he got back there to Askew. As a result when the vote came, Askew said that the Governors had agreed to support Article 10." What made this vote meaningful was that in the next election cycle, "all of these liberals were booted out of office—Frank Church, Birch Bayh" (in other states). "We lost a lot of good people because of that, but we survived."

In 1976, when Singleton accepted a paying job as Director of Elections in the Secretary of State's office, the black community began looking for a replacement. In a July meeting at American Beach, Girardeau, along with other leaders in the local Urban League and NAACP, came up with a list of 19 possible candidates. "Teachers and preachers were the people that our community respected," he said, but it came down to which ones could make a living while they ran for office. None did. As they were leaving, someone said to him, "Doc, you've got to run."

"So I went over the morning of the last day of registration and qualified. The interesting thing here is that a friend of the black community," Andrew Johnson, who was white, also decided to run. "His mother and father are said to have met at an Urban League meeting some years back in the '20s, which said in essence that they were liberals," Girardeau said. Johnson believed that if he could get elected, he could help blacks. "But my attitude was blacks needed to represent blacks. They needed somebody who knew what it meant to be black," Girardeau said.

Both men went after the same votes, making it a tough campaign. Girardeau won

Figure 3.63. Sen. Arnett Girardeau peruses bills laid out on the fourth floor of the Senate Office Building East. In his day, bills were printed on paper and photocopied for legislators and their staffs to read. Photograph courtesy of Florida Senate Archives, October 6, 1987. http://archive.flsenate.gov/data/Publications/Archive/Photos_on_display/SenatorsandEvents1980s.pdf.

the primary and then the general election. "I went to the Legislature with the attitude that my job was to help change things or make them better for minorities in the state, pretty much full-time. My dental practice was pretty much put on hold." Every morning, instead of seeing patients, he attended meetings on legislative business.

"That's when I really learned why we were so far behind," he said. "Because the business community, and I'm talking about the white business community, pretty much ran the government." As business people, "they supported each other, they saw ahead and planned ahead, and as a result, we blacks were always playing catch up."

His first successful bill was an amendment to the Sunshine Law, which said that "in all actions of government, whether it's local or all the way up the state, any action that was to be voted on had to be done in the public view, or public arena. And some nice, smart Republican tried to derail it by adding on to it that even the discussions between the attorneys and the judge in chambers had to be open to the public," which should have killed the bill. But "I'll be darned if the people didn't go and vote for it," he said. "I've thought about it ever since, any time a case came up whereby plea bargaining and that sort of thing was done. I thought about that—that we had a hand in making sure that the public had access to that."

When Girardeau entered the Legislature, a number of blacks had moved into important government positions. Trailblazers Joe Lang Kershaw (1968–1982) and Gwen Cherry (1970–1979) were fellow House Democrats. They "were neighbors, but they didn't get along. By the time I got to the Legislature, I found it important to try to bring Gwen Cherry and Joe Lang Kershaw together. Couldn't do that. So I went ahead and did what I could with one, then I did what I could with the other, and that made a bridge in the gap between the two," Girardeau said. When Kershaw was a student at Florida A&M University, back in the '30s, "he used to clean up the Capitol.

He had a job working for the Sergeant-at-Arms. He relished the idea that now he is a Representative," but he had no agenda, Girardeau said.

Gwen Cherry, on the other hand, was trying to encourage other blacks to run for office, Girardeau said. Her term was cut short, however, in the first week of the 1979 session, when she died in a car wreck.

After Girardeau had been in the Legislature for two years, trailblazer Carrie Meek became a member of the House. "She and I immediately began to work together. In fact, as we used to say, 'the Black Caucus met in the phone booth.'"

Trailblazer Jesse McCrary, a black attorney from Marion County and Secretary of State at the time (1978–1979), had Girardeau's respect. "He was a good appointee and he worked well—and he was mindful of his heritage," said Girardeau. He "was not one of those self-righteous persons. He was recognized and made it known he was an African American. And he represented his people."

Trailblazer Joseph Hatchett had already been on the Florida Supreme Court for a year when Girardeau went to Tallahassee. "I sat and talked with [Justice Hatchett] about some things I was trying to do, and he gave me advice as how to do it, the legality of it," said Girardeau. "I followed his advice; it worked."

In 1980, a black Republican and trailblazer from Miami, John "Gus" Plummer, was elected to the House, but nobody knew much about him, Girardeau said. He quoted Plummer as saying, "The world will know that Gus was here." "So, Gus was there. He didn't do anything, but Gus was there. And so he lasted only one election. He just wanted to run for office. That was the only thing. He had no agenda. He had no commitment, no nothing."

In Girardeau's third and last term in the House, another redistricting occurred, making it an opportune time for him to run for the Senate. He spent much of his last eight months of the House legislative session drawing districts on the computer. "In some instances where in the previous administration they had just had a little sliver to join two groups in order to avoid the black community, I reversed that and took strips to join black communities. Because we had 15 million people by then, but I think 2.7 million were black. Fortunately we had in our favor that blacks were congregated in urban centers."

"We had to draw just urban centers. Miami. Second, Jacksonville. Next, Tampa. And so forth on down. So what we did was, I started out in Jacksonville because Miami was under the Voting Rights Act, and as a result, they had sufficient numbers to have 60 percent or better blacks in one district. And Miami was considered a liberal area, so we didn't have to worry about that. But in Jacksonville, we had 23 percent blacks in the overall voting population by this time," he said. "Now, that meant that we had to bring it up to where it would be closest to 65 percent black population in order to meet the possibility of what they call a black majority-minority access district." To accomplish that, "we went to Fernandina and connected them with Duval County, then just went down the coast to St. Augustine. And from St. Augustine we went on down toward Orlando and continued to splice those together." Trailblazer Corrine Brown would ultimately be elected to Congress from this district.

The district map underwent many changes, "but the important thing is we had good leadership who supported it." At the time Democrats Harry Johnston who presided over the Senate, and H. Lee Moffitt and Steve Pajcic were vying to become House Speaker. (Pajcic wanted to be Speaker in order to run for Governor at the next election, and Moffitt wanted to establish a cancer center at the University of South Florida.) Girardeau remembered Pajcic saying (about himself and Democratic House Speaker Hyatt Brown): "We're going way out on the limb creating a district that you might be able to win. Are you thinking if we make a district that you all can win it?" Girardeau replied, "Yeah, you make the district right and we can win it." "Now, in fact I drew all of those districts myself," he continued, "but the main thing is I was in leadership at the time and leadership supported what we did." Furthermore, the Civil Rights Division of the U.S. Justice Department gave its approval.

In the next election, legislative leaders "were on pins and needles as to whether or not we could really win it," Girardeau said. Sure enough, "it wasn't only in Jacksonville," he said. It was "Jacksonville, Miami, Tampa, Fort Lauderdale, St. Pete, Orlando—all of those areas began to get elections." That was when he and trailblazer Carrie Meek gained seats in the Senate.

In the primary leading up to his Senate victory, Girardeau faced a previous contender. "Andy Johnson had campaigned that he and I were good friends, and that on some issues he was blacker than me, which was a ridiculous statement but that's what he did. And I tried to explain to him that it was not against him but just the fact that blacks needed to have visible representation in government." Girardeau won again. "That's when we really began to make progress politically because as a Senator, I could do a lot more than I could as a House member."

Valuing his moderate to liberal leanings, Senate colleagues elected him President Pro Tempore in 1989. Looking back on his legislative leadership, he said, "We made so many changes. It was pretty much understood that this segregation was gone. We had to do away with that."

Campaigning changed dramatically from his first race in 1970 to his races for the Senate in the 1980s. From the beginning, he had handed out campaign literature at grocery stores, sporting events, and other places, and not just in the black community. "I would hand a white person my literature. Some of them started to reach for it and saw it was political and took their hand back. They would not accept the literature of a black man. I said, 'I'd appreciate your support.' And when I said that, that's when they said, 'Oh, no, no thank you.' Then they'd go on. That was in 1970. By the time that I left the Legislature, there was a total change. Whites and blacks both accepted the literature," he said. "On top of that I had campaign workers—as many whites as I did blacks."

One form of campaigning in the black community was the "ticket." Blacks who held a certain amount of power would encourage fellow members of the community to vote for the candidates on their tickets. Girardeau remembered an east side ticket put together by Ed Holt, a west side ticket by Lee Haines, one by Frank Hampton, Sr., and another by Isadore Singleton (Mary Singleton's husband). To get on a ticket, a candidate had to pay money. "Frank Hampton and Isadore Singleton were always at each other for leadership," said Girardeau. He gave this example: To get on Hampton's ticket, you had to go through the Rev. Dallas Graham, the pastor at Mt. Ararat Baptist Church. The pastor directed the candidate to Hampton, as the church Board of Deacons chairman, whose business was conveniently located across the street on Myrtle Avenue. The candidate would tell Hampton he wanted to run for office, and Hampton would say, "Well, stranger, if you're a good man, we'll do what we can to help you. How much are you willing to contribute to our effort?" The larger the contribution, the more likely the candidate would get on the ticket. "If you couldn't make Hampton's ticket, and maybe you had money but not quite enough money, you could be on Isadore's ticket. And if you didn't have enough money for the Isadore ticket, you might be on the Ed Holt ticket, and on down the line."

Girardeau added: "Quite frankly, I admired the blacks for learning at least the way to get involved with the political process." Not all churches participated in the ticket process, and candidates did not always understand how it worked. As a result, black candidates began to use more conventional methods of campaigning.

When Girardeau first ran in 1970, he had no money. "Actually, you didn't know that you had to have money to run," he said, but he believed his cause was right.

His first campaign manager, Richard Bradley, was a black contractor. "We were very innovative," Girardeau said. "We got ourselves a lighted sign, hooked it up on the trailer and connected it to the car's electric system and slowly towed it to the community." They also drove through the community with an electric microphone mounted on a car, through which they would extol Girardeau's virtues. Cars were also used for bumper stickers, signs plastered on the sides, and placards on top (the placards were suspended on a triangular shaped platform and strapped to the car roof).

Girardeau was also innovative in distributing literature. John Farmer, who ran a program giving black children constructive things to do, "would bring his kids over to my campaign headquarters and load up the campaign literature, which we sometime had to print ourselves." Farmer had the blessing of Clanzel T. Brown, Urban League president, who said, "Anything that Doc and his group wanted, help them." Farmer sent the kids, who ranged in age from 12 to 16, out in the black community to distribute the campaign flyers. "I called them the little army," Girardeau said. "I mean they covered the black community. All over. And they did this time after time, every day during the election season."

In one election, "Business people in the black community were interviewed by the FBI because my fundraising didn't show that I should have that kind of a visible campaign." Black business people went to L. C. Lucas who had a printing press and had been involved in elections a long time. Lucas told them, "Look, I don't know why you all are bothering that man. Everybody knows him and his family. His mother has been a teacher in Duval County for 40 years, his uncles have been barbers and businessmen ever since I can remember, and as a result, the total community's supporting him. So you're wasting your time" looking for misuse of campaign funds. "As a result, they dropped that investigation," Girardeau said. "From that time on we didn't have a problem with that."

Every day of a campaign was "a full day of meetings with the black community or the white community or both," he said. "What happened was the white community had tried to spread the idea of the Civil Rights Movement as being a black ragtag group of people who were doing these sit-ins. Well, when I came here as a local and a doctor, they couldn't identify us as being ragtag and misguided people." He tried to get other medical professionals to join the NAACP's effort, but "I was the only medical doctor or dentist to be admitted for 10 years." Dr. James R. Henderson, also a dentist, had been the previous one. "Dr. W. W. Shell, Jr., was the chairman of the Urban League, but the Urban League was not looked upon as a civil rights group," said Girardeau. "That came later."

The most rewarding thing about serving in the Legislature was that he was accepted by the leadership and put in a position to make a difference. "You can be a member of a Legislature and your name hardly be heard. But because I was part of the leadership, I had people who supported the ideas." Reapportionment was an example. By "leadership," he was referring to "the group that led for those changes, not I as an individual, but they took my advice."

If a young black man asked about running for office, "I'd advise him, unless he was committed to the cause, don't run. Because the minute that you run for office, you're running as a part-time legislator. You have to have an income," he said. "Mary Singleton learned it the hard way. She had her husband's business as a barbecue place, but when she ran for office, she found out that their business has dropped off and of course you have to be there to build a business."

"The other thing is you look at politics and it looks good. But there are a lot of heartaches involved in politics. You don't win everything. The most important thing to learn is that there are two sides to every issue. I didn't really know that. But I mean I really didn't know that some people believed in segregation," he said. "Therefore, it was our responsibility to see that that was changed, which I worked hard to do."

Arnett Girardeau was interviewed in person by the author Oct. 4, 2013.

Carrie Meek (D)

First African-American woman elected to the Florida Senate, 1982

First African-American woman elected to the U.S. Congress from Florida, 1992 [a first shared with Corrine Brown]

Personal: Born April 29, 1926, Tallahassee, Florida; divorced with three children.

Education:

- Florida A&M University, B.S. (1946)
- University of Michigan, M.S. (1948)

Occupation: Teacher

Trailblazer Elections:

- Senate District 36 (Part of Dade County) *Dem Primary* 1982
  - Carrie Meek—*Unopposed*
- Senate District 36 (Part of Dade County) *General Election* 1982
  - Carrie Meek—*Unopposed*
- U.S. House of Representatives District 17 (Dade County) *Dem Primary* 1992
  - Carrie Meek (82.5%), Darryl Reaves (9.2%), Donald Jones (8.2%)
- U.S. House of Representatives District 17 (Dade County) *General Election* 1992
  - Carrie Meek—*Unopposed*

For the full Carrie Meek story, see the Congress section, page 452.

Figure 3.64. Sen. Carrie Meek, Democrat from Miami (*left*), is sworn in as the first black woman to serve in the Florida Senate. Meek said she "came to [the Senate] with a strong sense of what was right and what was fair" and pledged that "whenever I feel someone is being mistreated, I'm ready to fight for those people." State Archives of Florida, *Florida Memory*, https://www.floridamemory.com/items/show/21274. Photographed on November 16, 1982. Also sworn in at the same time are Sens. Frank Mann (D-Ft. Myers) and Roberta Fox (D-Miami).

Ileana Ros-Lehtinen (R)

First Cuban woman to serve in the Florida House of Representatives, 1982

First Cuban woman to serve in the Florida Senate, 1986

First Cuban American and first Hispanic woman to serve in the U.S. House of Representatives, 1989

Personal: Born July 15, 1952, Havana, Cuba; married with one child and two stepchildren.

Education:

- Miami-Dade Community College, A.A. (1972)
- Florida International University, B.A. in education (1975)
- Florida International University, M.A. in educational leadership (1986)
- University of Miami, Ph.D. in higher education (2004)

Occupation: Teacher

Trailblazer Elections:

- House of Representatives District 110 (Part of Dade County) *Rep Primary* 1982
  - Ileana Ros (48.3%), Raul Pozo (40.2%), S.J. Rand (11.5%)
- House of Representatives District 110 (Part of Dade County) *Rep Runoff* 1982
  - Ileana Ros (55.6%), Raul Pozo (44.4%)
- House of Representatives District 110 (Part of Dade County) *General Election* 1982
  - Ileana Ros-R (58.5%), William (Bill) Oliver-D (41.5%)
- Senate District 34 (Part of Dade County) *Rep Primary* 1986
  - Ileana Ros-Lehtinen (88.0%), Bettina Rod-Inclan (12.0%)
- Senate District 34 (Part of Dade County) *General Election* 1986
  - Ileana Ros-Lehtinen-R (58.2%), Steve Zack-D (41.8%)
- U.S. House of Representatives District 18 (Part of Dade County) *Rep Primary Special Election* 1989
  - Ileana Ros-Lehtinen (82.8%), Carlos Perez (11.05%), David M. Fleischer (3.39%), John M. Stembridge (2.76%)
- U.S. House of Representatives District 18 (Part of Dade County) *General Special Election* August 29, 1989
  - Ileana Ros-Lehtinen-R (53.25%), Gerald F. Richman-D (46.75%)

For the full Ileana Ros-Lehtinen story, see the Congress section, page 415.

Figure 3.65. No cell phones back then! Sen. Ileana Ros-Lehtinen (R-Miami) was using a phone in a conference room at the back of the Senate chamber when the call for a vote came up. She dragged the phone with her onto the floor and signaled her support for the proposal with a "thumbs-up." State Archives of Florida, *Florida Memory*, https://www.floridamemory.com/items/show/103193. Photograph by Donn Dughi (Donald Gregory), May 10, 1989.

Roberto Casas (R)

First Republican Cuban man elected to the Florida House of Representatives, 1982
First Republican Cuban man elected to the Florida Senate (a first shared with Javier Souto), 1988
Personal: Born April 25, 1931, Havana, Cuba.
Education: Havana Business University, B.A. (1954)
Occupation: Real Estate Broker/Investor
Trailblazer Elections:

- House of Representatives District 107 (Part of Dade County) *Rep Primary Special Election* 1982
  - Roberto Casas—*Unopposed*
- House of Representatives District 107 (Part of Dade County) *Special General Election* 1982
  - Roberto Casas-R (53.7%), Ed Cardounel-D (46.3%)
- Senate District 33 (Part of Dade County) *Rep Primary* 1988
  - Roberto Casas (52.5%), Rudolfo "Rudy" Garcia, Jr. (47.5%)
- Senate District 33 (Part of Dade County) *General Election* 1988
  - Roberto Casas—*Unopposed*

Figure 3.66. In the Senate, Roberto Casas, first Cuban Republican elected to both the Florida House of Representatives and the Florida Senate, found the Senate a quieter chamber. With fewer members, it was easier to work out issues and pass legislation. Although he was Senate President Pro Tempore, he had no ambition to be Senate President but was always ready to help others he deemed good leaders to secure that post. Photograph courtesy of Roberto Casas.

THE ROBERTO CASAS STORY

Roberto Casas became involved in politics in Cuba when he was 12 or 14 years old. "A friend of my family was running for Mayor of Havana, and I got involved in that campaign. He won, and then after that, I was very close to him. I helped him in different campaigns and I was involved in almost every campaign that came after that. When I was 21 years old, I was going to run for state Representative there, but it happened that Batista came to power in 1952 and everything fell." A few years later, he wanted to try again but could not because of the revolution led by Fidel Castro.

A few years after coming to the United States, "I started getting involved in different campaigns—Nixon campaign [1968], Reagan campaign [1980]—and that's how it started. I was the treasurer for the Republican Party in Dade County, which I served for about five years."

Originally he and other Cubans were Democrats, but because of the Bay of Pigs fiasco (1961), they started switching to the Republican Party. "I guess that was the party that we chose because that was more in line with what we wanted." Indeed, the Bay of Pigs invasion had a huge impact: "I would say 65 or 70 percent of the Hispanics or Cubans that were registered Democrats switched to the Republican Party. And I was one of those."

Involvement in political campaigns whetted his appetite for running for office himself. He ran for state Representative in a special election in 1978 and lost. When a special election came up in January 1982, he ran again. This time he sought the seat vacated by A. M. "Tony" Fontana (Democratic state Representative 1972–1982), who had accepted a Governor's appointment to the Florida Parole Commission. "I was looking for an opening and that was the opening." At the time the district was a multi-member district that occupied about a quarter of Dade County. "That was a big district: Overtown, Liberty City, Opa-Locka, Sweetwater, Hialeah, Miami Springs."

He raised only about $20,000 for the race. Raising money was always the most difficult part of running for office. But "I was lucky to have many people involved in my campaign," he said, especially in canvassing for votes.

"I campaigned mainly in my district," he said. "At that time, there were no single-member districts, so we had to work with my friends and family. I was helped by the City of Hialeah Mayor Raúl Martinez and several council members."

Voter turnout was 10 or 12 percent, "but the large number of people who voted were in Hialeah, Sweetwater and Fontainebleau Park—a lot of Hispanics there. The blacks didn't come out to vote, just 3 or 4 percent, and the Anglos the same way."

When single-member districts were created later that year, candidates had to run in another election in November. In this race, the district was confined largely to the Hialeah area. Even though the Republicans were not in power at that time, Casas won because he had been involved in many prior campaigns and knew lots of people in Hialeah. "I was lucky enough to have the people coming out to vote for me."

Going to Tallahassee for the first time was confusing: "I was new, I didn't know anything there, I didn't know anybody there, just a few people that I knew from Dade County and that's it." He began at once to mix with people. "After a few days I was in place. I had made a lot of new friends. We had people, John Cosgrove [Democratic state Representative 1981–1984], for example, who were from Dade County. Bob Reynolds [Democratic state Representative 1978–1984] from Dade County, they all helped me out, and people from the north too. We had good people working there." Even though the Republicans were a minority at the time, "I was able to mix with the Democrats and the Republicans."

Reapportionment was a top priority. "I was in the middle of a session when I went there and the reapportionment was being worked out that time," he said. "It took a long time, like three or four months." The configuration of the county created more chances for Republicans to be elected, he said. "In 1982, for example, from Dade County we got about five or six new members." Among those arriving with him were Cuban Republicans Ileana Ros and Humberto Cortina.

In the 1983 session, the Florida Legislature passed a unitary tax, which assessed multinational corporations with operations in Florida on a portion of their worldwide income. "That was good for the state," Casas said, and "I voted for it." Critics, however, argued it would hurt the state's economy by forcing corporations to go elsewhere. Because of the huge outcry, the legislators came back the same year and repealed it.

During the regular session in 1987, the Legislature passed a tax on services, including services performed outside the state but used in Florida, as well as local and national advertising used in the state. Casas was one of the few Republicans to vote for it. At the time, he felt "frustrated." "I thought it was the right thing to do, but I was a little confused on that. Then when we voted for it and we passed the bill, we heard all the outcry there. Everybody was complaining about the service tax, and then they called the special election. We had to go back and vote again." Gov. Bob Martinez (1987–1991) "was the one who really pushed for the service tax. I think that was the issue that killed him really. He was a good Governor. He did a good job for the state, but I think it's that single issue that killed him." A second fatal issue involved abortion. That "was another issue that was against him 100 percent. That was bad."

The Legislature ended up raising the sales tax instead, which Casas thought was "worse." "I think if we had passed the service tax at this time, we would have plenty of money in the bank right now. The state of Florida would have money to pay for all the services."

When Democrat Elvin Martinez (House member 1966–1974, 1978–1997) was the chairman of the Criminal Justice Committee, "I was able to pass a couple of good pieces of legislation," he said. One involved latent prints (fingerprints left by oil or perspiration and not visible to the naked eye). Another involved military training: "I was able to pass an amendment to the bill sponsored by Elaine Gordon [elected to the House in 1972] that would allow [individuals] who were [engaged in] training to [do so to] fight communism and terrorism."

State business was not so serious as to prevent playing pranks on each other, however, especially on freshmen legislators. "At that time a lobbyist would send you a note: 'I'd like to contribute to your campaign. Come out, I have a check.' So we sent this guy out for a check." He went out looking for someone with a paper in his hand, and finding no one, he came back. "We sent him another note. 'I'm with the blue suit, the red tie.' You know, most of the lobbyists wore a blue suit and red tie." Again he returned with no check. "So finally we sent this guy to the Governor's office [Democrat Bob Graham 1979–1987] looking for Mr. Till. He went to the door and said, 'I want to see Mr. Till.' The receptionist said, 'We don't have any Mr. Till here, and the Governor is having a meeting there with the Cabinet.' Nobody knew Mr. Till." So he came back to find the pranksters hiding in a room and enjoying a good laugh.

Another time in the House, someone pretending to be a lobbyist sent this note to a new female Representative: "I would like to take you to dinner tonight. I'm upstairs in the gallery. Please wave at me if you are interested." The woman started waving, but no one in the gallery responded. Then she saw her fellow members laughing and realized it was a joke.

In 1988, he decided to run for the Senate. "John Allen Hill [Democrat], who was the Senator in my district, was a very close friend of mine. He wasn't doing too well in health," Casas said. "We went to lunch one day, and I said, 'If you run, I will never run against you.' That seat was going to be won by a Republican because of the configuration of the district at that time."

"One day he called me and he said, 'Roberto, I am not going to run for the Senate. I want you to run, and I will help you.' And that's when I opened my campaign account right there and ran for the Senate. Then Rudy Garcia, Jr., who was a member of the House, ran for the Senate too. We went head to head [in the Republican primary] and I was able to win the election." (Garcia stayed out of the Legislature for a year, ran for the House again and won, and was elected to the Senate in 2000.)

Casas found the Senate a quieter chamber than the House. With fewer members, it was easier to work out issues and pass legislation. At first, Democrats held the majority, but by 1992, the Senate was split: 20 Republicans and 20 Democrats. That year, the Legislature created majority-minority districts, which changed the political landscape in Florida.

In the Senate, as in the House, "All you have to do is be good. Try to make friends. When you make friends there, you get along with everybody there, with the staff, with the members. You can do whatever you want, whatever you want to pass. If it's logical, they will help you to do it," he said.

Casas spoke with particular fondness about a fellow Senator, Democrat Pat Thomas (Senate President 1993–1994): "He was a very good Senator. He always helped me when I was in the House. He liked to hear about Cuba because I gave him a couple of books about the history of Cuba. He was always kidding around with me." He also invited Casas to spend weekends in a small cabin near Tallahassee: "We went there on Sunday once in a while. We had a good time, wonderful time."

"Sen. George Kirkpatrick [Democrat 1980–2000] helped me in the Senate every time I went to him. He was there for me, really. Dempsey Barron [Democratic state Representative 1956–1960, state Senator 1960–1988] also. I was able to meet with him in a couple of places and he helped me too." Casas ignored warnings to avoid the famously powerful Barron: "I say I don't care, I talk to him and see what happens. And every time I went there, he opened the door for me. He was a very nice guy."

He spoke highly of Democratic Gov. Bob Graham (1979–1987), whom he knew from Dade County, and Gov. Lawton Chiles from Polk County (1991–1998). "Every time I called Lawton Chiles for something, he would say, 'Come down, talk to me,' and I went there and talked to him." "He was a very nice person, very nice, and very good Governor too. I've got good memories about him."

Casas expressed hope that Sen. Toni Jennings would run for the Governor's office. "I think she will run and she has a good chance. She is smart, she knows the issues, and I think she can be a good Governor." She would be appointed Lieutenant Governor in 2003 by Jeb Bush to replace Frank Brogan who resigned to become President of FIU. Jennings was sworn in on March 3, 2003. He admired her greatly: "I tell you she was able. When anybody went to her with an issue, she'd study the issue and if she said, 'I'll go for this,' she would. If she didn't like it, forget it, she would not do it. She was like that. When she thought something was not good for the state, no way. She was honest. When she gave her word, that's it. You could go and rest and knew you won't have any problems."

In 1996, Casas was elected President Pro Tempore under Jennings (Senate President 1996–2000). "Everybody was coming to me, 'I need help, I need help.' And I tried to help everybody and I was able to help a lot of people," Casas said.

He had little or no ambition for the Senate's top leadership post but was ready to help others. Ander Crenshaw, for example, "didn't even have in his mind that he was ever going to run for President of the Senate." Casas invited him to dinner and urged him to run. He did and was elected the first Republican Senate President in more than a century in 1992. He shared the Senate Presidency with Democrat Pat Thomas due to a tied vote, 20/20, during the 1992 Organization Session. (He would be elected to Congress in 2000.) After Jennings, "Doc Myers wanted to be President, and I said give it to him. I had no desire. Give it to him. He deserves it. He's been there for a long time." Myers was elected President Pro Tempore in 1998.

Giving the position up was not hard: "You get tired because everybody comes to you. They need help from Dade County, from different places. They think you can do whatever they want—you want, and it's impossible. You help a lot of people, but they all come to you. Lobbyists and everybody come to you, 'Help me with this,' and, it's hard to do it. It's not an easy job. It's not an easy job!"

A perennial issue for Casas was the Hialeah Park Race Track. The state allowed it to operate on exclusive dates to fend off competition from the Gulfstream and Calder race tracks. Opponents wanted "to cut the days" and force the closing of Hialeah Park. Every time the issue came up, Casas got help from his friends. Sen. Kirkpatrick, for example, would say, "Well you know, this is Roberto's issue. I can't go against him." As a result, "I got 37 or 38 votes for Hialeah. So, they weren't even coming to the

Figure 3.67. Sen. Roberto Casas and Senate President Toni Jennings (R-Orlando) take a moment to pose with Macaw parrots, native to Mexico and parts of Central and South America. Casas, who served as Senate President Pro Tempore under Jennings, greatly admired her and hoped she would run for Governor. (She would become Lieutenant Governor under Jeb Bush in 2003.) Photograph courtesy of Roberto Casas, ca. 1996–1998.

Senate anymore. They went and worked on the House because that was a dead issue for them in the Senate."

In addition to protecting the park's operation schedule, "I was able to get the simulcast for Hialeah Park which they didn't have before." (Simulcasting allowed betting on Hialeah races from other tracks and off-site locations.) In addition, "we cut the taxes to almost nothing. They were the lowest in the state, and I was able to keep that race track going on for many years."

But getting the simulcast required cutting a deal. "Some members in the House wanted some deals for Jacksonville, for the dog tracks, and they wanted to kill Hialeah Park," he said. "The last few days they held my bill hostage in the House. So I went to Toni Jennings and said, 'Madam President, I have this problem.' She said, 'Well, don't worry. We'll see what we can do.' So at six o'clock, they were coming to me and saying, 'We have to make a deal, we have to make a deal.' I said, 'Well, unless I get what I want for Hialeah Park, nothing is going to happen in the Senate.' So they made an agreement between the House and the Senate. And we were able to get the simulcast for Hialeah Park on the dates."

The track provided jobs for 300 or 400 people and was good for the area's economy. "Right now [2004], there is nobody working there, maybe 20, 25 people." In its heyday, Hialeah Park had a far-flung reputation: "I remember I was in Cuba and somebody was living in the United States and sent me a postcard with the flamingos 'Hialeah Park.' It was well known all over. It's a shame that it's closed."

The Equal Rights Amendment, which he voted against, "was a nightmare, believe me." Getting out of the chamber required special police, he said.

He made decisions about bills in a simple way: "If I think it's good for the state; if I think it's good for the people, if I think it's going to help a great number of people in the state, I would vote for that."

The final three or four days of a legislative session were always frantic. Some bills were stuck either in the House or Senate. "Everybody was running from the Senate to the House, from the House to the Senate. It was a nightmare. One time when Gwen

Margolis [a Democrat] was the President of the Senate [1991–1992], we stayed in session the last day I think it was until five o'clock in the morning. From nine o'clock to five o'clock in the morning. That was a long, long, long day," he said. "Everybody was exhausted, everybody—you know, the bills were coming. You don't know where you were—what you're voting on because your mind was completely out. That was crazy, completely crazy."

As the first Cuban American elected to the Senate, "I was very happy that I was the first one." No one treated him differently because of his heritage. Once you get elected, he said, you are "on the same level." Despite some who warned him about discrimination, "I never felt that in my skin, never." People always treated him with respect and helped him: "They always were there for me. I was very lucky. Either I was lucky or I did know how to treat people."

If he were to give advice on how to be a good legislator, he would say: "First of all, make friends. Be helpful to everybody there. Try to mix with the staff. They're very helpful for you too and besides that, when you help people, they are going to help you. Make friends. Study their issues too. When you have something that you have to vote for, you study the issue. Read the bills as much as you can and then you'll be successful in life."

To minorities contemplating a run for public office, he would advise them "to do the same things that I did—work hard and have a good team in your campaign," he said. He added, "Get endorsements from unions and businesses, and most important, meet the people of the district."

Reflecting on his legislative career, he said, "I want to be remembered as an honest person, a person who worked for his district, a person who was able to be friends with everybody in the Senate and the House." His parents, both of whom were born in Spain, emphasized the value of personal reputation to their two sons. His father "was always telling us, 'Never smear your name. Never do anything wrong. Never take any money from anybody.' And we followed that. I was able to be here today without any problems, without any spot in my record. Throughout the years, honesty, friendship—that's what I want the people to remember me for."

Information for this story was taken from an interview with Roberto Casas conducted June 1, 2004, and recorded for the Legislative Research Center and Museum. He also answered questions by e-mail from the author July 31, 2013.

Javier D. Souto (R)

First Cuban Republican man elected to the Florida Senate (a first shared with Roberto Casas), 1988

Personal: Born December 15, 1939, Sancti Spiritus, Cuba; married with three children, eight grandchildren.

Education:

- Villanova University (in Havana)
- The University of Havana
- Miami-Dade College
- University of Miami School of Business (1967)

Occupation: Commissioner, Burroughs Wellcome Pharmaceutical Company

Trailblazer Elections:

- Senate District 40 (Part of Dade County) *Rep Primary* 1988
    - Javier Souto (69.4%), Theodore (Ted) Lyons (30.6%)
- Senate District 40 (Part of Dade County) *General Election* 1988
    - Javier Souto-R (52.7%), Dick Anderson-D (47.3%)

Figure 3.68. Sen. Javier Souto (*left*), Vice Chair of the Agriculture Committee and from an agricultural family in Cuba, shows three types of fruit grown in South Florida—a papaya, mamey sapote, and mango—to North Florida Sen. Pat Thomas, D-Quincy (*center*), and Sen. Donnell "Don" Childers, D-West Palm Beach (*right*). Souto also played a key role in the creation of the Senate Tourism Committee. State Archives of Florida, *Florida Memory*, https://www.floridamemory.com/items/show/102910. Photograph by Donn Dughi (Donald Gregory), May 16, 1989.

THE JAVIER SOUTO STORY

Voters supported Javier Souto in his successful races for the Florida House and Senate for many reasons, one of which was his participation in Brigade 2506, the invading force in the Bay of Pigs operation that sought to free Cuba from Castro in 1961.

As he described his participation:

> I served under Rogelio "Francisco" Gonzalez Corzo, a young engineer at the University of Havana, the national coordinator of the anti-Castro Movimiento de Recuperación Revolucionaria (MRR)—[the Cuban Revolutionary Recovery Movement]. In 1960, Francisco was appointed national coordinator of the Democratic Revolutionary Front (FRD), a coalition of the main underground resistance groups. Francisco and his team, which included me, a 21-year-old college student, would enter and leave the island on U.S.-sponsored missions to provide the people with weapons so they could support their own fight for independence and support the Bay of Pigs invasion.
>
> On the afternoon of Saturday, March 18, 1961, less than a month before the Bay of Pigs invasion, a number of leaders of the underground were meeting in

> a supposedly "safe house" to discuss plans to intensify the sabotage campaign in advance of the planned U.S.-backed landing at the Bay of Pigs. Castro's agents stormed the meeting and captured Francisco and the rest of the group. The morning of April 20, three days after the failed invasion, where 114 brave men were killed and over 1,100 captured and imprisoned, a young 28-year-old Francisco was executed. His last words were "¡Viva Cuba, Viva Christ our King!" We lost many members of our teams including my dear friend Francisco.
>
> My wife, Berta, who was a teenage girlfriend at the time, and her young sister were captured by Castro's thugs and imprisoned so that they would reveal my whereabouts. I was able to evade capture and seek refuge in the Brazilian Embassy and later spent half a year living in Brazil, which is why I have strong affinity for the Brazilian people and the country of Brazil.[83]

Souto, who was born in Sancti Spíritus in Central Cuba, came to Florida in 1960, after Castro had taken control of Havana and forced the Batista government to flee. He obtained CIA-sponsored military training from the U.S. Army and Marines as part of invasion planning that had started in the last days of the Eisenhower administration and continued under President John F. Kennedy.[84] After the failed invasion and exile in Brazil, Souto returned to Florida, went to college at the University of Miami, and began working in the pharmaceutical business.

He bought his first house near the Dolphins' stadium "because it was my days in the CIA. I wanted to be away from all the Cubans and far away where people wouldn't trace me because I was going back and forth to Cuba on clandestine trips. I wanted to be really low key, super low key." Meanwhile, Brigade members formed a veterans association, of which he was later persuaded to serve as vice president. "They sort of adopted me because I was raising the family and in the business world," he said. Among other things, the veterans began talking about getting Cubans involved in politics.

In the early 1980s, the first wave of Cubans, including Roberto Casas, Humberto Cortina, and Ileana Ros, had been elected to the House. By that time, Souto had begun helping candidates of both parties who were friends of friends. One was Bob Graham, a Democrat who had served in the Florida House in the 1960s and the Senate in the 1970s and was elected Governor in 1978.

"I was raised Republican, and we got some of our guys—all Republicans—to run for office," Souto said. In 1984, he decided to run for the Dade County Republican Party Committee. "In those days the elections to the committee were big elections, and it was like any election," he said. Before announcing his candidacy, he got an OK from his bosses at Burroughs Wellcome, which later became GlaxoSmithKline. His responsibilities at the pharmaceutical giant were varied: "I did a bunch of stuff there: I sold, trained, traveled, was all over the place with all kinds of people."

He won election to the Committee and so did a young Jeb Bush, a Florida newcomer and second son of then-Vice President George H. W. Bush. "Then we elected him to be the chairman of the party, and the Cubans in the party wanted me to run for vice chairman. I knew I wasn't going to make it, but they insisted," Souto said. He lost by three or four votes to Mary Collins, "a revered person in the party" who would become a close friend. The night of the election, "Jeb Bush said, 'I want you to be close to me, want you to be one of my guys, and working with me.' So we started, and he had, I don't know, how many guys working with him." At that time in Miami, "the Republican Party was nothing," he said. "We met almost weekly in Coral Gables in an office on Salzedo Avenue. He appointed me the guy in charge of elections and research for the party."

One morning, Souto, Bush, Collins, and other colleagues were meeting at a Marriott Hotel. On a break over coffee, Collins said to the group, "I've been telling Javier that he should run for the state House." It was not a complete surprise because she had mentioned it to him a couple of times. Bush looked at him and said, "Yeah, that's a good idea." Souto thought about it for a week and decided to go for it.

In the general election, he faced incumbent Democrat Tim Murphy, a Harvard lawyer in line to be Speaker. "I was the new kid on the block," Souto said. Despite the challenge, he gained widespread support. "The Cuban thing was very active in those days. People knew me and knew about my background in the Brigade and the things that they saw. We had a lot of support. I mean, it could not have been done without that support. If I'd only been [focused on] the Republican Party, I would not have won that election."

He described his campaign as "neighborhood oriented, family oriented," connecting with people he knew from his work with drug stores, his children's scout troops, and community groups. "I had people in Cuban radio, for instance, who put me in programs. I knew a lot of folks in the media. That's how I got to know Tomás Regalado, who's now Mayor of Miami."

Campaign money came in small donations. "We campaigned like hell," he said. "We did what a lot of people thought was impossible. We won by 1 percent, I think it was. But we won."

Souto was reelected for a second term in 1986. That same year, his friend Jeb Bush was named Florida's Secretary of Commerce under Republican Gov. Bob Martinez. While in the House, Souto served on Appropriations, Finance and Taxation, Judiciary, Criminal Justice, and Higher Education committees, and he held the party committee post until 1986.

In Tallahassee, Souto made friends on both sides of the aisle and in both houses of the Legislature. Democratic friends included Rep. Gene Hodges, Agriculture Commissioner Doyle Conner, and Sen. Dempsey Barron (who later switched parties). "I was the only guy from my group that would go and ride horses with them in the

Apalachicola National Forest. I really enjoyed it. It's a beautiful place," he said. "I used to drink beer with the guys, and go to the countryside and get together in Tallahassee. It was nonpartisan. There were people from both parties there in that group. We used to get along really well. I was sort of like the Cuban redneck guy, or the Cuban semi-redneck, if you can call it that."

One night friends invited him to an informal dinner to eat grouper. "I was the only member of the House. Everybody was a Senator there, and a couple of lobbyists that brought the grouper." While the fish was cooking, Sen. Dexter Lehtinen took him aside. (Lehtinen and his wife Sen. Ros-Lehtinen had become friends with Souto in the House.) "I thought he was going to talk to me about a bill that we were doing," Souto said. Instead, Lehtinen said that President Bush would soon appoint him to be U.S. Attorney for the Southern District of Florida. "I want you to be one of the first ones to know about that. I think you should run for my seat." That weekend Souto went to Miami and talked to friends about the proposition.

One friend at the time was State Rep. Lincoln Diaz-Balart (R). "We used to sit in the back row next to each other. We talked a lot," Souto said. Both represented Miami districts and felt that the Legislature often neglected the area in favor of other parts of the state. "Plus we were sort of guiding the Cuban Caucus." Souto said he was considering a run for Lehtinen's seat in the Senate. Diaz-Balart indicated his support, but added, "Well, what about my brother [Mario]?" They made a deal on the spot. "OK, fine, and I'll support your brother," Souto told him.

In the Senate race, he faced Democrat Dick Anderson, a former safety for the Miami Dolphins. "He had been a Senator, and he left and he wanted to come back," Souto said. "We got in there and we fought like hell." Anderson thought he was going to win. But "at midnight when they counted the votes—Poof! We won by 1 percent."

By winning in 1988, he, along with Roberto Casas, became the first Republican men elected to the Senate since Reconstruction. His friend, Sen. Ros-Lehtinen, had become the first Republican woman two years earlier. All three were Cubans from Miami.

On taking the oath of office, he realized the tremendous power of the Senate. "There are 40 guys who control the state. They can do things," he said. "By the way," he added, "I was part of the electoral vote when George W. Bush became the President [2000]. It was the Senate of Florida that decided with the Supreme Court here who was going to be the President of the USA. Just to show you the power of the Senate."

"The state of Florida is a powerful state in many respects," he continued. "A state loaded with military bases of all kinds. The Gulf War was controlled from Tampa, from MacDill Air Force Base." The state has Miami, Miami Beach, and Disney World, places known all over the world. In addition, its geographic location and culture give the state an important connection to Latin America and its 400 million people.

Figure 3.69. Javier Souto, as a House member, is recognized after passage of his resolution honoring veterans of the Bay of Pigs in 1985. Behind him are Reps. John Renke, R-New Port Richey (*left*), and Jim Frishe (R-St. Petersburg). A former veteran himself, he had a background in chemistry and pharmaceuticals that spurred him to work for passage of the AIDS Information Bill, making Florida the first state to establish voluntary and confidential HIV testing and counseling in all its counties. State Archives of Florida, *Florida Memory*, https://www.floridamemory.com/items/show/20359. Photograph by Donn Dughi (Donald Gregory), 1985.

"I know Latin America because I've traveled there," he said, citing his origin in the old Cuba, residence in Brazil and Guatemala, and frequent visits to Colombia, Peru, and other countries. "We need to take care of this state—no doubt, one of the most important states."

While in the Senate, he served as vice chair of the Agriculture Committee. "In those days the vice chair was like the chairman because the chair [a teacher] didn't know anything about agriculture," he said. "I came from an agricultural family in Cuba," he explained.

"I was one of the guys who created the Tourism Committee, which was something new because we're trying to get Miami going with Brazil. And we did that." He became knowledgeable about pollution and protection of environmentally sensitive areas. "I did some parts of big bills in those days in the Senate and the House. I got really involved with the Natural Resources Committee in the Senate, and we got our hands in everything." He also chaired a subcommittee of Finance and Taxation as well as the Personnel, Retirement and Collective Bargaining Committee.

Of his legislative service, he said, "I was never disappointed. I like to learn. To me, everything was a learning experience." He had had some familiarity with politics growing up in Cuba because one uncle, a physician, had been a mayor and a congressman, and another uncle, a lawyer, had been a councilman. "As a young boy I was always helping people. It's always a learning experience. Both in the House and in the Senate, I was lucky to be close to people who knew a lot."

"My biggest challenges were when I was the vice chair of the Reapportionment Committee in 1992. It was when we created the districts for minorities. I had to go all over the place. I saw congressmen in Washington, all these big people came to see me, and I saw people crying because we were going to change their representation, and we did change a lot of it. So I learned a lot from the reapportionment."

He counts among his legislative accomplishments the passage of the first-ever AIDS bill. In the mid-1980s, "People were dying of HIV and nobody knew what HIV was," he said. With his background in pharmaceuticals, he led the way in gathering information about the virus that caused AIDS. "I guess in a way I'm a frustrated doctor maybe because I like medicine and what makes people live. I've been with so many doctors in my life, around the family and in the business." At the same time, because he was a Republican, "people with the wrong ideas were calling me, 'What are you trying to do?' 'I'm not trying to do anything. I'm just trying to find out what is this thing killing people,'" he said.

Gov. Bob Graham (1979–1987), who created an AIDS task force in 1985, put together "a group of researchers from the University of Florida in Gainesville, working with me, helping me, guiding me, and we came up with the AIDS Information Bill," he said. In 1987, Florida became the first state to establish voluntary and confidential HIV testing and counseling in all its counties.[85] Funding was also provided for prevention and education in communities. In 1988, he helped Rep. Lois Frankel, who "knew nothing about AIDS," to draft the Omnibus AIDS Act that passed the Legislature. "It was the first thing to try to guide this disease that was killing people," he said.

Another national first dealt with precursors, the materials used to manufacture drugs and explosives. The bill "caused me a lot of trouble to pass," he said, noting "the power of the Mafia is working in there." Passage occurred in reverse: instead of House to Senate, the bill went from the Senate to the House.

"The thing was that Miami was the cocaine capital of the world." He remembered a house that exploded about two blocks from where he lived. "I heard the explosion, and the house caught on fire and the house next door because they were stashing ether in the garage." Ether and acetone are needed to manufacture cocaine, he said, which he knew because "I took about two years of chemical engineering before I got into the Bay of Pigs and before I came here." Consequently, "the idea was to control ether and acetone. You could buy a gallon or 200 gallons of ether, just like that."

"When we passed that bill, the manufacture of cocaine died in Miami. Died," he said. "It's funny because when we got into the books about cocaine and the *Cocaine Cowboy* [2006 documentary film] days and all that, it was wild in Miami in those days. Not that we didn't have cocaine, but by this time the cocaine wars were as bad as they were before. It's like the *Scarface* movie. The bankers involved and realtors involved and people laundering money—it's a whole industry." He recalled a pharmacy by the Miami River that was selling bottles of ether. "The boats used to come and load the bottles and take them to Colombia and other places."

While in the Senate, he was friends with Republican Gov. Bob Martinez (1987–1991) and near the end of his Senate term with Democratic Gov. Lawton Chiles (1991–1998). "Lawton Chiles used to call me to his office because I was a Republican who would be the mediator. For instance, the creation of the Elder Affairs Department was because of me." Voters had approved a referendum in 1988 to address the issues of the elderly.[86] Democrats, including Chiles, wanted to create the agency, and Republicans were against it. Souto thought it was a good idea. "My vote tied up the whole thing," he said. The bill went to a conference committee, where it passed. "I was the only Republican that went to the signing ceremony of the bill that took place at Broward Community College. I was the only Republican invited to that event because I was a guy who did the move," he said.

While he derived satisfaction, even "exhilaration," from passing important legislation, he found that legislative service could wreck one's physical well-being. "I got tired of the kinds of foods that were available around there, got tired of pizza and got tired of the greasy stuff. There was a time when I almost didn't eat. Tallahassee could be very dangerous in many ways, if you don't adhere to the basic principles of things. You could end up being a mess in different ways—drinking or losing your family," he said.

He changed his routine. "Instead of going to Clyde's, where I used to go before and drink a lot of beer," he started going to the YMCA across from the hotel where he lived. He would quit work at 6, work out in the gym, and then run a mile. He did that almost every day, Monday through Friday, and sometimes afterward, "I would just drop dead in bed and get up the next morning." As a result, "I really got in shape."

If he were giving advice to someone interested in going into politics, "I would say that in politics, you have to be well-anchored." A legislator has to avoid "misguided" lobbyists, he said. "You have to pretend that you're stupid, and yeah, you don't know what the hell they're talking about. You're swimming with the sharks."

In addition, "You have to get your feet wet, get to working with some political members, get to work in the Capitol." But don't let that work get out of hand, he warned. He explained: "In the Senate I had a bunch of young guys working with me, and the girls would come from FSU at lunchtime, and it was like a party in my office. I would say, 'Hey guys, we are at work here.' You've got to have your principles."

"Temptations are all over the place. People will come and either buy your vote or control you. You've got to be very careful with all kinds of different influences. I'm not better or worse than anybody, but you've got to be careful. There are moments that you need to get control over the whole thing." He gave living arrangements as an example. Sharing an apartment doesn't work because you have to contend with roommate activities. Having your own apartment doesn't work either: "People would come to my apartment and knock on the door in the middle of the night: 'Hey I need something to drink.'" His solution was to live in a hotel. "It was right next door to the clerk. If anybody knocked on my door in the middle of the night, everybody would know about that."

"I've met the good, the bad, and the ugly. I had all kinds of moments," he said.

After leaving the Senate in 1992, Souto was elected to the Miami-Dade County

Commission. "Miami is a capital of Latin America," he declared. "Miami is a global city. Would you believe that there are two members of the Russian Parliament who own condos here in Miami?" The Miami airport "moved over 41 million passengers last year, and we have direct flights all over the world—not only passengers, also cargo." In June 2014 Qatar Airlines inaugurated direct flights between Doha and Miami. "Unbelievable! But it's happening here. So for better or for worse, we are in a place in the world today that is a place to be reckoned with. And I've been very fortunate to be part of this adventure."

Javier Souto was interviewed in person by the author July 31, 2014.

Frederica S. Wilson (D)

First woman of Bahamian descent to serve in the Florida House of Representatives, 1998
First woman of Bahamian descent to serve in the Florida Senate, 2002
First woman of Bahamian descent to serve in the U.S. House of Representatives, 2010
Personal: Born November 5, 1942, Miami, Florida; widowed with three children.
Education:

- Fisk University, B.S. (1963)
- University of Miami, M.S. (1972)

Occupation: Teacher
Trailblazer Elections:

- House of Representatives District 104 (Part of Dade County) *Dem Primary* 1998
  - Frederica S. Wilson (50.7%), Shirley Gibson (22.3%), Jacques Despinsosse (19.1%), Bernard W. H. Jennings (3.6%), Kevin A. Fabiano (2.3%), Judith Goode (2.0%)

Figure 3.70. State Sen. Frederica Wilson, one of Florida's 27 presidential electors, signs her Electoral College Certificate of Vote for President-elect Barack Obama in Tallahassee. Standing at right (*L-R*): Florida Department of State staff members Amy Woodward, Nolah Shotwell, Donald "Don" Palmer, Sarah Jane Bradshaw, and Shelby Bishop. State Archives of Florida, *Florida Memory*, https://www.floridamemory.com/items/show/23669. Photograph by Darryl Jarmon, taken December 15, 2008.

- House of Representatives District 104 (Parts of Dade County) *General Election* 1998
  - Frederica S. Wilson-D (85.2%), Clyde Pettaway-R (14.8%)
- Senate District 33 (Part of Miami-Dade County) *Dem Primary* 2002
  - Frederica S. Wilson (72.3%), M. Tina Dupree (17.6%), John D. Pace, Jr. (10.1%)
- Senate District 33 (Part of Miami-Dade County) *General Election* 2002
  - Frederica S. Wilson—*Unopposed*
- U.S. House of Representatives District 17 *Dem Primary* 2010
  - Frederica S. Wilson (34.5%), Rudolph "Rudy" Moise (16.1%), Shirley Gibson (11.9%), Yolly Roberson (10.3%), Phillip J. Brutus (8.4%), Marleine Bastien (6.0%), Scott Galvin (5.6%), James Bush III (5.4%), Andre L. Williams (1.7%)
- U.S. House of Representatives District 17 *General Election* 2010
  - Frederica S. Wilson-D (86.2%), Roderick D. Vereen-NPA (13.8%)

For the full Frederica S. Wilson story, see the Congress section, page 497.

Oscar Braynon II (D)

First man of Bahamian and Jamaican descent to serve in the Florida Senate, 2011

Personal: Born February 1, 1977, Corpus Christi, Texas; married with two children.

Education:

- Florida State University, B.S. in political science (2000)

Occupation: Consultant

Trailblazer Elections:

- Senate District 33 (Miami-Dade County) *Dem Primary Special Election* 2011
  - Oscar Braynon II (41.8%), Phillip J. Brutus (37.7%), James Bush III (12.0%), Darryl Franklin Reaves (8.5%)
- Senate District 33 (Miami-Dade County) *General Special Election* March 1, 2011
  - Oscar Braynon II-D (73.6%), Joe Celestin-R (26.4%)

Figure 3.71. Oscar Braynon II, the first man of Bahamian and Jamaican heritage elected to the Florida Senate, served as the chamber's Minority Whip in the 2013 session and Minority Leader Pro Tempore in the 2015 session. He calls himself the "special election king" for running for—and winning—vacated seats in House and Senate elections. Photograph by Meredith Geddings, January 14, 2009. http://www.myfloridahouse.gov/Sections/PhotoAlbums/photoAlbum.aspx?MemberId=4427.

THE OSCAR BRAYNON II STORY

Oscar Braynon II, the first man of Bahamian and Jamaican heritage elected to the Florida Senate, remembered that as a child in the early 1980s, he went to neighborhood meetings with his parents. At that time, people in his neighborhood, led by community activist Betty T. Ferguson, were trying to keep Joe Robbie (later Sun Life, now New Miami) Stadium from being built in their backyard.

When Braynon asked what was going on, his father showed him articles in the newspaper. "I started reading the newspaper. I got all my friends involved in painting signs, and then I was very excited," Braynon said. He thought that because it was their neighborhood, "we should have been able to get what we want." But the stadium was built anyway.

"I'm going to say we didn't win, but that's not exactly true. We got a lot of concessions, but as a 10-year-old, I thought we didn't win." When he asked his mom why they didn't win, she said something like, "It's politicians, baby. They don't care about us. They only care about themselves and who is lining their pockets." Braynon then resolved to himself, "I'm going to be a politician because I want to look out for my neighborhood and I want to make sure that whatever I want happens."

He's been politically active ever since.

When he was in the 10th and 11th grades, he interned with Ferguson, who by that time had been elected to the Miami-Dade County Commission. After graduating from high school, "I decided to go to Florida State mainly because I wanted to be closer to the Capitol." There he interned for State Rep. Kendrick Meek during his first year in the Florida House.

Braynon finished a degree in political science and was about to enroll in law school when it occurred to him that he might run for the City Council of the newly incorporated town of Miami Gardens in 2003. "At the time most of the people that were running were my grandparents' age," he said. "But I said, why not be the voice of my peers? I grew up in this community. I grew up in this area. I have a million friends that have not come back because they don't see any opportunities and they don't have anybody that they feel like is representing them. I said, why can't I, why not me, and why not now? And so I ran and I got elected." He defeated another young resident, Oliver Gilbert, a 2000 honors graduate of the University of Miami School of Law, with 57 percent of the vote. Braynon also served as Vice Mayor from 2005 to 2007.

In 2007, the state Representative for his district, Wilbert Holloway, was appointed to the Miami-Dade County School Board. In the special election that followed, Braynon ran for the vacant House seat. In the Democratic primary, he ran against Myra Taylor, an educator and former Mayor of Opa-Locka, and won with 62 percent of the vote. He went unopposed in the general election. In the next regular election later that year, he ran unopposed and won, and repeated the victory when he ran for reelection in 2010.

In his first House term, Braynon served on four committees: Administrative Procedures, Economic Development and Community Policy Affairs, Government Operations Appropriations, and Governmental Affairs Policy.

Before he finished the last House term, State Sen. Frederica Wilson resigned to run for Congressman Kendrick Meek's seat when he ran for the U.S. Senate. That opening in the Florida Senate required a special election, and Braynon ran for it. "I am the special election king," he quipped. In that election, he faced serious competition from three former state Representatives: James Bush (1992–2010), Phillip Brutus (2001–2007), and Darryl Reaves (1990–1992). Braynon won the primary by a slim margin of 42 percent, and managed a landslide (74 percent) victory in the general election against former North Miami Mayor Joe Celestin.

In 2012, after the state's redistricting moved the lines of his Senate district, he ran unopposed in the primary and general elections.

In 2014, as the incumbent, he ran for reelection against Haitian-born Anis Blemur, an accountant, realtor, and director of two private schools. At a candidate forum sponsored by the NAACP, some Haitian candidates accused African-American candidates of not representing the entire community. But Braynon outraised his opponent in financial contributions and was publicly endorsed by Haitian-American former North Miami Mayor Andre Pierre. Braynon won with 70 percent of the vote amidst sluggish voter turnout. In the general election, he easily won over a write-in candidate.

In campaigning and serving in office, Braynon never really encountered racism because "my district is the most African-American, black district in the state, and the most Democratic district in the state. So we didn't have the [black-white] racism," he said.

"What we did have was the cultural struggle between the Haitians and the African Americans—the immigrant population versus the native blacks in the community." That struggle was "sad" because "we all have the same problems. What happens in North Miami are the same problems that they have in Miami Gardens. I would say that, for us in Miami, when you deal with the majority population, which is mostly the Cuban population, it doesn't really make a difference between a Haitian and an African American. You're just a black person. Especially when you come to somewhere like Tallahassee, we're all the same, we are black people. Like I said, our problems are not different, so why would we be fighting each other?" he said. "When I've run against Haitian candidates, there are very few, if any, topics or issues that we separate on, that we'll say, 'Well, as an African-American candidate you feel this way, but all the Haitian-American candidates feel that way.' We are almost locked in step when it comes to issues."

The perceived tension between blacks and Haitians in elections may be resolved through assimilation. "I think that maybe minorities or even immigrant populations go through this where they feel that it's more about someone who looks like or is from the same background as I am, rather than someone who is more qualified or is a better candidate. It just comes down to 'Oh, I just need somebody there that looks like me.'" As Haitians engage with their non-Haitian elected officials, they will learn more about the political process and "at some point there will be someone that will transcend the vibe between Haitian and African American or Bahamian." People of Haitian descent who were born in Miami "have a much better understanding of the political process here, and I think once that starts to happen you'll see a different type of Haitian candidate."

Miami has a large Jamaican population as well, but that's an English-speaking group. "It really is much easier to campaign or much easier to speak to, much easier to deal with, when you speak the same language," he said.

Braynon has not always followed the traditional campaign path. "I've actually never done TV, and that's because I feel I can spend my money better in touching specific voters that I want to touch. And that's worked. It's worked a lot," he said.

One particular campaign focus has been absentee voting. "Turnout in our community is really not high," he said, "and you have to go and almost drag people out to vote. And one of the ways to do that is making sure they vote absentee or making sure they vote early. And the way you do that is very labor intensive. So I do a lot of door knocking. I do a lot of canvassing, also direct mail, things like that."

The 2014 campaign was a reelection effort, and in a reelection, "one of the things that you mainly do is talk about the things you've done. I thought it was really good. This was a great year for me to be able to talk about the things that I've done because I've done so much," he said "That's my way, my style of campaigning. I try to talk to people about what I have done and because I've been working for my community for so many years, the list is pretty long."

Even when he ran for City Council, he was able to talk about what he had done while working as the community liaison for the County Commissioner, such as adding a red light at a major intersection and adding speed bumps and sidewalks in places where they were needed. Consequently, instead of "making promises, I could talk more about what I have done. I've always been able to do that. I always thought that made my message a little different than a lot of the people I ran against. The thing was I always said I am experienced and I am always the youngest and I'm always running against someone older than me. But I think I always seem to have more experience than the people I'm running against."

"The reason I do absentee and all that is I'm driving the vote. People are only going to vote for me, so I have to make sure that they show up. I can't depend on them coming to vote for Barack Obama and 'Oh, we like Oscar too.' I have to make people get up out of their house and go vote specifically for me."

In addition to citing his experience in his most recent campaign, he followed five themes: (1) Foreclosure—"Keep families in their homes"; (2) Jobs—"Bring jobs to District 36 through the economic development of main corridors"; (3) Education—"Ensure that Miami-Dade County receives proper funding from the state for our public schools"; (4) Crime—"Encourage neighborhood Crime Watch programs so that we can take an active role in the safety of our community"; and (5) Government Employees—"Protect the pension and retirement of our government employees."

What he has enjoyed most about being in the Legislature "is being able to bring legitimate resources back to my community. I mean, to be able to see something or see a road paved and know that I did that, that's what I asked for, I worked it through committee. Being able to see changes in things has been the most enjoyable part of being in the Legislature."

Bringing about change became easier when he moved to the Senate. "When I ran for the House, Congressman Kendrick Meek, who was a mentor of mine, he always said, 'Look, man, what you really want to do is you want to go to the Senate because when you're in the minority, you have a voice in the Senate. When you're in the House, it is very hard to have a voice in the minority.' Once I got to the Senate, I understood exactly what he was saying. I've been able to do so many things that I would have never been able to do in the House."

For instance, in a Republican-controlled House, he had to be creative, such as proposing a transportation tax that gave Miami Gardens a percentage rather than a line item. "When I got to the Senate, I think last year we probably got about $10 million in actual line item appropriations" because he specifically asked for it. Of that, $5 million went for rebuilding a run-down gym at a local community college. "Miami Gardens has a little bit of a crime problem, and they're going to get a half million dollars for this ShotSpotter (technology) program that the city wanted that was going to help them find out who was shooting. Like all these things that you can actually make happen, even though I'm a Democrat in a Republican-controlled Senate."

What has been the most disappointing thing is the "tone of the government in Florida" emanating from a rigid philosophy. "I believe I'm pretty flexible with what I believe. I do believe, unlike my colleagues on the other side of the aisle, that there is a place for government in our society. I think there is such thing as social contract. I'm not a socialist, but I agree with the social contract. I believe that there is a place for government like building roads, picking up garbage, education. Even when we talk about it, they believe in a national defense and there's a reason they believe in a national defense."

"Again, there are some things that an individual cannot do. I don't think that we

Figure 3.72. Sen. Oscar Braynon II (*center*) presents the Miami-Dade College Board of Trustees with a $5 million check to repair and renovate the gymnasium at the school's north campus, where as a young man he played his first game of basketball and attended summer camp. The renovation will include the creation of a tactical training facility for the college's School of Justice. Trustees are *(L-R)*: Jose K. Fuentes, Bennie Navarro, Marili Cancio, (Sen. Braynon), College President Dr. Eduardo J. Padrón, Helen Aguirre Ferré, and Armando J. Olivera. Photograph taken at Miami-Dade College, February 5, 2015. http://www.sfltimes.com/news/local/sen-braynon-gets-boost-for-mdc-north-campus.

can build and maintain bridges on our own. I think the private sector only does it for profit and I think that we have to depend on government service workers. These people do it for service. They don't get paid millions of dollars. All they get is a pension and a retirement and at least the promise that they'll be able to survive and live and have a reasonable lifestyle. In my opinion that's been the backbone of America. That's what made the great society. It's because those people have had good middle-class jobs. That's what my parents did. My parents were government workers. My grandparents were wanting to be a teacher, a nurse, what most of the people that live in my district are. There's like an attack going on from the other side on those people as if they did something wrong. But they're people who are just making gobs of money in the private industry and cutting all kinds of corners and not, in my opinion, doing things with a moral compass."

In taking the oath of office in the Senate, Braynon reflected on his heritage as a fifth-generation transplant from the Bahamas, plus the Jamaican heritage of his mother's father. "I have such a long litany of family that are here in Florida and that have done so many great things in South Florida and to be so proud to be one of those, to continue the legacy." For example, a great-grand-uncle, Harold Braynon, Sr., was a civil rights lawyer and one of the first black judges in Florida. An aunt, Lenora Braynon-Smith, the first African-American Teacher of the Year, had an elementary school named after her. Cora Braynon, a Registered Nurse, served on the North Broward Hospital District Commission. "Thinking that I get to join the ranks of them as somebody that in my family people are going to look back and say, 'Oh you remember little Oscar. He was a Senator and that's somebody that we strive for.' That the little kids in my family are going to want to look up to, and they're going to have a standard that the Braynons are supposed to do great things. So I felt very proud to be one of those people in my family, that's what we're supposed to be like."

In the Senate, he serves on six committees: Ethics and Elections, Health Policy, Higher Education, Regulated Industries, Transportation, and the Joint Legislative Budget Commission. At the beginning of the 2013 session, he served as Vice Chair of the Regulated Industries Committee and as a member of the committees on Children, Families, and Elder Affairs; Ethics and Elections; Gaming; and Health Policy.

If a young African American wanted advice about running for office, "I would ask them why they want to run for office. I always tell people that I totally do it for the service aspect. I do it to make sure that my area is a better place. With that in mind, I don't think I would ever run for statewide office because I am very focused on my neighborhood, on my area, on my people, and that was my goal," he said.

"The next thing I would tell them is something that many people don't tell you about the political process: If you want to get your message out, you have to raise the money. I think traditionally African-American elected officials do not raise money and because they don't, we don't get to move up in the structure of our Legislature [much]. We don't get to control the conversation. We don't talk to the movers and shakers because we make no effort to try to fundraise, and you know you should fundraise; you should learn how to fundraise."

In January 2015, Braynon was selected to lead Democrats in the Florida Senate. His predecessor Sen. Arthenia Joyner said, "Sen. Braynon is fond of saying that the only way to make a difference in the lives of others is to be an active participant in the political process. His commitment to improving the lives of Floridians is unshakeable, and our state will have a true champion for the people under his leadership."

Oscar Braynon II was interviewed by telephone by the author Mar. 5, 2015.

Darren Soto (D)

First Puerto Rican man elected to the Florida Senate, 2012

Personal: Born February 25, 1978, Ringwood, New Jersey; moved to Florida in 2001.

Education:

- Rutgers University, B.A. in economics (2000)
- George Washington University Law School, J.D. (2004)

Occupation: Lawyer

Trailblazer Elections:

- Senate District 14 (Parts of Orange, Osceola, Polk counties) *Dem Primary* 2012
  - Darren Soto—*Unopposed*
- Senate District 14 (Parts of Orange, Osceola, Polk counties) *General Election* 2012
  - Darren Soto-D (70.0%), William McBride-R (30.0%)

Figure 3.73. State Sen. Darren Soto's most rewarding moment came in 2014 when the Senate passed a bill allowing certain undocumented immigrants to become licensed lawyers. The impetus for the legislation was Jose Godinez-Samperio, a 27-year-old man who had come to the United States with his parents at age nine, graduated from the Florida State University College of Law, then passed the Bar exam only to be told he could not practice law in the state because he was not a citizen. Photograph courtesy of Sen. Soto, n.d.

THE DARREN SOTO STORY

Without a doubt, the most rewarding part of Darren Soto's Senate career so far occurred in May 2014, when the chamber passed a bill allowing certain undocumented immigrants to become licensed lawyers.

The impetus for the bill was Jose Godinez-Samperio, a 27-year-old man who had come to the United States with his parents at age nine from Mexico, graduated from law school at Florida State University, and passed the Bar exam in 2011. A month before the Senate passed the bill, the Florida Supreme Court had ruled that he could not practice law in the state because he was not a citizen, and the Court called on the Legislature to remedy the "injustice."[87]

"The backdrop was that we were already that chamber that was being more hostile toward in-state tuition," Soto said, referring to another measure that would allow in-state tuition rates for undocumented students, commonly called DREAMers.[88] The House had passed the bill, but the Senate was dragging its feet.

Advocates for Samperio were looking for a way to help him get a law license. Former Florida State University President (1994–2003) Sandy D'Alemberte, who had argued Samperio's case before the Florida Supreme Court, asked for Soto's help. "I was honored to be able to work with this guy. He's a legal giant," said Soto. "I met with Jose a couple times, and I had an ally in Sen. John Thrasher [Republican, elected to Senate 2009] because he's very close with D'Alemberte and he's kind of a moderate on the immigration issues. As the Rules chair, that was a strong ally to have in the Senate."

Soto decided to attach the provision as an amendment to a family law bill he had introduced. "That morning I ended up trying to just float it on, you know—the shorter the explanation of the amendment, the better the chance," he said. On the Senate floor, he said, "Mr. President, this amendment would expand discretion and admit members to the Florida Bar." The President knew what was going on and asked if anyone had any objection. "Right before he's about to say it was approved, a staffer runs to Majority Leader Lizbeth Benacquisto [Republican, elected 2010] and tells her. I'm like, 'Uh oh, this is going to be tough.' She stands up and says, 'Senator, do you want to tell the membership what this really is about?' So, of course, I quickly mentioned this would allow the [Florida] Supreme Court discretion to admit undocumented law students. Then all these microphones started jumping up and everybody starts asking questions. We were about to break for lunch, and we get the first vote actually right after some questions, but there was some confusion. Even Thrasher had voted against my amendment because a lot of people didn't realize it was happening at that moment," Soto said. The bill lost by two votes.

D'Alemberte chided Thrasher: "You were supposed to vote with us." Thrasher then moved for reconsideration, and the chamber broke for lunch. "We come back, and a two-and-a-half-hour debate ensues. It just so happened to be Puerto Rico Day, and we had 100 constituents up in the audience at that moment for the entire debate, including the editor of *La Prensa* and several reporters from *El Sentinel* and others," he said. Sen. Thrasher, Sen. David Simmons [Republican elected 2010], and others argued in favor of the bill. "It was one of the best debates, if not the most historic debate, we had in the Senate this past year. And it really foreshadowed the in-state tuition debate and everybody knew it. Almost every member of the Senate stood up and debated that day, which almost never happens. Then it passed—when that morning it looked like I was crazy and there's no way it would happen."

"We even turned around State Rep. Greg Steube [Republican elected 2010], who wasn't initially happy because he voted against the in-state tuition bill and he didn't want this on his family law bill in the House. But after D'Alemberte talked to him and after he read the opinion of Florida Supreme Court Justice Jorge Labarga—and he is an attorney—and Thrasher and others, he even had to turn around and defend the amendment and voted for the bill and got it passed. Then the Governor, obviously in line with his turnaround on Hispanic issues, signed the bill [May 12]."[89] (Gov. Rick Scott would also sign the in-state tuition for undocumented students bill in June.[90])

One persuasive segment of debate testimony came when Republican Sen. David Simmons discussed the opinion of Justice Labarga, who had observed similarities between his own family's escape from Cuba and Samperio's flight from economic persecution in Mexico. "He asked the Legislature to act, and so we acted on it."

Soto, the first Puerto Rican state Senator in Florida, had lived in the state only a few years before passing legislation favorable to fellow Hispanics. He was born in Ringwood, N.J., to a Puerto Rican father and an Italian mother. After earning an economics degree at Rutgers University in 2000, he began working toward a law degree at George Washington University in Washington, D.C.

"My parents moved here in 2000. I was going to law school for that first year, and then in December 2001, I interned down here. Even though I never thought I'd get into politics, I knew I was going to work down here because I really liked it." He went back and finished law school and moved to Central Florida. "I took the Bar in 2004 and was getting sworn in to the Legislature in April of 2007, so it was a pretty quick thing."

In November 2004, right after U.S. Sen. John Kerry lost the race for President, Soto attended a Young Democrats meeting. "Even though I always voted, it never occurred to me that all of them were volunteers and all the work that goes into it because I was never an activist. But I joined the Young Democrats to meet people because I didn't know a lot of people down here." His theory, which he had learned as social chair and rush chair at the Alpha Chi Rho fraternity in college, was to attend an event every month. "I would call it the steamroller theory, where if you can get into people's routines, you can get them to join and do things."

At that first meeting of Young Democrats, only 25 members showed up, all discouraged because of Kerry's loss. At the second meeting, because he was "new blood," he got elected vice president of communications. "I came up with this idea for an event called a Speak Easy, where on the last Friday of each month, we'd have an elected official come in, speak for a maximum of five minutes, and it would be happy hour after that. We expanded our membership in four or five months from about 25 to 120 people." One of those speakers, Democratic State Rep. Scott Randolph (2006–2012), would become a significant figure in Soto's future political activity.

"I went from being this outsider who didn't know anybody to being the person who literally was in the core inside group that recruited all these young-minded progressive Democrats from Orange County," he said. The county already had a majority of Democrats, 1.2 million people. "That group made all sorts of connections. Even today, the group that started back then, they are legislators, they're elected officials, they're lobbyists, they're staff, they're all throughout Tallahassee and Washington, D.C." As examples, he named Christine Biron and Tracy Brooks, his legislative assistants; Natalie Kato, a lobbyist for the trial lawyers; Kenneth Pratt, a lobbyist for the bankers association; Mallory Wells, lobbyist for Equality Florida; and Joe Saunders, state Representative (elected 2012). "So a lot of people who met back then have gone on to do these amazing things."

That political activity "compensated for the fact that I wasn't from around here, that I was one of the founders of the modern movement of people who ended up getting all these people elected, including Scott Randolph [elected Orange County tax collector 2013], [Anthony P.] 'Tony' Sasso [elected to House 2008], myself, and others."

In their zeal to get Randolph elected to the Florida House in 2006, "a couple of us filed in other seats to make sure that the Republicans would have more races to spend on." Soto filed to run against incumbent Republican Andy Gardiner. "So my first race I actually lost, but I had no intention of winning. I didn't raise any money. I didn't walk for myself. I contributed money to Scott Randolph's campaign and walked for his campaign. But I did do interviews with the press and then managed a Kissimmee mayor's race right after that and got pretty close to winning for Democrat John Cortes[91] [later elected to the House in 2014]. And then four months later this special election happened because John Quiñones decided he wanted to run for County Commission."

At that point, Soto filed for real. In running, he stressed his Puerto Rican-Italian heritage, even though the district was predominately Puerto Rican. In doing so, he took a page from the election manual of Quiñones, a Republican Puerto Rican, who had defeated Democrat Jose Fernandez, a Nicaraguan, in 2002. "You have to be a student of history and of local politics in order to shape your own campaign, so we learned a few things from that."

In addition to highlighting his father's birth in Manatee County, he referred to himself as *coquí,* the name of a tree frog native to Puerto Rico, in his campaign literature. When Puerto Ricans want to express their nationality, he explained, they say, "*Soy de aquí como el coquí* [I'm as Puerto Rican as a coquí]"

"I'm also proud of being of Italian descent," he said, "and it was just part of my family's story. It would've been odd to just describe my father without describing my mother."

The hardest part of his campaign was "overcoming youth, but it was a double-edged sword," he said. "At first everybody kind of looks at you like, 'Uh, aren't you a little young? Shouldn't you wait a little bit?' I was 28, turning 29 during that election. But if you're on the level, then it becomes an advantage to you because people are like, 'Wow! If you're doing this now, what are you going to be doing five years from now?'"

"The metaphor is to create your own hurricane, to create this momentum. You have to, through the momentum of each of these moments, create this great push that by the end is unstoppable. It starts with all these days of walking doors, all these days of making phone calls and raising money, getting all these different endorsements. Momentum begets more momentum, begets more momentum. So the biggest obstacle is starting and getting up that first day you're running. It's making that first phone call and knocking on that first door."

In April 2007, he beat back other Democrats in the primary and narrowly won against Republican Tony Suarez in the general election. He was easily reelected in 2008 and 2010.

Near the end of his third House term, "I had heard early on that because of the huge demographic shifts, there would likely be a Hispanic congressional and Senate seat. I knew that probably better than most people because my House seat was so overpopulated." The area he represented originally consisted of cow pastures and orange groves, he said, but during the 1980s and 1990s, after big developments went up in southeast Orange County and north Osceola County, people began moving

Figure 3.74. From the beginning of his political career, Sen. Darren Soto maintained close ties to Puerto Rico. While in the House, he welcomed Puerto Rico Secretary of State Kenneth McClintock-Hernández (*left*) to the House chamber, then read a resolution honoring the 65th Infantry Regiment—the "Borinqueneers"—who served during World War II and the Korean War. State Archives of Florida, *Florida Memory*, https://www.floridamemory.com/items/show/254848. Photograph by Meredith Hill Geddings, April 22, 2009.

in, many of them New York retirees of Puerto Rican or Hispanic descent, as well native islanders who responded to marketing in La Plaza de la Americas, a big mall in Puerto Rico.

"I didn't know what the district was going to look like other than it would probably be in that area. So the race for the Senate really began at least vaguely the moment I walked into session during the redistricting year," he said. He decided to stay out of drawing the districts. "I didn't get involved at all because what I saw was people who tried to get their districts the way they wanted, they ended up having to sell out and promise all these favors. So I did nothing, asked nothing, and got everything. But I contemplated the seat, so obviously—I met with a lot of different folks during that session, everybody from party activists to other legislators to lobbyists to community groups, already foreshadowing that if there was a seat created, I would run for it."

When the districts were finally redrawn, he filed to run for the newly created District 14. In the Democratic primary, he ran uncontested. In the general election, he ran against Republican Will McBride and won.

He began campaigning after the Fourth of July weekend. "Even though my entire House district was in the Senate district, there was still between a third to half of the people who I had never represented before, so we had a lot of catching up to do in Poinciana and Haines City in the south part of the district. But in the north part, it was saying hello again for the fourth election to many friends. That helped out a lot."

His staff and volunteers canvassed 160,000 households. They bought commercials on Hispanic TV and Hispanic radio and sent mailers "but nowhere near what my opponent had," he said. "The district, most of my neighbors, they worked two to three jobs and they have a lot on their minds. They could have a big family, maybe financial problems, so we try to get them directly." With that in mind, "I led by example by walking every weekend and that's how I started and that's what I continue to do. But that was the big difference."

The first year in the Senate was tough because he had lots to learn about the budget process. "In the House if you're a Democrat, you don't get any budget, and if you do it's because some Republican Senator helped you out," he said. By contrast, "in the Senate everybody's in play. Now, I wouldn't get as much potentially into the budget as a Rules chair or the President would, but a savvy Democrat can get projects in the budget as can savvy Republicans," he said.

"Money talks. Money is like two-thirds of the power of the Legislature, and it's the thing that people care about the most. In my first year I had a lot to learn and I got a few things into the budget initially and stayed the first weekend of budget talks and watched over the projects, and then it went on to the budget chairs. I didn't stay around that next weekend, nor did a lot of my peers, especially the new guys, and I proceeded to come back to everything wiped out before the final budget." Other members who were around all weekend got in. "Keep in mind when I say 'my projects,' I mean projects that my local officials have given me to try to get."

"I never seek any project that it's just my idea. There'll be county staff preparing usually water projects or PECO [Public Education Capital Outlay] dollars for education institutions. So that first year I wasn't really able to get much into the budget, and then the Governor vetoed my primary bill, the DREAM Act driver's license bill. Now he took the biggest lumps of the last two years for doing that, so I was a hero in the Democratic Party, but I would rather have had my bill passed, than giving a black eye to the Governor. But we made up for it this year because I had a very good year in the budget. I got a million dollars in for a Poinciana campus of Valencia College that the Governor just approved, so we'll start a whole new Valencia campus in the district, as well as 1.5 million dollars' worth of water projects to help clean water going into the Kissimmee River, which eventually goes into the Everglades, as well as flooding issues in Kissimmee."

In his campaigns, he never encountered discrimination because of ethnicity or race. "We enjoy—even with some power fights here and there—pretty good relations in the district because the district is mostly Hispanic and Anglo with about 10 percent African American, and it's not very segregated between them." For example, "where I live in East Orlando, my neighbor on one side is of Cuban descent, and my neighbor on the other side is an Anglo family that's lived there for 20 years and works for the State Attorney's office. The guy in front of me, he's an Anglo and he's lived there forever, and then a Puerto Rican on this side and a Puerto Rican on that side. They all socialize. It's not unusual to hear, you know, 'Hey, Jose, you coming over for the barbecue?' '*Sí*, Señor John, I will be there.' You see that intermixing, even among families of different backgrounds. It's not as gentrified an area," he said. "It is truly a mix of Hispanic and Anglo with some African American there. I think that plays a lot into the fact that most people who chose to stay there who were the original Southern white residents were OK with it, or else they would have moved."

He was careful to point out that a single nationality can have subgroups. Among Puerto Ricans, for example, there are the *Puros*, who are from the island, and there are "New-Yorkians" or "New-Jerseyans," who were born in New York, New Jersey, Pennsylvania, Connecticut, or other Northern cities.

Furthermore, one cannot assume that those coming from the Northeast bring their staunch Democratic credentials with them, or that the *Puros* require more persuading to join a party. "Even though they have their political alliances at home, they come here with more of an open mind and have been, as a result, swing voters," Soto said. "The critical aspect is that for many years they don't view Central Florida as their home, whether they're from New York, New Jersey or Connecticut, or from Puerto Rico. That is, in my personal opinion, the real essence of why they were swing voters and are still to a certain extent.... They're more concerned about who is going to be Mayor of New York or Governor of Puerto Rico back home than they are about who's going to be their state Rep or state Senator."

"I can remember talking to a woman when I was walking door-to-door [for] my first election in the district, saying, 'I'm a lifelong Democrat. I'm born in New York and we're dyed-in-the-wool blue Democrats, but I voted for John Quiñones the past couple of years because, you know, he's a Puerto Rican like me and he came by and he asked for my vote and I really didn't feel that strongly either way, so I voted for him.' That, to me, was such a symbolic comment about how they would be very staunchly Democrat, but down here because they're not from around here, it's not as deep of a feeling that their guy has to be a Democrat or a Republican."

Puros, while aware of Democrats and Republicans, experience some confusion because "their whole political system is based upon status of the island, whether it's going to be a state, a commonwealth, or independent. And to further compound it is the fact that the PNP [Partido Nuevo Progresista—pro-statehood] are also known as the *Republicanos*, but they're not associated with the Republican Party at all. So because they want to be part of the republic, they'll come up here and say, 'Oh, I'm PNP. I'm from the People's New Progressive party, and so I must be Republican up here because I'm *Republicano* down there.' That caused confusion as well because of the fact that they shared similar names, even though they had nothing to do with each other."

"So you had a lot of these outside issues coming in, whether it'd be a lack of familiarity with the political system or the fact that the 'New-Yorkians' still felt at home up in New York and to a certain extent the *Puros* still felt at home in Puerto Rico, so they're more pliable because they were less staked in this community."

"While the African-American community has a long history, obviously, post-Lincoln era, of the Democrats helping them out with civil rights and things like that, and so there's that historical connection that the Puerto Ricans and the Spanish in general don't have, but this immigration issue is developing it. I think that's what the

President [Barack Obama] has taken advantage of—that they have seen over the past five years that immigration issue is their civil rights issue. So I think it is changing, but I don't think it's said and done that the Hispanic community's going to be Democrat in Central Florida, absolutely not."

Party affiliation aside, country of origin can play a part in state politics, he said, although he was proud that Cubans and Puerto Ricans, neither of whom have immigration problems, "led the charge to provide in-state tuition to undocumented students." Furthermore, "while I view the Puerto Rican thing as a matter of cultural pride, my platform is in a large part a pro-Hispanic platform regardless of country of origin. In fact, a lot of the platform has a lot more to do with Hispanics who are not from Puerto Rico."

A case in point: the western part of his Senate district, agricultural Haines City in particular, is heavily Mexican American, many of whom are second- and third-generation. "Those who aren't in my district in Polk County still look to me to lead," including those in Lake County and Apopka, where they don't have Hispanic representation.

Consequently, in 2013 he worked on a driver's license bill for DREAMers, which Gov. Rick Scott vetoed after near-unanimous passage by the Legislature. "That was a huge deal last year setting off protests across the state." That helped set the stage for the undocumented attorney and in-state tuition bills in 2014. When the in-state tuition bill came to the Senate Judiciary Committee, of which Soto is vice chair, he presided over the hearing because the chair, Republican Sen. Tom Lee (elected 2012) was otherwise occupied. Then Soto, along with Republican Senators Anitere Flores (elected 2010), René García (elected 2010), and Miguel Díaz de la Portilla (elected 2010), pushed to get a coalition big enough to pass the bills for DREAMers.

When Soto was honored recently for his work on the Judiciary Committee, "my speech focused on how we have cultural pride, but we have to lead the entire Hispanic community through our position. It was met with robust applause," he said. "The main point is while a lot of us as Puerto Ricans who have been elected have cultural pride in being Puerto Rican, we look out for the entire Hispanic community. That is a big part of our message," he said. "A lot of Puerto Ricans have the same issues as everybody else because they don't have that immigration problem, but they do have discrimination problems and heavy lack of health care and things like that."

If asked for advice on running for political office, "I would say if you want to run, run. The only times I ever asked people should I run or should I be a lawyer, I got bad advice that I shouldn't run. I never listened to it."

"But I'd also say it may be helpful for you to sit out one or two election cycles and volunteer for others. One of the biggest mistakes I see of candidates is that they didn't see anybody else do this before them, so they make mistakes that they would have known about if they had seen another candidate lose. They learn how to walk doors, they learn what it's like to make phone calls, they learn what it's like to be in a debate, to be interviewed by the press. If you sit there as a staffer or a campaign volunteer, you see your candidate rise and fall on the various occasions and can learn from them. Then when you're there, you can learn from the mistakes that they make."

In addition, he would ask: "Have you read the newspapers across the state for the past three to four years? Because you have to know stuff to run for office. To me, one of the biggest things I've always seen candidates fall on in addition to these mistakes of not having experience, is that they don't know anything. They don't have a platform, and they end up having to talk about themselves because they don't have any ideas." Because he constantly read newspapers from across the state every day for years, he knew the full history on issues going back at least the past five to eight years. "If you're going to run and you've never picked up a paper in your life or you've read only the sports section, you are going to be crushed by your editorial board, you're going to be crushed by voters who are educated and know what they're talking about, and you're going to lose before you ever win."

His newspaper reading habits helped him get the endorsement of the *Orlando Sentinel* for every election except the first pseudo campaign against Republican Andy Gardiner. "They said that I had a future in politics and to look out for me, and then four months later they wrote the future is now. But I've always met with my editorial board. I have lunch with them once or twice a year. I speak fluent *Sentinel*, which is that I know about what they're saying. Like any other, they want to know that I'm listening to them. I don't have to agree on everything but if I'm disagreeing I'd better know my stuff, and better be able to bring it back to the district of why I just disagree on that subject. You have to know the newspapers in particular, then the TV stations to a certain extent. You've got to know the history of how they feel on the issues and what their opinions are."

"It takes a lot of work. I must read at least 15 minutes to a half an hour, maybe more each day," he said. Consequently, when he gets asked about an issue, "I have an opinion and have background on it. They may disagree with me, but no one's going to say I don't know what I'm talking about. That's been probably the biggest source of confidence for me is that I'm prepared."

During his career, Soto had two kinds of mentors—legal and political. "You have to start with the legal because I didn't come here thinking I was ever going to run for politics, but those gentlemen shaped my ability to debate and to think on my feet." Those mentors include Luis Gonzalez, a cousin of an uncle by marriage, who was born in New Jersey but worked for 20 years in Puerto Rico as a lawyer. "He was very influential in teaching me about the culture of the island. He helped me get admitted to federal court in Puerto Rico down there and to meet certain contacts. I also had Lee Dura, who was sort of his law partner at the time, an old self-proclaimed 'Cracker.' So I got to learn the ways of the South as well. Both those aspects really gave me a balanced approach to dealing with two major cultures in the district," the Hispanic and the Southern.

On the political side, an early mentor in the House was Democratic State Rep. Ron Saunders (1986–1994 and 2006–2012). "He had just gotten elected to his second term in the House and he was a self-styled social moderate, fiscal conservative. He never voted straight on Democrat issues. And that was kind of my way," he said. As a freshman legislator, "I would sit in his office and seek his counsel a lot."

Democratic Sen. Dave Aronberg (2002–2010) "was pretty influential as far as learning how to be—how can I say—bigger than life as a Democrat in getting some things done." In the Hispanic Caucus, Soto found several strong mentors, "who now I can mention but it was kind of quiet back then because they were mostly Republicans." They included Sen. Alex Díaz de la Portilla, who served in the House (1994–2000) and then the Senate (2000–2010), where he was Majority Leader. With his help, House Speaker Marco Rubio (R) appointed Soto to the PSC (Public Service Commission) nominating board. "He was a big influence in really honing my political shrewdness," which lay, for example, in discerning the wants of the party's base and knowing how to wedge an issue by picking the 50–60 percent who are on your side. He worked with Soto on bills dealing with veterans and helped him develop relationships with other Senators who helped him pass bills, like Republican Senators Carey Baker (2004–2010) and Lee Constantine (2000–2010).

Another mentor, René Garcia, a state Representative (2000–2008) who was elected a Senator in 2010, was a moderate Republican whom everybody liked. "I'd say out of anybody in the Senate, he and I are probably the closest alike, just on opposite sides of the center."

Finally, the late [Eliott] "Rico" Piccard, a Puerto Rican and long-time human rights activist in Orlando, was a mentor on "street politics." A Vietnam veteran and former social worker, Piccard was remembered for his cry for equal justice: *¡Arriba los de abajo!* (Lift up the downtrodden!)[92]

Darren Soto was interviewed in person by the author June 3, 2014.

Leadership—Speaker of House; President of Senate

FLORIDA LEGISLATURE

Figure 3.75. President Pro Tempore of the Senate Louis de la Parte (*right*) stands with House Speaker Terrell Sessums (*left*) as Gov. Reubin Askew signs a bill. When de la Parte became Senate President, it meant that the leaders of both houses were Democrats from Tampa. State Archives of Florida, *Florida Memory*, https://www.floridamemory.com/items/show/19278. Photograph by United Press International, December 1, 1972.

Marco Rubio (R)

First Hispanic man chosen Speaker of the Florida House of Representatives, 2006
Personal: Born May 28, 1971, Miami, Florida; married with four children.
Education:

- University of Florida, B.S. (1993)
- University of Miami, J.D. (1996)

Occupation: Attorney/Professor
Trailblazer Elections:

- House of Representatives Speaker, 2006–2008
    - *Unanimous vote of colleagues November 21, 2006*

Figure 3.76. Marco Rubio, R-Miami, challenges his House colleagues to begin adding to the blank pages of a book titled *100 Innovative Ideas for Florida's Future* that he presented to each member upon being selected by Republican colleagues to be the first Hispanic Speaker-designate. He then collected ideas from people across the state and created a blueprint for issues to tackle. The project turned out to be his most rewarding experience as Speaker. State Archives of Florida, *Florida Memory*, https://www.floridamemory.com/items/show/135178. Photograph by Mark T. Foley, September 13, 2005.

THE MARCO RUBIO STORY

Marco Rubio, the first Hispanic Speaker of the Florida House of Representatives, chose to run for that position because at the time that's where he thought he would be most effective.

"When I got to the Legislature, it took me about three days to figure out that in the House, the real decision-making happened on the third floor, in the Speaker's office," he said. "Even more so than the Senate President, the Speaker of the House has control over the agenda in the House and the ability to move forward. So my thinking was, if that is the most effective legislative post in the House, and I want to be as effective as possible in serving the state, and I think if I have a serious opportunity to do it, I should consider it."

The opportunity came in his fourth term. He received support from colleagues, primarily Stan Mayfield from Vero Beach and Rafael Arza from Hialeah, both Republicans who entered the House with him in 2000.

The previous Speaker, Republican Allan Bense from Panama City, had served in the post from 2004 to 2006, having defeated Gaston Cantens from Miami. "When Gaston didn't succeed, I think there was this idea that Dade County hasn't had a

Speaker, there's never been a Cuban-American Speaker, Gaston almost did it, and you might be uniquely positioned to do it now," Rubio said. "Of course that's a unique office to run for because the voters are your colleagues."

At Speaker selection time, several House members usually announce they're running. "Once a couple of people drop out and it narrows down to two people, they usually wrap up pretty quickly," Rubio said. In the fall of 2006, after Republican Rep. Dennis Ross (elected 2000) dropped out, "many of his supporters had me as their second choice and they came on board, which at that point triggered an avalanche. All the other members were thinking, 'We'd better sign up with a guy who's going to win.' That led to me getting elected two years ahead of time."

Taking the oath as Speaker, "I really felt like in a small way it was important for the Cuban exile community," he said. In his acceptance speech, he acknowledged the many Cubans who had fled to the United States a half century ago, some of whom achieved great success and others who didn't. "They were happy and they were grateful to be here. They made extraordinary sacrifices for their children and their grandchildren," he said. "I remember the speech became a really big deal in Miami. I mean, it was even broadcast live by Radio Martí[93] into Cuba."

Rubio's parents came to Florida in 1956 to seek a better life. His father worked as a hotel bartender, and his mother as a maid and clerk in Miami,[94] where Rubio was born. When he was eight years old, the family moved to Las Vegas to get away from the cocaine and crime that plagued the city at the time. The family moved back in 1985, and he attended West Miami Middle School. "I spoke like a kid from Nevada," he said, and "a lot of my friends didn't even realize that I was of Cuban descent." It was something of a shock because his family had always spoken Spanish at home and celebrated holidays as Cubans did. Once he got to South Miami High School, which was more racially and ethnically mixed, he was able to assimilate better.

He first got involved in politics when he interned for U.S. Rep. Ileana Ros-Lehtinen in her congressional office in 1991. "She had been elected in '89 to replace Claude Pepper. So in 1991 I was a college student and I basically just called up her office and said, 'Do you guys do internships?' At that time they didn't have a formal internship program, but I just started going over and helping out and I literally did what our interns do now. I mean, I was responding to constituent letters, answering phones, making copies, doing all of that," he said. Actually, "I think Ileana runs one of the best constituent service programs in the country, so I think a lot of that has stuck with me in terms of my expectations for our own office [as U.S. Senator]."

The next year he worked in his first campaign. "I was a college student and I volunteered in a local congressional race for Lincoln Diaz-Balart. I knew I had some interest in politics. I didn't have a master plan or anything, but I thought I'd just dabble on the edges of it and eventually maybe one day figure out if I wanted a career in politics, but not yet."

Four years later, in 1996, "I ended up volunteering in U.S. Sen. Bob Dole's presidential campaign[95] and then enjoyed it so much, they actually hired me to run Dade and Monroe County for his presidential campaign."

That same year he finished law school at the University of Miami and joined the firm of Tew Cardenas, under the tutelage of lobbyist Al Cardenas (who served two terms as chair of the Republican Party of Florida during the Jeb Bush years). Living in the municipality of West Miami, he seized an opportunity to run for the City Commission in 1998. Two years into his four-year term, he seized another opportunity to run in a special election for the Legislature. "I liked public service, I liked what I was doing on the City Commission, and with term limits kicking in, I knew . . . that I would have to wait another eight years to run for a vacant seat [if I didn't run then]." He ran for a seat vacated by Carlos L. Valdes (R-Miami, elected 1988). After a close primary, Rubio easily won the general election. He was only 28.

"I always felt like the legislative process wasn't responsive to the daily lives of people, so most of the issues that came across the table in the Legislature happened for one or two reasons. Either a lobbyist group created the issues—we had a lot of industry food fights—or something broke in the press, some major crisis and then you scrambled to address it. I felt we needed to be more proactive."

Consequently, "once I'd won the pledges for Speaker, I decided let's go out and let's collect ideas from people from all over the state. Let's ask them: 'What would you do if you were in the Florida Legislature?' From that, we gathered thousands of ideas, but we culled it down to about 100, which were published in a book, *100 Innovative Ideas for Florida's Future*." The project turned out to be his most rewarding experience as Speaker.

It was "the opportunity to go out and talk to people and identify what exactly was on their minds, craft an agenda that responded to that, to be in a position as Speaker to make that our agenda, and to actually execute it, to make things happen. And so, of our 100 ideas, over 50 of them became policy or law in our state. I mean, they passed the House, passed the Senate, and the Governor signed them. Many of them are only coming to fruition now."

One example was the Miami Children's Initiative, based on "a trip I took to New York to see the Harlem Children's Zone, where they're basically taking kids in a geographic area who are at high risk of economic and educational failure and intervening in their lives to make sure that that doesn't happen. While there's been some struggles in getting that off the ground here in Miami and now in Jacksonville and Orlando, they've actually identified geographic areas where that's happening."

More than half of the 100 ideas were related to education, including vocational education and expanding vocational opportunities so that a high school diploma leads to employable skills.[96]

Another idea was the Healthy Choices Program, basically a health care exchange without mandates and subsidies. "We didn't call it an 'exchange,' we called it a 'health care marketplace,' where individuals could go online and shop for health insurance that met their particular needs at a price they could afford," he said. "Unfortunately, Gov. Charlie Crist (R) didn't fund it after I left and that kind of slowed it up, so that only now has it gotten off the ground."

"Again, that was part of the *100 Ideas*. So that was rewarding, to be able to put a lot of them in play."

By contrast, one of the most disappointing experiences was not getting enough done on property tax reform. A hot real estate market had raised property taxes for many, while others were protected with a constitutional cap. He wanted to eliminate property taxes on primary homes and offset those revenue losses with a 2.5 cent increase in sales taxes.[97] "We were forced from a pragmatic perspective to accept half a loaf, in my opinion, maybe a quarter loaf."

His last decision as Speaker was also disheartening. Halfway through session he came face-to-face with what autism meant to a family. "We have a personal friend who was struggling to get services for their child. So we started studying all the different programs that are out there that help children with special needs, whether it's a McKay scholarship[98] or Medicaid dollars, or what have you. We decided that not only do we need to expand it to include autism services, but we needed to somehow consolidate them [with other special needs including Down Syndrome] so that we provided a one-stop shop for all of these services and really make it most effective," he said.

At the time, Democratic Sen. Steven Geller (elected 1988) "had his own proposal, which was much more limited. It was basically just an insurance mandate that certain insurance companies had to include autism coverage. We actually accepted that but went much further. But the Senate played a game where they passed it as their last bill and sent it over to us as a take-it-or-leave-it proposition. You either pass it or nothing happens at all. So the decision I had to make is: Do we help 1,000 kids or do we blow the whole thing up because it doesn't help 10,000 kids. That was a tough decision because I felt passionately about it and all of our members did as well." He worked with Democratic Rep. Loranne Ausley and Republican Rep. Andy Gardiner (House members 2000–2008), and ultimately decided to support it. "That's one that still strikes me as a missed opportunity. But it's better than not having done anything at all."

After his fourth term and speakership ended in 2008, he briefly thought about running for Miami-Dade County Mayor, but decided against it. "I had really made the decision to come back home and become a private citizen at least for a while. I always held open the option of running for something in the future, but I thought I'd spend a couple years out of office." He began teaching at Florida International

Figure 3.77. Marco Rubio gives the victory sign to the House chamber after his closing remarks as House Speaker, May 2, 2008. Lt. Gov. Jeff Kottkamp and Gov. Charlie Crist (*right*) applaud. State Archives of Florida, *Florida Memory*, https://www.floridamemory.com/items/show/135225. Photograph by Mark T. Foley, May 2, 2008.

University, opened a small law practice on his own, and worked as a political commentator for Channel 23, the Univision affiliate in Miami.

In late 2008, Mel Martinez decided not to run for reelection to the U.S. Senate,[99] prompting Marco to consider the U.S. Senate race. At the time "I really felt strongly the country was heading in the wrong direction. Primarily the stimulus[100] that had just passed—I thought it was really the wrong approach," he said. "I looked around the field and when Jeb [Bush] decided not to run for the U.S. Senate, I felt there's no one else running that stands for what I stand for, and I should consider doing that. Then we started working on it for a few months and got some momentum. Gov. Crist then decided to run, which was unexpected at the time." Rubio decided to move forward, "thinking that at the minimum I would force him to be more conservative, and perhaps I could even win depending on whether our campaign could catch fire, which it did." As Rubio's numbers went up, Crist decided to run without party affiliation, to no avail. In November 2010, Rubio easily won the general election, trouncing Crist and Democrat U.S. Rep. Kendrick Meek (2003–2011).

"To think that just two years earlier I literally had no chance—I mean, it was such an improbable victory. Everything that I knew about politics up to that point told me that I couldn't win, and a lot of people reached that same conclusion," he said. "It happened so quickly that to me it was more of an affirmation that if you believe in something strongly and you're willing to go out there and advocate for it, you have a chance to actually make something happen, especially in a country like this."

At the same time, "I understood the magnitude of the issues and the challenges that we face as a nation," he said. "What worries me the most is not that America's going to collapse or crumble. I don't believe that. But I do worry that we have some extraordinary opportunities before us that we're not taking advantage of and that we're going to look back at it with regret if we don't. I think the 21st century has the real opportunity to be much better than the 20th century was."

Having been involved in politics for more than two decades, he has seen changes in Miami's status on the world stage and in the area's population.

"Miami has really grown up over the last 20 years to become a real international city. I mean, it now is beginning to establish all the institutions that great cities have—cultural institutions of world-class importance." At one time, Miami sprawled westward, "but now you're starting to see a lot of the development is happening vertically." As many as 20,000 people live in downtown Miami, which means they can go downstairs and just walk to work, he said.

Migration to Miami from Cuba has changed over the past 50 years. The first wave of people who came around 1960 "were professionally and politically established in Cuba that fled when a new government took over. The second wave were people that just didn't want to live under communism," he said. The Mariel boatlift[101] in 1980 was a unique situation in which Castro allowed 125,000 Cubans to board boats bound for Florida. "Now it's just a steady trickle of 20,000 to 30,000 people that come a year who have grown up their entire lives under that system, but now want to live in the United States for a better life and more opportunities, and in some instances to flee the repressive nature of that society," he said. Cuba itself is different after 50 years, he noted.

Apart from Cuba, people have come from Nicaragua, Venezuela, and other Latin American countries. "It's a much more Pan-American Hispanic community in South Florida than it was just 20 or 25 years ago." People have also come from Haiti and other countries in the West Indies. "Many African-American families in South Florida track their lineage back to the Bahamas, the Bahamian immigrants that came at the turn of last century."

"On top of that, you continue to have people that live here on a part-time basis. I mean, everywhere I go, it's amazing to me how many people I run into. I always joke if they're over 40, they have a place in Palm Beach, and if they're under 40, they have a place in South Beach." People from the Northeast come to Florida "for the weather for sure, but also because we have no state income tax, and that's also provided a level of diversity."

"In the Hispanic community, country-of-origin politics still matter," he said. "When you drive around now, you're going to see a lot of cars that have 'S.O.S. Venezuela'[102] written on them. Or flags. I mean, what's happening in Venezuela has importance." He cited an example: "On Election Day they had old-fashioned poll workers outside handing out punch cards asking people to vote for them on the way into the Consulate in the Venezuelan elections. Venezuela closed the Miami Consulate so that Miami Venezuelans couldn't vote. They had huge caravans leaving from here for Doral, which is kind of the center of Venezuelan Miami. They were getting into huge chartered Greyhound busses and driving to New Orleans to go vote over there in the last couple of elections." Venezuelans are also getting involved in politics here.

"I mean, the first Venezuelan-American politician in the country I think, was elected Mayor of Doral [Luigi Boria in 2012], so you're beginning to see that as well."

Another example is Colombia. "Just a couple of weeks ago we were in Coral Gables on a Sunday and there was a huge line outside the Consulate because there was an election in Colombia and people were going to vote. In fact, one of the congressional seats in Colombia is for a Colombian Congressman that lives abroad representing Colombians living abroad. The largest vote for that district happens in Miami. So Colombian congressional candidates campaign in Miami for votes here," he said.

Unfortunately, Latin and South America have been neglected at the national level: "That's a trend that's just continued to get worse," he said. "Obviously, some of it is because of the situations we've had with Afghanistan and Iraq and now of course with Iran. Then we've got real challenges in the Asia-Pacific region. Interestingly enough, Europe felt that way. I was in London in December and their feeling was the U.S. has kind of forgotten about the trans-Atlantic partnership, paying attention to Asia and to the Middle East. So, I think negligence has consequences and I certainly think the U.S. from a diplomatic policy perspective is much less engaged in the Western Hemisphere than it should be. I think eventually that will trigger some crisis or conflict that will force us to refocus on it, but I hope we can avoid that by focusing on it now."

"That's why I've been so involved and engaged on the issue of Venezuela because I think it's actually part of a broader trend toward growing totalitarianism in the region. A growing number of governments are headed away from democracy now in the way they govern their people. You see that already in Ecuador and Bolivia, increasingly in Argentina, certainly already in Venezuela, for a long time in Cuba. But now there are questions about El Salvador and what direction they're going to take. Nicaragua is already there in some respects. So it's a real troubling trend."

Events that occur in other countries can be directly affected by what U.S. leaders, particularly the President, say and do, he said. "If you take a bad vote or you're wrong on a policy item as a U.S. Senator or as a Congressman or as a Speaker of the House, it has significance. But for a President that has not just executive functions but the power to send the young men and women to war, as one example, or who has to make very difficult decisions on foreign policy or matters of intelligence gathering and so forth, it has life and death consequences that are immediate in some cases."

The presidency "is literally the most important political office in the world," he said, and "no one is ever fully prepared for the office because there's no comparison to it. But I think the most important job that the President has in the current era is the ability to convince the country that this is what the future can be like, and here's how we can get there, and then provide the leadership that guides our republic in that direction. In order to achieve things in a republic, you've got to work with and achieve outcomes working with people that have strong disagreements with you on a bunch of issues."

"That's gotten harder to do in the modern era for multiple different reasons, not the least of which is the polarization of our politics, but also the way politics is now covered, almost like a sporting event, 'Who won and who lost?' And since politics is largely covered by political reporters. They're much more interested in the political aspects of a story than of its policy implications. I think that's seeped into how we make policy now, and as a result I think some important things haven't happened."

Political reporting and campaign communications have changed because of technological advances. Compared to 20 years ago, "it's easier to communicate with people, and it's also easier for people to communicate against you," he said. Furthermore, more people are watching and covering campaigns. "Some of them don't have editorial restrictions. If a newspaper reporter misquotes you in an interview, you have someone you can appeal to. But if a blogger misquotes you, there's no one for you to appeal to. I'm not saying blogging is illegitimate. On the contrary, I think it's been a very positive perspective. Just know that you are now in a process and unfortunately some people may disagree with me, but I think it's even harder for someone who is running from the right versus someone from the left, that every word you say could potentially be spun by your opponents into what you didn't intend to say. There's very little room for error with regard to that, and you have to recognize that when you get into it. The coverage is a lot more intense. The attention span that people have for the news cycle is much shorter than it used to be. There are literally stories that will dominate the headlines for a week and then just completely drop off the radar screen the next week."

In addition, "There's a premium placed on conflict because of the competitive nature of mass media today. I think the media is under increased pressure to deliver conflict and scandal and outrage because that's what drives clicks on a website or viewers to a television station. As a result, just know that if you're going to put out a 10-point plan to solve the world's problems, it's the right thing to do, but it may not get a lot of attention. But if you're going to stand up on the floor of the Florida House and accuse someone of being a whatever, then you're probably going to get a lot of attention. But long term, that's probably not the way you should behave. That's the nature of politics today. It's probably tougher than it's ever been because of that, and it's a lot more personal than it once was."

Rubio's political words and behavior have been shaped by at least four mentors. After Ros-Lehtinen, for whom he interned as a college student, Mayor Rebeca Sosa helped him get elected to the West Miami City Commission. "When I got into the state Legislature, [Speaker] Allan Bense (R) was very helpful to me, especially the two years before I became Speaker," Rubio said. "I really learned a lot by just watching him operate and the things he did." Jeb Bush was a big influence, especially in his last couple of years as Governor: "I really admired his governing model, which was you identify big issues and you come up with big solutions, and then you use the power and position that you have to advocate for those things and to bring people along."

If he were advising a young person going into politics, "First, I would say people have to decide why they want to be involved in politics. If you simply want to be involved in politics because you want to be somebody because you like the acclaim that comes with it or the power that comes with it or the standing that comes with it, that's not a good enough reason to do it. In fact, it's the wrong reason to do it, and you'll end up regretting it. In politics, you can be up one day and down the next and up again, and especially given the nature of our politics today, you're never going to make everybody happy. It's increasingly impossible to do that. If you want to just become popular and have people love you, go into charity. That's a valid way of serving people."

On the other hand, if you really want to make a difference, elected office is "one way that you can do that. It's not the only way." Other options are getting appointed to office, working for a government agency, and running campaigns.

A second bit of advice: "When you get into government service, recognize you are walking away from economic opportunities. You are walking away from time that you could spend on leisure or family. There are consequences to that."

Nonetheless, "It's also very rewarding to be in a position to wake up in the morning and read about something that upsets you, and then have the opportunity to actually go out and do something about it or be part of finding a solution for it. If that's what motivates you to get into public service, then I think you should pursue it."

He added, "You shouldn't do it your whole life. I think it's important to have a perspective from having done something apart from government. That's why I'm glad the Florida Legislature is part time. You still have to make a living, and it requires you to still live like everyone else does. And that's why I'm grateful for the couple years I had out of office as well because it gave me a perspective."

In 2016, Marco Rubio ran unsuccessfully for the Republican nomination for President of the United States. In announcing the suspension of his candidacy shortly after suffering defeat in the Florida Presidential Preference Primary (March 15, 2016), Rubio told his supporters, "I know firsthand that ours is a special nation—because where you come from here doesn't decide where you get to go. That's how a 44-year-old son of a bartender and a maid . . . that's how I decided that in fact I, too, [could] run for President."

Marco Rubio was interviewed in person by the author Mar. 20, 2014.

Louis de la Parte, Jr. (D)

First Spanish man elected to the Senate, 1966
First Hispanic President Pro Tempore of the Senate, 1972
First Spanish man to serve as President of the Senate, 1974
Personal: Born July 27, 1929, Ybor City (Tampa), Florida. Died September 28, 2008, Tampa, Florida.
Education:
- Emory University, B.A. (1950)
- University of Florida, LL.B. (1953)
- University of Florida, J.D. (1967)

Occupation: U.S. Air Force (1953–1956), Lawyer
Trailblazer Elections:
- Senate District 22 (Hillsborough County) *Dem Primary* 1966
    - Louis de la Parte (67.4%), R. M. (Dick) Ayers (20.3%), Jack Flynn (12.3%)
- Senate, District 22 (Hillsborough County) *General Election* 1966
    - Louis de la Parte—*Unopposed*
- Senate President, 1974

Figure 3.78. Sen. Louis de la Parte (*left*) stands with Senate President Verle Pope, one of the state's most prominent legislators. Little did de la Parte know that he would one day wield the gavel as Senate President. After the swearing-in ceremony on July 1, 1974, de la Parte, age 44, reflected on the accomplishment: "After 12 years in the Legislature, eight years in the Senate, to be able to achieve this is the highest goal of any Senator." State Archives of Florida, *Florida Memory*, https://www.floridamemory.com/items/show/29757. Photograph taken April 4, 1967—the opening day of the regular session.

THE LOUIS DE LA PARTE STORY

As President of the Senate in 1974, Louis de la Parte enjoyed a unique vantage point in Hispanic politics in Florida. Bridging an older generation with a younger, more diverse generation, he saw dramatic changes in the state's population and government.

His view of generational differences included a knowledge of local history dating back to the 1890s, when Tampa was a small, predominately commercial fishing town of a few thousand people. "A guy named Martinez-Ybor,[103] who was a New York/Key West cigar manufacturer, came to Tampa and wanted to put his factory there. They were having trouble in Cuba with cigar factories and there was this strike in Key

West. He bargained for and bought acreage that was in the eastern part of this county [Hillsborough]," de la Parte said. In addition to establishing a factory, he built houses and other accommodations for his workers. Other cigar manufacturers followed.

"In the early 1900s, maybe 50 percent of everybody in Tampa worked in the cigar factories," he continued. "There was a mass migration between 1890 and 1920 of Spaniards, Cubans, and Sicilians to work in these factories." All came seeking better economic opportunity; the Cubans were also fleeing Spanish colonialism.[104]

"They formed their own clubs, the Centro Español, Centro Asturiano, Circulo Cubano, and they had their own hospitals. In Tampa, for example, we had these HMOs [Health Maintenance Organizations] before Kaiser.[105] I was talking to Mr. Kaiser once, and I said, 'We were doing this a long time ago. We had our own hospitals.' I paid $98 a year and I have hospital privileges for as long as I want to. I could stay here forever. It's a hospital approved by the National Hospital Association, it isn't just a little rinky-dink clinic."

"The Italians became very assimilated with the Spanish and the Cubans," he said. "The owners were Spanish, the workers Cuban, and so most Italians speak Spanish in my community." One man who personified this combination of ethnicities was Dick Greco, twice Mayor of Tampa, who was first elected to the office in 1964. "Dick is trilingual," de la Parte said. Greco's father was Italian in heritage, and "his grandmother on his mother's side was Spanish."

Of his own heritage, de la Parte said his father's parents came to the United States from Spain. "They were very poor," he said. "They had lived in Asturias, which is the northern part of Spain. It's mountain country, tough for farming. No opportunities. I mean, I was there 15 years ago and they still don't have plumbing in their farm." His mother's parents came from Cuba. "Grandfather was a maintenance man, a janitor in the schools, and very poor. My grandmother used to work in a cigar factory," he said.

For both families, the incentive was the same: "When they got here, there wasn't anything but just an opportunity to work. And they had nothing. They struggled through a generation of getting on their feet and always remembering that the key was their children going to college, getting an education. A lot of them just didn't make it. They just stayed in very low, depressed economic circumstances."

The Great Depression of the 1930s didn't help. "When I grew up, FDR's picture was in our homes, and we loved him." De la Parte grew up in Ybor City and graduated from Jesuit High School in Tampa. He fulfilled his family's dream of higher education by earning a bachelor's degree from Emory University in Atlanta and two law degrees from the University of Florida.

As he was getting established as a young lawyer in the late 1950s, Cubans began fleeing Castro's revolution. They consisted of both poor laborers and affluent professionals. "There must be 3,000 Cuban doctors in Florida, almost 1,500, maybe 1,800 that are practicing and licensed in Florida, which is an unbelievable number," he said.

"The same goes for lawyers, veterinarians, nurses, you name it. They were professionals, and they were businessmen and they had money."

The older generation, having assimilated, looked at the recent immigrants and wondered, "Why is it that they get monies? Why do they get public assistance? We don't, and we still have problems." Having heard that sentiment from some older residents, de la Parte said: "It's really a horrible thing. I don't know how widespread it is. It exists." And that resentment "is a political force now [1974]," he said.

Many Cubans registered as Republicans, first because of the disastrous Bay of Pigs invasion in 1961, and second "because of the enormous efforts of President Nixon to make them feel a part of what he was doing, and the fact that he stood for a strong attitude toward isolating Castro. I think as those issues fade, that it's more likely that they will go to the Democratic Party."

He clarified that opinion by distinguishing between the two parties along economic lines. "When you get rid of the strong influences of Bay of Pigs and the President, I think it will shake out in the same manner in which most Americans make their choice between being a Democrat or Republican, which has to do with, in my judgment, economics—your own protection of the status quo."

"To the extent that they experienced firsthand the loss of a country to an ideological force that was contrary to ownership of property and that sort of thing, to that extent, they're going to remain conservative because that's something you can pass on to the children. I think in terms of the racial, religious types of things that they'll probably be more tolerant anyway on those issues."

Assimilation into American culture would have a huge influence, he believed. For one thing, fewer younger Cubans would feel the need to recapture the island. "As you get the younger Cubans, they don't want to go to Cuba. There's no way in this wide world," he said. "And their daddies aren't either. So they're not going to leave their sons and their daughters and their grandchildren here."

In addition, members of the younger generation would want to make their own mark as professionals and public servants. "In Miami they're unhappy because they're not getting enough representation in their own metro government at this time," he said. As an example of a potential public servant, he cited a young community college professor who was studying for the Bar exam and writing for *Diario las Americas* in Miami, the largest Spanish-language newspaper in the United States. With time, more Cubans would be appointed to local and state government boards, de la Parte said. Gov. Reubin Askew was "conscious of that and he wants to do that, and he needs to do that. But I think they will become a very interesting force. I don't know what will pull them together."

Furthermore, "I expect that we'll see Cubans permeate all of the facets of state government, and certainly be a very dominant political influence in Dade County," he said. "Four years from now they'll be very important. They are already important.

Dave Kennedy [Miami Mayor 1970–1973] told me once that there were 30,000 to 40,000 registered Latin Americans in Miami, so that's a pretty healthy number of people. In any election, that is equivalent to maybe the size of the 10 or 15 smallest counties combined."

With that large constituency, he predicted more Cubans would seek election to public office. "You're seeing candidates. You're going to see them in Hialeah, which is very heavy in Cuban. I would be very surprised if we don't have a state Representative or a state Senator from the southern part of Dade, because it's a very conservative area and there's a lot of Cubans there. I think Dade's liberal hue is going to begin to go through a change because they're very conservative." (His prediction would prove correct beginning in 1982 with the election of Republicans Ileana Ros, Roberto Casas, and Humberto Cortina to the state House.)

A factor influencing a shift to the Democratic Party, he thought, was the Watergate scandal.[106] "But you have to remember they had a lot of their people involved in Watergate, and, if anything, Watergate might polarize defense of their guy. But sooner or later, they're beginning to realize more and more that these guys were duped."

Youth itself was an important factor. He believed a greater number of younger Cubans would register as Democrats: "You know, you're more liberal when you're young."

Older voters identified with him when he entered politics in the 1960s. While in Miami as a state Representative, testing the waters for a Senate run, "I received instant acceptance. There was no question in my mind that I would have carried those areas heavily. The ability to speak fluently their language—language is an unbelievably binding thing. Their discovery that there was somebody in government in a position of some influence who did the same things that they did—they grew up drinking Cuban coffee and reading the *Bohemia*, which is the Spanish magazine in Cuba, and listening to Cuban radio. I was aware that José Martí[107] was the great liberator in Cuba. That community of feelings with the guy who had black beans and rice was very binding."

Aside from changes in political attitudes, state government was changing as well. "We were so poorly apportioned in '65, and for so long, we just had been dominated by the influence of legislators from rural Florida. They, together with those interests from the rest of Florida, liked to have things stable, understandable and predictable. When you reapportion, it was a really unbelievable thing. All of a sudden some of us found ourselves meeting in phone booths representing the majority of the people."

He ran his first political race in 1962 for a seat in the Florida House. "I had a very heated, very tough race," he said. "I had a very heavy vote in my district in the Latin precincts, and I had a very heavy vote in the black precincts. In my runoff, I carried my precinct front and back, by unbelievable margins."

"Of course, there was good reason for that, too. I mean, my family had been in

Figure 3.79. Sen. de la Parte had served in the House before being elected to the Senate in 1966. He described his time in the Legislature as the transitioning of Florida away from a rural-dominated Legislature. "It became an active body. We knew that we had to reform government and make it responsive to people and to the growth of this state." Senators at oath-taking ceremony administered by a justice on the Senate floor. Senators *(L-R)*: Henry B. Sayler, Louis de la Parte, Jr., T. Ruett Ott, Ray C. Knopke, David H. McClain. November 12, 1968. State Archives of Florida, *Florida Memory*, https://www.floridamemory.com/items/show/43376.

Tampa since the 1890s and I've got an unbelievably large family and they're all there." His father, for example, was a popular businessman. "I did very well in areas where people with Spanish and Italian names predominated, I'm sure. And to the extent that that happened, I won. I was not endorsed by the local papers, so they didn't hurt me."

In 1964, he ran for reelection against no opposition. In 1966, as the Legislature struggled to reapportion seats that would satisfy the U.S. Supreme Court, he ran for the Senate. "I was elected, and the courts threw that out. Then I picked up two or three guys and I won in the first primary. Then they threw that out. Then I picked up one guy and I won." As he explained, "I ran three times for the Senate in the course of several months, but that is reapportionment fights." He won with nominal opposition and little money and was reelected for three more terms.

When he entered the Senate in 1966, his class included Lawton Chiles, who would eventually serve as U.S. Senator (1971–1989) and Governor, Wilbur Boyd (state Senator 1966–1972), Dick Stone (state Senator 1966–1970), and Bob Shevin (state Senator 1966–1970). "The old man, Verle Pope [state Senator 1948–1972], became Senate President in 1966 followed by Jack Mathews [1969–1970], Jerry Thomas [1971–1972], and Mallory Horne [1973–1974]."

It was an "unbelievable turnover" in both the House and Senate. "Not only did those of us that had been in the House leave, and leave vacancies under us, but other seats had opened up for new people to move in. All the frustrations that had been pent up in the House during those years, realizing the tremendous needs that the state had and growth—it was very easy then for it to come out in the form of governmental reorganization, constitutional revision, judicial reform and the Sunshine Law."

With changes in its composition, the Legislature "became a very active body," he said. "We knew that we had to reform government and make it responsive to people and to the growth of this state. We talked about reform at length," he said, referring to Chiles, Mallory, and Matthews in the Senate and Terrell Sessums (1963–1974) and Dick Pettigrew (1963–1972) in the House.

De la Parte's own accomplishments included helping to create the Department of Health and Rehabilitative Services, improving educational programs in prisons, extending homestead exemptions to working families, and enacting environmental water legislation.

"We still have a long ways to go," he said. He urged a greater emphasis on out-of-session activity, better control of calendars on the first day of the Senate session, a filing cut-off for bills, computerization of all bills, more openness on the amendment process, professional rather than political staffs, directing fiscal policies by state priorities, and performance audits.

He argued against 12-month legislative sessions. Why? "Because the nature of man would not want to do a damn thing until we have to," he said. "If we had 12 months, we wouldn't put it on the calendar until November. And in the meantime, we'd screw around and we'd have time for whatever the hell happens to be a current national thing." By contrast, a 60-day session pressures legislators to act.

He suggested restructuring the process in this way: "Come up here a month before and do nothing but committee work and getting those bills on the calendar. Then spend a week before the session on the Rules Committee because that's the fallacy now of the whole process. The Rules Committee has got to do a fair and objective job in placing bills on the calendar in accordance with the state priority and considerations and not each taking care of his own pork barrel."

After the first day of the session, no bills would be introduced, he continued. Only those bills that are in the hopper the first day of session would be considered that session, except by two-thirds vote. "Then you can begin to put in priority the bills that have statewide application and necessity." With committee work done 30 days in advance, the net effect would be a 90-day session.

He gave an example: "When I was chair of Ways and Means, I had the appropriations bill out three months before the session, so the appropriations bill would be on every Senator's desk on May 3rd. And for two years on May 3rd, or whatever day I said, that bill was on every Senator's desk," he said. "It was on his desk and we passed it that day." He concluded: "That tells you it can be done. You set a target and you say this is where you're going to go, Senators, and everybody knows it. No public hearings were held after the first of the session. And when the session started, that was the end. There were no public hearings on the appropriations bill. Then it was the Senators working on the bill, on a timetable."

"The legislatures around the country have just atrophied," he observed. In the budgetary process in California, the legislators "get in a fight with Reagan [Governor 1967–1975] and they don't even pass the budget in terms of the fiscal year and get snarled up in all kinds of terrible fiscal problems, when you know that they could if they had to," he said. "The Congress is the worst, it was absurd. The Congress of the United States is the most antiquated, inadequate, pompous organization, I guess, in this country. They are completely incapable of dealing with the problems of this country. I think that had it not been so damn incompetent, some of the messes that we're in wouldn't occur. They couldn't balance a budget if they had to."

He attributed government reforms in Florida largely to reapportionment but also in some measure to legislators who were studying law at the University of Florida in the 1950s and 1960s. "The heads of both houses were University of Florida graduates, and I would suspect that a profile of each house would reflect on an awful lot of members of the University," he said. He did not consider himself part of that elite group, even though he earned law degrees from the same university, served on the law review staff, was student body president, and was president of the John Marshall Bar Association.

"I think my desire for public service was stirred up there, but my interest was stimulated more when I came up here in 1953 as a special assistant attorney general," working for Attorney General Dick Ervin (1949–1964), who would later serve on the Florida Supreme Court. "That was the first time I'd ever been in Tallahassee. I'd never seen the Legislature before then. I'd just graduated from law school. Then I went into the service [U.S. Air Force] for three years, then I came home and prosecuted. But I knew I would come back."

"I don't know that any of these thoughts were a part of my life when I was in school, and I think they came about after I was elected. The friendships that I had made in school made it easier for me to trust and know and like colleagues," he said. They included Pettigrew, Horne, Mallory and Askew. "Actually, our closeness began to occur in the Senate, not even in the House."

"I catch myself now watching Senators or reform ideas that were liberal and reformed six years ago, and they ain't liberal reforms anymore," he said. "Those that were obvious somebody came up with and, hell, they were pretty good for the time, but times have changed. Other efforts, even liberal thinking or reform thinking has got to be updated and you've got to have fresh ideas."

Reflecting on his time in the Legislature, he said, "I think the legislators of Florida enjoy a fair reputation with the public generally. I think we have been relatively scandal free. During the Kirk [Governor 1967–1971] administration, this Legislature took a very active role in directing state government."

"The press generally has been good," he continued. "The *Miami Herald*, they don't even know that state government exists, except when they want to kick it in the ass. But most of the others—the *Florida Times-Union*, the *Tampa Tribune*, the

St. Petersburg Times—they are all quite active in terms of reporting the Legislature." In particular, "the *Tribune* supported and fought like hell for the $12,000 pay raise. They're alert. They know what's going on. The Capitol Press Corps is good and they keep us on our toes. It takes that. It takes a combination of the public wanting it and people who are desirous of doing that." He singled out two reporters as "very knowledgeable people": Bill Mansfield, bureau chief for the *Miami Herald*, and Hank Drane, the *Florida Times-Union*. "These men know more than most legislators about what the heck the story is."

As one example of the press's tenacity, he described a time when legislators planned to go into executive session to consider a matter, possibly a confirmation or an expulsion. "The press got the idea, 'Hey, they're going in there to talk about strategy,' which really wasn't true. They staged a sit-in in the gallery, and we had to get the Sergeant-at-Arms to kick them out. We saw men up there we knew and liked. Really, it was a terrible trauma because of that. They were wrong in what they were doing, and yet they were your friends. That was the last session we ever closed. We have never conducted, since I've been in the Senate, a hearing on the confirmation or expulsion of a public official."

"We have kicked out state attorneys, county solicitors, local sheriffs, you name it, always out there in the open," he continued. "And in that regard, we built up a body of law that's unbelievable." He cited a law review article by Fred Karl (state Representative 1956–1964, state Senator 1968–1971) on due process for a public official under consideration for an expulsion by the House and the Senate. "By and large, to sit there in the open, it's just an unbelievably good thing. I wouldn't want to serve in a legislature that wasn't open."

"People tend to minimize the intelligence of the voters," he said. "But they know. They understand when you're posturing. They understand your BS-ing. I mean, they'll take a blunt comment on the floor of that Senate about something. They understand. And you can say what you want to say. Hell, they're just like you, they'll accept it, if you're saying it and actually doing it." Legislators feel the pressure "to follow the merit and the logic and the argument and the cause because then it's going to be recorded."

SENATE PRESIDENT

In July 1974, de la Parte, who had been Senate President Pro Tempore for two years, was sworn in as Senate President. Having already announced that he would not run for reelection in the fall, he served as a transition between Mallory Horne, who had resigned to run for the Democratic nomination for the U.S. Senate, and Dempsey Barron, who had been designated by the majority to become the next President in November.

As it turned out, de la Parte never presided over a Senate session. But he served in the role and his portrait hangs in the Senate chamber.

The swearing-in ceremony took place in the President's office, with Supreme Court Justice Richard Ervin officiating. De la Parte took the oath on a white Bible given to him by Senate Secretary Joe Brown and Sergeant-at-Arms John Melton.

"After 12 years in the Legislature, eight years in the Senate, to be able to achieve this is the highest goal of any Senator," he said after the swearing-in.[108]

It was a warm family event, recalled Catherine Real, his staff director at the time. His children were young and hadn't seen him for several days. "They came running at him. Hugs. He was so warm and so caring. His children just adored him."[109]

Real remembered that the *Tampa Tribune*, which historically had not been kind to Hispanics, had consistently supported de la Parte. "My impression was that they thought, first of all, he represented his people and the Anglos, yes, but he wanted a fair shake for his people, Hispanics." As an example, she remembered a judge running for office who asked for the Senator's support. De la Parte agreed only if the judge would "be fair to my people." "Now if that doesn't show his dedication to his cultural heritage, nothing does," Real said.

As another example, she remembered when Health Maintenance Organizations (HMOs) were looking for health care alternatives. "One of the things he wanted to do was to grandfather in the existing health care programs they have in Ybor City (such as the Centro Español). He saw that they were grandfathered in," she said. Who else would have been willing to treat poor Hispanics and "have them jump through hoops to get certified when they had been doing it for a century?" Their continued existence made sense not only for Hispanics but also the general public.

Not only was he sensitive to different cultural groups in the community but also he was an effective politician. "He knew how to legislate. He knew what somebody wanted and how he could help them do it in return," Real said. He knew how to make compromises, knowing that a future session provided an opportunity to improve a less-than-perfect bill. At the same time, however, "I never saw him give up a principle. I never saw him take a position that would hurt the Hispanic community."

Moreover, he made sure his office responded to constituents. "The greatest thing that I can say about him, if you really want to know his character, look at what that office did for the people that called in. He cared. He was adamant to get briefed regarding the calls. He would see what happened," Real said. He always had a bilingual staffer "to make sure they got the right message with what the problem is. Some problems can't be resolved. But if they can be resolved honorably, he did it."

Coming to the end of his term, de la Parte had definite opinions on key issues of the day.

On the subject of minority political organizations, he said: "Let me just make this point clear: I think any group that attempts to polarize that group and then use that group for elections, is creating a real disservice to that group. I don't think any group can benefit if it sets itself apart and is in competition with the majority. No minority group ever beat a majority. Ain't no way. I have a feeling a lot of those are created at election time by presidential candidates." Such organizations, he said, "are very loosely held. It doesn't mean anything."

"As a matter of fact, the Cubans' problem is they've got so many organizations." Lots of organizations means lots of leaders, which results in fragmentation and disorder. "Now there seems to be a merging, an easier consensus of who the guys are, and that is being measured by activity in the community. You're beginning to see who is serving on which committees."

On the subject of a political coalition of Latin Americans and blacks, he saw an economic conflict. "At this point it's not a natural coalition. They don't have anything in common. It would be a coalition of convenience if there were. The blacks, I gathered, were being sort of resentful of the fact that the Cubans had moved in and taken a lot of their jobs—all the bellhops in the hotels and all the waiters in restaurants."

In his campaigns, the Spanish, Italian, and Cuban Americans served as a de facto coalition. "They were all economically depressed and they knew that collectively they could have a chance to beat the establishment. So in most instances you would find a Spanish-Italian-Cuban candidate faring well with black precincts. But I don't know that that alliance exists in Miami right now."

His main regret on leaving public office: "I know that I'm going to miss it terribly, because I love it. It excites me like nothing else that I could do. I'm as stimulated now in thinking of all the things that I still wanted to do and that I like to do."

"But I can't stand the political hassle anymore. It's become too expensive. Financially, I've just got to get out. I can't afford this anymore. It just takes too much of my time and I have my family commitments. I have a standard of living that I want to continue."

He felt troubled about the election system and the way that candidates raise money. Public financing of campaigns could be a solution but it was not without its problems. "If our democracy is worth anything, if the ability to have men who can make personal and objective and fair decisions as it relates to our lives and our children's lives, it may be hard, but it's that important. We ought to be willing to pay the price to get that because that is more important than money. The problem comes in avoiding a proliferation of candidates who will be running for reasons other than the desire for public service." They may be running to promote their insurance company or automobile dealership, or other business. "Until a man can come to office without having to amass a huge sum of money by asking people who have an interest in his actions, who have expressed or implied it's there, and they're the only ones that give money. And nobody's going to give big money who doesn't have an interest. How many brothers and sisters, uncles and aunts and close friends do you have that are going to contribute because they love you?"

He also deplored the practice of getting editorial endorsements by first finding out an editor's views and catering to that. Until all those things change or are somehow subdued in importance, candidates will come to public office unable to judge issues except by aligning with their donors and friends. "Now maybe that's the democratic process and maybe that's the guts of what we're talking about, I don't know. But at least remove the money part of that. Because if you've got to raise a million dollars to run for House or state Senate, where do you get it?"

When people complained to him about campaign funds from big companies, he would ask, "What did you give?" Typically, "they didn't give anything. They probably didn't even put a bumper sticker on the car," he said. "Damn right the insurance companies give and the banks give. After all, the only thing they're promoting and what makes it right is because we are for free enterprise. Making money is good. And all they want is for you not to pass any law that keeps them from making money or to pass a law that helps them make more money."

He expressed no interest in a higher office: "I want to be a civilian in the worst way," he said. "I don't want to have to worry about anything but just my family and the things that I want to do and I want to say—what I want to say when I want to say it and to heck with 'em. I'm seeking to be liberated. I can't do that as long as I'm making this money from these offices. And they don't pay anything. You know I make more money now than a Supreme Court Justice or a Cabinet officer, and I'm working part-time. I work four months out of the year in my law firm."

He was proud that he kept his law practice separate from public office. "I have no clients that have any interests in the legislative process. I have never appeared before a state agency. As a matter of personal self-discipline, I have never appeared before any County Commissioners, or city council or state agency. I've never represented anybody that had anything to do with government because I didn't want it to be a political practice and I just thought that it wasn't the thing to do in public office anyway."

"The accolades are great," he said. He felt fortunate to be voted into office without opposition. He enjoyed good rapport with newspapers. In fact, the Capital Press Corps had nominated him Most Valuable Senator each of the past seven years, and elected him for the honor three times. He and his colleagues treated each other with mutual respect: "I love them, it's just a beautiful thing."

But public office also comes with scorn. "People don't realize what these men in public office go through," he said. "When we got our $12,000 raise, one newspaper in this state had a picture of a pig wallowing in money and that was supposed to be us. Hell, I think I have more overhead than that in my office."

At the same time, the demands on public officials continued to increase. "Now we're talking about financial disclosure and filing this and filing the other. Presumptions almost, that you're going to do bad things and so you have got to be on public display. I think that's bad," he said, because it adds another layer of aggravation to public service.

"The campaign finance law that we passed last session is just replete with felony counts for this or the other. You have to be very careful and worry about something that you ordinarily wouldn't have to worry about," he said. "If your personal affairs are all screwed up because you're over here too busy doing other things, and some people don't get that. Hell, you take a chance that you file something inadvertently wrong or forget to file it and then you will become a criminal."

"What you're doing is you're catching the bad guys maybe, because I don't think Agnew[110] brought on the disclosure law. It's going to pass. I think the people expect it. I think if you don't do it, it's going to look like you've got something to hide or we're impervious to their desires. But I don't see that as correcting the process."

"People need to understand that this is not just a game we play," he said. "People talk about it as a 'game.' Well, it ain't no game with me. I've got to tell you that it's the most important thing in my life. Elections are the most important, the decisions I made are the most important. It isn't just a matter of just jumping in so you can get a name so you can get business. It's a matter of very fundamental issues."

"The men that I have worked with and have known in my public life in Tallahassee, believe me, are better men than the men and women that I have met outside of public life," he said. "You won't find, even in the professions, the higher-caliber men day in and day out making tough decisions oftentimes well knowing it can defeat them." He had special praise for Panhandle Democratic Sen. Dempsey Barron, credited with helping break up the "Pork Chop Gang" of powerful rural Senators who brought government projects to their counties. "This guy had more courage than any 10 people," de la Parte said. "His sheriff tried to beat him every year he was up. It took a tremendous amount of courage."

"Really, people get better government than they deserve." He guessed that only 60 percent of eligible voters turn out to vote, "or they don't register because they don't want jury duty. Then after they register, they don't vote because the weather's bad. Where do they get off complaining? They never give a damn about what's happening except when it affects them personally. They vote for people on the basis of looks and what the image maker says or whether they can raise money to be on TV." He realized that his comment was unfair to regular voters. "There are many responsible, committed, dedicated people, but by and large the answers to the problems we have today don't rest in Tallahassee or Washington. They rest at home."

Louis de la Parte was interviewed May 21, 1974, as part of the Samuel Proctor Oral History Program on behalf of the University of Florida. The author interviewed attorney Catherine Real, de la Parte's Staff Director on Mar. 5, 2015, about his time as President of the Senate.

4

Trailblazers

State Executive Offices—Governor, Lieutenant Governor, and Cabinet

There have been few minority candidates for statewide executive offices, and their success rate in holding on to those positions has not been good. To date, Hispanics have been more successful at winning the top offices (Governor, Lieutenant Governor[1]) than African Americans, who have garnered more Cabinet posts through gubernatorial appointments. Just a note: under the Constitutions of 1865 and 1868, Florida had an elected Lieutenant Governor who served as the presiding officer of the Senate. But the position was eliminated with the adoption of the 1885 Constitution. It was reestablished in 1969 as a result of the 1968 constitutional revision approved by Florida voters.[2]

Figure 4.1. Crowd attending the inauguration of Gov. Bob Martinez. State Archives of Florida, *Florida Memory*, https://www.floridamemory.com/items/show/95225. Photograph taken January 6, 1987.

Florida Minority Trailblazers—State Executive Offices: 1960s–2010s (Dates Served)

Time frame	Governor	Male Lieutenant Governor	Female Lieutenant Governor	Male Cabinet Member	Female Cabinet Member
1960s					
1970s					1971–1973 M. Athalie Range—D Secretary, Dept. of Community Affairs Bahamas—Miami Appointed by Gov. Askew—D
				1978–1979 Jesse J. McCrary, Jr.—D Secretary of State African American—Miami Appointed by Gov. Askew—D Filled vacancy	
1980s	1987–1991 Robert "Bob" Martinez—R Governor Spain—Tampa				
1990s				1993–1995 Douglas L. "Tim" Jamerson—D Commissioner of Education African American—St. Petersburg Appointed by Gov. Chiles—D Defeated running for full term	
2000s					
2010s			2011–2013 Jennifer S. Carroll—R Lt. Governor Trinidad—Jacksonville Elected statewide Scott-Carroll Ticket Resigned March 12, 2013		
		2014–Present Carlos López-Cantera—R Lt. Governor Spain (Born); Cuba—Miami Appointed by Gov. Scott—R Filled vacancy			

Note: Consult Appendixes B and C for a full listing of minority officeholders in Florida.

The new Constitution strengthened the hands of the chief executive by allowing the Governor to serve two consecutive terms, consolidating the number of executive departments, and granting budgetary responsibilities to the chief executive. At the same time, it formally recognized the Cabinet as a constitutional body and granted certain Cabinet officers authority over the consolidated executive agencies.[3]

Governor and Lieutenant Governor

Florida's first minority Governor was Hispanic Bob Martinez, former Mayor of Tampa, elected in 1986 as a Republican. He had previously been a Democrat[4] but became a Republican at the personal urging of President Ronald Reagan, who invited him to the White House to discuss the possibility of a party switch. Martinez was defeated by Democrat Lawton Chiles in his bid for reelection but later was appointed the nation's "Drug Czar" by President George Herbert Walker Bush (R). He remains an important fundraiser and policy analyst for Republican presidential and gubernatorial candidates.

Daryl L. Jones, a state Senator from South Florida, was the first African American to run for Governor. He finished third in the 2002 Democratic gubernatorial primary behind Janet Reno and Bill McBride (the nominee). In 2006, Democratic gubernatorial candidate Jim Davis selected Jones as his running mate. Had the Davis-Jones ticket won, Jones would have been the state's first black to be elected statewide to a nonjudicial post. But that honor went to Republican Jennifer Carroll, a former state legislator from Jacksonville, who was elected Lieutenant Governor in 2010 as the running mate of Gov. Rick Scott (R). Carroll was not, however, the first black woman to be on a gubernatorial ticket. That was Mary Singleton, a former Democratic House

Figure 4.2. Mary Singleton was the first black woman selected to be on a gubernatorial ticket. The former Democratic House member from Jacksonville was selected by Republican Gov. Claude Kirk as his running mate in 1978. The ticket performed abysmally, however, placing fifth out of six tickets in the primary. http://jacksonville.com/news/columnists/2010-11-15/story/look-back-another-woman-almost-beat-carroll-florida-milestone. By permission of the *Florida Times-Union.*

Figure 4.3. Annette Taddeo, the first Hispanic Democrat selected as a Lieutenant Governor candidate, celebrates with gubernatorial candidate Charlie Crist as they win the Democratic primary for the Florida Governor's race in 2014. They lost to the Republican Rick Scott and Carlos López-Cantera by 1 percent, the closest gubernatorial race in Florida history. Photograph by Brian Blanco, courtesy of the Florida Democratic Party.

member from Jacksonville, who was Republican Claude Kirk's running mate in 1978.[5] (The Kirk-Singleton ticket received only 6 percent of the vote and placed fifth out of six tickets in the Republican primary.)

When Lt. Gov. Carroll resigned at the request of Gov. Scott over a contract her firm held with a fraudulent veterans group (she was never charged),[6] the Governor appointed the state's first Hispanic Lieutenant Governor (Jan. 14, 2014, took office Feb. 3) to replace her—Republican Carlos López-Cantera, a Cuban former state legislator from Miami.

The first Hispanic Democrat, Colombian Annette Taddeo, was gubernatorial candidate Charlie Crist's running mate in 2014. The Democratic pair lost to the Scott-López-Cantera ticket in November 2014 by 1 percent—the closest gubernatorial race in Florida history. These choices signified that the days of an all-white gubernatorial ticket were once and for all, gone.

Figure 4.4. Former State Sen. Daryl Jones (*right*) was the running mate of Democratic gubernatorial nominee Jim Davis in 2006. Four years earlier, Jones was the first black to run for Governor; he came in third in the Democratic Primary, behind Bill McBride and Janet Reno. Photograph by Pat Carter, © 2006 Associated Press.

Cabinet

African Americans have been more successful than Hispanics at securing Cabinet positions, primarily through gubernatorial appointments. The state's first black Cabinet member, Jonathan C. Gibbs, was appointed Secretary of State, then Superintendent of Public Instruction, during Reconstruction. (The Superintendent position was later renamed Commissioner of Education in 1968 under Florida's newly revised Constitution.) Reflective of the period in which Gibbs served, both of his appointments came from Republican Governors.

Fast forward to the 1970s. Democrat Gov. Reubin Askew was greatly responsible for expanding the role of African Americans in both the executive and judicial branches during his tenure. He appointed Miami activist and City Council member M. Athalie Range as Secretary of the Department of Community Affairs to the "Little Cabinet" in 1971. She made history as the first African American to head any state department[7] and became the highest paid woman ($22,500 annually), as well as the top member of her race in state government.[8]

Historically, the "Little Cabinet" was an informal but influential group of advisors that initially included the Chairman of the Industrial Commission, Chairman of the State Road Department, Motor Vehicle Commissioner, Hotel Commissioner, Conservation Supervisor, and Beverage Director.[9] These were full-time gubernatorial appointees whose terms expired with that of the Governor. Over the years, other positions were added—Chairman of the Turnpike Authority, Chairman of the Development Commission, Chairman of the Racing Commission, and the Governor's own Executive Assistant.[10] Gov. Askew added the Secretary of the Department of

Figure 4.5. Jonathan Gibbs was Florida's first minority Cabinet member. Gibbs served as Secretary of State, then Superintendent of Public Instruction during Reconstruction. http://www.blackpast.org/aah/gibbs-jonathan-1827-1874.

Community Affairs to his "Little Cabinet."[11] With passage of the constitutional revision of 1968 and the restructuring of the formal Cabinet (six posts elected statewide), the once-powerful "Little Cabinet" gradually faded away.

Askew also appointed African American Jesse J. McCrary, Jr., a Democrat from Miami, as Secretary of State in 1978 to fill the unexpired term of Bruce Smathers, who resigned to run for Governor. With the appointment, McCrary became the first black in the Cabinet since Reconstruction. Prior to his appointment, McCrary had served for many years as Assistant Attorney General (the first black to do so), and represented Florida at the U.S. Supreme Court—the first black lawyer to speak there for a Southern state. His task: asking the Court to uphold a state law permitting defendants in non-capital criminal cases to be tried by juries of 6 rather than 12. The case was *Williams v. Florida*, and he won.[12] Gov. Askew, in reflecting on the swearing-in ceremonies for McCrary (and Supreme Court Justice Joseph Hatchett), recalled that "I was thinking about their mamas. How they must have felt seeing history breaking."[13]

In 1993, Gov. Lawton Chiles (D-Lakeland) appointed African American Douglas L. "Tim" Jamerson, Jr., former state House member from St. Petersburg, to a full-fledged elective Cabinet post—Commissioner of Education, after the resignation of Democrat Betty Castor (Tampa) to become President of the University of South Florida. "A standing-room only crowd of about 300 family members, friends, elected officials, and educators packed the media center at Cobb Middle School [in Tallahassee] as Jamerson, 46, was sworn in as Education Commissioner."[14] Jamerson had served many years on education reform committees in the House. But Jamerson lost his 1994 electoral bid for the Commissioner of Education post to Republican Frank Brogan (who would later successfully run for Lieutenant Governor as Jeb Bush's running mate). After Jamerson's loss in November 1994, Gov. Chiles appointed him Secretary of the state's Department of Labor. Jamerson's legacy and passion for education live on in the Douglas L. Jamerson, Jr., Elementary School and the newly named Douglas L. Jamerson Midtown Center Campus of St. Petersburg College, both in Pinellas County.[15] Personal friend and former State Sen. Al Lawson (D-Tallahassee), in speaking of Jamerson's lasting impact on education said, "It's not how many years we live, it's what we accomplish in the years we have."[16]

In 2014, Thaddeus Hamilton, an African American, ran for another Cabinet post—Commissioner of Agriculture and Consumer Services. Although he won the Democratic nomination, the Florida Democratic Party gave him little support—financially or publicity-wise in his race against incumbent Adam Putnam—a popular Republican Commissioner. Hamilton had sought the same position in 2010—but as a No Party Affiliation (NPA) candidate.

In 2014, Perry E. Thurston, a former state House member of Bahamian descent, lost the Democratic primary for Attorney General to George Sheldon, former Secretary of the Florida Department of Children and Families. However, Thurston did receive editorial endorsements from two newspapers—the *Orlando Sentinel* and the *Sun Sentinel*.

No Hispanic or Asian has held any Cabinet posts.

Executive Trailblazers Hail from Populous Areas

Overall, most state executive office trailblazers—African-American and Hispanic—have come from the populous Miami and Tampa areas. With the exception of Republican Gov. Bob Martinez, Lt. Gov. Carroll, and Lt. Gov. López-Cantera, the trailblazers have secured their executive positions through gubernatorial appointments. Of the two who sought reelection (Gov. Martinez-R and Education Commissioner Jamerson-D), neither was successful.

Given the opportunity for gubernatorial appointments and a more consolidated executive branch, one might ask: Did minorities want executive office enough to run on their own? Did the prospect of running seem to be too ambitious? Or were executive positions simply less desirable than legislative ones? Five African Americans—Daryl Jones, Doug Jamerson, Perry Thurston, Jennifer Carroll, and Thaddeus Hamilton—clearly wanted an executive office and chose to take the risk of running.

Governor and Lieutenant Governor

Robert "Bob" Martinez (R) (formerly D)

First Hispanic man elected Mayor of Tampa, 1978

First Hispanic man elected Governor of Florida, 1986

First Catholic Governor of Florida, 1986

Personal: Born December 25, 1934 in Tampa, Florida; married with two children and two grandchildren.

Education:

- University of Tampa, bachelor's degree in social science (1957)
- University of Illinois, master's degree in labor and industrial relations (1964)

Occupation: Business labor consultant and economics instructor at the University of Tampa

Figure 4.6. Republican Gov. Bob Martinez signs into law a bill establishing a state holiday in honor of slain civil rights leader Dr. Martin Luther King. Applauding the document's signing are *(L-R)* House Speaker Pro Tempore James Burke (D-Miami), Rep. Willie Logan, Jr. (D-Opa-Locka), and Sen. Carrie Meek (D-Miami). State Archives of Florida, *Florida Memory*, https://www.floridamemory.com/items/show/103247. Photograph by Donn Dughi (Donald Gregory), May 31, 1988.

Trailblazer Elections:

- Mayor of Tampa 1979–1986
- Florida Governor, *Rep Primary* 1986
  - Bob Martinez/Bobby Brantley (43.8%), Lou Frey, Jr./Marilyn Evans-Jones (24.7%), Tom Gallagher/Betty Easley (23.5%), Chester Clem/Tom Bush (8.0%)
- Florida Governor, *Rep Runoff* 1986
  - Bob Martinez/Bobby Brantley (66.3%), Lou Frey, Jr./Marilyn Evans-Jones (33.7%)
- Florida Governor, *General Election* 1986
  - Bob Martinez/Bobby Brantley-R (54.6%), Steve Pajcic/Frank Mann-D (45.4%)

THE ROBERT "BOB" MARTINEZ STORY

Bob Martinez, Florida's first Hispanic Governor, blazed a trail to the state's highest executive office through a local position—Mayor of Tampa. His eight years as mayor of a large city prepared him in many ways for the governorship of the state. But the step up was neither short nor simple.

His grandparents had immigrated to the Tampa area from Asturias, a province in northern Spain, in the early 1900s. They came to work in the cigar factories but mostly worked as dairy farmers and restaurateurs. Martinez grew up in a rural area known to his grandparents as *Los Cien*, named for the 100 Spaniards that first lived there.[17] His grandparents and parents told him stories about their early life in West Tampa, a tightly knit community where Spanish was spoken in business and in the schools.

The family had land enough for a garden, a few cows, and chickens. Because both of his blue-collar parents worked, he was cared for largely by his mother's parents who lived with them. As a schoolboy living close to Drew Army Airfield, "I constantly saw the weapons of war flying over the house and the soldiers marching all through the neighborhood as part of their required marches."[18]

Cultural influences were strong. He grew up speaking Spanish because that was the language spoken at home. His family belonged to a mutual aid society, Centro Español, which provided cultural facilities, medical care, and burial benefits for a small monthly fee. The society held fundraising events, such as a dance on Sunday evenings in Ybor City for all the Latin teenagers.

"*Latin* was a collective term for Spanish, Cuban, and Italian in Tampa. I'm not sure it carries elsewhere," he said. "I never had heard the word *Hispanic* in my life. It never was used in our community."

He attended Thomas Jefferson High School—fed by students from two junior high schools located in two different areas described collectively as the "Latin quarter." Streetcars were the common mode of transportation, carrying students to high school and workers to jobs downtown. Martinez lived along one of the streetcar lines that in earlier years had taken Latins from West Tampa to cigar factories and all of Tampa.

"I was the first one in my family to go beyond the ninth grade," he said. He knew he would go to college but didn't give serious consideration to a major until after high school. By that time, he had fallen in love with Mary Jane Marino, the woman who would become his wife, and chose to attend the University of Tampa to be near her. They married when he was a sophomore.

At that time, the university held classes in the historic Henry B. Plant Building, which had no air conditioning and used fireplaces for heat.[19] "It was almost an extension of high school," he said. Among the 700 or 800 students, "Everybody knew one another." To pay his way through school, with his parents' assistance, he worked as a bookkeeper for the hotel and restaurant bartenders union and, during tax season, filed tax returns.

Knowing he would need a job and recognizing a healthy job market for teachers, he chose education as a career. After graduation, he taught for three and a half years at Oak Grove Junior High School. "When I got my bachelor's degree [in social science], I had a lot of emphasis on economics and labor, and it sort of got my interest, so I went back to school, the University of Illinois, and got a master's degree in labor and industrial relations." At that time in the South, no school offered a degree in that subject, he explained.

When he returned to Tampa in 1963, he represented the unionized Spanish Restaurant Owners, but, without a large enough client base, he turned to full-time teaching at Chamberlain High School where he taught social studies (world history, then Problems of American Democracy and economics). "That's when the whole teacher movement started to change," he said. Teachers, himself included, wanted to refocus the mission of the Hillsborough Classroom Teachers Association from one generally discussing education to one advocating for teachers before the County School Superintendent and School Board. Glenn Barrington, an Association Board member, recommended hiring Martinez to represent them. As a result, he quit teaching—"You can't be on two sides of the fence. You're basically a hired gun, that's what they hire you for"—and also phased out his labor relations consulting business.

"The 1960s was a period of trying to shake off the establishment in every fashion you can think of," he said, referring to Vietnam War protests, civil rights struggles for women and minorities, and union strikes. Throughout the United States, particularly in Florida and New York, teachers demanded such things as more funding for schools and collective bargaining rights. In 1968, nearly half of Florida teachers walked out of their classrooms. Although the walkout had little immediate impact, it did make education an issue that the Governor and the Legislature could no longer ignore. Martinez managed to get a local act passed that allowed Hillsborough teachers to bargain collectively, helping to pave the way for all public employees to do so just a few years later.[20]

"Of course, most of public sector negotiation is politics," he said. "So that's where I honed my skills in terms of dealing with political issues and races and lobbying and all the rest of it."

Martinez continued to represent the teacher association until the spring of 1975. "I had gotten tired of it, frankly." While having dinner at his uncle's restaurant, the Café Sevilla in West Tampa, his uncle told him about plans to sell so he could retire. "I didn't say anything at the time," but Martinez later said to his wife, "I'm tired of going to Washington, I'm tired of going to Tallahassee, and maybe I need a change." Because his family had been in the restaurant and dairy business, "they had kept me away from those two tough ways of earning a living. So I never worked in either one of them growing up." At this point, he needed not only a change but also a challenge. He partnered with a brother-in-law and bought the business.

Actually, he had grown tired enough of lobbying for the teachers that he let his attorney, J. Clint Brown, talk him into running in a special election for Mayor the previous year [1974]. Brown had first suggested that he run for a seat on the County Commission, but Martinez refused: "I don't like the legislative side. I respect it and I lobbied it and I still deal with all that now, but that's just not me. I'm on the executive side of it." He lost the nonpartisan Mayor's race to Bill Poe, who ran an insurance agency.

Another political opportunity presented itself a month after buying the restaurant. Gov. Reubin Askew (D), whose campaign Martinez had been involved with, asked him to be on the Southwest Florida Water Management District Board. "I said, 'Governor, I just bought a business that I don't know much about and I don't know that I could handle that. I can't spare the time.' The Governor responded, 'They only meet once a month.' He wouldn't get off the phone. And it was in the middle of lunch, so finally, I said, 'All right, I'll do it.'" It turned out they did meet once a month, but it was for two days, and because the District's basin boards,[21] three of which Martinez chaired, met on separate days, he ended up spending three-and-a-half days a month on water business. As a result, he learned a lot about water use, permitting, and conservation.

Meanwhile, he worked at the restaurant seven days a week, from 6 a.m. to after midnight most days. The business thrived, attracting well-to-do clients mostly by word of mouth. That business plus his involvement in the community increased his visibility among voters.

When the next mayoral election came up in 1979, Brown again talked him into running. "There was no plan," Martinez said. They didn't hire a political consultant or a professional pollster.

A bit later, however, someone from the University of South Florida offered to conduct a poll. It wouldn't cost anything, it would take two or three days, and they would need an office with lots of phones and volunteers to make the calls. Martinez agreed. "The poll comes back showing I was going to win in the first primary in the high 50s."

"I still had like $40,000 in the bank and I had not committed anything for the run-off. We talked about that into the wee hours of the morning." Finally he decided, "All right, I'll roll the dice. We'll spend the whole amount on TV just to lock it down." He believed the poll was "probably not accurate because it was a bunch of amateurs that did it, and it was one night of systematically made calls, but the gap is huge enough that it's worth the gamble." Sure enough, he won over the field in the first primary.

In those days, Tampa, like many cities across the country, had experienced an exodus of businesses and residents to the suburbs. His goal was to revitalize the downtown, bringing people back to live, work, and attend cultural events, all of which required strong infrastructure. To explain his views, he published a series of white papers on labor relations, economic development, and public safety. He also pushed for building a multimillion-dollar performing arts center, which turned out to be a popular campaign topic.

Martinez won the election over four opponents. He won reelection in 1983. Under his leadership, the city improved the water and wastewater system, expanded the airport, reconstructed the Lowry Park Zoo, and restored the 1915 City Hall, the refuse-to-energy plant, the Performing Arts Center, and the Convention Center.

When he ran for reelection, he announced he would not run for a third term. His attorney immediately asked why. Martinez told him it was because he had promoted passage of a referendum imposing term limits on future mayors and City Council members. "I always felt you shouldn't roost in an office," he explained. Brown said, "Well, you've got to make it clear, you're talking about Mayor, because there's other things to run for." "Such as?" Martinez retorted. When Brown mentioned the Governor's office, Martinez laughed: "Are you kidding?" But it was enough to start a conversation. Brown's fellow attorney, Mac Stipanovich, who had managed the mayoral reelection campaign, became campaign manager for the gubernatorial race.

Up to that time, although the mayoral race was nonpartisan, Martinez was a registered Democrat. "But I knew that after the way I had governed that I didn't fit in the Democratic mold. I had tangled with the unions, I had dropped property taxes, I had reduced the size of the staff. None of that fit in to a primary for the Democratic Party." He was already grabbing attention from prominent Republicans at the national level, several of whom, including Sen. Paul Laxalt (1974–1987) from Nevada, and Sen. Orrin Hatch (elected 1977) from Utah, worked hard at getting him to change parties.

In the spring of 1983, during his second term, Martinez received a call from the White House inviting him to come for a visit with President Ronald Reagan. Martinez

Figure 4.7. Martinez, once a Democrat, changed parties at the personal urging of President Ronald Reagan. The President said, "We've been watching you operate in Tampa [as Mayor], and we don't know why you are registered Democrat. You should be a Republican." Martinez and his wife, Mary Jane, changed their party affiliation soon after (1983). State Archives of Florida, *Florida Memory*, https://www.floridamemory.com/items/show/19507. Photograph ca. 1987–1991.

had met with the President before as part of his involvement with the U.S. Conference of Mayors and the National League of Cities. "But I never had spent any time with him, other than being in a group of maybe eight or nine mayors or something like that. So I figured this wasn't about city business." He bought his own ticket and flew to Washington for the meeting.

"I walked into the Oval Office. Vice President George H. W. Bush was there as well. We started chatting and then the President says, 'Mayor, I'd like to talk to you about your party affiliation. We've been watching you operate in Tampa, and we don't know why you are registered Democrat. You should be a Republican.' I thanked him for his comments. He said, 'Well, in many ways we're sort of similar. I was once a Democrat, and I was once the head of a union. I saw you had a strike there in Tampa, and you handled the strike much like I handled the air controllers. So you really, really need to think about becoming a Republican.'" The meeting lasted about 30 minutes, and Martinez got his picture taken with the President and Vice President. (Reagan later invited Martinez to speak at the 1984 Republican National Convention in Dallas.)

"I did not announce I was going to Washington, but I knew that if this is what it was, I suspected the media would be waiting for me when I left the White House," he said. "Sure enough, when I left, there was a whole bunch of Florida media out there waiting. Back then, the press corps was bigger than they are now. 'Why are you here?' 'Who paid for your way here?' 'What was the conversation about? Are you changing parties?' I obviously just kept giving the generic answers." Another group of reporters accosted him at Washington National Airport, but still he said nothing.

In the summer, "Mary Jane and I walked down to the Supervisor of Elections and changed parties. Right before I changed, I called the White House, the Chief of Staff, and let him know I was doing it. And that was it. Then I got a lot of flak, obviously, from both sides."

By early 1983, Martinez had sold the restaurant and began thinking seriously about running for Governor. "In the early stage of the campaign, you're looking at money centers," he said. He talked to a number of people about a possible run and got commitments from 30 people. "I announced, got on the phone—that's before e-mail and all that stuff and everything's by phone—called those 30 people the same day and said, 'I need all the money you can raise for me in the month of March [1985].' I gambled that I could raise a nice amount and—great news, I did. I raised almost $400,000 in one month. So instantly you were a legitimate candidate. And nobody was close to me in the primary at that time. So we took some gambles in terms of trying to bring attention to the campaign by doing things that became newsworthy. Raising that amount of money in 30 days was worthy—not of front page news—but among the political class it was big enough."

From that point on, he went to visit people that had a history of raising money. "It was all one-on-one," he said. "I didn't hold fundraisers 'til almost maybe into August 1986, before the primary." Once he had money in the bank, his campaign hired pollsters and media consultants.

Because of his recent conversion to the Republican Party, "I wasn't necessarily welcome with open arms by the state Republican leaders, and so I went after the county leaders"—all 67 counties. "I knew what I was doing with a county party because a state party normally doesn't spend that much time with the county leaders, at least in those days they didn't. So I worked those 67 chairs and executive committees and even held fundraisers for them where I was a speaker and they kept the money. That's how I was able to become an establishment Republican, despite the fact that I was a recent Republican."

Those opposed to his candidacy included Dick Langley, a Republican leader in the Florida Senate. "He came up with ABM, Anybody But Martinez, an anti-ballistic missile kind of thing. But then four or five months before the primary, he calls me. He says, 'I made a mistake. You are the candidate, and I want to hold a news conference with you.' And he did."

In the primary, Martinez faced three established Republicans: Louis "Lou" Frey, Jr., who had served in Congress for 18 years, State Rep. Tom Gallagher (1979–1987), and State Rep. Chester Clem (1972–1976). Martinez finished first in the primary, and then defeated Frey in the runoff. In the general election, he defeated Democrat Steve Pajcic, who had served in the Florida House since 1975.

Looking back on the campaign, he noted that he had identified regional leaders for the statewide campaign, but "I never gave titles or anything like that, but there were people in every area that were well respected, well connected." For example, in Jacksonville, Pajcic's hometown, businessman and former State Sen. Tom Slade helped raise money. "But it's always a very—it still is—cohesive group in the Republican Party there. Tom did a fantastic job of managing that part of the state's campaign." One of his early supporters, State Rep. Bobby Brantley (1978–1987) from the Orlando area, became his running mate. A young man in his mid-30s who headed the Dade County Republican Party would become his Commerce Secretary—Jeb

Bush—whom he later described as an energetic young man, respected by the business community, and with much expertise in the area of international trade.

In selecting campaign stops, "you've got to go where the registration is," he said, and each trip had a mission for reaching a particular group. "When you go to Dade County, you go there for the Anglo campaign, the Cuban campaign, or the Jewish campaign. You never go there to campaign in Dade County."

At one point, his campaign conducted a benchmark poll to find out what constituted the largest ethnic voting bloc. "Guess what it was. It was the Italian Americans. And we catered to them. There were all kinds of chapters in Pasco, all the way down to Charlotte County. Of course, my wife Mary Jane is of Italian extraction. So we worked that group real hard. Most of them were from up north that came down here to retire."

The Cubans composed only a small percentage (9 percent or so) of the registered voters back then, and many were still not citizens. The Puerto Rican population had not grown much in the state at that time, and the Mexican Americans were still a migrant population, he said.

In choosing campaign issues, "It's like the Olympic rings. There are five big buckets in government and they just take turns having priority—whether it's transportation or education or human services of one kind or another, or the law enforcement/judicial all grouped in one, and then all others." Selection becomes a question of the most pressing problem at the time. But "basically it was jobs, environment, tax levels."

A candidate's political history is fair game for opponents. As Mayor, Martinez said, "I made sure all the enterprise funds were well funded and paying for themselves, which meant fee adjustments. So you always had to watch your back on fees because water, sewer and solid waste, you run off of revenue and not property taxes. And I did the refuse-to-energy plant, which meant you had to adjust prices to cover higher technology to get rid of garbage that isn't going to the landfill. But that never came up, the whole fee thing. The only reason I don't think I got hit on that is Pajcic had advocated a lot of taxes in his years in the House." Actually, spokespeople for Pajcic, like State Rep. Sam Bell (1974–1988), had alluded to the need for a personal income tax. "I had dropped the property tax from $9.75 to $4.65, so I knew that tax issue wasn't going to 'get me' in the campaign."

Today campaign attacks have become "more graphic and more instantaneous," he said. "When I ran for Governor in '86, the brick cell phones had just come out. You had some reception in Tampa and you had some reception in Miami to just north of Palm Beach and that was it. And there was no Internet. The 24/7 news stations were not really around, so there was nothing to really highlight conflict, or the gaffes or anything else simply because you were locked into broadcast TV and the print cycle."

Martinez ran a traditional campaign. It included debates before the primary and one before the runoff. "Talk radio was just beginning, so I did a lot of talk radio." He had plenty of money for TV ads, and he received newspaper endorsements. "I think I had about half of the major dailies the first time around."

On newspaper endorsements: "I think the less money you have, the more it helps if you have them. If you're well-funded, you can go over that noise. Back then, I think, because the circulation was greater, they probably had greater influence than they may have now with their circulation in decline." A candidate for a state House seat who raises a quarter million or half million dollars will likely get endorsements. "A lot of candidates will use them for advertising," he said.

Throughout the campaign, Martinez led in the polls. He won 54 percent of the vote compared to Pajcic's 46 percent. Pajcic attributed his loss to several factors—a divided Democratic Party and being outspent.[22]

"I had all the money I could spend," Martinez said. But he was careful to point out that "I never used soft money, ever. It was all hard money. I never had a committee account, never had a PAC [Political Action Committee]. Even to this day I don't like soft money. I'd rather see higher limits with tighter disclosure, and you answer for those who gave you the money."

He recalled no incidents of discrimination. "I never heard a slur of any kind." But he did incur skepticism among many of those from his old neighborhood about how well his ethnicity and religion (he was Florida's first Catholic Governor) would play in other parts of the state. "I would go to people who had known me all of my life. They were the hardest ones to convince." The guys who called him Bobby rather than Bob told him "You are crazy. How can you run statewide when you change parties, you were in a teachers' strike, you are a Catholic, and your name is Martinez?"[23]

The fact that his name was Martinez resulted in a couple of other interesting episodes during the campaign.

One day early in the campaign, he received a call from Miami. "You got to come down here and get on the radio stations," the campaign worker said. "Why?" asked Martinez, who was still busy raising money and organizing county teams. "They're saying you can't speak any Spanish, and you're going to have to come down here and get on these talk shows to show that you can." Martinez went to Miami, aware that his childhood Spanish had faded. "I remember he sat behind me at all the stations to whisper to me when I didn't understand something. We hit all the big radio talk show stations there. They were friendly, obviously. There were no hostile questions—all about my background, how I liked being Mayor, things of that sort," he said.

Another episode occurred when State Sen. Dempsey Barron (1961–1988) invited Martinez to his ranch for a fundraiser. Barron and four or five other Democratic Senators, including Malcolm Beard (1980–1996) and Curtis Peterson (1972–1990), had endorsed him over Pajcic. "Dempsey was a character. Man, I loved the guy," Martinez said. "Of course I had lobbied him for years for the teachers and then with the water management district and all that, so I wasn't a stranger to him. He knew who I was." After a social period with a country band playing outside, they went inside the ranch house. Barron "calls everybody's attention and he says, 'There's somebody here that I want to introduce.' Dempsey always goes on about himself for a little while, but he's always funny. Finally he segues into my introduction. He says, 'Now some of you are probably confused because you think there's more than one person running for this office with a similar name. When this candidate is in Tampa, they call him Bobby Martinez, but when he's down in Miami, they call him Roberto Martinez (he tried to say it in Spanish—you know, he was trying to give it a roll), but up here he's Bubba Martin.'"

A candidate running for office today could benefit from speaking Spanish in some cases. What voters do, once they understand a candidate's positions on policy, "you start looking for separation—which university they went to, what their profession is. You start looking for connecting the dots with who you are. I think most people do that once they get beyond this person and the policies. If you're still uncertain, somebody says, 'Well, he's a Gator,' or whatever it may be. That adds another point on your side. I think that clearly does happen. There's no doubt that if, in fact, you are in a room full of people who are still not comfortable speaking English or that's just not their native [language] yet and they're registered to vote, clearly that can be helpful in getting those voters there because they connect by an affinity."

In reflecting on his inauguration day, the accomplishment overwhelmed him. Thoughts of his ethnic blue-collar background, his nearly 100-year-old grandmother at home watching him take the oath on television, and twin six-month-old granddaughters gave him "a tremendous sense of gratitude and belief in a system that allows that to occur."[24] At the time, there were five generations of the Martinez family in Florida.

Coming into office, Martinez recognized that Florida's population had been growing over the past two decades and would soon become the fourth most populous state in the nation. That meant dealing with water needs, disposing of wastes, building highways, educating more children, and protecting the environment. At the same time, he realized that "unlimited good intentions have to give way to the reality of limited resources," as he said in his inaugural address.[25]

He set about meeting the challenges much as he had as Mayor, except that now he had to deal with legislators in the two parties. "When I took office, the Democrats had majorities in both Houses, and we had six Cabinet members, all Democrats. You had to maneuver differently than if you had Republican majorities to get something done. I ended up with a [bipartisan conservative] coalition in the Senate [including Democrats] Dempsey Barron and Malcolm Beard. They did not confirm Democrat Ken Jenne as President, and they sided with the Republicans and got [Democrat] John Vogt [1986–1988] to be the President.[26] So the Senate was my favorite of the two Houses because this is where I could get things done."

Another challenge upon taking office was administrative related, specifically the selection of staff. "The difficulty was that it was not easy to find the staff you wanted. There were not an awful lot of Republicans to select from for government service, particularly with experience in running an agency."[27]

"You always have to look at what the terrain is, and where there is a passageway to get between two points. It's all make-believe until you get there. But I had my areas of interest," he said. "You serve basically who you are. You take the issues that are out there and you figure out from your background how you want to address those."

One of his issues was the environment because of his growing up in a rural area and serving on the Southwest Florida Water Management Board. His environmental focus helped bring Republicans back to a pro-environmental stance. "For those Republicans who thought that they were not environmental, I said, 'Well, who lives along the coast? Who lives on the water?' They're generally people who can afford to live there. Would that be a greater tendency to be conservative and Republican or not? Do you think they bought property on the water to see it destroyed? So that's the argument I was making to them. It's not that we Republicans aren't as sensitive to environmental issues as anybody else. Now they may want to do it in a different way."

In that respect, he was a Teddy Roosevelt Republican. "There's a difference between *conservation* and *preservation*. Preservation, you can't use it. Conservation, you use it with care. I set myself to be a conservationist, although I did call it Preservation 2000 and came up with a land-buying program. But basically I believe resources are to be protected and cared for but used. Otherwise you'd have no friends. If you can't use something, how do you build a base to support it? I've always been an advocate for conservation, but at the same time, I wanted to make sure the public had a right to access it and to utilize it, not just simply have it fenced off and not use it. You know, there's nothing worse than seeing a library with nobody between the stacks."

In addition to the agenda he had in mind for his administration, "You always have to be prepared for the unscheduled events because they dominate often. Scheduled events are easy to handle. You've got them planned, you study them, and you have time to execute them. It's the unscheduled events that make you or break you in terms of how they occur, whether it's a hurricane or if it's a civil disturbance, it doesn't matter what." One of his unscheduled events was a prison crisis. "The Feds had shut down the [state's temporary housing units] and released all those kinds of people—something you didn't even run on, that had priority." When events like that occur, "you've got to prep instantly and get it and execute it instantly. There's a lot of excitement in that, too. It keeps the adrenaline going."

In 1990, Martinez ran for reelection against former Democratic U.S. Sen. Lawton Chiles. Chiles had resigned his Senate seat early out of frustration and burnout, but supporters convinced him to run for Governor. Going into the campaign, Martinez faced the hurdle of having signed a law placing a state sales tax on services during his first months in office. The furor over the tax plus Chiles's iconic status with voters put Martinez behind in the polls. But despite campaign appearances by President George H. W. Bush and former President Reagan, he lost the election 45 percent to 55 percent.[28]

"You always hate losing, there's no question about it. It goes back to the service tax that had passed before I got there. But in hindsight, I should have asked for more time to study the issue that wasn't mine and then left it there to be implemented. Same thing as growth management. It got left to be implemented the year that I got sworn in. It wasn't implemented before that. And so hindsight smartness would've been you want an extension for further study of the impact it would have, and we didn't do that. Almost did that, and then at the very last moment I got talked out of it. But that was the main thing," he said.

The campaign raised plenty of money. "I think for the Governor's race, each time I ran I must have raised some $10–11 million. I had all the money back then that you could have ever spent. You know, we had planes, the whole bit." Most of it went for television and radio. "Most of our ads on our opponents had to do with contrasting records—the old 'here's mine, here's yours.' They were not nasty like they are now. I don't recall other races back then that appear to be as mean-spirited as today's ads are."

TV ads today have higher quality and can be produced much faster. "Back then, to get a nice looking video, you had to use film. But that takes time because you have to take a lot of film" to have enough to edit. "And it wasn't until you got into combat at the very end that you did the video and it didn't look as good but it was quick." The improved video and introduction of digital media "allows this instant comeback on something that you want to strike back on real quick. Back then, it just took a little bit longer. But the official campaigns back then, I think, were a lot more timid."

In addition, there were no outside groups that could produce their own ads and pay for broadcast time. "I don't recall an outside group that was involved with any of my campaigns." Those ads are hard to control, whether for you or against you, he said.

Politics has changed dramatically since he left office in 1991. "I think it has gotten more vicious," he said. "I shouldn't say this because I have been out of the business a long time, but I think too many consultants think only of the negative campaign, and the positive message is lost basically. Maybe they haven't learned to create an effective positive message or maybe they're going with the blood and guts that you see on the evening news. That's what people like, so therefore that's what you've got to give them. As a result, almost all campaigns that are contested end up being negative. And a lot of it is not at all negative about policy. It's negative about the individual. I don't see anything turning that back."

It is a far cry from his earliest memories as a child of going to Democratic political rallies in West Tampa with his uncle—back then, all the rallies were for Democrats. He recalled that "hundreds would show up, and they were throwing out ice cream to the crowds that were there, and the signs and the demonstrations. It was politics like it was intended to be, with people there listening to the message directly and not getting it filtered or getting it on the tube."[29]

After the failed reelection, President George H. W. Bush (R) appointed Martinez Director of the National Office of Drug Control Policy, commonly known as "Drug Czar." In that post, which he held for two years, he emphasized prevention and treatment of drug abuse. He returned to Tampa in 1993 and later joined the Holland & Knight law firm as senior policy advisor with an emphasis on Florida government affairs.

In the two decades since leaving public life, his single term as Governor "is often overlooked," wrote one political writer for the *Tampa Tribune*. Actually Martinez made significant accomplishments in such areas as the environment, transportation, higher education, and criminal justice.[30] In that respect, he stayed true to his often-quoted inaugural promise: "I did not come here to be different. I came here to make a difference."[31]

Bob Martinez was interviewed in person by the author Feb. 21, 2014.

Jennifer S. Carroll (R)

First black Republican woman elected to the Florida House, 2003

First black person and woman to be elected Lieutenant Governor of Florida, 2010

Personal: Born August 27, 1959, Port of Spain, Trinidad, West Indies; married with three children.

Education:

- University of New Mexico, B.A. in political science (1985)
- St. Leo University, M.B.A. (2008)

Figure 4.8. An enthusiastic Jennifer Carroll interacts with a crowd as gubernatorial candidate Rick Scott's (R) running mate. The Republican ticket won the 2010 race and Carroll became Florida's first *elected* woman Lieutenant Governor. She shared Scott's interest in bringing jobs to Florida, having served as chair of the House Economic Development Council. Photograph by Joe Burbank, *Orlando Sentinel*, September 3, 2010. Photograph courtesy of the *Orlando Sentinel*, 2010.

Occupation: Retired U.S. Navy Lieutenant Commander, Business Owner
Trailblazer Elections:

- House of Representatives District 13 (Parts of Clay and Duval counties) *Rep Primary Special Election*, April 15, 2003
    - Jennifer Carroll (65.5%), Linda Sparks (34.5%)
- House of Representatives District 13 (Parts of Clay and Duval counties) *General Special Election* May 13, 2003
    - Jennifer Carroll—*Unopposed*
- Florida Governor/Lieutenant Governor *General Election* 2010
    - Scott/Carroll-R (48.9%), Sink/Smith-D (47.7%)

THE JENNIFER CARROLL STORY

Jennifer Carroll left Trinidad with her parents in 1967 when she was eight years old. Little did she imagine that she would one day make history as a black woman elected to state public office in the United States.

Her immigrant status led to membership in the Republican Party by default. "When my parents received their naturalization, they registered as Republicans," she said. At the time, they lived in Hempstead, N.Y., and her parents "were told that if they weren't Republicans, if something happened on their street, that whether they needed the snow shoveled or a water main broke or something like that, they weren't getting that fixed if they weren't Republicans."

After Carroll was naturalized as a citizen, she became a Republican too. "When I ran for Congress [in 2000], I was meeting with a dentist [Arnett Girardeau, who was black and a Democrat] in town, and he asked, 'Are you conservative or liberal?'" She didn't know. "That was a lesson to learn." She would learn many lessons about the realities of politics on her life journey.

As a child, she learned to cook and clean house from her mother, but she preferred hanging out with her dad, a mason and dental technician, who liked to work on cars. Her affinity for tinkering under the car hood influenced her job choice as a jet mechanic in the U.S. Navy, when she enlisted in 1979. While in the Navy, she was selected for the enlisted commissioning program, which allowed her to go to college and become a naval officer. She started out majoring in chemistry at the University of New Mexico. At the time she was newly married and not able to spend much time with her husband because chemistry classes and labs kept her busy.

One day she asked herself what she would do with a chemistry degree. "I didn't plan on being a doctor or anything like that, didn't plan to work in the medical field. And I thought I'm just getting a degree to get a degree." Talking to other military students in the same ROTC unit, she heard one student describe what he was learning in political science. She found it fascinating. "Most important was how we got to where we are," she said, and how philosophers like John Locke shaped ideas about human rights. "So that gravitated me to that degree."

After graduating, she became an aviation maintenance officer and was assigned as an aide to Admiral Kevin Delaney at the Naval Air Station in Jacksonville. He was in charge of 17 major commands, including Pascagoula, Mississippi, and the base in Panama. "Typically admiral's aides were those who get the coffee and sit out there and wait until I call you, do a couple of letters and that's about it. But my admiral had me very involved with decision making, with sharing ideas and being a liaison to our elected officials for our needs for the base." In addition, he recommended her for Leadership Jacksonville and Project Blueprint of Jacksonville, which gave her grounding in issues facing local leaders.

The base was in the congressional district of Democrat Corrine Brown (U.S. House, elected 1993), who "was not very responsive to a lot of our needs and concerns." By contrast, Republican Tillie Fowler (U.S. House 1993–2001), who was in Congress at the same time, "loved the military, never served in the military and didn't have this base in her district, but she was interested in helping us." Consequently, Carroll confirmed an OK with Brown's office to use Fowler as a conduit to Congress.

At the time, the district was one of the poorest in the state. It "had health disparities, high crime, high failure rate in schools, low economic development. I'm thinking, 'Well, if the surrounding county districts can have a spur of economic development and A schools and B schools, why isn't this district, which has a Representative, afforded the same opportunities as the surrounding districts?' And I decided that when I retired, I would run against [Brown]."

In 2000, and again in 2002 after the district was redrawn, Carroll carried out her decision. She lost both times with 42 percent of the vote, not too bad for a political newcomer in a congressional race. The vice chair of the state Republican Party at the time, Jim Stelling, from Seminole County, said publicly she shouldn't run against Brown because it was a losing battle. Additionally, Republican John Peyton (Jacksonville Mayor 2003–2011) contributed to her opponent.

The Republican Party's strategy at the time was this: "Number one, don't stir up a hornet's nest because we don't want the black voters to really have a reason to come out. Number two, [Brown] has full access to Bill Clinton and although she's outlandish, we'll put up with that." Carroll disagreed: "If you are representing the people and getting the public dollars, then you ought to be doing the work for the public and not just benefitting yourself."

Her first campaign in 2000 coincided with the presidential race between George W. Bush and Al Gore. Her observations of the Florida election did not endear her to fellow Republicans: "I was critical of [Bush] getting elected. For example, during that time, it was during the paper ballots, and the paper ballots were in my district, particularly in the black precincts, we had never had Republican poll watchers in those precincts. But I had some poll watchers in those precincts, and they experienced things where people from years past were able to come in and just cast a vote without showing any documentation. So this happened where bands of people would come in to try to vote. We had some areas at 10 o'clock in the morning where ballot [boxes] were so stuffed that the supervisor had to bring more ballots. And we had precincts that had over 100 percent voter turnout. . . . Well, you never see 100 percent voter turnout. But the question mark didn't pop up then. Then, down in Orlando, we had information which we shared with Bill Cowles, who at the time was the [Orange County] Supervisor of Election, of dead people voting—family members of my volunteers who were dead since May and now voted in November—and he didn't do anything about it. So, when people were being bused to the polls, it was a mantra of 'Gore/Brown, Gore/Brown, Gore/Brown.' If nobody was running against Corrine Brown—it so happened at the time I was running against Corrine Brown—there would be no need to say 'Gore/Brown,' it would've been 'Vote Gore.' Twenty-seven thousand ballots in Duval County were thrown out because they were spoiled because two presidential candidates were voted for. That was Harry Browne, Libertarian, and Al Gore. Twenty-seven thousand. At the end of the day, after a recount, Bush won by a little over 500 votes."

"That was in 2000, and you would think that here it is after the 2008 election, where President Obama wins the election and shows no race or ethnic group ought to be left out from reaching for a campaign, that we [the Republicans] would have learned a lesson. But that mentality still exists today," she said, even among the consultants that advise party officials.

Her party also made it hard to raise money. In the first campaign, "I outraised Corrine Brown each step of the way with hard-core dollars. These were some people, not from the lobbying core or the special interest groups or anything, these were hard core dollars. Every time I would go to the RNC [Republican National Committee], they always asked me to raise more. They always moved the carrot. 'Oh, let's see what you raise next quarter,' and I'm coming out here busting my butt. Tillie Fowler would tell me, 'Have them put it in writing, get a commitment from them.' She even went with me to the RNC," and the response was the same. Fowler "was very supportive of me, even took me to Denny Hastert [Republican U.S. House Speaker 1999–2007] at the time, and Denny came down and was a guest speaker at one of my fundraisers here. But if you don't have the machine behind you, it's very difficult."

Learning about the redistricting process proved eye-opening. District lines had been redrawn before Carroll faced Brown in the second contest in 2002. Carroll chose to run again because "I still had the passion in my belly. I knew that this district could do better." She also thought that this time she would have her party's support. She learned otherwise at a meeting of a select committee, made up of members of the Florida Senate and House, in Tallahassee. At one point, Brown, a Democrat, "begins to praise John Thrasher, who is a Republican and was in the House at the time doing redistricting, praise him for making her seat more Democratic . . . and my mouth fell to the floor." Carroll had no idea that Republican officeholders helped redraw the lines that worked against her. She also remembered the words of Tom Slade, a former chair of the Republican Party of Duval County, who said that running against Corrine Brown was like beating your head against the wall and expecting different results. Hearing that from a member of her own party, Carroll wondered, "If you thought that, why say it in public? You're already stopping me from having an opportunity out the door."

Carroll chose to run for the Florida House in a special election in 2003 after being approached by Republican State Rep. Mike Hogan, who was giving up his seat to run for a county office. She was skeptical about receiving party support, but he told her not to worry. "The party still wasn't with me. As a matter of fact in Tallahassee, the word was that I wouldn't be able to win this seat" because the opponent was a white woman who was chairman of the school board and had won election several times. Furthermore, "the rednecks would not vote for a black female there in Northeast Florida."

Fortunately, a friend invited a lobbyist to Jacksonville to walk door-to-door with her. When people came to the door and she introduced herself, they would say, "THE Jennifer Carroll? Are the cameras here?" "He came out of there flabbergasted. He said, 'These folks know you, they love you, they think you're a celebrity. He goes back to Tallahassee saying, 'You guys have it all wrong. She's going to win. I saw firsthand how these people regarded her and loved her.'"

Her prior candidacies also worked in her favor: "People got a chance to know me as an individual, see my credentials and see my passion, plus I still continued my work in the community with the YMCA, the YWCA, the Clay Behavioral Center, and Junior Achievement." Her critics "were just looking at, again, sheer numbers, what the consultants were telling them." And she got no editorial endorsements. But she had friends who believed in her and walked with her door-to-door. They included Brian Graham and Matt Justice, Marie McGee and Mary Ellen Ludeking and her husband Bill from Duval County, and people on the west side, Edith Davidson and her husband and family.

She received 80-plus percent of the votes in Clay County (the redneck area) and more than 60 percent in Duval County. "I never had an opponent after that election for the time that I was in office. I firmly believe I didn't have an opponent because I stayed connected with the voters."

As a woman and as a minority, she had to challenge a perception that a woman's place is in the home. "I am not a Suzy homemaker, stay-home-and-bake-your-food sort of person." Yet, in the Legislature, the perception prevailed. Typically the leadership assigns women to education, health care, and the Department of Children and Families. Some suggested a spot for her on military affairs because of her Navy background. "I said there's nothing much in military affairs. You just do a ceremony here and there." Instead, she wanted structure and substance "so that I can see the fruits of my labor, whether it be with policy or the finances that we put forward to make things happen." With that attitude, she ended up on committees dealing with transportation and economic development.

Legislative service brought rewarding experiences. As examples, she cited the following bills:

- Allowing people with disabilities to come into public buildings with their service animals. "When I was presenting my bill before a Senate committee, disabled individuals with their service animals were restricted from coming into the Capitol to hear my testimony. I immediately called my office and I said . . . get them in this committee room right now."
- Strengthening the power of law enforcement to remove people who were harassing women in shelters. Previously a law officer could ask offenders to leave but could not arrest them unless they committed a crime, such as breaking a window.
- Providing additional funds to the Florida Export Finance Corporation. Exporters, many of whom were small businesses, would have to wait to get paid until after their products were received. The corporation assisted the exporters by giving them short-term loans. "They were running out of money, and I was able to get a match of two million dollars to be put in the corporation for these businesses to stay afloat. That's where we really saw jobs maintained and increased our revenue coming into the state."
- Revamping the Black Business Investment Corporation. This agency was created 20 years ago to help black businesses grow. The director of the corporation's board "was holding money to give to the [businesses], so they were going on a shoestring budget," with the only help coming from municipalities. Businesses were also having trouble getting the required certification. Carroll recommended halting the agency's funding and called for a study by OPPAGA (Office of Program Policy Analysis and Government Accountability) along with an auditor general inspection. "Now, when I defunded it, the board director that was causing a lot of the problems, he left because now he had no salary. So that created a level playing field." Companies getting state money had to show measurable results, and the agency needed to spread money among more companies, instead of giving loans to the same ones every time. Within the first year, the agency reported increases in payrolls and black businesses. "We didn't just do it for black businesses, we left it for black and minority businesses. And it was not just in an area like Duval County, we expanded it regionally so we can cover more areas."

- Improving incentives for the film industry to produce films in the state. The idea was to give film companies a tax credit if they met certain conditions: "They had to film here, they had to hire Floridians—and it couldn't be just somebody coming and getting an I.D. card and that's the end of that. It had to be an established Floridian . . . and they had to show their receipts." The plan worked. "That brought in millions of dollars into the state coffers and kept jobs and brought more film production here," including digital film production.

Staying in touch with voters was essential: "When I was in office, I had both before– and after–town hall meetings, and I encouraged my constituents to share with me what their issues and concerns were. Some of my bills came from my constituents." She also communicated with them via e-mail. "When we were in session, if I was going to vote against the establishment and things sounded well but it wouldn't be good for my district, I would send them information as to why I voted the way I voted," she said.

"I never turned anyone away, even if it was a constituent from another member's district. My office had a standing order, even my Lieutenant Governor's office, anyone that needs help, we will help them and we will follow up to make sure. They may not get the answers that they want, but at least they got an answer to resolve whatever their issues and concerns were," she said. "It's not just a one-way street, it's two-ways."

What advice would she give someone considering a run for public office? "When I told a cousin of mine in Trinidad that I was going to run for office, he said, 'But Jenny, you're a nice girl. Politics is a dirty, dirty place.' I said, 'Oh no, we need good people in politics.' But it's a cutthroat place and in many instances I was blindsided with how cutthroat it really is."

First, she would advise a potential candidate to develop a base. "That base of support can get the message out about you, tell your story so you don't seem like you're self-serving and handle any negatives that may pop up." Having supporters counter negative publicity is better than holding a press conference to refute it.

Second, "Get it into your heart as to why you want to run," she said. Do something "that would give you some leadership and managerial experience before you get into office. I see many people that get into office that never had any title, any position, any leadership, so now this is their opportunity and they just let it go to their head and forget the reason. The humility just goes out the door. After a couple of years you [may ask of yourself]: 'Where'd you come from? You're a monster.' Humility needs to stay with you throughout your time."

Third, "Get involved in the community. If you want to serve the community, you have to have a basic understanding as to what the community needs are. What you think they may need may be totally different than what their needs are. So, for example, Clay Behavioral Center is a center where a lot of needy families that have troubled children come to get services. Being on that board afforded me an opportunity to see that my life is good and my kids' lives are good, but my neighbor's next door may not be."

Another valuable experience came when she was U.S. Navy liaison for Junior Achievement, encouraging Navy personnel to volunteer their time in schools to talk about the value of an education. "The kids hear it from their teachers all the time, and after a while it goes in one ear and out the other. I went to the inner city schools because most of the time they would've never seen someone like me. And I would show up in uniform." While speaking at one inner-city school, she noticed that some of the girls were putting on their makeup and others were not paying attention. She told them, "I'm spending my time to come here and share something I believe that's valuable to you so that you can have a better life for yourself. So pick your head up from the desk. You will listen, we will have interaction, don't turn around." And they responded.

Community involvement sharpens one's instincts for conducting a campaign, she learned. As an example, when she ran for Congress, she was told to hire a Washington, D.C., consultant. "I spent lots of money on those idiots. They didn't know the district." They told her not to walk door-to-door, but she disagreed. In a meeting with one political consultant, Republican Tom DeLay, she was told that she was "spending her money in the wrong place" and shouldn't be going to certain precincts. She replied, "Let me tell you something. You guys haven't put a dime in my race. I'm raising all the money. How dare you!"

Friends in the House like Democrats Hazelle Rogers, who was born in Jamaica, and Perry Thurston, whose family came from the Bahamas, seemed eager to open the racial/ethnic categories in the census to include national origin rather than just black or African American. "I don't think we ought to be called African Americans at all," Carroll said. A citizen by naturalization, "I consider myself an American. I don't consider myself anything but. So once you put that tagline on there, it seems as if you're separating yourself and don't fully want to assimilate into this country." She also pointed out that some African Americans, including a friend she served with in the Navy, are actually white. "To separate it, then it makes the black community seem like we're not part of America."

At the same time she acknowledges the cultural differences between countries in the Caribbean and regions of the United States. She still connects with her Caribbean countrymen but "that's a culture that's very in line with conservative principles. So, if the Republicans really wanted to have a full tent, you would think that this would be a community that you go to," she said. "But to totally ignore them, I don't think it's an option."

Public office is all about serving the people. "Before I got into office, I was against term limits because I thought the citizens will be the one to say if this person represents them well or not. After I got into office, I said, 'Thank God we have term limits.'

Because some of these members that are in there, you want them gone. You don't want them sticking around for life because within a short order, it isn't about the people anymore."

In 2009, Rick Scott asked her to be his running mate, but he was not the first to consider her for the post. She had been approached in 2006 by Republican Charlie Crist's campaign. That experience had turned her off because her information had been made public. "If you want me to submit all my financials and information, personal information, just keep that in-house until you make a decision," she said.

Consequently, she didn't trust the call that came from Susie Wiles, Rick Scott's campaign manager, on the candidate's behalf. "I've been down this road before and I really don't want to," she told Wiles. In fact, she had already filed papers to run for re-election, unopposed, to the House. As chair of the Economic Development Council, she had spent most of the summer traveling to ports, getting additional information from various industries about how to build the state's economy.

"I told Susie, if that short list is five, ten people, I am not interested." Carroll had a full calendar of speaking engagements, including ones at Yale and the University of Florida. "I don't want to interrupt what I'm doing just to come and talk to somebody." Wiles responded, "It's a really, really short list." Finally, Carroll relented. "They flew me down and I spoke with the lawyers," she said. "So I'm sitting there in the hotel room, and it went into late hours, and then the lawyers came back." After she answered their questions, they said, "Well, it's yours to lose."

At breakfast with Scott the next morning, "we hit it off." They shared their common experiences in the Navy and their focus on the economy and jobs. She pointed out her ability to deal with people and gain bipartisan support, which she had on all her bills that passed. "I said, 'I think it's important for us to work across the aisle, and if the betterment is for the state of Florida and its people, we will get there.' He liked my legislative experience, he liked what I was saying. I said, 'I'm not a bump on a log, so if you just want somebody to hold a title and sit behind a desk, it's not me.' He said, 'No, I want you to be involved. I want you to be working hard like I do.' So, we left it at that."

On her way to the airport, she got the call. She accepted Scott's invitation, assuming that he had chosen her because of her experience and views. "It wasn't until after the election, actually it was toward inauguration, then it really hit me." He was choosing a black woman and the chance to make history. Later she learned that few had been interested in the job.

Once selected as a running mate, she heard from many blacks of both parties "because, just like Obama, people wanted to be part of that experience." That's when "I started seeing the responsibility. I then had to try to pave a way for somebody else to come behind me."

During the campaign, her ideas for reaching out to blacks and minorities were

Figure 4.9. Lt. Gov. Jennifer Carroll descends the steps of the Old Capitol in Tallahassee with her husband, Nolan, during the inauguration ceremony for Gov. Rick Scott in January 2011. But the pomp and circumstance would give way to conflict and frustration with the Governor and his staff. After little more than two years, she would be asked to resign because of fraudulent activity by a group to whom she had been a public relations consultant. The irony was that she was never formally charged. State Archives of Florida, *Florida Memory*, https://www.floridamemory.com/items/show/96198. Photograph by Roy Eugene Lett, January, 4, 2011.

nixed because of fear they would vote against the Scott-Carroll ticket. She retorted: "Well, if you never go to them to share who you are, what you are, what you want to do, and most importantly get their input and let them know that they have a value to you, how the heck would you know you wouldn't get their vote?" Furthermore, if a minority outreach effort failed to get the desired results, it would not be a waste of money. The relationship with voters "takes time to build, and you can't come just during campaign time."

She encountered a similar sentiment when a businessperson wanted to contribute $10,000 solely to her. But because it was a combined ticket, the money had to go to Scott. The potential contributor objected. The solution was to print a pamphlet that showed how Carroll's earlier actions in the Florida Legislature had benefitted the African-American community and minorities in the state.

Minorities typically don't have the money and the donors needed to run for office. "I think that's why people gravitated to Rick Scott and why I never had that feeling, whether it was real or not, of inclusivity in his team because I wasn't that rich," she said. "If I was a millionaire they'd probably be kissing my toes, too." Money is needed "to get your message out there and run for office. So now you have to try to go and share your story with someone that you don't know," she explained. "You're encouraging them to give you $500, $1,000 or whatever dollars depending on the race you're running, and what are their bets that you're really going to get elected if you've never been on a trail before?"

Another demographic that Carroll wanted to reach was the Jewish community. She befriended some Jewish Democrats in West Palm Beach who "didn't care for the Governor, but wanted to help me, and they did." One prominent Jewish person, for example, made the robocall for her.

Her campaign efforts included going into black churches. “There was a candidate forum at Bishop Curry’s church in Miami, which is staunchly Democrat, solely black. You had all the candidates there, with the exception of our opponents, Alex Sink and Rod Smith.” Carroll wanted to participate, but the campaign said no. “It’s going to be hostile,” they said. She responded, “I can handle that.” It was a little hostile, she said, “but people respected me and appreciated that I valued them enough to come and present my side.” The fact that some candidates did not attend the forum disappointed the congregation. The pastor, who “was about to endorse Sink,” felt let down. “The next day on his radio program, he blasted them for taking them for granted and not showing up.”

“We cannot ignore any demographic, whether it’s Asians, Native Americans, blacks, Hispanics, no matter who, even our Middle Eastern communities,” Carroll said. “Our state is so cosmopolitan now.” Political consultants are “ignoring these demographics because of numbers. They feel the numbers are so low that they don’t have to go after them. But they really do. Because when you’re governing, you’re impacting these people as well and you need to understand where they are.”

She described an experience with a Miami program, Urgent Inc., which had been operating for 13 years in Liberty City. “Their whole plan was to get the youth involved in cleaning up their area and lessening crime, getting the kids more engaged and involved in the arts.” The program never received any state money, only contributions from personal donors. At one point someone asked her whether the Governor had an urban policy. She took the question to the Governor’s Chief of Staff, Adam Hollingsworth, thinking the Governor could adopt the Urgent program or at least help raise funds for it. Three weeks later, word came back that the Governor didn’t have an urban policy and wasn’t going to develop one.

“You cannot have a one-size-fit-all when it comes to policy,” she said. Not just cities, but also rural areas could benefit from an economic development plan. Increasing funding for teachers and K-12 education is great, she said, “but what about these other segments here of a population that are out of work, have given up looking for work, and you don’t even tabulate them anymore because they’ve given up? You need that job skill training along with encouraging businesses to go into those areas so a tax base can be established and have them grow from the ground up. But you’re not hearing that.”

As second in command to someone new to politics, “I thought my job was to make sure I gave [the Governor] 100 percent of what I knew, to watch his back and give him information so that if the press came in his face, he would have knowledge of it.” But she was often excluded from meetings with his staff. “A couple of times I didn’t go, and a couple of times I just bucked and I just went. And the look on their faces was like who the hell let her in here?” In this uncertain atmosphere, “I had to walk that fine line and balancing act, so I knew where I stood with his folks and what they thought of me."

"At that time I didn't really know I didn't have his support . . . 100 percent," she said. The fact was that she was expected to serve in a ceremonial role. As she had promised the Governor, however, she pushed forward on economic issues, which resulted in at least two rewarding experiences:

- Strengthening the space industry at a time when the shuttle program was ending. Because the state was threatened with the loss of 8,000 jobs, "I worked with my Space Florida board to look toward next-generation space opportunities." She met with counterparts in the other seven states involved in space about how to collaborate in drawing back space activities lost to France and other countries. She consulted with NASA administrator Charles Bolden in Washington, D.C., and with Robert D. "Bob" Cabana, executive director at the Kennedy Space Center, who saw opportunities for commercial space operations. "Our U.S. Sen. Bill Nelson [and staff] was absolutely wonderful to work with to help me to get Boeing to expand here for their CTSD [Crew and Thermal Systems Division]." She also worked with the Economic Development Commission of Florida's Space Coast, particularly Lynda Weatherman, to explore possibilities.
- Bringing Air Force missions during a time of base closures. Assistant Air Force Secretary Terry Yonkers, now retired, "helped me to get missions here to the state of Florida." Bases were consolidated elsewhere, but Florida managed to bring troops to the state. "Once you reduce a mission and you have the military personnel go, their houses are vacant, they're not spending the money here, the revenue decreases. Yonkers got more F-35s to come over here, F-22s to go down in Homestead. So, again, that was really, really huge for this state that people will probably never see."

Carrying out her ideas for the economy required travel, and getting a travel budget proved difficult. Although she finally got it, with limitations, she felt she had to defend it: "If you're not seeing people face to face, and you're not having that dialogue on a regular basis, you're not going to get anything. It's going to go somewhere else."

Her history-making firsts proved emotional for many women. "I had some women crying and I realized how important it was to them because they saw a way and I was creating that way," she said. At the same time, "I have to be a bit careful in being a woman and being a minority because how I present myself is how all others will be viewed. So, if I come across aggressive, then I'm known as the witch with a 'B.' If I come across as angry or vocal, 'Oh, she's just being an angry woman. It's that time of month.'"

Discrimination against women was often overt. She related one incident in which a female staff member was ridiculed by the Governor's Chief of Staff at a public function. Surprised to see the woman there, he ordered her to leave and "really cussed her out in front of everybody." When Carroll heard about the incident, "I pulled this young lady aside and I said, 'Don't ever let a man, regardless of how powerful you think he is, talk to you and denigrate you like that ever again.'" Aware of the young woman's qualifications and experience, Carroll advised, "There are many others that will come after you, and if you don't do something about it and nip that in the bud now, he will treat others the same way again."

Carroll had seen the same thing happen in the military: Junior enlisted women in discussions with their male counterparts would be treated "like they were lower than dirt." She admonished women to put a stop to that treatment, noting, "If a guy comes across aggressive, he's strong. A woman comes across aggressive, she's on a rag."

Frustration with the Governor's staff mounted as time went on. Eventually she realized that "they didn't want me there because I shouldn't have been there to begin with being a woman. I shouldn't have been there being black. I shouldn't have been there not being one of those 'good ol' boys' because I wasn't their pick to be in that position. So the jabs would come."

The final jab came March 12, 2013. On that day Florida Department of Law Enforcement agents questioned her about her previous public relations consulting work for Allied Veterans of the World, a Florida nonprofit that operated Internet cafes selling access to online sweepstakes games mirroring slot machines. The veterans group made national headlines when nearly 60 of its people were arrested on charges of illegal gambling, racketeering, and fraud. Fearing a scandal, the Governor's staff forced her to sign a resignation letter. She issued a statement saying she did not believe she was targeted by the investigators for any wrongdoing. Shortly thereafter she explained to the Associated Press why she had resigned so abruptly before clearing her name: "In my military time, when the Commander in Chief makes a demand or a request, you say 'Aye, aye sir,' and you march on. And that's what I did. I thought it would be better to remove myself from being a distraction."

She remained grateful for having had a wonderful job that "afforded me to make history, to show many minorities and women that they too can reach high levels, they have to just be prepared when the door opens."[32] In December, the Allied Veterans group's national commander obtained a plea bargain, and in February 2014, the group's attorney was sentenced to prison. Carroll was never charged with any crime.

She published her side of the story, *When You Get There*, in August 2014. She also took a job as a political commentator for WJXT, an independent Jacksonville television station. Several times she has been asked whether she would ever run for office again and has kept the door open by replying "No, not yet. . . ."

Jennifer Carroll was interviewed in person by the author Sept. 20, 2013.

Carlos López-Cantera (R)

First Hispanic (Cuban) man to serve as Lieutenant Governor, 2014

Personal: Born December 29, 1973, Madrid, Spain (Cuban parents); married with two children.

Education:

- Miami-Dade Community College, A.A. (1994)
- University of Miami, bachelor's degree in business administration (1996)

Occupation: Real estate broker

Trailblazer Elections:

- Lieutenant Governor *Appointed by Gov. Rick Scott (R)* 2014
- Florida Governor/Lieutenant Governor *General Election* 2014
    - Scott/López-Cantera-R (48.1%), Crist/Taddeo-D (47.1%)

Figure 4.10. Gov. Rick Scott escorts newly appointed Lt. Gov. Carlos López-Cantera from the Governor's Mansion to a news conference after his swearing-in during a private ceremony at the Governor's office in the Capitol earlier in the day. Scott touted López-Cantera's "great legislative background, being Majority Leader, Majority Whip, building great relationships," along with his business background and local government experience as property appraiser of Miami-Dade County. López-Cantera succeeded Lt. Gov. Jennifer Carroll, who resigned in March 2013. State Archives of Florida, *Florida Memory*, https://www.floridamemory.com/items/show/266719. Photograph by Bill Cotterell, February 3, 2014.

THE CARLOS LÓPEZ-CANTERA STORY

Florida's first Hispanic Lieutenant Governor comes from a successful Cuban family. Born in Madrid, Spain, to Cuban parents, Carlos López-Cantera grew up in Miami where his family had gone after fleeing the Castro takeover in 1960.

"At the very beginning my grandfather started selling cigars at the old Dinner Key Marina, saving pennies. They owned a gas station early on. Once they sold that, they started the business that they had in Cuba—bookkeeping and tax services," said López-Cantera.

While growing up in the 1970s and 1980s, he heard stories from the family about how they had sacrificed. "There was a decade that they didn't go out: not to dinner, a restaurant, or a movie. No luxuries. No entertainment. It was all save, save, save, so they could invest in a business that would then produce."

"They started in a small office on Southwest First Street right by the intersection on 12th Avenue, which was made famous by a restaurant on the corner called La Esquina de Tejas, where Ronald Reagan went in the '80s," he said. "The business grew and they bought a larger building just down the street and became one of the go-to bookkeeping companies for the Cuban exile community."

By the time he was grown, "the family was doing well and was in a good financial situation, but that didn't prevent my grandparents and my father from constantly reminding me about the sacrifices that they went through."

His family helped other Cubans get started in business by helping them navigate local regulations and get loans. "My grandfather (Carlos López-Aguiar) would personally guarantee loans at the corner bank, back when you could do it on a handshake. He would personally guarantee them and if they didn't pay the bank, he would. He also lent money himself to help people get their business started. And there are a lot of those businesses that are still operating today. I've encountered people, throughout not only my political career but while I was working for that same company in the '90s, who are very fond of my grandparents and appreciative of the opportunities they helped them get."

"I think that it was the experience working in that family company that helped lead me into politics," he said. "My grandfather was very supportive and almost insistent about the idea of me going into public service."

López-Cantera earned an associate degree at Miami-Dade Community College in 1994 and a bachelor's degree in business administration, with a minor in political science, from the University of Miami in 1996.

When young people ask him for advice in seeking a political career, he tells them: "I've used my business degree more in my political life than I've used my political science degree. Politics—you'll learn [by] doing politics." He advises taking courses like accounting, management, and economics—"the arithmetic of dollars and cents." In addition, "Make sure you have a good job, and make sure that that's not something you'll have to worry about."

The summer after graduation, he and friends traveled to the Republican National Convention in San Diego. He remembered seeing Marco Rubio, now a U.S. Senator. "He had a specific role at the convention and we all thought, 'Man, Marco's made it! He's the floor leader!' He was out there mingling with all of the leaders of our party, and here we were just trying to get in, sneak peeks and snap pictures with whoever we could."

Apart from going to college and getting involved in politics, López-Cantera worked in the family business. "I did real estate with my dad and we had done all right. We weren't the foremost in real estate in South Florida, but we did fine. My dad was very conservative—he still is—with family investments and what we did," he said. The philosophy was "eat what you kill," which meant that they wouldn't overextend themselves. The office stayed small and was staffed primarily by family members.

Politics was never far from his mind, however. In 1997 he was a facilitator for the Florida Senate's Criminal Justice Committee. In 2002 he ran for a seat in the Florida House, but lost. He ran again in 2004 and won and subsequently was reelected three times. He was House Majority Whip from 2008 to 2010 and House Majority Leader from 2010 to 2012. In addition, he served on the Governor's Property Tax Reform Committee and chaired the Committee on Business Regulation and the Government Affairs Policy Committee.

The most rewarding thing about serving as a legislator was "the ability to fix things, the ability to solve people's problems," he said. In both the 2002 and 2004 campaigns, "I knocked on thousands and thousands of doors; many at the homes of elderly citizens. One of the big, recurring issues was property taxes." As a result, when he went to Tallahassee, "I filed a constitutional amendment to double the homestead exemption. We ended up being able to get a constitutional amendment on the ballot in 2006 to double the homestead exemption for low-income seniors." Today he looks back at that experience "as one of my favorite legislative accomplishments because I knew we had accomplished something for people that made a difference."

"As I advanced in my political career, I was given more responsibility. I had knowledge of the process and was more effective, and I enjoyed being able to solve problems. I learned that it didn't have to be through stand-alone legislation in the form of a bill before the Legislature. There was an amendatory process and there were agencies that one could call." When constituents, both individuals and institutions, would contact his office about an issue, "I enjoyed being able to work through the process with them. First giving ideas and suggestions on how they could accomplish their goals, and then helping them actually achieve them."

In August 2012, he was elected Property Appraiser for Miami-Dade County, a geographic area of more than 2.5 million people and almost a million properties. He had campaigned on a platform of making it easier to interact with the Property Appraiser's office, to increase community outreach, and to be more responsive to residents. In the short time he served, he renovated the Property Appraiser's office. "I wanted to create a more customer-friendly environment," he said, "I wanted the space to be open and inviting." He also stepped up enforcement of homestead exemption fraud.

In December 2013, he met with Gov. Rick Scott about the Lieutenant Governor position. López-Cantera had heard rumors that he might be considered for the position and when the phone call came, "the gravity hit," he said. "In those 24 hours a lot of stuff goes through your mind."

When the Governor called the next day, "we spoke about many of the issues that he had been championing—jobs, turning Florida's economy around." Then the Governor asked if he would be interested in becoming the Lieutenant Governor. He said yes.

"I remember having the first truly sleepless nights of my life, contemplating the gravity of the opportunity, not only as it related to being part of the administration but how it would affect my family."

"My wife was wonderful. She said, 'Whatever makes you happy.' She's been so supportive of me and the work I've done serving Florida not only as a legislator, but also now as Lieutenant Governor—and even when I was Property Appraiser because there were nights I wouldn't come home until 9 o'clock or later."

As Property Appraiser, "I was running an organization of 350 employees. I was really running it. It took time and energy and commitment. She's been wonderful throughout our marriage."

In early January, he and his wife were invited to lunch with the Governor and First Lady. López-Cantera remembered sitting down beforehand with his oldest daughter, who was then six, and explaining what a Lieutenant Governor was. "I explained it to her in terms of President and Vice President because every kid knows who the President is," he said. "I told her, '*Papi* would be like the Vice President of the state and would be helping the Governor.' And I remember hearing back from my father-in-law that my daughter had told him that I was going to be the President's helper."

Up to that time, "I guess her only impression of her father throughout her whole life was, 'Well, he goes to a place called Tallahassee every once in a while,'" he said. Now, after having been home for a year as Property Appraiser, he asked her permission to be gone again on weekdays. He said lightheartedly, "I don't know if I did it so that if she ever complained I could tell her, 'You told me I could do it.' But I did want to sit down with her. I thought she was old enough to be able to participate in a decision that would affect the whole family, and she did."

When the time came for the lunch, his wife was a little nervous about the impression that she would make. "I said, 'Honey, if you were just yourself and the Governor was going to make the decision based on you, I've got this in the bag. I mean there's no problem. If it's decided based on you, I'm fine.' And we had a very pleasant lunch with Governor and Mrs. Scott."

The lunch was in Coral Gables, close to where the Governor had just finished taking part in a parade. The Governor offered him the job, and López-Cantera accepted. Two days later, on January 14, 2014, Gov. Scott announced the appointment at a press conference in Miami, where his family was in attendance.

López-Cantera was officially sworn in at 10:30 a.m. in a brief private ceremony that took place in the Governor's office in the Capitol. Judge Joseph Lewis of the First District Court of Appeals officiated. Standing with López-Cantera were his mother, wife and two daughters, the youngest not yet a year old.

Speaking to reporters afterward, Gov. Scott said, "He's got a great legislative background, having served as Majority Leader, Majority Whip, and having built great relationships. He's been in business. He's got local government experience."

At 5 p.m. the same day, Ricky Polston, Chief Justice of the Florida Supreme Court,

Figure 4.11. The Lieutenant Governor's grandfather, Carlos López-Aguiar, planted the seed of a political career. López-Cantera said: "I still remember the day my grandfather sat me down—I was studying political science at the time—and he said to me, 'You're going to go into politics.' And it wasn't like a question, it was a direction." López-Cantera keeps a photograph of his beloved grandfather on his desk in the Capitol. Photograph courtesy of Carlos López-Cantera, who was four or five years old at the time it was taken.

conducted a ceremonial swearing-in in the Florida House. López-Cantera addressed House members in English and Spanish.

"It was surreal to be in that chamber for a ceremony that was focused on me. I had participated in some, I had spoken at a few, but I had never been in a position to have that type of honor," he said.

He added, "I had to go back and watch the replay on the Florida Channel to take it all in. Because while it is happening, time is flying by and it's hard to really take it in."

His grandfather, who had been the greatest influence on his political life, had died in 2005. It was a presence sorely missed. But his grandfather had been alive when López-Cantera had taken his first oath as state Representative. "Every time I had the honor to accept a higher level of responsibility, not only in the legislative process but throughout my career, I thought a lot about him. I actually keep a picture of him on my desk."

"He was a very, very big influence on my life. I would, almost on a daily basis, especially when I was working in the same building, just sit with him and listen. He taught me a lot about life," both business and personal. "He gave me profound advice that I still think about to this day."

But the most significant remembrance of his grandfather came when he first saw the signs with his name printed below Gov. Scott's for the 2014 campaign. To explain, López-Cantera described his experience as a freshman legislator at a bill signing with Gov. Jeb Bush. "I was nervous and so I tried to make a joke, I guess, to hide my nerves. When he was about to sign the bill, I made a joke somewhere along the lines of, 'Would you like me to sign that for you, Governor?' He teased, 'No, Carlos, you need to run statewide and be elected Governor to be able to sign one of these.' I remember responding, 'Well, I don't think that's ever going to happen for me.' When he asked why, I responded, 'Well, because I have a hyphenated last name, and I don't think that a hyphenated last name would ever be viable on a statewide ballot.' He immediately responded, 'Don't be so sure, Carlos.'"

Consequently, when he first saw the campaign sign, "It hit me that this is real. It's not just a Hispanic name, it's a hyphenated name. There's no getting around it. It hit me that my name would be on a ballot throughout the entire state of Florida." Late in the campaign at an event with Bush, López-Cantera reminded the former Governor of the exchange. "I was wrong, you were right," he told Bush. Having his name on the sign "was special, not just to me but to my community, to my family."

In a similar vein, he discovered that running for statewide office differed from running countywide, and both were vastly different than running in a House district. For Property Appraiser, "I was running on a single issue, which was property taxes, and everybody saw property taxes the same way—nobody liked them. But campaigning for the executive branch in a state like Florida, where every issue permeates debate and decision making, is very different."

The main difference he noticed in campaigning now versus 10 years ago is that "technology and the Internet have become a huge part of the political process," he said. "It's not just at the local level; it's all the way up and down the ballot." When he entered politics, campaign news appeared in the newspaper and on TV. Blogs were just starting. "Now, you look at Twitter to see what's going to be in a blog and then what's going to make a story."

Another difference, in South Florida at least, has been the large influx of South and Central Americans. "The communities that I've seen that have more impact on the political process are the Venezuelan, Colombian, and Puerto Rican communities. We saw a lot of support from those communities."

"When we were in South Florida, we did several events with the Venezuelan community, in order to attract more attention to what had been taking place in regard to the Maduro regime and what the regime had been doing to not only their country but their citizens. There is a parallel between the Cuban and Venezuelan communities because it's widely known that the Cuban regime is involved with the Maduro regime, helping them conceive and execute the strategies that are having such negative effects on that country," he said. "It was like the stories my grandfather would tell me about Cuba were being replayed in Venezuela today."

Figure 4.12. Seeing the 2014 campaign sign bearing his hyphenated Hispanic name really made an impact on the Lieutenant Governor. As a freshman state legislator, he told then-Gov. Jeb Bush that he did not think "that a hyphenated last name would ever be viable on a statewide ballot." He later recounted that having his name on the sign "was special, not just for me, but for my community, for my family." Photograph by author.

The Republican ticket of Scott and López-Cantera won the November 2014 election by a slim margin of 1 percent. They defeated former Florida Gov. Charlie Crist and his running mate Annette Taddeo, Miami-Dade Democratic Party chairwoman and a Colombian-American small-business owner.

By the Florida Constitution, the Lieutenant Governor would step in to replace a Governor should the office be vacated. Otherwise, the person in the No. 2 office assists the Governor with the duties of the executive branch. A bipartisan move has been underway, however, to give the Lieutenant Governor more defined duties, such as heading a state agency.[33]

Gov. Scott, for his part, has made it clear what he wants López-Cantera to do: "We want $500 million (in tax cuts) back to Florida families, but on top of that, he's going to work with job creators around the state. He'll be traveling the state, making sure we continue to build the state where your kids and grandkids can get a great job."

The Governor said to him early on: "You can be a part of whatever you want to be a part of." The Governor "recognized that I had good relationships with the Legislature. He wanted to make sure that I had good relationships in his administration. He has allowed me to participate in anything and everything. And there were times when we were here last year that, for instance, he'd be interviewing a judge and he would say, 'Carlos, have you sat in on one of these interviews before?' I hadn't and he said, 'C'mon, you should.' He's been great. He's been really great."

In a meeting with the Hispanic Legislative Caucus, the Governor and López-Cantera spoke with legislators about their priorities, including in-state tuition for U.S.-born children of undocumented immigrants. "I know the Governor cares about all Floridians and he cares about the individual issues that you guys have brought up," said López-Cantera. "To whatever extent I can act as a conduit for any of you to talk about your individual priorities, talk about your pieces of legislation, I'd be happy to. I know the legislative process."[34]

He has remained loyal to his Cuban heritage. In an op-ed piece in the *Miami Herald* on the occasion of Veinte de Mayo (marking Cuba's independence from Spain), he reflected on recent victims of the Cuban government's brutality.[35] "It is from these modern-day *Mambises* [freedom fighters] that the children of exiles find today's inspiration to never forget. This is a sentiment that will never be captured in any opinion poll. The generosity of spirit and meritocracy that is the United States of America allows the son of a refugee to become the first Hispanic Lieutenant Governor of Florida."

Carlos López-Cantera was interviewed in person by the author Feb. 3, 2015.

Cabinet

M. Athalie Range (D)

First African-American woman to serve on the Miami City Commission, 1965

First African-American woman to serve in a "Little Cabinet" position (Secretary of Department of Community Affairs), 1971

Personal: Born November 7, 1915, Key West, Florida. Died November 14, 2006.

Education:

- New England Institute of Anatomy and Embalming; funeral director certification

Occupation: Funeral business

Trailblazer Election/Appointment:

- Miami City Commission, *Appointed by Mayor Robert King High(D)* 1965, then elected
- Secretary of Community Affairs, *Appointed by Gov. Reubin Askew (D)* 1971

Figure 4.13. Athalie Range walks with Gov. Reubin Askew, who named her Secretary of the Department of Community Affairs. The first African-American woman to head a major state agency in modern times, she served in Askew's "Little Cabinet"—an influential group of agency heads that met regularly with the Governor. State Archives of Florida, *Florida Memory*, https://www.floridamemory.com/items/show/129054. Photograph taken December 30, 1970.

THE M. ATHALIE RANGE STORY

Athalie Range, the first black person to hold a top-level executive office in Florida since Reconstruction, had many accomplishments in a public service career that began in the late 1940s. "There were so many inequities in those days that you could just reach out and pick something and change it," she said.

Range's grandparents had come from Nassau in the Bahamas, but she and her parents were born in Key West. She remembered Key West as "a very beautiful little peninsula, surrounded by water, so you went swimming almost every day."

"We did not know segregation in Key West, not in the days when I lived there," she said. Her neighbors included two older white women and a Spanish-speaking family. "We all went to the same Catholic church up on Rocky Road in Key West." When the Ku Klux Klan made its presence known in the area, however, her father decided to move the family to Miami on the mainland.[36]

In 1923, when she was seven or eight years old, they settled in Overtown, an all-black area bordered north-south by Northwest Fifth Street to about Northwest 21st Street and east-west by two railroad tracks—the Florida East Coast Railway (First Avenue) and the Seaboard Railway (Northwest Seventh Avenue). Her father worked as a stevedore for a cement company, then taught himself to cook, and worked as a cook in Miami Beach hotels.

As a child, Range remembered the difficulty black people had in venturing outside Overtown. "Black people could not go across the beach to work unless they had an identification card," she said. "If you worked, you did not approach the front door, you went around to the back." At the Catholic church the family attended, blacks sat in the back pew. White children received their First Communion in the main body of the church, while black children received theirs in the basement.[37]

During this time, construction began on Booker T. Washington High School that was to serve black students. When it was about half completed, it was bombed. "Even though they tried to play that down, there are a few of us who are living witnesses to know that this actually happened," she said. The bombing set back the construction and delayed the opening by several months. In addition, "We knew of police brutality, but no one dared speak of it because it was just a no-no," she added.

After graduating from Booker T. Washington in 1935, she worked as a clerk at Christian Hospital, a small hospital for blacks. She left Overtown in 1937 and married Oscar Lee Range, who had worked in a funeral home in Valdosta, Ga. Together they opened a funeral home in Liberty City in 1953 at Northwest 15th Street and 67th Street. A few years later they relocated to 5727 Northwest 17th Avenue.

"We had a motto when we started the business, and it said, 'A living service for the living.' That means serving those persons who are bereaved in every way we possibly can, not taking advantage of their bereavement and being aware of the fact that people are not at their best when death occurs," she said.[38]

At first, the new location proved difficult: "There were some threats from people who did not want us in this area," she said. One neighbor complained about an odor, but funeral homes don't smell, she said. Only one older white woman who lived with her son "who was not quite normal" was friendly. "Several people called and said some unkind things, but we didn't let that bother us," she said. When her youngest child was ready to go to school, the Archie Miller School was being integrated, "we received some rather nasty threats about that, but we didn't really stop because we went right on."

In 1960, her husband died of a heart attack, leaving her a widow with four children. Although she had apprenticed with her husband, she needed formal training and a license to continue operating the funeral home. So she studied at the New England Institute of Anatomy and Embalming in Boston, finished the apprenticeship, and got her license. Her eldest son Patrick studied at the same school, obtained his license in 1965, and went into partnership with her.

Range's public service career had begun a dozen years earlier, in 1948, while she was a PTA president. Her children attended a segregated school, Liberty City Elementary at 60th Street and 17th Avenue, which enrolled 1,200 children. The school had no permanent building—only portables—no lunchroom, no trees, and no grassy areas. It had 12 toilets for girls and about the same number for boys, so students started lining up to use them at 10:30 in the morning. The only water fountains were outdoors and were fed by pipes merely laid on the ground—"not a blade of grass anywhere to keep them cool." The water was so undrinkable that some parents gave their children ice in Thermos® bottles or mayonnaise jars to take to school.

In a 1991 interview, excerpted in a book by Marvin Dunn,[39] Range recalled:

> Some of the parents began to suggest that we write the school board and tell them that we were not satisfied with the conditions under which our children were being educated. I felt that writing letters never helped, so I said rather than writing letters let's all get together and go down to the school board as a group. The parents were all very cooperative with this idea.
>
> That PTA meeting was on a Tuesday, and the school board met on Wednesday. We decided we would go that Wednesday and we went to the school board unannounced. About 125 people went to the meeting. It was a very great surprise to the school board members. We got there very early because we did not know when the meeting started. We filled up every seat in the auditorium; consequently, the other parents who were accustomed to going and talking were left without a seat. They delayed the meeting for an hour hoping that maybe we would go away.
>
> Finally, the superintendent called the meeting together, and I shall always remember what he said: "We have an unusual situation here today. In order to

> get our meeting moving, we have a large group of Negroes here so we are going to hear what they have to say. If there is a spokesman among you, you may come up." I went up and spoke for 15 minutes without a note. One of the school board administrators walked out of the meeting afterwards and asked our school principal, "Who was the silver-tongue derringer they sent down here to hang us?"

As a result, the Board promised a new permanent building with a cafeteria. In the meantime, a large portable was brought onto the grounds as a temporary lunchroom, and hot lunches were delivered from the all-white Miami Jackson High School. When the new school was built (in a different location), it was the first school built for black children in 21 years.

Over the next decade, civil rights activity increased in Miami. CORE (Congress of Racial Equality), of which Range was a member, trained activists in conducting nonviolent demonstrations. The NAACP campaigned to integrate the city's buses. One leading civil rights activist, the Rev. Theodore Gibson, a black Episcopalian priest, was fined and jailed for six months for refusing to identify NAACP members.[40]

Public attention to civil rights was often diverted to immigrants arriving from the Caribbean and Cuba. "I can very easily recall when there were no black clerks in stores like Burdine's, no black front-desk people in any of the hotels on the beach or here in Miami or anywhere else," Range said. "It was said on any number of occasions that the Cubans had come over and taken our jobs. The Cubans got jobs that we never had, and I think people ought to remember that."

In the midst of this activity, a vacancy opened on the City Commission in 1964. Alice Wainwright, the first woman on that body, decided not to seek office again. A group of black ministers visited Range and urged her to run. She won the primary by 500 votes. In the runoff, however, she faced a white candidate, Irwin Christie. "The evening before the election, there was a big sound truck going around the white sections of town saying, 'Unless you get out and vote in tomorrow's election, you may have a Negro deciding your fate on the Commission,'" she recalled. In addition, some blacks, who were unaccustomed to voting and politics, were told they could not leave their jobs to vote. "'You voted for Mrs. Range the first Tuesday. They will count it this time.' There was a lot of bitterness in the community," Range said.[41] Christie won by about 18,000 votes to Range's 17,000.

In 1965, Miami Mayor Robert King High (D), who had his eye on the governorship, wanted to increase his popularity in the black community. He persuaded one City Commissioner to give up his seat and appointed Range to fill it. (High ran twice for Governor but lost both times.) Range thus became the first black to serve on the Miami City Commission and twice won reelection in her own right.

Her office on the Commission "meant a lot to the blacks of Miami because prior to that time, black people expressed no interest in what was going on. The laws were passed, we were overlooked, our garbage was picked up whenever they got around to picking it up—many, many things that may not seem important now were just thrust upon the black community. Street lights were very sparse, no sidewalks throughout most of the area, and so when I became City Commissioner and began to learn of what it would take to get certain things done for the community, naturally I went after those things," she said.

Shortly before she took office, the city had approved the construction of a new expressway, Interstate 95, that was to go right through the heart of Overtown. Plans for the highway had been underway since the end of World War II. Originally the highway was to follow the Florida East Coast Railway, but slum clearance advocates objected and the Florida State Road Department rerouted it. "Residents who lived in the path of the new highway were given little warning that their homes were to be razed and few options for where to go. Some tenants had notice of fewer than 24 hours before their homes were boarded up and torn down."[42] Planners promised residents to bring new development to Overtown, but nothing much happened. "It was just a community completely destroyed," she said.

Once she was in office, black people became more interested in city affairs. "They would come to my home and bring their complaints, and I naturally would invite them to come to the Commission meetings," she said. "I would be sitting there with four white men—they were all men at that time—they had the feeling that whatever I proposed was what my constituents wanted. I was very fortunate that in most instances they followed my lead, such as if I brought an issue to the table, they would just look at me and everyone, whichever way I voted, they would vote."

In one instance, a fire in a black area of the city claimed the lives of 11 people. When an investigation found the cause to be a space heater, she led the way in passing an ordinance that banned space heaters in the city.

In 1967, she took on the issue of garbage pickup. "Can you imagine having to sit in a governmental body and fuss about whether your garbage is picked up or not? Well, that is what was happening. They had regular routes in the white areas for a pick-up twice a week. And in the predominantly black sections, you were lucky if you got your garbage picked up once in two weeks." She introduced an ordinance requiring twice-weekly garbage collection throughout the city. After the vote was postponed twice, Range came up with an idea. At the next meeting, Commission members found their chambers packed with black people holding bags of garbage. The ordinance quickly passed.

She encountered conflict when she proposed that black police officers serve as funeral escorts. "It struck me that we were paying out all of this money—we as funeral directors had to pay for this service of course, and there were always white officers escorting our services, so I got the idea that it could very well be that we could use black officers in the same capacity." When she approached City Manager Mel Reese

Figure 4.14. Athalie Range's appointment as Secretary of the Department of Community Affairs in 1971 came with a $22,500 annual salary. The *Tallahassee Democrat* (February 16, 1971) reported that made her "the highest paid woman, as well as the top member of her race, in state government." She was passionate about housing issues and the difficulties experienced by migrants, stemming from her days of service on the Miami City Commission, where she had been the first black woman elected to that body. State Archives of Florida, *Florida Memory*, https://www.floridamemory.com/items/show/243853. Photograph ca. 1971–1973.

about the idea, he said this was one section of the police department "that was not going to be a checkerboard." About that time the city was trying to acquire land for a park near Vizcaya, and Mayor High asked for her support. Not until you train blacks as motorcycle policemen, she said. Her bargaining worked.[43] The first black motorcycle officer to escort funerals was Robert Ingram, who would later become Police Chief and Mayor of Opa-Locka and vice chair of the Miami-Dade School Board.

Through the early 1960s, Miami had been spared from race riots. But after the assassination of Martin Luther King, Jr., in April 1968, rioting erupted in Liberty City, as it did in many other cities across the country. Range urged calm: "I think it is incumbent upon every leader, every citizen, and every follower to emulate the man who has become a martyr for the cause of non-violence," she said. "I think we cannot afford to let this man have fallen in vain."

The following August, the Republican Party held its national convention at Miami Beach. Representatives of CORE, SCLC (Southern Christian Leadership Conference), and the Black Panthers met at SCLC headquarters in Liberty City to plan a demonstration. What was intended as a peaceful vote rally blew up into a riot. An investigation later found that the riot had its roots in local frustrations, such as job losses and displacement from homes.

Appearing in the public spotlight as a black woman meant taking personal risks. But Range, who stood only 5 feet tall and weighed barely 100 pounds, felt she had to keep going. "I never thought anybody had the nerve to come up and to try to attack me. I wasn't afraid."[44]

In 1971, Gov. Reubin Askew (D) appointed her Secretary of Community Affairs, a state agency that included the divisions of Economic Opportunity, Technical Assistance, Migrant Labor, Emergency Government, Veterans Affairs, and Training and Professional Development. Her $22,500-a-year salary made her the highest paid woman in state government at that time.

Upon joining the Governor's "Little Cabinet," she saw housing as the most pressing need of her department. Expressing concern because "we have been limited in our thinking," she hoped to deal with the housing needs not only of low-income people but also of the middle class in densely populated areas. "I find this subject crops up more and more," she said. "Prices are exorbitant, people in any price range have to pay far too much for what they get." She advocated a stringently enforced statewide housing code.[45]

Modular homes were not the answer. She pointed to some that had been built in Dade County: "They're very expensive so they don't supply the needs of low-income families. In addition, the builders are concerned only about putting homes in and they provide none of the supportive services needed in a community."

Clearing ghettos was an important issue at that time. "We must erase the ghettos from within. We can no longer afford to live within the double standard of the law which has made all the difference between neighborhoods."

Shortly after taking office, she toured a migrant camp at Pahokee. The experience "enlarged my concept of suffering," she said. "I'd read of the plight of the migrants and know that it has been said things are improving for them. However, I cannot see how their situation could ever have been worse. If it isn't at its lowest ebb now, it is incredible. Some of the experiences I've observed were heartbreaking."

In 1970–1971 Florida suffered a severe drought, causing massive crop failure. Fire broke out in the Everglades and burned uncontrollably. At the request of farmers, she visited the hard-hit agricultural areas. At her suggestion, Gov. Askew sent a team of specialists with Range to survey the damage by helicopter. As a result, more than $8 million in state and federal money was allocated to help alleviate the situation.

Federal aid was helpful in the drought, but she had reservations about it in general. "Too much federal money goes into studies, executives to conduct the studies, and the things that relate to the man on the street but [do not reach] him." The Democrats were just as bad as Republicans in this criticism. She described the effect on people by alluding to a quote from a Bible inscription: "We live in hope and sometimes die in despair."

She left state office in 1973 but continued to work in public service, often behind the scenes. In the late 1970s she was one of the first blacks in Florida to support Jimmy Carter (D) in his campaign for the presidency. In 1978, he appointed her to a two-year term on the national board of AMTRAK.

She remained active in the community in the 1980s and 1990s and continued to run the funeral business with her son. Among her community interests was the preservation of Miami's beaches. "Every grain of sand is owned by some hotel. You more or less have to go through their lobbies to get to the beach. I think those kinds of things are not good for the future of Miami, if it's to be the paradise that it's touted to be all over the country. People come here for vacation and they see more of the same thing that they left at home—just tall buildings and nightclubs."

She was equally pessimistic about class divisions. "You can legislate and change laws, but you just can't change the hearts of men. I think the rich are always going to be richer and the poor are always going to be poorer. I don't see a whole lot of change coming." Nonetheless, she believed blacks must encourage their children to seek a broader education, including learning about other languages and cultures.

She died in 2006 at age 91. After her death, accolades came pouring in with a common theme—"her quiet but forceful presence as a tireless and trusted advocate of the disadvantaged."

"She knew more about politics than anyone I knew," said U.S. Rep. Carrie Meek. "She taught me humility, first and foremost. She taught me to go out and talk with the little people in the community, who no one else thought about."

"Athalie Range was a beacon who showed the way for us in fighting for the rights of others," said State Rep. Kendrick Meek. "The magnitude of her courage and the strength of her heart defined her will to end inequality and discrimination everywhere she found their evil vestiges."

Information about Athalie Range came from two interviews—"Tell the Story," University of Florida Oral History, Aug. 28, 1997, and the Turner Tech History Archive, Mar. 22, 2002—as well as news clippings.

Jesse J. McCrary, Jr. (D)

First black lawyer to argue a case before the U.S. Supreme Court on behalf of a southern state, 1969

First African-American man to be on the Florida Cabinet since Reconstruction, appointed as Secretary of State, 1978

Personal: Born September 16, 1937, Blitchton, Florida. Died October 29, 2007.

Figure 4.15. Gov. Reubin Askew appointed Jesse J. McCrary, Jr., the first black Secretary of State in Florida since Reconstruction. A lawyer and former Assistant Attorney General, McCrary often served as an advocate on behalf of poor African Americans and saw himself as "the link between the establishment and the ghetto." On the wall behind McCrary is a portrait of Jonathan C. Gibbs, the first black Secretary of State, who served from November 6, 1868, to January 17, 1873. State Archives of Florida, *Florida Memory*, https://www.floridamemory.com/items/show/43654. Photograph taken July 19, 1978.

Education:
- Florida A&M University, B.A. (1960)
- Florida A&M University, J.D. (1965)

Occupation: Attorney

Trailblazer Appointment:
- Secretary of State, *Appointed by Gov. Reubin Askew (D)* 1978

THE JESSE J. MCCRARY, JR., STORY

"None of us is free until all of us are free," Jesse McCrary once told the *Miami Herald*.[46] For Florida's first black Secretary of State since Reconstruction, the recurrent themes of freedom, equality, and justice guided his life from cradle to grave.

McCrary's earliest influence was his father, a Baptist preacher. The Rev. Jesse McCrary, Sr., made it clear to his eldest son that he must rise above the limits of a segregated society as it existed in the South in the late 1930s. The young McCrary, growing up in Blitchton, a hamlet northwest of Ocala, attended Marion County public schools. He had thought about becoming a doctor but changed his mind when he realized he couldn't stand the sight of blood.

In high school, at the all-black Howard Academy in Ocala, he participated in choral and dramatic productions as well as sports, playing quarterback on the school's championship football team. He enrolled in the historically black Florida A&M University as the Civil Rights Movement was gaining momentum. In 1956, for example, blacks boycotted the buses in Tallahassee, and students held demonstrations. At Florida A&M, McCrary met Elbert Hatchett, who later observed that McCrary was "always in the middle" of civil rights demonstrations.[47]

McCrary majored in political science and also took part in student government, debate, and drama activities, experiences that helped build the oratorical skills he would use as a lawyer. He graduated in 1960, and as an ROTC cadet, entered the military as a second lieutenant. He served in army intelligence at a time when the United States was increasing its military presence in South Vietnam.

When he left the Army, he returned to Florida A&M to study law. At that time, the law school was small, having been created in 1949 as a separate school for blacks. His old buddy Hatchett (who would graduate from the law school in 1966) called McCrary "a shot in the arm to the whole law school," making everyone feel as though they "had special destinies to fill." For his part, McCrary once said he developed "a feel for law and order" while serving on Florida A&M's Honor Court.

Apart from immersing himself in the U.S. Constitution, civil and criminal procedure, litigation, and the intricacies of property, torts, and contracts, McCrary got his first glint in the national media spotlight when *Ebony* magazine named him one of the most eligible bachelors in the country in 1963. After all, he was a military veteran, handsome, intelligent, and headed toward a great future.

He earned his law degree in 1965, only a few years before the Legislature would close the school. (The Florida A&M law school would reopen in Orlando in 2006.) He worked briefly in the law offices of Allen and Hastings, Fort Lauderdale. (His boss, Alcee Hastings, a 1963 Florida A&M law graduate, would later become a U.S. Congressman.) McCrary was admitted to the Florida Bar in 1966.

He began the practice of law during a time of widespread racial and antiwar violence in the United States. In 1967 alone, for example, 159 race riots erupted across the country,[48] including one in Tampa. In April 1968, violence broke out after the assassination of Dr. Martin Luther King, Jr., and in August, antiwar protests resulted in brutality at the Democratic National Convention in Chicago.

One summer during this period, McCrary spoke out during racial unrest at Pompano Beach. "You tell us that you have a job opening for a machinist, but where in hell can we find a Negro machinist if you don't let him go to school?"[49] He warned of a long, hot summer, noting "the germ of discontent has been sown and inequities exist."

In the midst of the turmoil, in 1967, Attorney General Earl Faircloth-D (1965–1971) appointed McCrary Assistant Attorney General and assigned him to Miami. In becoming the first black to that post, he said, "I don't think my race imposes any particular burden. I interpret this as an appointment made to a man who happened to be qualified."[50] Recognizing that some might disagree with him, he said, "I believe in America and I believe in democracy. A great deal of progress has been made, but there are many areas where a lot still has to be done."

In the Attorney General's office, he handled criminal appeals and advised the state Racing Commission. In 1969, at age 32, he represented Florida before the U.S. Supreme Court, becoming the first black lawyer to argue a case before the high court on behalf of a Southern state. In *Williams v. Florida*, he asked the Court to uphold a state law allowing defendants in non-capital criminal cases to be tried by juries of 6 rather than 12. "There is nothing magic about the number 12," he said. "It doesn't ensure a fair trial."[51] A jury is designed to be a buffer between an oppressive government and the people, and all that is required is that the jury be large enough to deliberate guilt or innocence. If 12 is the number, then it can also be argued that 24 or 36 jurors are better, he said.

He won the case, saving the state millions of dollars a year in jury costs. He expressed his satisfaction matter-of-factly: "We in Florida are abiding by constitutional standards. This is the real reward of the whole thing, it strengthens the whole administration of justice as it relates to jury trials in Florida." Georgia Ayers, a long-time community activist, called the reaction typical of his perspective: He was not selfish for himself. "It was what he could do for the community as an attorney."[52]

In 1971 he went into private practice as senior partner in McCrary, Ferguson, Lee, Adderly, Culmer, and Long. (One partner, Wilkie D. Ferguson, Jr., would later be

Figure 4.16. Jesse J. McCrary, Jr., takes the oath of office from Florida Supreme Court Justice Joseph Hatchett—the first black to serve on the Supreme Court. McCrary's father, the Rev. Jesse J. McCrary, Sr., holds the Bible. McCrary received many congratulatory letters and telegrams, including one from the Rev. Ralph David Abernathy of Atlanta who wrote: "You serve as an example to our young people lately so turned off by the political processes. . . . We are fully aware that you have done what you have done on your own." State Archives of Florida, *Florida Memory*, https://www.floridamemory.com/items/show/43652. Photographed on July 19, 1978.

appointed a federal judge.) At the same time, McCrary became the first black attorney to represent the Dade County School Board (1971–1972 and 1973–1978).

He often served as an advocate on behalf of poor African Americans and considered himself as "the link between the establishment and the ghetto." In 1971, for example, he headed a commission to study the cause of riots in Opa-Locka's black community and issued a report critical of the city's government and police department.

By this time, he had become involved in politics, working, for example, on Democrat Reubin Askew's campaign to unseat Republican Gov. Claude Kirk. The newly elected Gov. Askew (1971–1979) appointed McCrary to a judgeship on the Industrial Relations Commission (1971–1973). As one of three judges, he heard appeals in workers compensation, unemployment benefits, and industrial safety. That position, paying $32,000 a year, made him Florida's highest paid black official in 1971.[53]

In 1973, McCrary returned to private practice as a partner in McCrary, Berkowitz, Davis, and Felg. He also served on state committees studying judicial reform, capital punishment, constitutional revision, and workers compensation.

In July 1978, Gov. Askew—the two were now friends—tapped McCrary to fill out the term of Secretary of State Bruce Smathers, who had resigned to run for Governor. (Smathers would lose to Bob Graham.) The appointment made McCrary the first black member of the Florida Cabinet since the end of Reconstruction. From the beginning, McCrary made it clear that he would not run for the seat in the upcoming election, so the historic appointment lasted less than half a year.

At the swearing-in ceremony, McCrary took the oath from the first African American to serve on the Florida Supreme Court, trailblazer Justice Joseph Hatchett (1975–1979). McCrary's father led the prayer. Many people sent him congratulatory letters and telegrams. The Rev. Ralph David Abernathy of Atlanta wrote: "You serve as an example to our young people lately so turned off by the political processes. In particular, you serve as an inspiration to the courageous and wonderful people of Marion County and Ocala who went through so much to be able to participate in government at all levels. We are all fully aware that you have done what you have done on your own."

Once in office, McCrary set two goals: simplifying the state's voter registration system and having all candidates file financial disclosure statements. "Voter registration and voter education are two important elements if we are going to take some steps to reduce election apathy," he said. "We have to seek ways to simplify the registration process so citizens can become active participants without feeling put upon. We make it easy for citizens to pay their taxes. We should make it easy to register to vote." Among other things, he sponsored a voter registration program for supervisors of elections and interested citizens.

One important duty was recommending judicial appointees to the Governor. "I used to kid that Jesse made the appointments, and I just signed them," Askew said. In general, the Secretary's office took charge of state records, receiving for safekeeping documents about legislation and returns of city elections involving charter changes.

True to his word, McCrary returned to private practice in 1979. Although he could have joined a deep-carpet law firm, "He preferred to stay on the ground and address some of the everyday issues that impacted have-not black people," said his former law classmate, Elbert Hatchett. "I don't think he ever considered abdicating that responsibility that he was born to."

McCrary argued several cases before the Florida Supreme Court. In *Neil v. State of Florida*, the court agreed with him that a juror cannot be dismissed on the basis of race. Much of his work involved community problems. For example, he represented a County Commissioner in a public corruption scandal (his defendant pleaded guilty to bribery and served 27 months in prison). He felt his greatest pride in saving JESCA, a Miami community services organization, from bankruptcy. He took over as the organization's chair—with no pay—and after 18 months, left it in the black.

Through the 1980s and 1990s, he enjoyed a vigorous civil trial practice, with an emphasis in governmental and administrative law. In 2001, he was named to a commission to make recommendations to Senior Judge Lenore C. Nesbitt (1983–2001) in a federal condemnation suit brought by the National Park Service to acquire land for the Everglades National Park.

In 2003, the Florida Legislature passed a resolution honoring him as a "living legend" and "a preeminent authority on constitutional law who had won 10 landmark cases presented before the Florida Supreme Court." One of that Court's Justices once said McCrary "was the best prepared lawyer in the state when he came before them."[54]

Many other honors, state and national, came his way, among them being voted Outstanding Black Lawyer in America by the National Bar Association, an organization of predominantly African-American lawyers and judges. He served on many boards, such as those of the University of Miami and Florida Memorial College.

When he died in 2007, at age 70, many stepped forward to commend him. "He was a great public servant that a lot of public servants can emulate," said former Gov. Askew. "He was one of the greatest warriors who never, ever hesitated to go to the civil rights battlefield," said U.S. Rep. Carrie Meek. "He left us a message, regardless of what happens to you in life, you keep pushing." Students at the Florida A&M College of Law named their chapter of the National Black Law Students Association in his honor, and an elementary school in Miami is named for him.

Throughout his career, McCrary accepted invitations to speak to groups, including students. As Secretary of State, for example, he spoke at a luncheon of the Dade County Bar on future developments in the legal system.

"We can predict that the law will continue to provide a link to the past, adding the dimension of human experience to the cold logic of science, and offering a welcome source of continuity in a radically changing world," he said. "Although the law doesn't change as rapidly as many other aspects of life, it must evolve if it is to remain a living, vital means of solving problems and resolving conflicts. One way in which it will change, I think, is that the body of laws and regulations will grow, as will our reliance on law and legal process, in response to technological advances, the growing complexity of life, and changes in society."[55]

He outlined changes in biomedicine, transportation, communication, corporate business, and government. Many factors will enlarge the role of law in the future, he said. "Some of these factors, such as improved legal services, should bring us closer to the goal of equal justice under law. Surely it is proper that the poor, the aged, and other disadvantaged persons should at last have the opportunity for adequate legal representation. Surely the cause of justice is served when the voiceless have at last a voice before the law."

In many of his speeches, McCrary read a short poem to challenge his audience to decide what role they might play in shaping the nation:

"A Bag of Tools" by R. L. Sharpe

Isn't it strange
That princes and kings,
And clowns that caper
In sawdust rings,
And common people
Like you and me
Are builders for eternity?

Each is given a bag of tools,
A shapeless mass,
A book of rules

And each must make—
Ere life is flown—
A stumbling block
Or a stepping stone.

Information about Jesse McCrary came from news clippings and archival materials.

Douglas L. "Tim" Jamerson (D)

First African-American man to serve as Commissioner of Education, 1993

Personal: Born October 16, 1947, St. Petersburg, Florida; married with one child. Died April 21, 2001.

Education:

- Pinellas County Police Academy (1977)
- St. Petersburg Junior College, A.A. (1977)
- University of South Florida, B.A. (1979)

Occupation: Police Officer/Occupational Specialist and Counselor/Teacher

Trailblazer Appointment:

- Commissioner of Education, *Appointed by Gov. Lawton Chiles (D)* 1993

Figure 4.17. Doug Jamerson, first black Commissioner of Education, strongly believed that education was the "great equalizer"—the vehicle for social change. He loved visiting classrooms and was committed to erasing stereotypes about black students and challenging young black men to take advantage of educational opportunities. State Archives of Florida, *Florida Memory*, https://www.floridamemory.com/items/show/23200. Photograph taken ca. 1994–1995.

THE DOUGLAS L. "TIM" JAMERSON, JR., STORY

Douglas L. "Tim" Jamerson, Jr., Florida's first African-American Commissioner of Education, said on many occasions that education was the "great equalizer," the vehicle for social change. But he made it clear that education was neither easily obtained nor dispensed. "School is not designed to be fun," he said. "It is designed to be hard work and perseverance. If you do those two things, you'll be rewarded later."[56]

Jamerson grew up in a poor black neighborhood of St. Petersburg known as Gas

Plant, named for the two giant fuel tanks that stood in the center. One of the city's oldest neighborhoods, it dated back to the late 1880s when black workers came to help build the Orange Belt Railroad. They settled there and built houses, churches, markets, hotels, and small businesses.

The city razed the neighborhood in the early 1980s and built the Florida Suncoast Dome that eventually became Tropicana Field. "My grandmother and others gave up their property on the expectation that people would have affordable housing. Light industry and jobs were promised. We still haven't seen that come to fruition," he said years later.[57]

His mother and grandparents, who cared for him while his mother worked, were probably the first to instill in him the value of education. His grandfather, Booker Timothy Bullard (the middle name accounts for Jamerson's nickname), would buy books and then read and discuss them with the boy. His grandmother, Gertie, stayed busy running a restaurant out of her home and expected the school to guide his grades and discipline: "Don't call me out there for nothing. Just whip him."

The man who would become the state's biggest advocate for public education went to private Catholic schools in his youth. He spent his elementary years in a school at the Immaculate Conception Mission Church that was started by two nuns to serve the city's blacks. (St. Joseph's, the sister Catholic Church, served the city's whites. The two congregations would merge in the 1980s.)[58] He graduated as valedictorian due in large part to Sister Elizabeth Anne's demands for perfect test scores.

He wanted to attend the all-black public high school named for Jonathan Gibbs, the black man who served as Secretary of State and State Superintendent of Public Instruction during Reconstruction. But Jamerson's grandmother persuaded him to attend Bishop Barry High School (now St. Petersburg Catholic High School). He was one of the first African-American students to attend the school in the early 1960s when the Pinellas County public school system was still segregated.

After graduating in 1965, he wanted to go to Howard University in Washington, D.C., but his family couldn't afford to send him. He started college at St. Petersburg Junior College, but it must have been a half-hearted effort. "I had the good sense to join the Air Force before my report card came out," he said.[59]

In the Air Force, he became a security specialist with top-secret clearance. He spent part of his service time in Turkey, where he served as a guard at a sensitive military installation.

Back home by 1971, he put his security experience to work as the first black campus police officer for the Pinellas County school system. He returned to junior college, earning an associate of arts degree and graduating from the school's police academy. He went on to the University of South Florida, earning a bachelor's degree in criminal justice in 1979. He would later became assistant director of the Criminal Justice Institute at the junior college.

He worked at St. Petersburg High School in a number of capacities—helping recruit minority teachers and assisting students as an occupational specialist and guidance counselor. One of his duties was supervising the time-out room for disruptive students. "I had the kids looking for jobs—kids that [some] thought [ought] to be kicked out," he recalled later. A student who attended the school at the time remembered Jamerson "as a big man with a big laugh and a bigger heart." That student would later become a Governor—Charlie Crist (2007–2011).

Jamerson was teaching social studies in 1982 when new single-member districts made it possible for blacks to be elected to the Legislature. His students said, "Why don't you run?" He said, "What? You know I don't have any experience." They said, "Well, why not? You've talked about how anybody can run." So he and his students worked on his campaign. All his signs were homemade.[60]

In the Democratic primary, he faced a prominent local lawyer who had fought for years to create just such a district. The man, Morris Milton, headed up the NAACP, received the endorsement of the *St. Petersburg Times*, boasted of the county Democratic chairman's support, and raised three times as much money.[61]

"I was dispatched to tell him this was Morris Milton's seat, and there was not much purpose in him running," said Peter Rudy Wallace, who worked for the Democratic Party at the time.[62] Many others felt the same way, not realizing Jamerson's deep roots in the community. But Jamerson stayed in the race, finished second in the primary, and then squeaked out a victory in the runoff by 48 votes.

In the general election, he won with 66 percent of the vote, becoming the first black legislator from Pinellas County. Over the next 11 years he chaired committees on housing, corrections, and education. According to one account, he "held down a prized seat on the Appropriations Committee, and made himself widely respected as one of the few inspirational, effective leaders in a generally lackluster Legislature."[63]

His accomplishments included obtaining $15 million in funding for construction of low-income housing, "the first significant investment by Florida ever in the area." He was also instrumental in establishing the $1.67 million Tampa Bay Black Business Investment Fund to help stimulate entrepreneurship in the black community.

But education was his passion: "From the very beginning of his legislative service, he made himself an education expert. It was his priority. He became knowledgeable about it, not only the substance but the funding," said Wallace,[64] who was elected to the House in 1985 and later was Speaker of the House (1994–1996). "Doug had stepped very naturally into the role of being the chair of the K-12 committee and had a great ability to work across party lines" and with the Senate.

As chair of the Education Committee, Jamerson became the principal architect of the Education Reform and Accountability Act, known as Blueprint 2000. The law was intended to shift control of education from the state to local teachers and parents.

In practice, it required the state's public schools to conduct needs assessments and develop school improvement plans.

A lifelong educator himself, he often focused on the classroom and in particular advocated for multicultural instruction. He wanted children to have a broader view of history—something more than "slavery was the beginning of black folks and that women had no contribution other than Betsy Ross that did the flag."

"He liked to go to classrooms," recalled Laurey Stryker, a former Assistant Commissioner of Education. "He was very much about challenging, especially black stereotypes and young black males, to take advantage of opportunity."[65]

He seemed to have a special affinity for middle school students. "They're really not little kids anymore, and yet they're really not even teenagers or close to adults," said Cathy Kelly, a former official with the Florida Education Association. "It's that age where it's very hard to fit in, and I think he just really understood that."[66]

He spoke at lots of high school graduations. On those occasions, he often read the following poem:

"Your World" by Georgia Douglas Johnson[67]

Your world is as big as you make it.
I know, for I used to abide
In the narrowest nest in a corner
My wings pressing close to my side.

But I sighted the distant horizon
Where the skyline encircled the sea
And I throbbed with a burning desire
To travel this immensity.

I battered the cordons around me
And cradled my wings on the breeze,
Then soared to the uttermost reaches
With rapture, with power, with ease!

In late 1993, when Education Commissioner Betty Castor (1987–1994) was tapped for the president's job at the University of South Florida (USF), Jamerson made it known that he was interested in taking her place. In short order, he received endorsements from the state's two largest teaching unions, the House Speaker (Peter Rudy Wallace), conservative Democrats, the NAACP, the Southern Christian Leadership Conference, the Florida Coalition of Black Churches, and Congressman Alcee Hastings.

According to insiders, another person also wanted the office—Lt. Gov. Buddy MacKay. It was a powerful position with oversight of a $10.3 billion education budget

Figure 4.18. Doug Jamerson (*left*) accepts the applause of Gov. Lawton Chiles (*second from left*) at the ceremony in which he was sworn in by Judge Joseph Hatchett (*third from left*) as Commissioner of Education, the first black to hold that position. As a State Representative, Jamerson had long been a champion of multicultural instruction—wanting children to have a broader view of history than just thinking black history began with slavery or that women's contributions consisted of Betsy Ross making the flag. Fittingly, the swearing-in ceremony took place at Elizabeth Cobb Middle School in Tallahassee. State Archives of Florida, *Florida Memory*, https://www.floridamemory.com/items/show/129040. Photographed on January 3, 1994.

plus, as a Cabinet member, a voice in developing state policy in a variety of areas. Some speculated that Gov. Lawton Chiles (D) would use MacKay to restructure the education agency and take credit for massive cuts. But the speculation ceased in early December when Chiles announced for reelection with MacKay continuing in the No. 2 spot.

While still waiting for Castor's hiring at USF and the Governor's decision on her replacement, Jamerson announced his candidacy for the Cabinet post, both for the interim and in the next election. "I know the Florida education system, its strengths and weaknesses, its failures and dreams," he said. "I know what it is like to light the spark that starts the fire of educational achievement. And I know what it is like to hug the child who has just learned that her best friend has died of a drug overdose."[68] He avowed: "I have no greater political ambition than to serve the children of this state."

He said he believed the state had failed to provide support to local districts and that teachers were trapped in a dysfunctional system. Moreover, the state had failed to teach "the values of service and sacrifice and love of country, the values of hard work and faith." Those were his values, he said, and "I believe you teach those values by example, not by spending a jillion dollars on curriculum and consultants."

On December 22, 1993, Gov. Chiles appointed Jamerson as Education Commissioner. Certainly, the Governor appreciated the historic nature of the appointment—"I think he did care about that," said Kelly. At the same time, "The fact that he really liked Doug and he trusted him and had confidence in him played a huge role in his decision. Chiles was not a man who bent to pressure."[69]

Jamerson was more than ready to take the reins. On January 1, 1994, he announced a New Year's resolution: "To begin to try to structure a department of education that recognizes the three critical themes that I intend to stress—classroom, family, and the community—and to build a collaboration between those entities that will provide each and every child in Florida with a quality education."

The swearing-in took place January 3 at Cobb Middle School in Tallahassee. Standing with him were his wife, Leatha, and son, Cedric Alexander. Federal Judge Joseph Hatchett, a former Florida Supreme Court Justice from Pinellas County, administered the oath. More than 300 Cabinet members, legislators, and others were on hand to wish him well.

Taking the podium, Jamerson said he wanted to return Florida's schools to an environment in which students respected their teachers and worked hard in class and were safe in school. Schools would also help restore families and resist welfare. "As Franklin Roosevelt warned us 58 years ago, welfare is a narcotic, a subtle destroyer of the human spirit. We—and I say we—must escape this web," he said. Florida could do that by "providing all of Florida's residents, traditional students as well as returning adults, a good quality education, one they can use to earn a high-paying job or continue on to a four-year college."

From the beginning of his appointment, he was not only running the Department of Education but also running for election. Public appearances became opportunities for stump speeches. In mid-March, while touring a Citrus County primary school recently renovated to provide students health services, he said the full-service approach showed how Florida could reestablish the link between the family and the community. "The idea is to relocate existing services to the one place we know we can find troubled children every day, and that is the schools," he said.[70]

He reaffirmed steps for school reform, as outlined in the fledgling Blueprint 2000 plan, but "he really wasn't ready to do that yet," said Joy Frank, his former legislative affairs director. He saw value in a lot of things the agency did and wanted to evaluate what needed to be cut. "So that was a real struggle of having legislation that looked like you were cutting the bureaucracy out of state government and were just really rearranging the deck chairs on the Titanic."

Speaking at a convention of teachers in April, Jamerson expressed frustration with the Legislature, which seemed more concerned about building prisons than educating children. He believed the prison problem would not be solved until the literacy problem was solved. "Sometimes I don't think they understand. It's prevention and intervention, stupid!" he said. "Prisons acknowledge our failures. Education celebrates our future. One is despair, the other is hope."[71]

By May, he sounded more positive, acknowledging that in the previous four months the Legislature had increased the education budget by 5.2 percent. That was necessary, given the state's phenomenal growth—70,000 new students in schools every year over the next several years. Furthermore, education was key to shifting the state from an agrarian economy to a technology-based economy in the 21st century, and Blueprint 2000 was bringing a "new spirit" to education in three important areas:

assessment, technology, and training of teachers, parents, and school boards in their respective roles.[72]

School reform was one accomplishment that bridged his legislator and commissioner roles, and another was the creation of two task forces on history as taught in K-12 classrooms. The Holocaust Task Force provided materials for teaching about the annihilation of six million Jews under the Nazis, and the African American Task Force promoted the contributions of African Americans to American society. Both were intended to raise awareness and increase tolerance.

As a former legislator, "he could walk on the floor of the House and Senate. He just walked in and got what he needed done," said Joy Frank. "And he was a great orator. When he would get on the stump, he was passionate and lyrical. One time on the floor he started singing. Occasionally he'd go, 'Free at last, free at last.'" He would poke fun at himself and yet take things seriously. "He was a gracious, inviting, comfortable-in-his-own-skin kind of guy."

"When he became Commissioner, he was very good at working with all the various groups," said Stryker. Shortly after Jamerson had been sworn in, Pat Tornillo, head of the Florida Education Association, came into the office and said, "Doug, one thing you got to remember. You're black and that's going to make a difference." Jamerson looked him straight in the eye and replied, "Pat, you know what? Something you're going to have to remember, you're short. And that's something you have to live with."[73] Stryker and others all agreed that Jamerson had a real self-deprecating approach to life. His humility was a trait that many found very endearing.

As the fall 1994 election approached, four candidates—one Democrat and three Republicans—ran for the Education Commissioner post. All called for school reform, citing low test scores, crowded classrooms, crime, and low teacher pay.

In the Democratic primary in September, Jamerson was expected to cruise over his opponent, retired naval officer John Griffin. But Jamerson won by only 50.2 percent of the vote compared to 49.8 percent for Griffin. Many believed that Jamerson had not campaigned hard enough, including holding off on TV commercials in order to save campaign funds for the general election.

The Republican primary winner, Frank Brogan, had been Martin County's School Superintendent since 1988 (and would later become Lieutenant Governor to Gov. Jeb Bush). Brogan criticized Blueprint 2000 as adding another layer of bureaucracy and opposed the use of too much money for social programs. Teachers' reactions were mixed, some praising Brogan's vision and others calling him an "autocrat." Brogan also received the endorsement of former U.S. Secretary of Education William Bennett and was favored by the Christian right.

Jamerson's campaign leaped into action, hiring a media consultant and pollster, creating statewide television ads, tapping into the teacher union's network, and securing help from the Democratic Party. But it wasn't enough. Jamerson lost as part of a tide that swept many Republicans into office. That year "was such a disaster for Democrats, from the top down," said Wallace. Jamerson "could have been George Washington, and he would have lost that election."

Another factor in the loss may have been race. Former University of South Florida President Betty Castor remembered a Brogan ad featuring "a sweaty, dark face, making sure that people knew that Doug was an African American."[74] At some level, Jamerson had his own doubts. That became evident to Joy Frank, when she mentioned at one point in the campaign: "Well, I think you have a chance. I'm feeling good about it." He responded, "Look at my face. I'm black, and I'm not just light black." According to his own polls, 5 percent of respondents said they wouldn't vote for him because he was black.[75]

"When he didn't win, it was really crushing," said Stryker. "He didn't win his own county, Pinellas County, and that really hurt." But "he was the type of guy that said, 'Look, we did the best we could, we've done good work, and we just need to move on.'"

Less than two months later, Gov. Chiles, who had won reelection after a challenge by newcomer Republican Jeb Bush, appointed Jamerson Secretary of Labor. "I kind of view life as a great adventure," Jamerson said. "You hate to lose, but this is a great opportunity to serve."[76]

In the new post, he oversaw the divisions of labor, employment and training, unemployment compensation, workers' compensation, and vocational rehabilitation. One of his top priorities, he said, was to broaden retraining of workers who lost jobs through military base closures.

After leaving the labor post, Jamerson decided to try for the Florida Senate. He faced Les Miller, a black state Representative from Hillsborough County and House Minority Leader. In the September primary, Jamerson criticized Miller for unproductive leadership, and Miller portrayed Jamerson as a has-been in a changed political environment.[77] Miller won easily, went on to win the general election, and served in the Senate until 2006.

Less than a year after the defeat, on April 21, 2001, Jamerson died, at age 53. Few knew that he had been battling cancer. At his death, Gov. Bush ordered the flags of all public institutions to be flown at half-mast. More than 800 people attended his funeral. U.S. Reps. Corrine Brown and Carrie Meek gave a tribute to him on the floor of the U.S. House that was published in the Congressional Record.

Most mourners remembered his passion for public education—a passion best epitomized by his own words at Martin Luther King Day ceremonies during his first month as Education Commissioner: "I believe education, as Martin would have said, is the great equalizer. Education will lead us to the promised land."[78]

Information for this story came from news clippings, letters, and speeches preserved by the State Library of Florida, and interviews with five of Jamerson's former associates.

5

Trailblazers

The Florida Supreme Court

It was not until the 1970s that minorities were successful at being placed on the state's highest court. As minority populations swelled, Governors came under more pressure to diversify their appointments to the Court. Consequently, by the early 2000s, Florida's Supreme Court was deemed one of the most diverse in the nation.

Figure 5.1. Florida Supreme Court Justices hold a ceremonial session in the Old Capitol. The Court had met in the Old Capitol Building from 1845 to 1912 and in an earlier Supreme Court Building (Whitfield Building) from 1912 to 1949. It moved to its current location, the Supreme Court Building, in 1949. Shown *(L-R)*: Charles T. Wells, Stephen Grimes, Ben Overton, Chief Justice Gerald Kogan, Leander Shaw, Major Harding, Harry Lee Anstead. State Archives of Florida, *Florida Memory*, https://www.floridamemory.com/items/show/47275. Photographed on May 9, 1997.

Florida Minority Trailblazers—Florida Supreme Court: 1960s–2010s

Time frame	Male	Female	Male Chief Justice	Female Chief Justice
1960s				
1970s	1975–1979 Joseph W. Hatchett Appt. by Gov. Askew—D African American— Clearwater Filled vacancy Last Supreme Court Justice to run statewide			
Merit Retention Judicial System put in place by Constitutional Amendment in 1976				
1980s		1985–1994 Rosemary Barkett Appt. by Gov. Graham—D Mexico (Born); Syria—Miami		
1990s			1990–1992 Leander J. Shaw, Jr. Appt. by Gov. Graham—D On Court 1983–1992 African American— Jacksonville	
				1992–1994 Rosemary Barkett Appt. by Gov. Graham—D On Court 1985–1994 Mexico (born); Syria —Miami
		1999–Present Peggy Ann Quince Jointly Appointed by Gov. Chiles—D and Gov. Bush—R[a] African American— Tampa		
2000s	2002–2008 Raoul G. Cantero III Appt. By Gov. Bush—R Cuba—Miami			
				2008–2010 Peggy Ann Quince Jointly Appointed by Gov. Chiles—D and Gov. Bush—R[a] On Court 1999-Present African American—Tampa
2010s			2014–Present Jorge Labarga Appt. by Gov. Crist—R On Court 2009-Present Cuba—Palm Beach	

Note: Consult Appendix D for a full listing of minority Supreme Court Justices in Florida.

[a]Quince is the only Supreme Court Justice to be jointly appointed by two governors. At the time of the appointment, Gov. Chiles was still in office but Gov. Jeb Bush had been elected to succeed him. Chiles died before his term was up and was succeeded by Gov. Buddy MacKay-D who served out Chiles's term before Bush took office. It was Gov. MacKay who signed her commission on December 8, 1998.

Merit Retention

The Florida Supreme Court, the state's highest court, is composed of seven Justices. When a vacancy on the bench occurs, it is filled by the Governor who selects the Justice from three to six nominees submitted by a Judicial Nominating Commission (JNC). At the next general election held more than one year after the initial appointment, a newly appointed Justice may choose to run for retention to a full six-year term. Voters are asked, "Shall Justice [name] be retained in office?" If a majority votes "Yes," the Justice is retained. There is no limit on the number of times a Justice can be retained, only on age. (The mandatory retirement age is 70.)

Judicial selection was not always done this way. Under various Constitutions in the 1800s, Justices were selected by the Legislature, appointed by the Governor and confirmed by the Senate, or elected.[1] But in 1976, Florida voters approved a constitutional amendment creating the merit retention method for selecting its appellate court judges.

The merit retention system, adopted in 1976, was first used in elections for the Supreme Court in 1980. Since the system's implementation, Florida voters have never voted to oust a Justice, although several times there have been organized efforts to reject justices—in 1990 and 2012 (although the latter effort really began in 2010). Each effort was soundly rejected by the voters.

In 1990, African-American Justice Leander Shaw, Jr., was subjected to such an effort (unsuccessful) from critics of his authorship of a majority opinion declaring unconstitutional a statute requiring unmarried females younger than 18 years of age to get written consent from a parent or guardian before obtaining an abortion. While 59.6 percent of the voters ultimately chose to retain Shaw, it was still the closest retention vote since the state began using retention elections.[2] Shaw's response? "The people want a fair and just legal system and [today] they said they don't want any single-issue group toppling that system."

Two decades later (2012), a conservative group (Americans For Prosperity) spent $100,000 on a website and one night of television commercials criticizing the Florida Supreme Court for keeping an "Obamacare" referendum off the ballot, although the group did not take a position on whether the Justices should be voted out.[3] (Florida is the only state that gives its highest court the right to remove a proposed constitutional amendment from the ballot if it is not clearly worded or addresses multiple subjects.)

In 2012, three of the Justices (Peggy Quince—an African American—Barbara Pariente, and Fred Lewis) who were part of the 2010 decision (5–2) to keep the proposed amendment off the ballot and up for a retention vote were targeted by two conservative groups—Americans for Prosperity and Restore Justice 2012—and by the Executive Committee of the Republican Party of Florida. Their complaint? The Justices

Figure 5.2. Florida Supreme Court Justices and Secretary of State Glenda Hood stand with a handwritten "secretary's copy" of the 1838 Florida Constitution, the only original copy of the first state Constitution known to exist. *Back row (L-R)*: Kenneth B. Bell, R. Fred Lewis, Chief Justice Harry Lee Anstead, Charlie T. Wells, and Raoul G. Cantero III. *Front row (L-R)*: Peggy A. Quince, Barbara J. Pariente, Secretary of State Glenda Hood. State Archives of Florida, *Florida Memory*, https://www.floridamemory.com/items/show/23286. Photograph by Caroline Ferguson on March 2, 2004.

were too liberal,[4] were "legislating from the bench," and therefore should be voted out of office (not retained). The targeted Justices were forced to hit the campaign trail and raise money to defend themselves, although the bulk of money for that purpose was raised by an outside independent group (Defend Justice From Politics).

Former Supreme Court Justice Raoul Cantero III heavily campaigned against the effort to oust the Justices: "My strong feeling is, if we start turning the merit retention process into a political vehicle, then we are turning the judiciary into another political branch of government, which the Founding Fathers of our country specifically intended to avoid."[5] In the end, all three Justices were handily retained, receiving over two-thirds "Yes" votes. But the episode left many convinced that judicial elections were becoming as politicized as the other elections in highly politically polarized ("purple") Florida.

African-American Successes

African Americans have had their statewide electoral successes in Supreme Court races. The first black Florida Supreme Court Justice, Joseph W. Hatchett, was appointed to the bench by Gov. Reubin Askew (D) in 1975 to fill a vacancy. In 1976,

Hatchett had to run for reelection in a statewide nonpartisan race because the retention system had not yet been put into place. By one account, "The seven-month campaign was the last in Florida in which any statewide candidate appealed overtly to racism."[6] Yet Hatchett won handily with 60 percent of the vote, carrying 45 of the state's 67 counties. *His victory made Hatchett the first African American to win a statewide election—not just in Florida, but in the South.*

Gov. Bob Graham (D) appointed Leander J. Shaw, Jr., to the Court in 1983. Shaw would later become Florida's first black Chief Justice. In 1998, in a rare joint appointment, Lawton Chiles (D) and Jeb Bush (R) placed the first African-American woman, Peggy Quince from Tampa, on the Florida Supreme Court.[7] She became the state's first black female Chief Justice in 2008. [Note: The Chief Justice position is normally rotated every two years.] Republican Gov. Charlie Crist appointed the third African-American man to the high court—E. C. Perry—on March 11, 2009.

Hispanic Successes

Raoul G. Cantero III was the state's first Hispanic Supreme Court Justice, appointed to the bench in 2002 by Gov. Jeb Bush (R). Cantero is the grandson of Fulgencio Batista, the former Cuban dictator who was overthrown by Fidel Castro. Justice Cantero resigned in 2008 citing family reasons (young children too far from their extended family). In January 2009, Gov. Charlie Crist (R) appointed Cuban-born Jorge Labarga to fill the vacant seat. On June 30, 2014, Labarga became the state's first Hispanic Chief Justice.

Some argue that Rosemary Barkett, appointed by Gov. Bob Graham (D) in 1985, was actually the first Hispanic Justice. She was surely the first Arab-American Justice. Barkett was born in Mexico to Syrian parents. The Barkett family moved to Miami when Rosemary was five. She became a naturalized U.S. citizen at age 18. Barkett was the first woman to serve on the Florida Supreme Court and the first female Chief Justice.

There have been no Asian state Supreme Court Justices.

Impact of Diversity on the Bench

In 2008, a Standing Committee on Fairness and Diversity was established to help advance the state court system's efforts to eliminate from court operations bias that is based on race, gender, ethnicity, age, disability, financial status, or any characteristic that is without legal relevance. That same year, the Committee submitted a report titled *Perceptions of Fairness in the Florida Court System*.[8] The report concluded that "significant improvements in reducing discrimination have been made over the past two decades" but that the task was unfinished. It was fitting that an administrative order for the Committee to extend its work was signed by then Chief Justice Peggy A. Quince on December 3, 2008.[9] The value of minority representation on the Court could not have been more evident.

It was made even clearer when new Chief Justice Labarga announced strong support for increasing the diversity of all the state's courts down to the county court level. At his investiture ceremony, Labarga said: "This is the way our judicial system should look," as he looked at his fellow Justices (three white men, one white woman, an African-American man and an African-American woman).[10] Ethnic pride was on display in the courtroom that day. Prior to his investiture, trailblazer Lt. Gov. López-Cantera offered his congratulations to Labarga: "From one Cuban-American who has achieved a first, to another Cuban-American who is about to achieve a first, let me just say, '*Felicidades* (congratulations).'"[11]

Not long after his investiture, Labarga created the first Florida Commission on Access to Civil Justice—a 27-member commission consisting of judges, attorneys, academics, and large employers whose goal was to improve the access of lower-income and middle-class Floridians to the court system in civil matters.

Improving the state's judicial system is essential. "Like everything else, the justice system is susceptible to human failings," said Rosemary Barkett. "So not everything that happens in the justice system is always going to be just, which means that they have a real obligation to try to improve it in every way they can. And I would point out that there are lots of ways to do that."

Justices

Joseph W. Hatchett

First African-American man appointed to the Florida Supreme Court, 1975

First African-American man elected to statewide office in Florida and the South, 1976

First black from the South appointed to a federal appeals court in the Deep South, 1979

Personal: Born September 17, 1932, Clearwater, Florida; married with two children.

Education:

- Florida A&M University, B.A. in political science (1954)
- Howard University School of Law, LL.B. (1959)

Occupation: Lawyer

Trailblazer Appointment and Election:

- Supreme Court Justice, *Appointed by Gov. Reubin Askew (D)* 1975
- Supreme Court Justice, *elected statewide in nonpartisan race* 1976
  - Joseph W. Hatchett (61%), Harvie S. DuVal (39%)

Figure 5.3. Joseph W. Hatchett, in addition to becoming the first black Florida Supreme Court Justice, was the first black to win a statewide election. In 1976, 15 months after his appointment, he had to run for office in the old election system. That race was highly contentious—with elements of racism—but it also was the last time a Justice had to run in a competitive race. That same year, voters overwhelmingly approved a constitutional amendment requiring merit retention elections (Yes or No) for Supreme Court and District Court of Appeal judges. State Archives of Florida, *Florida Memory*, https://www.floridamemory.com/items/show/19895. Photograph by James L. Gaines, ca. 1975–1979.

THE JOSEPH W. HATCHETT STORY

Joseph W. Hatchett, the first African American on the Florida Supreme Court, earned his law degree in 1959 from Howard University Law School in Washington, D.C. "That was the correct place to go because that was the civil rights law school in the country," he said. "All of the people that worked on the *Brown* case[12] were there, and it was all about desegregation and the Constitution and rights for African Americans, so it was a very great place for one who wanted to be a civil rights lawyer."

From Howard, he went to Daytona Beach to practice law with Horace Hill, who had offered him a job. "Our only connection was that our families knew each other from Clearwater, where we were both born." After a few months, realizing that he wasn't doing the kind of things he wanted to do, he opened his own law office in Daytona. The move was "one of the bravest things I ever did in my life, and probably it could've been pretty foolish, but somehow I made it, I made enough money."

His law practice consisted of "civil rights law, small criminal cases, small estates—everything I did was small. I didn't have any major cases other than large civil rights cases." As a cooperating attorney with the NAACP Legal Defense Fund, he was one of many fighting the on-the-ground legal battles to end discrimination in public accommodations, housing, employment, and voting.

"I was on a team of three lawyers—Horace Hill was one, the other one was a lawyer in Tampa named Rodriguez. I was just out of law school, so my job was to work with the demonstrators—teach them not to fight back when they got arrested, what to say, how to conduct themselves," Hatchett said.

In Daytona, the demonstrations focused on restaurants and drugstores on the mainland side of the city. "We were protesting, but we weren't crazy. For example, in Daytona Beach we'd never protest on the beach because we would close the motels down. All the African Americans in Daytona Beach worked in the motels or in the restaurants on the beach. So there was some sense to this madness." Daytona Beach didn't have a speedway at that time, and Bethune-Cookman College was the largest employer in the county. "So if you drove away the tourists, the whole county would've died, and so we didn't want to do that."

In handling cases, he focused more on getting people—many of whom were college students—out of jail than winning. "I lost more cases in one day than any lawyer in the world because we would have sit-ins and wade-ins and all of the demonstrations. Of course the kids would get arrested as they were supposed to get arrested, and the team would have to get them out of jail. So I'd have 10 on trial in St. Augustine, 10 in the afternoon in Daytona Beach, 20 in Cocoa the next day, 25 in Titusville the next day. It only took one police officer to prove the case: 'They were there, I told them to disperse, they did not disperse, then I arrested them, therefore they were guilty of trespassing.' Those were the facts, and I couldn't say those were not the facts.

So the judge would find all 10 of those guilty, and then I'd go to the next place and another 10 would be guilty. Some days I'd end up with 50 clients guilty."

In most cases, the clients were assessed fines. The community held mass meetings and took up collections to pay the fines. "Back in those days, there was more understanding than people realized," he said. "We wanted to open lunch counters. For example, in Daytona at least, there was always a group that was ready to open the lunch counters. The question was, who's going to do it first? You had the local lunch counters and they couldn't do it. And finally, Walgreens, a chain, could do it. Walgreens decided they were going to open all of their lunch counters. In all of that area of Florida they opened, and that was the end of it."

"There was a lot of understanding like that," Hatchett said. "For example, my kids were being arrested in Daytona Beach, and there was no place for them. The county jails couldn't keep them. It was burning up the budget. I knew the city judge, of course, and so I would remove the cases to federal court. All it took was a motion filed in Jacksonville in federal court, and all those cases would be removed. Well, if the cases are going to be removed, then there was no reason to have kids in jail; so all the kids could be released, pending the hearing in the federal court. And we'd do that month after month after month because we were just cooperating."

As he explained, jailing large numbers of people presented problems. "You had to separate children from adults; you had to separate girls from boys; and they didn't have the guards; they didn't have the cooks; they didn't have anything. So, we would overcrowd the jail and the officials would have to close the jail or they'd have to go rent another place or send the arrestees out of county. So it wasn't a great burden by the kids being arrested, because nobody wanted them out of jail more than the people who had put them in jail."

"But they couldn't say that to the community. It was left to people like me to find a way to let the officials off the hook and get the arrestees out of jail. So that was the kind of cooperation you had."

Many cities in which he worked had biracial councils that met without press coverage. "You couldn't do that today, of course—just sit and talk with each other. People on the councils tried to work out whatever the dispute was about, which helped keep down rioting and other bad things that could've happened," he said. "We were pushing, and the public officials had folks that were not going to let them do what we wanted them to do, or they had to do it very slowly; and we had to be patient enough to go through that process with them if we wanted to get what we wanted."

Demonstrations were also held by the opposite side—segregationists and the Ku Klux Klan. "In St. Augustine, the Klansmen would march, and we would march too. I mean, that was just the way it was. All of us would march to the old slave market. It was just a question of who was going to do it first; the sheriff's office decided. The KKK would be on one side of the street, demonstrators would be on the other side.

The KKK would march and that would be their march, and they'd stand on the side and we'd march. Then nothing happened."

But the atmosphere was often tense and sometimes downright scary. It was not uncommon for Hatchett to receive phone calls from hate mongers, for example, and one night in St. Augustine, he feared for his life.

As he told the story: A judge had ordered demonstrators to reform school, which was a type of penal facility for law-breaking juveniles, and a riot had broken out at the jail. "I had a bail bondsman, an African American, who always rode with me because he was the only one in the area who could write bail bonds or who would write the bonds for the kids. So, we pulled away from the jail, and we were going back to Daytona Beach, and we noticed we were being followed. There had been Klansmen all around the jail, too. Unfortunately, I was driving and we had a pistol, but I did a silly thing. I had locked the pistol in the glove compartment and had the key on the same key ring as the ignition key. So, I couldn't cut off the ignition. We were going down Highway 1, and I sped up and made a U-turn and went back to the jail and got a Highway Patrol escort. The Klansmen went away."

Hatchett had first gone to St. Augustine "to get into the rally way before Dr. King came" (for a 1964 rally during the city's 400th anniversary celebration). A local movement leader, Dr. Robert B. Hayling, "decided one night that he was going to go to a Klan rally. He got in his car, he knew where they were meeting, went through the woods, and was watching the meeting." All of a sudden, Klansmen seized him and "took him out into the middle where the cross was burning. They knew him because he was a local—he was the only black dentist in town—and they didn't know what to do. They became afraid because it was so stupid of an African American to come to a Klan rally, so they thought it was a setup by the FBI. So they hit him on his hands a few times because he was a dentist and needed his hands. They put the cross out and all of them left him standing out in the middle of this area. They just couldn't believe it. I couldn't believe it either. I said, 'You did what?'"

Hatchett had seen the Klan as a child in Clearwater. "I went to a baseball game in a new city park. Cars came in, people got out wearing white robes and hoods. They told all of the black people to leave. So we left. That was the Klan. They were running us out of the city park."

Born into a working-class family—"My father was a fruit picker, mother was a maid"—he attended public schools in Pinellas County during the Great Depression and World War II. By the late 1940s, as the NAACP began pushing for equal treatment of blacks in employment and education, Hatchett's high school civics teacher told him: "America is going to be changed by the law and by lawyers, and if you want to be a part of that change, you try and be a lawyer."

That idea stuck in the back of his mind for the next several years—through high school, where he "did a little debating, played basketball, played in the band." It was the band experience that led him to choose Florida A&M for college: "They had the best band that I'd ever heard of."

"They had 99 in the band, and I came and I was number 100, so they named the band after me—The Marching 100," he said. "Of course, there are about 600 other people in the world who claim the same thing. Maybe 800."

At Florida A&M, he majored in political science, which was a brand new major at the historically black university at that time. Because the Korean War had erupted, "I went into the Reserve Officers Training Corps and therefore got a deferment until I finished college." He spent two years (1954–1956) as a lieutenant in the Army, including 18 months in West Germany.

Back in civilian life, he was finally able to turn his attention to studying law at Howard University. "I married on the way to law school, so I didn't work on Law Review, although I qualified for it. But I went to work. I worked at the post office at night and then went to law school, and somehow I got through that OK."

After passing the Bar exam, he practiced law and worked on civil rights cases. "If you had a civil rights case that involved a pattern or practice, you could ask the government to intervene in the case with you. I was suing chain restaurants like Big Daddy's Barbecue in Cocoa, which were all through Brevard County." He asked the Justice Department to intervene, which meant he worked with department lawyers. Soon he was offered a job. "At that point, there were no African-American lawyers working for the Justice Department in the South."

He got assigned to Jacksonville as an Assistant U.S. Attorney. He worked there for two years and, because of the turnover in the office, became the Chief Assistant Attorney in 1968, and thus started running the Jacksonville office. (The main U.S. Attorney's Office was in Tampa.)

In 1971, he became U.S. Magistrate for the federal Middle District of Florida. While a magistrate judge, "I applied for a Florida Supreme Court vacancy, never expecting to get it." In reality, "I wanted to be a U.S. District Court judge, and I felt that if I could simply make the list for the Supreme Court, just get interviewed, it would look good on my resume when I applied for the district court."

"Much to my surprise, I got a call from Gov. [Reubin] Askew [D], who invited me to Tallahassee for an interview. Well, I didn't take that very seriously. I had a very fine interview. I was just as happy as I could be. Back in Jacksonville, my neighbors had a big party. They had a big sign out in front of my house," touting the interview that made him a "big shot."

During the interview, the Governor never mentioned the historic nature of the appointment, but "of course we both knew that." One thing the Governor did ask, however, was whether Hatchett would be willing to run for office if appointed. "I knew that you had to run—I didn't know when—but I said, 'Sure, I'll run.'" At this point, Hatchett thought an appointment unlikely, "so I said yes to anything. And lo and behold, then the next thing that happened was I was appointed."

He quickly learned that he would have to run in the next general election, which was 15 months away, to stay on the Court. "I didn't know anything at all about running for office. I had never run for any office at all, but was willing to do it. Some lawyers formed a little group and chose me a campaign manager, and off we went." Two of the chief campaign organizers were aides to Gov. Askew—campaign manager Howell Ferguson and attorney [Eugene] Gene Stearns.

"The Governor was fully behind me, and he said so," Hatchett recalled. The Governor never went on the campaign trail, but "every chance he got, he said that it was the most important thing that I get elected. And I think Ferguson got his campaign list and plugged into it. We had people in every county, and I sure didn't know anyone."

The first time Hatchett met with an editorial board, at the *Tampa Tribune*, Ferguson arranged for the reporters to give him copies of the questions when the interview was over. Then the campaign team reviewed all the questions, wrote answers, and came up with a position book. "I studied that and studied it and studied it so that I could recite it in the middle of the night in a thunderstorm. And that pretty much got me through the campaign."

In addition, "I had to sit down and memorize a script so I could go on Spanish radio in South Florida. And I did that. I learned to do greetings and small talk in Spanish. I can't do it anymore. But I learned the script and practiced it and practiced it."

In Miami, he received training on how to appear on TV. Making a commercial "was much harder than I thought. I had my speech and I had to walk down steps and time the steps with the speech. I think we did 40 takes before I finally got it right."

The election turned out to be contentious from the first day. "The best thing that happened was my opponent, who was Harvie DuVal [a white candidate from Dade County], announced on the day that I was appointed that he was going to run against me. I had never met him. I had never written an opinion. I had never appeared in his court. He knew nothing about me at all. And, of course, I hadn't done anything as a Justice on the first day when I was sworn in, so there was nothing he could criticize me for, but he declared that he would run against me that day. From there on, it got pretty dirty, not from my side, from his side. The good thing about that is, it got dirty very early and there were a lot of good candidates out there that would have defeated me easily, but they stayed away from the race. It just was not the kind of thing any person wanted to get into, and that probably saved me."

The "dirty" part was in the things his opponent said. For example, when Miami attorney Stephen N. Zack announced he was supporting Hatchett, "DuVal asked him what in the world was a good white boy like him doing supporting me? And when asked why DuVal had announced the day I was sworn in, his only answer was that he knew I was not qualified. When pressed on why he knew it, of course, he didn't say it was about race, but that was what was implied."

"I was sure I was going to lose," Hatchett said, so he took the attitude of having fun as he traveled all around the state. "I had a great campaign team," he said. "I generally did whatever the campaign people said do because I'd never done it before and had never worked with anyone who had done it before."

Like many African-American politicians at the time, he spoke at black churches, but he also spoke at Bar Association events, League of Women Voters meetings—"anyone that would invite me." For example, "I remember I was going to a garden club meeting and I was wondering why in the world am I going to a small garden club meeting down in South Florida somewhere. Well, I went and there were about six women there. But a guy showed up with a tape recorder, and I gave my usual speech. That night all over the radio I could hear myself." Then he realized: "Oh I get it, that's why they send me to these locations. They record it, then they take it to the radio station and the broadcast reaches hundreds of thousands of people."

Traveling back and forth between campaign stops and the courtroom in Tallahassee was often difficult. "I'd catch the early morning plane out of South Florida and just make it in time to get to the Court before it started. So I was very, very busy," he said. "I lived through it. Of course, I was very young then. I was 43 and could do that kind of thing." To Hatchett, the multiple campaign stops "seemed like running for sheriff in every county."

Ferguson came up with a media strategy after consulting with an advertising agency in New York: "Don't buy a single billboard and don't buy any bumper stickers. Raise the money and we're going to spend it all on TV." No one had ever done that before, Hatchett said. He went along with the plan even though it irritated his supporters. "I'd be down in South Florida and I'd be meeting with the people who were raising the money, and they were asking me, 'Well, what are you doing with the money?' And I couldn't tell them. I kept telling them, 'Something's going to come out, you'll see it.' And they said 'Well, what is it?' It got me into big trouble, especially with the African-American community that was working on my campaign" because they couldn't see anything and the opponent's signs were going up everywhere. "Finally we did come up with a handout," he said, "but I almost lost some very good friends over that."

A couple of weeks before the election, his TV spots flooded the state, and in the nick of time. "I didn't know anything about any of that, so I was worried. But my team had already bought the spots ahead of time, and so I was coming on the air right after Walter Cronkite. They were great spots, and so it was a very successful campaign."

In addition, while talking to Ferguson, Hatchett learned that every newspaper in the state, except for a small one in Miami Beach, had endorsed him. "Oh, really?"

Figure 5.4. Joseph W. Hatchett dons his ceremonial robe prior to taking the bench and is joined by Mrs. Hatchett and daughters Brenda and Cheryl. He resigned on July 18, 1979, when President Jimmy Carter nominated him for a seat on the U.S. Court of Appeals for the Fifth Circuit, a position he held for 20 years. State Archives of Florida, *Florida Memory*, https://www.floridamemory.com/items/show/34337. Photograph by Mark T. Foley, September 2, 1975.

he said. "And every labor union," Ferguson added. "Then it really scared me because then I really did want to win. I had been having fun thinking, 'Well, this is going to be over and I'm going to go back and practice law.' And then when he told me that, I realized, 'Oh my God, I think I'm going to die if I lose now.'"

The possibility came as a surprise to his wife too. She was a school teacher, their children were in elementary school, and they had just built a new house in Jacksonville. As victory appeared possible, "we had to worry about what in the world we were going to do now. We're going to have to move to Tallahassee."

He won the election, becoming the first African American elected to statewide office in Florida. "Even until today, only President Barack Obama has won a statewide election in Florida as an African American," Hatchett said.

After being sworn in on the bench, he was often recognized and celebrated as a "first," but the sensation was not entirely new. "When I went into the military as a military officer, there weren't many African-American officers. I had been noticed because of my color before," he said. "But after a while, you don't feel like a trailblazer. You've been there before. You've been a first at so many things." And later, "You say who gives a damn what they think. You just go on and do whatever you're doing. You stop thinking about the fact that 'Oh, there's no one here like me.'"

At the same time, he had to deal with the unsavory parts of being not only black but also a judge. "The whole time I was on the bench, I got all kinds of things, death threats," he said. He cited the case of Robert S. Vance, a federal appeals judge who was assassinated by a mail bomb in 1989.[13] "In that case all of us got threatening letters saying that the guy's going to kill all of us, and he did kill Judge Vance. Then there are the crazy prisoners that send you all kinds of foolishness. Every time you deny something that they send you, they write you back and tell you, curse you out, or something. But that happens every day."

In 1978, Gov. Askew appointed Jesse McCrary Secretary of State. Hatchett swore him in to office. There was "no place else in America that could have happened at that time—that an African American as a Supreme Court Justice could have sworn in a Cabinet member, a Governor's Cabinet member. It doesn't happen any place."

Hatchett counted other Florida trailblazers among his circle of friends and acquaintances. Peggy Quince, for example, appeared before Hatchett when he was on the Court. Leander J. Shaw, who joined the Court in 1983, had been in law school with him. "We were very, very tight friends."

In 1979, Hatchett decided to leave the Supreme Court. Although a Justice was a "great, great, great position," he wanted to get back into the federal system. "I liked the federal system, and many of the cases that I'd tried before as a civil rights lawyer were in federal court. We went into federal court a lot, so I got very pleasant and comfortable in federal court." When he ran for the Florida Supreme Court in 1976, Jimmy Carter was running for President. "So when I was out campaigning for the Florida Supreme Court in all of those condos down in South Florida, all of the President's people were there, too. I got to know all of them. To make a long story short, I had a gut feeling that I could be appointed a federal judge—and that's a lifetime appointment."

In 1979, President Carter (D) appointed him to a new seat on the U.S. Court of Appeals for the Fifth Circuit. That appointment marked another first: He became the first black man from the South on a federal appeals court. He was reassigned to the 11th Circuit in 1981 and served as Chief Judge from 1996 to 1999. He retired in 1999 after 20 years.

Even before he had left the Florida Supreme Court, he had formed a definite opinion about appointing versus electing judges. His election to the Court in 1976 marked the last time appellate judges were elected in Florida. Voters had approved the merit retention system the same year, and it was first used in 1980.

"I went through that last person-to-person, run-for-sheriff-in-every-county election, and you do not want your Justices doing that. If you tell your Justices to go out and raise money, they will raise it and guess who they'll raise it from? They'll raise it from the law firms. My group tried to avoid any impropriety when I ran, and so we set a $100 contribution maximum. I can't tell you how many times I was in a lawyer's offices where somebody dropped down money on the table for the campaign. I said, 'No, $100. You have to send it to Tallahassee. I am not going to take it. You cannot give it to me. I'm not supposed to even know who's giving the money.'"

When Justices run for election, "after a while they're going to build up constituencies. Yes, they're going to have to if they keep their job. And the longer they stay there, the more they need the constituency because they're too old to go out and practice after they've been on a court 10 or 12 years. So it gets rougher and rougher every time. Every six years they've got to go out and really work. And if you haven't done anything for anybody, nobody's going to give you the money. If one Justice is doing something for a group and you're not, then you're at a disadvantage. That's the way the system was. So, no, you don't want to go back to that." He mentioned Alabama, where Justices must raise $12–$14 million for an election: "No, you know something must be wrong in that system."

In addition, Justices would find it hard to ignore contributions by lawyers. "I would spend the weekend down in Miami at a big fundraiser and I'd be at some lawyer's house, a successful lawyer, at a lawn party and I'd disappear when money was collected. Well, guess what? The next morning, half of the lawyers that I was down there with would be on the plane flying to Tallahassee. I'd go on the bench and they would argue their cases. You can't stop that if you're going to send your Justices out to be politicians, just straight-out politicians. That's going to happen."

Moreover, running for office limits what a Justice can say. When Hatchett ran for office, "there was nothing I could talk about. I couldn't talk about any pending case. I couldn't talk about any case that could come before the Court or a case that had been heard, except to say, 'Go read it.' So what do you talk about? Well, you talk about how happy you are to be on the Court."

One thing he did talk about was merit retention because it was on the ballot when he ran: "I'd say to groups, 'I shouldn't be here, I should be in Tallahassee. I should be there doing what you pay me to do, but I'm spending half of my time down here running for office.'"

As a judge for nearly three decades, Hatchett had 63 law clerks who assisted him. Six of them became judges. To those interested in becoming a judge someday, he would say, "Go at it. Keep working. Work hard. It's a very rewarding profession. Not only does it pay well, but you have an opportunity to do good rather than simply think about it."

Looking back on his career, the civil rights work stands out as the most rewarding. "It was all during that period when America was trying to find its way with school desegregation and the segregation in public places and golf courses and swimming pools and all of those kinds of things that I decided what I wanted to do. Just being involved in changing America because that's what I went to law school for. It's the most pleasing thing that I've ever done, civil rights work, in spite of being on the Supreme Court and deciding some very important issues. Those nights I spent in St. Augustine are still the ones that I love the most."

"When you are a Justice on the Florida Supreme Court, you may not be able to prevail, but you can preserve the issue. You can always dissent, and dissents are important because they plant seeds in the minds of other lawyers for the next case. I didn't always win, but I like to think, too, that little by little I was convincing my brothers that what I was saying was right even though I lost the vote. But I at least took everybody through the process of thinking through it and not just jumping to a conclusion and saying it's always been this way."

"That was one of the advantages that I had by being a judge. Other people wanted to do good, but I had something they didn't have. I could write published opinions. I could say what the issue was in the case. I could suggest why the Court may have wanted to go in a certain direction rather than another. And that's powerful. Words are powerful. And if you can send out an idea or suggest a course of action, that's very important."

Joseph Hatchett was interviewed in person by the author July 24, 2013.

Rosemary Barkett

First woman appointed to the Florida Supreme Court, 1985
First female Chief Justice, 1992
Personal: Born August 29, 1939, at Ciudad Victoria, Tamaulipas, Mexico; naturalized January 22, 1958, Fort Pierce, Florida.
Family: Born in Mexico, but parents were Syrian
Education:

- Spring Hill College, B.S. (1967)
- Levin College of Law, University of Florida, J.D. (1970)

Occupation: Lawyer/Teacher
Trailblazer Appointments and Elections:

- Supreme Court Justice, *Appointed by Gov. Bob Graham (D)* 1985
- First retention election 1986
    - Yes (76.8%), No (23.2%)
- Supreme Court Chief Justice (elected by her colleagues on the Court), 1992–1994

For the full Rosemary Barkett story, see the Supreme Court Chief Justice section, page 377.

Figure 5.5. Rosemary Barkett, born in Mexico to Syrian parents, poses with Gov. Bob Graham, who appointed her to the Florida Supreme Court in 1985—making her the first woman to serve on the Court, the first "Hispanic" (by place of birth) and the first Arab American. She later was appointed by President Bill Clinton to the federal 11th Circuit Court of Appeals, then by Pres. Obama to an international court (the Iran-United States Claims Tribunal in The Hague). Barkett saw her heritage as a big asset on the bench: "It has been a huge advantage to have come from a tri-cultural background. It gives you a global perspective on shared values and an appreciation of the world as a whole." State Archives of Florida, *Florida Memory*, https://www.floridamemory.com/items/show/133902. Photograph by Mark T. Foley, October 14, 1985.

Peggy A. Quince

First African-American woman appointed to the Florida Supreme Court, 1998; jointly selected by Gov. Lawton Chiles (D) and Gov.-elect Jeb Bush (R) in 1998—four days before Gov. Chiles' unexpected death

First African-American woman elected to statewide office in Florida (in retention election), 2000

First African-American female Chief Justice of the Florida Supreme Court, 2008

Personal: Born January 3, 1948, Norfolk, Virginia; married with two children.

Education:

- Howard University, B.S. in zoology (1970)
- Catholic University of America Columbus School of Law, J.D. (1975)
- Stetson University College of Law, Honorary Doctor of Laws degree (1999)
- St. Thomas University School of Law, Honorary Doctor of Laws degree (2004)

Occupation: Lawyer/Assistant Attorney General

Trailblazer Appointments and Elections:

- Supreme Court Justice, *Appointed by Gov. Chiles (D) / Gov.-elect Jeb Bush (R) 1998*
- First retention election 2000
  - Yes (71.1%), No (28.9%)
- Supreme Court Chief Justice (elected by her colleagues on the Court), 2008–2010

For the full Peggy A. Quince story, see the Supreme Court Chief Justice section, page 389.

Figure 5.6. Peggy A. Quince (*center*) was appointed to the Supreme Court on December 8, 1998, by a group of officials she referred to as "the Trinity." She was jointly selected by outgoing Gov. Lawton Chiles (D) and Gov.-elect Jeb Bush (R), but the actual commission placing her on the Court was signed by Buddy MacKay (D), who became Governor for three weeks after the unexpected death of Gov. Chiles. Her investiture was on March 5, 1999. Here she leads her colleagues into a gathering of the Florida Legislature. Behind her is Justice Barbara Pariente. At left is State Rep. Carlos López-Cantera (R), and at right is State Rep. Will Weatherford (R). State Archives of Florida, *Florida Memory*, https://www.floridamemory.com/items/show/23919. Photograph by Darryl Jarmon, ca. 2007–2011.

Raoul G. Cantero III

First Hispanic (Cuban) appointed to the Florida Supreme Court, 2002

Personal: Born August 1, 1960, Madrid, Spain (Cuban parents), married with three children.

Education:

- Florida State University, B.A. in English and business (1982)
- Harvard University, J.D. (1985)
- Fulbright Scholar

Occupation: Lawyer

Trailblazer Appointment and Election:

- Supreme Court Justice, *Appointed by Gov. Jeb Bush (R)* 2002
- First retention election 2004
    - Yes (70%), No (30%)

Figure 5.7. Raoul Cantero III felt a strong sense of responsibility as the first Hispanic Justice on the Florida Supreme Court. "The whole time I was on the Court [2002–2008], I felt I was representing a community, a culture, and that I had to make sure that my behavior was outstanding, that everything about what I did was outstanding so that people wouldn't feel remorse about having appointed me." State Archives of Florida, *Florida Memory*, https://www.floridamemory.com/items/show/23210.

THE RAOUL G. CANTERO III STORY

For Raoul G. Cantero III, who would become the first Supreme Court Justice of Hispanic descent, a law profession was not his first career goal. "When I went to law school [at Harvard], I wanted to be a writer. I majored in creative writing [at Florida State University]. But I liked law, too, and I was going to be a lawyer until I could make a living from writing." No, he has not yet penned the Great American Novel, but the training proved useful.

In a recent article in an appellate law journal, he explained that writing a good brief requires a mastery of the writing craft: "All writing is re-writing. The first draft should never be the final product—nor the second, or the third, or the fourth." In addition, "Excellence does not come easy. It takes a lot of work."[14]

Cantero was born in 1960 in Madrid, Spain, to Cuban parents who had fled the island when Fulgencio Batista was overthrown by Fidel Castro. The family immigrated to Miami in 1961, when he was nine months old.

After graduating from law school, he clerked for U.S. District Judge Edward B. Davis in Miami. For the next 14 years, he practiced law, specializing in civil and criminal appeals, in South Florida. During that time, he handled more than 300 appeals and 150 oral arguments in the state's appeals courts, the Florida Supreme Court, and several U.S. Courts of Appeals.

When Justice Major B. Harding retired from the Supreme Court in 2002, colleagues urged Cantero to apply for the opening because of his extensive experience in appellate cases. "There were rumors that the Governor [Jeb Bush] wanted to appoint the first Hispanic to the Florida Supreme Court, and people wanted to make sure that we had somebody appointed that was qualified and people applying that were qualified," he said. "I felt almost an obligation or duty."

Nonetheless, it was "a very grueling decision to make because we had all of our family here [in Miami]," he said. His wife was less than enthusiastic to say the least, and the three children, ages 12, 9, and 7, were in elementary school, with the eldest just going into the seventh grade. Moving them into new schools in Tallahassee would be difficult, and they expected the commitment to be fairly long term.

After conferring with his wife for a few weeks, he decided to apply—just before the deadline. For a solid week, he prepared the application, which required specific information on his last five cases and answers to questions about his background and practice.

The Florida Constitution, he explained, requires one Justice to come from each of the five districts in Florida in the interest of geographical diversity. Because Justice Harding, who was from Jacksonville, was leaving and the Court already had someone from the First District Court of Appeals, there were no restrictions on who was eligible to seek the judgeship.

In all, 21 people applied. Applications went to the Judicial Nominating Commission, which vetted the applicants and nominated five candidates for interviews with the Governor.

When Cantero met with Gov. Bush, "there were maybe six or eight people in the room asking questions along with him." Cantero had met with Gov. Bush once before, when he had interviewed for the Governor's General Counsel position two years earlier. (Charles Canady got that position.)

"I wasn't even a Republican," Cantero said. Nor was he a Democrat. He had always been No Party Affiliation (NPA) because "I had always thought maybe I'd want to be a judge and I always thought that a judge should be politically neutral."

During the interview, "The Governor asked me who I thought the greatest political figure of the 20th century was. I said, Winston Churchill. Then he said, 'If you had one question to ask him, what would you ask him?' I said I would ask, 'How did you inspire your country to come back and win the war after the bombing of London?'"

Another person asked which of the Founding Fathers he most admired. He said he really couldn't pick just one.

He also remembered questions from Philip A. "Phil" Friedin, a plaintiff's attorney: First, "What has prepared you for the responsibility of ruling on a death penalty case?" Cantero's answer: "I don't think that anything you do in life will adequately prepare you for determining who lives or dies, but the juries have to do it and I have to do it, and I'll follow the law. Whatever the law is, that's what I will apply."

Next Friedin asked whether Cantero could be fair to plaintiffs since he had mostly represented defendants. Cantero replied that even though his firm did mostly defense work, it had started as more of an independent firm. He joined the firm when it was still small. "I didn't go there to practice defense law. I just went there to practice law," and the defense practice grew. "I didn't have any philosophical antipathy toward plaintiffs. And, in fact, one of the reasons I wanted to be a judge was to be able to look at things objectively."

During the interview, the Governor said nothing about an intent to appoint a Hispanic to the Court, Cantero said. In talking to reporters after announcing the appointment, Gov. Bush said he had considered Cantero's qualifications, while also trying to add diversity to the Court. It was not about gaining support among Hispanic voters. "It's not based on politics," he said. "It's based on principle."[15]

The appointment, while applauded by many Hispanics, drew criticism because some 20 years earlier Cantero had represented Orlando Bosch, an anti-Castro extremist labeled as a terrorist by the U.S. government. Cantero called his connection to the Bosch case "bizarre because, No. 1, I was just an associate at a firm and told to work on the case. No. 2, we were involved in his immigration matter. We weren't defending him on any criminal charges. No. 3, he had been acquitted of the terrorist charge of bombing a Cuban airliner. And, No. 4, that's what lawyers do is defend others. So under that theory, no criminal defense lawyer could ever be appointed to the Court."

"But for some reason," he continued, "they thought—they wanted to believe—that I was a right-winger. And these are people that I had never met before. I was never in any political organization one way or the other, so it wasn't like I was involved in any kind of political cause."

As Cantero understood things, the Governor had the choice of appointing either the first Hispanic or somebody he knew would be a conservative judge. "I was nominated along with four judges, so those judges had a track record." Because Cantero had had no experience as a judge, Gov. Bush had no idea about how he might rule. "About me, he knew next to nothing." Cantero didn't contribute to either Republican

Cantero: First Hispanic Justice

"We are full shareholders"

Still asleep after returning from a vacation in Sanibel, Ani Cantero was awakened in her Coral Gables home on July 9 by an early morning phone call. She picked up the phone, then turned to her sleeping husband, Miami appellate lawyer Raoul G. Cantero, III.

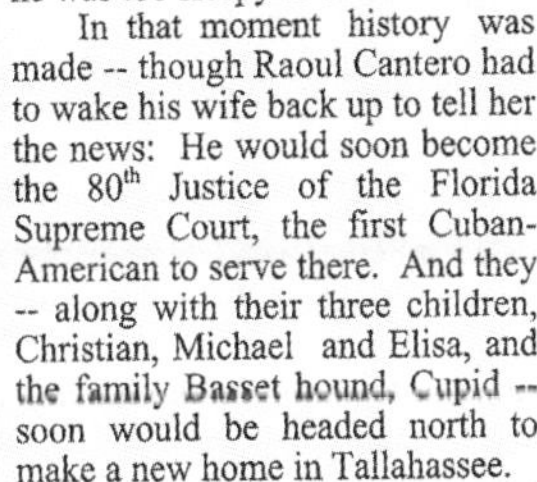

"Raoul," she said, "it's for you. It's the Governor's office."

Her husband later recalled that he was too sleepy to be nervous.

In that moment history was made -- though Raoul Cantero had to wake his wife back up to tell her the news: He would soon become the 80th Justice of the Florida Supreme Court, the first Cuban-American to serve there. And they -- along with their three children, Christian, Michael and Elisa, and the family Basset hound, Cupid -- soon would be headed north to make a new home in Tallahassee.

Justice Raoul Cantero

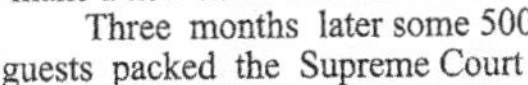

Three months later some 500 guests packed the Supreme Court Building, filling it with applause and cheers, as Cantero took the oath of office after Gov. Jeb Bush presented his credentials to Chief Justice Harry Lee Anstead.

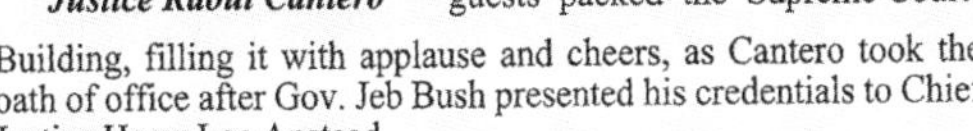

Figure 5.8. Raoul G. Cantero III's appointment to the Florida Supreme Court on July 10, 2002, by Gov. Jeb Bush made headlines. In a statement about his appointment of Cantero, Gov. Bush said: "I am proud to say that Raoul will be the first Hispanic ever to serve on the Florida Supreme Court. . . . Raoul's achievement is important because it proves that service on our state's highest court is open to men and women of excellence from all backgrounds." Courtesy of Florida Supreme Court Historical Society, *Historia Juris* (December 2002).

or Democratic campaigns and he wasn't a member of the conservative Federalist Society.

At the investiture, "There were hundreds of people in that courtroom," he remembered. "I mean, it was really like a community thing. Hundreds of people came up [from Miami] for me and just for the investiture," he said. "It was a great feeling, but it was also a feeling of immense responsibility. I knew everybody was counting on me to make it work."

During his remarks, he offered a moment of levity by telling about a retiring judge giving some advice to a new judge coming in. The retiring judge says to the new one, "On your first day of oral arguments, you're going to sit at the bench with your colleagues and you're going to look down that bench and you're going to say, 'What am *I* doing here?' But, you know what? A year is going to pass by and you're going to sit on that same bench and you're going to look down at your colleagues and you're going to ask, 'What are *they* doing here?'"

Before his appointment, he had served on a city planning and zoning board in Coral Gables, which "helped me a lot as far as presiding over meetings. I was the chair for four years, and it really taught me the importance of, and the dynamics of, group decision making." He and another board member "had very different philosophical views about development. My view was the owner of the property should be able to do whatever he wants with that property with certain exceptions and regulations, and his view was more we need to keep Coral Gables beautiful."

The two were "personally good friends," and the other board member had encouraged Cantero to offer himself as chair. "It really taught me the value of no matter what your philosophical views vis-à-vis the other members of your group decision-making body, it's always important to make friends and not to make things personal that are just professional."

"When I got on the Court, one of my best friends on the Court was Barbara Pariente [appointed 1997], who spoke at my retirement ceremony. She and I differed a lot on the cases. But because we were friends and we trusted each other's integrity, we did sometimes change each other's minds. We were able to talk, intellectually working through a problem." That was better than not talking to each other at all or talking at each other without trying to understand the other's viewpoint, he said.

As a Justice, Cantero wanted to develop better relations with the Legislature. When applying to the Court, "I had kind of a philosophy of what I would do if I was on the Court, and it was really three parts. One, I wanted to increase the collegiality on the Court because it had really, at least from the public's perspective, splintered after *Bush v. Gore*. So this was less than two years after that."

"Two, I wanted to promote the concept of professionalism in the profession. And, three, I wanted to improve the relationship with other branches of government. I felt that my philosophy then and now is that once you get to know somebody, you're less likely to ascribe evil motives to what he does," he said.

In carrying out that philosophy, "I would invite the Miami delegation to the Court for Cuban coffee and a tour of the Court. We also sometimes would just have lunch with the Hispanic delegation together, not necessarily on a regular basis, but several times. Also, I was good friends with Dan Gelber [Democratic state Representative 2000–2008 and state Senator 2008–2011]. We knew each other from when we were in law school and played basketball together in the summers. He was a Representative back then and so was [John P.] Jack Seiler [(D) 2000–2008]. He [Gelber] would invite me to eat lunch with the Representatives in their lunchroom while they were in session, two or three times during the session. I would go over there and just socialize with them," he said, and play basketball with them on Wednesday nights at the Leon High School gym.

In 2004, Cantero and fellow Justice Kenneth Bell had to go on the ballot to keep their jobs, as part of the state's merit retention requirement.[16] "I had to deal with the signs in front of my house that my wife was holding up, saying, 'Vote No on Cantero,'" he joked. "There was no campaign or anything like that," he said. The only thing related to the merit retention election "was my wife got some calls from parents at our school asking her what my position on abortion was. She said that I couldn't give them my position because I was a judge and I wasn't allowed to give positions on political subjects. So that was dropped."

He was also interviewed by the media about the election. "They would tell me,

'Well, nobody's ever been removed under that process of merit retention.' And I would tell them, 'Well that's like saying that this field goal kicker hasn't missed an extra point all year.'"

In 2012, after he had stepped down from the Court, he rose to the defense of three Justices[17] who had come up for merit retention because of a challenge by a conservative group. As he said at the time, "if we start turning the merit retention process into a political vehicle, then we are turning the judiciary into another political branch of government, which the Founding Fathers of our country specifically intended to avoid."[18]

As it turned out, all three Justices were retained by large margins. "They had to raise money and all that, and that was inconvenient, but ultimately the process did work. I know a lot of conservatives wanted to vote them out. My position was, this shouldn't be the way we do things with judges. You don't vote them out because you differ with their opinions. If we could do this now with justices we think are liberal leaning, then 20 years from now when the demographics in Florida change, then people are going to seek to remove those justices because they're too conservative. And I didn't think that was a good way to have the judicial system in Florida."

His most memorable and challenging case on the Court was that of Terri Schiavo[19] in 2005. "It was one of my first major cases after my appointment to the bench and one of the most contentious. Not only did the case attract significant national and international media attention, but it also became a rallying point for pro-life and disability groups, as well as politicians, including members of the Florida Legislature, U.S. Congress, and the President of the United States."

"In all, the Schiavo case involved 14 appeals and numerous motions, petitions and hearings in the Florida courts, in addition to five suits in federal district court. The Supreme Court of Florida overturned legislation by the Florida House and Senate known as 'Terri's Law' to keep Terri Schiavo alive. We found that the law unconstitutionally attempted to reverse lower court decisions."

"The case was challenging because I had to put aside my personal and religious views, which could have counseled for a different result, and focus only on the applicable law. Our Court deliberated the case dispassionately and focused only on our duty under the law and the Constitution, which was difficult given the amount of publicity and emotion surrounding the case. In the end, our opinion was unanimous, which I think helped to quell any lingering doubt that the decision was based on political or personal considerations."[20]

One role of the Court that doesn't get much publicity is issuing advisory opinions on matters affecting state government. "The advisory opinions are very formalized. When there's a constitutional amendment for the ballot, the Attorney General has to ask for an advisory opinion on certain things. That's where we would get most of the advisory opinions."

The work on the Court was fulfilling, but the most rewarding part was meeting with a group of elementary school children, talking to a law class, or interacting with people who came to visit the Court. It's not just meeting with Hispanic students, he said. "Every once in a while I get an e-mail from a university student or a law student or a young lawyer, and they just want to have lunch and talk about the career and get some advice. I'll meet with them and help them along."

For young Hispanics who might want to follow in his footsteps, he said, "I think it's important to be involved in different kinds of groups. It's good to be involved in Hispanic groups really depending on where you are in the profession. If you're a young Hispanic lawyer, it's good to get mentoring from older Hispanic lawyers. If you're an older Hispanic lawyer, then it's good to give mentoring to the younger lawyers." At the same time, "I don't think you should join Hispanic groups to the exclusion of joining other groups."

The biggest change in the law over the period he was on the bench occurred in technology. "I felt like [Rip Van Winkle], when I got back and my physical inbox was empty, but my electronic inbox was overflowing. When I left the practice of law, it wasn't like that. It's not like we were getting pleadings by PDF, by e-mail. Everything was physical and so it had totally changed. Now my physical file drawer is virtually empty but I have everything on my computer."

Other changes included the growing number of lawyers and smaller firms. In addition, "there's not the professionalism that there was before. I think there's a lot more vituperative language in briefs than there used to be." He felt strongly enough about this problem that he chaired the Florida Supreme Court's Commission on Professionalism for six years.

Legal problems unique to Miami as a melting pot of Latin Americans include immigration and undocumented immigrants. In particular, he referred to Jose Godinez-Samperio, whose case had gone before the Florida Supreme Court in early 2014. "This person had gone to high school over here, gone to college here, gone to law school here, passed the Bar here, and he was undocumented, not because of him but because of his parents," he said. The issue was "whether somebody who was an undocumented immigrant could be a member of the Florida Bar." (At the Florida Supreme Court's urging, the Legislature changed the law and the young man was admitted to the Florida Bar in 2014.)

Another issue in South Florida was the legal rights of migrant farm workers, he said. "I think they're really the ignored population."

"The whole time I was on the Court I felt I was representing a community, a culture, and that I had to make sure that my behavior was outstanding, that everything about what I did was outstanding so that people wouldn't feel remorse about having appointed me," he said.

In September 2008, Cantero resigned from the Court, citing the family's desire to

Figure 5.9. Cantero resigned his position on the Supreme Court, returned to Miami, and joined the White & Case firm. When he returns to the Supreme Court to argue cases before his former colleagues, Cantero says he has to be on his A+, not just his A, game because he doesn't want them to be disappointed with his advocacy. Here he attends a Legal Services of Greater Miami, Inc., Campaign (fundraiser) event. Campaign Co-Chairs Cantero and Tracy A. Nichols (*left*), a partner at Holland & Knight, stand with former Chief Justice Rosemary Barkett (*center*), who received the Legal Services 2012 Equal Justice Judicial Leadership Award. Photo courtesy of Legal Services of Greater Miami, Inc., Fall 2012.

return to Miami. "Certainly the longer we stayed there [Tallahassee], the more my kids wanted to return to Miami. When we returned, my oldest son was graduating from high school, and he ended up at FSU. My second son was going into his sophomore year of high school, and my daughter was going into eighth grade."

"I think Hispanics in general and Cubans in particular are very much family oriented. We have a big extended family down here. My wife is one of five siblings and there's now like 15 grandchildren from that family. So we're used to going to birthday parties and things like that." In Tallahassee, "we went from all these activities to basically zero, so that was a big shock."

In addition, "In late 2007 my daughter got sick and it took months and months to diagnose what she had, so we were going through this whole thing alone up there [Tallahassee]. Finally we found out it was a tumor in her adrenal gland and we had it removed. But just going through that whole process alone really struck home that we wanted to be where we would have family support when these kinds of things happen."

When he was on the bench, the Florida Supreme Court was one of the few courts in the country that required Justices to live in the capital. When the economy collapsed in late 2007, the newly appointed Justices didn't move to Tallahassee. Cantero indicated he might have stayed on the bench longer had he been able to commute from South Florida.

After leaving the bench, Cantero joined the firm of White & Case in Miami. He renewed his involvement with Legal Services of Greater Miami, having served on its Board before he became a Justice. Since 2009, he has been cochair of a committee to raise funds for the nonprofit group. When the economy tanked, he said, the clientele increased and the funding decreased.

Going back before the Court now and arguing from the other side of the bench has become "routine because I think I've argued there at least eight to 10 times since I've left. It definitely is an interesting dynamic. First of all, it's more pressure on me because I know that I have to be on my A+ game. Not just my A game, but my A+ game because I'm going back before my former colleagues, and I don't want them to be disappointed in my advocacy. Whether or not they rule in my favor, I want them to be able to say, 'Wow, he's really doing well. He's a great lawyer.'"

"It also furnishes some good repartee with my former colleagues. I had an argument there in February (2013) that had to do with statutory interpretation. I was making my argument and Justice Pariente said, 'Well, when you were on the Court, you always argued for looking just at the plain language of the statute without looking at the legislative history.' I said, 'Yes, but mostly in dissent.' The seven Justices just started laughing. That's the kind of thing that would never have happened to anybody else."

In 2007, the Cuban American Bar Association created an endowment in his name at the Florida State University School of Law. "That was very flattering. While I was on the Court, a lot of times we'd have college students come and watch an oral argument. One time the University of Florida came up, they were watching an argument—I forget which class—and during our midmorning break, the Marshal came up to me and said there's a student there that wants to say hello and meet you. So I went out there and I met him. It was a kid who had arrived from Cuba maybe three years earlier. He had gotten a scholarship to Florida, and he was just so proud that there was a Hispanic on the Court and he felt that was something that he could aspire to. To me, it really validated what I had done and said. I did this so people could feel that they could do it too."

Raoul G. Cantero III was interviewed in person by the author Oct. 8, 2013.

Chief Justice

FLORIDA SUPREME COURT

Figure 5.10. Justices Leander Shaw, Jr., and Rosemary Barkett made history as the state's first black and female Chief Justices of the Florida Supreme Court (*center*). State Archives of Florida, *Florida Memory*, https://www.floridamemory.com/items/show/47077, Photographed on December 8, 1988.

Leander J. Shaw, Jr.

First African-American male Chief Justice of the Florida Supreme Court, 1990

Personal: Born September 6, 1930, Salem, Virginia; divorced with five children. Died December 14, 2015.

Education:

- West Virginia State College, bachelor's degree (1952)
- Howard University, J.D. (1957)
- West Virginia State College, honorary doctor of laws degree (1986)
- Florida International University, honorary doctor of public affairs degree (1990)
- Nova University, honorary doctor of laws degree (1991)
- Washington and Lee University, honorary doctor of laws degree (1991)

Occupation: U.S. Army Artillery officer/Assistant Public Defender/Lawyer

Trailblazer Appointments and Elections:

- Supreme Court Justice, *Appointed to the Court by Gov. Bob Graham (D)* 1983
- Supreme Court Chief Justice (Elected by his colleagues on the Court), 1990–1992

Figure 5.11. Leander Shaw, Chief Justice of the Supreme Court 1990–1992 (appointed to the Supreme Court by Gov. Bob Graham [D], 1983), recalled working as a civil rights lawyer in the 1960s. When he arrived in a town to get activists out of jail, the local townsfolk—who had never seen a black lawyer before—would often "be sitting out in front of the courthouse, like the circus was coming," he said. He and other black lawyers would be spat upon, chased by the Klan, and denied lodging in hotels. The Florida Supreme Court in 1991. *Seated (L-R)*: Ben Overton, Chief Justice Leander Shaw, Parker Lee McDonald; *standing (L-R)*: Gerald Kogan, Rosemary Barkett, Stephen Grimes, Major Harding. State Archives of Florida, *Florida Memory*, https://www.floridamemory.com/items/show/47219. Photograph ca. 1991.

THE LEANDER J. SHAW, JR., STORY

Leander J. Shaw, Jr., the first African American to serve as Chief Justice on the Florida Supreme Court, chose a career in law because "I could see that this country just had to change. It was inevitable that it would change, and that change was being brought about by lawyers, many of them black lawyers. I had never seen a black lawyer until I started seeing them in the paper," he said. "I wanted to be part of that movement and part of that change."

Shaw, who can trace his ancestry to slavery in his great-great-great-grandmother's family, was born in Salem, Va. Both his parents were in education: His mother taught at a high school in Lexington, and his father was principal there. Shaw attended public schools in Virginia and received a bachelor's degree from West Virginia State College in 1952.

In college, he went through ROTC. "You graduated two ways," he said. "If you were a Distinguished Military Student [DMS], you got a regular army commission. You could not be rolled back, and if you were not a DMS, after the war was over, they could bust you back to a sergeant or something like that."

As a DMS, he went into the Korean War as an artillery officer. At one point, when a black group was coming to entertain the troops, a white colonel told him to go and greet them. Shaw asked why only he was being sent instead of the general practice of sending a committee. The colonel said, "They'd be happy to see you." Perceiving that he was being used as a token, Shaw refused. "Leander, you need to toe the line a little better," the colonel said. "You could have a great career in the military, and you don't want to hurt it up front." Shaw retorted, "Listen, let me tell you something. The only career that can be hurt here is yours. I'm putting in two years and I'm gone." And he left.

"I knew I didn't have the temperament to stay in the Army. I would've gotten in trouble. I would've stayed in 10 years, been hooked on it, felt I had to put in the other six. But sooner or later somebody would've done something to get me out, or I would've popped off to the wrong person. I just didn't have the temperament to survive."

He took that temperament to Howard University School of Law in Washington, D.C., where he graduated in 1957. That was an era when communities in the South were reacting to the U.S. Supreme Court's decision in *Brown v. Board of Education* (1954).

At that point, his father, who had become Dean of the Graduate School at Florida A&M, told him the law school was looking for professors. Shaw saw the opportunity as "heaven sent." He had not yet taken the Bar exam, and he knew he didn't want to practice in the Northeast because he didn't like the weather there. So he began teaching at A&M's law school, which had been created in 1951 to satisfy the "separate but equal" principle guiding education at the time. "A&M of course then had a law school—a black law school to keep blacks out of the white law schools," he said.

He soon realized, however, that the law school could not long survive economically. "One of the first questions I asked when I came here was, 'How can they afford to keep a law school open and have about eight students in it?' You had as many professors as you had students." Besides faculty, a school needed a library and classrooms. "The cost is astronomical to keep a law school going."

"I asked a black legislator the very question. I said, 'How can you afford to keep the school open, and how long do you plan to keep it open?' The man's answer was quite frank: 'As long as it takes, and whatever it costs.' But I saw the handwriting on the wall, so I went ahead and took the Bar and moved to Jacksonville," Shaw said.

Taking the Bar exam provided an example of Jim Crow practices prevalent at the time. "Somebody from the hotel came through and whispered something to the Bar examiners. We were all sitting there ready to take the Bar then. The Bar examiner said, 'The hotel has informed us that the white applicants and the black applicants cannot take the test in the same room.' So some of us left, some stayed, and just—you know, that just blew it to pieces right at that point."

In Jacksonville he formed a partnership with Earl Johnson, Sr., another Howard law graduate. Both had met Thurgood Marshall and other civil rights leaders when they had come to campus. "We knew them by face, and they came and inspired us." Marshall knew Shaw well enough to greet him by name. "He was just somebody I admired tremendously."

They met other soon-to-be famous civil rights leaders, such as Ruby Hurley, NAACP Southeast Regional Director, as they began working in the Civil Rights Movement. "A lot of them were traveling all through the South and going through the abuse that they had to take. When they would come, they couldn't stay in a decent hotel, and so people in the community were kind enough to keep them at their homes. They would meet at the black churches and organize whatever they were organizing at the time."

Of course, Jacksonville had its own civil rights leaders. One was Rodney L. Hurst, Sr. "He headed the youth movement there in Jacksonville at the time in the '60s. He was the object of a lot of hate and scorn. There was one particular juvenile judge, Judge Marion Gooding, that just was determined he was going to put Rod in prison for life." In one incident, Hurst was arrested for "contributing to the delinquency of a minor" by recruiting young people to engage in demonstrations. Johnson and Shaw represented Hurst at the hearing. The case was dismissed when the minor could not identify Hurst as the person who told him to demonstrate.[21]

Another local leader they knew was trailblazer Arnett Girardeau, who served as captain of the Axe Handle Saturday sit-in demonstration and would become the first African American to serve in the Florida Senate since Reconstruction (1982–1992).

"Jacksonville was bad. It was terrible," Shaw said. "You had Governors and Mayors that were just determined that it wasn't going to change." The town had biracial councils in which activists and townspeople met to work out solutions. "But it was all a charade," he said. As soon as the meeting was over, the other side would say, "Ain't nothin' going to happen here in Jacksonville, not while I'm alive."

Fifty miles south of Jacksonville was St. Augustine, a hotbed of the Civil Rights Movement. The police "were arresting black youth by the bus loads. They arrested so many, they were just holding them in the armory. The jails wouldn't hold them," Shaw said. Among those arrested was Mary Parkman Peabody, mother of Massachusetts Gov. Endicott Peabody, who came at Dr. Martin Luther King, Jr.'s, request to lead a sit-in at a segregated dining room of a motel.[22]

"The youths would go to the beaches and get arrested there. They'd go to hotels and say they want to register or they want to swim in the pool and so forth. This is when the guy came and just—in one hotel—stood and poured acid in the pool."

When such things happened, Shaw and Johnson would drive to St. Augustine to get activists out of jail. Dr. Robert B. Hayling, a local dentist and activist, "would call and say, 'We've got 30 kids and mothers in my office. Com'n up.'"

"I guess Dr. Hayling's the bravest man I've ever seen in my life because he just was with it every day. He couldn't leave. He lived right there. His dental practice was there, and everybody knew that he was the driving wheel for black organization and movement there. So his life was on the line all the time. Fortunately, he survived and nothing really tragic happened to him. He had a lot of protection. But still, you can only protect a person so much."

"We had bondsmen, two or three black bondsmen that we knew at that time—a lot of the white bonding agencies just wouldn't bond out blacks," Shaw said. One black bondsman was always on call. "We'd call him and have him either come himself or make arrangements with another bonding agency to get the kids out."

Driving back and forth to St. Augustine "got to be sort of a hazardous trip because Klansmen would start following your car," Shaw said. "One day they got behind Earl, and he had just bought a brand new Buick. He wrecked his Buick coming back because they were chasing him. I think he caught a deer, or something jumped out in front of him. But that was the kind of thing that you ran into."

Once Shaw and Johnson arrived, the townspeople would flock to the courthouse to look at them. Few had ever seen black lawyers before. "They'd be sitting out in front of the courthouse, like the circus was coming. 'Oh, here they come. Look, here we come.' As you came down the aisle, they'd be spitting at you and that type thing. Having the kids spit at you—more and more of that." When one local man was interviewed by the press, and "they asked him what his favorite occupation was, he said, 'Raisin' hogs and killin' n_____s.'"

Shaw remembered one incident that illustrated the institutional resistance to change: "I went over to St. Augustine to file some papers to get some kids out of jail. The person at the desk told me, 'No, you can't file no papers. Those are not the right papers.' I said, 'I'm a lawyer. I'll determine what the right paper is and what papers I want to file.' They said, 'Well, you can't file those here.' I said, 'You'd better go over and talk to your judge and see what he has to say about that.' The person disappeared and came back about 15 minutes later. I was just sitting there cooling my heels waiting on him. The person said, 'The judge said you can't file those papers here, so you can just get on out.'"

"I'd never heard about anything like this in law school. Where do you find out what to do in this instance? If you can't file your papers, a lawyer's cut off at the pass. He's cut off at the knees if he can't file anything. So you're completely useless. I don't know what to do, so I say, 'Well I'm going to go right to the horse's mouth.' I called the Supreme Court of Florida, and I happened to get Judge Adkins."

"'Yes, this is Mr. Jimmy Adkins,' he said. I said, 'Mr. Justice, I know I'm not supposed to be calling, but I'm a young lawyer and I ran into this problem, and frankly it's beyond me. I know you've heard about what's going on down here in St. Augustine. I tried to file some papers and was told by the clerk's office that I could not file the papers and I just don't know what to do past this point.' Justice Adkins said, 'Well, the case is probably going to end up here in my court anyway, so I can't be advising you how to practice law. But I'll tell you what: Go on back in about 10 minutes. They might have a change of heart.'" When he went back, "there were a lot of red faces, but I didn't have any problem about them filing my papers at that point."

Years later when Shaw was appointed to the Supreme Court, he asked his then-fellow Justice Adkins about the incident. Adkins said, "I called the judge and told him, 'You can't stop a lawyer from filing papers. Are you out of your mind?' So that got filed. But that was kind of ironic that I would end up on the Court with him." Adkins served on the Court from 1969 to 1987 and Shaw from 1983 to 2003.

In addition to working in civil rights, his private practice was growing. He would get clients almost anywhere. Even when he would pass by a saloon at night, he might find someone waiting with a civil case they wanted him to handle. But most were criminal cases, not just from blacks but also from whites. "They started telling their cousins and all that I was their lawyer. 'You got to talk to my lawyer.' And then they took that over to the civil side. If they got in an accident, they would come to see 'their lawyer.' And then they started using me on the divorces and probate."

The first time he had a white client with a divorce case, "I was sitting there with my client and the judge finally came out and asked me, 'Leander, when are your clients going to get here?' I said, 'They're sitting right here.' He couldn't believe it. After a while they got used to it. I mean, like everything else, it went on."

While in private practice in Jacksonville, Shaw also worked part-time in the state's

Public Defender Office on non-capital cases. That connection would lead to his next job in the State Attorney's office.

Ed Austin, a former Public Defender with Shaw, got elected State Attorney and invited Shaw to join him. At first, Shaw declined. "At that point we were opening up golf courses, we were suing school boards, we were going up to Live Oak and Lake City and places like that, so we had our hands full. Then he gave me an offer I couldn't refuse. Criminal law was my specialty then. He said, 'You know more about our criminal practice than most lawyers, so I'll make you head of Capital Crimes Division. You'll probably be the only one in the South because I don't know of any other blacks to head the Capital Crimes Division in the South.'" Then came the clincher: "'You'll do more doing this than some other things you might do in practice. It'll open up some things.' He said, 'It's just minds have to be opened.'"

When word got out that Austin was planning to appoint Shaw, "All sorts of forces descended upon his office, the police department and all. They came and said, 'No, that can't happen. Yeah, he's a good lawyer and so forth, but if he's going to head the Capital Crimes Division, he will be in charge of rape cases, and white women would be uncomfortable coming to him and telling him what happened to them.' They gave all sorts of other excuses and reasons. Ed politely listened to them, and then he said, 'I'll tell you who's going to head my Capital Crimes Division, and there will be no cases prosecuted if they can't come before him.' It was just that simple."

As time passed, homicide lawyers and policemen started coming by his office for information and assistance. That's when Shaw knew he had made it. "A lot of times I would go to the crime scene myself," he said, and "we developed a rapport."

"By the time I left the State Attorney's office, I had a lot of friends," he said. "In fact, they used to make book on when I was going to lose a case." His record turned out to be 42 wins and one loss. "Ed was right. It showed that given an opportunity, blacks could perform. So I think it was a good choice going with the State Attorney's office as opposed to just staying in private practice because I was still doing other stuff, too. And, as I say, working in the State Attorney's office came kind of easy to me because it was stuff that I liked and I was familiar with criminal law."

In 1972, he and two white attorneys from the State Attorney's office went into private practice together. "We decided that it was time for us to get out and go ahead and do something else. So we got together and talked about it, and it appeared that all of us were making approximately the same amount of money, some a little more than others, but we all had good practices. We know each other, we like each other, so we did. So there was Harrison, Finegold and Shaw."

Theirs was probably not the first law firm in Jacksonville to integrate, however. That distinction may belong to Henry Lee Adams, Jr., who joined William J. "Bill" Sheppard and others. Adams later became a U.S. district judge.

With his reputation growing, Shaw ran for judge and for the school board but lost both elections. "One of the lawyers that was running against me, his platform was 'Looks Like a Judge.' I couldn't understand that. Then I talked to one of my campaign workers who was white and I said, 'What does he mean 'Looks Like a Judge'? He said, 'You haven't seen any black judges here in Duval County, have you?' No. 'That's what he's saying. It's code for you need to elect the black and white judges. It's code words for that.'"

"By that time I had become political to the point that when politicians were in town, they would come by my office and see me." One of the first was State Sen. Verle A. Pope, known as "the Lion of St. Johns County." Shaw could hardly believe it: "Where'd you get my name?" he asked Pope. "Are you sure you're in the right office?"

Without his realizing it, Shaw's career was shifting into high gear. In 1974, he received a call offering him a seat on the Industrial Relations Commission, a statewide appellate body that handled workers compensation cases. "We had a very good Commissioner there in Jacksonville, Thomas Carroll. I had handled workers' comp cases, but you couldn't lose because Carroll was not going to let you hurt your client. If you didn't know what to do, Carroll was going to spoon-feed you through it," Shaw said. "I thought he was going to get the seat, and to this day I don't know why Tom didn't get it. He certainly deserved it, more so than I did."

Shaw was appointed to the Commission by Gov. Reubin Askew (D, 1971–1979). Just five years later, in 1979, the Legislature abolished the Commission as part of a reorganization effort and shifted workers comp appeals to the First District Court of Appeals. At least two of the five Commissioners, Shaw and Winifred "Winnie" L. Wentworth, along with others, went before the nominating commission for two open seats on the Court.

"Everybody thought Elmer [O.] Friday, Jr., was going to get it," Shaw said. Friday, a former Secretary of the Senate, "was sort of a legend here." But Gov. Bob Graham (D, 1979–1987) appointed Shaw and Wentworth. "It came as a sort of a surprise to both of us."

In January 1983, Shaw took the big step up to the Florida Supreme Court, again appointed by Gov. Graham. During the next 20 years, he would contribute to opinions in a number of important cases.

One opinion, *Gore v. Harris*, led to what might become the legal case of the century. In the 2000 presidential election, the outcome came down to the vote count in Florida. Secretary of State Katherine Harris had declared that Republican George W. Bush received more votes than Democrat Albert Gore, although a few counties had not finished their manual recounts. The conflict came before the Florida Supreme Court, which on December 8 ruled to allow the manual recount to proceed. Shaw had concurred in that opinion, later explaining that the process "lacked sufficient guidelines and could not be completed promptly and fairly."[23]

Figure 5.12. In one high-profile case in 2000, *Gore v. Harris*, the Court ordered a manual recount of ballots in certain counties. But it was soon overturned by the U.S. Supreme Court, making George W. Bush President. "All the king's horses and all the king's men could not get a few thousand ballots counted," Shaw said. "The explanation, however, is timeless. We are a nation of men and women and, although we aspire to lofty principles, our methods at times are imperfect." State Archives of Florida, *Florida Memory*, https://www.floridamemory.com/items/show/47184. Photograph ca. 1983–2003.

Days later, the U.S. Supreme Court overruled the state court's opinion, making Bush the winner in *Bush v. Gore*. The Florida Court met again in late December, calling on the Florida Legislature to develop standards for counting votes. Shaw lamented the difficulty in assessing the will of voters: "All the king's horses and all the king's men could not get a few thousand ballots counted. The explanation, however, is timeless. We are a nation of men and women and, although we aspire to lofty principles, our methods at times are imperfect."

Another case, *Provenzano*,[24] ruled that the electric chair could continue to be used for executions in Florida. "In my dissent I did something that apparently was so unusual, nobody'd ever done it before that anybody could remember." He added graphic color pictures of an executed man in the electric chair "with all the blood and described all the smell and parched skin and flames jumping off of his legs and all of this gore. We got stuff from all over the world on that."

"I ain't going to say it's not cruel and unusual with flames jumping out of the man's head and all this type of stuff. But the Legislature abolished the electric chair rather than let it go up to the U.S. Supreme Court. They went to lethal injection, so that muted the issue of electric chair in Florida. I can't say it was because of my dissent, but that's what happened. Chances are, it had something to do with it."

A third case, *DiGuilio*,[25] "is supposedly the most cited case in Florida. It establishes what we call a 'harmless error test' to be applied in criminal cases," he said. Basically, it requires that whoever benefits from the error must prove that there is no reasonable possibility that the error contributed to the verdict.

In addition, Shaw served as Vice Chair of the Court's Racial and Ethnic Bias Study Commission. The Commission found, among other things, that "minorities are significantly underrepresented as judges in proportion to their numbers in the general population," and that "minorities are not included in the selection process and are underrepresented in the pool from which judges are drawn."[26]

Shaw noted that the court system had been integrated some years before he was appointed. "Joe Hatchett [Supreme Court Justice 1975–1979] would've been the one to start that because Joe was on the Court before I was. Then I kept it up and kind of kept an eye to see that there's some diversity there," he said. But "it was not unusual even after we had done it at the Supreme Court to go through different counties and see their circuits, see their court system, and the woeful lack of any diversity."

He served as Chief Justice from 1990 to 1992. "You could tell that there was a lot of ambivalence about having a black Chief Justice, ranging from 'A black just can't handle this job' to 'Lee, is there anything I can do to help you?'"

In November 1990, a conservative group led a merit retention challenge against Shaw because he had written a controversial opinion the previous year that overturned the state's parental consent abortion law. "That was a chance to get rid of me without saying we're doing it because he's black. They were going after Raymond Ehrlich also. Well, Ehrlich's a Jew," Shaw said. "They didn't prove any points there necessarily. But there were people of goodwill that got behind us. They put money behind us, put expertise, put their friendships on the line and so forth." Voters approved his retention on the Court.

About the same time, the Legislature passed an austerity program in which all state agencies had to cut 10 or 20 percent off their budgets. "I took the position that the court system is not an agency. It's a branch of government. It's one of the three branches of government." In talking to legislators across the street, "I told them the reality of it. I said, 'Now you can cut money from the system if you want to, but we'll end up like California. It'll take five years to get a civil case to trial. If that's what you want in Florida, that's what you're going to have. In the criminal cases, you've got to do certain things in certain timeframes. You don't have to do that on the civil side, so that's what's going to suffer. But the criminal cases, we're going to have to process them. The Constitution mandates that.' So that seemed to ring a bell, and we got our money."

Shaw often made speaking trips to encourage young people to enter the law profession. "I was up in Fernandina buying some bait, and eight or nine black kids around high school age came up and started looking at my car. 'That's a good car you have. You must be somebody big.' I said, 'Well, I don't know about that. I'm a lawyer.' They wanted to know what a lawyer did. I said, 'Actually I'm a judge.'" They asked his name, and he told them. They didn't recognize it. "I said, 'I'm on the Supreme Court.' 'The Supreme Court of the United States?' they asked. I said, 'No, the Supreme Court of Florida.'" Not a single one knew there was a black on the Supreme Court of either Florida or the United States.

"That inspired me to go around and speak more than I'd intended to do, quite frankly. Because I was just shocked that here were kids that have graduated from, or should have graduated from, high school that had no idea that there was a black on the Supreme Court of Florida."

In 2003, facing mandatory retirement age, he left the bench. People asked why he did not join a law firm where his time could be billed at large hourly fees. "But, no, when I retired, it was all over for me. I was ready to retire. And there's such a thing as staying too long. I've seen prize fighters stay too long. I've seen politicians stay too long. I was determined that Leander wasn't going to stay too long. And I've enjoyed my retirement," hinting that he might have done it sooner if he had known it would be so pleasant.

If he were advising a young minority man or woman today about going into law, he might be cautious: "The times are different. I understand that a lot of young lawyers are struggling now, and a lot of them are changing professions and this type of thing, so there seems to be a problem. When I first started out, certainly if you were a black lawyer, the black community welcomed you. They were glad to have you there."

Over his career, Shaw has seen massive changes in America. "There has been a lot of change but there's been a lot of resistance, too. I worry about some of the things, some of the attitudes that are surfacing now. There seems to be some kind of retreat in some ways. I don't know what it is. What happened?" May be a loss of civility. "I put my faith in the Lord. I believe that we're going to win in the end."

Leander Shaw was interviewed in person by the author Apr. 14, 2014.

Rosemary Barkett

First woman appointed to the Florida Supreme Court, 1985

First female Chief Justice, 1992

Personal: Born August 29, 1939, at Ciudad Victoria, Tamaulipas, Mexico; naturalized January 22, 1958, Fort Pierce, Florida.

Family: Born in Mexico, but parents were Syrian

Figure 5.13. Rosemary Barkett made history when her colleagues chose her to become Florida's first woman Chief Justice of the Florida Supreme Court in 1992. "There was always vigorous debate" among the Justices, but "the nice part about the Florida Supreme Court that I served on is that it seemed really familial." She saw disagreements on issues as if they were between siblings: "It was a family fight over an issue and it never carried over into enmity or resentment or anything like that." State Archives of Florida, *Florida Memory*, https://www.floridamemory.com/items/show/144573, n.d. No. 35225.

Education:

- Spring Hill College, B.S. (1967)
- Levin College of Law, University of Florida, J.D. (1970)

Occupation: Lawyer/Teacher

Trailblazer Appointments and Elections:

- Supreme Court Justice, *Appointed by Gov. Bob Graham (D)* 1985
- First retention election 1986
    - Yes (76.8%), No (23.2%)
- Supreme Court Chief Justice (Elected by her colleagues on the Court), 1992–1994

THE ROSEMARY BARKETT STORY

Born in Mexico to Syrian parents,[27] Rosemary Barkett had four "firsts" on the Florida Supreme Court: first woman Justice, first woman Chief Justice, first "Hispanic" Justice, and first Arab-American Justice. From the Florida Supreme Court, she was appointed to a federal appeals court, and from there to an international court, the Iran-United States Claims Tribunal in The Hague, in 2013.

"It has been a huge advantage to have come from a tri-cultural background. It gives you a global perspective on shared values and an appreciation of the world as a whole,"[28] she said.

The shaping of her global perspective began in Ciudad Victoria in the Mexican state of Tamaulipas. She spoke only Spanish when her family (surname Barakat) moved to Miami in 1945, when she was six years old. At age 17, she entered a convent and taught school, hoping to accomplish more for humanity in the outside world. In 1970, she graduated from the University of Florida College of Law, where she became the first woman to receive an award as the outstanding senior graduate.[29]

After practicing for eight years with a small firm in Palm Beach, she began her public service career when Gov. Bob Graham (D, 1979–1987) appointed her to a state circuit court judgeship in 1979. He appointed her to a state appellate court in 1984 and then to the Florida Supreme Court in 1985.

While on the state's high court, she deliberated a number of significant cases, including at least two dealing with the termination of life of incapacitated people. In 1990,[30] the Court ruled in *Browning* that caregivers could abide by wishes to remove artificial life support, as expressed in a living will. That case preceded the 15-year legal battle over prolonging life support for Terri Schiavo, a cardiac arrest patient who had no living will.

More numerous were the search-and-seizure opinions, some of which had been "unanimous on our Court," and went to the U.S. Supreme Court. One example was *Riley*,[31] "where the issue was whether or not an anonymous tip could support the police use of a helicopter dipping way down, to 25 feet or so, above someone's yard to observe if they were growing marijuana. I wrote the opinion holding that helicopters would have to stay at the same level the FAA requires for planes and not go below that point," she said. The Attorney General appealed to the U.S. Supreme Court, which reversed the state's ruling 5 to 4.

"The opinion came out when we were at the annual meeting of all the state chief justices, which was being held in Florida. I was not Chief Justice at the time, but because the meeting was held in Florida, all of the justices were attending to help host the event," she said. On the day the opinion was issued, Barkett had been playing tennis with Justice John Paul Stevens and his wife and fellow Florida Justice Ben Overton (1974–1999). "When we finished our doubles game, we sat to have a drink, and I asked him to autograph one of the tennis balls for me. He took the tennis ball and on one side he printed out our tennis scores for the sets we played. On the other side he drew a little helicopter and printed the name 'Riley' with a 5–4 after it."

"The Attorney General at the time was Bob Butterworth [1987–2002], whom I had known for many years. I would see him regularly at all of the functions we would have in Tallahassee—the social functions, political functions, and so forth. Bob was an easy man to get along with—not stiff; not an ideologue. So I felt very comfortable teasing him about appealing the *Riley* decision to the U.S. Supreme Court. When I saw him at some event, I asked him how he could possibly appeal a decision that was so right. Then I added that the police hovering over people's backyards were nothing but voyeurs checking to see whom they could see sunbathing nude in the privacy of their backyards. He laughed. Well, when the opinion came out, as I said, it was during this meeting of the state chief justices. I was sitting in back of the room listening to the speaker when somebody delivered a box to me. Of course, I was curious and since I was over in the corner in the back, I thought I could open it unobtrusively." She opened the gift-wrapped box and read the card from Butterworth: 'Dear Justice Barkett: Sorry that the Court's opinion was reversed, but I thought you might find this particular item handy.'" It was a black bathing suit.

As Chief Justice from 1992 to 1994, she "got in trouble over judicial salaries by not advocating enough for them," she said. "Circuit judges were trying very hard to get a raise but at that time, we were suffering the worst budget crisis and the Legislature was cutting the money needed to operate the court system. I felt obliged as Chief Justice to push for the monies that were necessary to run the court system, rather than push for judicial salary increases."

"There was always vigorous debate" among the Justices, she recalled. But "the nice part about the Florida Supreme Court that I served on is that it seemed really familial. We were all living in Tallahassee. Tallahassee is really a small town with the Legislature there and the Court was constantly attending social functions pertaining to the Legislature, or pertaining to the University. Many times, one or the other of the Justices would insist on picking me up to take me along. They were very brotherly about making sure that I had a ride or was going."

As the only woman on the bench at the time, she felt the other Justices were "a little too brotherly sometimes because one of them—I will not name names—would always come in on Monday morning wanting to know exactly what I had done that weekend. I'd say, 'Never mind what I did this weekend.' Because of this familial relationship, I think it carried over into the debates in conference over cases." Having grown up in a large family "with people vociferously expressing their views" and not taking offense, Barkett saw disagreements on issues as if they were between siblings: "It was a family fight over an issue and it never carried over into enmity or resentment or anything like that." Of course, she admitted, "the passage of time may have made the situation rosier than it actually was. But I remember it very fondly as a group of people that I felt very comfortable agreeing and disagreeing with and whom I believed to be comfortable disagreeing with me. There was never a feeling that you had to be careful about how you said something because people knew you and would be able to filter what was said through that knowledge."

Moreover, there was no horse trading of votes, as sometimes happens in legislative bodies, she said. "But you certainly wanted to be accommodating about compromising where you could in order to remain collegial—like changing language in an opinion or leaving a section out that someone asked you to delete if it was not necessary to the opinion."

Relationships among Justices had not always been so collegial. From a historical viewpoint, "there were instances where the Florida Supreme Court was terribly fragmented. Justices didn't get along. Some didn't speak to each other, although the Florida Supreme Court was never as bad as some other state courts," she said.

Before going on the bench, she didn't know any of the other Justices. "But they were so welcoming. I remember Jimmy Adkins, whom I grew to love. He was an irascible character," she said. "He came into my office the first day I came to work and said: 'Now, I want you to listen to me. You've only been here a day, but you are one-seventh of this Court as of the day that you were appointed and you should never feel that you are too new or something, not to participate fully in this Court.' I thought that was amazing."

She also had great affection for Justice Raymond Ehrlich (1981–1990). "He was the greatest gentleman and a gentle man—old-world courtly and courteous. But he loved to tell risqué stories and jokes and was always teasing me. He sat next to me in the courtroom and would sometimes pass me funny notes during the argument."

From time to time, the Justices would gather socially. At the home of Justice Parker Lee McDonald (1979–1994), for example, the group would have dinner and then sing, accompanied by McDonald's wife at the piano.

Collegiality on the Court kept her from feeling excluded because she was a woman. "I think there is a point in the beginning when you join any group when you feel like an outsider," she admitted. "I do believe that sometimes the already constituted group just doesn't think of you. Or it doesn't occur to them that you might want to participate. But then there's a mechanism in some people that just refuses to recognize slights—if they are slights, you don't see them as clearly because you have a sense of self that sort of blocks you from seeing that, I suppose. Or maybe some are readier to see slights when perhaps they are not really intended." When women join a new group, "you have to work really hard at overcoming awkwardness. I don't think men who have always 'belonged to the group' or feel like they are part of a group have to worry about it."

Collegial relationships did not exist on the federal appeals court, 11th Circuit, to which she was appointed by President Bill Clinton (D) in 1994. The judges were spread over three states and saw each other only sporadically. It was "a different dynamic," she said. There was more reserve—"more care taken not to be disagreeable when you're disagreeing," which she found "somewhat inhibiting."

On the federal court, she authored several landmark opinions in constitutional law, sexual harassment, disability rights, labor rights, privacy rights, rights of speech and association, and immigration—opinions criticized by conservatives as "judicial activism," a term that Barkett finds "unfortunate." Because the term "seemed to have a negative connotation," she determined in speaking and writing about the issue that "I should know exactly what it means. So I tried to parse the meaning by trying to define it the way a jury instruction would—that is, in terms of its component elements. Beyond an act by a judicial officer, however, it seemed that the remaining element was that the speaker using the term disagreed with the judge or opinion they were talking about. I was trying to make the point that as a shorthand phrase, the only thing it does is signal that you disagree with what a judge did. That doesn't explain your complaint with a judge or an opinion, which is not to say that you shouldn't criticize judges or their opinions. I think by all means you have every right—and even an obligation to do so."

But, she continued, "A critic of the judicial opinion should be required to have reasons for criticizing an opinion, such as the facts were wrong, or the opinion did not recognize precedent, or the logic of the opinion was flawed in that the major and minor premise did not lead to its conclusion. You should not be able to get away with criticizing a judge or an opinion by simply calling them 'judicial activists.' It's like writing a dissent. You just don't simply say, 'I disagree,' period. You explain why the majority's position is flawed."

In examining issues, "You have to be loyal to the text of the Constitution. The problem is that much of the text of the Constitution is ambiguous. When the 14th Amendment talks about *due process*, what does that mean exactly? When you talk about the Eighth Amendment's prohibition against cruel and unusual punishment—what does that mean? What is cruel and unusual in a given point in time? So, of course, you start with the text of any document. But the text itself does not always answer the question presented. Then you have to look to more than the text. You look at precedent if there is any. You look at the intent of the drafters, if you can discern it fairly in the context of the problem presented." In examining the document, "you may have to look to the broad intent and apply it to present-day situations. The right of privacy, for example: How can you not say that the framers believed there was an area of personal autonomy that was sacred and immune from governmental interference?"

She traced the right of privacy to a line of cases beginning with *Griswold v. Connecticut*.[32] The attorney in that case argued that a Connecticut law prohibiting the use of contraceptives was unconstitutional because of a right of privacy. "The state cannot tell us that we cannot use contraceptives. That's government action that goes too far," she said. "The U.S. Supreme Court agreed. Then the state tried to distinguish the case by saying that *Griswold* involved married people and argued that they could prohibit the use of contraceptives by single people. The Court said, 'No, no, you knuckleheads, you missed the point. It's not about whether people are married or whether they're single, but about every individual's right to privacy or autonomy within a limited sphere involving intimate decisions. It's a personal right that you have whether you're married or single.' And that led to the protection of *Roe v. Wade*."[33]

"That was followed by the gay rights question in *Bowers v. Hardwick*,[34] in which the Court deviated from the analysis used in *Griswold* and its progeny," she continued. "Instead of asking whether homosexuality involved an intimate right, the Court asked whether homosexuality was named in the Constitution and protected explicitly. Of course, when you look at the Constitution, there's nothing about homosexuality, but there was nothing there about contraceptives either. When the Court was faced with homosexuality again in *Lawrence v. Texas*,[35] it said the opinion in *Bowers* was flawed because it had not asked the right constitutional question and reverted to the *Griswold* analysis: Does this involve a decision pertaining to personal and intimate relationships? The Court in *Lawrence* said yes and overruled *Bowers*." The point is that "in those cases and many, many others, the Court takes a look at the language first, and then the intent of all of the provisions of the Constitution taken as a whole, and the whole history of the relationship between citizens and the limitation of government."

To those who criticize certain judicial remedies as judicial activism, Barkett said: "I can see that criticism of some remedies might be legitimate and should be debated. But sometimes, if you cannot fashion a remedy, then you really have not addressed a complaint that you have conceded has value and merit. It's hard to discuss this in the abstract because you have to target a lot of particular cases. For example, the

Court ordered busing after *Brown v. Board of Education*.[36] Was that a correct remedy? I don't know. I think that's a debatable question. Should the Court have said that 'separate but equal' is not equal? Absolutely, yes." In that situation, "nothing was happening to remedy the practices of past segregation. So they were confronted with the question of how do we implement our judgment? Should the Court consider how various states will react? If the Court sees a wrong and believes the state legislatures will not act to enact remedies, does that give the Court additional grounds to craft remedies? If the Court says, 'separate but equal will not do,' the Court can either stop there or fashion a remedy." Whether the Court fashions a remedy depends on the issue.

As an example, she referred to a state constitutional provision that requires that every child in the state receive a quality education. "That's a constitutional mandate. Then a lawsuit is filed alleging that the Legislature refuses to fund a quality education. What can the Court do? And we're talking in the abstract, so I'm not sure that there is such a case and I don't know how it would be decided ultimately. But I would think a Court would have to at least ascertain whether the Legislature was funding education, and then deal with the question of what a 'quality education' meant, and then perhaps grapple with a remedy: What has the Legislature done? What resources are available? How must a quality education be prioritized when considering all of the needs of the state? How does the separation of powers play out in considering these questions? Those are very hard questions."

Dissents are an important part of the judicial process, and almost all the dissents she wrote "were important to me or I wouldn't have written them. I'm not being flip. I mean, you try to reach consensus and you try in a collegial court not to dissent just to be argumentative. You dissent because it is an important issue that warrants the exposition of what you see as the errors of the majority position."

When she found herself in the minority, she often tried to persuade colleagues to change their minds. "Sometimes you can't because there are two legitimate sides to an issue or interpretations of precedent and a colleague just views an issue differently. What I find difficult to accept is a colleague who will not respond to the substance of an argument or the specific language you might point out in a precedential opinion by simply saying, 'Well, we just don't agree.' That just doesn't cut it. I mean, that's not what we are there for. We are there to engage in a discussion, to explain why an argument is being rejected or a position is being espoused as logically preferable or at least viable. That's the point of having three people on a panel or seven or nine people on a Supreme Court. The idea is to subject an argument to multiple views. Each judge should engage in testing his or her position against the logic being advanced by another."

She admitted that there were times when conservative colleagues persuaded her to take their view, "even if I didn't like the result—because the law called for it."

One of the most memorable experiences on the 11th Circuit "was an *en banc* session where we heard four *en banc* cases in one day, all of which were extremely important, at least in my view. The cases had all been decided by a panel, but one of the judges might have asked for an *en banc* [whole court] vote to have the panel opinion reviewed."

One case, *Faragher v. City of Boca Raton*,[37] "had to do with a female lifeguard in Boca Raton who was sexually harassed by a supervisor. The question was what kind of notice was necessary in a situation like that to hold the city liable in a sexual harassment case." Barkett had requested the *en banc* vote because she thought the panel opinion was wrong.

"The second was a case called *Davis v. Board of Education*,[38] where I had written a panel opinion saying that a fifth grade student had a right under Title IX to bring an action for sexual harassment when the school did absolutely nothing to protect her from sexual harassment after they had been noticed about the situation. She ended up being sexually attacked in the stairwell of the school."

The third was *Shahar v. Bowers*,[39] in which the plaintiff, Shahar, had been hired by the Attorney General of Georgia but was fired when the Attorney General discovered that she was gay.

The fourth case was "one of our very first cases under the AEDPA [Antiterrorism and Effective Death Penalty Act, 1996], the *habeas* statute."

"It was an amazingly intense day. I have to confess, I was very optimistic about the outcome of the cases as I thought that once we all sat around the table, everything would be very clear and everyone would agree with the way I saw those cases. I remember Judge Joe Hatchett saying to me, 'Rosemary, you are so naive.' Anyway, we were in oral argument and in conference from 9 in the morning until about 7 or 8 that night discussing those cases."

In *Faragher*, "I could not persuade the Court that the panel opinion should be reversed, and I wrote a dissent," she said. "In *Davis*, the *en banc* court reversed my majority decision and I wrote a dissent. In *Shahar* the *en banc* court reversed Judge Phyllis Kravitch's opinion granting relief to Shahar, and I dissented." Ultimately, Barkett's dissenting positions in *Faragher* and *Davis* were vindicated by the U.S. Supreme Court. *Faragher* established new rules for reporting sexual harassment grievances and establishing the responsibilities of employers in Title VII[40] claims.

"*Shahar* had not originally been my case. Three of our senior judges had ruled that *Shahar* had a cause of action and that she was wrongfully terminated on the basis of sexual orientation and the majority reversed *en banc*. That did not go up on appeal to the United States Supreme Court, although I wonder how that would have ended up, actually considering *Lawrence v. Texas* now."

Another important case in which she wrote a dissent was *Chandler v. Miller*.[41] "That case involved a Georgia law that required every candidate for public office to

Figure 5.14. Chief Justice Rosemary Barkett (*right*), along with U.S. Attorney General Janet Reno, attend the installation of Patricia A. Seitz (*center*) as the first woman President of the Florida Bar. Barkett recognized the significance of being the state's first woman Chief Justice and was happy to accept invitations to events touting the accomplishments of women lawyers. Each year, two awards are given in her honor: the Rosemary Barkett Outstanding Achievement Award given by the Florida Association of Women Lawyers and the Rosemary Barkett Award, presented by the Academy of Florida Trial Lawyers to a person who has demonstrated outstanding commitment to equal justice under law. State Archives of Florida, *Florida Memory*, https://www.floridamemory.com/items/show/37909. Photograph taken June 25, 1993.

pass a drug test. I thought the law unconstitutional. The U.S. Supreme Court agreed with me—8 to 1, I think, reversing the majority."

As a judge, "I worry about the impact of all decisions on people. I worry that wrong decisions can do so much damage. I think we have an obligation to be extraordinarily careful to listen and understand the arguments both sides are making and approach each side of the case with a really open mind. You may ultimately reject a position but you have to understand it first. You have got to put yourself in the shoes of both parties, in order to see the issue from both sides."

Barkett believes that most cases touch the everyday lives of people. "Every criminal search-and-seizure case or probable-cause case or stop-and-frisk case really touches a lot of people in terms of what police are able to do under what circumstances. Cases regarding your rights to control your own body and medical decisions are hugely important and directly affect all of us at some point or another."

Issues dealing with equality of women in the workplace have been especially troublesome. "The workplace has been traditionally and historically the place where women were not granted equality in many ways, not just in how they were treated but in terms of equal pay. We're still struggling with how we should balance the responsibilities of parenthood with the right of each parent to work and be fairly compensated. The problem is that we haven't yet equalized the responsibility of parenthood between men and women and we also haven't accommodated the rules of the workplace for one of the most important functions we can have, that of parenting. That's certainly an area which touches everyone," she said. Even patent law and intellectual property law affect everyone "when you think about accessing movies and books and downloading music from the Internet."

In sexual harassment cases, "because we didn't always have Title VII [of the Civil Rights Act], the idea of being able to sue for a hostile environment in the workplace was shocking to many people. So applying a new congressional remedy was harder because it was new. And there was a huge volume of cases because so many employees who lost their jobs attributed the termination to a discriminatory motive."

Some were frivolous lawsuits. "At the same time, legitimate lawsuits were being rejected because the concept of a sexually hostile workplace environment was hard for many judges—who had never experienced one—to understand," she said. "It's hard to convey what a woman may suffer in some of these places where women are the butt of sexual jokes and comments and innuendoes that men do not have to be subjected to. I think it's hard sometimes for people who have lived a more privileged life to understand what life is like in the places which gave the impetus for the passage of Title VII."

Nonetheless, employment opinions led to changes in the workplace. Having taught an appellate law seminar for 25 years, which brings in employees and employers, she has observed "corporate lawyers describing the extensive training programs throughout the big corporations to eliminate sexual harassment in the workplace and workplace rules to make it clear that sexual harassment won't be tolerated. You would not see that absent Title VII. So I think it has made a huge difference in the workplace—just like, I think, for example, requiring *Miranda* warnings changed the landscape in terms of advising defendants about their rights."

Some workplace issues, like equal pay and promotion opportunities for women, have been more difficult. "I don't think that our society has yet figured out how to give women the opportunity to pursue both a professional life and a family life. I think that's wrong. We make women choose whether they want to be a mother or a professional. I don't think that that's a fair choice because fathers get to be fathers and professionals," she said. "I'm not talking just about leave because leave is only a band aid. Maternity leave or paternity leave for a matter of a few weeks isn't going to solve the problem of the longer term, such as losing one's place on a partnership track for example. I mean, we have to rethink how we're going to deal with women and families," and it's something that "should be addressed by everyone with a stake in our society—the Legislature, the Bar, private employers."

"While we are talking about families, we also need to restructure our courts and how they should handle the separation of a family—in divorces, domestic violence, and juvenile courts," she said. "I haven't been in the trial court and certainly not in the state court for a long time, but I always felt that there was tremendous discrimination in the way our society treated women in court. There always seemed to be an inequality because of the assumptions people made, because women were less able to articulate their concerns or were so terribly emotionally shattered by facing a completely different life without the ability to generate income in many cases. The whole idea of divorce court seemed to me a very poor way to deal with the separation of a family unit. Even requiring mediation was sometimes difficult for women, even though it seemed a better way than the adversarial system. But it too had its drawbacks because, again, women were not used to negotiating in those days. There was always the danger of manipulation or coercion."

"The whole adversary system, at least as it used to be, is horrendous and ill-suited to family matters," she said. "The adversary process only seems to exacerbate the hostilities generated so often in divorce. Trying to maintain two homes on the same income that was used for one seems insoluble and has to be addressed in a better and more comprehensive way. In addition to economic issues, there are questions of who gets to live in the house pending the divorce, how to address the psychological damage that is occurring to all of the parties, how to deal with issues of physical abuse, all while the process generates many more problems in a family that's already troubled to begin with."

Throughout her legal career, she has demonstrated a commitment to children. "They are a fragile group that needs protection," she said. "I also think that we are not very enlightened about how to deal with juvenile delinquency issues and dependency issues, and we can't get people to devote enough legislative and judicial attention to issues pertaining to children or to families. They get very short shrift and very little thought." She became involved in juvenile affairs through a juvenile judge in Fort Lauderdale, Frank Orlando, who helped teens who had violated probation get temporary jobs on research ships. "We rejected the 'boot camp' model, which we felt might work for the few months," she said. But when they returned to their neighborhoods, "there wouldn't be a sergeant overseeing every aspect of their conduct."

Her commitment to children evokes experiences during her early years as a teacher. A former student recently wrote her out of the blue, saying that Barkett was "a superhero nun" who showed that she cared about the students. The letter also said that Barkett played sports in her habit and wouldn't put up with disrespect or slouching. "I did love teaching, and I loved the students," Barkett said. "I think I loved their earnestness and their innocence and their desire to be good—even the kids who were bad wanted to be good—and their enjoyment of life. They were still at a point in time where life was not as complicated as it would be later on for them."

Youthful innocence diminishes as people grow older, she said. "They experience loss, they experience disappointment, they experience responsibility which sometimes weighs exceedingly heavy on them, and then they focus on all of those things and they lose the ability maybe to enjoy life as much as they did when they were children or younger. Then sometimes they get exposed to people who are making less of an effort to be good and that entices them into doing things that they maybe otherwise would not do."

She has continued teaching as a lawyer and a judge. One reason is that teaching

Figure 5.15. What's so funny? According to Supreme Court librarian and archivist Erik Robinson, Justice Rosemary Barkett caught her heel on the carpet and fell into Justice Raymond Ehrlich's lap, startling both of them. Others wanted to suppress the photo but Barkett insisted on sharing it because she said it showed the humanness of the Justices. The Justices *(L-R)* Ben Overton, Parker Lee McDonald, Stephen Grimes, Gerald Kogan, Barkett, and Ehrlich were in the lawyer's lounge of the Supreme Court Building prior to a scheduled formal *en banc* portrait. State Archives of Florida, *Florida Memory*, https://www.floridamemory.com/items/show/47054. Photograph taken 1987.

"makes you much more knowledgeable about the area of law you are teaching because you are forced to understand it thoroughly in order to convey it to others and be prepared to answer their questions." Another reason is that teaching "enables you to engage with other judges when they are not in a real situation with their real colleagues. They are not threatened so that you can have really wonderful exchanges of views about how the law has developed in a particular area or discuss candidly the result of a particular case or line of cases or talk about the future of a particular area of the law."

She has participated in judicial education activities at prestigious U.S. law schools and in dozens of different countries, including Syria, Qatar, Dubai, Algeria, and Kuwait. Going to the Middle East was "a terrific opportunity to use the little bit of Arabic that I can speak, and also to touch the roots of the place where my parents originated." Topics cover many areas: the need for judicial independence and judicial training; the question of how judges should be chosen; and what should be covered in a code of ethics for judges, for example.

If law students asked her for advice about a career, "I would tell them that the way to succeed is to do every job that you're given really, really, really well. Don't worry about how you are going to do the next job well. But rather concentrate on whatever task you've been given and really excel at it. Then you'd be surprised at how many people notice that and then give you more responsible jobs to do."

If asked about a future in the justice system, "I would tell them that we have to temper our expectations because like everything else, the justice system is susceptible to human failings. So not everything that happens in the justice system is always going to be just, which means that they have a real obligation to try to improve it in every way they can. And I would point out that there are lots of ways to do that." But advice goes only so far: "I'm not one to tell anybody else what to do with their lives. People really have to discover that kind of thing by themselves."

"I have been fortunate in that I've always been happy doing whatever it was that I was doing until I wanted to change it for whatever reason. I had wonderful parents; I have wonderful sisters and brothers and nieces and nephews. I have a very loving and supportive family. I was lucky enough to have been given the intellectual abilities to be a teacher, so that I could be a lawyer, so I could then have the opportunity to become a judge. There are many, many people who could certainly do this job but didn't get the opportunity to do it."

Information for this story came from interviews in Women Trailblazers in the Law Project by the American Bar Association Senior Lawyers Division, conducted between 2006 and 2009, and from email correspondence with the author.

Peggy A. Quince

First African-American woman appointed to the Florida Supreme Court, 1998; jointly selected by Gov. Lawton Chiles (D) and Gov.-elect Jeb Bush (R) in 1998—four days before Gov. Chiles' unexpected death

First African-American woman elected to statewide office in Florida (in retention election), 2000

First African-American female Chief Justice of the Florida Supreme Court, 2008

Personal: Born January 3, 1948, Norfolk, Virginia; married with two children.

Figure 5.16. Taking the oath as Chief Justice in 2008 gave Quince "a wonderful feeling," she said. "I was glad that my colleagues felt that I could do it. I felt that it was another opportunity to show the citizens that you can't judge a book by its cover." No other black woman had ever been a Chief Justice of the Court, and for that matter, no other black woman had ever headed any branch of government in the state. *Back row (L-R)*: Raoul G. Cantero III, Barbara Pariente, Fred Lewis, Kenneth Bell; *Front row (L-R)*: Charles T. Wells, Quince, Harry Lee Anstead. Photograph taken in 2008 courtesy of the Florida Supreme Court.

Education:
- Howard University, B.S. in zoology (1970)
- Catholic University of America Columbus School of Law, J.D. (1975)
- Stetson University College of Law, honorary doctor of laws degree (1999)
- St. Thomas University School of Law, honorary doctor of laws degree (2004)

Occupation: Lawyer/Assistant Attorney General

Trailblazer Appointments and Elections:
- Supreme Court Justice, *Appointed by Gov. Chiles (D) / Gov.-elect Jeb Bush (R)* 1998
- First retention election 2000
  - *Yes (71.1%), No (28.9%)*
- Supreme Court Chief Justice (elected by her colleagues on the Court), 2008–2010

THE PEGGY A. QUINCE STORY

Peggy A. Quince, the first African-American woman on the Florida Supreme Court, might have become a doctor had it not been for the civil rights and antiwar protests of the 1960s.

"We had so many things going on in this country. Just prior to my going to undergraduate school, Dr. Martin Luther King did his 'I Have a Dream' speech," she said. "And during the time I was in undergraduate school, we had the murder of the students at Kent State,[42] the Vietnam War was going on, the whole Black Panther[43] movement was going on, and it just appeared to me that all of these things had a legal underpinning."

"But even as I started getting more and more interested in law school and the law, I continued my undergraduate degree [in zoology] because, quite frankly, I could not afford to change majors. I had to finish undergraduate school in four years. I had a four-year scholarship."

She participated in civil rights marches and sit-ins but not in the leadership. "I was never really interested in the hierarchy of the Civil Rights Movement, so I didn't get into it to that degree. I was more interested in the underpinnings of it and what was being used to move it along, and that to me was the law."

Reared in Virginia by her father, a civilian Navy employee, she had lots of responsibility as the second-eldest of five children. "But we pretty much grew up like most kids. We were not privileged at all. We were basically a poor family, but my dad worked hard and gave us the basics."

When she was growing up in Virginia, the U.S. Supreme Court ruled segregation unconstitutional in *Brown v. Board of Education* (1954). "When the decision was announced, my father said to us, 'Now you can attend any school that you want to.' But it wasn't that easy. So in the fall of 1954, when I went off to the first grade, I went to John T. West Elementary School in Norfolk, Va., the segregated school. In

1954, only the cities of Washington, D.C., and Baltimore, Md., began a desegregation program."[44]

The next year, the U.S. Supreme Court decided "*Brown II*," she said, saying that integration should take place "with all deliberate speed." "But therein lies the rub. What is, in fact, 'all deliberate speed'?" Many Americans opposed integration. In 1956, "100 members of Congress from the 11 Southern states penned what they called the Southern Manifesto, whereby they determined to fight integration with all means necessary." In Virginia, that meant the schools shut down until a federal court decision opened them again. In 1965, Virginia offered the "freedom of choice plan," which the U.S. Supreme Court threw out in 1968. It took many years for schools to finally be integrated.

In July 1964, President Lyndon Johnson pushed the Civil Rights Act through Congress. That fall, when she was midway through high school, he campaigned on a platform that included a "War on Poverty," which he hoped would challenge Americans to support programs that would improve life for the nation's poor. "I was what we called a 'Johnson girl,'" she said. "Even though I was pretty young, we were out campaigning for Lyndon Johnson."

She had no women lawyer role models growing up. When she started college at Howard University in Washington, D.C., in 1966, however, she became aware of civil rights lawyer Constance Baker Motley who was appointed to a federal judgeship in New York, the first black woman to sit on a federal bench. "When I went to law school [at Catholic University of America in D.C.], I did not know any lawyers, did not know any judges. I was just interested in the law."

One influential professor was Lawrence Velvel, now Dean at the Massachusetts School of Law. "We had some just really interesting talks about constitutional law. He was always in the forefront of my mind because he was really such an interesting person and was very interested in human rights and civil rights issues. So I would say that he was one of the people who kept me going."

After graduation in 1975, she worked as a city hearing officer on rentals in D.C. and then briefly in private practice in Norfolk, Va. In 1978, she and her husband moved to Bradenton, Fla., where she practiced general civil law. In February 1980, she joined the Attorney General's office, Criminal Division. That's where "I really got my mentoring," she said. She handled numerous appeals, including death penalty cases.

"A lot of people have asked me, how could you really get involved, and how could you deal with those kinds of cases? But the death penalty in this state was an act of the Legislature, of course, and has passed constitutional muster. So it was my obligation as an Assistant Attorney General to help to make sure that that law was executed properly. And that's what I did. I cannot say that any case I ever worked on that I felt uncomfortable with it or felt that this person had not actually committed the crime, because if that had been the case, I would've talked to someone about it. So if you follow the statute, follow whatever constitutional provisions are applicable to any case that you're working on, then I think you have discharged your obligation as a lawyer. And I don't have to agree or disagree with the particular statute."

After about 10 years, she began thinking it was time for a change. She applied for a state judgeship but was unsuccessful. "The next time around, there were actually three openings on the Second District Court of Appeals, and so my name was again submitted to the Governor." In her interview with Gov. Lawton Chiles (D, 1991–1998) and his staff, "we just talked about different aspects of the law, and actually, we talked about Lakeland a little bit because that's where the Second District Court of Appeals is headquartered."

During that conversation, nothing came up about the historical importance of appointing someone of her race and gender. "Whether or not that played into his decision, I don't know," she said. At that point, the Court had one African-American man but no woman. When she was appointed in 1994, she made history as the first black woman on the appellate court.

Within a couple of years, she set her sights on the Florida Supreme Court. The first time she applied, she lost out to Barbara Pariente, who joined the bench in 1997. The next time an opening came up, she was interviewed first by outgoing Gov. Chiles and later in the day by incoming Gov. Jeb Bush. Her term on the Court was to begin on the first day of the new Governor's taking office. "Rather than have any kind of acrimony about it, the two decided that they would both interview all the candidates, the names that were submitted to them, and sit down and make a joint appointment," she said.

Because she had met with Gov. Chiles a year or two earlier and they had seen each other on other occasions, "the interview was a much more relaxed, personal kind of interview." Gov. Bush, who was making his first appointment, "really went through more of the kinds of things I had done in the law before—the kinds of briefs I'd done with the Attorney General's office and the kinds of cases I had written opinions on at the Second District Court of Appeals."

As it turned out, Gov. Chiles died in mid-December, which meant that his Lieutenant Governor, Buddy MacKay, became Governor for three weeks before Bush took office. As a result, MacKay signed the commission placing her on the Court. It was "a mixture of all of them," she said. "I call it 'the Trinity.'"

Quince was on the Court in the decisions leading up to *Bush v. Gore*, "or as we call it '36 days of pre-Christmas festivities,'" she said. "Even though the United States Supreme Court eventually overruled what we had said, I'm still very proud of how this Court handled itself. I think we did exactly what courts are required to do. But, I also am very proud of the fact that the people of this state and of this country accepted the final product, whether we agreed with it or not. Because when you have contested elections in some other countries, you end up with tanks on the street, guns, and all of that, but we allowed the system to run its course."

In addition, the Court struck down a private school voucher program and reversed a law ordering the reconnection of a feeding tube to Terri Schiavo, a woman described as "in a vegetative state." In the latter, the Court deliberated such issues as whether a person's life should be ended on the basis of relatives' recollection of her wishes, and whether the law violated the separation of powers between the three branches of government.

But the most important—and heart-wrenching—cases throughout all her years as a judge were those involving children. "They are difficult cases," she said. "We don't see a lot of them at this Court. I saw a lot more of them when I was on the Second District Court of Appeals, but especially those involving termination of parental rights. To me, those are serious, serious cases when you're talking about taking children away from their parents. Of course the state has to step in and help raise these children," she said. "I think that it requires the best of everyone in the judiciary—and even those who are not a part of the judiciary but are bringing these cases—to really consider what is in the best interest of these children."

Taking the oath as Chief Justice in 2008 gave her "a wonderful feeling," she said. No other black woman had ever been a Chief Justice of the Court, and for that matter, no other black woman had ever headed any branch of government in the state. "It really brought home to me how important it was for people to see that. I had people from elementary school and high school who came for that occasion, people from college and from all these other associations that I have been a member of over the years."

In addition, the appointment made her realize the "awesome responsibility" of deciding the direction of the judicial branch. During her time in the position (2008–2010), the country was in recession. "There were times when I had to make some really tough economic decisions and cut back on things that we had been doing in the judiciary," while preserving the core functions. "I was glad that my colleagues felt that I could do it. I felt that it was another opportunity to show the citizens that you can't judge a book by its cover."

She extolled the Court's transparency in allowing its proceedings, from ceremonial to trial sessions, to be televised and recorded. That's something the U.S. Supreme Court does not allow. "Quite frankly, I don't understand why because it is not intrusive. The cameras are up, and it doesn't intrude on what we're doing at all. I don't even think about them, the fact that they're there. I don't do anything differently. Every now and then, I do think back on it and wonder if I picked my nose that day. But other than that, I honestly never think about the fact that it's being recorded."

Recordings can enhance instruction about the law in schools and give the public a window into the judiciary. In addition, "When we're making our decisions on cases,

I'll go back and watch and try to pinpoint what a lawyer may have said on a particular issue."

Quince has found herself on a retention ballot three times—once in 1996 while she was on the state Circuit Court, again in 2006 and 2012. The latter two occurred while she was on the Supreme Court. "You never had to go out and campaign. Your name was on the ballot. You had to get a majority of yeses, but basically if the public hadn't heard anything bad about you—your name wasn't involved with any scandal—that was the end of it," she said.

She survived the first two ballots with virtually no opposition, but the prospect of a challenge on the third began to emerge as early as 2010. In that year, "a group started pretty much a low-level social media campaign against Justice Jorge Labarga and Justice James Perry," who were considered liberal judges. The other two Justices on the same ballot, Charles Canady and Ricky Polston, were considered conservative. "Justice Perry and Justice Labarga got lower numbers [percentages] than the other two. A group out of Orlando actually took credit for it, saying that they were the people who were running this low level social media campaign," she said. The group also boasted they would do the same in 2012 against Quince and her colleagues Barbara Pariente and Fred Lewis.

"Quite frankly, I decided that I'd see what was going to go on and see what I needed to do from there. Well, the rhetoric continued, and outside money started coming in—*Citizens United*.[45] Plus, in 2010, three justices in Iowa lost their positions on the court in a retention election where big money came in and they did nothing, basically."

Quince, Pariente and Lewis "decided that we were not going to sit back and let this happen. We pretty much began in 2011 trying to come up with a strategy for what to do. So we decided that we would campaign." Judges cannot personally raise money, but a campaign committee can, she explained. Each of the three had a separate committee that raised money. "We didn't have the kind of money you would need to run TV ads, but we did do social media" as well as robo telephone calls, literature, and editorial endorsements.

"We went to editorial boards because we believed that a lot of people still read those editorial pieces about candidates and what they should do in elections. The thing is, people don't really understand the judiciary. It's probably the least understood branch of government because unless you have a case, you don't really know about how the system works. We wanted to make sure people understood what a retention election was all about. We could explain that to editorial boards, and they could explain it to the public."

Their educational campaign included speaking before community groups. Calling for a judge to be removed from the Court in the retention process should not be about disagreeing with a judge's opinion, she said. "People are not going to agree on

Figure 5.17. Supreme Court Justice Peggy A. Quince administers the oath of office to State Sen. Christopher L. "Chris" Smith, with his son, Christopher Leveorn Smith, by his side. Quince, who had no women lawyer role models growing up, believed it important for blacks to get involved in politics: "With diversity of people we get diversity of ideas." State Archives of Florida, *Florida Memory*, https://www.floridamemory.com/items/show/23921. Photograph by Darryl Jarmon, November 18, 2008.

everything. The real issue is a judge's character and behavior. In the federal system, for example, the question is: Are judges doing what the Constitution requires a judge to do?"

"I've dissented on opinions, which means I disagree with my colleagues, but that doesn't mean that they did not do what they felt the law required them to do. It was incumbent, I believe, upon the three of us who were up for retention to try to reach as many people as we could to explain what retention was all about."

"I really was very, very disappointed when the Florida Republican Party came out in opposition to our retention because first of all, it's a nonpartisan election. That had never happened before." In addition, she deplored the big quantities of money that came in from the outside.

In arguing against retention, opponents referred to opinions they disagreed with. In one opinion, for example, the Court said a man on death row should be retried. "The Supreme Court of the United States reversed us on that, but it was our view that the law required him to have a new trial." The opposition, instead of focusing on the reasons for a new trial, claimed that "we were going to let a murderer go."

In another example, the Legislature had proposed an amendment to the state Constitution that would ban mandatory participation in a health care plan. The Court refused to allow the measure to be placed on the ballot. "We said that the ballot summary that the Legislature had done was misleading. Well, they spun that around and said, the Court was in favor of Obamacare."

Voters approved retaining all three Justices by 60 percent or more. "I hope that it sends a signal to these outside groups that we're not going to let you come into the state of Florida and take over our elections," she said.

She praised the racial and gender diversity of the Florida Court. "I think we have to have diversity because with diversity of people we get diversity of ideas. There are things that come up that, in a case you may not have ever experienced, whereas I may have experienced that just because I'm black. Or something comes up that I may not have experienced but you have because you're white. Or Justice Labarga, for example, may have experienced because he's Hispanic."

"While it may not necessarily change the outcome of the case, at least it changes the discussion sometimes, and you think about if that makes a difference in a particular case. I think that makes a world of difference in just the dynamics of how cases are decided and the discussion of the cases. When the oral arguments are over, we discuss those cases and talk about what decision is going to be made in the final analysis. Even cases that no party has asked for oral argument on, we bring those to a conference and discuss those cases. It doesn't happen on every case, but there are cases where I can say, 'Yes, this happens in this community.'"

Not having known lawyers in her youth, Quince has worked to serve as a role model among young people. "There were not a lot of black lawyers around when I was in law school. And often we were not welcome in the majority associations. So it was very important for us to get together and to maintain some kind of contact with each other so that we knew that there was someone we could go to if we had any kind of difficulties, or even if it wasn't a difficulty, but to socialize with, to know that there were others who shared a common goal." While in law school, she belonged to the Phi Alpha Delta Law Fraternity and the Black American Law Students Association.

"Even today I believe these associations are still important. I belong to the black associations, and I belong to the majority associations, but it is not the same feeling often of really being welcomed." In addition, black sororities and black church groups have helped foster interest in politics and leadership in young men and women. She belongs to Alpha Kappa Alpha Sorority (founded by women at Howard University in 1908) and New Hope Missionary Baptist Church as well as the Urban League and the NAACP.

Apart from the socialization such membership offers, "It's the whole idea that you have an opportunity to influence other blacks to continue their education, to open their own business, to get involved in politics, to try to develop our communities economically. Those are the kinds of issues that we discuss in these kinds of groups and hopefully it resonates. You're not going to reach everyone, but if you can reach a couple of people in all of these groups so that they decide, 'Yeah, I do want to do more than my bachelor's degree,' or 'Yeah, it's time for me to start saving for the future so that when I leave this Earth, I'll leave something for the next generation.'"

Young minority women and men often need somebody to help them along. As an example, she explained the activities of The Links group in Tallahassee, of which she is a member. "Over a six-week period, we do a lot of things with them," such as college tours, basketball games, and museum visits. "Some of these young people, while they are smart kids, just have not been exposed to some things. And so we try our best to help them in that way and to encourage them: 'You are smart. You can do this. You can continue on with your education.'" For young men, the group hosts a beautillion. "You know, instead of a cotillion for girls, we do a beautillion for boys."

Quince enjoys talking to groups about the state Constitution and the judicial system, as she does on Law Day (May 1) every year. "One of the things that's troubled me in the last couple of election cycles has been the constitutional amendments. First of all, there have been so many of them that it is hard, I think, for the public to get a handle on all of them. Maybe there should be a limitation on how many you can have in any election cycle. I don't know."

Another issue is the length of the amendment on the ballot. "The Legislature can put the whole amendment on the ballot, and that's what they did in this last cycle. That's why it was so long. In a citizen's initiative, you are limited to 75 words to try to explain what the amendment means. Seventy-five words is hard. And then there's always someone who is trying to say, for the most part, that those 75 words are misleading."

Among her public service initiatives on the Court was the compilation of a history on the black lawyers of Florida. The book covers 110 years—from 1869 to 1979, the year that Virgil Hawkins became a member of the Florida Bar. "A lot of black lawyers actually helped me with this project. My very good friend, Judge June [C.] McKinney, who is an administrative law judge here in Tallahassee, spearheaded this for me."

When the book was published in 2009, "we had a big gala in Orlando to unveil the book," she said. "It really is a great part of history. So often these things are lost. I mean, a lot of people never even knew that James Weldon Johnson, for example, wrote the Negro national anthem ['Lift Every Voice and Sing']. People have no idea that he was a lawyer and a lawyer here in the state of Florida."

In 2019, Quince will reach the mandatory retirement age of 70 for Justices. The Legislature recently proposed raising the age to 75, but the measure did not pass both houses. "When you think about it, 70 was put in years ago when the life expectancy was lower and people were not in as good of health as they are now," she said. "I know some 80-year-olds that I'd feel very comfortable with the decisions they make, and I know some 60-year-olds that I wouldn't. So it's very difficult to say that 70 really ought to be the cutoff age."

In a judicial career spanning 20 years, Quince has studied and argued the "legal underpinnings" of civil rights and human rights, striving for equity, balance, and fairness. "It's not a black or white thing, a man or woman thing, or a rich or poor thing," said her daughter Peggy Laverne. "She's been poor. She's been a woman when women weren't allowed anything. She'll always be black, another minority hurdle. But no matter what, she will always be fair. She will take all the information and create an informed, fair decision."[46]

Peggy Quince was interviewed in person by the author Apr. 14, 2014.

Jorge Labarga

First Hispanic (Cuban) Chief Justice, Florida Supreme Court, 2014

Personal: Born October 21, 1952, Cuba; arrived in the United States at age 11, married with two children.

Education:

- University of Florida, B.A. (1976)
- University of Florida, J.D. (1979)

Occupation: Assistant Public Defender/Circuit Court Judge

Trailblazer Appointments and Elections:

- Supreme Court Justice, *Appointed by Gov. Charlie Crist* (R), 2009
- Supreme Court Chief Justice (Elected by his colleagues on the Court), 2014–2016

Figure 5.18. Jorge Labarga (*left*) accepts the gavel as Chief Justice of the Supreme Court from his predecessor, Ricky Polston. Labarga became the 56th Chief Justice of the Florida Supreme Court when he took the oath of office on June 30, 2014. When asked about the significance of being the first Hispanic to hold the position, Labarga replied: "If I learned anything from my experience in Cuba, it's to appreciate the freedoms and the rights that we have, and I'm here to protect those rights." Born in Cuba, Labarga remembered the incredible heartache of his family having to flee the island to Mexico when Castro's promises of an American-style democracy "turned into a Marxist nightmare." Photograph courtesy of the Florida Supreme Court, 2014.

THE JORGE LABARGA STORY

Jorge Labarga, the first Hispanic Chief Justice of the Florida Supreme Court, views the judiciary as the guardian of democracy:

"I was born in Cuba and I came to this great nation in 1963 when I was 11 years old. I was old enough to have remembered a lot of things that happened back there. I was old enough to still recall the day that Batista left and Castro came in with all his promises of democracy, the American-style democracy. I remember helping my father tie a Cuban flag to the antenna of his 1956 canary-yellow Bel-Air Chevrolet, and I remember driving around with him honking the horn. They were so happy because they were finally going to get this American-style democracy that was supposedly promised to them," he said.

"And I was also old enough to remember the incredible heartbreak when that dream they had turned into a Marxist nightmare. And I remember the executions, the fear. I remember my father having to flee the country. He left two years before we did and we were caught behind because of the Cuban Missile Crisis and President

Kennedy pretty much enacted the embargo, and you could not leave Cuba directly to the United States. My dad just got on a Pam Am flight, and he was in Miami. Two years later, after the Cuban Missile Crisis, we could not. So we had to fly to Mexico and live in Mexico for six months, and then we came to the United States."

"So if I learned anything from my experience in Cuba, it's to appreciate the freedoms and the rights that we have, and I'm here to protect those rights."[47]

Labarga, his two brothers, and his mother were reunited with his father in rural Pahokee, Fla. There his father had found work with a former employer at the Osceola Farms sugar company run by the Fanjul family, who had grown sugar cane in Cuba since the 1850s and moved their business to Florida in the 1960s. Growing up in Pahokee, Labarga was grateful for liberty but found it strange that signs denoted separate facilities for White and Colored.

"It was a period in the early '60s when our country was still struggling with the question of racial justice, when women were not provided with the same opportunities as men, and when a young and inspiring president [John F. Kennedy] almost failed to get elected simply because he was Catholic," Labarga said at his investiture as Chief Justice. "While it can be said that we still have a ways to go, we have certainly come a long way since those dark days, and it is absolutely imperative that we continue to strive to be a country and a state of inclusion and not exclusion."

Labarga started the fourth grade in Pahokee speaking only Spanish, but within the year he was speaking and writing English well enough—without the benefit of a bilingual program—to learn and do well. After graduating from Forest Hill High School, he earned a bachelor's degree in political science (1976) and a law degree (1979), both from the University of Florida.

He had known he wanted to be a lawyer from the time he arrived in Florida, after having democracy ripped out from under his feet. "I always figured that being a lawyer was the profession that best suited my goal to preserve this democracy because it has been lawyers all along that have really been pushing our democracy," he said. He noted that 25 signers of the Declaration of Independence were lawyers[48] and that lawyers were instrumental in *Marbury vs. Madison* (affirming the constitutional separation of the judicial and executive branches of government), the Emancipation Proclamation by Abraham Lincoln (a lawyer), *Brown v. Board of Education* (ruling that segregated schools were unconstitutional), and the Civil Rights Act of 1964 (outlawing discrimination based on race, color, religion, sex, or national origin).

He began his own career as a lawyer in 1979 as an Assistant Public Defender in West Palm Beach assigned to the appellate, misdemeanor, and felony trial divisions. In 1982, he joined the West Palm Beach State Attorney's office, where he tried cases ranging from theft to homicide. In 1987, he did an about-face and began practicing personal injury law, first with a private firm and then as a founding partner in Roth, Duncan, and Labarga in West Palm Beach.

In 1996, Gov. Lawton Chiles (D) appointed him a judge on the 15th Circuit Court, in and for Palm Beach County, where he served in the family, civil, and criminal divisions. In 2000, he found himself in an election dispute that would eventually determine whether George W. Bush or Al Gore would become President of the United States. At first, Bush appeared to have won, but the margin of victory was less than the required minimum of 0.5 percent of the vote. After a machine recount reduced Bush's votes even further, the Gore campaign requested manual recounts in four counties, including Palm Beach County where it was alleged that the ballot design may have confused voters. Lawyers filed motions for and against allowing the recount to proceed, and Labarga, as the presiding judge, reviewed them.

"Everybody just wanted their candidate to win," he said later. "They didn't want to hear about what the Constitution required. They didn't want to hear about counting the intent of the voters. None of that! They just wanted me to rule in a way that their candidate will win. It was extremely important that a judge would be sitting there, above that, cutting through the chaff and looking at what the Constitution and what the law required and let the chips fall where they may."[49]

Labarga ordered Palm Beach County to review the irregular ballots by hand to determine voter intent. He ruled against a new election because, under the Constitution, an election must be held on the same day everywhere in the United States. Before the recount was finished, the U.S. Supreme Court stepped in and gave Bush the victory. Labarga later said, "I somehow feel that I may have done the right thing, because I completely irritated both major political parties. I must have done my job."

Of course, *Bush v. Gore* created a media circus. The night before Labarga was to issue orders, he was working in his 11th-floor office in the Palm Beach County Courthouse. About 10 p.m. he decided to take a walk to clear his head. Looking down at the media trucks and satellite dishes, with reporters ready to pounce, he decided to venture outside anyway because he was dressed in jeans, sweatshirt, sneakers, and a University of Florida cap. Sure enough, no one recognized him. He passed by one reporter talking to the studio, saying, "All we know about him is he was born in Cuba and came as a little boy." She had no idea that he was passing behind her at that moment on live TV. He didn't hang around long, however. When he spotted a couple of local lawyers, he went back inside.

In 2008, he applied for two judgeships that were open at the time: the Fourth District Court of Appeal and the Florida Supreme Court. The Judicial Nominating Commission assigned to each court nominated him, and both nominations went to Gov. Charlie Crist (R). Labarga had interviews with the Governor's staff and then the Governor, for each court—first for the District Court, later for the Supreme Court. In December, Gov. Crist appointed him to the Fourth District Court, Criminal Division.

"I was pretty much completely resolved" to that appointment, he said, even to the point of selecting his new office. Because Christmas was near and he was going to leave, he took his division staff out to lunch as a gift for their work during the holiday season. As they were eating, his phone rang. It was the Governor's General Counsel Jason Gonzalez. He said, "I have Gov. Crist on the speaker phone and Lt. Gov. Kottkamp, and the Governor would like to talk to you." To get away from the restaurant noise, "I went back in the alley and I spoke to Gov. Crist. He asked me, 'Are you still interested in the Florida Supreme Court?'" Labarga said yes, and Gonzalez called again later in the day to arrange the second interview.

The interview took place Dec. 23 in the Governor's office with Crist and Kottkamp, both their general counsels, and the Governor's Chief of Staff. Kottkamp did most of the talking, but at one point Gov. Crist asked, "What character traits are important to have as a judge?" Labarga said there were four.

The first two traits, he said, are determined by the Judicial Qualifications Commission: legal qualifications and judicial temperament. "At the appellate level, temperament is more pointed to collegiality with the other six justices and our ability to disagree and still get along," Labarga explained.

"The last two are the ones that are typically decided by the Governor," he said, noting that Gov. Crist at this point was sitting on the edge of his seat. "The third one is humility," Labarga said. "This job is not about me. It is me doing a public service during my time on the Court." If he were to die tomorrow, the Commission would nominate someone else, and life would go on.

The fourth trait he listed was "A judge needs to have compassion for everyone." Having compassion is hard in a murder case, for example. "But think about it for a second. That person has a mother and father who raised their child and somewhere along the line that child fell off the track," he said. The parents suffered through that, and "they're sitting in that courtroom today listening to you sentence their child to death." For the next 15 years, they "will be counting the days when their son is going to be marched down to the execution chambers and be executed."

The need for compassion extends further, he continued, referring to the victim, the victim's relatives, and the lawyers. "We need to figure out what's going on with people's lives. Why are you doing this? Obviously some people need to be punished severely, but there's a story behind everyone."

Within a matter of days, on January 1, 2009, Gov. Crist elevated Labarga to the Florida Supreme Court.

As he was sworn in, "I'm thinking about what happened in Cuba, me being in this country and everything it has done for me, and that I have an obligation to make sure that the same thing doesn't happen here." He was careful to point out that in 1940 "Cuba ratified a constitution that was practically identical to the Constitution in the United States," he said. Then came the military *coup d'état* in 1952, which was followed by Castro's takeover in 1959.

"We're caught up in discourse right now about the U.S. Constitution, but we forget

Figure 5.19. Justice Jorge Labarga stands by a framed copy of the bill passed by the Legislature in May 2014 that contained a provision allowing noncitizens in Florida to become lawyers if they were "brought to the country as a child, have lived here at least 10 years, have a work permit and a Social Security number, have registered for the draft, and have satisfied other requirements for Bar admission." (Debra Cassens Weiss, "Florida Lawmakers Pass Bill.") A short time earlier, Labarga had "reluctantly" concurred with the Court ruling against licensure for noncitizens and urged the Legislature to pass a bill making it legal. Photograph by Susan A. MacManus, March 16, 2015.

that there has always been discourse in politics," he said. As examples, he cited the bitter disagreement between Aaron Burr and Alexander Hamilton that ended in a duel and Hamilton's death, laws that Franklin D. Roosevelt rammed through Congress and his unsuccessful attempt to pack the Supreme Court, and President Dwight Eisenhower's regrets in nominating Earl Warren and William Brennan to the Supreme Court. "And of course we know what Warren did for this country," he said. "In a sense, that is democracy. It is not organized. Sometimes it's not even pretty—it's downright ugly. But that's just the way it is when you have 300 million people who may have different beliefs trying to get along with each other."

Labarga approached the Justice position with gravity: "The Supreme Court Justice's job is much different than the job of any other judge. Just on the appellate level, the decision making level, it is much different than anything else," he said. "Our opinions are far more encompassing. And everything we say becomes the law of the entire state."[50]

In 2010, the Supreme Court upheld a circuit court ruling to remove an amendment from the November ballot that sought to nullify part of the Obama administration's Affordable Care Act. The Court said the 20-word statement would be confusing to voters. Observers noted that the amendment would have been useless anyway because, according to the U.S. Constitution, the states do not have veto power over federal laws. Nonetheless, social conservatives targeted Labarga and Justice James Perry as not deserving retention on the Court. Both Justices survived, however. Labarga kept his seat by winning 59 percent of the vote.

In 2014, in another significant case, the Florida Board of Bar Examiners requested an advisory opinion on whether Jose Manuel Godinez-Samperio, the son of undocumented immigrants from Mexico, could be admitted to the Florida Bar because he was not a citizen. The Court ruled him ineligible, and Labarga concurred but only "reluctantly."

In that opinion, he wrote: "Indeed, in many respects, [Godinez-Samperio's] life in the United States parallels my own. He and I were brought to this great nation as young children by our hard working immigrant parents. We both learned to read, write, and speak the English language within a short period of time. We excelled scholastically and graduated from college and law school—[Godinez-Samperio] from Florida State University and I from the University of Florida. Both of us were driven by the opportunities this great nation offered to realize the American dream. Sadly, however, here the similarities end and the perceptions of our accomplishments begin. When I arrived in the United States from Cuba in 1963, soon after the Cuban Missile Crisis—the height of the Cold War—my parents and I were perceived as defectors from a tyrannical communist regime. Thus, we were received with open arms, our arrival celebrated, and my path to citizenship and the legal profession unimpeded by public policy decisions. [Godinez-Samperio], however, who is perceived to be a defector from poverty, is viewed negatively because his family sought an opportunity for economic prosperity."[51]

The Court noted that the state could allow eligibility to the young man if the state Legislature enacted a law to that effect. In April, Rep. Greg Steube (R-Sarasota) worked such a bill through the House, while Godinez-Samperio watched from the gallery. In the Senate, Sen. David Simmons (R-Altamonte Springs) worked a companion bill,

Figure 5.20. Jorge Labarga, new in his position as Supreme Court Chief Justice, officiates at the ceremonial swearing-in of Jose Manuel Godinez-Samperio to the Florida Bar November 20, 2014, in Tampa at the Hillsborough County Hispanic Bar Association annual gala. The young man had come to the United States at age nine with his parents on a tourist visa, stayed after they left to continue his schooling, graduated with honors from law school, and passed the Florida Bar exam. It took an act of the Legislature to clear the way for his licensure. Photograph courtesy of the Florida Supreme Court.

reading Labarga's opinion on the Senate floor. Labarga watched the proceedings on his office computer. In May the bill passed both houses, and the Governor signed it. Senate President Don Gaetz (R) and House Speaker Will Weatherford (R) framed an enlarged copy of the bill and presented it to Labarga, who hung it on the wall in his office lobby for everyone walking by to see.

Godinez-Samperio was officially admitted to the Florida Bar in September, but the climax was still to come. Sandy D'Alemberte, the lawyer who had represented the young man, called Labarga and said, "You've got to come swear him in." At a ceremonial swearing-in at the Hillsborough Hispanic Bar gala in November, Labarga, who by that time had become Chief Justice, administered the oath to Godinez-Samperio. Among those attending were the young man's family who had been allowed to come from Mexico just for the occasion.

At his own ceremony four months earlier, Labarga accepted the gavel as Chief Justice. From his new seat in the center of the dais, flanked by his six colleagues—three white men, one white woman, an African-American man, and an African-American woman—he said, "It is imperative that every effort is made to ensure that this Court's members, the true face of America, appears at every level of our judicial system."

The festivities surrounding the historic occasion reflected his Cuban heritage. The day before, the Florida Bar hosted a Cuban-style pig roast for 200 people. Ray Abadin, a Cuban-American attorney who grew up in Miami, served as head pig roaster, and a local Cuban restaurant handled the catering. At the ceremony, Carlos López-Cantera, the first Cuban-American Lieutenant Governor, represented Gov. Rick Scott. "From one Cuban American who has achieved a first, to another Cuban American who is about to achieve a first, let me just say, 'Felicidades.'"

A Chief Justice is elected by other Justices on the Court and serves for two years. As Chief Justice, Labarga serves as the top administrative officer of the court system and lead questioner in oral arguments. The toughest part of the job, Labarga said, is "having to manage the judicial branch," which has many "tentacles," including the Florida Board of Bar Examiners and the Judicial Qualifications Commission.

In January 2014, when his selection was announced, Labarga said he and his predecessors, Ricky Polston and Charles Canady, had been working for some time on the same goals—to increase funding for the judiciary and to increase access to legal help for people who can't afford it.

On the first issue, Labarga explained that funding for the judiciary has slipped in recent years from seven-tenths of 1 percent of the state budget to six-tenths of 1 percent. Ideally, he said, it should be 1 percent[52] because of the crucial role the judiciary plays in preserving democracy. He recalled his days as a prosecutor when wiretapping was used to combat organized crime. But he warned against more extraordinary measures in pursuing criminals. "I think our Constitution is here to protect us from overzealous reaching," he said. "The judiciary decides when it's appropriate to knock down someone's door by first issuing a search warrant. "The first thing Fidel did, the first thing Hitler did, the first thing Stalin did—they got rid of the judiciary and put in their own so-called judiciary. And that should tell us something about our society—the need for us to be here."

As a practical matter, the Court lacks funding for security of judges. State marshals provide some protection and coordinate with local law enforcement when he goes out of town, he said. But he has not been overly concerned about his safety, despite a busy schedule of public functions. Moreover, he said, "The judiciary is pretty much unknown to people," so it is possible for a Justice to go unnoticed when wearing street and casual clothes.

On the second issue, Labarga signed an order in November 2014 creating the first Florida Commission on Access to Civil Justice. In criminal cases, defendants are guaranteed access to an attorney, but in civil cases they are not. "Access to civil justice for lower-income citizens and Florida's middle class has become a critical challenge for the legal system, especially in difficult economic times," he said. "Simply put, those who can afford it will have access to civil justice; those who cannot afford it, will not."

In Florida, as in other states, the poor may seek legal help from nonprofit legal aid societies that are funded by the interest accrued on lawyer accounts held in trust for their clients. But the recent drop in interest rates has drastically cut this source of income. In addition, Bar members reported 1.7 million hours of pro bono work to low-income clients and donations of $4.8 million to legal aid organizations. Some states provide public funding to legal aid groups, but in Florida the Governor has vetoed extra legal aid funding every year. "We can't expect government to be the only fix," Labarga said.

The 27-member Access to Civil Justice Commission consists primarily of judges, attorneys, and academics, but it also includes the general counsel of two of the state's largest employers, Publix Supermarkets and Walt Disney Company as well as the CEO of Cheney Brothers food distributors. Labarga pointed out the importance of access to justice for business owners—namely, that employees who are dealing with a foreclosure or divorce without legal help are likely to have more absences and be less focused and thus less productive.

In January 2015, as part of a seminar panel on access to justice at the University of Miami School of Law, he emphasized how the issue affected the working middle class who are not eligible for legal aid programs for the poor. Recalling his 15 years as a Palm Beach trial court judge, he said, "Every other case had one unrepresented party. Today, it must be even more. There is nothing more heartbreaking than to have a foreclosure case, and the bank's lawyer comes in all polished, well-dressed, and he knows exactly what to do, and you see a husband and wife all by themselves with a file. As a judge, you can't say, 'This is what you have to do so I can rule in your favor,' but you want to."[53] If they had a lawyer, "the lawyer can go with them and perhaps get it all done in one phone call or maybe even just one court hearing, and it's done, they get back to work, 100 percent attention to their job."

Other states have tried solving the problem in various ways. New York requires law school graduates to perform 50 hours of pro bono work before they are admitted to the Bar, for example, and California allows nonlawyers to help litigants. Perhaps the most innovative is Louisiana, which gives recent law school graduates a $36,000-a-year internship to represent indigent clients. The program is a win-win for new lawyers, for whom the unemployment rate once stood at 47 percent and is now nonexistent. In addition, every courthouse and library in Louisiana has kiosks staffed by volunteers who provide information and forms to litigants without lawyers.

Recognizing the past efforts of the Florida Bar to address the issue, Labarga said, "We must now take it to the next level, bearing in mind that the question of access to our civil justice system is a societal question and, as such, the solution rests with all segments of society." Although the Commission submitted its report to the Supreme Court in mid-2016, the issue "is not something that we're going to study, do a report and shelve it," he said. It will continue to exist. "Is it a panacea where all of a sudden we're going to have a lawyer for everybody? No," but it will address problems as they come up.

In addition to the Access to Civil Justice Commission, he has urged the Florida Bar to host a retreat on the future of the legal profession. "Globalization of the legal community is happening, and either we start looking at it and try to control it, or it's going to control us," he said. Florida has 100,000 lawyers and jobs for only 60,000. Every year another 40,000 are graduating from law schools. They have learned how to think like a lawyer but don't know how to practice law, something that usually comes with mentoring but often does not happen.

If he were advising a young person interested in becoming a lawyer, he would say, "Before you invest your time and your debt" in law school, work for a time in a private law office or volunteer in a State Attorney's office or Public Defender's office so you can actually see what a lawyer does and whether you like the work. "There's a big misperception about that. The legal profession is very stressful. It's 75–80 hours a week," and that deprives you of a social life, not to mention having little or no time for your spouse and children.

When he makes speeches to law students and to others around the state, he often says, "The Constitution basically is just words on paper." Yes, lawyers and public officials debate its different sections, but in the end, "It's up to us, the citizens, the people, to make it work and to make sure that we don't deviate from it and to uphold it."

Jorge Labarga was interviewed in person by the author Mar. 16, 2015; additional information came from news reports.

6

Trailblazers in Congress

U.S. House and U.S. Senate

Figure 6.1. The U.S. Capitol Building. The U.S. Senate is to the left of the Rotunda; the U.S. House of Representatives is on the right Photograph by the Architect of the U.S. Capitol. http://www.aoc.gov/capitol-buildings/about-us-capitol-building.

Florida Minority Trailblazers—U.S. Congress: 1960s–2010s

Florida members of Congress appear in chronological order. If elected the same year, they are listed alphabetically.[a]

	Senate		House of Representatives	
Time frame	Male	Female	Male	Female
1960s				
1970s				
1980s				1989–Present Ileana Ros-Lehtinen—R Cuba—Miami
1990s			1992–2010 Lincoln Diaz-Balart—R Cuba—Miami	1992–2003 Carrie P. Meek—D African American—Miami
			1992–Present Alcee Hastings—D African American—Miami	1992–Present Corrine Brown—D African American—Jacksonville
2000s			2002–present Mario Diaz-Balart—R Cuba—Miami (Younger brother to Lincoln Diaz-Balart)	
			2002–2010 Kendrick Meek—D African American—Miami (Mother-Son)[b]	
	2004–2009 Mel Martinez—R Cuba—Orlando			
2010s			2010–2012 Allen West—R African American—Miami	2010–Present Frederica Wilson—D Bahamas—Miami
			2012–2014 Joe Garcia—D Cuba—Miami	

Notes: Consult Appendix E for a full listing of minority members of Congress in Florida.

[a]Members of Congress are elected in the November of even-numbered years but assume office in the January of odd-numbered years. The dates given are dates of election.

[b]In 2002 Kendrick Meek became the first African American to directly succeed his mother (Carrie Meek) in Congress.

Table 6.1. Florida seats in the U.S. House after census

Census	Number of seats
1950	6
1960	8
1970	12
1980	15
1990	23
2000	25
2010	27

The election of minorities to the Congress came much more slowly than in the Florida Legislature in spite of the population explosion beginning in the 1950s and the continued increase in the number of seats in the U.S. House accruing to Florida after each census.

Not until 1989 was a minority elected to the U.S. House (Cuban-American Republican Ileana Ros-Lehtinen). It was not until 1992, with redistricting and the creation of majority-minority seats, that African Americans were thrust into Congress—the first since Reconstruction (Carrie Meek, Alcee Hastings, and Corrine Brown).

It was more than a decade later (2004) before Floridians elected a minority to serve in the U.S. Senate—Cuban-American Republican Mel Martinez from Orlando, who narrowly bested Democrat Betty Castor from Tampa.

From 1989 to 2014, 11 minorities have been elected to the U.S. House from Florida: six Democrats and five Republicans; among them seven men (4-R, 3-D) and four women (3-D, 1-R).

Only two minorities (both Cuban-American Republican men) have represented the state in the U.S. Senate (Mel Martinez and Marco Rubio). (See Appendix E for a list of Florida minorities serving in the U.S. Congress post-Reconstruction.)

The biggest impetus for the increase of minorities in Congress has been redistricting, an always contentious process—and one driven by congressional acts (Voting Rights Act of 1965, amended in 1975 and 1982) and federal court rulings.

Figure 6.2. Mel Martinez greets supporters in his race for U.S. Senate in 2004. The former Orange County Mayor narrowly defeated Democrat Betty Castor, a former state Senator and Education Commissioner, to become the first Hispanic from Florida to serve in the U.S. Senate and also the first Cuban-born U.S. Senator. Photograph courtesy of Mel Martinez, 2004.

The 1982 Redistricting

The 1982[1] redistricting created a strong minority candidacy pool ready to take the next bold step and run for Congress.

Minorities achieved their goal of capturing more *state legislative* seats with the 1982 elections, in many cases winning seats not only gerrymandered to create minority opportunity but open after incumbents had been switched to single-member districts (SMDs). Democratic State Rep. Carrie Meek of Miami and dentist Arnett Girardeau of Jacksonville became the first black state Senators since 1887. Ten African Americans were elected to the House in 1982[2]—twice the number two years earlier. Among these was Corrine Brown of Duval County. The number of Hispanics (usually Republicans) in the House increased from one in 1980 to three in 1982 and seven in 1984. Ileana Ros (later Ros-Lehtinen) became the first Hispanic woman to serve in the state House and in 1986 she became the state's first Hispanic Senator.[3]

All three of the minority women state legislators became Congress members. Ros-Lehtinen was the first. In 1989, she won a special election to fill the vacant seat created when long-time Congressman Claude Pepper (a white Democrat) passed away. By then, the district had become much more heavily Hispanic. Actually, Ros-Lehtinen was the first Hispanic in Congress from Florida in 166 years. Joseph Marion Hernández, who served from 1822 to 1823, was the first—and that was before Florida achieved statehood in 1845.[4]

African-American Democrats Meek and Brown, along with Alcee Hastings, all won election to the U.S. House after the 1992 redistricting, as did Cuban-American Republican Lincoln Diaz-Balart. All but Brown from Jacksonville were elected from South Florida districts, with large concentrations of minority voters. Each of these trailblazers cited the importance of the federal Voting Rights Act to the redistricting process that yielded their election.

Figure 6.3. Ileana Ros-Lehtinen was the first Hispanic woman elected to Congress from Florida. She won a special election in 1989 and was soon followed by the Diaz-Balart brothers—first Lincoln (*left*), then Mario (*right*) as congressional districts with sizable Hispanic populations were drawn in response to the federal Voting Rights Act and court rulings. Photograph courtesy of Chris Simmons (*to right of Lincoln*)—a counterterrorism expert. http://humanchess.co/the-author/, n.d.

The 1992 Redistricting

Entering into the redistricting session, both African-American and Hispanic legislators were strongly committed to increasing their presence in the Florida congressional delegation.[5] From the outset, it was obvious the major struggles would be over how best to enhance minority participation to prove compliance with the 14th and 15th Amendments to the U.S. Constitution and the federal Voting Rights Act of 1965, as amended in 1975 and 1982.

Heated battles ensued as legislators disagreed on the percentage of minority voting-age population to place in a district to ensure approval of the plan by the U.S. Justice Department (preclearance requirement—Section V of the federal Voting Rights Act) and the federal courts. Significant debates took place, even among minority legislators, about what type of minority district—majority or influence—would be best to increase minority representation.

This intense discussion came on the heels of the U.S. Supreme Court's landmark 1986 *Thornburg v. Gingles* ruling that instructed courts to determine whether "if as a result of the challenged [voting] practice or structure [redistricting plan] plaintiffs do not have an equal opportunity to participate in the political process and to elect candidates of their choice." In the end, the Legislature, with a Democratic majority in each house, failed to pass a congressional redistricting plan, leaving it to a federal court to draw.[6] The three-judge panel consisted of U.S. Circuit Judge Joseph W. Hatchett, a trailblazer, who was the state's first black Supreme Court Justice, and U.S. District Judges William Stafford and Roger Vinson. The plan, approved by the federal court in May 1992, created four majority-minority districts[7]:

District 3: 50 percent black voting age population (VAP); a controversial U-shaped district connecting black populations in Gainesville, Jacksonville, Daytona Beach, and Orlando; won by Democrat Corrine Brown.
District 17: 54 percent black VAP; in Miami; won by Democrat Carrie Meek.
District 23: 52 percent black in population (46 percent black VAP) connecting black neighborhoods north of Miami, through Fort Lauderdale and Palm Beach; won by Democrat Alcee Hastings.
District 70: created as the second majority Hispanic district in the Miami area, with 70 percent Hispanic VAP; won by Republican Lincoln Diaz-Balart.

The judges concluded that this plan "overall substantially increases the level of participation and electoral representation for the members of minority groups in Florida."

In 1996, the congressional plan had to be redrawn on the heels of a U.S. Supreme Court ruling challenging a Georgia congressional district. In *Miller v. Johnson* (1995), the Court ruled that race could not be the "predominant factor" in redistricting. In April 1996, a three-judge panel ruled against the Third Congressional District. This

Figure 6.4. This painting, titled *The Florida Empowerment*, features the first African Americans elected from Florida to the U.S. Congress since Reconstruction—all from majority-minority districts. *Top row (L-R)*: Carrie Meek, Alcee Hastings, Corrine Brown. The painting was commissioned by the Florida Local Host Planning Committee for the Congressional Black Caucus Foundation's Florida Public Policy Conference held in Miami, March 18–19, 1994. For many years it hung in Congresswoman Carrie Meek's Washington, D.C., office. She later gave it to the Carrie Meek-James N. Eaton, Sr. Southeastern Regional Black Archives Research Center and Museum at Florida A&M University, where it is now displayed. Photograph by Susan A. MacManus, August 2014.

time, the Legislature successfully redrew the district, reducing the number of black voters in the district; it was approved by the courts in May 1996. The reconfiguration of the district had little impact on the performance of the district as Representative Corrine Brown was reelected. However, the general issue of what proportion of minority population to place in a district continued to be debated even among minorities over next two redistricting cycles—2002 and 2012.

Passing the Torch to Family

Much is made of white political "dynasties," Democrat and Republican alike—the Kennedys and Clintons, the Rockefellers and Bushes. There are also strong family ties among Florida's minority congressional trailblazers—the Meeks (Democrats) and the Diaz-Balarts (Republicans).

When Congresswoman Carrie Meek decided to retire in 2002, her son, Kendrick, who had served in the Florida Legislature from 1994–2002 in both the House and the Senate, successfully ran for her seat. In 2010, the younger Meek gave up his seat when he ran, unsuccessfully, for the U.S. Senate against Republican Marco Rubio and independent Charlie Crist. The following year, President Barack Obama (D) appointed Kendrick as a U.S. representative to the United Nations.

Mario Diaz-Balart followed big brother Lincoln to Congress after winning one of the two new seats Florida gained after the 2000 Census. Mario's District 25, created during the 2002 redistricting, covered portions of Miami-Dade, Collier, and Monroe counties. The Diaz-Balart brothers served side by side until 2010 when Lincoln announced he would not seek reelection. In 2010, Mario ran unopposed for his brother's seat (District 21). After the 2012 redistricting cycle, he ran for and was elected to the newly reconfigured 25th Congressional District, including portions of Miami-Dade, Broward, Collier, and Hendry counties—friendlier territory for Republicans than the altered District 21.

Open Seats and Rematches

Kendrick Meek's decision not to seek reelection in 2010 created a rare open seat, won by Frederica Wilson (a former state Representative, then Senator). After the 2012 redistricting, the district was renumbered and became District 24. It stayed a majority African-American district and included the southern parts of Broward County and the eastern parts of Miami-Dade County.

Mario Diaz-Balart's decision in 2010 to run for his brother's District 21 seat left District 25 open. Cuban-American Republican David Riviera was elected and served but one term. The 2012 redistricting altered the district's composition. District 26 (the new number) now stretched from the Miami area to Key West—a more Democratic district. In a rematch of the 2010 race, Cuban-American Democrat Joe Garcia beat rival Rivera by nearly 10 percentage points. Garcia became the first Cuban-American Democrat to be elected to Congress from the Sunshine State. In 2014, the seat flipped back Republican as Cuban Carlos Curbelo bested Garcia.

Figure 6.5. Congresswoman Frederica Wilson (*second from left*) presents a Congressional Proclamation to constituent Desaline Victor, a 102-year-old woman who waited for more than three hours to vote in the 2012 presidential election. Wilson had been in office only two years, having run for the U.S. House seat vacated by Kendrick Meek. http://wilson.house.gov/about/full-biography.

Allen West: Black Congress Member, White District

In 2010, retired U.S. Army Lt. Col. Allen West became the first black Republican to represent Florida in Congress since Rep. Josiah T. Walls, who served during Reconstruction.[8] As of this writing, West is the only congressional minority trailblazer to have been elected from a predominantly white district. He won 55 percent of the vote, defeating Democratic incumbent Ron Klein, with the strong backing of Tea Party activists and conservatives in District 22 and across the country. (In 2008, West had lost to Klein by a similar margin.)

Like most other post-Reconstruction black Republican trailblazers, Congressman West was raised in a family of Democrats but was initially attracted to the Republican Party during his military service. The 2012 redistricting altered West's old district so much that he switched to the 18th Congressional District, narrowly losing to Democrat Patrick Murphy. He would later leave Florida and move to Dallas to head a nonpartisan think tank—the National Center for Policy Analysis.

Common Ground

The congressional trailblazers' successes, particularly those winning U.S. House seats, have been heavily influenced by three factors: (1) every redistricting since 1982 (and related court rulings centered on the Voting Rights Act), (2) minority population growth and changing residential concentration patterns, and (3) party affiliation and, to a lesser extent, family ties and prior state legislative experience.

"Florida is a very complicated state to run a statewide race in," said Sen. Mel Martinez, reflecting on population diversity and the contrasting political issues in different parts of the state. Running for office has become even more complicated by changes in technology, fundraising, and professional management of campaigns. "These are things you do because it's the right thing to do," he said, "but also when you're in political life, you think about the political benefit of those kinds of things. It's sort of a two-fer, if you will—good policy and good politics go hand-in-hand."

House

Ileana Ros-Lehtinen (R)

First Cuban woman elected to the Florida House of Representatives, 1982
First Cuban woman elected to the Florida Senate, 1986
First Cuban American and first Hispanic woman to serve in the U.S. House of Representatives, 1989
Personal: Born July 15, 1952, Havana, Cuba; married with one child and two stepchildren.
Education:

- Miami-Dade Community College, A.A. (1972)
- Florida International University, B.A. in education (1975)
- Florida International University, M.A. in educational leadership (1986)
- University of Miami, Ph.D. in higher education (2004)

Occupation: Teacher

Figure 6.6. Cuban-born Ileana Ros-Lehtinen became the first Hispanic woman to serve in the U.S. House of Representatives (101st Congress). In 1989, she won a special election to fill the vacancy caused by the death of longtime Congressman Claude Pepper (D-Miami). State Archives of Florida, *Florida Memory*, https://www.floridamemory.com/items/show/20775. Photograph taken in 1989.

Trailblazer Elections:

- House of Representatives District 110 (Part of Dade County) *Rep Primary* 1982
  - Ileana Ros (48.3%), Raul Pozo (40.2%), S. J. Rand (11.5%)
- House of Representatives District 110 (Part of Dade County) *Rep Runoff* 1982
  - Ileana Ros (55.6%), Raul Pozo (44.4%)
- House of Representatives District 110 (Part of Dade County) *General Election* 1982
  - Ileana Ros-R (58.5%), William "Bill" Oliver-D (41.5%)
- Senate District 34 (Part of Dade County) *Rep Primary* 1986
  - Ileana Ros-Lehtinen (88.0%), Bettina Rod-Inclan (12.0%)
- Senate District 34 (Part of Dade County) *General Election* 1986
  - Ileana Ros-Lehtinen-R (58.2%), Steve Zack-D (41.8%)
- U.S. House of Representatives District 18 (Part of Dade County) *Rep Primary Special Election* 1989
  - Ileana Ros-Lehtinen (82.8%), Carlos Perez (11.05%), David M. Fleischer (3.39%), John M. Stembridge (2.76%)
- U.S. House of Representatives District 18 (Part of Dade) *General Special Election* August 29, 1989
  - Ileana Ros-Lehtinen-R (53.25%), Gerald F. Richman-D (46.75%)

THE ILEANA ROS-LEHTINEN STORY

"We had a wonderful life in Cuba," said Ileana Ros-Lehtinen. "But Castro took it all away, and thank goodness there is this great country, the United States of America, that opened its arms to us."

She and her family left Cuba when she was eight years old, but she remembered a bit of Fidel Castro's revolution: "We would be driving down the streets of Havana and all of a sudden, my parents would say, 'Duck!'" She and her brother "knew something strange was going on."

"My family and I came in one of the last commercial flights of Pan American Airlines. We thought, 'Oh, maybe this so-called revolution will be over in a few days.' So we came with practically nothing, maybe we packed a little bag. We bought a round-trip ticket because we said we were going to be in Miami a few days or a couple weeks and then we'll be back home." She still has that round-trip ticket. One day she hopes to cash it in "because Cuba holds a special place in my heart and I fight every day for a free Cuba, and hope that one day that will happen." She did not find it difficult to say goodbye: "I was just a kid, so anything is fine with me." Her family arrived in August, and two months later it was Halloween. "My brother and I thought, 'Wow! This is an amazing country. You go around with a little grocery bag and people give you candy.' We didn't celebrate Halloween in Cuba, so I remember that was one of the best impressions that we had of this country."

Her parents found work—her mother in a Miami Beach hotel kitchen, and her father, who had been a teacher in Cuba, in a laundry. "They were glad for the work, very happy, and to me, they taught me that there's dignity in all work and that nothing is beneath you. It doesn't matter what you do. It's a clean, honest living." Even though her father had graduated from a university in Cuba, he went to Miami-Dade Community College and then graduated from the University of Miami. (He ended up becoming a Certified Public Accountant and a pharmaceutical representative.)

"My mom took many bus rides and did bus transfers to get to Miami Beach because we had only one car," she said. They rented a home in Little Havana that became a virtual refugee center. "Families would come and go, and maybe they'd stay with us for a week or two weeks or two months," she said. "It was great. I just have wonderful memories growing up in Little Havana and seeing people come and go. It was a wonderful time. I can't say that I suffered as a refugee. We had lots of fun, and my parents were very patriotic Americans at the same time that they were very loyal to the cause of a free Cuba."

"In the early exile years, you really had a sense of community," she said. "Everybody was in the same boat. You had very little money, very little food, and you helped each other," she said. "Everybody we knew was poor."

"My parents helped me with a can-do attitude to know that even when you have obstacles and some stumbling blocks, they're really just challenges and that you can overcome them. If the will is there and if your desire to learn and to persevere and to advance yourself and to succeed is there, then anything is possible because this really is the land of opportunity. They may be clichés for many people. If you've lived here many generations, maybe you take all these things for granted, but when you're a hungry refugee—hungry in all senses of the word—then you are eager to get ahead."

Learning English was difficult. "When we first came in 1960, there were no bilingual programs. Or if there were, they weren't in any of my schools. So it was sink or swim, and you did the best you could," she said. "For a while, many teachers thought there was something not quite correct with you because you couldn't understand the concepts. But leaning a new language at the same time you're learning the subject matter, that's quite a challenge." Her parents couldn't help because they were working two jobs, plus her dad was going to school. They had no money to hire a tutor. They learned English by watching TV: "It was homework."

"I always liked learning," she said. Some might have called her a nerd. "I liked doing schoolwork and homework assignments and earning extra credit." She dreamed about becoming a teacher. She went on to earn bachelor's (1975) and master's (1985) degrees in education from Florida International University and a doctorate from the University of Miami (2004).

She started her career as a teacher and founded a private bilingual elementary school in south Hialeah, a working-class area of South Florida. "I got to know the parents of the schools and all the problems they had, and I would help them with their individual problems." Then a fellow teacher suggested that she could run for office where she could set policy and help the families in bigger ways.

Nobody in her family had come from a political background, and she had never participated in student government in school. But her family and their friends talked about human rights and democracy around the kitchen table. "My parents were very involved in the anti-Castro movement when we came over to the United States," she said. "In that sense I grew up, not in a political atmosphere, but in a sense that America's role in the world is an important topic of discussion." "Foreign affairs were domestic issues for us," she said.

The more she thought about the teacher's suggestion, the more interested she became. She mentioned the idea to her father, and he thought it was great. But how does one learn how to run for office? "We found a campaign school run by the GOP, and I think it was in Orlando," she said. In the weekend session, they learned about printing brochures, mailing literature, getting endorsements, and canvassing voters.

At that time, the early 1980s, Florida was converting multi-member districts to single-member districts (SMDs). She decided to run for one of the new House seats that would be created. "There was no incumbent, and that's where I lived, and so I decided to run for it." With the district lines still in litigation, her father reasoned that "this little chunk of real estate would be in the district and that's where we would run. So for a year and a half, but before they had the lines drawn up, we were already walking door-to-door," she said.

The race attracted important people in both the Republican and Democratic primaries, but her family said, "Let's go for it, and let's work harder than anybody else." In meeting people while walking door-to-door, "I think people thought: 'Well, I don't think she's going to make it, but well, let's vote for her. She came to our door.' And we got lucky. Hard work makes you lucky."

During the campaign, her dad suggested a trip to Tallahassee, where they had never gone before: "We should go to Tallahassee because somebody is going to ask you, 'What do you think of Tallahassee?' It's not good if you've never been." So they went to Tallahassee and saw the capitol, the Governor's Mansion, and other government sites, and came home the same day.

With grassroots support, she won enough votes in the primary to be in the Republican Party runoff. She faced a man who was better known, better funded, and older than she was. Although he was expected to win, she outworked him and came out ahead. "We had wonderful volunteers from family and friends," she said. "My father was just the best campaign manager, and my mom was a volunteer coordinator."

In the general election, she ran against a Democratic candidate who had won outright in the primary. He knew that Republicans were a minority and not used to winning, so he took victory for granted. With the election only four weeks away, she and

Figure 6.7. House members applaud as State Reps. Ileana Ros and Dexter Lehtinen announce their engagement. They were married on June 9, 1984. State Archives of Florida, *Florida Memory*, https://www.floridamemory.com/items/show/20191. Photograph taken in 1984.

her supporters redoubled their efforts. She won, becoming the first Hispanic woman to serve in the Florida House.

At that time, "you weren't supposed to win if you were Republican. In fact, when you registered to vote in South Florida, and you went to the elections department, and you registered there as a Republican, usually the lady would tell you, 'You know, you probably won't be able to vote because most of the races are decided in the primary.' She wasn't trying to steer you to the Democratic Party, and literally you would have very few positions that you could vote for."

In Tallahassee, she met State Rep. Dexter Lehtinen, who had already been in the House for two years. "He was a Democrat then, and he switched over to the Republican side" in 1985, shortly before they were married. They served together in the Florida House for four years, and then both ran for separate seats in the Florida Senate in 1987.

At that time, President Ronald Reagan was nearing the end of his second term, and Florida Republicans were gaining power and influence. She defeated Democrat Stephen Zack[9] for a seat vacated by Democrat Joe Gersten, who resigned to run for attorney general. Meanwhile, her husband defeated incumbent Democrat Roberta Fox in a hard-fought campaign.

Their opponents "were very upset that we were both running for the Senate because we had single-member districts. They said, 'You can't do that.' We said, 'Well, we have two homes. We spend some time in his house, which is in his district, and some time in ours'" in her district, she said. "We found out from walking the district, people didn't care whether we lived in this house so many days and lived in the other." While their opponents focused on the residency question, "We kept talking about the issues," which included low taxes, few regulations, and constituent service, she said. Their strategy worked. "Paying attention to your constituents, paying attention to your district—that's what matters a lot to people."

While she was in the House, "Republicans were such a small minority we were actually almost just cast aside." In the Senate, with only 40 members, "You could really get things done. And by then the Republicans were already taking hold." Many of her constituents had become fiscal conservatives. "They were very worried about government spending money that we did not have [at local, state and federal levels]. Thank goodness in Florida, as in most states, you have to have a balanced budget," she said.

One "awful time" in the state Legislature occurred in 1987 with the public outcry against the service tax. Legislators came back in session with the idea of repealing the tax, but Republican Gov. Bob Martinez embraced it. "There are better ways of balancing the books, and that is cutting expenses, not raising taxes," she said. "Gov. Martinez inherited the problem and he thought he could blame somebody else for the tax and use the revenue to build schools and satisfy other public needs. But people were not in the mood for a tax on services. He tried to talk me into voting for it, but I said, 'No thank you.' 'Dance with the ones that brung you,' as Ronald Reagan said."

In the Senate, one of her proudest pieces of legislation was the Prepaid College Tuition Program. She and Sen. Curtis Peterson from Lakeland wrote the bill, modeling it after the only other plan in existence at the time. "We did it more or less as an experiment. We never thought that it would catch on in the way it did, and we did not think that it would be the biggest, most financially sound get-ready-for-college program in the United States." Many other states modeled their programs after Florida's. "It's a layaway plan for college," she said. "And I tell you, I could do 20,000 things from there on, but it will never have as big an impact as that bill." The program "has changed the lives of a million families in Florida," she said, and she still gets thanks from parents for it. (Stanley Tate was the program's first Chair of the Board and made it such a success that the program now rightly bears his name.)

She expressed gratitude for the work of her grassroots supporters: "I was very happy mostly for the wonderful volunteers and for my family because they worked so hard, and it wasn't supposed to happen. I was just so gratified for them—and still to this day, my family is the unit that helps me the most, and this core group of volunteers. They're so loyal and reliable and dependable. It's amazing that I've kept this team together for so many years."

She and her husband had many mentors, both Republicans and Democrats, in the Legislature. "We served with incredible people like Tom Gustafson [Democrat]," she said. "We had great Representatives like Dale Patchett and Ron Richmond [Republicans], just incredible folks that I remember so well that we served with. All of them were great role models for me." In addition, "We had many women legislators in the Senate. We had Toni Jennings, Mary Grizzle and just incredible women who were leading the charge for the Republican Party."

Some of her best memories were serving with members of the South Florida Republican delegation. "People like Tom Gallagher. He was a state Representative who was elected before Republicans were anything. He was the only state rep who was a Republican from South Florida, probably south of Orlando, for many years." Two others were Jim Brodie and Scott McPherson, Republicans elected to the House in 1980. "That's one of the nicest memories—folks like Tom, Jim, and Scott who helped me get elected," she said.

In getting elected to the Legislature, she made history as the first Hispanic woman in both the House and Senate. That feat "was a source of great pride for my community. That's when the Cuban-American community was starting to flex its political muscle." They were becoming naturalized Americans. "With great pride, we would become registered to vote, and then we would vote very eagerly. We were proud, proud voters. For so many in our community, this was a sign of 'Wow! We really made it in the United States now when we're able to elect one of our own to the Florida Legislature.'" Her election "really opened up a lot of eyes about the potential for the Cuban-American vote and the Cuban-American public official and how far we could all go."

When Congressman Claude Pepper (D-Miami) died in May 1989, she decided to run for his seat. As much as she loved serving in the Florida Senate, "I was missing the foreign policy aspect of what motivated me," she said.

"Foreign affairs was really like a domestic affair" because while she was growing up, her family's kitchen-table discussions focused on "freedom and democracy and human rights and my native homeland of Cuba and this terrible communist dictatorship that took over the island," she said.

Her husband, who had become a U.S. Attorney, encouraged her to run for Pepper's seat, saying, "This is your time. You've got to do it." Her dad, who had always been a source of great encouragement for her political aspirations, also urged her to run. With children ages two and three, she was concerned about their care. At that time, however, "Congress was more of a Tuesday-to-Thursday club," she said. "You could come up on Tuesday and leave on Thursday, so we thought it would be doable. And in the early years, our little kids came up with me because they weren't in school." (When they were in school, her parents moved into a house across the street in Pinecrest and helped care for the children.)

The special election attracted more than a dozen candidates vying to fill out the term of the lionized Democrat who had served in the U.S. House for more than a quarter century. "It was a hard, nasty, no-fun campaign," she said. "I was running against a liberal Democrat who, in my point of view, had made statements that seemed to be anti-Hispanic. His slogan was, 'This is an American seat.' I don't know what he meant by that. It didn't sound like the correct thing to say because I'm an American too." Two weeks before the election, Republican President George H. W. Bush came to Miami to support her.

On election night, suspense hung in the air. "The election results were coming in late," she said. "Our election official had actually passed out from the tension, and the computers came back up at like 3 in the morning and we got to find out that I was the winner."

She won by 6 percentage points. "I promise to carry on the work of Claude Pepper: to take care of the old, educate the young and keep this country free," she said.[10] Her supporters, still smarting from the opponent's slogan, chanted, "Viva the Cubans!" They formed conga lines and sang along with Celia Cruz, a celebrated Cuban-born salsa singer. Later Ros-Lehtinen attributed her victory to uniting the different Hispanic communities in response to the "American seat" slogan, although she drew votes from non-Hispanics as well.

The morning the election results were final, the *Today* show called. "Katie Couric, who was interviewing, says, 'How does it feel to be the first Hispanic woman elected to Congress?' I said, 'Well, Katie, I'm very happy that I won but I don't want to correct you on the air but I don't think I'm the first Hispanic woman.' And she says, 'Oh yes, we've got a good research team. You are the first Hispanic.' I said, 'Wow, that's pretty good, I like that. Well, just being in Congress is good enough for me.'"

When she arrived in Washington, D.C., Dante Fascell, a Florida Democrat and chairman of the House Foreign Affairs Committee, invited her to sit in on the committee even though it didn't have an opening at the time. She accepted: "I told him that's the one committee I want to be on." Sure enough, Fascell managed to get her a bona fide seat on the committee within a short time. Fascell "was a great role model and a mentor for me," she said. "Not only was he from my area [Dade County], but he worked in a bipartisan way," she said. "He ran the committee in a very even-handed way and helped Republican presidents quite a lot."

Fascell retired in 1993, and Ros-Lehtinen continued moving up in seniority until she became committee chairman in 2011. Among the chairmen serving in the interim was Democrat Tom Lantos of California. "He was the first and only Holocaust survivor ever to serve in Congress," she said, noting that she and Lantos held the distinction of being two naturalized Americans who chaired the Foreign Affairs Committee.

"This is a great country, I always say," she said. "The privileges and the responsibilities and the honors that we have in this great country, you wouldn't have that in other places. Where else could you come as a refugee, a penniless refugee, and be able to serve in a legislative body like this, and be able to chair the Foreign Affairs Committee, setting the tone for our policy when you're not even from this country. Is this a great country or what?" She was succeeded as chair by Ed Royce, a Republican from California, in 2013.

As chairman emeritus of Foreign Affairs, she has continued to oppose Castro's dictatorship in Cuba, an effort that prompted Castro to call her *La Loba Feroz* (the ferocious she-wolf). "He thought he was insulting me," she said, but she relished the nickname.

"I hope and I pray and I work hard so that one day Cuba will be free." She denounced Cuba's state-controlled media and oppressive politics: "The Communist Party is the only party that's allowed to exist. They don't really have elections because they don't have any parties. Nobody is debating the issues because if you do that, you'll go to jail. So there's no dissent. There are no labor unions. There are no freedoms. There are no opportunities, and that's why people literally die through the Florida Straits trying to come to the United States."

"It is incomprehensible to us that so many years have gone by and that there's still the communist dictatorship in Cuba that controls every facet of one's life. I think the unfortunate thing for Cuba is that it's so close to the United States. Maybe if it were in the Middle East, maybe it would already be free. I don't know," she said. "I am very confident that I will see a free and democratic Cuba. It's going to happen."

Other foreign leaders, besides Castro, attacked her in the press. After helping free a former Venezuelan political prisoner, she was quoted as saying: "I take it as a badge of honor that tyrants like Chávez and Bolivian leader Evo Morales and the Castro thugs say bad things about me," she said. "That means I'm doing my work and attacking them for their record."[11]

"Every time I put out a press release or I make a statement in favor of freedom and democracy and against dictatorships, these dictators take it very personally. If I've managed to poke them in the eye and make them upset, that makes my day, because I talk about freedom and democracy and human rights. That's what I live for."

She added, "I'm the most senior Republican woman in Congress and it just means I'm an old hag and I last a long time. Stick around long enough and you get to be that." In March 2014, as dean of the Florida Republican delegation, she had the honor of introducing Republican David Jolly as the newest member of the U.S. House of Representatives.

Her work in foreign affairs has included assistance to Israel, measures to combat Islamist extremism, and support for free trade with Colombia, Panama, and South Korea. On defense, she has sought to improve the nation's military and veterans' health care.

A former educator, she has worked to strengthen Head Start and make student financial aid more accessible. She has supported legislation to reduce Medicare fraud and domestic violence.

Both foreign and domestic issues sometimes involve conflict with the administration. "I've served under Democrats and Republicans, both in the Florida Legislature and in Congress. You just do your job, and you try to work out the differences with the executive branch. Sometimes it doesn't really matter whether it's a Democrat or a

Republican. There are just those kinds of traditional problems you have with leadership whether it's Democrat or Republican. I have found in every combination I've served that it's still a hassle. And the rank and file, we still believe that we're right. No matter who the lead dog is, we think we are the lead dogs."

Despite representing a fairly liberal district, she has continued to win as a conservative. "Those legislators keep drawing districts for me that are very tough because they say Ileana can win," she said. "I have my principles and stands that I take, but it doesn't mean that I'm the owner of the truth," she said. "I give the opportunity to the other side to voice their point-of-view."

In addition, "My district is a majority-minority district, so most of the population and the voters are Hispanic. The majority of our campaign ads are in Spanish on television and radio. But we spend a good chunk also in English because people younger than I am may be labeled as Hispanic, but to them, English is a far easier language."

Her campaigns also rely on local Spanish-language newspapers. "They're very helpful. They circulate in the cafeterias and places like Versailles [a Cuban restaurant in Miami], the *commedores*—lunchrooms at elderly group homes. So we have about seven *periodicos* [newspapers], so we spend money on those, too." She does not advertise in local churches because political ads could damage their tax-exempt status.

She finds it hard to generalize about which political party Hispanics choose: "You could say Puerto Ricans tend to be more Democratic, Cuban Americans tend to be more Republican, and I think the community of Venezuelans, Nicaraguans and Colombians is up for grabs." In addition to those groups, other immigrants are coming to South Florida from Russia, Israel, Iran, and India. "We don't have as many folks from Asia as California and New York would have." Overall, "it's getting more cosmopolitan and more international."

Haitians were in her first congressional district in 1989, but districts have changed since then. "Now my district does not have that vitality of the Haitian Americans," she said. "Haitian Americans and Jamaicans are making Miami their home, so black Caribbean voters and residents are changing in a positive way, the character, and the richness of our culture in South Florida."

Because of the growth and diversity of immigrant groups, "we should pass comprehensive immigration reform. It's important to help our communities. As an immigrant myself, I'm sensitive that it's not right for me to say, well I came over and I'm glad the United States let me in, but now don't have anybody else come in."

Apart from the influx of Latin Americans, Florida's population has changed in other ways. Snowbirds from northern states are less likely to winter in Florida, and many elderly people are going elsewhere to retire: "People come and go. They come in and make Florida their home, but they don't stay in one place as much as they used to. Florida and the country have changed a lot because we tend more to follow

Figure 6.8. Congresswoman Ileana Ros-Lehtinen at Key West High School answers questions from a reporter after the highly destructive Hurricane Wilma. State Archives of Florida, *Florida Memory*, https://www.floridamemory.com/items/show/100007. Photograph by Dale M. McDonald, October 25, 2005.

our jobs rather than we get a job and keep it forever, or we buy a home and that's our home forever. Now we are more of a transient population."

Being a woman candidate has pros and cons, she said, and gross generalizations on this topic, as well as others, are often inaccurate. "Most people tend to think of women as fair, more honest, more open, and more trusting—at least polls and surveys have indicated that. But still we're at a disadvantage, and that's why there are not enough of us here in Congress or in the Legislature. Not enough of us run, first of all. We're our own worst enemies because we think we can't do it. We're used to fundraising for the Red Cross but not fundraising for ourselves." Men are better at raising money, she said. Nonetheless, women need to "go for it no matter how hard the obstacles are." What's more, "I think that voters don't see enough female candidates, so you sort of have an advantage. It really depends on the personality because it doesn't so much matter the gender. So I'm just making a gross generalization based on surveys. But women think that they can't get elected because they say, 'Look around, there are hardly any women elected.' Well, it's because they're not running." For herself, she said: "I have never found my gender to be a liability in the least, not in the least."

When she goes to schools and talks to students, she says, "This is a great country where the only barriers sometimes are the ones that you set for yourself because anything is possible. I mean, you look at Barack Obama, the first office he holds is a U.S. Senator and then he goes to the presidency. You talk about the phenomenal political success of Hillary Clinton and so many good Republican candidates as well who have been trailblazers. I think there's still room for many firsts, so I don't want people to ever give up and say, 'Oh boy, everything that could possibly be achieved has already been achieved.' No, there's still a lot more that we can do."

She tries to encourage young women to think about a career in public service. "To so many of them, it's the furthest thing from their minds." As a former teacher, she explains how women can combine public service with teaching. "They don't have to do it full-time, and they don't have to do it for a long time. It's something that gives you a great sense of satisfaction." As examples, she explained how she, through her district office staff, helps people with immigration problems, Medicare and Social Security issues, and veterans' benefits. Without that help, those people "would've been deported or they would've been in difficult legal limbo," she said. "It's a real sense of satisfaction when you can help people. I think it's an extension of when I was a teacher. It's the same kind of mission—to help people."

She also derives great satisfaction from training the next generation of leaders. "Marco Rubio used to be an intern for me, and now look at him, Mr. Big Shot, a U.S. Senator. René Garcia, another former intern, is now a state legislator. It's incredible. They are now judges, they are lawyers, they are running the world. I make it a point of highlighting internships with our office, and we hope we encourage young people to come."

Political campaigning has changed greatly since she first ran for office in 1982. "Outside groups have really made an unfortunate difference in campaigning. Now it doesn't matter how much cash on hand you have. I'm a pretty good fundraiser. I raise it in little chunks at a time with different groups, but on Foreign Affairs I don't have the clout that somebody in Appropriations or Ways and Means would have. I meet with ambassadors, I don't meet with the titans of industry," she said. "Now no matter how good you are at fundraising, you have outside groups that you have no control over who would come in to help you or to hurt you. I do not like the growing influence that outside groups have in campaigns." She admitted that candidates are free to accept money from almost anyone, "but I lament their growing influence in campaigns. It's no longer A versus B, it's A versus B and all outside groups. You'll never know who's involved because it's uncoordinated and unbeknownst to you."

"I would've never thought that this would happen when I was running in '82, '84, '86, '89 and every year since," she said. Outside groups "sometimes spend more money for or against you than you are spending on your campaign. Somebody can come from outside, and then just out of the blue they start sending mailers and you don't even have time to respond."

"I know that politics in America at all levels has gotten a little more bitter and a little more nasty. Back in the day, in the golden age, people would get along and there was not all this bitterness and harshness with each other. What's happened is that the balance of power has shifted dramatically. Now in any one election, the other party can be in control, whether in the state House, in the state Senate, or here in Congress. Every election matters, and so we play a lot of 'gotcha' politics. It's a shame because—not that I want a complete takeover from one party in any chamber—but it means that every seat and every bill and every vote is important. You've got to be very careful because somebody is watching."

"I'm always fussing, even about a journal vote, even about an attendance vote. I worry all the time because every vote is sacred. Even though it may not be important to you, it's going to be important to somebody else. It's not that they have a special interest group, it's that everybody has somebody who has a special interest in special education or has a special needs child, or in health care. There are no throwaway votes."

Once she has voted, however, she feels no regrets. "I move on and live to make another mistake the next day. We all could be better people, but only God is perfect. We aspire to greatness and to be good, and if you are kind to people, then you'll meet them on the way down because we'll all go down."

If giving advice to prospective legislators, "I would say to them this too shall pass, and don't sweat the small stuff, but it all matters. It's not that it's all small stuff. I believe everything matters. If you're not here to make a difference, if you're not here to make someone's life better, then you've got no business being here. If you don't have the guts to make those tough decisions knowing that you are going to make somebody mad because whether you are in Congress, whether you are in the state House or the state Senate, you make tough decisions every day. You're going to vote yes, or you're going to vote no, and half the people are going to be angry with you."

"There are few motherhood-and-apple-pie issues where you can say, 'Oh, yeah, that's an easy vote.' Most of the votes are 'Ugh!' and you've just got to vote your conscience because you can't really reflect a hundred percent of your district. Here in Congress, we represent almost a million people. There's no way I can do an instant poll and find out how my district feels. So what I say to my constituents is, 'You know me. You know my record. You know what I stand for. I will vote my instincts and my principles, and then I have a responsibility to explain it to you why I voted a certain way.' They're not always going to like it, but maybe at the end of the day, they will disagree with some and agree with others. Or 'I don't agree with her but I understood why she voted that way.' So you have to have principles. You have to have a sense of purpose. You have to know why you're there, and that you're there to make a difference, to lead this world, to leave our state a better place than the way you found it."

Public service can be hard on family and personal life. "It's not easy to say goodbye and come up here and do your work and then go back home at the end of the week. It takes a special person, whether a spouse or significant other, to be in this crazy life. It's not easy," she said. "Being a mom and being a spouse and being a daughter and being whatever you do in your life, it gives you a good perspective because you're not just a public official. You're also a member of this community, and you have the same kind of issues that anybody would have."

Serving in Congress from 1989 to the present, she has almost matched the length of service of her predecessor. For all her accomplishments, she still sees much to do:

"Fix the deficit, balance the budget, stop spending money we don't have, get jobs for every American, help the Cuban people and all the oppressed people have freedom and dignity and human rights and free elections."

Ileana Ros-Lehtinen was interviewed in person by the author Mar. 14, 2014. Additional information came from an interview conducted in 2003 for the Oral History Project of the Florida Legislative Research Center and Museum and from two videos published on YouTube: "Ileana Ros-Lehtinen—Falling in Love with America," July 2, 2012, https://www.youtube.com/watch?v=v_4NcR35wHM; and "Ileana Ros-Lehtinen—Congresswomen Cuban Refugee Community," Oct. 12, 2012, https://www.youtube.com/watch?v=dVcnOeok4t4.

Corrine Brown (D)

First African-American woman elected to U.S. Congress from Florida, 1992 [a first shared with Carrie Meek]

Personal: Born November 11, 1946, Jacksonville, Florida; divorced with one child.

Education:

- Florida A&M University, B.S. (1969)
- The University of Florida, M.S. (1971)
- The University of Florida, Ed.S. (1974)

Occupation: Teacher at Florida Community College/Guidance Counselor/Owner: Springfield Travel Agency

Trailblazer Elections:

- U.S. House of Representatives District 3 (Parts of Alachua, Baker, Clay, Columbia, Duval, Flagler, Lake, Marion, Orange, Putnam, Seminole, St. Johns, Volusia counties) *Dem Primary* 1992
    - Corrine Brown (43.2%), Andrew E. "Andy" Johnson (31.0%), Arnett E. Girardeau (18.3%), Glennie Mills (7.5%)
- U.S. House of Representatives District 3 *Dem Runoff* 1992
    - Corrine Brown (63.8%), Andrew E. "Andy" Johnson (36.2%)
- U.S. House of Representatives District 3 *General Election* 1992
    - Corrine Brown-D (59.3%), Don Weidner-R (40.7%)

Figure 6.9. Congresswoman Corrine Brown described her first decision to run for office as a calling: "It's just like a minister has a calling. It's that you can help people. You can make a difference." She had an influential role model—Gwendolyn Sawyer Cherry (the first black woman elected to the Florida Legislature). Of Cherry, Brown said: "She saw something in me and she thought I should run for office. She got me interested in politics and opened doors for me." The two met while students and sorority sisters at Florida A&M University—Brown an undergraduate and Cherry a law student. Official congressional portrait of Congresswoman Corrine Brown.

THE CORRINE BROWN STORY

Corrine Brown owes her trailblazing path in Congress, at least in part, to fellow trailblazer Gwendolyn Sawyer Cherry. "She got me interested in politics and opened doors for me," Brown said. It wasn't just going to meetings but actually getting involved in causes. The two belonged to the Sigma Gamma Rho Sorority at Florida A&M University, and Cherry, who was a bit older and studying law at the time, got Brown involved in activities of the NAACP, the League of Women Voters, and other organizations. "She saw something in me," Brown said, "and she thought I should run for office."

Cherry would become the first black woman to win a seat in the Florida House in 1970, and two of her classmates, Arthenia Joyner and Alcee Hastings, would later win legislative offices as well. These alumni were but a few of the state's black leaders schooled at Florida A&M. "If it wasn't for Florida A&M, I would not be here because they gave me the nurturing and support that I needed," Brown said.

It was nearly 10 years after her graduation from Florida A&M when her mentor Cherry died in a terrible car accident (1979). Soon thereafter, Brown, a faculty member at Florida Community College-Jacksonville, decided to make her first run for office. "I'll never forget when I went to see my provost, Dr. Ezekiel W. Bryan, and I told him that I was going to run for the [Florida] House of Representatives. He looked at me like I was crazy. He said, 'Why would you want to do that? You've got the perfect job, you work at the college.'" She described her decision as a calling. "It's just like a minister has a calling. It's that you can help people. You can make a difference," she said.

Brown lost her first race in 1980 but ran again in 1982 and won. "A lot of people run one time and they think everybody knows you, but they don't," she said. "I never stopped running." She was reelected in the next four consecutive elections.

By 1992 she was ready to run for Congress in one of the four seats created after the 1990 Census. Three seats were won by black Democrats, all trailblazers: Brown, Carrie Meek, and Alcee Hastings. "We had not had an African American in Congress in 129 years," Brown said. The fourth seat was won by a Republican and native of Cuba, Lincoln Diaz-Balart.

Brown's district, drawn with African-American representation in mind, took an odd shape that included Jacksonville, Gainesville, Orlando, and Ocala. Of her eight opponents, Brown faced the stiffest competition in Andy Johnson, a white radio talk show host from Jacksonville. Brown defeated him in the primary and the runoff, and then won the general election in November. After the U.S. Supreme Court ruled in 1995 against race as a predominant factor in redistricting, the Florida Legislature redrew the district. Brown won in the redrawn district, despite its smaller number of blacks.

In Johnson, Brown faced an opponent who seemed to relish running for office. He had lost to trailblazer Arnett Girardeau for a Florida House seat in 1976, got elected to the House in 1979, lost again to Girardeau for a Senate seat in 1982, and challenged Brown for the congressional seat in 1992. "Oh, God, it was a tough race," Brown said. Johnson "thought he could represent us just as well [as a black person], so that was fine. But it was a real tough race because that's all he did on his radio [show], run for office." It wasn't racist, Brown said, maybe just "obnoxious."

During that same time, Brown also faced a candidate who owned a black newspaper. He claimed that he had been giving jobs to the community, but he printed only "police reports and stuff like that," she said. "It was difficult running against people that controlled the media."

"I really view the media as the fourth branch of government," she said, and that's something that minorities need to master. The new Internet media may provide the opportunity. At any rate, "you have to come up with innovative ways to get yourself on TV or get yourself out there."

Media that she used included television news shows, radio, and newspapers. She received endorsements from papers in Orlando, Daytona, and Gainesville, but not the *Florida Times-Union* in Jacksonville. She found it irritating that the *Times-Union* would not only withhold its support but also hoped someone would run against her. "Here I get 80 percent of the vote or whatever, and you're talking about you want somebody else to represent the district?!"

Perhaps her most important way of "getting out there" is attending church services. "Even to this day I try to do two services every Sunday," she said. People often ask: "You mean they let you just come in the services?" She responds, "I don't just come during election time. I come all during the year, and I stay through the services." She visits different denominations and makes the rounds in different cities. "I don't just go in the services and wave. I mean, I stay the entire service." She compared her church participation to the practice by others of going to civic groups such as the Rotary Club. "My people go to church," she said. Her strong support from black churchgoers is a far cry from what she experienced during her first run for office: "This minister told me that whenever possible he liked to support black men. I told him 'Well, that's nice but in our small community, we need to support whoever wants to run.' And I made it my business to carry [win] every house around his church."

She dismissed those who question whether political matters belong in church. For example, when someone on the U.S. House floor, who claimed to be a churchgoer, said there's no politics in the church, she retorted, "What church you come from? Every church has politics in it."

When she first ran for office, her daughter Shantrel, who was in high school at the time, said to her: "Now how am I going to feel if you lose? I'd be embarrassed to go to school." Brown suggested that she help by going door-to-door. That worked well

Figure 6.10. In reflecting on changes in campaigning, Congresswoman Corrine Brown admitted she was constantly devising inexpensive and creative ways of reaching voters—from passing out lollipops and candy bars with her name on them to a photograph of herself with President and Mrs. Obama. "One of the things I learned is that you've got to pass out something they're [voters] going to keep." Photograph courtesy of Corrine Brown.

because her daughter could visit more homes in the same amount of time. "If I go, they've got to talk with me," Brown said. On one occasion in Gainesville, her daughter went to a house where people were sitting on the porch. She introduced herself and described how her mother worked for them. "When she walked away, all she could hear was 'Corrine does this.' 'Corrine does that.' So she knew my commercial got to them," Brown said.

Brown's mother, a beautician, helped campaign by inviting customers in beauty salons and barber shops to sign petitions. "A petition drive is very good because it makes you get grassroots organized," Brown said. Circulating petitions at other local functions, including flea markets, gets a candidate engaged in the community and can be especially effective for those with little funding.

"I didn't have a lot of money, so I used to give out lollipops [with my name on them]," she said. For Valentine's Day one year, a woman pasted Brown's photo from campaign literature on 20 candy bars.

"One of the things I learned is that you've got to pass out something they're going to keep. I don't give anything out that they're going to throw away," she said. Examples of such keepable tokens included Jacksonville Jaguar schedules, college football schedules, and church fans. In fact, a man saw her fans at a funeral and remarked, "I don't know who she is, but she's coming." One especially popular item was a photograph of Brown with President and Mrs. Obama. "We printed at least 50,000 of them. People love that picture," Brown said.

As a black woman, Brown found it difficult to raise money. "The idea of going into a room and sitting up there five hours making calls, asking for money, I don't like doing that. Because you're either doing that or you're serving, and I prefer to serve," she said. It's different when groups drop by her office and leave contributions, but if you're making calls from the Democratic Club, "then you're not receiving people." Because money is so essential in politics, "it's perceived as a weakness when you don't have money," she said. "I have had to try to come up with creative ways to raise money."

She did that by hosting theater parties. "I get about five people to give me $100, or whatever [the rental price] is. We buy the theater and then I invite [people] to go to the movie." Brown passes a basket, and the audience members give whatever they want to give. "So it's a date night with me. We did it for Valentine's, and we do it for all of the great movies that we like to watch."

One thing she learned from the Obama campaign was that people with low or fixed incomes would give him five dollars a month. "I'd never thought they could afford to give me anything," she said. "So I never asked them. I just didn't feel like they could afford it."

Funding is critical, considering the huge amount of money required nowadays to run a campaign. When Republican Jennifer Carroll challenged Brown in the early 2000s, "she had a million dollars, and as usual, I probably didn't have $100,000. However, I had [President] Bill Clinton," Brown said. "Clinton came to Jacksonville at 2 o'clock. I mean, it was packed. People took their kids out of school, everything. He said, 'They brought me in early and I traveled around, and I saw those big billboards [showing Carroll] all dolled up, you know, those glam shots. I want to clear something up before I begin.' He said, 'Corrine is the prettiest one in the race.' That's Bill Clinton," Brown laughed. He also said, "In addition to that, when we see her coming, we just say give her what she wants." "Well that was the end of the race," Brown said. "They had a million dollars, I had Bill Clinton. So that was a great equalizer."

Watching political celebrities on stage or screen gives some people the idea of running for office. "A lot of young people, they only see your name in the paper, or they see you on TV," she said. What they don't see is the work, the grind, and the preparation. "You've got to know how to start it and take it to the end. And that is not glamorous." Moreover, potential candidates need training. She herself had attended boot-camp-type events put on by the Democratic Party and Congressional Black Caucus for candidates. When Alvin Brown, an African American, ran for Mayor of Jacksonville, "I told him he had to go to boot camp before I would support him." Not only that, she expected him to go to City Council meetings and sit in on committee and subcommittee meetings. "I don't have time to train you," she said. "I think it's very important that you know why you're running and the dos and don'ts of how to run."

When people approach Brown about their interest in running for office, she asks them, "Well, what do you want to do? Why do you want to be in the room?" Knowing why is important: "You're not just in that room because you're smart, because you're good looking. You're in that room to make a difference."

"I do think over the course of my career, I have made a difference just being in the room." As an example, she described how she obtained funding for a program

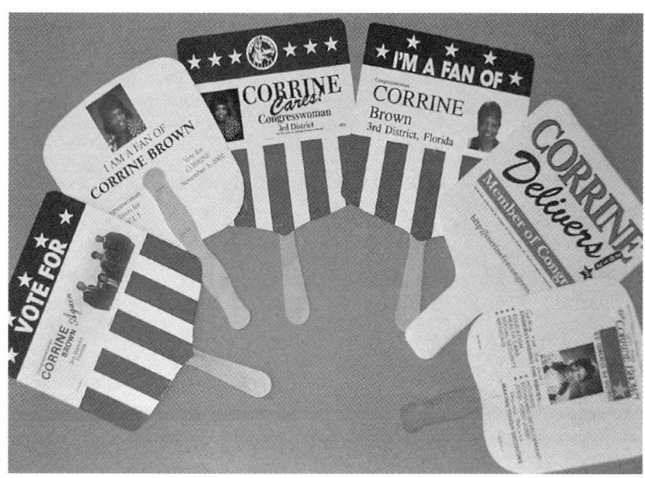

Figure 6.11. Corrine Brown passed out fans like these in churches when campaigning for office. "My people go to church," she said. "I don't just come during election time. I stay through the services." She was elected to Congress in 1992, the same year Carrie Meek was elected, making the two of them the first black women from Florida to serve in the U.S. House and friends for life. Fans courtesy of Corrine Brown; photograph by Susan A. MacManus, 2014.

at Florida A&M University. Congress had just killed funding for the supercollider, and it seemed that NASA might be next. "A lot of people from NASA were coming to talk to me. I had done my homework. I said, 'Well, get those people from California to vote for [your funding] because that's who you've given [all the math and science program monies to].' They said, 'We've got to have your vote.' And I said, 'Well, the only way I will give you my vote is that the Presidents from FAMU and Bethune-Cookman and the University of Florida give me a call.'"

The next Monday morning, she received a call from Dr. Oswald P. Bronson, President of Bethune-Cookman College. He said, "Corrine, you made me somebody today." Sure enough, NASA had called him and asked for his help [and told him he needed to call her]. A little while later, she received a text from Dr. John Lombardi, President at the University of Florida, saying, "Let's give them [NASA] one more chance." Then the phone rang. It was Dr. Frederick Humphries, President of Florida A&M: "Corrine, I'm in town. Where do you want me?" "He came to my office and we called NASA and they gave FAMU a program for five years, where they worked with their kids in math and science. So I decided to vote for NASA. When I'd made that decision, I went to my colleague, Sanford Bishop [Jr.] from Georgia. I asked him to vote with me because I'd been voting with him on peanuts. It passed by one vote. One vote saved it."

Brown connected with college presidents and other influential leaders through community involvement, beginning with her college days and continuing through her education career. While a student at Florida A&M, she worked in student government and for the band director's wife. After graduating, she taught at Edward Waters College in Jacksonville, Florida State College in Jacksonville, and the University of Florida. She also worked with women's groups and served on a number of boards.

Campaign issues "really don't change," she said, citing education, health care, and the economy. The key is "whether or not you work with the community, with the community needs." "I mean, I've been here. They get to know you, they know that you care about them." When Democratic campaign strategist David Heller came to Jacksonville to begin working on her campaign, he asked, "How are we going to get people to know you?" She told him, "David, they know me. Everybody knows me." He looked doubtful. She added, "Now I don't know that they like what they know, but they know me." They made a bet. Seeing a police car with white police officers nearby, he went up to them and, pointing to Brown, asked, "Do you know that lady?" "That's Corrine Brown," they said. So the real question is not whether people know you, she said, but rather "how to get them to know what I want them to know."

She stays in touch with community needs by going home to Florida every weekend. Staying in Washington can be a big mistake. She explained how one Christmas she encountered a colleague in a Washington, D.C., gift shop. No, he said, he wasn't going home for the holidays. "I mean, you're talking about Christmas and you are here?" she thought to herself. Meanwhile his opponent was busy in the district, shaking hand and making speeches. The congressman lost that year.

To her, a politician who understands the need to continue making human contact is Republican-turned-Democrat Charlie Crist, a former Governor who ran again for that post in 2014. "I went to a football game at the University of Florida, and everybody was there," Brown said. "He hugged me, he was soaking wet. He had kissed every baby and shook every hand."

In addition to staying in touch, she gives "personalized service," she said. As an illustration, she described two incidents that occurred at the airport. In one incident, "this white lady came up to me, and she says, 'My daddy who lived over in Palatka, he's dead now, but he told me to always vote for you.'" He had had a problem with the Veterans Administration that Brown got resolved. Another woman working in security thanked Brown for recommending her son to West Point. "At one time, unless your daddy was a banker, you didn't get recommended to West Point," Brown said. "I don't care that whether they're black or white or whether they're rich or poor," all requests get personalized service. "That's something they've never had before. Never had before. This is their Capitol. This is their White House. And so they need to feel that government is a part of them. That is the real problem."

One issue in which she felt the government has worked against people is the "stand your ground" law in Florida and other states, which allows people to defend themselves against perceived threats. The law generated national attention when a young black man, Trayvon Martin, was killed by a neighborhood watch volunteer, in Sanford, Fla., in 2012. "People don't feel that the government works for them when you're talking about the way things are going," Brown said.

Another issue is direct filing. The direct file process gives prosecutors the discretion to file criminal charges against juveniles directly in criminal court.[12] "We have a 70 percent increase in direct filing of black youth in Duval County. Well, they're no worse than the youth in Tampa or Miami," she said. She talked to a judge who had a program that held juveniles accountable for their wrongdoing, without branding them as felons for life. "Do you know the prosecutor sent the money back, wouldn't put one kid in the program?" It took a phone call, but "the next day I had somebody over there. Personalized service."

Issues like these make many blacks believe the government is not on their side. "I feel that when America gets a cold, the African American gets pneumonia and now we're on life support," she said. While sensitive to issues affecting minorities and women, "I just feel like if you work with the major problem, you'll help all of the people." Two examples are Head Start and the National School Lunch Program. "I care about all of the children. I don't care what color they are," she said. "If you don't have that lunch or that breakfast, you can't learn. One of the reasons we started the program was because the military said that our people weren't strong enough to go in battle because they didn't get the right food in the richest country in the world."

Working together with congressional colleagues has become challenging in recent years. "The difference between Democrats and Republicans is that if we had shut down the government and caused a loss of 29 billion dollars [in revenue over the next 10 years], we would all be indicted and it would be in the news every day, every moment," she said. She was referring to the GOP's attempt to block Obamacare, which could have partially shut down government in the fall of 2013. "But Democrats ain't that way," she said. "We're too nice, and a lot of times they take kindness for weakness. I mean, we want to get something done. We want to work together, and they have no intentions of doing things like that."

One exception was Republican Congressman Bill Young (1971–2013). "He was from the old school. He believed in getting things done," she said. "He was a kind man. I'll never forget he helped me with the courthouse in Orlando." It happened to be under construction in April 1995 when two conspirators bombed a federal building in Oklahoma City. Architects "had to turn it around because the way it was [off I-4], you could shoot right in," she said. Consequently, the cost ran $100 million over budget. "He worked with me to get the additional money we needed."

Perhaps Brown's most reliable source of support came from Carrie Meek, who shares the trailblazer title as the first black women from Florida to go to Congress. Until 2003, when Meek chose not to run again, the two worked together on issues and built a strong friendship. They stuck together "because there was just the two of us," Brown said.

They also share many of the same values—hard work, tenacity, compassion, and humility. "Black women work harder because we see being elected is like a calling. And so we serve, we're servers. And no matter how big or important you are, you have to go home and wash your laundry. That keeps you humble. You know, men go home, their wives do their laundry. We do our own."

Like Meek, Brown believes her path to Washington, D.C., came from a higher source. "I've always known that it was God. Yeah, it was the grace of God that brought me all the way to the United States Congress."

Corrine Brown was interviewed by the author Apr. 15, 2014, and participated in a joint interview with Carrie Meek Apr. 21, 2014, also conducted by the author.

Lincoln Diaz-Balart (R)

First set of brothers since 1890s to serve in Florida Legislature, 1988
First Cuban man elected to the U.S. Congress from Florida, 1992
Personal: Born August 13, 1954, Havana, Cuba; married with two children.
Education:

- American School of Madrid, Madrid, Spain (1972)
- New College of Florida, B.A. (1976)
- Case Western Reserve University, J.D. (1979)

Occupation: Lawyer
Trailblazer Elections:

- U.S. House of Representatives District 21 (Part of Dade County) *Rep Primary* 1992
  - Lincoln Diaz-Balart (68.6%), Javier D. Souto (31.4%)
- U.S. House of Representatives District 21 (Part of Dade County) *General Election* 1992
  - Lincoln Diaz-Balart—*Unopposed*

Figure 6.12. "It was always my dream to be elected to Congress," said Lincoln Diaz-Balart. His dream came true in 1992 when took office as the first Cuban-born man in the U.S. House of Representatives. Once a Democrat, he switched to the Republican Party in 1985 after becoming disillusioned with Democratic presidents for not decisively stepping in to "end the Castro nightmare." He had earlier served in the Florida House and Senate. From the Library of Congress, https://www.loc.gov/rr/hispanic/congress/diazbalart.html.

THE LINCOLN DIAZ-BALART STORY

"It was always my dream to be elected to Congress," Lincoln Diaz-Balart said. He achieved that dream in 1992, becoming the first Republican Cuban man elected to Congress from Florida. Before retiring 18 years later, in 2011, he accomplished key legislation that benefitted fellow immigrants—and became the first Hispanic appointed to the powerful Rules Committee.

His dream began when, as a six-year-old, he and his family had appealed for help in obtaining green cards from Congressman Victor Anfuso of New York.[13] "I knew how he had helped our family," said Diaz-Balart. "I knew, even as a child, the importance of being a member of Congress."

His father, Rafael Diaz-Balart,[14] had been a legislator in Cuba, and the two always talked politics when they were together. "My father never left Cuba spiritually and in his heart." At the same time, his father was "very nomadic" and the family was always moving. In the last decade of life, his father divided his time between Miami and Madrid.

Diaz-Balart came to love Miami because it was the home of his maternal grandparents, Juan Caballero and Maria Brunet. "I loved spending vacations with them, and they really are like my second parents." It was only natural then that after attending New College in Sarasota, Fla., and law school at Case Western Reserve University in Cleveland, he and his wife settled in Miami.

As a young lawyer in 1979, Diaz-Balart immediately got involved in politics, first as a member of the Young Democrats. "The Cubans who had arrived here in 1959, 1960, the overwhelming majority supported Kennedy in the election in 1960 because Kennedy criticized Nixon for not being tough enough and not doing enough to help the Cubans who were fighting against Castro."

Support for Kennedy did not last long, however. If the President had been Lyndon Johnson, Dwight Eisenhower, or Richard Nixon, "I'm convinced that Castro would not have survived," he said. Kennedy "had various opportunities to decisively step in and help the Cubans and end the Castro nightmare, but he did not. So it's ironic that we were rooting for Kennedy."

He switched to the Republican Party in 1985, three years after losing to Republican Humberto Cortina for a seat in the Florida House. "I felt very uncomfortable as a Democrat. But it wasn't just me—millions of Democrats changed." Many American voters had become disillusioned with President Jimmy Carter (1977–81) and turned to Ronald Reagan, who had also started out as a Democrat. "His language was genuinely welcoming," Diaz-Balart said. He also admired former Democrat Jeane Kirkpatrick,[15] who served in Reagan's Cabinet and became the first woman Ambassador to the United Nations.

Diaz-Balart began his steady climb to Congress, first with his election to the Florida House in 1986, then to the Florida Senate in 1989, and finally to Congress in 1992. He was elected to Congress with three other Florida trailblazers: Carrie Meek, Corrine Brown, and Alcee Hastings. Ileana Ros-Lehtinen was already there, having been elected in 1989.

"The Voting Rights Act really made possible my political career," he said. That 1965 federal law and subsequent amendments prohibited racial discrimination in voting and division of districts that prevented the election of minority candidates. That was done with African Americans who generally voted Democratic and with Cuban Americans in South Florida, for example. "These last 40 years in American history, I'm convinced that the Voting Rights Act was a very positive step forward because it really made possible the election of a number of minority candidates."

Congress had passed the Voting Rights Act, and its predecessor, the Civil Rights Act of 1964, because of President Lyndon Johnson. "Johnson was an extraordinarily successful President," said Diaz-Balart. Having read the fourth volume of Robert Caro's biography of Johnson, Diaz-Balart was impressed with the President's "brilliance as a strategist, as someone who would get things done in our system."

He based that admiration on his own experience as a member of the Rules Committee in Congress. "Remember, the Rules Committee prepares the agenda for the next day on the House floor and sets the terms of debate for all the bills." If a bill has gone through all the committees of jurisdiction and gets stalled in the Rules Committee, a member can still get it to the floor by using a parliamentary procedure called a discharge petition. With enough signatures, the member "can take it away from the Rules Committee and go straight to the floor without amendments, and it will get 40 minutes of debate."

President Kennedy's civil rights bill got stalled. President Johnson—upon taking office after Kennedy's assassination—decided to use the discharge petition to go around the Rules Committee. Its chairman, Howard W. "Judge" Smith (D-Va.),[16] opposed the bill. "He put it in a drawer," Diaz-Balart said. To get it to the floor, Johnson needed 218 signatures, ordinarily an impossibility, "because it's basically an instrument that allows the minority to show that they're doing something." But "the majority doesn't give away its prerogative over the floor to the minority."

What did Johnson do? "He calls [Democrat Richard W.] 'Dick' Bolling of Missouri, who was a lone wolf, a maverick. He says, 'Dick, I need you to file and start getting signatures. I'll put the whole power of the White House behind you, and I'll call myself to get signatures for the petition.' Think of that! Then Johnson himself starts calling folks, 'I need you to sign the discharge petition.' Then he goes to the Republicans and he starts making speeches: 'You're the party of Lincoln, the founder of civil rights, and the liberator of the slaves.' At first the Republicans didn't want to sign because Judge Smith shared power with the Republicans and the conservative Democrats." Eventually, however, Judge Smith was persuaded to release the civil rights bill to the floor, and it passed.

Johnson "was a master legislator," said Diaz-Balart. "I don't agree with some things he did, but I recognize that he was a very effective President. I felt affinity toward him and especially toward people like Scoop Jackson[17] and the strong, pro-defense, anti-communist Democrats. That all changed when the Vietnam War came and then [George] McGovern[18] took over the Democratic Party and they became isolationists and they became something completely different."

Just as civil rights legislation in the 1960s had made it possible for him to run for office, radio made it possible to reach out to voters in the 1980s. "Traditionally, Cubans and Cuban Americans get their information from the radio. They listen to the radio more than anybody I know, more than any other nationality. Radio was key." In particular, radio commentator Armando Pérez Roura[19] "was instrumental in allowing us access to the radio to get our message across, just to talk about what our ideas were, our proposals, what was on our mind," said Diaz-Balart. "During my entire political career Radio Mambí was decisive. Armando would always let us call in and just say, 'This is what we're working on' and inform the voters."

The *Miami Herald*, which served as a major news source for English TV and radio, generally didn't cover his political activity. Consequently, "What I was able to do here in the state Legislature and in the Congress in those 24 years, and my constant battles and the fight for this community—to a great extent the English-speaking community never found out about." He recalled a statement made by former Miami Mayor Maurice Ferré in the early 1980s: "As long as this community depends on the *Miami Herald*, we will not be a community."

Diaz-Balart felt that when the *Miami Herald* endorsed him, it was because they knew he was going to win. In 2008, when it looked as though he might lose to former Hialeah Mayor Raúl Martínez, the newspaper endorsed Martínez despite corruption charges against him. That year Diaz-Balart won reelection to Congress by 18 points.

Once he was elected, *El Nuevo Herald*, a Spanish-language newspaper in South Florida, and reporter Maria Travierso provided good coverage. "That was a big breakthrough because then the non-Cuban community saw what the two Cuban-American members of Congress [he and Ros-Lehtinen] could do for the non-Cubans."

One early fight on behalf of his constituency was NACARA, the Nicaraguan Adjustment and Central American Relief Act of 1997. "That's where my community got to see not only where our heart is, but that we were really getting something important accomplished."

As he explained it, a significant group of Nicaraguans had begun coming to South Florida under the Carter administration and continued arriving under Reagan. They had deferred deportation under a concept called *color of law*, which meant that it gave the appearance of being legally right. "But they were progressively facing more concern and getting near to a point where they were going to be deported." In early 1997, Diaz-Balart and Ros-Lehtinen hosted a meeting with Republican House Speaker Newt Gingrich and the Nicaraguans. "At that time I started working on this legislation to get them legalized, to give them clear legal status—in other words, green cards."

Gingrich felt sympathetic but knew that any immigration bill would have to go through Rep. Lamar Smith (R-Texas), who chaired the Immigration Subcommittee. Smith "had been the author a year before of a major immigration reform that I and

Figure 6.13. Congressman Lincoln Diaz-Balart was greeted by a crowd of happy Nicaraguans upon his arrival back in Miami after having led the fight for passage of the Nicaraguan Adjustment and Central American Relief Act of 1997. Speaking for himself and other Cuban Congress members about the Act, he said: "That's where my community got to see not only where our heart is, but that we were really getting something important accomplished." Photograph courtesy of Lincoln Diaz-Balart, 1997. That photo was a gift to Lincoln by the late Cristobal Mendoza, President of the Asociación de Nicaragüenses Pobres en el Exilio. (He is in the photo in the crowd.)

Ileana had opposed because it took some steps that we thought were very negative. But Lamar hadn't sat down with me to talk" about the bill for the Nicaraguans.

In October, with the bill still in limbo, "I went to the Rules chairman, my dear friend [Republican Gerald B.H.] Jerry Solomon of upstate New York, and I said, 'The year is ending and I really need to get this heard and on the floor.'" Solomon asked the Majority Leader, Republican Dick Armey of Texas, for help. "Armey spoke to Lamar right there on the floor and said, 'You've got to talk to Diaz-Balart and sit down and reason with him.' Then a miracle happened because Lamar and I, within a few minutes, came to an agreement on legislation that ended up legalizing status for about 500,000 people. That was possible, that miracle was possible, because Lamar needed something. The legislation that he had passed the year before had been subject to a couple of court rulings which he disagreed with. So he needed to remedy, from his vantage point, the court rulings. That gave me leverage."

Diaz-Balart was able to get to the point of negotiation because he had worked long and hard for the prior three years on the Rules Committee. "That allowed me to acquire 'political capital' or 'pity capital,'" which means that "the leadership appreciates the fact that you're loyal, you're there until sometimes 2:00 or 3:00 in the morning," he said. "That attitude that I had, that respect, if you will, from leadership, especially Newt Gingrich, gave me leverage." It was a two-way street: "Just like they weren't giving me what I wanted without working it out with Lamar, they weren't going to give Lamar what he wanted without working it out with me."

Even with that breakthrough, there were details to work out with key members of Congress, including Republican Sen. Spencer Abraham from Michigan, chair of the Senate Immigration Subcommittee. Florida Sen. Connie Mack III provided "decisive" support as did Ros-Lehtinen. "I can't emphasize that enough, from the moment I got to Congress, Ileana was supportive. She was already extremely well known and respected, and she used that respect to help me. I'll never be able to thank her enough."

The next year, in 1998, he worked with Rep. Carrie Meek (D-Miami) to get a similar bill passed for the Haitians. He also persuaded the Obama administration to grant temporary protective status to Haitians after the 2010 earthquake.

On the issue of immigration in general, the challenge is "to be heard." As he explained, "there's so much static created by the immigration issue that unless and until that static is brought down, allowing the other issues to be discussed and allowing the communities to listen to the points of view of the Republicans, that challenge is going to remain." He said the static comes from "those who do not want the Republicans to get their message heard, to keep the message precisely from being heard."

"I still hope that immigration legislation can be passed, and I know Mario [his brother and successor to his seat in Congress] is working very, very intensely on this issue," he said. In 2009 and 2010, the last two years Diaz-Balart served in Congress, he helped found a bipartisan working group that drafted legislation, which he called "extraordinary" and "very persuadable for the people." "It's still there. If this issue ever gets to the floor, the work product of the bipartisan working group will be a great contribution to the legislation. It's a contribution in waiting."

Mention of Mario called to mind the brother's election to the Florida House in 1988: "The joy I felt when he got elected was by far more than the joy I felt when I was elected" in 1986.

"We're four brothers and we inherited different things from our parents," he said. "My dad was a masterful legislator and he only had a four-year legislative career in Cuba because then the Republic ended. But when I see Mario in action, I see a lot of the talent in my dad in him, and the ability to give credit to others." He likened that quality to a saying President Reagan had on his desk: "You'd be surprised how much you can get accomplished if you don't worry about getting the credit."

His eldest brother Rafael became a banker and consultant, and brother José, an anchor for the Telemundo TV network and for MSNBC. By the way, José "makes a point of not covering his brothers. It's part of his journalistic ethics," Diaz-Balart said. "He's very clear about the fact that he's nonpartisan, and I respect that."

His own inherited talent was "the love of public service" and the concept that politics "is the most noble of human endeavors," he said. "My father always said politics is a lay priesthood. He said unless you're willing to devote yourself like a member of the priesthood devotes himself to service, don't go into politics." It's a 24-hour-a-day, 365-days-a-year job. That concept was well understood and supported by his wife Cristina, a banker, who worked to help support the family from the time they first moved to Miami.

His most rewarding work in Congress was negotiating agreements. "A negotiated agreement is a beautiful manifestation of democracy." Most people don't understand

Figure 6.14. Lincoln Diaz-Balart attributed his political successes and those of other minorities to the passage of the federal Voting Rights Act of 1965. Button from the Library of Congress collection.

that, he said. "If you don't sit down with people who disagree with you, you can't get anything done in democracy." He contrasted that with a dictatorship, in which one person could have all the power.

Also rewarding were the relationships he developed with colleagues. He especially loved and admired fellow trailblazer Carrie Meek (D-Miami). "She was very busy and she was on the Appropriations Committee from the moment she got to D.C. Yet she was always pleasant, always upbeat. I have never met anybody with more charisma, in the sense that she always immediately filled you with optimism and joy, whenever you'd come across her, whether twice a week or twice a day. She would uplift us. She would uplift me."

He repeated his praise for Ros-Lehtinen: "I feel as though I have a sister in Ileana. She's wonderful and very intelligent. I don't know anybody in an elected office who will go out of his or her way to try to help you like she does. She helps her constituents like no one who I've met."

Although politicians get lots of criticism, "the most noble people that I've met, the most honorable and admirable people that I've met have been politicians." The bad ones are a minority. "In any human community, there are some bad people. But there's just so many good people in politics."

The most disappointing thing about serving in Congress was "being away from the family, thinking back to all the baseball and soccer games that I missed."

One thing he never got used to was fundraising. In other countries with parliamentary systems, party leaders get all the funding and make all the decisions, including who's going to run where, which means that citizens may not know who represents them. "In our system, you've got to raise money to get your message across," which means that citizens get to know who you are and can later ask you for help with problems.

"The negatives make possible the positives. When you want to get something done in the United States, when you want to lobby, for example, have your voice heard in Congress, it's not enough to go to three or four leaders because those three or four leaders can't tell the member of Congress how to vote. Our system, where the member of Congress is genuinely sovereign, representing a sovereign constituency, a sovereign people, is a system not reproduced anywhere else."

If things change in Cuba, he would like to go back: "I have a lot of good friends there, a lot of former political prisoners and people who I admire who I'd like to see." He would also like to see "where my grandma's buried, my father's mom in eastern Cuba, in Banes. But I'm not going to go back while the dictators are there. I have deep hope that this chapter, as long as it's been, is coming to an end soon."

"Old Fidel Castro will be 88 in August [2014]. He has been the brain for evil, and all of the decisions that his brother has made have been Fidel Castro decisions." He likened Castro's Marxist ideology to that of extremist groups such as the Taliban and Al-Qaida: "What do they have in common? They hate the United States." He attributed that observation to his uncle Waldo Diaz-Balart,[20] an artist in Madrid, who said: "The era we're living in now in history is not the era of left and right and the ideologies of the 20th century. The era we're living in now is what is your view of the United States?"

Retiring from Congress was "the toughest decision of my life," he said. "I can't find anybody who loves politics more than me and who loved it more since an early age." That decision was essentially this: "Am I going to be here in a very honorable way like Claude Pepper [Dem. U.S. Senator (1936–51) and U.S. Representative (1963–89) or Bill Young (Rep. U.S. Representative 1973–2013)], who I admire very much, or do I leave? And if I leave, when? It's got to be now. Life's finite, and so I want to go back to the law practice. It doesn't mean that I'm not involved in the issues that I care about."

When he told his brother Mario he was leaving, "I had no doubt that he would announce" for the same seat Lincoln had held [District 25]. Mario did, and he was elected. (Mario had previously held the District 21 seat but switched to his brother's vacant seat—a more heavily Republican and Cuban-American district.[21]) Lincoln, the older brother, "liked the idea of Mario representing my old constituency . . . It gives me great satisfaction because I know he's a great legislator and he's going to give it his all."

If asked for advice by a young person wanting to run for Congress, "I say get involved in the community and get to know the community. And that way the community will get to know you." He pointed out, however, that "You don't need to be an elected official to serve," he said. "There are so many charities, so many needs that you can help alleviate."

"Then, if you're interested in partisan politics, you can get involved in the political party and in campaigns and volunteering. You've got to learn so much in terms of how even elections work and campaigns work." What's more, he said, don't be in a hurry.

"When you hear that America is exceptional, you bet it is. Because I know it!" he said. The proof is his own life story. "If you have a dream and you work hard and you persevere, you can turn your dream into reality in the United States. But that's so difficult in other countries of the world. In other countries, they often ask, 'Where are your grandparents from?' In some countries, you don't even acquire citizenship for generations. Here you can be an immigrant and you can be a Congressman."

Lincoln Diaz-Balart was interviewed in person by the author June 2, 2014.

Alcee L. Hastings (D)

First African-American federal district judge in the state, appointed by Pres. Jimmy Carter (D), 1979

First African-American man elected to U.S. Congress from Florida since Reconstruction, 1992

Personal: Born September 5, 1936, Altamonte Springs, Florida; married with three children.

Education:

- Fisk University, B.A. (1958)
- Florida A&M University, J.D. (1963)

Occupation: Attorney/Judge

Trailblazer Elections:

- U.S. House of Representatives District 23 (Parts of Broward, Dade, Hendry, Martin, Okeechobee, Palm Beach, St. Lucie counties) *Dem Primary* 1992
  - Lois Frankel (34.6%), Alcee L. Hastings (28.2%), Bill Clark (27.3%), Kenneth Donald Cooper (5.2%), William Bill Washington (4.7%)
- U.S. House of Representatives District 23 (Parts of Broward, Dade, Hendry, Martin, Okeechobee, Palm Beach, St. Lucie counties) *Dem Runoff* 1992
  - Alcee L. Hastings (57.5%), Lois Frankel (42.5%)
- U.S. House of Representatives District 23 (Parts of Broward, Dade, Hendry, Martin, Okeechobee, Palm Beach, St. Lucie counties) *General Election* 1992
  - Alcee L. Hastings-D (58.5%), Ed Fielding-R (31.1%), Al Woods-NPA (10.3%)

Figure 6.15. Alcee Hastings was elected to Congress in 1992—the first male African-American Representative from Florida since Reconstruction. He attributed his victory, along with that of Carrie Meek and Corrine Brown, to redistricting and the drawing of majority-minority districts. When someone asked him if it was fair that the Legislature drew districts so that blacks could win, he replied: "Hell, yes, it was fair. It had been *unfair* for 129 years [when] they drew them so the blacks could *not* win." Official photograph, House of Representatives 111–112th Congress.

THE ALCEE HASTINGS STORY

When he was growing up in Seminole County, Alcee Hastings remembered that men would engage in *bolita*,[22] a popular lottery game imported from Cuba. "They were men who somehow or another had influence in politics, even though we were terribly segregated and they paid the sheriff and the local city person," he said. "I had an uncle that was involved in that activity and he commented to me, 'The one thing you have to understand is that politics controls everything about your life.'"

That statement influenced his views about education, economics, and race and stayed with him throughout his career as an attorney, civil rights activist, judge, and member of Congress.

Born in Altamonte Springs, he graduated from Fisk University in Nashville, Tenn., in 1958 as the Civil Rights Movement was gaining momentum. During those college days, "I worked for a sheriff candidate in his office. I was the only black person there folding letters and doing grunt work as a campaign worker with students from Vanderbilt [University] and Scarritt [and] Peabody [colleges], and I was the only one that was involved in that Davidson County Sheriff's race. The guy won, and I thought it was kind of neat. He was a racist but everybody else in the race was a racist—it wasn't anything new. I just picked the best of the lot and he won," he said. That experience was a matter of "cutting my eye teeth in real politics."

After finishing law school at Florida A&M University in Tallahassee, he came to Fort Lauderdale in 1963. "At that time I partnered with [W.] George Allen, who was the first black to graduate from the University of Florida." In those days lawyers could not advertise, and, knowing only five people in the town, "I determined that one good way to let people know that I'm here is to run for the Legislature. Well, it cost $84 to do that, and I gathered together the $84. Sure enough, the *Sun-Sentinel* ran a story with the headline, 'Negro Runs for State Legislature.'"

He didn't win, of course, but the technique worked so well that he used it again in city and state races. "The pivotal race that I think helped an awful lot of change in our state was the 1971 election in which Lawton Chiles became our United States Senator and Reubin Askew became Governor." Hastings and three other candidates ran against Chiles in the Democratic primary. This was the race in which Chiles gained media coverage for walking 1,003 miles across the state and earned the nickname "Walkin' Lawton."

"It was the hardest thing I've ever done in my life," Hastings said. "I knew that I could not win. And it didn't matter whether I had the magic bullet to solve all the problems—being black was going to be the [biggest] factor. Interestingly enough, I carried Alachua and Broward counties."

In that race, "I did a unique thing: I spread the word that someone named Hastings was my great-grandfather in the old sawmill town of Hastings up in Putnam

County. I never showed my face there, and I didn't carry the county, but I ran second in Putnam County just on the basis of name alone."

"During that election I got to know Reubin Askew extremely well," he said. "We would stand in corners at meetings, and folks wouldn't talk to either of us because we weren't popular." But Askew (D) managed to unseat Republican Gov. Claude Kirk by 14 points and went on to become one of the most highly rated Governors of the state. He appointed the first blacks to the Florida Supreme Court (Joseph Hatchett) and to state executive posts (Athalie Range, Secretary of the Department of Community Affairs, and Jesse McCrary, Jr., Secretary of State).

In 1977, Askew appointed Hastings to the Circuit Court in Broward County, and, in 1979, President Jimmy Carter (D) appointed him a federal district judge, the first African-American federal district judge in the state. In 1983, after more than a decade of service on the Court, he was indicted for perjury and bribery, tried, and acquitted. A new probe shortly afterward resulted in his impeachment and removal from the bench in 1989.[23]

"I was removed from office on a Friday, and I went to Cleveland, Ohio, to speak on Saturday, as I had promised the people that I would for a housing program. I went to Tallahassee, and on the *Today Show* I announced that I was going to run for Governor, but wound up running for Secretary of State. Then that Tuesday I was back in Dade County, and before I left the Dade County courthouse, I had three cases and I began the practice of law again."

Three years later, with new districts being drawn, State Rep. Peter Deutsch, a Democrat, "called me about 5 o'clock one morning from Tallahassee and told me, 'I see a race that's developing here, a district that you could win, a congressional seat.'" At first, Hastings was doubtful, but Deutsch persisted. "So I got involved then with the NAACP and we looked at the configuration and demographics. And I decided, 'Yep, I can do this.'" (Deutsch also ran for Congress the same year, was elected, and served from 1993 to 2005.)

In that election, "I had one hell of a race with Lois Frankel, who ultimately became Mayor of Palm Beach County," he said. Neither won a majority in the Democratic primary, forcing them into a runoff. "We had a knock-down-drag-out, and people would normally think we were bitter enemies, but as professionals we reconciled our differences in light of the fact that I was representing Palm Beach County. I went on then to become friends with her and actually participated in helping her to get elected. We now reciprocate in more ways than one." (Frankel was elected to the U.S. House in 2012.)

Hastings upset Frankel and easily won the general election in the mostly Democratic district. His victory meant that he became the first African-American man from Florida in Congress since Reconstruction.

That election had racial undertones. "Lois's people did a push poll and in the push poll they said, 'Did you know that Hastings was a crook?' A lady from Hallandale that became one of my biggest supporters commented, 'I don't know that he's a crook, but evidently you all think he is, so if he's black and he's a crook, I got my crook and you got yours.' And so she stumped for me."

"But here's the thing," he continued. "For 129 years blacks had been excluded from being able to be elected. Therefore they drew congressional districts that allowed for at least three African Americans to be elected and that was Corrine Brown, myself, and Carrie Meek. Someone asked me, 'Well, is it fair that they drew the districts so that blacks could win?' Hell, yes, it was fair. It had been unfair for 129 years—they drew them so the blacks could not win."

"It's sort of like when I became a federal judge. Someone asked me, did my being black have something to do with my becoming a federal judge? I said, 'Yes, just like being white had something to do with everybody else that became a federal judge at a given time.' What's so unique about that?"

In many respects the role of race in redistricting was the dominant factor in the election. "The news media, of course, talked about the squiggly districts and how much territory and what have you. But if you look at gerrymandering all over the country, including this year, politicians drew districts that they thought were going to be favorable to them, and it didn't seem to be too much of a problem. I started out representing five different counties, but upstate people were representing 14 different counties and that was all right, you understand," he said.

"Florida doesn't lend itself, I might add, to square districts the way Montana could, which doesn't have many districts anyway, but the square states geographically are easy to deal with. But in Florida with its peninsula, it would be very difficult, even under the fair districting formula, to draw unitary districts in other than in the metropolitan areas. So race matters. It always has, and regrettably it always will in my lifetime."

"Now I wish that was not the case. I wish people could see the content of folks' character and what have you. But even now, we did our own little mini study in Broward County and what we learned is that 20 percent of white Democrats do not vote for black people seeking public office. And these are the people we are seeing every day and participating with, and, I might add, are very white. They come to us and say, 'Help me get out the black vote.' And I say to them all the time, 'Well, when are you going to help me get out the white vote?'"

"From a transactional point and from an acculturating point, I believe that there are a number of people, white and black, who perceive that I am a good legislator and a dynamic force in politics writ large. So, toward that end, you would think that we would have come to a point where 20 percent of the white Democrats would think favorably about me. Well, they don't. And I haven't done anything other than try to be a good Representative. I represented them as well, I believe, as I have African Americans. So it will take time."

He campaigned in various ways, traditional and unorthodox. "Got in an automobile and went all over the state and did everything that I could. I made presentations at all the editorial boards. Shocked people by getting the endorsement of the *Lakeland Ledger*, the *Gainesville Sun*, the *Daytona Beach News-Journal*, and then the *Sun-Sentinel*. So I must have been making some kind of favorable impression."

"The reason I carried Alachua was I went to the University of Florida, and a young black fellow and a young white fellow that were in the student council took a liking to me and they took it upon themselves to assist in organizing. Well, we didn't have social media, but what they had was telephone and letter writing, and they contacted students at other schools—at Stetson and St. Mary's and places where you would normally not expect that a black person would be invited to speak. And so I received an invitation. I got 99,000 votes in that election and Lawton Chiles didn't get but 139,000 in that primary."

"A student at FSU did her master's thesis on that election," he continued. "It turns out there were 319,000 registered blacks and by all accounts she could only identify about 33,000 that actually voted for me. So the majority of my vote came from whites throughout the state, and I don't think it was as much a protest as that I was making noise and appealing to people."

"But I did some interesting things. For example, I learned that if you go to Tallahassee and you appear before the Capitol Press [Corps], you'll get your name popped out there around different places, as through the Associated Press and then UPI [news services]. So about once every two weeks I would drive to Tallahassee and have a press conference. Then I learned that I could call in to the Associated Press, and say, 'In Cocoa today Hastings says that he believes that we should power up the space program.' Well, hell, I was in Gainesville when I made that statement."

"It's sort of like in the old Civil Rights Movement. We used to issue press releases: 'In a mass meeting last night, Negro says such and such.' The mass meeting consisted of one white person that was a media person and Rev. Samuel George of the NAACP. We didn't have no damn meeting. But the press printed it as a mass meeting."

Another campaign pitch: "In those days, you could actually get paged at an airport," he said. "We had people call 10 airports in Florida every day and ask for Sen. Alcee Hastings."

He had to rely on such ploys because he had raised only $19,000 for the whole election, which was not enough for a full-fledged effort of printing and mailing literature and buying radio and TV ads. But he was quick to add: "No sir, I never did any dirty or underhanded or negative kinds of stuff."

The mere fact of running unsettled traditional political power brokers. In his 1971

U.S. Senate campaign, for example, the head of the Longshoremen, said to him, "Well, you didn't ask me about running for the United States Senate." Hastings replied, "I didn't ask my momma either. You go to hell. I'll talk to you later."

As he explained: "It was very confusing to them because they hadn't been accustomed to African Americans running statewide, and they certainly weren't accustomed to anybody 29 years old doing it. And so it kind of shook up the establishment in the black community as well as the white power structure."

In campaigning, he took advantage of his community involvement, such as membership in church, fraternity, Elks, and Masons, which he called "political infrastructure." His legal work also stood him in good stead. "I filed the original school desegregation case in Broward County. Well, almost anybody that was in town at that time from the children to their parents to the teachers knew who I was and knew that I was fighting for change. And I filed the juvenile delinquent desegregation case and sued hotels and restaurants about discrimination. That gave me a forum and I would attend faithfully to those duties."

"I say even now, when people talk about geography, I don't represent geography, I represent people. While it is true that there are parameters to the district, the more important thing to me is that we have good constituent services and that we help people, and my office is known for that. And it doesn't matter that I don't represent the people in certain locales, white or black. I try to do everything I can to help people."

Taking the oath of office in Congress brought back the memory of his impeachment. "I was coming off of being thrown off the bench, and having perhaps an historic impeachment—all of them are—but in its own right. It came after a not-guilty verdict.[24] Never in the history of Western civilization had that occurred." He cited a similar case of a Judge Cook in Australia, in which the Legislature did not consider impeaching him after he had been found not guilty in a court of law. "I still think that they should not have here either."

"However, having said that, my thoughts were how ironic: I am now in the body that said that I should be removed from office." Adding to the irony, he sits on the powerful House Rules Committee that determines conditions under which legislation is considered.

"Periodically I will run across people, you know, when you ascend to Congress or the Senate and you come from a City Commissioner, a Governor or a state Senator or what have you, you keep your title. So I have people that pass me that voted that I should be removed from office, that call me 'Judge.' I still find that very amusing."

"But the best way I could put it is my momma said when I was sworn in that she got all of her money back. By that she meant all of the sacrifices that she had made, she got all of her money back. So when I was sworn in, I was thinking about my momma and I was thinking about my daddy, who never went to school a day in his life and always told me, 'Boy, be your own boss man.' And I have fulfilled both of their

Figure 6.16. Alcee Hastings (*left*) shakes hands with South African President Nelson Mandela, with Congressman Kweisi Mfume and later CEO of the National Association for the Advancement of Colored People (NAACP) standing by. One exciting thing about being a Congressman for Hastings was "having an opportunity to be on the world stage and to make a difference." In 2007, he became the first African American to chair the Commission on Security and Cooperation in Europe—an independent federal agency that monitors human rights and democracy building. Photograph taken June 30, 2009. Posted on https://www.flickr.com/photos/repalceehastings/sets/72157620637813875.

desires for me to do better than they did. And hopefully I can instill in others, black and white, to do likewise, to try to leave the world a better place than they found it."

If asked for advice by a young minority person about running for office, he would say: "Broaden your horizons and don't get caught in niches. And don't commit to the notion that you have to stay in certain lanes. Try to grab knowledge. Read everything that you can. And don't ever say I am bored. If you're living, you can take a walk and watch insects and learn something. When you're about acculturating in a society and assimilating in a society, wherever you land, go to the home show, the dog show, the cat show, go to the country and western music and the blues and the jazz and the gospel and the opera, and don't limit yourself. When you limit yourself, when you say, 'Oh, I don't like hip hop,' then you are limited because you don't know what hip hop is and you have not broadened your horizons. Be a greedy reader. Read everything! I pick up stuff like the scientific magazines. One time I attended a marketing strategy for grocers. I just happened to be at the hotel—was waiting to speak [to another group]. I went in at the tail end of their meeting, sat down next to a gentleman, and made one of the largest fees I ever made as a lawyer by virtue of being willing to explore. Open your mind and keep it open all the time."

Having come out of the state and federal judiciary to Congress, he more fully recognizes that "when I vote, I'm carrying the weight of a substantial number of people. But you know, I don't even like to use the term 'I.' For example, people that work with me, I say they work with me, not for me. When I talk about the congressional district, if you looked at the sign on the door, it says, 'This office belongs to the people of the 20th Congressional District of Florida.' And you rarely will hear me say 'my congressional district.' It's the district that I'm privileged to serve and therefore I'm not too full of myself. I'm more into trying to get things done, and I don't wear titles all that well. I prefer to be called 'Al' or 'Alcee' than to be called 'Congressman' or 'Judge' or a lawyer or any of those kinds of things. I've always been that way. Therefore I don't get excited too much about too many things because there's always something else to do, and something else to be exciting."

The most exciting thing about being a member of Congress is "having an opportunity to be on the world stage and to make a difference." He mentioned, in particular, meeting world leaders like the Pope, Nelson Mandela, the Dalai Lama, Xi Jinping, Angela Merkel, Hosni Mubarak, the King of Jordan and his son, and King Abdullah. "Every Prime Minister in Israel since I have been in office, I've gotten to know personally. Now that's saying something, when you think about it." He said he could also call Sergey Lavrov and have him call back: "There's not many people who know the Foreign Minister of Russia on a first-name basis, and I've had that privilege."

Hastings has a voice in international affairs by virtue of serving on the Commission on Security and Cooperation in Europe,[25] an independent federal agency that monitors human rights and democracy building. In 2007, he became the first African American to chair the Commission.

The most disappointing thing about serving in Congress is "the dysfunction and the fact that people don't get to know each other as friends. We're like ships passing in the night. That's not only Democrats and Republicans, that's internal. We operate in little cliques and klatches. I don't like that. I believe that we should be a better people."

Also disappointing is "to have people more concerned about wealthy people than poor people. I just find that an anathema, in addition to the fact that people don't want to support the National Institutes of Health and the Centers for Disease Control. They want to cut back on the inspection of food and cut back on the quality of air and water. That is extremely troubling to me. And also those who would cut Early Start programs and Head Start programs and after-school programs. I've deemed them critically important for those who are the most vulnerable in our society, children and the elderly. I see that as a terrible disappointment that this institution is controlled by those who are the wealthiest in our society, be they Democrats or Republicans, and I think that that's horrible. Congress is returning itself to an elite institution. If it stays on the course that it is on now, then only the wealthy can afford to serve here."

"I feel much of my life has been involved in trying to bring a dramatic change to benefit black people and white people," he said. "But the upshot of it all is wanting to make a difference." In his unsuccessful race for the U.S. Senate back in 1971, "I wanted white children and black children to know that there really were African-American people who were concerned about their education and also concerned about the world balance of trade and ongoing circumstances in the lives of people as it pertains to housing, education and jobs. It has been my view, and still is, that the inseparable triumvirate of inadequate jobs, inadequate housing, and inadequate educational opportunities are what create the disparity that exists in our society as it pertains to race. I see that as a continuing struggle and not something that I will ever be able to finalize, but I do believe that I will have made a difference. That was my objective from the time that I had that conversation with my uncle about politics."

Alcee Hastings was interviewed by the author in a telephone conversation June 24, 2014.

Carrie Meek (D)

First African-American woman elected to the Florida Senate, 1982

First African-American woman elected to the U.S. Congress from Florida, 1992 [a first shared with Corrine Brown]

Personal: Born April 29, 1926, Tallahassee, Florida; divorced with three children.

Education:

- Florida A&M University, B.S. (1946)
- University of Michigan, M.S. (1948)

Occupation: Teacher

Trailblazer Elections:

- Senate District 36 (Dade County) *Dem Primary* 1982
  - Carrie Meek—*Unopposed*
- Senate District 36 (Dade County) *General Election* 1982
  - Carrie Meek—*Unopposed*
- U.S. House of Representatives District 17 (Part of Dade County) *Dem Primary* 1992
  - Carrie Meek (82.5%), Darryl Reaves (9.2%), Donald Jones (8.2%)
- U.S. House of Representatives District 17 (Part of Dade County) *General Election* 1992
  - Carrie Meek—*Unopposed*

Figure 6.17. Meek viewed her trailblazer role somewhat as destiny: "For me to get there [to Congress] and to try to break down some . . . discriminatory practices and . . . discriminatory laws was to me God's way of putting me there so that I could be there at the time to make a contribution. . . . I think I brought strength to the black community as a whole." Photograph from http://www.famu.edu/headlines/UserFiles/Image/cmeek.jpg.

THE CARRIE MEEK STORY

Congresswoman Carrie Meek, who served in both houses of the Florida Legislature, spent her childhood within walking distance of the Capitol in Tallahassee.

"I grew up one block down the hill on Van Buren Street from the Capitol, and those were the grittiest days of segregation," she said. "We were not welcome in the Capitol. The only time we got to even go near it was every four years when the Governor was inaugurated. My father used to call it 'when the Governor took his seat.' We were sort of like welcome at that time. But otherwise you could not see a black face in the Capitol. Now, if you saw one, it was probably someone who was a maid or who was a yard man. I never once thought in all of my life that I would ever enter that Capitol in any other way but in a capacity like that."

Meek entered the Capitol as a state Representative after teaching for 30 years, first at Bethune-Cookman University in Daytona Beach and later at her alma mater, Florida A&M University in Tallahassee.

In that first race, "the reason I won was because of the black church. Had I not been a strong church member, it probably would've been harder to get to be known as much as I was," she said. As a church member, "you weren't intimidated, by the so-called white community." It felt safe and respectful. "The strength was in the church, particularly in the African-American communities." But her status as an educator was a big factor in her victory.

Taking the oath of office in 1978 felt "overwhelming" and "scary." "Can you imagine me, a little black girl from Tallahassee where blacks weren't that welcome during those days? We were intimidated by the crowds and especially white people," she said. She had felt intimidated during the campaign: "You could feel the animosity in the room and wherever I was, it was particularly with the white Americans," she said.

Figure 6.18. One of Carrie Meek's role models, Mary McLeod Bethune, started a school for African-American girls that later merged with an all-boys school and became Bethune-Cookman University. The school gave Meek her first job out of college, as a basketball coach and biological sciences teacher. State Archives of Florida, *Florida Memory*, https://www.floridamemory.com/onlineclassroom/marybethune/photos/page2.php. Photo No. PR0075, ca. 1920.

Back then, African Americans were called Negroes, and violence against them was still fresh in memory. "I had a brother who was killed because of the hate," she said. One brother "had been jailed because he was a little mouthy and spoke out, said too much at the wrong time."

When she took office, she joined trailblazers Joe Lang Kershaw, who had been in the House for 10 years, and Gwen Cherry, who had been there for eight. Although they had blazed the trail for blacks, the path was by no means clear. The two were "given second-class citizenship," Meek said. "As a matter of fact, Joe Kershaw revealed a lot of things to me that made me cry," Meek said. He "was treated more like a boy than a man. He was able to pass one bill, as I recall, which they called the 'Cane Pole' [which allowed a person to fish with a cane pole without having to buy a state fishing license]. But Joe Lang, in himself, was a very smart man. He was not the kind of man that would've been given the treatment he was given," she said.

"Gwen had a much higher status, in that she had a law degree," Meek said. "She was very strong in terms of civil rights. She was a leader in the NAACP. So in my opinion, she was treated with much more respect, and she was a stronger legislator when it came to equal rights, so she was treated very well. She was a fighter. She did not cringe, she did not hang back. She was really, really a person who set the pace for what African-American men or women would aspire to in the Legislature."

Meek thought of Cherry as a role model. "I used to help in her campaign, and I thought that she was the kind of legislator I would like to be." She had introduced and passed significant legislation, including some affecting child labor.

Meek took part in the House debate on ratifying the federal Equal Rights Amendment, which Cherry had introduced. "I will never forget the fact that women came from all around the smaller cities in Tallahassee—women were against the Equal Rights Amendment—who said to me, 'You have no business up here. Why are you here? You have no business interfering in this,' as if this were the domain of only white women. So I said equal rights is a domain of all women, and I have as much right to participate in this as anyone." Women who took part in the struggle included Roxcy [O'Neal] Bolton, an avid feminist, and Democrat Elaine Gordon, who was elected to the Florida House in 1972. Florida never ratified the ERA. "There were fighters there, and of course I joined them in that fight," Meek said. It "was a privilege to be involved in that."

Among those opposing the ERA was Democrat Dempsey Barron, a conservative and long-time chairman of the Senate Rules Committee. Despite his stance on the ERA, Meek said, "I have a very good feeling in my heart for Dempsey Barron. He was the epitome of a good ol' boy, and a good ol' boy with power and with feeling. Dempsey Barron was very sensitive to the needs of African Americans. I think he had grown up around them. He knew what some of their struggles were." Unlike some Senators, he kept his word and would not trick someone into thinking he favored a cause when he didn't, she said. "Dempsey was an honest man and he was very forthcoming and I had a lot of respect for him."

Actually, it was Barron who set up the opportunity for Meek to win a Senate seat. She was in the House during the 1980 redistricting, when there was no Senate district for an African American. At that time, "we had over 104,000 African Americans in the central core of this city. Yet, their Senator was all the way across Biscayne Boulevard over in one of the islands on the Miami Beach side," she said. "This is really something to have all of these people not being represented when they have enough in the district to have a Senator," she thought. She showed a map to Barron, who also could not believe a white Senator across the bay represented so many blacks. He said to her, "Draw me up something and bring it back tomorrow morning." She did, and he brought it to his committee. "I tell you to this day, that bill would not have been heard had it not been for Dempsey Barron," Meek said. It passed in the Senate against the wishes of South Florida Senators, including Democrats Jack Gordon and Gwen Margolis. "Dempsey never put anything forward that didn't get any votes, and he had the votes."

When first elected to the Legislature, Meek represented a multi-member district (MMD) that included Hialeah, parts of North Miami, the inner city in Liberty City, and Overtown. "That was one person representing a broad array of different people. Many times they didn't have the same community of interest," she said. For example, "Hialeah was not interested in what was going on over in the central core of Liberty City. And down south, being an agricultural area did not have the same interest. Multi-member districts meant, however, that every Senator in the Florida Legislature from Dade County owed every member of every community something. That was the attribute or the good point of multi-member districts—that is, Gwen Margolis had to answer and Jack Gordon had to answer to African Americans as well as the people who lived in the environs in which they lived. That was an asset," she explained.

When MMDs were replaced in 1982 with single-member districts (SMDs—the one-person, one-vote principle), her constituents "were able to vote for the person they wanted, and that person was someone from the African-American community. They had not had that before." As she explained, "Naturally a person who lives in your own neighborhood would know more about your needs and be able to represent you better. It isn't that the others outside your district didn't try, but they had a much broader scope to try and cover."

Before election to the Senate, Meek served in the Florida House from 1978 to 1982. "It took me two years to really know what was going on in the House. It's very, very important to build some institutional capacity." By that, she meant knowing what went on before, what the statutes said, which government agencies handled which programs, and where the stumbling blocks were in the process. For example, "You may come there as a doctor or you may come there as a nurse, but you're not that familiar with state agencies that govern this. You don't know who HCFA (Health Care Financing Administration) is. HCFA sounds like a hiccup to you because you don't realize that that's a state agency that has a lot to do with health and the amount of money that goes into health programs."

Because that institutional capacity has to be developed, "I think term limits is a big mistake." Term limits can determine benefits to constituents. If you don't understand the transportation system, for example, your district may not get the roads or bridges it needs, she said. The same is true of health care. "On the other hand, I don't think that people should come to the Florida Legislature and stay 30 some-odd years. I think they should stay a reasonable amount of time, and on their own, move up to something else. [But] I don't think they should be mandated to move."

Like other legislators, she had to learn the process of filing a bill and guiding it to the Governor's desk for signing. "It isn't hard to file a bill if you researched it well and Bill Drafting has drafted it in a plausible fashion. At the same time, you should go to the other body and get someone else over there to file and sponsor the same bill." A lot of legislators will file bills but won't work them. They expect the bills to die. "So you have to be very intuitive about the people you get to sponsor your bills." When bills are assigned to committees, "you have to go and meet with the staff on both sides of the aisle," she said. "You have to write letters, you have to go and beg, you have to go and cajole to get your bill agenda'd in the committees."

Getting bills before committees isn't enough. "You've got to have some anecdotal information as to how this situation affects the general populace. You've got to have people who come up to testify who experienced this because legislators listen to people from their district." She gave an example of a child adoption bill she worked on. "Adoption, by the way, is one of the hardest kinds of legislation to get out of the Legislature," she said. People from all over the state who had been adopted came to testify because they wanted to know the identity of their birth mothers, information that is kept confidential. In such situations, it's important to get support from outside groups, like the PTA or trial lawyers, who deal with the issue every day, she said.

Another example was her experience on the Growth Management Committee. "There were people who just really wanted to fill Florida up with all kinds of buildings instead of knowing that the environment needed to be protected." In that instance, it was important to get testimony from people dedicated to protecting the state's water, land, and other resources. "You need proponents of what you are trying to do. If you don't, the enemies of the bill will come forward and kill your bill."

"If you can get that bill out of committee, you are doing very well because usually that's where most of the bills die." Amendments added by committee members in many cases can water down or dilute the bill's real purpose. Getting it out of the Rules Committee is critical. If stalled there, "you won't get your bills agenda'd no matter

Figure 6.19. State Sen. Carrie Meek meets with Rep. Elaine Bloom (D-Miami Beach) to plan a strategy for moving a bill through both chambers. Meek firmly believed that women sticking together could make a difference in the legislative process. State Archives of Florida, *Florida Memory*, https://www.floridamemory.com/items/show/21275. Photograph taken September 29, 1987.

how good they are," she said. Another tactic for killing a bill was to insert implementing language before it went to the Governor. "They took the Florida A&M Law School out of the implementing language. I got that passed when I was in the Florida Senate, and they took it out" and gave it to a study committee.

"One of the hardest fights is getting a bill that has passed committees to get ruled and made eligible for the floor." At this point, you must "still work to be sure that the President or the Speaker puts it on his or her agenda and brings it forward. And even after that, you have to work with the Governor's staff." A veto could happen because the Governor's staff "didn't really understand your bill or they did not feel it was something worthwhile. But if you find out early enough, you may be able to intercede and explain to the Governor's staff what this bill is all about," she said. "The lesson to be learned here is to follow that bill from beginning to end, never feel confident that the bill is going to be passed until it is passed and until it gets out of the House and into the Governor's hand."

As a side note, she explained "greasing," a practice used by the highest part of the administration to slip measures through the Legislature. "You know that it's destined to pass, and they're just putting it in that committee as a matter of procedure. That's all it is, procedure. You know when it comes, it's been greased and it came down from the Speaker's office or it comes down from the President's office and it's meant to slide through." In committee it may receive little or no deliberation, or it may not even go to committee. "The Speaker and the President, when I was there, had enormous power to get things done. Things that they didn't want on the calendar didn't go on the calendar. Things that they didn't want to get passed didn't get passed. Chairmen that they didn't want to have a nice office didn't have a nice office. And it just happened that way."

Meek found the House and Senate operated differently. "The House is a crazy place. I mean, you really have to be on your toes all the time," she said. There are so many Representatives, and they all have different issues. But "the House is a fun place," she admitted. "You get to know people from other areas real fast. That is, someone from the northern end of the state who has agricultural interests would certainly know the people on the south end because the delegation from Dade County at that time was the biggest delegation and it still is." Despite that advantage, "You could not get as much passed in the House as you could in the Senate. After all, you had more people to deal with than you had in the Senate."

The Senate "is a more deliberative body. That is, they deliberate longer on things and they get bills passed faster," she said. A bill in the House might be referred to several different committees, whereas a bill in the Senate would go to no more than two committees. Furthermore, a bill sponsor would have only 40 people to deal with. The Senate "also gave me a better chance for leadership. I got to be over an appropriation subcommittee in the Senate in education thanks to Democrat Gwen Margolis, who was then the President. Not only Gwen Margolis [1990–92] but Democrat Betty Castor [first woman President Pro Tempore 1985] as well. The two of them gave the women a chance to be chairpersons of committees. We had not had that kind of opportunity before those two women were in the leadership in the Florida Senate."

Another difference between the two chambers was that "it's easy to have a niche" in the Senate. "My area was pretty much education. That is, they sort of looked to me for things that were very, very substantive in the field of education" and in civil rights in general. It was also easier to reach agreement: "You don't have as many with whom you must negotiate to get a deal cut, and when I say 'deal,' these are good things for the people of the state of Florida."

Meek and trailblazer Arnett Girardeau started the Legislative Black Caucus in 1982 when both were elected to the Senate. "It was minimal, but at least we were recognized," she said. "We started for the sake that in numbers we had strength and we could articulate things better as a group than as just one person standing up on either side of the House." The 10 legislators in the House "were much stronger than we were, so we decided to get together and have a mutuality of interests and a mutuality of procedures the way we did things. We were able to get some things done by getting together and being able to reach out to the other legislators. They began to respect us as having a cohesive group that worked together instead of being bifurcated all over the place."

The real power brokers—and memorable characters—in the Senate included Rules Chairman Barron, as mentioned earlier, and W. D. Childers, a Democrat who had been there many years (1970–2000). "Dempsey was able to get coalitions between Democrats and Republicans." Jim Scott, a good friend of Barron's, represented the Republican side almost all the time. Dempsey had power "in such a way that whatever he wanted done on that Senate floor, got done, because he had this coalition of Democrats and Republicans."

Childers "was sort of an enigma then. He could reach out to poor people, and he spoke with a kind of accent that they speak in North Florida. He was just a good ol' boy and he would always help you regardless of what part of the state you were from. You could be from South Florida, he didn't care, if you felt strongly enough about what you were doing."

Democrat Curtis Peterson (1972–90, Senate President 1982–84) "was just the opposite," she said. "I won't say he was mean, but he was very hard. It was very hard to cut a deal with him." He chaired the Education Committee for many years, and "he knew it very well. And he was not one to want to meet you halfway. That's the only way I can place Sen. Peterson. He knew his field, he worked very closely with Dempsey. He was one of Dempsey's lieutenants."

One Senator who "never ever forgave me for having my feelings about civil rights" was Republican Richard H. "Dick" Langley, who was elected to the Senate in 1980. "He felt that that was something that he could not condone, nor did he respect my willingness to provide that kind of equity for African Americans." She always got along with Langley, "yet I fought him vehemently on all the issues he had against women and against African Americans."

Ken Jenne (Senator 1978–98) "was an outstanding Democrat, an outstanding moderate who did everything he could at all times to help everyone. He was one that didn't get caught in that partisan stuff," Meek said.

Two powerful Republicans were Senators Warren Henderson (1963–66, 1967–84) and Mary Grizzle (1978–92). Henderson "was the wittiest man in the whole Senate," Meek said. "No matter what you said, he was a standup comedian. But it didn't mean that he was any kind of a joke. He was able to combine his knowledge with being funny and being full of wit. Everybody liked him."

Mary Grizzle had power "because of her knowledge and her ability to just hold back until it was time to work," Meek said. "What made her good was her compassion, her sincere compassion. Mary was not a glad-hander. She was not a hot shot, you know, to grab people and pat them on the back. She was very bright," and she "was an expert in all areas of the Legislature." "I went to her when I was trying to pass a bill on comparable work, which would equate what women do to what men do. I was surprised to find out that Mary Grizzle had such a command of what had gone on in the Florida Legislature regarding women and comparable work. She was very, very thorough. She was very astute. She didn't talk a lot. She didn't stand up on the floor every minute. But whenever she stood, she was listened to."

Having a personal relationship with fellow members increased the ability to influence them. "They will listen to you, and you can badger," Meek said. "You never give up, you just keep badgering, badgering, badgering constantly bringing this to their attention. Sooner or later they say, 'Well my God, this must be very, very important,' and they will at least give you a chance to be heard," she said. "If you can be heard, you feel you've been treated fairly. You may lose, you may not have the votes, but if you're not heard before the committee, that means they're not even giving you a chance. That's why I think that a personal relationship at least gives you a chance to be heard and that's all you can ask for. You can't make people agree with you. You can't be angry because they voted against you."

At the same time, it's critical to know beforehand whose votes you have. "If you haven't counted them, you're in for a rude awakening." She remembered that as a freshman legislator, she put up a bill that would create a state commission on the status of women. "During those days, if they wanted your bill to fail, they sent it to Agriculture, but I didn't know that," she said. "I was just full of vinegar, I was just sure I was going to this committee with my first bill." She explained the bill seriously, and they listened. "They didn't say one word, and the minute I finished, Democrat Sid Martin [1974–88] said, 'We're going to call for a negative roll call on this little sucker—and he was using his best North Florida language—because we don't want these kinds of bills passing.' I was so crestfallen. I was about to cry." But after a while, Martin said, "I move that we reconsider the vote by which this bill failed." The committee reconsidered and voted it out. "So I thought then, all is not lost. I do have a chance up here."

"You can go to school for 25 years and not learn what you would learn in one session in the Legislature in terms of just human behavior and human dynamics," she said. "There are people in the Legislature who will tell you things that they know will not happen, but they do it to snooker you or to fool you. If you're not smart to the process, you will go along thinking that what you've already introduced will pass, when really it's going to have three or four different committees of reference on it."

Meek worked on several issues that strengthened equal rights for blacks. One bill prohibited the dismissal of people who had been active in the Civil Rights Movement from serving on juries. Another did away with limiting judgeships to only those who had already been judges. "That would certainly just protect the ones who were there and never gave an African American a chance to get in," she said.

She introduced some bills that, while they didn't pass, laid the groundwork for the future. One such bill, supported by the ACLU and the NAACP, would have allowed blacks to serve on juries. "It was sort of like I was a forerunner and it sort of softened the hearts and the minds of the Senate and the [House], and later on it passed."

Two of her successful, and hard-fought, efforts dealt with business. One required a set-aside for minority contracting to make sure that some money spent by state government went to minority-owned businesses. "There were people who felt that why did African Americans need a set-aside. Why couldn't they just be thrown in the general population of business people and let the marketplace take care of them?" she said. "But all the statistics showed that there had been very little business for African Americans. State business just had not gone to them." After a long fight, the bill passed.

Another effort created the Black Business Investment Board, in which funds were granted to assist blacks with capitalization of their buildings or businesses. She credited an outstanding lawyer in a Miami law firm with helping the bill pass. The man, known as Big John, "was what we would call a very, very liberal white man who stayed on the floor of the Legislature and worked very much with the Governor at that time to be sure that that bill passed." Another who helped was Frank Scruggs, an influential black lawyer with strong ties to the business community. It was the influence of such outsiders that civil rights moved through the Florida Senate.

A setback for African Americans, Meek said, came in November 1999 when then-Gov. Jeb Bush (R) issued an executive order for the One Florida initiative, which ended affirmative action in the state. She explained her opposition to the order by recounting her own tribulations with higher education. When she graduated from college at Florida A&M, a historically black school, she could not pursue graduate study at either Florida State University or the University of Florida because of a prohibition against blacks attending state universities. "Yet, my parents had long been citizens of the state of Florida, all my family, and there were African Americans all over this state who paid their taxes that went into higher education. It was very hurtful and very disappointing to me." Instead, for those who wanted a master's degree, the Florida Legislature would pay tuition and train fare to go out of state. "When you think of it, what they were doing was just shipping us out to prevent us from going to the state universities here," she said. She remembered the day in 1947 when she left Florida. From her house, she went down the hill to the Seaboard Railway Station on Gaines Street. "I wore a little derby hat, I had a little box with chicken in it, I had a little envelope with a $350 voucher for the University of Michigan." Going away to Michigan, where by the way, "I did get a superior education," opened her eyes to the unequal schools, including the lack of books and equipment, for children in Florida.

In a similar incident, Virgil Hawkins, a faculty member at Bethune-Cookman College, was denied admission to law school at the University of Florida in 1949, even though he had the academic and experience qualifications. He appealed to the Florida Supreme Court and lost. The Court then ordered the state to create a law school for blacks at Florida A&M.[26]

From Meek's perspective, then, "Florida has a very, very stricken history" on higher education for blacks. When the first fight for affirmative action occurred, "I was happy to see that Florida was going to follow the federal law to go with 'all deliberate speed' to be sure that schools and colleges were integrated. But of course, Florida dragged its feet on that," Meek said. "So you can imagine all the things that we went through back then." The experience left "rage in our hearts toward the way Florida mistreated us."

"When my son [Kendrick Meek, as a state Senator in 2000] took up the cause for affirmative action, it did not surprise me at all because he knows the history. I've told him what happened during those days, and he knows what's fair and what isn't fair," she said. When the Governor used an administrative act instead of going through the Legislature and getting input from people throughout Florida, "he chose, and I think wrongfully so, to wipe out affirmative action." She thought "he felt that he could do the job for higher education that the state university system has not. And I think it's leading to a dismantling of the higher education system in the state of Florida." Disturbing was the decision by University of Florida President Dr. John Lombardi to step down from the presidency in 1999, and the replacement of the state university system Board of Regents with trustees at each university. That change "leads to a kind of Balkanization of the university system. I think it's wrong."

Meek's experiences in education influenced her service in the Legislature, which "was not as much anger as it was caring, and as it was to being sure that equal justice happened." As an illustration, she explained that when she first went to the Florida Senate, someone had introduced an amendment to keep Vietnamese fishermen from fishing off the coast of Pensacola. "To me that was a gross wrongdoing. Why? Because the Vietnamese fishermen had some acumen in fishing, and they were going to keep them from fishing. That was wrong. So I came to that body with a strong sense of equal rights and a strong sense of what was right and what was fair," she said. Her background enabled her to assess what was right, "even just a tingling of it—I could feel it," and that sense went beyond race, gender, ethnicity, and religion. "Whenever I feel someone is being mistreated, I'm ready to fight for those people."

Her early work for blacks included Haitians. The reason was that Miami had more Haitians than any other place she knew of in the South. "I got to know the Haitian leaders, and they got to know me. I respected them for their leadership in their own country as well as here." That mutual knowledge and respect "had a lot to do with my early success in the Legislature," she said.

Another example of doing what she sensed was right was fair housing. Congress had passed the Fair Housing Act in 1968 and added amendments in 1988 that strengthened enforcement. "It had to pass the states before the states could implement the fair housing regulations, so that was fought very strenuously by many people" in the Senate and House, she said. It meant that landlords could no longer tell prospective renters they didn't have any space when they really did. In addition, the government "could send whites there to test it to see if there were space, and then African Americans and others who were kept out would be allowed. It's all a matter of equality, being fair and being equal," she said.

Of all the legislation she sponsored or worked on in the Legislature, she was proudest of Documentary Surtax Housing, which placed a small tax on commercial real estate transactions. It "brought about a whole different housing policy in the state of Florida," she said, because people who could not afford a house could now afford one. "Usually, the very, very poor get housing either through rental housing or through some subsidized housing," she explained, "but it's the middle income person, the person that I call the working poor who have jobs but still can't afford a house." The bill also contributed to economic development because it encouraged developers to build in areas where they would not have tried before.

The sales tax was another matter. "I felt that the sales tax was a regressive tax and particularly for the people I represented because most of them were poor or near poor. The sales tax was just a way of taxing them on the few pennies that they did have," she said. "Florida has a very poor tax base. It's one of the states in the nation that has no income tax. It has very little taxes when it comes to supporting its programs, and as a result of it, some of the social programs that Florida should be supporting they can't because they don't have the income base to do it." As a result, Florida ranks among the lowest states in the nation in the Medicaid program for children. Furthermore, women in the TANF (Temporary Assistance for Needy Families) program don't get full benefits. She voted against the sales tax in committee, but if the measure got to the floor, and if it contained earmarks that would benefit the poor and the near poor, she would vote for it.

By contrast, she supported the proposed tax on service transactions, "and I got hosed down real good for that," she said. "The business community certainly did not want the service tax. If you were one of the legislators that received most of your support from Associated Industries or some of the large business lobbyists [Meek did not], you could not vote for the service tax." Some legislators "started out with all good intentions of supporting the service tax, but they backed down. They took a walk when it came time for the heads to be counted." In the end, the issue "left blood on the floor." Many people were hurt by the controversy—"they either didn't come back or the business community really, really hit them very hard in terms of their contributions to their campaigns or to what they did for their community."

Apart from winning acclaim for her work on equal rights, Meek achieved notoriety for adding two phrases to the legislative lexicon: "Black Flag® dead" and "love it to death." The first one came about with a proposal to require Haitians to have identity cards "as if they weren't citizens," she said. "Any bill that I felt went contrary to equal rights or to people being treated fairly, I had this little saying: 'I want this bill killed and I want it killed Black Flag dead.'" Black Flag is an insect spray, she explained. "When you spray it on a bug, that bug turns its legs up and falls on its back," as illustrated on the front of the spray can. Meek also had a little flag with an emblem of the Jolly Roger on it: "I would wave this flag just before I got up to say something. It was just my way of adding humor to a situation that the amendment or the bill really was one that needed to be killed."

The second phrase, "love it to death," meant adding so much to a bill "that you just make it top heavy, that you know it's not going to pass," she said. "There is something that you want to add to it because you know if you add that to it, that no one will vote for it. So you're just loving it to death."

What she liked most about being in the Legislature was working for equality. "If you weren't successful the first time, if you kept upgrading their consciousness, consistently pricking them with facts, consistently showing them the disparate treatment, sooner or later [they would come around]," she said, "and this included people from the farthest end of North Florida all the way to Miami."

There came a time when being a woman and an African American didn't matter so much anymore. Meek attributed that to her hard work, the respect she earned among her colleagues, and "from not throwing the race card around every day." What's important in a body as small as the Florida Senate is the ability to get along with people. "It doesn't mean you have to give up any of your beliefs. Philosophically I disagreed with them on many things, but I respected their right, and they respected mine."

Balancing a part-time legislative position with an education career was difficult but doable, she said. At Miami-Dade Community College, where she had worked as a teacher and administrator since 1961, she gave up teaching classes every day because of legislative committee meetings. Her administrative duties gave her a broad view of community needs. "You understand policy better." In addition to addressing needs of schools, for example, "you understand why it's so important that day care workers have some regulations so that they will learn how human growth and development works on children," she said. You also understand health problems—"why it's so important that the populace should be educated, why they should have insurance, why they should be protected." In the Legislature, she considered herself a generalist "with a sharpened point toward education. Having been an educator, having been research-oriented, it was much easier for me to look into problems and be able to see problem solving," she said. She was also glad to work with the "extremely good staffs" in the Legislature.

"I was not someone in an ivory tower," she added. "An ivory tower educator in higher education would be unable to really know the needs of people" and unable to work with PTA groups, parent groups, and school boards. "You must be able to work with people in all walks of life to be a good legislator and be able to listen to them." In many cases, constituents have more experience in an area than does a legislator. "For a policy maker to feel he or she has a corner on everything is wrong. That's a one-sided person."

A young person thinking about running for a public office must have a base of support. "You just can't decide that after all, you're the big Oracle at Delphi and you know everything and you're going to run. You can't do that. You've got to have somebody who will say you'll do a good job. Or, I served with him in the military. Or, I served with him in the police department. Or, I served with that person as a parent in the PTA. I know that that person is honest, I know that person has integrity, and I know that person is unafraid. It really takes courage to be an elected official."

"Most of us run because we think that this gives us a better chance to help other people. That's why I ran." Helping one group sometimes hurts another one, however, and those it hurts deserve to know why you voted as you did. "You must explain to people, look, I voted for NAFTA [North American Free Trade Agreement] whether I was ill-informed or misinformed because I felt it would bring more trade to my state of Florida. It would provide more jobs. But in the end you can't do something without letting the other side know that this is important." So candor is a must.

Wanting to be helpful goes hand in hand with humility. "Because the minute you get there, if you're not careful, your head can just get bigger and bigger and bigger and the brain doesn't go to meet the head," she said. "It's important that humility follow that person into public office."

"It also takes a very, very thick skin," she said. "We all have egos, don't get me wrong. Everyone you see elected to office has an ego, otherwise they would not be there."

In addition, a legislator must find out what the facts are. "I think the entire ability to be a good elected official is being able to research and to find out what's going on and be able to try to solve problems, not make more problems," she said. "You don't have to be a college professor or a jet scientist to be a legislator, but you must be curious enough to find out how can this problem be solved which is facing you. So you must have some research skills."

Related to research skills is the ability "to reach out and ask people. You'd be surprised the amount of information we get from other people." Sometimes elected officials look wise because they carry a briefcase around, but their information comes from the populace. "My information on agriculture comes from the farmers. My information on communications comes from the communications industry. It doesn't mean that I have that kind of expertise." Sooner or later, a legislator learns what an industry is all about and how it affects people. But it begins with an eagerness to help others.

"You must have some integrity. That's very important because that teaches you that you don't lie to people and you don't misrepresent the truth, or you don't come forward and say one thing at this time and another thing the other time. So you must be courageous is the best word. That is, you can't just flop about, fish flop on one side today and tomorrow you're on the other side. The legislators, your other colleagues, will stop believing in you and will stop having you carry things and your word is not worth anything."

A legislator needs perseverance. "You must be very tenacious. You can't give up once you find out that that your bill is perhaps on the list to fail. There are other ways

Figure 6.20. Carrie Meek entered Congress at age 66 and immediately pushed an agenda that belied her southern accent and grandmotherly demeanor. "Don't let her fool you. She's not a little old lady from the ghetto," one Florida political observer told *The Washington Post*. She asked for and got a seat on the powerful Appropriations Committee, a rare feat for a freshman legislator. The framed clipping of Meek's accomplishment that appeared in the *Miami Herald* (January 5, 2013) hangs in the Carrie Meek-James N. Eaton, Sr. Southeastern Regional Black Archives Research Center and Museum on the campus of Florida A&M University. http://www.famunews.com/?p=2469.

of getting things passed other than through a bill. There are amendments. There are resolutions. There's more than one way to get the policy or the tenet across."

In a nutshell, legislators need "to have some causes and have a conviction on causes and know their constituency," she said. "They've got to know the people they serve when they go up there, they must have conviction and a conscience and most of all they must be smart."

"America is a wonderful country," said Carrie Meek. In "what other country could a woman from my background get to the Congress where I can make laws and set regulations that influence the entire country and the entire globe?"

After 14 years in the Florida Legislature, Meek was elected to Congress in 1992 from a newly created minority-majority district in Miami. She and fellow Democrat Corrine Brown share the trailblazer honor as the first black women elected to Congress from Florida.

In the wake of the 1992 redistricting, Meek ran for the seat long held by Democrat Bill Lehman (1973–93). She won in the Democratic primary and faced no opposition in the general election. In an astonishing feat for a freshman legislator, she contrived to get a seat on the powerful Appropriations Committee. One of her first tasks was securing federal aid for areas wracked by Hurricane Andrew.

The first way to make things happen, she said, "is to get along with the people who were there, to understand how you got here, and then get other people to work with you. I don't think there's one African American in the Legislature that doesn't understand that it takes more than African Americans to make things happen in the Florida Legislature or in the United States Congress. It takes reaching out. It takes working with others. It takes educating others."

Getting along with people, researching the issues, working together in caucuses, overcoming obstacles—these were skills she brought to Congress. "If you can get past the Florida Legislature, you can go into any legislative body," she said. "Congress is no big deal to me because I know the process and I know what it takes to make things happen. I learned all that in the Florida Legislature."

Besides hurricane relief, she managed to bring millions of dollars to South Florida colleges, seaport and airport projects, mass transit, and jobs and housing programs.[27] On a national level, she sought to create jobs, improve opportunities for black entrepreneurs, and cover household workers by Social Security. She worked with Republicans for years to increase research funding for lupus, a chronic autoimmune disease that killed her sister.

She was able to accomplish so much because "I have a strong intuition about people and which way I should go," she told a reporter after leaving Congress. She compared her ability to a coaching tip used in basketball, a sport in which she excelled at Florida A&M: "If you're guarding someone, you look at the belt buckle so you don't go for the fakes. You know which way they're going to go. You study them and know what they'll do."[28]

In 1995 Meek criticized Republican Speaker Newt Gingrich on the U.S. House Floor over a $4.5 million advance for his book that was to be published by a company owned by media mogul Rupert Murdoch. At the time Murdoch was in a licensing dispute with the government for his Fox TV network. Meek said the potential conflict of interest would put millions in the Speaker's pocket, "and that's a whole lot of dust where I come from." Republicans declared her remarks too personal and had them struck from the *Congressional Record*. Gingrich gave up the advance but kept the royalties.[29]

She also criticized Republicans for cuts to the welfare system. "The spending cuts that the House approved today fall mainly on the weakest members of our society, on the sick and on the elderly," she said in June 1997. "Tomorrow we will be voting on tax cuts that mainly favor the wealthy. . . . Today, the House voted to rob from the poor so that tomorrow the majority can help the rich."[30]

Her biggest disappointment was failing to pass a bill that gave Haitians the same rights as Cuban refugees. She filed a bill during her last week in office on the same issue, even though the bill had no chance of passage. "I wouldn't want to leave here after 10 years without trying to make Congress conscious of Haiti and the plight of its people," she said at the time. "This issue has to be kept alive."[31]

Her election to Congress was at once humbling and thought provoking: "It made me think back to the hundreds of people who should've been there before me." No black woman had come before her "because of the system, the system which was unfair, the system which was discriminatory. But for me to get there and to try to break down some of these discriminatory practices and some of these discriminatory laws was to me God's way of putting me there so that I could be there at the time to make a contribution."

Her climb up the political ladder brought much personal satisfaction. "One thing is to just be acknowledged, as a woman," she said. Some people today would be surprised at "how little esteem we had." "To be acknowledged as a woman and a black woman in particular was a great achievement." She gave part of the credit to role models, such as Mary McLeod Bethune[32] and trailblazers Athalie Range and Gwen Cherry. Meek also acknowledged colleagues, especially Corrine Brown. "I think that we have had more experience in the struggle than a lot of other people. We look forward to helping each other regardless of the circumstance. And that's what has happened. It happened in race relations even though we were sometimes the most hated. We looked out for each other because we had to."

In addition, "I think I brought strength to the black community as a whole," she said. Along with strength came respect, "because we didn't have a whole lot of respect . . . from the greater Miami community. But I think that the fact that when I got involved and, like Corrine, I have a big mouth, so that mouth helped me a lot to become stronger in the greater Miami community. The black community received a stronger sense of purpose because I was involved because whenever I said something, they knew that I was going to stand behind it and that I would have the respect of both the white community as well as the black community."

"It wasn't that I was just another African American," she continued. "It was some kind of attention being paid to me. The white community had respect for me as a black person who didn't mind going out and being aware of things and speaking out and being respected and not always being a rabble-rouser, but someone who really demanded respect by the fact that I always took a stand."

"If I had one real strong thing in my regard, it was my respect for the vote." She didn't mind speaking out about how African Americans should be respected in the voting process. "That was one of the main things why the white community liked me or respected me because I didn't mind taking a stand when it came to things that made us proud."

Meek left Congress in 2003, after 10 years of service. Her son Kendrick took her place, not unlike the similar patterns set by the Roosevelts, the Kennedys, the Rockefellers, and the Bushes. Her feelings when her son won election: "To say I was proud is not strong enough," she said. It was more that "God had something to do with this."

The information for this story was taken from an interview of Meek by reporter Mike Vasilinda on Apr. 9, 2001, for the Florida Legislative Research Center & Museum Oral History of Florida Lawmakers project and from an interview conducted by the author (with Carrie Meek and Corrine Brown), Apr. 21, 2014.

Mario Diaz-Balart (R)

First set of brothers since 1890s to serve in Florida Legislature, 1988
Youngest person elected to the Florida Senate (31), 1992
First Cuban man elected to the U.S. House of Representatives with a brother already there, 2002

Personal: Born September 25, 1961, Fort Lauderdale, Florida; married with one child.

Education:

- University of South Florida, studied political science

Occupation: Political Assistant to then-Miami Mayor Xavier Suárez (1985)/Public Relations, GDB & Partners

Trailblazer Elections:

- U.S. House of Representatives District 25 (Parts of Collier, Miami-Dade, Hendry counties) *Rep Primary* 2002
    - Mario Diaz-Balart—*Unopposed*
- U.S. House of Representatives District 25 (Parts of Collier, Miami-Dade, Hendry counties) *General Election* 2002
    - Mario Diaz-Balart-R (64.6%), Annie Betancourt-D (35.4%)

Figure 6.21. When Mario Diaz-Balart went to Congress in 2003, "I had the huge advantage of having [brother] Lincoln there," he said, as well as Ileana Ros-Lehtinen, who had been there since 1989. "Foreign policy continues to be a huge issue in South Florida," he said, but Cubans are no longer the primary Hispanic group. "We have the largest group of Colombians in the country, Peruvians, Nicaraguans, Dominicans, Puerto Ricans, you name it." Official photograph, U.S. House of Representatives.

THE MARIO DIAZ-BALART STORY

In a political family, is the aspiration to elected office passed down through the genes, or is it acquired by growing up in a political environment? For Mario Diaz-Balart, it was the environment.

First of all, he had grown up listening to family lore about two Balart brothers, Manuel and Rafael, who had fought in Cuba's war of independence from Spain at the end of the 1800s. They had fought on the side of the Cuban-born sons of Spanish colonists against Spanish soldiers. Only Manuel survived. "One of the most precious things that I own is a picture of him [as an old man] in my office in D.C.," Mario said.

The family never forgot Rafael. When babies were born, they were named after the fallen hero, either the first or the middle name. Mario's middle name, for example, is Rafael.

Second, Mario had family role models who had held political office in Cuba and in Florida. A grandfather (Rafael Jose) and an uncle on his mother's side had been members of the Cuban national Legislature. His father (Rafael Lincoln) had been Majority Leader in the national Legislature under Cuban President Fulgencio Batista. By the mid-1950s Rafael had begun to oppose the violent activities of a former classmate, Fidel Castro. On New Year's Day, 1959, when Rafael had taken his family on a professional business trip to Europe, they got word that Castro had gained control of the country. They did not go back.[33]

"My family's second life started in January 1959," said Mario. "We bounced around a lot of different places." Although he was born in Fort Lauderdale, "I grew up as a kid for many years in Spain along with my brothers. Eventually we made it back to the United States and created our lives here."

Third, and perhaps the most important of his environmental influences, was his immediate family. "The one thing that was really pushed on us by our parents was not what to do or where to do it, but just to serve," he said. "You have to help others. You have to believe you can help others."

Two of his brothers followed their parents' admonition in their own ways. The eldest, Rafael, "who is a very private guy," serves through the banking business and as a civic leader, and brother José, a news anchor at Telemundo and MSNBC, serves through the media, Mario said.

Most important among his family influences was his brother Lincoln, who preceded him in the Florida Legislature and in Congress. "He's seven years older than I am. Now seven years is nothing, but when you're a kid, it's a big deal."

While Lincoln was beginning a law career and getting involved in politics, Mario was studying political science at the University of South Florida. He also joined the Young Democrats and helped with campaigns, which led to a position as an aide to Miami Mayor Xavier Suarez.

Then began a series of elected offices that marked the beginning of a family political dynasty. Lincoln got elected to the Florida House in 1986, and Mario, in 1988. Lincoln got elected to the Florida Senate in 1989, and Mario, in 1992. Lincoln got elected to Congress in 1992, Mario, in 2002. Lincoln blazed a trail as the first Cuban-born man from Florida elected to the U.S. House of Representatives. Mario's election to the U.S. House marked the emergence of the first Hispanic political family from Florida.

But neither of their political careers could have been possible without the 1982 amendments to the federal Voting Rights Act, which made it more difficult to split up minority communities in districts: "That was a game changer," Mario said. After the

Figure 6.22. Brothers Lincoln (*left*) and Mario Diaz-Balart visit on the floor of the U.S. House before a session begins. For Mario, big brother Lincoln had always been a role model: "He's seven years older than I am. . . . Seven years is nothing, but when you're a kid, it's a big deal." They served together in Congress only a short time before Lincoln retired. In 2010, Mario ran unopposed for his brother's old seat. Photograph courtesy of Lincoln Diaz-Balart, ca. 2003–2011.

1992 redistricting, "we went from zero African Americans being able to get elected to Congress to three, and we went from one Hispanic to two."

Mario's first race for the Florida House in 1988 was tough, despite the advantage of the family name. "I had, I think, three or four people in the primary," he said. But he knew what to do. "It was personal contact, it was door-to-door. I literally walked the entire district more than once, and I may have lost 25 pounds. I looked like I was dying because I was a thin guy to start with," he said.

In the Hispanic community that he hoped to represent, he knew that campaigning was about meeting people, shaking hands, staying accessible, and making sure that the people knew what you were doing and why you were doing it. "It's a very personal kind of relationship," he said. "It's like they say, 'Showing up is half the battle.'"

He found those relationships critical in tough campaigns. He noted, for example, that in 2008, opponents spent 5 million dollars in campaigns against him and Lincoln, and all of it was negative. "I think what allowed us to do well was the fact that people knew us." They knew the two brothers, and they knew the family.

In his early days in the Florida House, Mario renewed ties with Rep. Art Simon, Democrat from Miami-Dade County, whose campaign he had helped with a few years earlier. Simon "had a huge influence on me. Just taught me a lot about, preparation, how to do it right. I'll never forget, for example, one day he told me, 'Look Mario, remember all this is artificial and back home is real. I mean, it's a good experience but remember that this is not real life and everybody has a job to do and you have a job to do.'"

In his campaigns, "radio was a big deal," he said. He also relied on weekly Spanish-language publications as well as *Diario las Américas*, the oldest Spanish-language newspaper in South Florida.[34]

The *Miami Herald* editorial board "has endorsed me quite a bit, but they haven't always agreed with me." In general, however, the *Herald* "has always been very fair in recognizing where I had been effective." Actually, in 1996 the *Herald* ranked him the most effective legislator in the state Senate.

When he got to Congress in 2003, "I had the huge advantage of having Lincoln there," he said. In addition, he found a strong ally and friend in Republican Ileana Ros-Lehtinen, the first Cuban and Latina in Congress, who had been elected in 1989.

As a working legislator, Mario served on Appropriations committees in both the Florida Legislature and Congress. In the Florida Senate he was the first Hispanic to chair the combined Appropriations/Ways and Means/Finance and Tax Committee. In Congress he sits on three Appropriations subcommittees, and serves as Chairman of the Transportation, Housing and Urban Development Subcommittee. In addition, as a member of the Transportation Infrastructure Committee, he secured federal money for widening I-75 and focused efforts on getting funding for the Everglades restoration.

When first elected to Congress, Mario represented Miami-Dade, Collier, and Monroe counties in the 25th District. In 2010, he ran unopposed for Lincoln's congressional seat. "I did that because our strongest base of support had always been Hialeah. I would always tell Lincoln, 'Man, if you weren't here, this is the position that I should have.' So when Lincoln decided to retire from politics, that was the goal—to represent a little bit more of what I used to represent in the state Legislature."

He took the necessary steps to comply with eligibility requirements for running, including moving into the district. As luck would have it, "When I moved into Lincoln's district, I lived in the district and then redistricting came and drew my house out of the district." After the 2012 redistricting cycle, Mario ran for the redrawn 25th district, which includes parts of Miami-Dade, Broward, Collier, and Hendry counties.

Like many Cubans in Florida, Mario started out as a Democrat. But in 1985 both he and brother Lincoln switched parties. "I was an activist" even in high school, he said. But it got to the point that he no longer agreed with the Democratic Party on foreign policy. As an example, he cited the foreign policy differences between Connecticut Sen. Thomas Dodd (1959–71) and his son Sen. Chris Dodd (1981–2011). Mario also deplored President Carter's weak response to civil wars in Central America and later presidential candidate Walter Mondale's stated reluctance to use force in the region.[35]

What really cinched the decision to switch parties was the turnaround of Jeane Kirkpatrick, Ronald Reagan's foreign policy advisor, in 1985. "When we realized that if she can't fight the fight anymore, it's time to switch," he said. "Whether you agree or disagree with her—and I mostly agreed with her—she was a giant."

"Foreign policy continues to be a huge issue in South Florida," he said, but Cubans are no longer the primary Hispanic group. "We have the largest group of Colombians in the country, Peruvians, Nicaraguans, Dominicans, Puerto Ricans, you name it. In South Florida, all those communities have very large numbers."

"The Nicaraguans are there because of the Sandinistas to a great degree. The Colombians are there to a great degree because of FARC [Revolutionary Armed Forces of Colombia]. The Venezuelans are there to a great degree because of Hugo Chávez," who died in 2013 and was succeeded by Nicolás Maduro. "Obviously you know the Castro regime is in the thick of that," he said.

These communities in South Florida maintain a vigorous interest in the countries they came from. For example, "During the Free Trade debate in Washington, the Colombian community here was organized, and they were working to try to see how they could help. Now, with the student movement in Venezuela trying to help the Venezuelan people recapture their sovereignty, and you have the atrocities being committed by the Maduro regime, that's a big deal."

At the same time, "they all share the same issues that everybody does, which is the desire for their kids to have the best possible education—they want to have opportunities."

"For Cuba, I think there are two possible scenarios for the future once the Castro brothers are gone. I really think it's once Fidel is gone, Raúl's going to have a really hard time," he said. One scenario is what happened in Spain, the Czech Republic, Hungary, and Portugal, which is democracy. The second scenario is what happened in China and Vietnam, "the new fascist dictatorship, where it's private sector investment, private sector money with no labor unions, no political parties, no freedom of press."

"Those of us who are involved in this issue very directly, we're going to do everything we can so that the Cuban people have freedom. Not slavery with big money involvement. I think it's going to happen relatively soon," he said, because of sanctions Lincoln codified into law when he was in Congress. In essence, "he got the same conditions in the law for sanctions to be lifted that the then-European Community, now the European Union, had imposed over Spain and Portugal for them to join the European community." The sanctions go away when three conditions are met: No. 1 is to free the political prisoners, No. 2 is to allow personal basic freedoms, freedom of press, independent labor unions, and political parties, and No. 3 is to start the process toward free elections, he said. The debate in Washington is whether to do that or unilaterally give the regime hundreds of millions of dollars, asking nothing in return.

Despite the integration of Hispanics into South Florida life, Mario experiences discrimination "every once in a while," he said. If he goes on the floor and speaks about what's going on in Venezuela, for example, his office may receive calls reflecting prejudice. "One of my favorite lines is people who say, 'Tell him to go back to where he came from.' My office always says, 'Sure, sir, but why do you want him to go back to Fort Lauderdale?'"

He also remembered as recently as 20 years ago a bumper sticker seen in Miami-Dade County that said, "Will the last American leaving Miami please bring the flag?" That attitude ignores the fact that the original Americans in Florida were the Native Americans, he pointed out.

Nonetheless, he finds Congress rewarding because of "what we can do in the district on a daily basis. The fact that you are literally in a position where you can help people swim through the federal bureaucracy and try to solve the problems," whether with Social Security or the Veterans Administration, is "exceedingly rewarding."

But there's a bigger picture too. To illustrate, he explained that he carries in his wallet a quote from Frederick Douglass, an African American who spoke out against slavery (1818–1895): "Find out what any people will quietly submit to and you will have the exact measure of injustice and law which will be imposed on them." For Mario, that means "to be able to be in the fight of trying to make us a more just, a more fair place is an incredible opportunity."

To that end, he has written immigration reform legislation that could give millions of undocumented immigrants a path to citizenship while requiring stricter enforcement of immigration laws along the border and inside the country. The current system is "broken," he said, because it hurts the economy and fails to serve national security.[36] The challenge is to obtain bipartisan support and to get it passed.

What he finds most disappointing about serving in Congress is the bickering. "That's just not my style. I'm very aggressive, but I am very proud that I am consistently ranked as the most bipartisan member in Congress." President Reagan "was a very principled person but still understood that you have to get things done, you have to deal with people. I always just tell people, 'Hey, other Americans are not the enemy.'"

As an example of the hostility, he described how he and colleagues had gathered in a sports bar on Capitol Hill to watch one of the final games between the Miami Heat and the San Antonio Spurs. The gathering included Ileana Ros-Lehtinen and Democrats Debbie Wasserman Schultz and Frederica Wilson as well as a few people from Miami-Dade County and from San Antonio. "It was all in good fun," he said. "We tweeted, we gave each other a hard time, and we did one of those fake bets, like oranges for cactus or whatever. The hate mail that the Republicans got from the right and the Democrats got from the left, from people out there was unbelievable," he said.

As another example, he explained how he and Wasserman Schultz have done events together. "I'm a Zionist on the Israel issue," he said. "We fight it out on the floor and we have debates and we don't vote alike, but we're friends." They get criticized for merely appearing on stage together. "That's a relatively new phenomenon that I didn't feel before." By the way, he said, "I think it's a minority in Congress and it's a minority among the American people. But in Congress it's a minority that, frankly, makes a lot of noise and has little tolerance for those who disagree. The essence of the legislative process is being able to communicate your thoughts and negotiate in order to advance what you truly believe in, your principles."

"That was not the case in the state Legislature when I was there," he said, "I still believe that the majority of the American people who have strong feelings want Americans to be able to sit down and work out our differences."

A new phenomenon in the last 15 years, perhaps because of social media, is the greater strength of outside unelected groups. "A lot of them are great because they're good on the issues, but some of them are just concerned about using different issues as fundraising tools. Those are the ones that, in my opinion, say you aren't even supposed to talk to anybody else because if you do you're evil. Just send me checks so I can fight those evil folks."

In recent years, many elected officials, at all levels of government, have been forced to leave elected office because of term limits. "The good side of it is that you have new blood," he said, noting, "I probably wouldn't be in Congress without term limits [in the Florida Legislature], and so for me they've been good."

But overall, term limits are "highly disruptive." He cited his personal experience in the state Legislature: "I think that I started coming into my own really in my sixth year. That is when I started to then realize, 'OK, yeah, got it. I know who the players [are] now, I know what their issues are, I know what makes them tick, I know who I can trust on separate issues. I know who the staffs are, I know how to talk to different staffs, I know what the committees do.' I think I started getting really good at understanding that."

At the same time, term limits "have empowered the lobbyists who are in many cases the only ones who have the institutional memory and the historic know-how. They have also empowered staff to a great degree," he said. Legislators "are now the inexperienced ones who frankly have very little time to learn." Consequently, term limits have "weakened the sovereign—the sovereign being the electorate, the people out there."

Although many new legislators are "very bright people, brighter than I am," the tendency is to act without regard for the future. He cited a recent state budget crisis, in which some "were intending to put non-recurring money into recurring issues. It's not only that, but they were doing it in bucket loads. Basically it's like, 'We have to solve this problem now and I'm not going to be around in three years anyway.' So there's basically no tomorrow."

"Look at Congress. Something like 60 percent of the Republican Congress has been there, I think, three terms or less in Washington. The turnover has been exceedingly high."

What would Florida be without having had Democrats Claude Pepper in Congress for 40 years, Dante Fascell, 38 years, and William M. "Bill" Lehman, 20 years, he asked. They couldn't have accomplished what they did in four years or six years or eight years. The same is true of the Florida Legislature, he said. One example was Jim

Scott (R), who served in the Senate for 24 years. "That guy was a huge mentor to me, and I remember him because it's precisely someone who had been there for many, many years."

If advising another young Hispanic interested in going into politics today, he would say, "The first thing is you have to care, to care enough to get involved. Then you have to be involved and be informed. But I think that you really have to know your community and know what issues are important to the community, and not just in a campaign season but to really get to know the community."

"Equally as important, make sure that the community knows you. The Hispanic community, all of the Hispanic communities, are exceedingly loyal. It wants to know you. It doesn't want to just elect people because they come out of nowhere. They like to know you. They want to make sure that they can touch you, talk to you, and see you."

"My dad used to say that politics is *un sacerdocio laico*, a lay priesthood," he said, reflecting advice gained in conversations at family gatherings. That means that elected office is about serving the public. When it gets to be about making money or being too tough on your family, "then you get out of politics."

Mario Diaz-Balart was interviewed by the author in a telephone conversation Mar. 24, 2014.

Kendrick Meek (D)

First African-American man to succeed his mother in Congress; elected to represent the 17th U.S. Congressional District, 2002

Personal: Born September 6, 1966, Miami, Florida; married with two children.

Education:

- Florida A&M University, B.S. in criminal justice (1989)

Occupation: Police Officer

Figure 6.23. Congressman Kendrick Meek grew up with a mother (Carrie Meek) who was a political icon within the black community. He did not decide to get involved in politics, however, until he became President of the Young Democrats at Florida A&M University. Like his mother, he served in both the Florida House and Senate before winning a seat in Congress. He gave much of the credit for teaching him how government really runs to Lt. Gov. Buddy MacKay, whom he described as "a brilliant man" but not flamboyant. Meek, a Florida Highway Patrol trooper at the time, was assigned to MacKay as his security aide. http://www.blackpast.org/aah/meek-kendrick-1966.

Trailblazer Elections:

- U.S. House of Representatives District 17 (Parts of Broward and Miami-Dade counties) *Dem Primary* 2002
  - Kendrick Meek—*Unopposed*
- U.S. House of Representatives District 17 (Parts of Broward and Miami-Dade counties) *General Election* 2002
  - Kendrick Meek-D (99.9%), Michael Italie-WRI (0.1%)

THE KENDRICK MEEK STORY

Kendrick Meek's election to the U.S. House of Representatives in 2002 marked the first time in U.S. history that an African-American man succeeded his mother in Congress.

Prior to that time, he had followed in her footsteps. Carrie Meek had served in the Florida House from 1979 to 1982, the Florida Senate from 1982 to 1992, and then the Congress from 1993 to 2003. Kendrick started his political career while his mother was still in Congress, serving in the Florida House from 1995 to 1998 and then the Florida Senate from 1998 to 2002, and finally replaced her in the Congress from 2002 to 2010.

His mother did not direct his career nor even urge him to go into politics: "She always left things up to me. She told me when I was in high school, 'Kendrick, if you want to go to college, I support you 110 percent. If you want to throw garbage cans off the back of a garbage truck, I'm going to support you.' It was good having that freedom and not that pressure," he said.

His earliest recollection of politics dated back to when he was 12 years old. "There was this big meeting in the small living room of our house in Liberty City where community leaders were trying to make a decision on who should run to replace Gwen Cherry in the state House of Representatives." The gathering consisted of lawyers, the publisher of the *Miami Times*, which served the Black community, and Athalie Range, the first black woman on the Miami City Commission. "It was very male dominated and the decision was made that my mother would not run," Kendrick said. "Athalie Range stayed afterward and said, 'Carrie, you really should run because you have the support of students at Miami-Dade Community College. You've run the Model Cities Program. You have the smarts to be a legislator.'"

"So, with no money, we decided to engage in this campaign. That was my first bite at politics, street-level politics, door-to-door politics, hand-to-hand combat, getting excited at someone writing a $25 or $50 check," he said. They made campaign signs using a head shot of his mother in black and white (color photos were too expensive back then). Students at the Miami-Dade College graphics department outlined the lettering and filled it in with markers. They covered the signs in clear plastic to protect them from the rain.

The Democratic primary attracted 12 candidates competing for Cherry's seat. Carrie and JoAnna DeLoach emerged with the most votes. In the runoff, DeLoach was so confident that she claimed to have already gotten an apartment in Tallahassee. That motivated Carrie's supporters all the more. After winning the primary, Carrie defeated Republican Roberto Casas in the general election.[37] "Then we moved to Tallahassee, and I had a good taste of politics there," Kendrick said.

In growing up, "I recognized but really didn't understand the contributions that my mother was making," he said. "I remember pushing a grocery cart at Winn-Dixie and people coming up to her and saying, 'Ms. Meek, thank you for helping me get into my first home.' 'Thank you for writing a letter for my daughter to be able to attend school.' And mainly, when she passed the Dade County surtax legislation, it made housing affordable. It also made a lot of millionaires amongst the home builders here in South Florida. But it was something that really helped a lot of working-class folks. So she got a lot of accolades for that along with her stands for social justice."

"When I got into college, I realized that I wanted to one day get involved in politics because I'd learned so much from pushing the grocery cart" and hearing about constituent services. "Back then there weren't as many black elected officials as you see now." He compared his mother to a present-day Barack Obama. "I ended up getting involved and I became president of the Young Democrats at Florida A&M's campus."

Going to college may not even have been possible but for the tutorial services provided by Florida A&M's Learning Development Evaluation Center, which Carrie helped create because of his dyslexia as a child. After college, Kendrick went to the Highway Patrol Academy, worked on the road as a DUI trooper for three years, and then was appointed by Gov. Lawton Chiles to work as a security aide to Lt. Gov. Buddy MacKay.

"Lawton Chiles really played an instrumental role in allowing me to see the executive branch," Kendrick said. That experience helped him understand how decisions are made—"and how small that circle is of the individuals who make decisions." He realized that the Lieutenant Governor is "out of the loop," and that "it's really the Governor, the Governor's Chief of Staff, his Budget Director, and the Special Assistant to the Governor. I mean, it's not someone that showed up on the ticket with him because that was a person of convenience within a three-month or four-month period. They weren't a part of the original kitchen-table design on how we're going to win. They weren't a part of the early stages of the campaign. That lives in the federal system, too."

"Lawton Chiles provided the appointment, but the real education came from Buddy MacKay. He had a great deal of patience with me. I considered myself a hard worker always. But being 24, a captain in the Florida Highway Patrol, and in my first year of marriage, I wasn't as sharp as I needed to be," Kendrick said. MacKay "was a brilliant man. He understood government up and down, he could run government, but he just wasn't the brimstone politician, the stump-speech-giving kind of guy. What got him excited was being a part of reinventing government."

Kendrick saw his first chance to run for elected office after meeting Democratic State Rep. Elaine Gordon at a political dinner. At the time, rumor had it that she was thinking about retiring. Kendrick went to her office and said, "I just want to let you know that I'm very interested in running. I don't know where you are in your decision, if you're going to retire or not, but when you do make that decision, I would love to follow you as the next Representative in District 104." She said, "Oh no, I haven't made any decisions yet." She welcomed his working as a volunteer in the black part of the district, however, and added, "I'll mentor you."

"After the meeting I go home, and we're sitting—I'll never forget this—at the dining room table where my mother is opening mail. 'How did the meeting go with Rep. Gordon?' she asked. I said, 'Well, it went well. She said she'll mentor me.' And she looked at me and she said, 'Mentor you? You're my son and she's going to mentor you?' It was on then. So she said, 'Well, OK.' After that, I started knocking on doors."

It wasn't long before Gordon called him. "Kendrick, I know you're thinking about running, but I've talked to all the lobbyists in Tallahassee, and we'll shut you down and I'll raise a mountain of money." He realized it was a "scare call." He said, "Madame Leader"—because she was the Majority Leader then—"with all due respect, I'm just going to keep doing what I'm doing, and we'll see how things work out."

One of his mother's sayings came to mind. "She would always say, 'Kendrick, the enemy sleeps in shifts, so that means you have to work harder.' I mean, she's a woman with metaphors. She is the beacon, the reason why I even had the will and the desire to serve the people of the state of Florida."

Although Gordon had not announced her retirement, it was clear that she was concerned about a reelection bid. Actually Gordon had called Carrie to dissuade Kendrick from running. His mother told him later, "I don't know why she's calling me. You're my flesh and blood." Carrie assured him that no matter what his decision, she would support him.

Then he got a call from Rick Sisser, "who is like the Ron Book[38] of lobbyists in those days," Kendrick said. Sisser said, "Kendrick, I just talked to Elaine. She's going to make a retirement speech in about an hour on the floor. I'm going to send you some checks in the morning." Kendrick was perplexed: "This was her No. 1 guy. This was her guy who, if you wanted to talk to her, you had to talk to Rick Sisser first." Later Sisser told him about a poll that showed Gordon had no chance of winning. People said that even though they didn't know Kendrick, if he was Carrie Meek's son, that was good enough for them.

Kendrick had great respect for Gordon. She had worked hard for the ratification of the Equal Rights Amendment for women in the 1970s, for example. "She was not just someone that was sitting and warming a seat. I mean, she was an active part of the legislative process." But the reality of politics is who can get the most support and raise the most money.

"She was in this district where all of these African Americans ran but lost." Money was key. "So if you've raised $5,000 and Elaine Gordon or Kendrick Meek raised $300,000, it would be hard for you to get your message out. You may be a wonderful person, but there's only so much of you that can go around, and that affects your support," he explained. "How many pastors are actually going to go out and do what they have to do to get the vote out for you? How many community leaders are going to side with you if you're not established enough to be able to even schedule an appointment? I mean, it goes back to the one, two, three of politics." With Kendrick running, Gordon had a problem. Rather than test the poll results, she retired.

He won the race and ended up being friends with Gordon. She became a Vice President at Florida International University, and "we did things together, so there was no bad feeling. And I understand because when you serve for a long period—and my mom went through this, too—you get institutionalized. You start thinking, 'If I don't do this, then what will this program do without me here?' So you have all these justifications for why you have to continue doing what you're doing."

Some public officials are wise enough to recognize when it's time to step aside. As an example, he cited an encounter with California Democrat George Miller shortly after he announced in January 2014 that he was retiring from Congress after 40 years. Kendrick said, "George, wow, man, I thought you'll be 'carried by six' out of this place." Miller replied, "Kendrick, there's more to life than Congress. I just realized that, but, you know, there'll be someone that will come behind me that will probably even be more talented than I was on the Education Committee as chair."

While they're in office, elected officials "have to stand up for folks and right wrongs when it's time to do so through legislative statute," Kendrick said. During the last year of his term in the Florida House, he introduced legislation that would compensate two black men, Freddie Pitts and Wilbert Lee, for wrongful imprisonment. They had been convicted of killing two gas station attendants in Port St. Joe in 1963, spent 12 years in prison, and received the death penalty. After new evidence was presented, including a confession by another man, they received a full pardon from Gov. Reubin Askew in 1975. In subsequent years, they had come to Tallahassee to seek compensation but were turned down 19 times.[39]

In 1998, when Lee presented their case to Kendrick in his South Florida district office, the young legislator had to take refuge in the bathroom to control his emotions. "I got back and I said I had to pull this stuff together because we got to get these guys compensation, and I got to let them know that it's for real. I said, 'Mr. Lee, I would be so angry. I would be so hurt. Twelve years on death row, wrongly accused.' Wilbert was contrite, like if he was a kindred spirit. He was very calm about it. It wasn't really about the money to them—it was about clearing them totally. And the courage of Gov. Askew. What he did was amazing back in that time—pardon two black men for a crime by a white man at the Mojo Gas Station. It's just amazing!"

Kendrick managed to get the bill through House committees, but it had not reached the floor by the closing days of the session. He tried to get the attention of the Speaker, Republican Daniel Webster (1996–1998), but was blocked on both sides of the rostrum by Sergeant-at-Arms officers. Kendrick later went to the Speaker's office to wait for him but was told, "Oh, Honey, I'm sorry, he left about 45 minutes ago."

Kendrick went back to Miami and met Pitts and his wife for breakfast at their house. He told them that the bill was on the agenda to be heard, but it needed second and third readings, which would require waiving the rules. Mrs. Pitts said, "Well, I don't understand all of that, but before you leave, I want you to stop back by here. I have something for you to give to the Speaker." When Kendrick returned, she gave him a letter. "It was sealed. This woman never was involved in the legislative process, and, you know, she's very, very, very religious and knew the Word. I took this letter. I saw the Speaker. I said, 'This is from Mrs. Freddie Pitts. We need this bill up.' So, next thing you know, the next day the bill was on third reading," and it passed. "Now, to this day, I don't know what that letter said."

"The big thing in the Legislature was that we didn't want to say that the State of Florida was wrong. But because we pushed hard, the Republicans came up with a way of saying we'll send it to an administrative law judge to make the final decision, but we'll do the parameters with the caps," he said.

Kendrick had arranged for Sen. Betty Holzendorf-D (1992–2002) to sponsor the bill in the Senate. When the bill came up in that chamber, the tension was palpable. Democrat Pat Thomas, former Senate President (1993–94), "stood up as a dying man in the Senate and cried like a teenager and looked up at Pitts and Lee in the gallery and apologized for standing in the door of them getting justice for all those years." Because it was a claims bill, it did not need the Governor's signature. Within two weeks, the administrative law judge signed it and sent it out, authorizing $500,000 each in compensation to the two men.

"Pitts and Lee was major in my book because it was about civil rights, it was about correcting a wrong," Kendrick said. "Just to think about what those guys went through. They had to first face the guys that wrongly accused them, beat them, and coerced them into confessing to a crime they did not do." For Kendrick, it was also about learning how to fight in the legislative process.

In 1998, Kendrick ran for his mother's old seat in the Florida Senate. He won, upsetting the incumbent Bill Turner, a revered politician who had made history in 1970 as the first black elected to the Dade County School Board.[40] In the Senate, Kendrick would once again challenge the status quo.

Jeb Bush, who had been elected Governor at the same time, called a special session for January 2000 on changing the death penalty by replacing electrocution with lethal injection and speeding up the appeals process.[41] Though not against the death penalty, Kendrick filed an amendment reflecting a finding of the Florida Supreme Court's Racial and Ethnic Bias Study Commission, chaired by attorney Frank Scruggs,[42] "that dealt with inequities of why African Americans are charged with death penalty more than Anglos, even though they did not carry out the majority of capital crimes in the State of Florida."

A University of Florida professor "testified during this special session about that Commission finding, saying that prosecutors, when it came down to black on white crime, filed for the death penalty almost eight times more than if that victim was black. And a white who killed an African American was just the reverse, very unlikely to get the death penalty," he explained. "Basically, what the amendment said was that there had to be a report when the death penalty is applied; the ethnicity, the gender—all this stuff was to be reported to the Attorney General's office. So it's public record to show the hypocrisy of the whole thing of why it's so easy to do it for African Americans."

"The Governor really hit the roof," he said. "The powers that be did not want this." The Senate "debated the amendment for an hour, they tabled the amendment, and then they went on recess. I'll never forget, the then-Majority Leader Tom Lee [R, 1996–2006] came over and said, 'Kendrick, in the Senate we do things differently. I know in the House you're used to fighting, but this is a little different body. You don't understand.' I said, 'Well, Mr. Chairman, you don't understand that I know this is the Senate, but it's still a democracy and we're going to vote on this amendment, period.' It was the moment where you could be meek and mild but you have to stand up for what you believe in because, believe me, the right never stops. Special interests never stop. So why should we stop on the legislative process? We came back, they did some sort of amendment to kill the amendment."

Sen. Daryl Jones-D (1990–2002),[43] who sat next to him, "was leaning back in the chair—he was always a very safe kind of policy maker, so he really didn't do the 'Rambo' approach that I would take sometimes," Kendrick said. Jones told him, "You know, you can refile it. It's a special session, the rules are waived, you can file the day before." Kendrick filed the amendment again. The next day, "they were like, 'OK, now we're ready to move,' and Senate President Toni Jennings [1996–2000] said, 'No we're not. Sen. Meek has just filed the same amendment. We can go through debate all over again.' So, of course, it was tabled and slowed the process down."

"I called the Governor's Mansion. Working for Lawton Chiles, I knew the security staff there. If you ever want to contact the Governor, you can call the Mansion if it's an emergency. So I called, and the security staff said, 'How are you, Kendrick?' 'I'm doing fine'—you know, same guys, it didn't make a difference. I said, 'Can I speak to the Governor?' 'Well, the Governor is working out now.' I said, 'OK, that's fine, have him call me.' The Lieutenant Governor, Frank Brogan, called me back maybe about an hour later. I stepped out of a Black Caucus meeting, and I said, 'I'd like to talk to the Governor about the death penalty piece.' Brogan said, 'Well, he can't talk right now. I'm handling all the legislative stuff.' I said, 'You know, Frank, you don't understand. I need to talk to him.' We ended up not winning that battle," Kendrick said, "and this is how the whole thing started on One Florida."

One Florida, a program to end affirmative action in college admissions and state government contracts, had been issued by Gov. Bush in an executive order the previous November. He did it without inviting public comment, nor talking with anyone in the Hispanic or Black caucuses. In late January, Kendrick and Rep. Tony Hill (state Representative 1992–2000, state Senator 2002–2011) went in to meet with him.

"We ended up getting a meeting with Frank Brogan—this was the day before the Governor was releasing his budget. Frank said, 'OK, you know, we're going to talk about education issues.' I said, 'Well, I really want to talk to the Governor about One Florida.' 'Oh, the Governor's working on the budget.' I said, 'Well, we'll be here when he's available.' 'Why don't we call you when he's available?' Frank said. 'No, no, we'll sit right here. We've been trying to meet with him for three weeks now, and it just can't happen.' Frank said, 'You're not doing this, are you?' 'Yeah, we're going to be right here.'"

Brogan left and the Governor came back. "He had a big ink blotch in his pocket, like he had just put his pen in his pocket I guess out of anger. He came in and he just looked directly at me, and he said, 'Kendrick, what's going on here?' I said, 'Governor, how are you doing?' He said, 'Listen, if you all expect for me to change my One Florida plan, then you might as well get some blankets, you're going to be here for a while.' So Tony Hill, being secretary-treasurer of the AFL/CIO at that time, just leaned back in the seat and put his hands behind his head. I said, 'Well, I guess we're going to be here.'" And so the sit-in commenced.

When word got out about the sit-in, scores of supporters, including 20 legislators, nationally known civil rights activists, state NAACP leaders, and college students gathered in front of the Governor's suite. Their singing and noise throughout the day resulted in an overnight lockdown of the office, and the ejection of nine reporters by armed security agents. When the protest started drawing national media attention, the Governor weakened and negotiations began.

After 24 hours, the Governor conceded to several requests from the 20-member Black Caucus.[44] One concession was that a 15-member select legislative committee would hold three public hearings on the proposal. Another was that the Board of Regents would delay a vote, which was scheduled for later in the week, on key parts of the plan affecting universities. The Regents ended up approving new standards not based on race or gender for college admission.

But Meek had kindled a flame. On March 7, an estimated 10,000 people, the largest in the state's history,[45] marched at the Capitol in protest. The march attracted the Rev. Jesse Jackson, Martin Luther King III, NAACP President Kweisi Mfume, comedian Dick Gregory, and other activists who made speeches, reminiscent of demonstrations from the 1960s.[46]

"This is not about black and white, but about right and wrong," Jackson said. "We're not fighting for privileges. We're fighting for access."[47]

What began in Florida as a request to talk to the Governor broadened into a national issue. It raised awareness among the people, "saying we're not living in kingdom politics," Meek said. "Because you got to think about it, Jeb Bush celebrated a Huey Long[48] kind of experience during that time—his father was former President of the United States, his brother was Governor of Texas and running for President of the United States, and so he was really coming into his own power and getting stronger."

In another conflict with the Governor, Kendrick led a massive citizen petition to reduce class size in Florida's public schools. Voters passed the amendment during a fall 2002 referendum.

"Florida families cannot be shortchanged," Meek said at the time. "They simply ask that their children not be packed into overcrowded classrooms. Instead of focusing on misguided priorities, Florida needs a long-term perspective to secure a better future for our children. Implementing the class size limits without delay is critical so our teachers can teach in classrooms where our students can learn. Moreover, it is important to note that our state needs to invest now in its human capital in order to reverse the tide of joblessness for tomorrow's workers."[49]

Since the amendment passed, the GOP has repeatedly tried to water it down. In 2010, when legislators put a changed version on the ballot, Kendrick, who by that time was in Congress, fought to retain the original measure. The voters stuck to their initial desire for smaller class sizes and rejected the Legislature's new amendment. Even so, efforts to get around reduced class sizes have continued.

After the battles to retain affirmative action and reduce class size, Kendrick remembered sitting with his mother in her bedroom. "She would always say 'Good job!' or something, but this is the first time she said, 'You don't have to prove yourself to me. I know you're a leader.' I mean, she just said it. We weren't talking about it. She knew my motivation was not only to serve the people, but to let her know that I was serious about the business of serving. That was a motivator for me. I never said it to her but she knew it. I remember getting in my car and driving home and it was such an emotional thing because you're trying to achieve something and you get confirmation from the very person that you idolize in that space."

By that time, his mother was in her mid-70s. "When I was in the state Senate, everyone—probably even the person that's in the drive-through window at McDonald's—knew that I would run for the Congress when my mom retired." She announced her retirement a couple of weeks before the qualifying deadline in July 2002.

Figure 6.24. Kendrick Meek's successful run for his mother's congressional seat marked the first time in U.S. history that an African-American man would succeed his mother in Congress. After his swearing-in, he came back to his House office only to find his mother, Carrie Meek, sitting at his desk. When he asked, "Who is this lady in my office?" she said, "Your No. 1 constituent." In describing what he learned from his mother, he said: "Through her, I learned how to be courageous." Photograph by Susan A. MacManus at Democratic National Convention in Chicago, 1996.

That decision generated enormous media coverage. "There were so many articles and news reports, people following me as I started to shake hands and tell people I'm running for Congress."

Other black elected officials had eyed the seat, but "it was hard for them to get out and do it because of the wave that was there," he said. No one challenged him in the primary, and he ran unopposed in the general election for four consecutive terms in the heavily black and Democratic district.

The day after he was sworn in, he was talking to staff in his front office. When he went back to his desk where his mother was sitting, he said, "Who is this lady in my office?" She said, "Your No. 1 constituent." They both laughed. Someone from the Smithsonian Institution came in and asked for both their voting cards. He asked why. That's when he learned that they were the first black mother and son to serve in Congress.

Succeeding his mother allowed him to hit the ground running. He already knew his way around the city, and he had often sought her counsel. But most important were the relationships his mother had developed. "Going to see the chair, may it be Republican or Democrat, of the committee, and the first word out of their mouth, 'How's your mom doing?'" he said. Those relationships were "beneficial to my constituents and to causes that I was working on."

Prior to the Democrats gaining the majority in the House and Nancy Pelosi from San Francisco becoming Speaker in 2009, Kendrick "worked with her on the message team, reaching young voters and raising money. But I had great relationships with the Republicans, too, because they knew my mother. My mother was like a grandmother figure to many of them. She was unlike any other member of the Congressional Black Caucus because of her uniqueness and the fact that she served on Appropriations, which, you know, never hurt."

The grandmother image reminded him of another metaphor his mother had used: "'You know, Kendrick, they see me all grandmotherly, as a 60-, 70-something-year-old woman, and they come to me'—excuse me, she used these very words—'and try to s—t me, but they don't know I carry a turd in my hip pocket.'"

While in Congress he championed the cause of the Haitians just as his mother, whom he called "the mother of the Haitian community," had done before him. He visited Haiti 26 times, worked to liberalize U.S. trade with the island and the federal government's treatment of Haitian refugees, and sought aid for them after the 2010 earthquake.[50]

"My mom stood for them when no one else would. They didn't have the numbers. It was only natural for me to follow suit. You know something? If it wasn't for Haiti, we wouldn't be who we are. Take a short trip up to Savannah and see how those free Haitian slaves fought on behalf of our independence against the Brits in the great battle in Savannah. There's a monument there. My name is there, my family's name, we gave to it. And if God would have it, my daughter would go to school in the very city where this took place. To make a long story short, because of their contributions way back when and because they're the poorest country in the Western Hemisphere, and they have such a footprint on South Florida and our economy, it made sense. It wasn't a black thing, it was a humanity thing."

Kendrick served on the powerful House Ways and Means Committee and met global leaders as a member of the NATO Parliamentary Assembly.[51] With his appointments and relationships, he could have stayed there until he was 70 years old, but he chose not to do that. Instead, when U.S. Sen. Mel Martinez (R) announced his resignation in 2009, Kendrick filed to run for the seat.

"I wanted to run for the Senate because I wanted to be able to be a part of the decision making," he said. House members tend to be like soldiers pointed in a given direction and told where to move, without much room for input. He wanted to be able to push for things he and his constituents felt strongly about. "If you look at my legislative history I didn't have a problem in upsetting or disappointing some people because I wasn't in line with everyone else." He wanted to stay grounded to his constituents and not "forget about that person who's catching the 5:30 bus to go clean someone's house."

He recognized the odds were against him because it was a midterm election. He also knew he would face a Republican opponent. "We knew it could possibly be Jeb Bush. But we did not think that Charlie Crist would leave the most powerful position in the state of Florida [Governor] just because he didn't want a break in service to run for the United States Senate." When Republican Marco Rubio, with Tea Party support, surged ahead in the polls, Crist dropped out of the Republican primary and ran as an independent, attracting support from South Florida Democrats.

"Once Charlie came over, it gave moderates and liberals a choice, which then left the conservatives with one choice, Marco Rubio," Kendrick said. Crist argued that Kendrick couldn't win, and former President Bill Clinton urged him not to run. "You had the whole thing with President Clinton being thrown in the middle by the White House because the White House was really saying that they didn't want Rubio to go up and become an opponent of the President." With Democrats and many independents split between Crist and Kendrick, Rubio won.

Kendrick viewed the outcome philosophically. "You'll never, including Barack Obama, who's the most powerful person on the face of the Earth right now as it relates to public policy, you'll never have the package that you need to succeed in every battle. If you are running for all the right reasons and you're willing to never give up, then you can be successful. But you have to build coalitions and it's more than just running for office. It's about building alliances with people of common thinking, and it's about engaging those individuals that oppose your efforts. Carrie Meek always said, 'Keep your hand on your enemy so at least you'll know which way they're moving.' It's important to live by that mantra and not be scared to fail."

Through it all, she was his biggest supporter. "I speak of her as Confucius, but, I mean, she's brilliant. She had real-life experience leading up to the job. You got to think, she was north of 50 when she first ran for office, and she was 66 when she went to Congress." He recounted key experiences in her life—growing up poor, going to the University of Michigan at age 19, working as a coach and teacher when physical education was a man's world, knowing the legendary Mary McLeod Bethune, educating people who are in education today, working at Miami-Dade Community College when it operated out of Northwestern Senior High School, building community development—all of that plus divorcing two husbands and raising three children.

"She was fortunate enough to be chosen with a little will and the desire to run. This was a gift to us here in Florida. A true gift," he said. Many people want to be elected to office, "but they didn't necessarily walk the walk and talk the talk, and understand what it means to make decisions, whether you're going to pay now or pay later—those kinds of life experiences. There are people out there that are punching in and punching out every day that need people elected that know what that means."

"I can go on and on about Carrie Meek," he said. "Through her, I learned how to be courageous."

Kendrick Meek was interviewed in person by the author July 31, 2014.

Allen West (R)

First Republican African-American man to represent Florida in the U.S. House of Representatives since Reconstruction, 2010

Personal: Born February 7, 1961, Atlanta, Georgia; married with two children.

Education:

- University of Tennessee (1983)
- Kansas State University, master's degree in political science (1986)

- U.S. Army Command and General Staff College, Master of Military Arts and Sciences degree (M.M.A.S.) (1997)

Occupation: Army/Teacher

Trailblazer Elections:

- U.S. House of Representatives District 22 (Parts of Broward and Palm Beach counties) *Rep Primary* 2010
  - Allen West (76.7%), David Brady (23.3%)
- U.S. House of Representatives District 22 (Parts of Broward and Palm Beach counties) *General Election* 2010
  - Allen West-R (54.4%), Ron Klein-D (45.6%)

Figure 6.25. Retired U.S. Army Lt. Col. Allen West had never considered getting involved in politics until a local political activist approached him about running for Congress. The suggestion was like "a poke in the chest," he said. But once he decided to run, being a novice did not hold him back. "Having been in the military and having been in combat, nothing is really that hard," he said. Photograph courtesy of Allen West. Source: http://allenbwest.com/meet-allen-west/.

THE ALLEN WEST STORY

Allen West, a retired U.S. Army Lieutenant Colonel and the first black Republican from Florida to serve in Congress since Reconstruction, said his preparation for a political career came from serving for 22 years in the Army, although he didn't know it at the time.

When he retired in August 2004, the idea of political office had never crossed his mind. "I got back from Iraq about the second or third week of December 2003, and we wanted to get the family moved because we wanted to get the girls in school. That was important so they could start school in the new term. At the time we had a gray Suburban, we got a U-Haul and we took what was necessary for them to be able to start out, and drove directly from Fort Hood, Texas, to the Sunrise Boulevard exit off of I-95 and headed west to Plantation, Fla." His wife, Angela, who was originally from Jamaica, was the one who had chosen Florida as their new home.

After getting the family settled, he went back to Fort Hood to finish retirement out-processing, but in 2005 he volunteered for a two-and-a-half-year stint of training with the Afghan army. In January 2007, while home on leave, a local political activist, Donna Brosemer, approached him about running for Congress. The Republicans had just lost the congressional majority in the midterm elections of 2006, and the party was looking for potential candidates for the 2008 cycle.

He said he wasn't interested because he was like many career military men who don't care for politicians. "As a matter of fact, when you get selected to be the escort officer for a politician, a congressional visit, normally it's because you've done something wrong and upset your boss, and it's a bit of a punishment." In addition, "as Commanders we remember congressional inquiries where we'd get these requests to come down because you had some soldier in your unit that was complaining and wrote a letter to the Congressman." Perhaps most important, "I was new to the area, so why would I think about running for political office? The other thing was that I still had to complete another full year of duty in Afghanistan."

Nonetheless, Brosemer's suggestion "was kind of a poke in the chest," he said, "because your oath of office does not have a statute of limitations, so you continue to see how you can serve your nation." When he returned from Afghanistan, the poke in the chest had become a clenched fist in the hand. He chose to run as a Republican for the congressional seat held by Democrat Ron Klein (2007–2011).

West did not register as a Republican until after he retired because of an unwritten rule that people in the military do not engage in politics. His wife, Angela, who had lived in New York and whose father was also career military, had leaned at first toward being a liberal but evolved as a conservative the better she understood the economy. "I didn't actually switch," she said. "It was an awakening."

Being new to politics did not hold West back from seeking public office. "First of all, having been in the military and having been in combat, nothing is really that hard. Understanding strategy, I mean, and tactics, and developing an operational plan, that's who we are, that's what we do every day of our lives."

He was already somewhat known in the region because as a retired army officer he had been invited to speak to various groups about the war in Iraq as well as his experiences in Afghanistan. Moreover, an army career "lends itself to the bigger picture of issues," he said.

"The great thing about a professional military education like what I received in my 22 years, you understand the economy. You understand foreign policy, international relations, national security. It's just about fine tuning some local issues a little bit more, and you can glean that by sitting around and talking to some of the preeminent business leaders and civic leaders in the area. For me, the most important thing was to try to establish a good ground game, good ground support, that type of thing."

As part of his fundraising, he went to the National Republican Congressional Committee: "The door was shut in my face because they have this paradigm of who they think is successful to run. The first question they ask you is, of course, how much money can you self-fund? Well, I looked at him to say, 'I've been in the military for 22 years and I'm just coming back from Afghanistan. I'm not a millionaire but what I bring to the table is a conviction, a commitment.' I tried to tell them my story of growing up in the inner city of Atlanta, Ga., and the history of the military and my family and that sense of service and sacrifice and commitment. For them, it was all about the money. So we didn't get that external type of support."

"But still, I mean, just running on our own, we raised, in that 2008 race, $583,000. We could only run one commercial on cable TV. Of course, Ron Klein was the incumbent. He had close to $3.1 million, and so he was just able to bombard us in commercials on TV." West ended up losing in a Democratic sweep that brought Barack Obama to the presidency.

"But the interesting thing was that here was a person that really had just put together maybe—you think March to November—a seven- to eight-month campaign," West said, referring to himself. "That's what really shocked a lot of people. It really incensed a lot of the local grassroots folks here to say if the establishment, the party structure, had given this guy a little support, guess what? He maybe could've overcome this thing and been an incredible story in the 2008 cycle. That inspired me to come back and run again because a lot of people said, 'You got to try this again.'" West immediately began preparing for another run.

For the 2008 campaign, he had focused on how he differed from the incumbent, especially on the economy. "We were coming off of that economic downturn, and when you really did the analysis of what brought that on, it was a big government going back to the Carter administration's Community Reinvestment Act. That created this mortgage bubble." West had studied and discussed the economy with his wife, a financial advisor with M.B.A. and Ph.D. degrees. "She was paying attention to the subprime mortgage crisis, so we used to talk about that all the time."

In 2008, his preparation proved valuable in a debate with Klein in Coral Springs. "He had a book prepared for him, and when they asked him a question, he flipped over and he like pretty much read a response. I had two 3 × 5 cards, just taking notes, and we did very well. Some people saw Klein chewing out his staff outside and, from then on, there were no more one-on-one appearances. I mean, he did not want to have that."

Military service trains you to prepare, West said. "You prepare by understanding the issues, having responses all in your head, and that was something different than I think a lot of people had seen. That's something that I still try to do today—to be very cognizant of the issues, to have solutions, and to be able to respond concisely."

"In December 2008 I pretty much told people that I would be back, and then in January after the holiday season, we started to put together that structure and everything so that we could be ready to go. Because, again, it's a campaign. So you took the lessons learned because I really believed that the only thing that hindered me in

2008 was time. Time is a factor of financial resources, getting your message out, so the more time that you had, the better it would be. So we went right back into it."

Sure enough, in 2010, he defeated Klein, riding a Tea Party wave of discontent with government and the economy. "The Tea Party is really a constitutional conservative grassroots movement," West said. "That's it. It is about people that are concerned about the excessive, onerous and expansive growth of government. Which, if you look at the Declaration of Independence, those were the grievances that Jefferson was talking about—the intrusiveness of King George III and the British government. They were concerned about fiscal responsibility."

Moreover, the nation's founders "talked about individual sovereignty and individual liberty and freedoms. Once again that's what we were established upon—the individual rights, their premises—life, liberty, pursuit of happiness. *Pursuit of happiness* originally was *property* as written by John Locke. They want to believe in the free market system, having the policies that enable the free market, private enterprise, to be able to grow so they can hire people and get them back to work instead of us seeing this explosion in the welfare society, the poverty and food stamp recipients in this country. Last, but not least, is national security."

The people in the district he represented were about 92 percent white. "I often tell people it was incredible that the year that I was born [1961] was when they had the wade-in down in Fort Lauderdale because blacks were not allowed to be at the beaches.[52] So 50 years later I'm getting sworn in as a Representative that covered all of those beaches."

Making history as the first black Republican from Florida in Congress since Reconstruction "never dawned on me until after I was sworn in," he said. "For me it's not about titles and making history and all of that. It's about really serving the country and providing the type of leadership that you believe can help get this nation back on track, especially when you look at some of the horrible paths that we have taken and where we see our country headed."

In Congress, West followed another black man, Alcee Hastings, a Democrat, who had been elected in 1993. But West was sufficiently interested in his own party's predecessor, Josiah T. Walls (1871–1876), that he read a biography of Walls as well as another book, *Capitol Men*, about the first black Representatives on Capitol Hill during Reconstruction. "It's an amazing story. There are many similarities between Walls's story and West's story because both of us really only served that one term and we had to fight the opposition and some forces within our own party to try to maintain that congressional seat."

As an Army veteran, he was appointed to the Armed Services Committee, where he sponsored or cosponsored bills dealing with military matters. As a member of the Small Business Committee, he promoted small business growth, which he said "was really the backbone of the country." The most common inquiries from constituents

Figure 6.26. Allen West takes the oath of office in the U.S. House of Representatives with House Speaker John Boehner officiating and his family looking on. It was a path he wanted his daughters to see. "That's why on occasion I took them out to campaign events so that they could see [the value of service] and understand that we as a family are working, campaigning to serve others, not for them to serve us." Photograph taken January 2011, https://gowestforallenwest.wordpress.com/.

dealt with government spending, the economy, and tax and regulatory policies. Spending was a huge concern, he said, noting, "We're now close to 17 trillion dollars in debt. That scares the bejesus out of somebody."

"When I was a young officer, you always had a sit-rep [situation report] up to your higher commander to let him know what you did in that week. That's the same thing I did to the constituents, so they always knew what I was voting on, how I voted, who I was meeting in that week, because we wanted to have true transparency, true openness." In addition, "every month we had two to three town halls throughout the district so we were always out and we were clearly visible. Again, it was about hearing their concerns, their issues, and going back and doing the best you could to have the right type of voting record and perspective."

For him, serving in Congress was "a dream come true." Having started as a ninth grade cadet in a high school ROTC program and going on to become an active-duty Army Lieutenant Colonel commanding a battalion in combat, and then to serve in the U.S. House of Representatives was "awesome." That kind of ascension is the legacy he wants his daughters to see. "That's why on occasion I took them out to campaign events so that they could see that interaction and understand that we as a family are working, campaigning to serve others, not for them to serve us."

What West liked best was "getting out and talking to people, understanding what their issues are, concerns, and being able to show them genuineness. I think that the problem in America is that we've got too many politicians and not enough statesmen and not enough people that understand that they're there to serve and not to be served. So that was the joy and the thrill. When I was in the office, waking up every day to take that morning run and running by the Capitol and knowing that once upon a time you fought to preserve that institution, that body, and now you're serving inside it—it's an incredible journey."

One thing he did not like about Congress was "that I would have to answer for other people's decisions." For example, in late 2010, when Republican Majority Leader

Eric Cantor sent out the calendar for the next session, "I looked at this and I said this is 150 some-odd days. That's when I wrote a letter to him and said this is not going to work. Think about all these things we have to take care of. How is 150 some-odd days in session going to get us to any type of end state? He kind of got angry about it, but I really didn't care," he said. "If it were up to me, I'd stay here because in the military you don't leave until the mission's done, 'til the job's done. We're in the leadership in the House. This is not a status quo thing. There's nothing written in law that says you got to leave for five weeks. So stay there and fight through these things."

"Our Founding Fathers never meant to have a permanent political class," he said. "They never meant for us to have this elitist structure. They meant for people that were from every other walk of life to come and do the business of legislating—locally, at the federal government level—and then go back and do your job. And now we've turned our Congress into this almost Soviet-like Politburo. That's what has happened with this health care law that members of Congress have an exemption from while the serfs, the little vassals, have to participate in it. We can draw a carve-out and say we're going to delay the mandate for the employers, but yet the individuals have to pony up. But that's the frustration that I think a lot of Americans have."

After his first term, the Florida Legislature redrew districts, making West's district more Democratic. He chose to move farther north up the coast into a different district that was more evenly split between the two parties. In 2012, he faced Democrat Patrick Murphy, a 29-year-old accountant new to politics, who had once been a Republican.

Because of his national following, West had raised $15 million by the end of September,[53] more than any other House candidate except Speaker John Boehner. Murphy, who raised little more than a third of that, benefitted from an appearance from former President Bill Clinton. West ended up losing by a close margin.

Bloomberg Businessweek called it the "Dirtiest Political Race in America."[54] One ad, paid for by Murphy's super PAC (political action committee), showed West punching two old ladies (alleging he voted for Medicare cuts) and flashing a gold tooth, a racial stereotype. West, his family, and his supporters were horrified.

When the issue of race came up, especially when other blacks disparaged black Republicans, West looked back to his upbringing and history: "It's all about truth. Truth always prevails," he said. "My parents, without a doubt, were registered Democrats, but they raised me as a conservative. When you look at the black community, it really is conservative at heart because it's about faith, it's about family, worshipping God, individual responsibility, education, self-reliance."

"I always talk to people about Booker T. Washington. His three-point plan was education, entrepreneurship, and self-reliance. That's conservative principle. He was perhaps the first conservative. When you look at what the black community was able to achieve even under the specter of segregation, Jim Crow, and everything like that, they were business oriented. They were people that strove for an education. They were families that were tight, and they helped each other out," he said. "The black family was the strength of our community. Now we're decimated."

"When you think about me, I'm the intersection of Dr. Martin Luther King, Jr., and William F. Buckley, Jr.," West said. "Conservatism and civil rights came together with me. My elementary school was right across the street from Ebenezer Baptist Church, and the principles that Buckley created for the *National Review* in 1955, that's what I've embodied and that's what my parents raised me on. So if you can be that example, which is what leadership is about—leading by example—then you can shine a light into the black community that maybe they need to hear and maybe now is the right time to hear."

"I talk to people about principle," he said. "I challenge them. I say when you go to church on Sunday, you're conservative. So what happens Monday through Saturday? It really gets a lot of people scratching their heads. I think that right now it's the right time for people to start to think: What are the foundational principles that made this country great and accessible? What has enabled a young man born in an inner city in Atlanta, Ga., and a young woman born in Jamaica to now be living here in this golf course community?"

"I'm not enamored with the Democrat Party. I'm not enamored with progressive socialism because when I go back to my neighborhood in Atlanta, I see what it's done—the low expectations," he said, alluding to the phrase "soft bigotry of low expectations"[55] coined by President George W. Bush. "And unfortunately, that was something that in this recent Trayvon Martin case with the young lady Rachel Jeantel[56]—I mean, people saw that in her testimony."

He doubts the tolerant attitude voiced by liberals: "I began to realize that the white liberals that were so accepting of people of all races and persuasions had only white friends," West said. Many whites speak to black men in a patronizing way: "I like the phrase, 'You're a credit to your race.' That's the one that always used to tickle me."

Nor is he satisfied with the Republican Party, which he said "is divided between the establishment and the mavericks." Those in the establishment "are the people that have no contact whatsoever with people outside of their own circles." The establishment side "is what you'd call politics as usual. You know, I say one thing to you and I'll say another thing to someone else. It's where they come up with that word *outreach* [to minorities]. You see, the establishment Republicans don't really mean for you to be included. They do outreach at voting time to make you believe that you're going to be included, and they have no intentions of doing so. They plan on going back to their sequestered corners, their quiet groups and pretty much keeping you out."

The mavericks in the Republican Party include Kentucky Sen. Rand Paul. "A lot of young people are going in that direction. I'm very excited to see that because that is a bold side to be on." At CPAC (Conservative Political Action Conference),[57] "we saw a wave, a movement. We saw Jewish kids, black kids, all kinds, 'Stand With Rand' buttons," he said. Moreover, "if the establishment side runs anybody this time, in 2016, they're going to lose because those kids are not going to vote for them." They won't because they're concerned about their future. "The recent statistics from last year, I think, 45 percent of college graduates are underemployed or unemployed," which has forced many grown children to live with their parents.

West's daughters, ages 21 and 18, have begun to recognize the government's impact on their own economic interests. West's older daughter Aubrey recently called him, upset by the amount of money taken out of her paycheck from her job as an intern at the Rand Eye Institute, a surgery center in Deerfield Beach. "She had in her mind a set amount that she would be able to save as she headed back to college after the summer." What amazed him was this statement: "Dad, you've got to get back in there. You got to get this right because this is about my future." She wants to be a doctor.

The establishment side has most of the money and is against the Tea Party. It has also managed to purge blacks, like West, and females, like Lt. Gov. Jennifer Carroll, from office, and they assume that Marco Rubio is going to appeal to all the Hispanics everywhere. "That's why the other side is able to exploit that and come up with the 'war on women' and all this identity politics," he said.

"The good thing about someone like Jennifer and me is that we don't serve a party, we serve the people. And we serve a country, or she served a state. She salutes the flag and moves on because it's that sense of character and integrity and honor that we're brought up with in the military where we don't start any fights, we just go ahead. When they did the redistricting thing for me, I just said, 'OK, obviously I got pushed further north.' We moved up here to Palm Beach Gardens, and, I mean, we uprooted ourselves to continue to try to do the right thing. But it's very disconcerting that there are people that want to play games in politics in the state and it's evident."

"People on our side really don't see race. They just see an individual. Do we need to get more faces like Jennifer Carroll and Allen West, whoever? Yeah! We do. Deep down inside I think that is who we are as a people. I think the big thing about the Republican Party of Florida, someone has to answer the question as to why would you take someone that has made this historic leap to become this first black Republican member of Congress from this state since Reconstruction, and redistrict him out of his district, when you have a super majority in the House and the Senate and you have a Republican Governor? I mean, what is the psyche?" He alluded to a complaint made by the Executive Committee Chairman of the Broward Republican Party that the redrawn district violated the constitutional requirement for compactness.[58]

He noted a recent feud between New Jersey Gov. Chris Christie and Rand Paul, both of whom are possible contenders for the 2016 Republican Party nomination for President. "That's not necessary. I mean, we need to find a common ground where we can move ahead." Young people "are looking for an image that can really connect with them, and that's what the Republican Party must come to understand. When you talk about me and who I am, I mean, I can connect. That's why I was a threat to the Democrat Party. Because when all of a sudden you have a black conservative, who grew up in the inner city who had parents that came from South Georgia, the third or fourth generation in the military, an educated couple, a stable family, two great young daughters, that's a threat not only a threat to the Democrats, that's a threat to some establishment Republicans."

Going forward, "It has to be about policy inclusiveness," he said. When you look at Detroit and the bankruptcies there, "this is where we can make a difference to say that those policies are failing, those policies don't get you anywhere. You think about school choice. Those are the type of policies that we're trying to promote. It is key to have the right type of faces, the right type of voices to be able to go into the community and talk about that. But if you start to cherry pick out and eliminate a lot of those faces and voices, it makes it real hard. Because what you saw in the 2012 election cycle, it was never about challenging Mitt Romney on policy, it was about attacking his image and making him disconnected from others. So that's what we have to start doing better. And, you know, Florida is a battleground state."

At the global level, West expressed concern about America's fading image in the eyes of the world. "When you look at Putin and what he has done to America, and China and their disrespect. Look at what Egypt is saying right now, who used to be a very strong ally of ours. We totally ruined that relationship. In the search of running around to be liked by others, we're not respected anymore. That's very important because a lot of our allies are confused and our enemies are emboldened all across the country."

"If you don't have your own house in order, especially your economic house in order, you cannot be seen as a world leader and you really can't go out there and try to—I don't want to say lecture—but be that 'shining city on a hill,' as Ronald Reagan said. That light is starting to flicker a little bit. It's not out but that light is starting to dim, and I think that's what a lot of people are concerned about. We can't be the generation that leaves less because we will be the first ones to do that. Because that's not the American way."

With some of his leftover campaign funds,[59] he started the Allen West Foundation. "What happened to me in 2008, I don't want to see it happen to anyone else that has a burning desire to serve their country in the political realm, to have the door closed to them. What we want to be able to do is to provide support, train them up on the issues, help them to be able to go out and talk to people, and show their ability to express thoughts in a clear, concise manner. I think the best asset I had was to show the competence and the conviction and the commitment. We have to do this from this level down here and not worry about party structures or whatever comes at the state level or federal level."

He compared the process to the farm team structure in baseball. "We have to get people here in local government, be it city and county, we have to get people on school boards because when you look at the situation of education in the inner cities, it's deplorable. We have to get people that challenge the status quo, and you can't do that unless you start to recruit and train people locally. You get them to go to that next level, and next level, and ultimately up to the major leagues."

"We've got to make sure that the education system is such that the people that take their place have actually a great deal of intelligence and are a bit more educated and able to think on their feet." He added, "They're going to have to be thick skinned, especially if they decide to be conservative. They're going to have to circumvent a lot of preconceived notions of the older set."

Allen West was interviewed in person by the author Aug. 10, 2013.

Frederica S. Wilson (D)

First woman of Bahamian descent elected to the Florida House of Representatives, 1998

First woman of Bahamian descent elected to the Florida Senate, 2002

First woman of Bahamian descent to represent Florida in the U.S. House of Representatives, 2010

Personal: Born November 5, 1942, Miami, Florida; widowed with three children.

Education:

- Fisk University, B.S. (1963)
- University of Miami, M.S. (1972)

Occupation: Teacher

Figure 6.27. When Frederica Wilson took the oath of office in Congress, all she could think of was her father, whose influence led her into politics. He had fled from the Ku Klux Klan after an altercation with a white man in Texas, hopped trains to Florida, and became active in the Civil Rights Movement, registering voters and pushing for sanitation workers' rights. Official portrait, U.S. House of Representatives, December 2010.

Trailblazer Elections:

- House of Representatives District 104 (Parts of Miami-Dade County) *Dem Primary* 1998
  - Frederica S. Wilson (50.7%), Shirley Gibson (22.3%), Jacques Despinsosse (19.1%), Bernard W. H. Jennings (3.6%), Kevin A. Fabiano (2.3%), Judith Goode (2.0%)
- House of Representatives District 104 (Miami-Dade County) *General Election* 1998
  - Frederica S. Wilson-D (85.2%), Clyde Pettaway-R (14.8%)
- Senate District 33 (Part of Broward County) *Dem Primary* 2002
  - Frederica S. Wilson (72.3%), M. Tina Dupree (17.6%), John D. Pace, Jr. (10.1%)
- Senate District 33 (Part of Broward County) *General Election* 2002
  - Frederica S. Wilson—*Unopposed*
- U.S. House of Representatives District 17 (Parts of Broward and Miami-Dade counties) *Dem Primary* 2010
  - Frederica S. Wilson (34.5%), Rudolph "Rudy" Moise (16.1%), Shirley Gibson (11.9%), Yolly Roberson (10.3%), Phillip J. Brutus (8.4%), Marleine Bastien (6.0%), Scott Galvin (5.6%), James Bush III (5.4%), Andre L. Williams (1.7%)
- U.S. House of Representatives District 17 (Parts of Broward and Miami-Dade counties) *General Election* 2010
  - Frederica S. Wilson-D (86.2%), Roderick D. Vereen-NPA (13.8%)

THE FREDERICA WILSON STORY

Upon arriving in the nation's capital to take her seat in Congress in 2010, Frederica Wilson "has distinguished herself with a daily display of head-snapping hats that blend church lady formality with rodeo queen panache," wrote a *Washington Post* reporter.[60]

For Wilson, wearing hats is a family tradition. Her Bahamian grandmother, also named Frederica, wore hats and gloves, and Wilson has continued the custom for more than 30 years with a wardrobe now estimated at 300 hats, coordinated with suits and jewelry. "I like to dress up," she said.

But wearing a hat on the floor of the U.S. House goes against a House rule dating back to the 1800s. At first she thought about challenging the rule but then reconsidered. "I really don't want to be distracted from what I've been elected to Congress to accomplish," she said. "The media has taken over, and it's almost as if I was going to Congress to wear hats."

"This would not be the first time that Wilson ran into roadblocks to her hats. When she wore Davy Crockett style hats in middle school, the dean called her father to complain, but she and her father didn't give in," the *St. Petersburg Times* wrote on May 11, 2009.[61]

Her father, Thirleen Smith, proved to be a big influence on her life. He was born in Timpson, Texas (near the eastern border with Louisiana), which had an active chapter of the Ku Klux Klan. "He would sit me on his knee, and tell me stories of what happened to him in Texas and how people were lynched," she said.[62]

As a young man, he ran afoul of the Klan by defending himself against a white man who had slugged him. With the help of neighbors, he and a friend fled to Florida by hopping on freight trains. When they arrived in Tallahassee, a white man picked them up at the train station, gave them a ride, and stopped in front of the old Capitol. He said, "How much money y'all got?" They said, "Two dollars." Thinking he had befriended them, they gave him the money. Then he said, "Get your n——r asses off my truck before I blow your goddamn brains out." So they jumped out, ran back to the train station, and made it to Miami.

In Miami, her father married, raised a family, and went into business. "Smith ran a restaurant and a billiard hall, but also became active in the Civil Rights Movement, registering voters and pushing for sanitation workers' rights. The couple's three children were sensitized to acts of injustice at a young age. Once, in high school, Wilson spied a classmate, a new kid in school, being teased for wearing torn clothes. Wilson, who weighed about 70 pounds at the time, stepped into the circle of bullies and ordered them to leave the boy alone."[63]

As a little girl, she would sit at the dining table where her father conducted political meetings. When she interrupted with a question, her father would tell her it was time for bed. Her mother suggested that before a meeting started, she could get her pillow and sit under the table, hidden by the draping tablecloth. "Just go under the table and listen," her mother said. "Take your little notepad if you want to write something down, and then after everybody leaves, you could ask your daddy your questions." That's how she got interested in politics.

After graduating from Fisk University in Memphis, Tenn., in 1963 with a bachelor's degree in elementary education, she worked as a teacher for a time and became an assistant educational coordinator for a Head Start program. While working, she earned a master's degree from the University of Miami in 1972. She took a leave of absence to raise her three children, and returned to the education field as an assistant principal.

In 1980, she became principal of Skyway Elementary School in a largely black and Hispanic neighborhood in North Miami. Among other things, she implemented a system in which teachers learned the name of every child in the school, making it seem more like a family.

The school had three goals. First, everyone would be drug free. During a time when the "crack cocaine cowboys" were flourishing, students and staff wore T-shirts printed with "I say NO to drugs" every Friday. Second, everyone would be college bound. Students were taken on field trips to county colleges, business people came to talk about their careers, and every student left fifth grade with a college savings account. Third, everyone would be bilingual. She had everything in the school from blackboards to water fountains labeled in two languages, and students recited the Pledge of Allegiance in Spanish and English. The goals worked. Skyway students had few problems with drugs. They scored higher on standardized tests than their peers in the area, and many students went on to college.[64]

In 1992, under her leadership, the school was honored as part of President George H. W. Bush's "America 2000" plan to upgrade national education standards. U.S. Secretary of Education Lamar Alexander (who would become a U.S. Senator from Tennessee) presented the award.[65]

Her leadership extended beyond the schoolyard. When a composting plant was built across the street from the school, the fumes were so bad that the children could not play outdoors during recess. It also caused a mold problem at the school and was polluting the community for miles around. Wilson led a successful campaign to shut down the plant.[66]

She ran for the Miami-Dade County School Board in 1992, and won. She attributed her victory to three bases of support: (1) her church family, branching out from St. Agnes Episcopal Church; (2) her sorority, Alpha Kappa Alpha, the oldest black sorority in the nation; and (3) her school community, which considered her a hero for having shut down the composting plant.

While on the school board, she founded the 5000 Role Models program to reduce dropout rates among high-risk minority boys. In 1997, it was honored with the Teaching Example for the Nation Award by President Bill Clinton at the Summit for America's Future.[67] In 2014, the program operated in more than 110 Miami-Dade County public schools, serving more than 6,000 young men. It had also awarded more than $5 million in scholarships.[68]

When State Rep. Kendrick Meek (D) left the Florida House to run for the Senate in 1998, Wilson ran for his seat, starting a pattern of succession for the two legislators. Appointed to the Criminal Justice Committee, she worked to have women inmates moved to prisons closer to their families. "If you have women in prison who are going to come out one day and be mothers to their children, you have to keep the connection going, otherwise it's not going to work," she said.[69]

According to the *Miami Herald*, the House Corrections Committee issued a report sharply critical of the prison system for ignoring inmates' families, failing to offer families a role in rehabilitation, and making it difficult for family members to stay in touch. The report cited impediments such as long distances to travel, varied visitation rules, and expensive collect phone calls. As a result of the report, prison officials began moving as many as 1,000 female offenders incarcerated in North Florida to prisons closer to their South Florida families.[70]

Wilson served two terms in the Florida House, serving as Minority Whip until 2002 when she was elected to the Florida Senate. Known for her willingness to take on controversial issues, she worked with Republican Gov. Charlie Crist to pass a bill

Figure 6.28. Congresswoman Frederica Wilson leaves a House Democratic Caucus meeting with President Barack Obama, House Speaker Nancy Pelosi (*far right*), and Congresswoman Terri Sewell representing Alabama's 7th Congressional District. In her run for Congress in 2010, Wilson had campaigned as a staunch backer of his administration. http://wilson.house.gov/about/full-biography.

that restored voting rights to ex-felons and worked with Republican Gov. Jeb Bush to remove the Confederate flag from the state Capitol. She also proposed a bill in 2007 that would ban the term "illegal alien" from state public documents.[71] She derived special satisfaction from passing two bills. One mandated that every person who leaves prison is tested for HIV and AIDS, and the other disallowed prison rapes to be defended as "consensual."

At that time Wilson and other black women were making their presence felt in the halls of government. In 1992, Florida State Sen. Carrie Meek and State Rep. Corrine Brown were elected to Congress. In 2002, when Carrie Meek chose not to run for reelection, her son Kendrick ran for her seat in Congress and won. A few years later, when he set his sights on the U.S. Senate, Wilson decided to run for his U.S. House seat. (He would lose to Marco Rubio.)

Her run for Congress put her in a contest with eight other Democrats—four other African Americans and four Haitians. The *Miami Herald* endorsed another African-American candidate, Miami Gardens Mayor Shirley Gibson. Running in Miami, which had given President Barack Obama 87 percent of the vote in 2008, Wilson campaigned as a staunch backer of his administration. Her website displayed photos of her with the President and First Lady.

She won, helped by the Haitian vote that split among four candidates, among whom were trailblazers Yolly Roberson and Phillip Brutus. She drew 16,653 votes, or 35 percent, and the second-place candidate, Haitian-American lawyer and doctor Rudolph Moise, had 7,769 or 16 percent. In the general election, she had no Republican opponent and won easily over an independent.[72]

In 2012, she ended up running against Moise again and this time beat him with 65 percent of the vote. In the 2014 general election, she defeated the Republican opponent with 86 percent of the vote.[73]

Running for public office every two years requires one thing she hates about public office—calling supporters and asking for money. "By the time you finish one race and you've won it, it's time to start over again."

But public office also has its poignant moments. After her first Congressional victory, in January 2011, more than 2,000 members of her local community gathered at St. Agnes Episcopal Church to bless the beginning of her service in the nation's capital.[74]

When she took the oath of office, all she could think about was her father. He had come to her first swearing-in in 1998 in the Florida House. A chartered bus had brought her parents, other family, friends, and sorority sisters to Tallahassee. He took them to the place where he had been thrown off the truck when he first arrived in Florida. By this time, the state had a new capitol in addition to the old one. Standing on Apalachee Parkway in front of the old Capitol, he said, "This is the spot where I stood, and just think that I'm standing here now because my child, my daughter, is going to be sworn in as a state Representative in this land."

As a member of Congress, Wilson has served on the Committee on Foreign Affairs, the Science, Space, and Technology Committee, and the Education and Workforce Committee. Her focus has continued to be children and education. She introduced a bill requiring each state to develop a plan for the prompt reporting of missing foster children and advocates for STEM (science, technology, engineering, and math) funding for public schools.

With her community in mind, she successfully worked to extend temporary protected status to Haitian nationals and requested that the U.S. Department of Justice's Civil Rights Division investigate the shooting deaths of several black men by police in 2010 and 2011.[75] She took a particular interest in the killing of a teenaged constituent, Trayvon Martin, whose family she had known all her life. She called the 2012 incident "racial profiling" and demanded the arrest of the gunman who claimed he was acting in self-defense under the state's "stand your ground" law.[76]

Today, if approached by a young black woman interested in running for office, Wilson would encourage her to run. First, however, it would be important to examine one's past for any incidents that could tarnish reputation. "There are no secrets in politics," she said, particularly today with social media like Facebook.

Having a thick skin is necessary "because one-third of the people will love you and adore you no matter what you have ever done. Another third will despise you. It doesn't matter what you do, it will never please them. And then you have another third that will be with you as long as you're on top. When you begin to falter, they will leave you," she said.

A prospective candidate needs to have a solid base of support, and that requires community involvement. One does not have to hold office to serve the community, she said. "Pick something you love, something that's your passion, and excel at that and let that be known. And you can win."

Running for public office is doubly hard for a black woman. The first roadblock is being black, and the second is being a woman.

Term limits have made public service even harder. It takes a while for an official to get grounded, especially a black woman, she said, and by the time she proves herself, she comes up against term limits.

She believes women have a definite role in public service: "There's an innate goodness in the hearts of women that God is having us be good stewards of the people's money and the people's trust, everything," she said.

Many women politicians, like her, started their careers in education. "I think that has a lot to do with women period. It's an innate love for children. We are the mothers of the community."

Frederica Wilson was interviewed in person by the author Feb. 17, 2015. Supplemental information came from news reports and her website as a member of Congress.

Joe Garcia (D)

First Cuban-American male Democrat elected to the U.S. House of Representatives, 2012

Personal: Born October 12, 1963, Miami Beach, Florida; divorced with one child.

Education:

- Miami-Dade Community College
- The University of Miami, B.A. in political science and public affairs (1987)
- The University of Miami School of Law, J.D. (1991)

Occupation: Department of Energy official

Trailblazer Elections:

- U.S. House of Representatives District 26 (Monroe and part of Miami-Dade counties) *Dem Primary* August 14, 2012
  - Joe Garcia (53.4%), Gloria Romero Roses (30.8%), Lamar Sternad (10.9%) Gustavo Marin (4.9%)

Figure 6.29. Joe Garcia, the first Hispanic (Cuban) Democrat to be elected to Congress from Florida, set his sights on running for office early on because "I always loved public debate. I loved discussion, and at our dinner table, that's what we did a lot of." Unlike his beloved Cuban grandfather who saw politics as a lowly profession, Garcia "always saw the wonder of it, that in America, rich and poor participated in politics alike. In fact, the rich wanted it more than the poor because they understood how important it was." Photograph, Office of Congressman Joe Garcia.

- U.S. House of Representatives District 26 (Monroe and part of Miami-Dade counties) *General Election* 2012
    - Joe Garcia-D (53.6%), David Rivera-R (43.0%), Angel Fernandez-NPA (2.3%), Jose Peixoto-NPA (1.1%)

THE JOE GARCIA STORY

Joe Garcia, the first Hispanic Democrat from Florida to be elected to Congress, said he had been interested in politics since his school days because he "wanted to have impact." As he explained, "The whole idea is if something's going to happen, you might as well steer it if you think you can do it."

Money can have great impact, he said, but a public life can have much more. He set his sights on political office early because "I always loved public debate. I loved discussion, and at our dinner table that's what we did a lot of."

That family dinner table often had seven relatives around it, all living in a two-and-a-half-room house. "We were tight. We were refugees."

"My dad arrived at 17 after his father died under house arrest in Cuba. My mother arrived at 18," he said. She worked as a waitress at a Howard Johnson's, and Father washed cars at the airport. His mother's father came to Miami to live with the family after Castro took over in Cuba. "He had been a bus driver, a union member his whole life, and was 58 or 59 when he retired. Lost everything because the revolution triumphed the year after. So he had not a penny to his name, and arrived in Miami to be with his only daughter," Garcia said. "Only a country as great as America would allow a man at the end of his life to immigrate, right? He was just so deeply grateful to the country." At his age, he could not get a job as a bus driver, so he worked factory jobs at night and cut lawns during the day.

Because his grandfather "didn't speak a lick of English," Garcia served as his translator. "We'd walk down the sidewalk, he'd push the lawnmower, and he'd say, 'See that man over there? Go tell him his yard is ugly.' I'm sure he was probably thinking it was a good marketing technique. So I got chased off of a lot of lawns." But gradually they built up a little business and worked several days a week and on weekends. "He did that well into his 80s, and I would work with him, every Saturday and Sunday at a minimum."

One day when Garcia was nearing the end of high school, his grandfather asked him what he would do after he graduated. "I turned to him and I said, 'Well, I'm going to finish high school, then I'm going to go to college, and then I'm going to get a law degree, and then I'm going to go into politics.' He looked at me, his eyes welled up with tears and I was thinking, 'Wow, this is one of those moments with your grandfather when he's immensely proud. He had been a lawn man, he had a sixth grade education—what a great achievement for a grandson!' But he looked at me and there was a scowl in his face suddenly and he said, 'Listen, politics is for the lowest people in society.' So my grandfather didn't know much, but he knew that a lawn man was above a politician."

Garcia understood that that was "how people saw politics." His grandfather blamed politics as the reason he was in his 80s and cutting lawns, and eventually would have to die in a foreign country. His grandfather cherished his native land. "He loved America—don't get me wrong—but he loved Cuba. I remember, as he got older, he'd sleep a lot and he'd wake up and say, 'You know where I was just now? I was walking on Cayo Coco Beach. I could feel the sand between my toes.' There was this hunger to be in his homeland," Garcia said. "Politics and that culture had failed him."

For Garcia, it was different: "I always saw the wonder of it, that in America, rich and poor participated in politics alike. In fact the rich wanted it more than the poor because they understood how important it was."

After high school, Garcia worked his way through Miami-Dade Community College and the University of Miami, where he was elected president of student government. "I always thought it incumbent that you should participate in politics, and that was like a driver to me." As president, "I had the incredible opportunity to meet with many of the top people." Through one of his best friends, Juan Carlos Mas, Garcia met his friend's father, Jorge Mas Canosa,[77] a political power broker in Miami and the Cuban-American community. "Of course, I loved politics and I soaked it up."

On one occasion, Jorge Mas Canosa invited his son and Garcia to come to dinner the next Saturday. "I'm thrilled. I just got invited by Jorge Mas. He realizes how important I am," Garcia thought. But when they got there, Mas handed them valet jackets and told them they were going to park cars. "But when we were finished, he sat us at a table. I'll never forget, I was sitting at a table where the President—the actual President of the University of Miami—was sitting, and some very important people in the community. Mas came and sat with us and we exchanged ideas. As the dinner was ending, we had to run out to get everyone's car. But I became very good friends with him."

After graduating from the University, someone suggested to Mas that Garcia might help him with a Cuban refugee resettlement program created at the behest of President Ronald Reagan who was trying to privatize different parts of the government. Economic studies had shown that many Cubans were stranded in other countries, which meant that "all this money was pouring out of Florida. But if you brought those people here, the money would stay in Florida," Garcia said. "I was getting ready to go to law school, I was taking a year off, and I'd been working for this group [a Salvadoran humanitarian organization] and Mas handed me this document. He said, 'I want you to read this and tell me how you'd change it.' I had no idea about refugee policy." The next day, Garcia came back with three recommendations. Mas asked what he was earning then, Garcia said $18,000 a year, and Mas hired him at that salary to run the organization.

"It was one of the greatest jobs I ever had," Garcia said. "I traveled around the world processing Cuban refugees. I was from a working class family, in essence, and suddenly I got to travel. By the time I was done, I had been to 18 different countries." He brought more than 10,000 Cubans to the United States at no taxpayer cost and helped them get resettled in the community. Today, some 30 years later, rarely a week goes by that he doesn't encounter someone in South Florida who says, "You got me out of Peru," "You got me out of Panama," "You got me out of Spain." Many were children when they came here, so "there's no way I can physically recognize them." One who recently spoke to him at a high school graduation had become a teacher. "It's an amazing thing and it's a great privilege to have done it," he said.

After earning a law degree from the University of Miami School of Law in 1991, he was appointed by Gov. Lawton Chiles (D) to the Florida Public Service Commission, the state agency regulating utilities. He left in 2000 to become executive director of the Cuban American National Foundation (CANF), an organization started by Jorge Mas to advocate for a free Cuba.[78] About that time, Garcia felt himself being drawn to the Democratic Party.

"I was already a known quantity in South Florida, but I had worked with the Republicans and felt very—I don't know about betrayed, but I just thought I was being used," he said. He enjoyed the fact that he could disagree with Democrats, "but it was an honest disagreement and I could affect policy." In his first elected office, as chair of the local Democratic Party, he "set about creating a voice for Democrats in South Florida—in other words, a voice that we'd lost."

Then followed a series of races for Congress: against incumbent Mario Diaz-Balart in 2008, against David Rivera in 2010, and against Rivera again in 2012. The third time he persevered. By then he had become more visible—President Barack Obama (D) had appointed him to a post in the U.S. Department of Energy in 2009, for example. The Democratic Party had also grown stronger, enabling him "to finally triumph in a seat that had been held by Republicans for a better part of over three decades."

He described that journey as "long and arduous." "I wasn't an ideological warrior in many respects [compared] to the Congress we have here today. My father was a committee man in the Republican Party. He's not very political, but someone asked him to join and because I was very well known in the community, he ran for committee chair and he won. Even though I wasn't a Republican, I wasn't a Democrat either. I had worked closely with figures like Lawton Chiles [Democratic Governor 1991–98] when I was on the Public Service Commission, and Dante Fascell [Democratic Congressman for nearly 30 years]—I worked in his campaign office, as a volunteer."

"Likewise, I had known a lot of Republicans and worked with them. Jeb Bush is someone that I still know. So my whole point was to try to be a voice for my community, to try to bring perhaps a new voice, because our community had become too ideological. I saw it as an opportunity to have a fresh voice not only about what I knew about the Cuban community but about the much more diverse community we were."

The voters in his district were nearly two-thirds Hispanic. The majority were Cuban Americans, and the rest were from Venezuela, Colombia, El Salvador, Guatemala, and Argentina. About 20 percent were Anglo, "a good percentage of those are refugees from New York and other places, but some of them are originals from Florida." About 10 percent were African American, "many of them historically middle class African-American neighborhoods as well as some of the poorest African-American neighborhoods in the southern part of the state." In addition to working-class suburbs, the district included "classic American suburbs like Kendall, agriculture and horse country like the Redlands and the outskirts of Homestead and Florida City, and a resort area like the Florida Keys."

In some parts of the district, "You can still find people who refer to Miami as 'Miama,' usually meaning that they are originals from the state," he observed.

"Because of my experience in South Florida, I know that our long-term linkage to South Florida is with Central and South America, and it's a linkage I try to make. It's a linkage that bothers some. But one of the other things I always say about South Florida, whether it's a guy who pronounces it 'Miama' or 'Miami,' is that those who stayed are people who are up for the adventure. Miami is an adventure, and South Florida is an adventure every day. Those tend to be the best kind of people you want to keep. Those who fear change and are bothered by it, I'm sure there are better places in Florida to live—it's just not South Florida. South Florida's a place that always renovates itself." As an example, he compared the skyline of Washington, D.C., to that of Miami. The skyline in Washington is permanent, but "in Miami you blink and the skyline changes." He referred to the title of a book by T. D. Allman, *Miami: City of the Future*: "Philosophically Miami is not a city about the past, it's a city about the future."

In Congress, when he met other Representatives for the first time, "some of the older guys and gals don't know who I am. But when you say to someone, 'I represent Key West,' you always get a smile. When you say, 'I represent Miami,' you get a quizzical look but interest because our brand is very strong, in spite of some of the crazy things that get done in Tallahassee." He told how comedian Jon Stewart once held up "a map of the size of individual states by weird stories they generate. Florida was half the size of the continental United States. So we're proud of our quirkiness and I represent a particularly quirky part of our state, when I represent the Florida Keys and the southern part of [Miami-]Dade County."

"Our interest was always to try to give a sense of a new Florida. A lot of people say my district is so far south, it isn't in the United States anymore. But the truth is we're so far south in many respects we're like the leading edge of what is happening in America. What is happening in Miami and south Dade is how major American urban centers are going to shift," he predicted. As an example, he cited the law

Figure 6.30. Democrat Joe Garcia celebrates his victory over Republican Congressman David Rivera in 2012. "In Miami, politics is a contact sport," he said. "I don't want to paint myself as some kind of Christ-like victim figure, but in politics life is brutal." At the same time, he found a "tremendous beauty" being around politicians because they have the ability to speak for the voiceless—the elderly, the poor, and the infirm. Photograph by Carl Juste, Associated Press, November 6, 2012. © 2012 Associated Press.

profession. "Most of the seminal cases in the country, or a good chunk of them, come from Florida. That's not just now—that's been probably for the last 50 years because we're a place where things happen. So what is happening in Miami and in South Dade and in the Keys, if we can get it right, it speaks to a lot of issues that are going to go on nationally."

One of those issues is the environment. "The single biggest environmental restoration project in the history of the world is in my district, which is the Florida Everglades. And even though we're only partially done, we've shown huge success." He called the rise in sea level "an issue of tremendous importance. In Florida, we don't have margin for error. In North Carolina, you get to move a little bit up the hill. But we are on the razor's edge."

His successful 2012 campaign was "very grassroots oriented," he said, and because of the large Hispanic population, many of his ads and brochures were in Spanish. Radio used to be a primary source of information because "Hispanics could not afford general market media. Radio still is an important part of it, but it's less so today," he said. "The Internet has become a very important thing, interestingly enough, because of texting." Hispanics and African Americans, in particular, who tend to have more than one job, use their cell phones to connect with their families on everyday matters such as who's picking up children.

He received newspaper endorsements but noted, "The way a newspaper today works is very different than when I first got involved in politics where they, in essence, were the arbiter of news. Today they create a sort of baseline information, but there is also today a huge amount of forum shopping that occurs by readers." In other words, a newspaper "says this is happening today and then other media sort of take a swipe at it," he said. "Part of the reason is that we've polarized politics so much because if you want to see the world in a conservative bent, well then there are conservative blogs and TV that you can go to. Likewise, the same happens on the liberal side. So the paper sets up the day, but rarely is it the final arbiter."

Did he face discrimination while running? "There's no question about it. You receive it all the time. You've got to realize that there are some who get it harder. Certainly my father got it harder than I did, and my grandfather and my grandmother before him. So you set forward a tone that you've got to sort of ignore."

To young people considering a political career, he would say: "It's a tough life. In Miami, politics is a contact sport," he quipped. "It's very hard on your family, and it's very hard economically—for me it's brutal. One of the advantages I have is that I had a career as a lawyer and so I could go in and out of it." He also advised: "Don't mistake the absurd life that we've made being the actual politician with a broader construct around politics," he said. "I don't want to paint myself as some kind of Christ-like victim figure, but in politics, life is brutal."

At the same time, he found a "tremendous beauty" being around politicians "that can be effective in policy—the ability to improve the environment [and] the ability to speak for the voiceless, because certainly those with money have voice. But the elderly, the poor, the infirm don't have a voice and many times the only guy or girl in the room is the politician. So it can be tremendously rewarding being a staffer to a politician, being a donor to a campaign."

"I've got some donors that I think get more excitement out of listening to me talk about my day because they'd love to do it, but their business won't let them; their obligations hold them back. Every time I find someone who is willing to get into it—I may not agree with them but I think that takes courage. But I also love the people who want to be in it and help. Because, believe it or not, when you show up and volunteer in a campaign, when you send a $10 check, you are having impact. And particularly if the person shares your views. Most people are sophisticated enough to know that they may not always agree with me, but I'll tell them where I am and I'll listen. I've always found that in arguing with someone, I have a tendency in a discussion to learn more and perhaps evolve my position toward theirs more than just sort of passively finding someone who I agree with and staying with them until I disagree with them."

He had many rewarding moments in Congress, including introducing legislation to reform flood insurance regulations and advocating comprehensive immigration reform. "I know how powerful immigration can be in creating a community. Cuban Americans have been treated very generously by the immigration system in some respects, and so part of our success I attribute to the ease that we have it. In fact, it creates a cultural aggressivity, right? If you're on your pathway to citizenship, almost immediately you tend to demand and fight for your rights much more than if you're hiding from the law, which happens to a lot of Hispanics."

On a personal level, one of his most wonderful memories occurred during his first week in the Capitol while he was giving his dad a tour. They had taken a back staircase and about halfway up, "I looked behind me and he wasn't there anymore. So I came down the stairs and he was standing at a sign that said 'Authorized Personnel Only.' My dad said, 'We can't go here, right? Because it says authorized.' I said, 'Dad, that doesn't apply to us anymore here.'"

In taking the oath of office, he realized that having "the ability to say I'm one of 435 people who represent 800,000 people in the community I grew up and live in, was just a tremendous honor."

"People assume that politicians want to agree with everyone. I represent people I don't necessarily agree with, but they don't have a voice, so I've got to put their voice forward. Sometimes I can't win with their position, but I will advocate that their position be recognized because that's what you're trying to do in this body."

"This is an imperfect system, but it's the most functional the world has found to date," he said. The nation's founders "were very skeptical of centralized power. They had just gone to war with one of the great societies—vertically integrated monarchy—on Earth, and they triumphed. As winners they weren't about to give up that space. If you wanted to take it from them, you had to fight."

"First they created the Articles of Confederation, which totally ignored the capacity of functioning as a government, and it collapsed," he said. "When the Tea Party talks about taking government back to its origins: Do you know what it looks like? It's the Articles of Confederation. Pretty much the same guys who created that said, 'OK, this doesn't work, now let's try this—limited centralized government that had the ability to bring us together for certain things and yet let us experiment on others.' It's a wonderful model, but it's not an easy model. No one, no matter how talented an individual or a party is, can hold power for very long before the system, by its own design, dissipates power."

To illustrate those shifts in power, he outlined a few presidential administrations of the past century: "FDR was elected with overwhelming majorities at a moment of national crisis. Within less than three or four years, he was fighting his own party to try to move forward, trying to stack the Supreme Court because he couldn't get exactly what he wanted."

Eisenhower, he said, came in as a "conquering hero," but eventually got stuck and "had to deal with the United States Senate to get anything done."

"Lyndon Johnson, probably one of the greatest masters of making government bend to his will, within three years, on the popularity of Kennedy's assassination, changed the social agenda in America in a marvelous way. Within three years he was so unpopular that he had to leave the White House, in essence, left almost in ignominy, a man who'd achieved things that today the middle class thinks are essential to our existence as a nation."

"Ronald Reagan, same thing."

"George W. Bush, at the surprise attack, went from being the least popular President to winning reelection in the short span, moving public policy to the right in important ways, whether you agree with it or not, and then also becoming tremendously unpopular because of the system."

"It is a very grinding system meant to preserve individual rights and in particular to preserve institutional prerogatives. And those institutional prerogatives keep power from ever being accumulated and centered in one place for too long."

"That is the history of our country, and it is one that I'm proud to be a little, little, little part of it, but it certainly gives voice to a new part of our country and a part of our country that I think is going to have even more effect and at a good time."

For his part, "I'm not here because I'm a particularly good politician," he said. "I am here because I was fortunate enough to receive the favor of a good number of people that live in my community. I will hold this position as long as I've got their favor and hopefully I keep their favor not by doing what they want but by doing what's right, and hopefully that will continue to converge. If it doesn't, I'll still go back and be a South Florida guy and love my part of the state."

He got the chance to return to being a "South Florida guy" after the 2014 election. Although he ran unopposed in the Democratic primary, he lost in the general election to Republican Carlos Curbelo, a member of the Miami-Dade County School Board, who received 51.5 percent of the vote.[79] Garcia took a job with an investment bank in February 2015.

What did he find most difficult to deal with in Congress? He responded this way: "As a politician I can fake almost anything, but when I'm negotiating with someone, I look in their eyes and I hope they're faking it, too. I find that some of my brethren on the other side aren't, that they have views that are anti-science, anti-rational thought, and I think that's dangerous for the Republicans, and that's what worries me. I don't worry that I disagree with someone, and I don't worry that they want to bend me to their will, as I will try to bend them to the will of the people of my district," he said. "I've always said there are two ways to do things: it's not the Republican way or the Democratic way, it's the right way or the wrong way."

"For most people 98.9 percent of each day, the thought of being a Democrat or Republican, a conservative or a liberal, doesn't cross your mind unless it's your business to make it that." With mowing a lawn, for example, it's "not a Republican mowing a lawnmower, or a Democrat. There's just a lawnmower. You get the job done, you do it to the best of your ability and move on to the next thing."

In the United States, pragmatism and compromise have always been essential, he said. "In fact, one of the debates I have with my Hispanic brethren is the word *compromise*. I've never found the exact word in the language in the same way. Compromise to the typical American means that I'm going to get some of what I want, you're going to get some of what you want, and because we're both getting something of what we want, we're going to agree to do this even though we don't necessarily agree with what we got, but we're willing to live with it." By contrast, when the word is translated directly to Spanish, it's *compromeso*, "which is more like a promise to do something." That's not what compromise has been in U.S. history.

He cited U.S. Sen. Henry Clay of Kentucky, who in 1850 presented Congress with a compromise over the spread of slavery in newly acquired territory.[80] "He was balancing slavery versus states' rights, and in that there was a horrible crushing human component that is unforgiveable. But nonetheless we recognized that compromise is what kept the country from devolving into civil war for a very long time. Some today may say that was a price too high to be paid. I'd probably agree with those. There is still, though, the recognition in this place that finding that pathway forward got us further along than it would've. There are those who argued that if we would've been uncompromising in the North or in the West, that had a war broken out, the South might have been the triumphant party, and evil would've lasted much longer in the heart of the American republic."

What is certain is that Clay championed a concept still preserved in the Congress, "although we're not acting too well on it today, you've got to try to find this middle ground. As a country, we've always done that. We fight tenaciously, we decide to take a step and then we go forward. And certainly there are more efficient ways to do things, but as a country as we clash, it gets rid of a lot of the under argument, but then the basis of what we've got to do gets done and we move forward, and we come together around big ideas."

Whatever his disappointment with the current Congress, he remains optimistic: "We're in a better position, better poised for the future than any nation on Earth. We should be proud to be Americans and proud of our history and certainly very, very forward leaning to what needs to be done because I think while we've gone through the 'greatest generation,'[81] there are greater generations and a greater American story yet to be told."

Joe Garcia was interviewed in person by the author June 18, 2014.

Senate

Melquíades "Mel" Rafael Martinez, Jr. (R)

First Cuban-born person elected to the U.S. Senate, 2004

Personal: Born October 23, 1946, Saqua la Grande, Cuba; married with three children and three grandchildren.

Education:

- Orlando Junior College, A.A. (1967)
- Florida State University, B.A. in international affairs (1969)
- Florida State University College of Law, J.D. (1973)

Occupation: Lawyer

Figure 6.31. Cuban-born Mel Martinez, influenced by his own rise from immigrant to attorney, worked in the U.S. Senate for immigration reform and supported the DREAM (Development, Relief, and Education of Alien Minors) Act to provide a path to citizenship for children of undocumented immigrants. His political path went from Orange County Mayor to U.S. HUD Secretary to U.S. Senator. Photograph courtesy of Mel Martinez.

Trailblazer Elections:

- U.S. Senate *Rep Primary* 2004
  - Mel Martinez (44.9%), Bill McCollum (30.9%), Doug Gallagher (13.6%), Johnnie Byrd (5.9%), Kare Saull (1.7%), Larry Klayman (1.1%), William Billy Kogut (0.3%)
- U.S. Senate *General Election* 2004
  - Mel Martinez-R (49.4%), Betty Castor-D (48.3%), Dennis F. Bradley-VET (Veteran's Party of America) (2.2%)

THE MELQUÍADES "MEL" MARTINEZ STORY

Melquíades "Mel" Martinez was the first Hispanic from Florida to serve in the United States Senate. He also enjoyed the distinction of three national firsts: the first Cuban-born Senator in the U.S. Senate, the first Cuban-born U.S. Secretary of Housing and Urban Development (HUD), and the first Hispanic to chair a major U.S. political party (Republican).

His rise to the nation's upper house was all the more remarkable, considering he came to the United States from Cuba in 1962 as a 15-year-old in Operation Pedro Pan, a Catholic humanitarian effort to protect children from Fidel Castro's policies.[82] Separated from his parents, who remained in Cuba for a time, he was placed with foster families and enrolled in high school, speaking no English.

As a teen alone and without family for four years, he experienced two events that would influence his path as an adult. The first was the Cuban Missile Crisis in October 1962, and the second was the presidential election in 1964.

In the missile crisis, Martinez and the world watched a Cold War standoff between the United States and the Soviet Union that could have erupted into nuclear war.[83] "The events before, during and after all of that really drew me to watch the news closely, to be interested in our governance because it impacted my former homeland and my hopes of reuniting with my parents," he said.

The second event, the presidential election pitting Democrat Lyndon B. Johnson against Republican Barry Goldwater, took place while Martinez was in a high school class, Problems of American Democracy. Because of the upcoming election, he and a classmate were assigned to create a presentation book of news clippings that followed the race. "I think that deepened my interest in the whole process," he said.

By the time his parents arrived in 1966, he was putting himself through college, first at Orlando Junior College and then at Florida State University in Tallahassee. "I actually never envisioned myself running for office, and a lot of that had to do with the fact that I wasn't American. I'd only been here a short time, my parents had just come, and we were busy making a living."

He remembered with pride his first time to vote—the 1972 election between Richard Nixon and George McGovern. "It was wonderful being able to vote in a presidential race. I remember standing in line and all of that. From then on, it was always a part of my life."

After finishing a law degree at Florida State University in 1973, he joined the Billings, Frederick, Wooten & Honeywell law firm in Orlando, where he eventually became a partner. "I had a wonderful mentor in [Willard] Bill Frederick," a founding member of the firm. When Frederick ran for Mayor of Orlando, "I got involved in his campaign a bit—I mean, going door-to-door and that kind of stuff. I wasn't a big strategist or something. But I remember Bill asking me to particularly try to focus on the Hispanic vote, which is the first time really—this is 1980—that anyone outside Miami was interested in the Hispanic vote."

Subsequently, Frederick appointed Martinez to serve on the Orlando Housing Authority and later the Orlando Utilities Commission. "That really got me into the whole political thing," Martinez said. When Frederick left City Hall, Martinez worked in the mayoral campaign of Glenda Hood, who was elected in 1993.

"I didn't see myself running but imbued with a sense of giving back to a country that's been so generous and good to me at a time when I had been able to succeed in life, if you will. I was a lawyer, I'd done OK, I was raising a family, lived in a nice house. My brother and I had helped our parents resettle in this community. A lot of good things had happened in my life, and I felt like I owed this country a lot and that if people who really believed in their country didn't really offer themselves to give back and whatnot, that we wouldn't be in a very good place."

In 1998, with the urging of friends and colleagues, he ran for Mayor of Orange County, and won.

"When I first registered, I was a Democrat, which in Tallahassee particularly in 1972, that was the only way to vote really. I remained a Democrat for about 10 years." His allegiance diminished during the Carter administration (1977–81), and "early in the Reagan years I switched to Republican. It felt much more comfortable. My wife did first, and Kitty, as often is the case, having a lot of wisdom in our family, said, 'I don't know why you're a Democrat.'"

Martinez got actively involved in the Republican Party, serving as cochair of George W. Bush's presidential campaign in Florida. After the election, President Bush named him to a Cabinet post—HUD Secretary. Among other things, he established a tax credit program for investors building affordable housing and a program to help low-income families make down payments.[84] Martinez chaired the U.S. Interagency Council on Homelessness—a collaborative effort between HUD, HHS (Health and Human Services), and the VA (Veterans Administration), with a long-range goal of ending chronic homelessness in 10 years by funding permanent housing and support services for the homeless.

He was first approached about running for the U.S. Senate in the summer of 2003. "Karl Rove asked me to come to the White House and talk to him about Florida politics. He said, 'Would you have any interest in running for the Senate?' I said, 'Karl, I really don't.' I was very firm in my response, and that kind of took care of that. There were a couple of reasons at the time. First, I was really enjoying what I was doing in the Cabinet, feeling I was doing things that mattered and had some purpose to them. Secondly, I didn't view myself as wanting to be in the Senate. I had been on the Washington scene long enough to where it just didn't seem to be the place for me."

A few months later, President Bush sent him to Russia to meet with officials on housing issues, as a result of an earlier summit with Russian Prime Minister Putin. "I was in St. Petersburg, Russia, and having dinner when I got a phone call from Matt Schlapp, who was the deputy political director of the White House." Florida Democratic Sen. Bob Graham had just announced he would not run for another term, and Schlapp wanted Martinez to come back and run for the seat. "I remember meeting in the White House at Schlapp's office with Sen. Rick Santorum [R-PA] and one or two other Senators. I started getting phone calls," he said, including one from Sen. Majority Leader Bill Frist [R-TN], encouraging him to run.

The fact that it was an open seat was critical. "I would not have even thought of it if Graham was running again," he said. In addition, he figured that his running could help increase the Hispanic voter turnout in Florida as well as win a seat for the Republicans that might easily be lost. Many observers believed that fellow Republican Bill McCollum couldn't win in a general election because he had lost to Democrat Bill Nelson in the Senate race in 2000.

The real question, however, was whether Martinez wanted to be a Senator or Governor. "I viewed myself probably more as an executive type," he said, referring to the county and federal HUD positions. "Whether I had a total focused desire to run for Governor or not, I'm not as clear, but I had enjoyed the role of Mayor and I thought I had done it well," he said. At the same time, he had always been interested in the foreign policy aspect of a senatorial role. He agonized over the decision for about two weeks. "Ultimately it becomes a very personal decision," he said.

After talking with his wife and friends, he decided to run. He called Gov. Jeb Bush with the news. "You're doing what? You're going to run for the Senate? Now? Really?" Bush said. Actually, Bush had just talked Republican State Sen. Daniel Webster into getting in the race. At this point in the game, Martinez had assumed everyone was on board, but clearly they weren't. Had he talked to Bush and Rove this time around, Martinez might have decided to wait for the Governor's election two years later. "Come to find out a little later that Schlapp was operating sort of without portfolio, and it was a good idea for me to do this, but it hadn't been thoroughly vetted by everyone."

"In any event, I decided to run because I wanted to continue to serve. I really thought that the balance of power in the Senate was important for things I believed in. I also thought that if I could help a presidential outcome, how could I not?" he said. In addition, the possibility that he might be one of a few Hispanics and clearly the first Cuban American ever in the U.S. Senate had some appeal.

"I thought I could be an effective Senator," he said. "By the way, in a decade that institution has been diminished greatly, by the extreme partisanship on both sides, which is very sad."

"But I had seen such titans over time that were figures in American history," he said. One was Democratic Sen. J. William Fulbright from Arkansas, who served more than three decades, including during the height of the Vietnam War. "He was such a significant figure in my youth, and I remember thinking that he was just an enormous person." Another was Republican Sen. Orrin Hatch from Utah, who took office in 1977. "I had such respect for him—and admiration." Being part of the Senate "would be an incredible opportunity. So, I jumped in, a little unsure that being a legislating Senator was really, really what I wanted to do, and, looking back, perhaps having been better suited to have made a stab at Governor."

Initially, some people discouraged Martinez from running for the Senate post against Bill McCollum in the Republican primary, saying, "McCollum has raised all the money there is to raise. You'll never beat him. This is done and you're getting in too late." Opening his campaign account in January 2004 left him only nine months in which to raise money for a statewide race, "a daunting task."

He also faced some naysayers when he was thinking about running for Governor in 2010—a while after his resignation from the Senate. "The truth of the matter is I think I might have done pretty well in that contest, given that I already ran a statewide race [Senate] and against a fairly formidable opponent. I felt like I might have done better than people forecasted, but that's water under the bridge and no sense in looking back at that. But I might have enjoyed the job more, clearly, of Governor than I would have of Senator, particularly as the gridlock in the Senate became more manifest."

He hired the same political consultants for the Senate race that had worked with him in the mayoral race: Tre' Evers and John Sowinski with Consensus Communications, who were friends. Although they brought in pollsters, TV consultants, and other staff, Martinez believed his late entrance in the race gave him a slight disadvantage in choosing the most seasoned staff, which may have resulted in costly and painful mistakes.

Drawing upon his experience as a Mayor, he sought to appeal to a diverse Hispanic population. "When I got elected, it was only like 8 percent Hispanic in Orange County. Today it's 15 percent, maybe more," he said. "It was not about Castro. It wasn't a typical thing that you did in South Florida campaigning. It was a whole different dynamic here—mostly Puerto Rican, some Mexican. It was people from all over the Latin American region." As Mayor, he had come to know Hispanic pastors in working on youth and community issues and he had gone on a trade mission to Puerto

Rico. "These are things you do because it's the right thing to do, but also when you're in political life, you think about the political benefit of those kinds of things. It's sort of a two-fer, if you will—good policy and good politics go hand-in-hand."

As HUD Secretary, he had played a role in the politics of the Bush administration by campaigning for congressional candidates, often in areas with a large Hispanic population such as New Mexico and California.

"I came to understand that the issues that concerned this population were education, health care, and jobs, but frankly, in Orlando, it was transportation to and from work. It was the ability to get to a low-paying job across town and maybe having public transportation so you wouldn't have to have a car, thus the importance of public transportation. It was the whole host of issues frankly that are not always identified as Republican issues and that are not always viewed as part of what politicians in Florida, back 10 years ago, would have been thinking of what was the Hispanic vote." In that regard, "I was in a way ahead of my time."

"I was celebrated as a Cuban candidate among the Cuban community, as Obama might have been in the African-American community. I was the first; I was unique. A lot of excitement was generated in the Cuban community in Miami, in Tampa, in Orlando, wherever there were Cuban communities of any substance. This was a big deal, and I had enormous support." It was so strong that "I outraised McCollum in the primary $5.3 million to $3-something million in just that short period of time. A ton of it was from the Cuban community. The point is that I campaigned in Miami as a Cuban Hispanic, and in other parts of the state as a more generic Hispanic."

"The biggest mistake of my campaign and one of the greatest regrets of my life, probably, because it still burdens me," was advertising that used homophobic slurs to disparage McCollum.[85] "It just got completely out of hand by a couple of people that were not long-time trusted persons of mine. I disposed of them and moved on, but the stain of it remained, and it was very painful and very, very disheartening. I don't know that I handled it well, and I don't know that I got it behind me as quickly or well as I should have," he said. "I didn't need that to win," noting that he had won by 14 points. "A campaign has to be well managed, and I think my campaign at times was not well managed, was not run tightly enough."

After defeating McCollum in the primary, he faced Democrat Betty Castor, who had served in the Florida Senate, been Florida's Commissioner of Education, then President of the University of South Florida (1994–99). "She was a very difficult candidate to run against. First, she was a person with a good history and background and had one or two statewide races under her belt. She was in many ways a last line of defense for Democrats." He named Bob Graham, Reubin Askew, and Lawton Chiles as the last highly respected representatives of the state's Democratic dominance, and placed Castor in that category.

Figure 6.32. The announcement by U.S. Sen. Bob Graham (D-Florida) that he would not run for reelection made Martinez's decision to seek the U.S. Senate post a little easier. He, like many other minority trailblazers, found open seat contests more inviting than running against a powerful popular incumbent. But the race itself was highly competitive—both in the Republican primary and in the general election. Photograph courtesy of Mel Martinez.

"But I think her gender posed some specific problems for me. You have to be very careful in debate," he said. Although he agonized about debating Castor, "I think the debates went very well for me. A big key was having the right tone, the right care, the right balance, and never overreaching." He cited as an example of overreaching in a Senate campaign the debate in 2000 between Hillary Clinton and U.S. Rep. Rick Lazio (R-NY). Lazio walked over to her podium and demanded she sign a pledge against accepting soft money.[86] "Being gentle and careful in your body language toward a woman candidate was always very important. Plus, I think the woman candidate has a certain constituency that's fairly well built in. I mean, women want to give that woman candidate a break."

"When the Broward County results came in on my election night, Jeb Bush called me and said 'You've won.' I am here to say the reason was that I was able to keep the margin-of-loss in Broward close—losing Broward is a given—but keeping the margin low is one of the keys to victory. I think the Hispanic population throughout Broward County, which is fairly extensive, supported me in great numbers."

He appealed to people with origins from various Latin American countries—Puerto Ricans, Colombians, Mexicans, Nicaraguans—because he had grown up with them, had represented them as a lawyer, and had been involved in community groups. "I was a part of that community, all kind of working together as one to try and improve our lives."

While he experienced no outright discrimination, "there was certain reluctance I think in certain power circles, money circles, to raise money and that kind of thing, particularly in the mayoral race. It took a little time to warm up to me and think of me running the county, particularly in rural areas," he said. In the Senate race, the counties he lost were "like a black hole," perhaps reflecting "a lack of understanding of ethnicity or the diversity of Florida. I'm sure it's changing and it will change, but in those days it was still a very, very challenging area for me." As he explained: "You begin to have a sixth sense of maybe something isn't right there." Nonetheless, "I have to say that in North Florida, I was pretty well welcomed and I was well received, which was kind of interesting, because that tends to be more rural. It tends to be a little different as well," he said.

"I had a lot of problems with the elderly," he said, which surprised him because he had also interacted well with seniors. "I remember going to pick up a date, and the mother would love me more than the girl." Toward the end of the campaign, he produced an ad that "focused on my three mothers—my two foster moms and my mother, all of whom were still alive then," and how important Social Security was to them. Seniors "were the last group to really move" to his side.

Moving from a county (nonpartisan) to a statewide (partisan) election posed significant challenges. "A big difference is the way you're treated by some in the media because you're now a Republican, and in local races you're not." Relationships with the African-American community were good in the nonpartisan mayoral race but "nonexistent in the other—the partisan U.S. Senate race," he said.

A second challenge was "the overwhelming amount of fundraising" required for a statewide campaign. Related to that were the state's size and diversity. "I don't mean just racial diversity, but just the diversity of the state. It's like running in three different countries." As an example of size, he pointed out that "the Orange County Mayor's seat had more voters than Sen. John Thune in South Dakota had vote for him." Martinez noted, in particular, the contrasts within the same areas of the state—Jacksonville and the rest of North Florida, and the I-4 Corridor and Lake County, for example. "Even within South Florida, Miami and Boca are not the same. It's like you're campaigning in Miami, you're in Little Havana, you're drinking the *cafecito*, and then you go into a synagogue in Boca [Raton] and it's a whole different world. I mean, you're talking about Cuba and Castro; you're talking about Israel now. And you go to Tampa and it's about jobs or whatever. Florida is a very complicated state to run a statewide race in."

Campaigning has undergone big changes since he first became active in politics. "I think it's gotten far more professional, too controlled by professionals," he said. Running for office in the 1980s "was about billboards, bumper stickers and shaking hands. The county sheriffs were a big deal, and the county chairmen were a big deal, and of course the party structure was a big deal. Today, the party structure means nothing. The get-out-the-vote effort better be done by your campaign in a statewide race, if you're in a nonpresidential year or in partnership with a presidential campaign in a presidential election year. There is no organized community leadership any more really that you'd go to that is going to drive votes. So then it becomes media driven."

In his campaign, the media complained about his schedule, which was controlled by fundraisers. "A breakfast fundraiser, a lunchtime fundraiser, an evening cocktail and an evening dinner, and in between those you'd do some politics. You'd go to a senior center; you go visit some children's project, or some big employer. But those were sort of incidental to what the day laid out in terms of the fundraising. In between those stops, you're on the phone raising money for the next one coming up. This was a daily grind. As a Republican, I'm not for public financing of campaigns, but I also have to tell you there's got to be a better way. Because even as a sitting U.S. Senator, I'd say 25 to 30 percent of the time is spent raising money for reelection, and that's just really not right. But it's also true. Nobody wants to talk about it, but it's a fact. I mean, every Wednesday night in Washington there'll be one fundraiser after the other."

He added that "while raising money is burdensome, it is a whole lot easier than people realize. People understand that if you're running, you've got to have money. They understand that giving money to politics is part of what people ought to and need to do. And I would say it's a whole lot cleaner than people think," he said. "Very few people are really giving you money with an angle that's very specific. I think a lot of times, you'd be surprised, more often than not, the people just want good government. They want you to do the right thing." He gave banks as an example: "I'm with a bank [Chase Bank Florida]. The bank may have a point of view, but the bank isn't trying to buy a candidate. The bank would like to see someone who is competent, capable, independent, who is going to go do a good job," he said. "Accepting a contribution doesn't bind you to anything and people know that going in."

Taking the oath of office in the U.S. Senate was memorable in several ways: "One was my very elderly mother was in the gallery. I remember looking up at her and she stood up and waved and blew me a kiss and that was very special. I had asked Paula Hawkins [U.S. Senator from Florida, 1981–87] to walk with me as the home Senator, and she was quite ill herself at the time. I had sort of braced myself for the bigness of the moment, and it was really a bigger moment than I even thought then. So, you walk into the Senate and you stand there and you raise your hand and the Vice President of the United States is giving you the oath. I was overwhelmed by the thoughts of gratitude to a country that would allow someone like me to do this. And how unlikely my path had been to come here as a kid, not even knowing the language, and to have risen to the opportunity of serving in the U.S. Senate was just an overwhelming feeling of just, 'Wow, I can't believe this is happening to me.' So it was a mixture of gratitude and awe."

While in the Senate, remembering his childhood experiences, he worked for immigration reform. Specifically, he opposed the building of a 1,500-mile wall along the U.S.-Mexican border and supported the DREAM (Development, Relief, and Education of Alien Minors) Act to provide a path to citizenship for children of undocumented immigrants.[87]

He helped individual constituents. "I enjoyed immensely having the opportunity to appoint young people to the service academies. It was such a thrill. I still hear from people. Someone this morning, said, 'My son is a captain in the Air Force, and you got him there.'"

He became friends with colleagues. "The camaraderie and collegiality among Senators is something that I still treasure to this day," he said. "That's something that is often not appreciated or thought of, particularly in the sense of what the controversies in Washington seem to be. But on both sides of the aisle there are friendships and there is camaraderie that go beyond the battles on the floor."

"Just the immense honor of representing a state as big as Florida, and having the chance to go all over the state as a Senator and then go to Washington and represent those views. I was Senator at a time when we were at war [with Iraq]. Visiting our troops overseas was very poignant. And at Walter Reed Hospital, those are bittersweet moments. To me, the magnificence of our people in uniform is what gives you that humility to really be so impressed by their competence and dedication."

"Taking a vote on the Senate floor each and every time was special, I have to say. It was sort of like being in the Cabinet and going through those gates that open and I was in the black car and I drove into the West Wing of the White House and walked in. Any time I did that it was like, 'Wow, I can't believe I'm doing this.'" Especially memorable was "voting for big deal moments like confirmation of Supreme Court Justices, which we usually did by everyone sitting at their desk as opposed to the usual milieu of just walking around and voting, but everyone at their desk in a very orderly fashion going through and alphabetically voting. Those were moments that you just remember, they're forever." Crossing party lines, he voted to confirm the appointment of Judge Sonia Sotomayor to become the first Hispanic on the U.S. Supreme Court.

If he were advising a younger person interested in running for office, "I would say first of all, be sure of yourself and your life and where you are in life. You've got to be able to have your life in order. If there's disorder in your life, don't think of it. But if your life is in order, you have a strong solid marriage, and your spouse is supportive of you doing this, you don't have a terrible consequential problem in your life, such as illness in your family, so you can devote the time and attention that it takes. I'd say a bit of financial security would also be prudent."

"Then I would say don't be dissuaded because of all the noise. Because it's very worthwhile. It's great to serve your country. It is necessary that good people want to serve their country and give back. We are a very blessed nation. You don't have to look any further than Egypt or Syria to realize just how very blessed we are." He warned against running on a single issue. "You need to have a broader purpose of serving and making your country better, your nation better, your state better, your community better, whatever it may be that you're running for."

"If you have a serious candidacy, you need to develop a network of people who believe in you enough to give you the seed money you need in order to build from there. But I would say it's essential—in just about any office—that you have some financial support and you have some professional guidance. I think the biggest mistake I see in people that get very enthusiastic about running for office is that they go in it unfunded and unguided. The professional class of people who do political consulting are as necessary to a political candidate as a doctor is for an illness. You can't decide that, 'Well, I'll just take care of this myself. I'm a smart guy and I know what I want to do.' Well, no, you don't know how to read an X-ray or whatever. The political techniques of modern political races, filtering down to the lowest levels, require professional guidance and advice."

In August 2009, Martinez announced that he would resign his seat, more than a year before his term would end, to return to private life and his family. He explained it as a confluence of family issues plus a lack of urgency in the Senate. Before leaving, he wrote an autobiography, *A Sense of Belonging: From Castro's Cuba to the U.S. Senate* (2008). His story was also chronicled in another book, *Immigrant Prince: Mel Martinez and the American Dream* by Richard Foglesong (2011).

In his farewell address in September 2009, Martinez said, "Having lived through the onset of tyranny in one country and played a part in the proud democratic traditions of another, I leave here today with a tremendous sense of gratitude for the opportunity to give back to the nation that I love—the nation not of my birth, but the nation of my choice."[88]

Mel Martinez was interviewed in person by the author Aug. 15, 2013.

7

Summary and Reflections

Push Factors at Work in Trailblazers' Lives

They came to Florida with dreams—to live in freedom, to escape war and violence, to gain economic prosperity. And some came to escape freezing weather in the North. Those native to Florida and long treated as second-class citizens wanted to achieve equality, the rights accorded to ordinary citizens. The minority trailblazers in this book managed to do something more—to gain a hand in governing.

By telling their personal stories, Florida's state and congressional trailblazers have revealed how various factors pushed them to run for office or accept a top-level appointment. The reality is that historical, demographic, structural/legal, political, and biographical factors *often worked in tandem* to help them blaze new trails. Individually and cumulatively, these risk-takers have helped make Florida's state and congressional officials much more diverse and more representative of its fast-growing multiracial/ethnic population.

"Push" Factors Evident among Florida Minority Trailblazers

Historical Factors

The first minorities were elected to state offices during Reconstruction. Seventeen blacks, mostly from the Panhandle (Florida's Black Belt), were elected to the Florida House in 1868 and three others to the Florida Senate. All were Republicans. Almost 20 years later in 1885, the first Hispanic, Fernando Figueredo y Socarrás, a Cuban from Key West, was elected to the Florida House (party unknown).

When the 1868 Legislature met for the first time under the state's new Constitution, the first actions were to ratify the 13th and 14th Amendments to the U.S. Constitution to abolish slavery and mandate equal protection of the law and due process regardless of race. "Florida's black legislators eagerly looked ahead to a new day in politics, law, and society. They foresaw rapid improvement for their race through legislative enactment and the power of the governor's office. . . . *It would take them only a few weeks to discover how hard a road remained to be traveled."*[1] Real change would happen nearly a century later.

Historical Times

Major advances in minority representation began with breakthroughs by African-American men in the 1960s on the heels of the Civil Rights Movement, minority women coinciding with the feminist movement in the 1970s, and Hispanic and Asian candidates in the 1980s and 1990s after large-scale population in-migration.

The African-American struggle for civil and voting rights culminated in passage of the federal Civil Rights Act of 1964 and the Voting Rights Act of 1965. Just four years later, in 1968, civil rights activist Joe Lang Kershaw became the first African American to be elected to the Florida House of Representatives since the Reconstruction era. In 1970, Gwen Sawyer Cherry joined him in the state House as the first African-American woman. Cherry proved to be an advocate for both her race and gender. In 1972, she introduced the Equal Rights Amendment in the Florida House and later chaired the state's Committee for International Woman's Year in 1978.

Florida's Hispanic heritage can be traced back to the state's beginnings. The Cuban population in the Tampa area grew substantially in the late 1800s with the emergence of the cigar industry in Ybor City.[2] Among those who worked in the cigar industry were the grandparents of Bob Martinez, who would one day be elected Florida's first Hispanic Governor.

Growth in Florida's Hispanic population during the 20th century came in spurts, initially from Cuba (1960s–1970s: the postrevolution exodus after Fidel Castro's takeover; 1980s: Mariel boatlifts), but more recently from other Latin and South American countries (Puerto Rico, Colombia, Venezuela, Nicaragua).[3]

The earliest Hispanic path-breakers, elected in the 1960s, were already citizens and long-time residents (examples are Maurice A. Ferré, Puerto Rican; Frederick Charles Usina, Spaniard; and Elvin Martinez, Cuban/Spaniard heritage). They were positioned to run at a time when the Hispanic population was growing because of the influx of immigrants from Cuba. In 1965 alone, the freedom flights from Cuba brought more than 100,000 Cubans to Miami.[4]

However, it was not until the early 1980s and expansion of the federal Voting Rights Act in 1975 (to include language minorities) that Hispanics began to enter the political arena in large numbers. The 1982 redistricting of the state legislative districts sped up the process considerably. In that year, when Roberto Casas, Humberto Cortina, and Ileana Ros (not yet married in 1982) became the first Cuban Republicans elected to the Florida House, a record-breaking "26 Cuban-Americans . . . opened accounts to run for a variety of 12 posts at all levels of government."[5]

Injustice and Racial Discrimination

The perception that a member of the African-American community has been attacked or treated unfairly by the government, media, or the white-dominated political establishment has been shown to energize black voters and activists. This occurred when Democrat Alcee Hastings ran for Congress in 1992, three years after being impeached and removed from a federal district judgeship in 1988. (Ultimately, his removal was voided by a federal district judge.) Hastings attributed his impeachment and removal to his frequent criticism of the Reagan administration as racist. He articulated this sentiment on the campaign trail, remarking to voters in the majority black congressional district he was seeking to represent in Washington that the government had conspired to "get this [n——] because he's outspoken," and citing the judiciary's long history of "institutional racism."[6]

Black voters reacted positively to this message, as reflected in the words of H. T. Smith, a lawyer and community activist: "I was born in Overtown [known in earlier days as 'Colored Town']. I never thought I would live to see the day when we could put forth a candidate who could not be broken. That is why the system fears him so much. You couldn't send a person more representative of the plight of the black person in this country."[7] Ultimately, Hastings's fiery rhetoric led to an above-average black turnout, which helped him prevail in his runoff race against fellow Democrat Lois Frankel, a white woman.[8]

Other firsts, like African-American icon Carrie Meek (state Representative, first African-American woman state Senator, then first black U.S. Congresswoman from Florida), recognize how much bitterness they still harbor toward racial discrimination and how much of a motivator it still is to remain engaged in politics: "When it's really broken down, it doesn't bring me any acclamation to be the first. There should have been someone long before me, and there should have been more than Carrie. I'm sorry we have to make such a claim over the 'first.' . . . I do have some rage and bitterness in me. In all candor, I do. . . . And it comes to the surface when I see discrimination against anyone. It doesn't have to be against black people. Anyone."[9]

Athalie Range began her political career as the president of the PTA at the local high school by fighting against racial discrimination in the community. She would continue this battle throughout her long distinguished public service career, including her time on Florida's "Little Cabinet."

Hispanics in Florida, for the most part, have not experienced the long history of racial injustice as have American blacks. Consequently, they have been less inclined to run on platforms of social or political injustice, with redistricting years being the exception. The more common pattern has been for immigrant Hispanic candidates like the Diaz-Balart brothers, Lincoln and Mario, and Ileana Ros-Lehtinen to run on issues of injustice in *other countries*, namely Cuba. Two other Cuban-born

Figure 7.1. Carlos López-Cantera kneels next to his six-year-old daughter Sabrina as she leads the Pledge of Allegiance in the House chamber at the start of his ceremonial swearing-in as Lieutenant Governor. The official ceremony took place earlier in the day in Gov. Rick Scott's office. To López-Cantera, "it was surreal" to be in the chamber where he had served as a legislator from 2004 to 2012. He addressed the House members in English and Spanish. State Archives of Florida, *Florida Memory*, https://www.floridamemory.com/items/show/266720. Photograph by Bill Cotterell, February 3, 2014.

legislators—Javier Souto and Humberto Cortina—were veterans of the Bay of Pigs invasion who ran and won on strong anti-Castro platforms.

On the bench, the opinions of, and statements by, Supreme Court Justices Jorge Labarga (Cuba), and Rosemary Barkett (Mexico, Syria) reflected similar concerns about racial/ethnic injustices stemming from their heritage.

Demographic Factors

The growth of the Hispanic population in Florida in the 1980s and 1990s greatly contributed to the increase in Hispanic political activity. Yet they still lagged behind blacks in capturing offices proportionate to their population size. This enabled other elected officials to use their appointment powers to bolster Hispanic representation. A prime example is Republican Gov. Jeb Bush's appointment of Raoul G. Cantero III to the Florida Supreme Court in 2002, making him the state's first Hispanic Supreme Court Justice. Cantero is the grandson of Fulgencio Batista, the former Cuban dictator who was overthrown by Fidel Castro. Cantero, who had no bench experience, saw his appointment as a sign that "the Governor, and through him the state of Florida, has confirmed that Cuban-Americans are exiles no longer. . . . We are full shareholders in the social and political life of the state, worthy of serving at all levels."[10] Bush, as a resident of the Miami area, was aware of what Cantero meant.

The most recent demographic shift within the black community has been the rapid growth of Afro-Caribbeans, especially Haitians in South Florida. With the help of the newly found political clout of the Haitian community, Phillip Brutus (D) was elected to the Florida House of Representatives in 2000 and Yolly Roberson (D) in 2002. Jamaican-born Hazelle Rogers (D) won election in 2008. Blacks with direct family ties to the Bahamas (technically not part of the Caribbean) have longer and deeper roots in Florida—trailblazers Edward Bullard (born in Nassau), Frederica Wilson, and Oscar Braynon II (Bahamas and Jamaica).

Structural/Legal Factors

The Civil Rights Movement forced the South to change laws and processes that discriminated against persons of color. Some of these changes came via the state Legislature while others were either mandated by Congress or imposed by federal court rulings. Of critical importance to minorities was removing barriers to their election to office. Single-member districts, redistricting, and term limits were each seen as ways to open up the political arena.

Elimination of Multi-Member Districts (MMDs to SMDs)

Several trailblazers explicitly mentioned the challenges of having to campaign in an MMD in rural and suburban parts of a county where they were unknown in addition to their own community. Elvin Martinez of Tampa encountered the Ku Klux Klan when he tried to campaign in a rural agricultural area of Hillsborough County—a place that was geographically and ethnically vastly different from the Latin-dominated West Tampa neighborhood where he lived.

Redistricting

In the mid-1960s, Florida had to change the way it measured equity in the drawing of its legislative districts from geographically based to population based—the one-person, one-vote principle.[11] Carrie Meek's election to the Florida Senate and then to the U.S. House of Representatives is an excellent example of how the redistricting process has been used by black legislators to advantage black candidates, including themselves. While still a House member (elected in 1979), Meek worked closely with former state Senate President Dempsey Barron (D) to create a black majority Senate district that she won in 1982.[12] (Sen. Arnett Girardeau was also heavily involved in fighting for black districts during the 1982 redistricting.)

Ten years later, Meek was a key figure in constructing the state's congressional redistricting plan that created a black district from which she was elected to Congress (1992). While in the Florida Legislature, Meek was referred to by some as "the most powerful black politician in Florida" and identified by a former House Speaker as "one of the five or six people who could turn votes."[13]

The congressional redistricting plan that was put in place in 1992 created three majority-minority black districts from which Meek (D), Corrine Brown (D), and Alcee Hastings (D) were elected—the first blacks sent to Congress from Florida since Reconstruction.[14] Nearly 20 years later, the only change has been that Carrie Meek's son Kendrick "inherited" her seat upon her retirement in 2002 and served until 2010, when he resigned to run for the U.S. Senate (unsuccessfully). Frederica Wilson then ran for the "Meek seat." Not only have these trailblazers held their seats, none has even faced a serious challenger.

The noticeable absence of any Hispanic Congress members from Florida rallied the Cuban community in the Miami area to fight for the creation of Hispanic-friendly districts during the 1992 redistricting cycle. The Republicans were happy to assist but it was ultimately the courts that made it happen. Lincoln Diaz-Balart ran for and won a seat in the U.S. House of Representatives in 1992 in a district that was created specifically for Hispanic voters.[15] He was a plaintiff in a lawsuit successfully challenging the congressional redistricting plan the state Legislature initially drew. Diaz-Balart's position was that "It [was] impossible for a Hispanic to compete in a district as it [was] placed [in that plan]."[16] The courts ultimately intervened after a number of lawsuits were filed challenging the congressional districting in South Florida. That same redistricting plan created a Hispanic district from which Lincoln Diaz-Balart was elected. With one election (1992), the faces of Florida's congressional delegation became much more diverse.

In later rounds of redistricting, after court cases limiting use of majority-minority districts, more minorities have been elected from access or influence districts, especially Hispanics. It has been more difficult to draw safe Hispanic districts because in many parts of the state, the Latino population is more geographically dispersed than the black population. The Tampa Bay area is a good example of this. Over the years its Hispanic population has become more assimilated into the Anglo community.

Term Limits

Early supporters of term limits were convinced they would create a lot of open seats, thereby encouraging more minorities and women to run for office without having to face an incumbent. While term limits have had less of an impact in increasing minority representation than expected, they did open up a seat that was won by Democrat Phillip Brutus, the state's first Haitian-American elected official. After incumbent Beryl Roberts-Burke, an African American, "termed out" in 2000, Brutus won the seat with more than 80 percent of the vote.[17] Brutus had come close to capturing the seat in 1998 when he ran against Roberts-Burke, losing by only 56 votes.[18] Approximately 700 ballots were disqualified because of voter error. Some experts surmised that the bulk of these disqualified votes were cast by Haitian first-time voters who were unfamiliar with the voting process.[19] To avoid a repeat of this in his 2000 bid for election, Brutus made voter training a priority of his campaign. He held workshops in churches and used Creole media to give detailed instructions on how to vote.[20]

Open Seats and Special Elections—Deaths, Resignations of Those Seeking Higher Office

Open seats created by deaths or resignations created opportunities for a number of trailblazers. For example, Ileana Ros-Lehtinen ran in a special election for the U.S. House seat that was left vacant by the death of Claude Pepper in 1989.[21]

The untimely death of State Rep. Edward J. Healey afforded Susan Bucher, his legislative aide of Mexican-American descent, an opportunity to run for the seat in a special election. Bucher was endorsed by a number of newspapers in the area, who saw her history with Healey and her knowledge of the legislative process and the needs of her district as strengths that made her more qualified for the position than her opponents.[22] Her familiarity with the voters in the district allowed her to run an effective grassroots campaign based more on contacts than money.

The resignation of Congressman Kendrick Meek to run for the U.S. Senate had a domino effect. It prompted Frederica Wilson to resign from the Florida Senate to run for his seat. In turn, Oscar Braynon II left the House to run for Wilson's Florida Senate seat.

Nine trailblazers in all won their path-breaking office via a special election: Democrats Edmond Gong, Maurice A. Ferré, Susan Bucher, and Oscar Braynon II; and Republicans Joseph M. Martinez, Roberto Casas, Ileana Ros-Lehtinen, Jennifer Carroll, and Mike Hill.

Gubernatorial Appointments to Vacant Positions, Boards

In Florida, as elsewhere, it is easier for minority trailblazers, especially African Americans, to be appointed than elected to top-tier executive and judicial posts. In the Sunshine State, vacancies created by resignations, removals, forced retirements (judiciary), and death have enabled several Governors to make such appointments. For example, in 1978, Gov. Reubin Askew (D) appointed African American Jesse J. McCrary, Jr., as Secretary of State, making him only the second black to serve in that capacity—the first since Reconstruction—and the first black to hold a Cabinet-level office in the 20th century. (Jonathan Gibbs was Secretary of State in 1868 and Superintendent of Public Instruction in 1873.) McCrary's appointment followed the resignation of Secretary of State Bruce Smathers to run for Governor. (He lost.) The headlines in the *Lakeland Ledger* the morning after McCrary took office read "McCrary Choice Symbol of New Day for Minorities."[23]

Another resignation, by trailblazer Lt. Gov. Jennifer Carroll, opened the door for Gov. Rick Scott (R) to appoint former state House Majority Leader, Carlos López-Cantera (R-Miami) to fill the spot. Regardless of whether the appointment was a political calculation by Scott aimed at winning more Hispanic votes in the fall 2014 election, Cuban-born López-Cantera took advantage of circumstances and made history as Florida's first Hispanic Lieutenant Governor.

In 1975, Gov. Askew appointed Joseph W. Hatchett, the first black Justice to the Florida Supreme Court, when a vacancy occurred due to an "extensive scandal at the court."[24] It was a dream come true for a black man from a poor family—"his mother [was] a maid, and his father a fruit picker"—who "leaped the hurdles raised by racial segregation" to become a lawyer.[25] Hatchett had served as U.S. Magistrate for the

Figure 7.2. Congresswoman Frederica S. Wilson (*center*) unveils a portrait and a plaque renaming the Little River Post Office in honor of trailblazer Jesse J. McCrary, Jr., Florida's second black Secretary of State and the first African-American member of the Florida Cabinet since the end of Reconstruction. McCrary's daughter, Jessica McCrary Campbell, and his widow, Mrs. Margaret McCrary, stand with Wilson at the February 22, 2013, ceremony. Music was provided by students from the elementary school named in his honor. Source: http://wilson.house.gov/about/full-biography. Also on South Florida Postal Blog: http://southfloridapostalblog.blogspot.com/2013/03/little-river-po-dedicated-to-civil.html.

Middle District of Florida prior to being tapped for the Supreme Court. He later (1979) became the first black man appointed to the federal appeals court in the Deep South.

A Supreme Court Justice reaching the mandatory retirement age of 70 afforded *two* Governors (Democrat Lawton Chiles and Republican Gov.-elect Jeb Bush) the opportunity to appoint Florida's first black woman, Peggy A. Quince. It was the first time a Justice had been appointed by "a joint agreement of an outgoing governor and a governor-elect."[26] Quince had been educated in a segregated school system in Virginia but took her father's advice to heart: "My father told me . . . get an education and work as hard as you can."[27]

Other trailblazers got a big boost ahead of their runs for office by having been appointed to key state boards and agencies by Governors. For example, Gov. Bob Graham (D) appointed Annie Betancourt to the South Florida Water Management District at a time when the Everglades became a high-profile issue.

It was a Governor who handpicked Joseph M. Martinez, Jr., for an opportunity to run for the House. He was part of a slate of community business leaders around the state drafted by Republican Gov. Claude Kirk to give him more support in the Legislature. Martinez did little, but he won, prompting the local paper to describe his victory as a "Cinderella story."

Political Factors

As Florida evolved from a one-party Democratic state to a more competitive two-party state, both major parties began "keeping score" on their diversity records. As the Republican Party grew, it began more aggressively recruiting and/or promoting minority candidates, mostly Hispanics. The party supported lawsuits challenging the 1982 redistricting plans drawn by Democrats who then controlled both houses of the state Legislature. Roberto Casas, the first Republican Cuban man elected to the Florida Senate, attributed his initial House victory to that effort: "Because of the Republican Party's help, the Cuban-American community in Dade County now, for the first time, has a direct voice in writing the state laws that affect our lives so much."[28] In 1992, when Republicans controlled both chambers and the redistricting process, they made sure there was no reduction in the number of GOP-leaning Hispanic districts.

As Florida's political clout on the national stage grew, the involvement of the *national* GOP in candidate recruitment became more intense. A perfect example is the party's successful 2004 courtship of Mel Martinez, former Mayor of Orange County, to run for the U.S. Senate as a Republican.[29] Martinez's candidacy was expected to "woo Hispanic voters."[30]

The GOP has had far less success in recruiting black Republicans, in spite of many efforts to do so. From the Great Depression when Democrat Franklin Delano Roosevelt was able to peel black support away from the "Party of Lincoln," African-American voters have remained solidly Democratic. There is still a stigma associated with being a black Republican. They are often labeled as "sellouts," "Uncle Toms," or "traitors to their race."[31] This phenomenon was quite evident in the 2000 race between two black women—Republican Jennifer Carroll and incumbent Democrat Corrine Brown—for a congressional seat in the Jacksonville area. The national Republican Party threw its support behind Carroll, a novice candidate, who raised $300,000 more than Brown to no avail.[32] Brown retained her seat in the heavily black district by a 16-point margin.

Ten trailblazers attribute their initial success to redistricting: Edmond Gong, John Quiñones, Juan C. Zapata, Arnett Girardeau, Darren Soto, Jennifer Carroll, Carrie Meek, Alcee Hastings, Lincoln Diaz-Balart, and Corrine Brown. Two lost reelection due to redistricting—Republicans Allen West and Ana Rivas Logan—prompting each to heavily criticize the Republican legislative leaders in charge of the process.

Florida's Supreme Court Justices sometimes find themselves in the political fray when targeted by groups unhappy with their court rulings. Social conservatives, for example, have tried to rally "No" votes for Justices Leander Shaw, Peggy Quince, and Jorge Labarga as not deserving retention on the Court because they were too liberal on specific decisions. But voters approved the retention of all three.

Party Competition

The parties' battle for the loyalty of minority newcomers to Florida, whether from abroad or another state, never ceases. Generational differences in party identification and the constant in- and out-migration of racial/ethnic groups have made it imperative for parties to micro-target by nationality/country of origin.[33] Race/ethnicity is a powerful component of a person's very being. It is often inseparable from feelings, beliefs, and customs that can be traced back to one's country-of-origin heritage.

Among Hispanics, Cubans have traditionally been the most loyal Republican voters, and to a lesser extent, Colombians and Nicaraguans, whereas more Mexican, Puerto Rican, Venezuelan, and Dominican voters identify as Democrats. Both parties have had success in electing Puerto Rican trailblazers—Democrats have sent Maurice A. Ferré to the state House and Darren Soto to the Senate, while Republicans tapped John Quiñones for the House. Colombian Juan C. Zapata and Nicaraguan Ana Rivas Logan—both Republicans—were elected to the House, along with Democrat Ricardo Rangel (of Ecuadorian descent).

Within the black community, the parties routinely compete for the votes of Afro-Caribbeans with ties to Haiti, Jamaica, and the Dominican Republic and for Bahamians. Democrats have been more successful in recruiting candidates with a Caribbean tie—Hazelle Rogers (Jamaica), Phillip Brutus and Yolly Roberson (Haiti), Oscar Braynon II (Jamaica and Bahamas)—and to the Bahamas (Ed Bullard and Frederica Wilson). Jennifer Carroll (Trinidad) is the lone Republican from the Caribbean.

Media Coverage

The tone and volume of media coverage of minority trailblazers has varied considerably, by the office, candidate, and the reporter(s) covering a contest. Some journalists choose to bring race into their news coverage of a candidate, while others focus more on what a candidate brings to the table insofar as experience or connections. However, when black candidates run for highly visible offices, their race or potential place in history is seldom left out of news articles. African Americans running for high-level executive and judicial posts also get more press attention than Hispanics or Asians because of many reporters' and editors' belief that discrimination is a bigger hurdle for blacks to jump over than other racial/ethnic minorities.

Media coverage can force a politician's hand when it comes to making top-level appointments on the cusp of a statewide election. Such was the case when African American Doug Jamerson (D) was in the running for an appointment as state Commissioner of Education, then a Cabinet-level post, to fill the vacancy created by the resignation of Betty Castor (D) in 1993. With the appointment, he would become the first black on the Florida Cabinet in almost 30 years and only the second since Reconstruction. He would also have an edge in running for a full term as Education Commissioner in 1994. (He won the Democratic primary but lost the general election.)

Prior to the appointment, the press made much of Jamerson's race, often by quoting other prominent blacks who were pressuring Gov. Lawton Chiles to choose Jamerson or face loss of black support in the 1994 election. For example, Alcee Hastings stated emphatically that "if the titular head and leadership of the party cannot support Doug Jamerson . . . then I cannot support Lawton Chiles."[34] Jamerson got the nod. In making the appointment, the Governor was well aware that having a black candidate on the statewide ballot for a Cabinet position could spike African-American turnout and help elect Democrats, including him.

Jamerson ended up losing the 1994 race to Republican Frank Brogan, supporting research showing that minorities often fare better via appointment than election when they make up a small portion of the electorate. (African Americans made up around 12 percent of all Florida voters then.) His loss also underscored the notion that too much media coverage of a candidate's race can be harmful—a fact that Jamerson himself worried about. He tried to minimize it by telling the press: "I am not running that kind of campaign, I need votes from everybody—black, white, Hispanic"[35]—although he acknowledged his race would be beneficial to his job as a role model to Florida's increasingly diverse school children. Later, another minority candidate, Phillip Brutus, a Haitian from Miami, expressed the same concerns. He lamented that "the media has seen fit to sort of taint my candidacy as a Haitian, to say that I'm going to be a Representative for Haitians only."[36]

In contrast, another pioneer, Korean American Mimi McAndrews, got very little press coverage of her successful run for the Florida House. Although she became the first Asian woman elected to the Florida House, newspaper articles covering that contest *rarely* mentioned her ethnicity or the historical nature of her run. This ethnically blind coverage might have occurred because of the relatively small Asian population in the district[37] and/or to her non-Asian last name—a situation in which many married ethnic minority female candidates find themselves. It could also have been because, as McAndrews acknowledged, "In Florida, minority is seen as Hispanic and black."[38] Interestingly, prior to her campaign, she had little awareness of her Asian heritage, having been raised in the Midwest by non-Asian parents. Her interaction with the small Korean community in South Florida in the course of her campaign changed that and she developed a stronger sense of ethnic pride. Still, she recognized the limitations of just focusing on Asian concerns: "If you really want to get involved in politics, you have to get involved in things beyond Asian issues. . . . You have to broaden your horizons."[39]

Trailblazer John "Gus" Plummer, a black Republican, intentionally chose to minimize media coverage in his run for a state House seat so as not to alert other Democratic minorities to his party affiliation.

Discontent with Policies and Issues of the Day

Issues that have driven minorities to seek office have ranged from immigration, election laws, health care, and criminal justice to the overreach of government and its stereotyping of racial minorities. Allen West, a black conservative Republican from South Florida who ran for Congress, railed against the overreach of the federal government and the economic policies of the Obama administration. He also ran against the hyphenation of racial groups: "I don't see myself as African American, black American. I see myself as an American."[40]

For Hazelle Rogers, concerns about problems affecting local communities—issues affecting homeowners associations, funding for community building in impoverished neighborhoods, and state-municipality interrelationships—pushed her into running for the Florida House.

Racial/Ethnic Pride and Bloc Voting (Group Cohesion)

Turnout and cohesiveness among specific racial/ethnic groups tend to be higher when someone from that group has a realistic chance of winning an office for the first time. Arnett Girardeau (D), the first African-American man elected to the Florida Senate, benefitted from this pattern. He acknowledged that "Given a choice, blacks are going to support candidates [of their own race] that are competent and have a chance to win."[41] Girardeau was a well-known dentist from Jacksonville (a city with a large black population), who had previously served in the Florida House of Representatives. He ascended into a major leadership post once in the Senate. Girardeau was the first black to serve as Senate President Pro Tempore.

Even though the Hispanic community has grown substantially in Florida over the past few years, Hispanic candidates are still most successful when they are supported by a voting bloc encompassing multiple Hispanic groups. For example, Ileana Ros-Lehtinen, in her run for Congress in August 1989, pulled the "Hispanic vote into a solid unit—irrespective of personal ideologies or party loyalties—and [delivered] it in numbers far exceeding its proportion of the voter roll," thereby giving her victory over a black and Anglo coalition that supported her opponent.[42]

In other instances, when Hispanics of separate nationalities compete against each other, such as in the race for a state House seat in a heavily Hispanic district in the Orlando area between Puerto Rican John Quiñones and Nicaraguan Jose Fernandez,

Figure 7.3. Cuban cigars create a bipartisan moment in the Florida House after an amendment to add cigars to the state's nine-cent cigarette tax failed. Rep. Susan Guber, D-Miami, called the exemption sexist, and a group gathered around to kid her. *Shown (L-R)*: Rep. Al Gutman, R-Miami, Rep. Guber, Rep. Luis Rojas, R-Hialeah, and Rep. Mario Diaz-Balart, R-Miami. State Archives of Florida, *Florida Memory*, https://www.floridamemory.com/items/show/103050. Photograph by Donn Dughi (Donald Gregory), May 1, 1990.

the Hispanic bloc splinters into groups defined more by country of origin than political party.[43] Quiñones was a Republican (the House's first Republican Puerto Rican) and Fernandez a Democrat. The district itself was primarily Democratic in its registration but composed of considerably more Puerto Ricans than Nicaraguans. Although Quiñones made an effort not to push his Puerto Rican roots too much, Puerto Rican voters easily got the message through statements like these: "I believe the Puerto Rican community as well as the Hispanic community are looking for a leader who can understand their culture and be sensitive to their specific needs. . . . If you are from Central America or if you're from Puerto Rico, such as myself, or if you are from Cuba, we've all got the same worries."[44] In summary, this contest is a reminder that national pride and loyalties may be more powerful voting cues than any abstract sense of Hispanic heritage or loyalty to a specific political party.

Multiracial/Ethnic Coalitions

Often the minority voting age population is not large enough to elect a minority candidate, even if the group votes as a bloc. This is the case in statewide races and for legislative or congressional seats that are not majority-minority districts. In such circumstances, successful minority candidates need to build coalitions with white voters. For minority Democrats, the most common coalition is with liberal whites; for Republican minorities, it is with conservative Anglos.

Racial/ethnic coalitions can temporarily fall apart, usually in contests where traditional coalition partners run against each other. For example, a white liberal with a history of supporting minority causes and candidates may run against a black in a district that is perceived by a minority group as "theirs." Such contests, usually Democratic primaries, become racially explosive, and the Anglo is demonized as "opportunistic" and faulted for "trying to take a seat that was meant for blacks."[45] Examples of contests featuring this type of racial politics include the 1982 Democratic primary for the Florida Senate between Andy Johnson (white) and his former mentor, Arnett Girardeau (black), and the Lois Frankel-Alcee Hastings race for Congress in 1992.

Multiethnic coalition-building is often difficult but critical to winning in diverse districts. Democrat Ricardo Rangel (D), whose grandparents are from Ecuador, ran from a largely Puerto Rican district in the Orlando area. Upon announcing his candidacy, he quickly encountered country-of-origin politics. He eventually bridged the gap via his language and his resumé—military service. Haitian Yolly Roberson (D) won from an even more diverse black ethnic district in the North Miami area. She described the major portion of the district as being composed of African Americans, Haitian Americans, Caribbean Americans, along with some Hispanics. Her victory was in line with studies showing strong support for women among minorities.

The two African-American Republican path-breakers in the Florida House, Jennifer Carroll and Mike Hill, had totally different kinds of experiences. Carroll ran for and won a state House seat in a district where white voters outnumbered blacks eight to one.[46] (She had previously been unsuccessful in two attempts to unseat Congresswoman Corrine Brown running from a larger, more liberal and more heavily black district). In the state House race, Carroll beat fellow Republican Linda Sparks by more than 20 points, aided by her military background that played well in Jacksonville, a city with a large military presence. Carroll was also helped by the desire of many Republicans to have racial and gender diversity on their ticket, especially a black woman who shared their conservative values. Hill won in a predominantly white (70 percent) district in the Pensacola area, also with a large military presence. (Hill received 42 percent of the primary vote and 58 percent of the general election vote.) Like Carroll, his military background appealed to white voters in his district, as did his conservative, religious, and business background.

Two Hispanics from the Tampa Bay area—Sen. Louis de la Parte (Spaniard) and Rep. Elvin Martinez (Cuban)—each represented a multiethnic constituency—persons of Spanish, Cuban, and Italian descent—referred to as "the Latin community." This geographically concentrated community, tied together for decades by Tampa's cigar industry, was more cohesive than other multiethnic parts of the state.

Biographical Factors

Biographies place people in context.[47] There are similarities in the backgrounds of successful trailblazers but some uniqueness as well. The patterns vary slightly by race/ethnicity, at least among Florida's minorities.

Candidate Qualities

While the path-breakers in Florida had incredibly diverse backgrounds at the time they broke the glass ceiling, there are also some commonalities in their biographies. Each had some college-level education; many had master's degrees or law degrees. Most were white-collar professionals, businessmen or women, or lawyers by the time they sought office or a high-profile appointment. Many held volunteer leadership positions that undoubtedly helped them achieve invaluable name recognition.

However, most trailblazers had backgrounds that starkly contrasted with those of most of their white counterparts. Black trailblazers grew up in poor, often segregated, neighborhoods and attended segregated schools. Hispanic trailblazers—a number of whom were first- or second-generation immigrants—came to the United States not speaking English—and with little money. They lived in ethnic-concentrated neighborhoods joined by culture and language.

Their strong ties to their communities began with their schooling. Ten of the trailblazers attended community colleges: Annie Betancourt, Susan Bucher, Hazelle Rogers, Juan C. Zapata, Javier Souto, Carlos López-Cantera, Douglas Jamerson, Joe Garcia, Mel Martinez, and Ileana Ros-Lehtinen. Nine of the black trailblazers went to Florida A&M University. Eight of the Hispanic trailblazers went to the University of Miami, and three went to Florida International University for at least one of their degrees.

Thirteen of the trailblazers were educators at some point in their careers: Annie Betancourt, Gwen Cherry, Joe Lang Kershaw, Ana Rivas Logan, Marco Rubio, Carrie Meek, Douglas Jamerson, Rosemary Barkett, Corrine Brown, Ileana Ros-Lehtinen, Allen West, Frederica Wilson, and Edward Bullard.

Several attributed their run for office to teachers—Congressman Joe Garcia, State Sen. Darren Soto, and House member Ana Rivas Logan. One, Commissioner of Education Doug Jamerson, gave credit to his students for urging him to seek office.

A number came from the business community, such as Hazelle Rogers and Carlos López-Cantera (real estate), Mike Hill (insurance), Humberto Cortina (media), Athalie Range (funeral home), Ricardo Rangel (marketing), Joseph M. Martinez (telephone utility), and Javier Souto (pharmaceutical industry), to name a few.

Twenty-one of the trailblazers came from the legal profession, including Gwen Cherry, Eddie Gong, Elvin Martinez, Mimi McAndrews, John Quiñones, Yolly Roberson, Marco Rubio, Louis de la Parte, Darren Soto, Jesse McCrary, Rosemary Barkett, Carlos López-Cantera, Joseph W. Hatchett, Jorge Labarga, Peggy Quince, Lincoln Diaz-Balart, Joe Garcia, Phillip Brutus, Raoul G. Cantero III, Alcee Hastings, and Mel Martinez.

According to Louis de la Parte, who would briefly serve as President of the Florida Senate, a number of his contemporaries studying law at the University of Florida in the 1950s and 1960s brought about big changes, including reapportionment, when they served in the Legislature. "We knew that we had to reform government and make it responsive to people and to the growth of this state," he said.

Some like Gwen Cherry and Leander Shaw were practicing attorneys and Florida A&M University law school professors. Leander Shaw became Florida's first black Chief Justice of the Florida Supreme Court in 1990. His experiences before being appointed a Supreme Court Justice in 1983 show the importance of context. Fellow African-American Justice Joseph W. Hatchett reminded a crowd gathered for Shaw's retirement of the struggles they both had as young lawyers during the Civil Rights Movement of the 1960s when they were "working for the public good for little or no pay. . . . We found out what pro bono practice really meant."[48] Shaw experienced considerable racial discrimination in his early career—resistance to appointing him as an Assistant Public Defender because of his race and racially discriminatory ads against him in a contest for a circuit court judgeship. Through it all, Shaw persevered with "gentility and wisdom." His role as a trailblazer cannot be understated for, as his friend Hatchett told him: "You took your bumps and bruises and turned them into your stepping stones."[49]

Figure 7.4. State Rep. Arthenia Joyner, D-Tampa, debates a measure on the House floor during the 2006 Legislature. Joyner along with Carrie Meek and Corrine Brown attended Florida A&M University, where they met, and were mentored by, trailblazer Gwen Sawyer Cherry. Joyner later became the Florida Senate's first black female Democratic Party Leader. State Archives of Florida, *Florida Memory*, https://www.floridamemory.com/items/show/134801. Photograph by Mark T. Foley 2006.

Age did not seem to be a commonality among the trailblazers. Some, like Republican Gov. Bob Martinez, decided to enter politics later than others, believing that their life experiences better prepared them for politics. (Martinez was a teacher, union leader, and restaurant owner before running for office.) He once said that "owning a restaurant was great training for getting into politics" because you had to interface with so many types of people, be disciplined, and have a strong work ethic.[50] And Carrie Meek made headlines when at age 66 she was elected to the U.S. Congress.

On the other end of the age spectrum were Juan C. Zapata and Oscar Braynon II. Juan C. Zapata, the first Colombian-born person elected to the state House, credited his expertise in international business and his status as a small business owner (Greenback Investments), along with his heavy involvement in the community for his election. He said it helped him garner a lot of votes from the Cuban community in spite of his Colombian heritage. Oscar Braynon II was also young when elected but had also been active in his community for years, beginning as an intern with a local government official, then a City Council member in Miami Gardens.

Maurice A. Ferré and Marco Rubio were also relatively young when they first entered the political arena. Rubio got on a fast track with help from his close relationship with another relatively young fellow conservative from Miami, Republican Gov. Jeb Bush. Rubio became Speaker of the Florida House of Representatives in 2006—the first Cuban to hold that post. Rubio's interest in politics stemmed from a home and community where politics was the focal point. Ferré, the first Puerto Rican elected to the House, would go on to be the nation's first Puerto Rican–born U.S. Mayor of a major city (Miami).

Chinese-American Edmond "Eddie" Gong had a unique background. He was a journalist, first in Hong Kong, then at the *Miami Herald*. His communication skills certainly helped him on the campaign trail. But the portion of his biography that had great appeal to voters in his district was being selected as Assistant U.S. Attorney for the Southern District of Florida by Attorney General Robert F. Kennedy, given the Kennedy family's popularity among the Miami area's Hispanic and Jewish voters. Gong was always able to fit in, while recognizing others saw him as different. Some of his ease can be traced back to his days at Miami High School—one of the area's largest and most diverse. He accepted his diversity as a state legislator: My "political career was an experience in which I felt a lot of eyes were watching me, but there was lots of good will. . . . I was never lonely. I was part of the system."[51]

Candidate Networks

The African-American trailblazers had vast networks at their fingertips that proved invaluable in their get-out-the-vote campaigns. Many were active in civic groups, such as the National Association for the Advancement of Colored People (NAACP), at the time they won. Most were educated at historically black colleges and universities, most notably Florida A&M University in Tallahassee. This concentration of future black state leaders had many benefits. It put Carrie Meek, Corrine Brown, and other black women, like Arthenia Joyner, in touch with Gwen Sawyer Cherry.[52] As their mentor, Cherry planted the idea of having a political career in their minds. She was the University's second African-American law professor. Throughout Meek's career, she would carry the path-breaker torch that Cherry handed her.

Other organizations important to many African-American leaders were black fraternities/sororities[53] and black churches. Unquestionably, active participation in these social and religious networks enabled extensive intragroup networking while on the campaign trail. It has been that way from the beginning:

> "Each successive wave of African American intellectual and political currents [has been] supported by organizations in the black community that enabled discourse, agenda-setting and collective action. All of these elements were fundamental to the unfolding of black freedom movements. The multiple intellectual, political and cultural sub-currents that emerged from these movements also led to the formation of a diversity of local organizations and efforts."[54]
>
> Likewise, "Black voice cannot be separated from the black church and its prophetic tradition—an unsparing, scripturally-grounded moral judgment against the immoral exercise of power and a calling to account of the government and powerful institutions for mistreating the powerless."[55]

Social and religious institutions also provided important networks to Hispanic and Asian path-breakers—religious networks (Catholicism) more for Hispanics, social and economic networks for Asians. Sometimes it was through mentors' connections that Hispanics gained access to political networks. A prime example is Marco Rubio, who was perceived as having "been anointed as Gov. Jeb Bush's favored successor at some point in the future."[56] Before that, Rubio had interned for Congresswoman Ileana Ros-Lehtinen and worked on Lincoln Diaz-Balart's campaign for Congress.

There are some gender differences as well. Women minority candidates, like women candidates generally, give a great deal more credit than men to social networks as a driving force pulling them into politics. For African American Corrine Brown, the building of these networks began in her college years at Florida A&M University. She became involved in Sigma Gamma Rho Sorority, one of a handful of traditionally African-American Greek letter sororities, and one in which she is still active. (Latina-based sororities are a relatively new phenomenon; the first was formed in 1975.[57])

For Cuban-American Democrat Annie Betancourt, critical social networks were forged through years of outreach to various community groups through her job as an administrator at Miami-Dade Community College, the state's largest and most diverse, and her activism in politically oriented organizations such as the League of Women Voters. Upon announcing her decision to run, she simply said: "I have served this community for the last 20 years and I've come to the conclusion that I am prepared to do it. I am ready to make a difference."[58]

Nicaraguan-born Ana Rivas Logan (R) also tapped into an extensive network built during her years as a Miami-Dade County School Board member. She was persuaded by some of her colleagues to run for the House because of her knowledge of educational policy—a top priority of Hispanics in her district.

Kinships

Elected officials of all races/ethnicities occasionally get pulled—or pushed—into politics by immediate family members. Such was the case for African-American Democrats Kendrick Meek (mother), Edward Bullard (wife), and Cuban Republican Mario Diaz-Balart (brother).

Carrie Meek, an icon in the black community, was an extremely powerful voice for her son Kendrick on the campaign trail: "She's calling in all her chits, she's calling all her friends for the campaign," he proudly announced when asked by a reporter about her role in his run for Congress.[59]

Rep. Edward "Ed" Bullard benefitted from the "hems" of his wife Larcenia Bullard, for whom he had campaigned several times in her runs for state Representative. When she termed out of the House in 2000, he successfully ran for her seat. She, in turn, ran for the Florida Senate. So both were on the campaign trail at the same time. When Edward termed out of the House in 2008, their son, Dwight Bullard, ran for and won the "Bullard" seat—held first by his mother, then his father.

Mario Diaz-Balart's brother Lincoln, elected to Congress 10 years before Mario, helped him make the decision to run and opened many doors. Not only did Mario recognize the potential of his brother's assistance, but Mario's opponent did as well: "I do not have a brother in Congress [who has a] connection and access to big money."[60]

Frederick Charles Usina benefitted from a family with deep roots and a long history of public service in historical St. Augustine. His grandfather, Domingo Usina, had served in the Florida House in the 1890s. The Usina name had been a prominent one for decades—associated with the Florida School for the Deaf and Blind and with the famous Alligator Farm, one of Florida's first tourist attractions.[61]

Reflections

This qualitatively based research demonstrates the value of such a methodological approach when applied to the study of minority path-breakers. From it, we can see and understand how specific factors have affected their candidacies. Over the 50-year period studied (a longitudinal time frame), several clear patterns are evident:

1. *Revolutions—political and demographic—do matter.* Many of the African-American trailblazers were elected in the late 1960s and early 1970s in lockstep with the Civil Rights Movement. Many of Florida's Hispanic barrier-breakers were elected in the late 1980s—on the heels of a massive in-migration of Hispanics, redistricting, and the Voting Rights Act of 1975.[62] A particularly telling example of this trend occurred in 1982. After redistricting, two Hispanics were first elected to the Florida House, and two African Americans first elected to the Florida Senate. But there was no clear gender-based pattern paralleling the feminist movement of the 1970s, suggesting that in the case of minority women pioneers, race/ethnicity was more important than gender. This latter finding is in sync with what other scholars have found.
2. *South Florida, with its influx of immigrants and in-migrants, whites and non-whites, has produced more minority officeholder "firsts" than any other part of the state.* The region's younger, more mobile, more diverse populations have prompted more risk-taking in South Florida than in other regions with sizable minority populations but with less educated, less tolerant, and more entrenched white voters. The South Florida region has also experienced more waves of in-migration by blacks and Hispanics than other parts of the state, with each wave attracting persons from different Latin American countries. The result has increasingly been a racial/ethnic politics often fragmented along country-of-origin lines, sometimes even within the same racial group (e.g., Haitians vs. African Americans; Cubans vs. Puerto Ricans or Colombians).
3. *The size of the group within a constituency base matters.* Legislative seats have smaller constituencies than executive or judicial posts. Redistricting (and

residential concentration patterns) make it easier to configure district constituency bases that have larger minority populations. Clearly, minority successes have come earlier in *legislative* seats (state House and Senate; Congress) than in state-level executive or judicial positions. At the district level, minority pathbreakers are more likely to win where the minority population is sizable, mostly in Florida's large metropolitan areas (Miami, Tampa, Orlando, and Jacksonville). Winning statewide executive and U.S. Senate races is difficult but more likely to occur when political party leaders (Governors; party officials) make the election/selection of a minority a high priority.

4. *There is some evidence that political party efforts to promote diversity are most intense when vacancies occur.* The pattern is most evident in the courts, where modern-day Governors have intentionally made appointments with diversity in mind. There is also evidence that minority candidates were recruited by party leaders to fill vacant legislative seats in special elections or to succeed a legislator who made a bid for higher office.
5. *Trailblazers have often experienced significant discrimination in their childhoods and in their adult lives.* As a consequence, their commitment to social justice is strong and their role as mentors is significant, thereby inspiring other minorities who are contemplating a political career. Their considerably higher-than-average education level gave them the tools to fight for justice and the networks (social, political, religious) to do so.
6. *Media coverage of their contests is most effective when the public is informed of a candidate being in a position to make history if elected by breaking down racial/ethnic barriers.* But too much coverage of their race/ethnicity may also backfire and make it more difficult to govern or get reelected, especially in areas where white crossover votes are needed to win.
7. *Gubernatorial appointments have been the most common path to office in the executive and judicial branches, while special elections are frequently the vehicles by which minorities first win legislative posts.* But one cannot ignore the impact that court-ordered one-person, one-vote legislative reapportionment in the 1960s and the switch from multi- to single-member districts in the 1980s each had on increasing minority representation in the state House. Minority women stepped onto the stage in the 1970s, aided by the growing clout of activists in the women's movement.
8. *In increasingly diverse states like Florida, the study of "firsts" will require scholars to focus more on specific nationalities to better understand the cultural and political differences between them.* It is no longer advisable to limit one's study to broad racial/ethnic classifications (blacks, Hispanics, Asians). Among the ranks of Hispanic elected officials in Florida (not limited to state and federal officeholders), there are now Cubans, Puerto Ricans, Colombians, Mexicans, and

> Dominicans. Asians include Chinese, Koreans, and Filipinos. Even the black population is becoming less monolithic. The election of Haitians and Jamaicans has caused uniform use of the term "African American" to be questioned. It is no longer acceptable to many politically active members of those communities. The results clearly show the emergence and impact of identity politics, as streams of new arrivals (black and Hispanic) from different Latin American, especially Caribbean, countries have poured into the Sunshine State and clustered in different geographical locations.

As these biographies have shown, Florida is truly a state where one-size-fits-all explanations for why citizens offer themselves up for elective office are not valid. That said, throughout this analysis we have seen almost universal agreement that an "I can't take us being excluded any more" attitude inspired these minority trailblazers to seek an office never previously held by someone representing their racial/ethnic-gender-party mix. And their hope is that telling their stories will encourage future generations to follow in their footsteps.

APPENDIX A

Significant Milestones: Florida

Left: Figure A.1. Cuban refugees on board a boat during the Mariel Boatlift Key West, Florida. State Archives of Florida, *Florida Memory*, https://www.floridamemory.com/items/show/98688. Photograph by Dale M. McDonald, 1980.

Below: Figure A.2. Multiple generations participate in an NAACP march in Tallahassee, Florida. The NAACP planned the demonstration to protest the U.S. Senate filibuster over the civil rights bill. The Civil Rights Act of 1964 eventually passed—signaling a new era in politics—the march forward toward racial equality. State Archives of Florida, *Florida Memory*, https://www.floridamemory.com/items/show/34860. Photographed on March 27, 1964.

1930s–1940s	The New Deal leads black voters to begin abandoning the Republican Party.
1937	Florida removes the poll tax as a prerequisite to voting.
1940	For first time, U.S. Census showes that more black Floridians lived in urban than rural areas.
1944	Florida Supreme Court invalidates the white primary.
1954	*Brown v. Board of Education of Topeka, Kansas* U.S. Supreme Court ruling; struggles over desegregation of schools begin.
1954	First Republican since 1885 elected to Congress from Florida; six Republicans elected to state House.
1960	U.S. Census ranked Florida 10th in nation, with population of 4,951,560.
1962	U.S. Supreme Court in *Baker v. Carr* ruling establishes one-person, one-vote reapportionment principle.
1963–1964	Racial protests and unrest; demonstrations in Daytona and Tallahassee (1963); black woman killed and other blacks injured at sit-ins in Jacksonville; St. Augustine—national political figures, including Martin Luther King, Jr., participate in activities (1964).
1965	Cuba's Fidel Castro allowes airlifts ("freedom flights") to begin on September 28; 48,000 Cuban refugees enter Miami each year, greatly transforming the ethnic makeup of Dade County.
1965	Three-judge Florida court orderes Florida Legislature to reapportion both the House and the Senate on a population basis by July 1. The U.S. Supreme Court rejects it, stating it underrepresents urban citizens.
1966	First Republican elected Governor since 1872 (Claude R. Kirk); Republicans win 3 of Florida's 12 seats in the U.S. House.
1967	Repeated efforts by the Legislature to devise an acceptable reapportionment plan fail; three-judge federal court draws the boundaries of Senate and House districts and orders new elections; Republicans win 20 of 48 Senate seats and 39 of 119 House seats.
1968	Voters ratify three broad-sweeping amendments to give the state a virtually new Constitution; directs Legislature to reapportion second year following a federal census; provides for a Senate of not less than 30 nor more than 40 districts and a House of between 80 and 120 districts.
	New Cabinet position, Commissioner of Education, created under 1968 Constitution; replaces the old Superintendent of Public Instruction post.

First Republican (Ed Gurney) elected to U.S. Senate; first popularly elected GOP Senator from Florida.

Joe Lang Kershaw (D) elected to the Florida House, becoming the first African American since Reconstruction to be elected to the Legislature.

1969 First Lieutenant Governor since 1889 appointed; the new 1968 Constitution reestablished the office.

1970 Gwen Sawyer Cherry (D) elected to the Florida House of Representatives—the first African-American woman ever to serve in the House.

1971 On January 14, M. Athalie Range appointed Secretary of the Department of Community Affairs by Governor Reubin O'D. Askew (D), becoming the first black woman to serve as a member of the "Little Cabinet."

1972 Florida Legislature successfully apportions itself; reduces the size of the Senate from 48 to 40 seats (25 Ds, 14 Rs, 1 I); House increases its membership from 119 to 120 seats (77 Ds, 43 Rs); first time Republicans ever elected from Dade County—one to Senate, one to House.

1973 Freedom flights from Cuba end on April 7 after seven and a half years; some 261,000 refugees.

1975 First black (Joseph W. Hatchett) appointed to the Florida Supreme Court by Gov. Reubin Askew (D).

1977 U.S. Supreme Court orders first black (Virgil Hawkins) admitted to the University of Florida College of Law.

1978 On July 19, Jesse J. McCrary, Jr., appointed Secretary of State (the second black to serve in that capacity) by Gov. Reubin O'D. Askew (D).

Mario P. Goderich, a Cuban exile who became a U.S. citizen in 1969, appointed a Circuit Judge for Dade County on December 12—the first exile to be appointed to a circuit judgeship.

1980 The "Mariel Boatlift" brings 125,000 Cubans to Key West; Some 30,000 Haitian and 15,000 Nicaraguan refugees enter the state as well.

1982 First elections for the Florida Legislature from single-member legislative districts (multi-member districts were abolished); two black Senators and 10 black House members elected, along with one Cuban-American (Ileana Ros of Miami); Carrie P. Meek nominated to be the first black state Senator since 1887 and the first black woman Senator ever. Dr. Arnett E. Girardeau elected to the Florida Senate—the first African-American man elected to that post. The first caucus of black legislators forms, chaired by Senator Carrie Meek.

1985	Rosemary Barkett becomes the first woman Florida Supreme Court Justice.
1989	Cuban-born Republican Ileana Ros-Lehtinen elected to Congress. She is the first Hispanic woman and first Cuban-American to be elected to Congress.
1991	Haitians flood South Florida after a coup in their homeland.
1992	Florida gains four seats in the U.S. House of Representatives; one new Republican—Cuban-born Lincoln Diaz-Balart, and three African-American Democrats—Carrie Meek, Corrine Brown, and Alcee Hasting.
1994	Violent protests in Havana and political turmoil in Haiti send more than 35,000 rafters across the Florida Straits toward Key West. Most are intercepted and detained at Guantanamo Bay and in Panama. Republicans gain control of the state Senate for the first time in the 20th century.
1996	Republicans gain control of the state House of Representatives for the first time in 120 years. Race riots in St. Petersburg.
1998	For the first time since Reconstruction, Floridians elect a Republican Governor and Legislature (House and Senate). Gov. Lawton Chiles (D) dies of heart failure with 24 days left in his term. The first female African American (Peggy A. Quince) appointed to the Florida Supreme Court.
1999	Young Elián González, found floating on an inner tube in the Gulf of Mexico, becomes the center of a long, highly publicized battle between his Cuban father and his Cuban-American relatives. Ultimately, he is sent back to Cuba.
2000	U.S. Supreme Court rules that there was no time to conduct a lawful recount of votes in Florida for president. George W. Bush becomes President, and election reforms become a high priority.
2001	Term limits adopted by Florida voters in 1992 kick in; there are 64 first-term members. For the first time since Reconstruction, the GOP controls the Governor's Mansion, the Cabinet, and Legislature.
2002	State Senator Daryl L. Jones becomes the state's first black gubernatorial candidate; he runs third in the Democratic primary. Cuban-American Raoul Cantero III becomes the first Justice of Hispanic descent (Cuban) to be appointed to the Florida Supreme Court.
2004	Republican Mel Martinez (Melquíades Rafael Martinez Ruiz) elected to the U.S. Senate, becoming the first Cuban-American elected to that body.
2005	Gov. Jeb Bush (R) appoints Dr. M. Rony Francois as Secretary of the

Florida Department of Health; he becomes the first Haitian American to head a Florida state agency.

2006 Former State Senator Daryl L. Jones, the first black gubernatorial candidate in Florida history, becomes the Lieutenant Governor running mate of Democratic gubernatorial nominee U.S. Representative Jim Davis (Tampa); the ticket loses. Republican Marco Rubio becomes the first Cuban American to serve as Speaker of the Florida House of Representatives.

2007 The Governor and the Cabinet, sitting as the Executive Clemency Board, vote to automatically restore the civil rights of felons who had served their time and paid restitution.

2008 On Friday June 27, Florida Supreme Court Justice Peggy A. Quince sworn in as Chief Justice of the Florida Supreme Court, becoming the first black woman to serve in that capacity.

2009 Gov. Charlie Crist (R) appoints his fourth Supreme Court Justice—African American James E. C. Perry. Gov. Jeb Bush (R) had appointed Justice Perry to the circuit court bench in March 2000.

2010 Jennifer Carroll, a Republican Caribbean black from Trinidad, elected as Lieutenant Governor, the first black woman to hold that position. Florida voters approve the Fair Districts amendments to the Florida Constitution.

2011 On September 8, the first nonstop commercial flight since 1962 between Tampa and Cuba is taken.

2012 African-American teen Trayvon Martin shot and killed by neighborhood watch member George Zimmerman; the incident raises concerns about Florida's "stand your ground" law.

2013 The Dream Defenders, an organized student movement, sit in and occupy the Florida Governor's office for weeks in protest of the "not guilty" verdict for George Zimmerman; they demand changes in Florida laws criminalizing young black people.

2014 Former Republican state Sen. Carlos López-Cantera becomes the first Hispanic (Cuban) to serve as the state's Lieutenant Governor; López-Cantera was appointed by Gov. Rick Scott (R) to fill the vacant position created by Jennifer Carroll's resignation and then elected on November 4. Jorge Labarga becomes the first Hispanic Chief Justice of the Florida Supreme Court. President Obama announces normalization of relations with Cuba (December 17).

2015 Extensive legal battles challenging the Legislature's drawing of the 2012 congressional and Florida Senate redistricting maps continue in several *state* courts (Circuit Court—Tallahassee, Florida Supreme

Court) and in *federal* court. At the heart of the controversies are implementation of: (1) the voter-approved Fair Districts constitutional amendments and (2) the federal Voting Rights Act criteria for protecting minority representation rights. The plethora of cases have not yet settled at the time this book was submitted for publication.

Sources: Abstracted from Morris and Morris, *The Florida Handbook* (biennial); Morris and Morris, *The Florida Handbook 2013–14*.

APPENDIX B

Black Members of the House of Representatives and Senators (Florida Legislature): 1960s–2016

Figure B.1. The Rosewood massacre was a rallying cry for many years for many black legislators. Finally, on May 5, 1994, 71 years after the 1923 Rosewood massacre in which white lynch mobs killed blacks and drove survivors into the swamps near a prosperous black community in Florida, Gov. Lawton Chiles signed House Bill 591 into law, providing for the payment of $2.1 million in reparations to the descendants of the black victims of Rosewood. Gov. Chiles (*seated*) shakes hands with descendant Arnett T. Doctor, Sr., who spearheaded the effort. Sharing the joyous moment *(L-R)* are Rep. Cynthia Chestnut (D-Gainesville), Rep. Tony Hill (D-Jacksonville), Rep. Addie Greene (D-Magnolia Park), Sen. Matt Meadows (D-Ft. Lauderdale), Rep. Miguel De Grandy (R-Miami), Lt. Gov. Buddy MacKay (D-Ocala), Rep. Willye Dennis (D-Jacksonville), Rep. Al Lawson (D-Tallahassee), and Rep. James Bush III (D-Miami). The bill sponsor (not shown) was Sen. Daryl Jones (D-Miami). Source: The Florida Legislature Research Center.

Black Members of the House of Representatives (Florida Legislature): 1960s–2016

Years	Name	Party	District
1968–1970	Joe Lang Kershaw	D	Dade County
1970–1972	Gwendolyn Sawyer "Gwen" Cherry	D	96
	Joe Lang Kershaw	D	99
1972–1974	Mary L. Singleton	D	16
	Joe Lang Kershaw	D	105
	Gwendolyn Sawyer "Gwen" Cherry	D	106
1974–1976	Mary L. Singleton	D	16
	Joe Lang Kershaw	D	105
	Gwendolyn Sawyer "Gwen" Cherry	D	106
1976–1978	Arnett E. Girardeau, D.D.S.	D	16
	Joe Lang Kershaw	D	105
	Gwendolyn Sawyer "Gwen" Cherry	D	106
1978–1980	Arnett E. Girardeau, D.D.S.	D	16
	John Thomas	D	17
	Joe Lang Kershaw	D	105
	Carrie P. Meek (elected Mar. 27, 1979)	D	106
	Gwendolyn Sawyer "Gwen" Cherry (deceased Feb. 7, 1979)	D	106
1980–1982	Arnett E. Girardeau, D.D.S.	D	16
	John Thomas	D	17
	Joe Lang Kershaw	D	105
	Carrie P. Meek	D	106
	John "Gus" Plummer	R	114
1982–1984	Alfred J. "Al" Lawson, Jr.	D	9
	John Thomas	D	16
	Corrine Brown	D	17
	Alzo J. Reddick, Sr.	D	40
	Douglas L. "Tim" Jamerson	D	55
	James T. "Jim" Hargrett, Jr.	D	63
	William A. "Bill" Clark	D	91
	Jefferson "Jeff" Reaves, Sr.	D	106
	James C. "Jim" Burke	D	107
	Willie F. Logan, Jr.	D	108
1984–1986	Alfred J. "Al" Lawson, Jr.	D	9
	John Thomas	D	16
	Corrine Brown	D	17
	Alzo J. Reddick, Sr.	D	40
	Douglas L. "Tim" Jamerson	D	55
	James T. "Jim" Hargrett, Jr.	D	63
	William A. "Bill" Clark	D	91
	Jefferson "Jeff" Reaves, Sr.	D	106

Years	Name	Party	District
	James C. "Jim" Burke	D	107
	Willie F. Logan, Jr.	D	108
1986–1988	Alfred J. "Al" Lawson, Jr.	D	9
	Betty S. Holzendorf (elected June 17, 1988)	D	16
	Donald George "Don" Gaffney (resigned April 4, 1988)	D	16
	Corrine Brown	D	17
	Alzo J. Reddick, Sr.	D	40
	Douglas L. "Tim" Jamerson	D	55
	James T. "Jim" Hargrett, Jr.	D	63
	William A. "Bill" Clark	D	91
	Jefferson "Jeff" Reaves, Sr.	D	106
	James C. "Jim" Burke	D	107
	Willie F. Logan, Jr.	D	108
1988–1990	Alfred J. "Al" Lawson, Jr.	D	9
	Betty S. Holzendorf	D	16
	Corrine Brown	D	17
	Alzo J. Reddick, Sr.	D	40
	Douglas L. "Tim" Jamerson	D	55
	James T. "Jim" Hargrett, Jr.	D	63
	William A. "Bill" Clark	D	91
	Jefferson "Jeff" Reaves, Sr.	D	106
	James C. "Jim" Burke	D	107
	Willie F. Logan, Jr.	D	108
1990–1992	Alfred J. "Al" Lawson, Jr.	D	9
	Betty S. Holzendorf	D	16
	Corrine Brown	D	17
	Cynthia Moore Chestnut	D	23
	Alzo J. Reddick, Sr.	D	40
	Douglas L. "Tim" Jamerson	D	55
	James T. "Jim" Hargrett, Jr.	D	63
	William A. "Bill" Clark	D	91
	Darryl Reaves	D	106
	James C. "Jim" Burke	D	107
	Willie F. Logan, Jr.	D	108
	Daryl L. Jones	D	118
1992–1994	Alfred J. "Al" Lawson, Jr.	D	8
	Anthony C. "Tony" Hill, Sr.	D	14
	Willye F. Clayton Dennis	D	15
	Cynthia Moore Chestnut	D	23
	Alzo J. Reddick, Sr.	D	39
	Douglas L. "Tim" Jamerson (resigned Dec. 31, 1993)	D	55

Years	Name	Party	District
	Rudolph "Rudy" Bradley (elected Mar. 1, 1994)	D	55
	Lesley "Les" Miller, Jr.	D	59
	Addie L. Greene	D	84
	M. Mandy Dawson	D	93
	Josephus Eggelletion, Jr.	D	94
	Willie F. Logan, Jr.	D	103
	Beryl D. Roberts-Burke	D	108
	James Bush III	D	109
	Larcenia J. Bullard	D	118
1994–1996	Alfred J. "Al" Lawson, Jr.	D	8
	Anthony C. "Tony" Hill, Sr.	D	14
	Willye F. Clayton Dennis	D	15
	Cynthia Moore Chestnut	D	23
	Alzo J. Reddick, Sr.	D	39
	Rudolph "Rudy" Bradley	D	55
	Lesley "Les" Miller, Jr.	D	59
	Addie L. Greene	D	84
	M. Mandy Dawson	D	93
	Josephus Eggelletion, Jr.	D	94
	Willie F. Logan, Jr.	D	103
	Kendrick B. Meek	D	104
	Beryl D. Roberts-Burke	D	108
	James Bush III	D	109
	Larcenia J. Bullard	D	118
1996–1998	Alfred J. "Al" Lawson, Jr.	D	8
	Anthony C. "Tony" Hill, Sr.	D	14
	Willye F. Clayton Dennis	D	15
	Cynthia Moore Chestnut	D	23
	Alzo J. Reddick, Sr.	D	39
	Rudolph "Rudy" Bradley	D	55
	Lesley "Les" Miller, Jr.	D	59
	Addie L. Greene	D	84
	M. Mandy Dawson	D	93
	Josephus Eggelletion, Jr.	D	94
	Willie F. Logan, Jr.	D	103
	Kendrick B. Meek	D	104
	Beryl D. Roberts-Burke	D	108
	James Bush III	D	109
	Larcenia J. Bullard	D	118

Years	Name	Party	District
1998–2000	Alfred J. "Al" Lawson, Jr.	D	8
	Anthony C. "Tony" Hill, Sr.	D	14
	E. Denise Lee (elected Nov. 2, 1999)	D	15
	Cynthia Moore Chestnut	D	23
	Alzo J. Reddick, Sr.	D	39
	Rudolph "Rudy" Bradley (changed party affiliation May 15, 1999)	R	55
	Lesley "Les" Miller, Jr.	D	59
	Addie L. Greene	D	84
	Christopher L. "Chris" Smith	D	93
	Josephus Eggelletion, Jr.	D	94
	Willie F. Logan, Jr.	D	103
	Frederica S. "Freddi" Wilson	D	104
	Beryl D. Roberts-Burke	D	108
	James Bush III	D	109
	Larcenia J. Bullard	D	118
2000–2002	Curtis B. Richardson	D	8
	Terry L. Fields	D	14
	E. Denise Lee	D	15
	Edward L. "Ed" Jennings, Jr.	D	23
	Joyce Cusack	D	26
	Gary Siplin	D	39
	Frank Peterman, Jr.	D	55
	Arthenia L. Joyner	D	59
	James "Hank" Harper, Jr.	D	84
	Christopher L. "Chris" Smith	D	93
	Matthew J. "Matt" Meadows	D	94
	Wilbert "Tee" Holloway	D	103
	Frederica S. "Freddi" Wilson	D	104
	Phillip J. Brutus	D	108
	Dorothy Bendross-Mindingall	D	109
	Edward B. "Ed" Bullard	D	118
2002–2004	Curtis B. Richardson	D	8
	Jennifer S. Carroll	R	13
	Terry L. Fields	D	14
	Audrey Gibson	D	15
	Edward L. "Ed" Jennings, Jr.	D	23
	Joyce Cusack	D	27
	Bruce Antone	D	39
	Frank Peterman, Jr.	D	55
	Arthenia L. Joyner	D	59
	James "Hank" Harper, Jr.	D	84

Years	Name	Party	District
	Christopher L. "Chris" Smith	D	93
	Matthew J. "Matt" Meadows	D	94
	Wilbert "Tee" Holloway	D	103
	Yolly Roberson	D	104
	Phillip J. Brutus	D	108
	Dorothy Bendross-Mindingall	D	109
	Edward B. "Ed" Bullard	D	118
2004–2006	Curtis B. Richardson	D	8
	Jennifer S. Carroll	R	13
	Terry L. Fields	D	14
	Audrey Gibson	D	15
	Edward L. "Ed" Jennings, Jr.	D	23
	Joyce Cusack	D	27
	Bruce Antone	D	39
	Frank Peterman, Jr.	D	55
	Arthenia L. Joyner	D	59
	Priscilla Ann Taylor	D	84
	Christopher L. "Chris" Smith	D	93
	Matthew J. "Matt" Meadows	D	94
	Wilbert "Tee" Holloway	D	103
	Yolly Roberson	D	104
	Phillip J. Brutus	D	108
	Dorothy Bendross-Mindingall	D	109
	Edward B. "Ed" Bullard	D	118
2006–2008	Curtis B. Richardson	D	8
	Jennifer S. Carroll	R	13
	Terry L. Fields	D	14
	Audrey Gibson	D	15
	Charles S. "Chuck" Chestnut IV	D	23
	Joyce Cusack	D	27
	Geraldine F. "Geri" Thompson	D	39
	Darryl Ervin Rouson (elected Apr. 15, 2008)	D	55
	Frank Peterman, Jr. (resigned Feb. 15, 2008)	D	55
	Betty Reed	D	59
	Priscilla Ann Taylor	D	84
	Perry E. Thurston, Jr.	D	93
	Matthew J. "Matt" Meadows	D	94
	Oscar Braynon II (elected Mar. 4, 2008)	D	103
	Wilbert "Tee" Holloway (resigned Nov. 28, 2007)	D	103
	Yolly Roberson	D	104
	Joseph A. "Joe" Gibbons	D	105

Years	Name	Party	District
	Ronald A. Brisé	D	108
	Dorothy Bendross-Mindingall	D	109
	Edward B. "Ed" Bullard	D	118
2008–2010	Alan B. Williams	D	8
	Jennifer S. Carroll	R	13
	Mia L. Jones	D	14
	Audrey Gibson	D	15
	Charles S. "Chuck" Chestnut IV	D	23
	Dwayne L. Taylor	D	27
	Geraldine F. "Geri" Thompson	D	39
	Darryl Ervin Rouson	D	55
	Betty Reed	D	59
	Mack Bernard (elected Sep. 22, 2009)	D	84
	Priscilla Ann Taylor (resigned Jul. 13, 2009)	D	84
	Gwyndolen "Gwyn" Clarke-Reed	D	92
	Perry E. Thurston, Jr.	D	93
	Hazelle P. "Hazel" Rogers	D	94
	Oscar Braynon II	D	103
	Yolly Roberson	D	104
	Joseph A. "Joe" Gibbons	D	105
	Ronald A. Brisé (resigned Jul. 23, 2010)	D	108
	James Bush III	D	109
	Dwight M. Bullard	D	118
2010–2012	Alan B. Williams	D	8
	Mia L. Jones	D	14
	Reggie Fullwood	D	15
	Charles S. "Chuck" Chestnut IV	D	23
	Dwayne L. Taylor	D	27
	Geraldine F. "Geri" Thompson	D	39
	Darryl Ervin Rouson	D	55
	Betty Reed	D	59
	Mack Bernard	D	84
	Gwyndolen "Gwyn" Clarke-Reed	D	92
	Perry E. Thurston, Jr.	D	93
	Hazelle P. "Hazel" Rogers	D	94
	Barbara Watson (elected Mar. 8, 2011)	D	103
	Oscar Braynon II (resigned Feb. 28, 2011)	D	103
	John Patrick Julien	D	104
	Joseph A. "Joe" Gibbons	D	105
	Daphne D. Campbell	D	108
	Cynthia A. Stafford	D	109
	Dwight M. Bullard	D	118

Years	Name	Party	District
2014–2016	Walter Bryan "Mike" Hill	R	2
	Alan B. Williams	D	8
	Reggie Fullwood	D	13
	Mia L. Jones	R	14
	Clovis Watson, Jr.	D	20
	Dwayne L. Taylor	D	26
	Randolph Bracy	D	45
	Bruce Antone	D	46
	Edwin Narain	D	61
	Darryl Ervin Rouson	D	70
	Larry Lee, Jr.	D	84
	Bobby Powell	D	88
	Gwyndolen "Gwyn" Clarke-Reed	D	92
	Bobby DuBose	D	94
	Hazelle P. "Hazel" Rogers	D	95
	Shevrin D. "Shev" Jones	D	101
	Sharon Pritchett	D	102
	Barbara Watson	D	107
	Daphne D. Campbell	D	108
	Cynthia A. Stafford	D	109
	Kionne L. McGhee	D	117

Black Senators (Florida Legislature): 1960s–2016

Years	Name	Party	City	District
1982–1984	Arnett E. Girardeau	D	Jacksonville	7
	Carrie P. Meek	D	Miami	36
1984–1986	Arnett E. Girardeau	D	Jacksonville	7
	Carrie P. Meek	D	Miami	36
1986–1988	Arnett E. Girardeau	D	Jacksonville	7
	Carrie P. Meek	D	Miami	36
1988–1990	Arnett E. Girardeau	D	Jacksonville	7
	Carrie P. Meek	D	Miami	36
1992–1994	Betty S. Holzendorf	D	Jacksonville	2
	James T. "Jim" Hargrett, Jr.	D	Tampa	21
	Matthew Meadows	D	Ft. Lauderdale	30
	William H. "Bill" Turner	D	Miami Shores	36
	Daryl L. Jones	D	Miami	40
1994–1996	Betty S. Holzendorf	D	Jacksonville	2
	James T. "Jim" Hargrett, Jr.	D	Tampa	21
	Matthew Meadows	D	Ft. Lauderdale	30

Years	Name	Party	City	District
	William H. "Bill" Turner	D	Miami Shores	36
	Daryl L. Jones	D	Miami	40
1996–1998	Betty S. Holzendorf	D	Jacksonville	2
	James T. "Jim" Hargrett, Jr.	D	Tampa	21
	Matthew Meadows	D	Ft. Lauderdale	30
	William H. "Bill" Turner	D	Miami Shores	36
	Daryl L. Jones	D	Miami	40
1998–2000	Betty S. Holzendorf	D	Jacksonville	2
	James T. "Jim" Hargrett, Jr.	D	Tampa	21
	M. Mandy Dawson	D	Ft. Lauderdale	30
	Kendrick Meek	D	Miami	36
	Daryl L. Jones	D	Miami	40
2000–2002	Betty S. Holzendorf	D	Jacksonville	2
	Alfred "Al" Lawson, Jr.	D	Tallahassee	3
	Lesley "Les" Miller	D	Tampa	21
	M. Mandy Dawson	D	Ft. Lauderdale	30
	Kendrick Meek	D	Miami	36
	Daryl L. Jones	D	Miami	40
2002–2004	Anthony C. "Tony" Hill, Sr.	D	Jacksonville	1
	Alfred "Al" Lawson, Jr.	D	Tallahassee	6
	Lesley "Les" Miller	D	Tampa	18
	Gary Siplin	D	Orlando	19
	M. Mandy Dawson	D	Ft. Lauderdale	29
	Frederica Wilson	D	Miami	33
	Larcenia J. Bullard	D	Miami	39
2004–2006	Anthony C. "Tony" Hill, Sr.	D	Jacksonville	1
	Alfred "Al" Lawson, Jr.	D	Tallahassee	6
	Lesley "Les" Miller	D	Tampa	18
	Gary Siplin	D	Orlando	19
	M. Mandy Dawson	D	Ft. Lauderdale	29
	Frederica Wilson	D	Miami	33
	Larcenia J. Bullard	D	Miami	39
2006–2008	Anthony C. "Tony" Hill, Sr.	D	Jacksonville	1
	Alfred "Al" Lawson, Jr.	D	Tallahassee	6
	Arthenia L. Joyner	D	Tampa	18
	Gary Siplin	D	Orlando	19
	M. Mandy Dawson	D	Ft. Lauderdale	29
	Frederica Wilson	D	Miami	33
	Larcenia J. Bullard	D	Miami	39
2008–2010	Anthony C. "Tony" Hill, Sr.	D	Jacksonville	1
	Alfred "Al" Lawson, Jr.	D	Tallahassee	6
	Arthenia L. Joyner		Tampa	18

Years	Name	Party	City	District
	Gary Siplin	D	Orlando	19
	Christopher L. Smith	D	Ft. Lauderdale	29
	Frederica Wilson	D	Miami	33
	Larcenia J. Bullard	D	Miami	39
2010–2012	Audrey Gibson[a]	D	Jacksonville	1
	Anthony C. "Tony" Hill, Sr.[b]	D	Jacksonville	1
	Arthenia L. Joyner	D	Tampa	18
	Gary Siplin	D	Orlando	19
	Christopher L. Smith	D	Ft. Lauderdale	29
	Oscar Braynon II[c]	D	Miami	33
	Frederica Wilson[d]	D	Miami	33
	Larcenia J. Bullard	D	Miami	39
2012–2014	Audrey Gibson	D	Jacksonville	9
	Geraldine F. Thompson	D	Orlando	12
	Arthenia L. Joyner	D	Tampa	19
	Christopher L. Smith	D	Ft. Lauderdale	31
	Oscar Braynon II	D	Miami Gardens	36
	Bullard, Dwight	D	Miami	39
2014–2016	Audrey Gibson	D		9
	Geraldine F. "Geri" Thompson	D		12
	Arthenia L. Joyner	D	Tampa	19
	Christopher L. Smith	D		31
	Oscar Braynon II	D		36
	Dwight Bullard	D		39

[a]Elected Oct. 18, 2011, to replace Anthony Hill.
[b]Resigned Oct. 1, 2011, joined Mayor of Jacksonville staff.
[c]Elected Mar. 1, 2011, to replace Frederica Wilson.
[d]Resigned Dec. 31, 2010, elected to Congress, 17th District.

APPENDIX C

Hispanic Members of the House of Representatives and Senators (Florida Legislature): 1800s–2016

Figure C.1. Ethnic pride and country-of-origin identity politics has long been an attribute of Florida's Hispanics. Here Florida State Rep. Mario Diaz-Balart wears his "Kiss Me, I'm Cuban" button. State Archives of Florida, *Florida Memory*, https://www.floridamemory.com/items/show/102663. Photograph by Donn Dughi (Donald Gregory), 1990.

Hispanic Members of the House of Representatives (Florida Legislature): 1800s–2016

Years	Name	Party	District or county
1822	Bernardo Segui (resigned)		East Florida
	Joseph M. (Jose Mariano) Hernández (resigned)		East Florida
	Joseph (Jose) Noriega		West Florida
1823	John (Juan) de la Rua (absent)		West Florida
	Joseph (Jose) Noriega (resigned)		West Florida
1824	John (Juan) de la Rua		Escambia
	Joseph (Jose) Noriega		Escambia
	Joseph M. (Jose Mariano) Hernández (President)		St. Johns
1825	John (Juan) de la Rua		Escambia
	Joseph (Jose) Noriega (absent)		Escambia
	Joseph M. (Jose Mariano) Hernández (resigned)		St. Johns
1826	Peter Alba		1

Years	Name	Party	District or county
1827	John (Juan) de la Rua		1
	Joseph Simeon "Jose" Sanchez	D	12
1828	Peter Alba (President)		1
	Joseph Simeon "Jose" Sanchez	D	12
1829	Joseph Simeon "Jose" Sanchez	D	
1831	Joseph Simeon "Jose" Sanchez	D	
1832	Joseph Simeon "Jose" Sanchez	D	St. Johns
1837	Stephen D. Fernandez	D	Nassau
1840	Henry A. Nunis	D	Escambia
1841	Stephen D. Fernandez	D	Duval
	Henry A. Nunis	D	Escambia
	Joseph Elzuardi		Monroe
1842	Francis Arnau	D	Calhoun
	Joseph Elzuardi		Monroe
1843	Francis Arnau	D	Calhoun
	F. E. de la Rua	Whig	Escambia
1844	Francis Arnau	D	Calhoun
	F. E. de la Rua	Whig	Escambia
	Joseph Simeon "Jose" Sanchez	D	St. Johns
March 3, 1845 Florida becomes 27th state			
1845	John J. Sanchez	D	Alachua
	Stephen D. Fernandez	D	Duval
	F. E. de la Rua	Whig	Escambia
	Bartolo Oliveros		St. Johns
1846	A. A. Canova		Duval
1847	Francis Arnau	D	St. Johns
1856	C. Gonzales		Escambia
	Paul Arnau		St. Johns
1860	A. A. Canova		Duval
1861	A. A. Canova		Duval
1863	Louis Deshong		Hillsborough
1864	James A. Pacetty		St. Johns
1865	Paul Arnau		St. Johns
1866	Paul Arnau		St. Johns
1871	B. F. Oliveros	D	St. Johns
1872	B. F. Oliveros	D	St. Johns
1879	George J. Arnow		Alachua
	George P. Canova		Baker
	Robert Gabriel		Monroe
	Paul Arnau		St. Johns
1881	R. B. Canova		St. Johns
1883	George P. Canova		Baker

Years	Name	Party	District or county
1885	Fernando Figueredo		Monroe
1889	M. P. Delgado	D	Monroe
	Manuel R. Moreno, M.D.	R	Monroe
1891	D. B. Usina		St. Johns
1893	Jose G. Pompez	R	Monroe
1899	A. T. Patillo		Volusia
1913	St. Elmo W. "Chic" Acosta (great-grandfather was a Spanish governor per oral history from WPA)	D	Duval
1915	Arthur Gomez	D	Monroe
1917	Arthur Gomez	D	Monroe
1918	Juan Francisco Busto	D	Monroe
1919	Juan Francisco Busto	D	Monroe
1921	Juan Francisco Busto	D	Monroe
1923	Juan Francisco Busto	D	Monroe
1925	Juan Francisco Busto	D	Monroe
1941	St. Elmo W. "Chic" Acosta	D	Duval
1943	Frederick Charles Usina, Jr. (Usina family in St. Augustine originally from Minorca per city government website)	D	St. Johns
	G. Warren "Bobby" Sanchez (descendant of one of three Spanish families that remained in St. Augustine after Florida was ceded by Spain to Great Britain per Robert F. Sanchez, cousin)	D	Suwannee
1947	Frederick Charles Usina, Jr.	D	St. Johns
1949	Frederick Charles Usina, Jr.	D	St. Johns
1951	Frederick Charles Usina, Jr.	D	St. Johns
1953	Frederick Charles Usina, Jr.	D	St. Johns
1955	Frederick Charles Usina, Jr.	D	St. Johns
1957	Frederick Charles Usina, Jr.	D	St. Johns
1959	Frederick Charles Usina, Jr.	D	St. Johns
1961	Frederick Charles Usina, Jr.	D	St. Johns
1962–1964	Louis de la Parte, Jr. (per oral history by Rep. Elvin Martinez)	D	Hillsborough
	Hilario "Charlie" Ramos, Jr. (parents owners of the oldest Spanish-owned Budweiser franchise in the country per obituary)	D	Monroe
	Frederick Charles Usina, Jr.	D	St. Johns
1964–1966	Louis de la Parte, Jr.	D	Hillsborough
	Frederick Charles Usina, Jr.	D	St. Johns
1966–1968	Ted Alvarez, Jr. (grandson of Spanish immigrants per obituary)	D	19
	Elvin L. Martinez (per oral history/Legislative Research Center & Museum)	D	63
	Joseph M. Martinez, Jr. (father from Spain per obituary)	R	88
	Maurice A. Ferré (born in Puerto Rico per Clerk's Manual)	D	91

Years	Name	Party	District or county
1968–1970	Ted Alvarez, Jr.	D	19
	Elvin L. Martinez	D	63
	Joseph M. Martinez, Jr.	R	88
1970–1972	Ted Alvarez, Jr.	D	19
	Elvin L. Martinez	D	63
1972–1974	Elvin L. Martinez	D	70
1978–1980	Elvin L. Martinez	D	67
1980–1982	Elvin L. Martinez	D	67
	Roberto Casas (elected Jan. 26, 1982)	R	111
1982–1984	Elvin L. Martinez	D	65
	Ileana Ros (later Ros-Lehtinen)	R	110
	Roberto Casas	R	111
	Humberto J. Cortina	R	113
1984–1986	Elvin L. Martinez	D	65
	Alberto "Al" Gutman	R	105
	Rodolfo "Rudy" Garcia, Jr. (youngest person elected to House as of Nov. 2012)	R	109
	Ileana Ros (later Ros-Lehtinen)	R	110
	Roberto Casas	R	111
	Arnhilda B. Gonzalez-Quevedo	R	112
	Luis C. Morse	R	113
	Javier D. Souto	R	115
1986–1988	Elvin L. Martinez	D	65
	Alberto Gutman	R	105
	Rodolfo "Rudy" Garcia, Jr.	R	109
	Lincoln Diaz-Balart	R	110
	Roberto Casas	R	111
	Arnhilda B. Gonzalez-Quevedo	R	112
	Luis C. Morse	R	113
	Javier D. Souto	R	115
1988–1990	Elvin L. Martinez	D	65
	Alberto "Al" Gutman	R	105
	Luis E. Rojas	R	109
	Lincoln Diaz-Balart (resigned Aug. 29, 1989)	R	110
	Miguel A. De Grandy (elected Aug. 29, 1989)	R	110
	Nilo Juri (resigned Nov. 7, 1989)	R	111
	Rodolfo "Rudy" Garcia, Jr. (elected Nov. 7, 1989)	R	111
	Carlos L. Valdes	R	112
	Luis C. Morse	R	113
	Mario R. Diaz-Balart	R	115
1990–1992	Elvin L. Martinez	D	65
	Alberto Gutman	R	105

Years	Name	Party	District or county
	Luis E. Rojas	R	109
	Miguel A. De Grandy	R	110
	Rodolfo "Rudy" Garcia, Jr.	R	111
	Carlos L. Valdes	R	112
	Luis C. Morse	R	113
	Mario Diaz-Balart	R	115
1992–1994	Elvin L. Martinez	D	58
	Luis E. Rojas	R	102
	Bruno A. Barreiro	R	107
	Rodolfo "Rudy" Garcia, Jr.	R	110
	Carlos L. Valdes	R	111
	J. Alex Villalobos	R	112
	Luis C. Morse	R	113
	Miguel A. De Grandy	R	114
	Carlos A. Manrique	R	115
	Eladio Armesto-Garcia	R	117
1994–1996	Elvin L. Martinez	D	58
	Luis E. Rojas	R	102
	Bruno A. Barreiro	R	107
	Rodolfo "Rudy" Garcia, Jr.	R	110
	Carlos L. Valdes	R	111
	J. Alex Villalobos	R	112
	Luis C. Morse	R	113
	Jorge Rodriguez-Chomat	R	114
	Alex Diaz de la Portilla	R	115
	Annie Betancourt	D	116
	Carlos A. Lacasa	R	117
1996–1998	Deborah Tamargo	R	58
	Elvin L. Martinez (resigned Aug. 31, 1997)	D	58
	Luis E. Rojas	R	102
	Bruno A. Barreiro	R	107
	Rodolfo "Rudy" Garcia, Jr.	R	110
	Carlos L. Valdes	R	111
	J. Alex Villalobos	R	112
	Luis C. Morse	R	113
	Jorge Rodriguez-Chomat	R	114
	Alex Diaz de la Portilla	R	115
	Annie Betancourt	D	116
	Carlos A. Lacasa	R	117
1998–2000	Bob "Coach" Henriquez	D	58
	Luis E. Rojas	R	102
	Gustavo A. Barreiro	R	107

Years	Name	Party	District or county
	Rodolfo "Rudy" Garcia, Jr.	R	110
	Carlos L. Valdes (resigned Jan. 25, 2000)	R	111
	Marco Rubio (elected Jan. 25, 2000)	R	111
	J. Alex Villalobos	R	112
	Manuel Prieguez	R	113
	Gaston I. Cantens	R	114
	Alex Diaz de la Portilla (resigned Jan. 25, 2000)	R	115
	Renier Diaz de la Portilla (elected Jan. 25, 2000)	R	115
	Annie Betancourt	D	116
	Carlos A. Lacasa	R	117
2000–2002	Bob "Coach" Henriquez	D	58
	Rafael "Ralph" Arza	R	102
	Gustavo A. Barreiro	R	107
	Rene Garcia	R	110
	Marco Rubio	R	111
	Mario R. Diaz-Balart	R	112
	Manuel Prieguez	R	113
	Gaston I. Cantens	R	114
	Renier Diaz de la Portilla	R	115
	Annie Betancourt	D	116
	Carlos A. Lacasa	R	117
2002–2004	John "Q" Quiñones	R	49
	Bob "Coach" Henriquez	D	58
	Rafael "Ralph" Arza	R	102
	Gustavo A. Barreiro	R	107
	Rene Garcia	R	110
	Marco Rubio	R	111
	David Rivera	R	112
	Manuel Prieguez	R	113
	Gaston I. Cantens	R	114
	Juan-Carlos "J. C." Planas	R	115
	Marcelo Llorente	R	116
	Julio Robaina	R	117
	Juan C. Zapata	R	119
2004–2006	John "Q" Quiñones	R	49
	Bob "Coach" Henriquez	D	58
	Susan Bucher	D	88
	Rafael "Ralph" Arza	R	102
	Gustavo A. Barreiro	R	107
	Rene Garcia	R	110
	Marco Rubio	R	111
	David Rivera	R	112

Years	Name	Party	District or county
	Carlos López-Cantera	R	113
	Anitere Flores	R	114
	Juan-Carlos "J. C." Planas	R	115
	Marcelo Llorente	R	116
	Julio Robaina	R	117
	Juan C. Zapata	R	119
2006–2008	Anthony Trey Traviesa	R	56
	Susan Bucher	D	88
	Eduardo "Eddy" Gonzalez	R	102
	Luis R. Garcia, Jr.	D	107
	Rene Garcia	R	110
	Marco Rubio	R	111
	David Rivera	R	112
	Carlos López-Cantera	R	113
	Anitere Flores	R	114
	Juan-Carlos "J. C." Planas	R	115
	Marcelo Llorente	R	116
	Julio Robaino	R	117
	Juan C. Zapata	R	119
2008–2010	Janet Cruz (elected Feb. 23, 2010)	D	58
	Eduardo "Eddy" Gonzalez	R	102
	Luis R. Garcia, Jr.	D	107
	Esteban L. Bovo, Jr.	R	110
	David Rivera	R	112
	Carlos López-Cantera	R	113
	Anitere Flores	R	114
	Juan-Carlos "J. C." Planas	R	115
	Marcelo Llorente	R	116
	Julio Robaina	R	117
	Juan C. Zapata	R	119
2010–2012	Darren Soto	D	49
	Janet Cruz	D	58
	Eduardo "Eddy" Gonzalez	R	102
	Luis R. Garcia, Jr.	D	107
	Esteban L. Bovo, Jr. (resigned Mar. 25, 2011)	R	110
	Jose R. Oliva (elected June 28, 2011)	R	110
	Erik Fresen	R	111
	Jeanette M. Nuñez	R	112
	Carlos López-Cantera	R	113
	Ana Rivas Logan	R	114
	Jose Felix Diaz	R	115
	Carlos Trujillo	R	116

Years	Name	Party	District or county
	Frank Artiles	R	119
2012–2014	David Santiago	R	27
	Mike La Rosa	R	42
	Ricardo Rangel	D	43
	Victor Manuel "Vic" Torres, Jr.	D	48
	Janet Cruz	D	62
	Manny Diaz, Jr.	R	103
	Carlos Trujillo	R	105
	Jose R. Oliva	R	110
	Eduardo "Eddy" Gonzalez	R	111
	José Javier Rodríguez	D	112
	Erik Fresen	R	114
	Jose Felix Diaz	R	116
	Frank Artiles	R	118
	Jeanette M. Nuñez	R	119
2014–2016	David Santiago	R	27
	Rober "Bob" Cortes	R	30
	Mike La Rosa	R	42
	John Cortes	D	43
	Victor Manuel "Vic" Torres, Jr.	D	48
	Rene Plasencia	R	49
	Janet Cruz	D	62
	Julio Gonzalez	R	74
	Manny Diaz, Jr.	R	103
	Carlos Trujillo	R	105
	Jose R. Oliva	R	110
	Bryan Avila	R	111
	Jose Javier Rodriguez	D	112
	Erik Fresen	R	114
	Jose Felix Diaz	R	116
	Frank Artiles	R	118
	Jeanette M. Nunez	R	119

Notes: 1925 and earlier: Members were generally included per appearance of the name in *People of Lawmaking* although ethnicity has not been confirmed by other sources.
1822–1837: Legislative Council (unicameral).
1840–1844: Legislative Council (House)—prior to statehood.

Hispanic Senators (Florida Legislature): 1960s–2016

Years	Name	Party	City	District
1986–1988	Ileana Ros-Lehtinen	R	Miami	34
1988–1986	Roberto Casas	R	Hialeah	33
	Lincoln Diaz-Balart[a]	R	Miami	34
	Ileana Ros-Lehtinen[b]	R	Miami	34
	Javier Souto	R	Miami	40
1990–1992	Roberto Casas	R	Hialeah	33
	Lincoln Diaz-Balart	R	Miami	34
	Javier Souto	R	Miami	40
1992–1994	Roberto Casas	R	Hialeah	33
	Mario Diaz-Balart	R	Miami	37
	Alberto “Al” Gutman	R	Miami	34
1994–1996	Roberto Casas	R	Hialeah	33
	Mario Diaz-Balart	R	Miami	37
	Alberto “Al” Gutman	R	Miami	34
1996–1998	Roberto Casas	R	Hialeah	33
	Mario Diaz-Balart	R	Miami	37
	Alberto “Al” Gutman	R	Miami	34
1998–2000	Roberto Casas	R	Hialeah	33
	Alex Diaz de la Portilla[c]	R	Miami	34
	Mario Diaz-Balart	R	Miami	37
	Alberto “Al” Gutman[d]	R	Miami	34
2000–2002	Alex Diaz de la Portilla	R	Miami	34
	Rodolfo “Rudy” Garcia, Jr.	R	Hialeah	39
	J. Alex Villalobos	R	Miami	37
2002–2004	Alex Diaz de la Portilla	R	Miami	36
	Rodolfo “Rudy” Garcia, Jr.	R	Hialeah	40
	J. Alex Villalobos		Miami	38
2004–2006	Alex Diaz de la Portilla	R	Miami	36
	Rodolfo “Rudy” Garcia, Jr.	R	Hialeah	40
	J. Alex Villalobos	R	Miami	38
2006–2008	Alex Diaz de la Portilla	R	Miami	36
	Rodolfo “Rudy” Garcia, Jr.	R	Hialeah	40
	J. Alex Villalobos	R	Miami	38
2008–2010	Alex Diaz de la Portilla	R	Miami	36
	Rodolfo “Rudy” Garcia, Jr.	R	Hialeah	40
	J. Alex Villalobos	R	Miami	38
2010–2012	Miguel Diaz de la Portilla	R	Coral Gables	36
	Anitere Flores	R	Miami	38
	Rene Garcia	R	Hialeah	40
2012–2014	Miguel Diaz de la Portilla	R	Coral Gables	40
	Anitere Flores	R	Miami	37
	Rene Garcia	R	Hialeah	38
	Darren Soto	D	Orlando	14

Years	Name	Party	City	District
2014–2016	Anitere Flores	R	Miami	37
	Darren Soto	D	Orlando	14
	Miguel Diaz de la Portilla	R	Coral Gables	40
	Rene Garcia	R	Hialeah	38

[a]Elected Aug. 29, 1989.
[b]Resigned, ran for Congress Aug. 1989.
[c]Elected Jan. 25, 2000.
[d]Resigned Oct. 27, 1999.

APPENDIX D

Florida Supreme Court: Minority Members

Years	Name	Appointed by	Chief Justice	Minority
1975–1979	Joseph W. Hatchett	Reubin Askew (D)	—	Black
1983–2003	Leander J. Shaw, Jr.	Bob Graham (D)	1990–1992	Black
1985–1994	Rosemary Barkett	Bob Graham (D)	1992–1994	"Hispanic"/Syrian
1998–Present	Peggy A. Quince	Lawton Chiles (D) and Jeb Bush (R)	2008–2010	Black
2002–2008	Raoul G. Cantero III	Jeb Bush (R)	—	Hispanic
2009–Present	Jorge Labarga	Charlie Crist (R)	2014–Present	Hispanic
2009–Present	James E. C. Perry	Charlie Crist (R)	—	Black

APPENDIX E

U.S. Congress: Florida Minority Members

House of Representatives: Black Members

Years[a]	Name	Party	Location	District
1871–1876	Josiah T. Walls	R	Florida At-Large	Statewide
1992–Present	Corrine Brown	D	Jacksonville	5
1992–Present	Alcee Hastings	D	Broward, Palm Beach, Hendry counties	20
1992–2002	Carrie Meek	D	Miami	17
2002–2010	Kendrick Meek	D	Miami	17
2010–2012	Allen West	R	Broward, Palm Beach counties	22
2010–Present	Frederica Wilson	D	Miami	24

House of Representatives: Hispanic Members

Years	Name	Party	Location	District
1989–Present	Ileana Ros-Lehtinen	R	Miami	27
1992–2010	Lincoln Diaz-Balart	R	Miami	21
2002–Present	Mario Diaz-Balart	R	Miami	21, 25
2010–2012	David Rivera	R	Miami	25
2012–2014	Joe Garcia	D	Miami	26
2014–Present	Carlos Curbelo	R	Miami	26

U.S. Senate: Hispanic Members

Years	Name	Party	City
2004–2009	Mel Martinez	R	Orlando
2010–Present	Marco Rubio	R	Miami

Note: [a]Years represent time of election. Members of Congress are elected in the November of even-numbered years but assume office in the January of odd-numbered years.

NOTES

Chapter 1. Florida: Population Magnet, Microcosm of America, Trailblazer Incubator

Epigraph sources: Smith, "Florida Population Growth: Past, Present and Future," 2; Schmidt et al., *Newcomers, Outsiders, and Insiders: Immigrants and American Racial Politics in the Early Twenty-first Century*, v.

1. See Bouvier, Leon, and Martin, "Shaping Florida: The Effects of Immigration, 1970–2020"; Smith, "Florida Population Growth: Past, Present and Future"; Mohl and Pozzetta, "Immigration and Ethnicity in Florida History," 470–96.

2. See chapters in Colburn and Landers, *The African American Heritage of Florida*; Winsboro, *Florida's Freedom Struggle: The Black Experience from Colonial Times to the New Millennium*; Balseiro, *The Hispanic Presence in Florida: Yesterday and Today 1513–1976*; MacManus, *Reapportionment and Representation in Florida: A Historical Collection*.

3. MacManus and Colburn, "Florida Politics: The State Evolves into One of the Nation's Premier Political Battlegrounds," 415–43.

4. *Caribbean countries*: Cuba, Dominican Republic, Haiti, Jamaica, and Other (Anguilla, Antigua and Barbuda, Aruba, Bahamas, Barbados, British Virgin Islands, Cayman Islands, Dominica, Grenada, the former country of Guadeloupe—including St. Barthelemy and Saint-Martin, Martinique, Montserrat, the former country of the Netherlands Antilles—including Bonaire, Curacao, Saba, Sint Eusstatius, and Sint Maarten, St. Kitts and Nevis, St. Lucia, St. Vincent and the Grenadines, Trinidad and Tobago, and Turks and Caicos Islands); *Central American* countries: Mexico, El Salvador, Guatemala, Honduras, Other (Belize, Costa Rica, Nicaragua, and Panama); *South American* countries: Brazil, Colombia, Ecuador, Peru, and Other (Argentina, Bolivia, Chile, Falkland Islands, French Guiana, Guyana, Paraguay, Suriname, Uruguay, and Venezuela). See Acosta and de la Cruz, *The Foreign Born from Latin America and the Caribbean: 2010*.

5. *Foreign born* excludes anyone who was a U.S. citizen at birth—those born in the United States, Puerto Rico, a U.S.-island area (U.S. Virgin Islands, Guam, American Samoa, or the Commonwealth of the Northern Mariana Islands), or born abroad to a U.S.-citizen parent or parents.

6. Private poll conducted by Dario Moreno and provided to the author, May 16, 2010.

7. Taylor et al., "When Labels Don't Fit: Hispanics and Their Views of Identity"; Marjorie Valbrun, "Haitian-Americans: Their Search for Political Identity in South Florida." Also see Ericson, *The Politics of Inclusion and Exclusion*.

8. Acosta and de la Cruz, *The Foreign Born from Latin America and the Caribbean: 2010*.

9. Pew Forum on Religion & Public Life, "Chapter 6: Social and Political Attitudes"; Asian American Legal Defense and Education Fund, "The Asian American Vote"; Fabrikant, "New Findings on Asian American Vote in 2012."

10. Olorunnipa, "South Florida Leading National Census Trend"; Norris, Vinces, and Hoeffel, "The American Indian and Alaska Native Population: 2010."

11. See Rivers, "Florida's African American Experience."

12. Brown, *Florida's Black Public Officials, 1867–1924.*

13. *Smith v. Allwright*, 321 U.S. 649 (1944).

14. For a good discussion of the role of the federal Voting Rights Act, see Lawson, *Running for Freedom.*

15. See Kent, "Immigration and America's Black Population," 8.

16. Audebert, "Residential Patterns and Political Empowerment," 53–68.

17. See Kent, "Immigration and America's Black Population."

18. Lawson, *Running for Freedom*, 54.

19. For a discussion of the similarities and differences between "Afro-Caribbean" immigrants and African Americans, see Reuel R. Rogers, *Afro-Caribbean Immigrants and the Politics of Incorporation: Ethnicity, Exception, or Exit.* New York: Cambridge University Press, 2006.

20. Valbrum, "Haitian-Americans."

21. The Bahamas are not technically part of the Caribbean. But they are often included in maps of the Caribbean "because of their cultural, geographical, and political associations with the Greater Antilles and other Caribbean Islands." See Graphic Maps, "Caribbean."

22. Mohl and Pozetta, "Immigration and Ethnicity in Florida History," 477. Florida legislators with Bahamian ancestry are included in the Caribbean Caucus. See Florida House of Representatives, H.R. 9077, "Caribbean Heritage Month."

23. Dunn, *Black Miami in the Twentieth Century.*

24. For studies focused on the political participation of the Miami Cuban exile community, see García, *Havana USA*; Grenier, Pérez, and Foner, *The Legacy of Exile*; Verdeja and Martinez, *Cubans: An Epic Journey*; Girard, Grenier, and Gladwin, "Exile Politics and Republican Party Affiliation."

25. For studies documenting the decline in Cuban political cohesiveness (rise of Democratic voting among younger generation) see Moreno, "Cuban American Political Power: Challenges and Consequences"; Bishin and Klofstad, "The Political Incorporation of Cuban Americans: Why Won't Little Havana Turn Blue?"; Krogstad, "After Decades of GOP Support, Cubans Shifting Toward the Democratic Party."

26. According to the 2012 Florida presidential exit poll, 34% of Hispanic voters were Cuban while 57% were non-Cuban. Among Cuban voters, the vote was split—49% supported Obama while 47% supported Romney. Among the state's non-Cuban voters, Obama won 66% versus 34% for Romney. Lopez and Taylor, "Latino Voters in the 2012 Election."

27. Lopez and Dockterman, "U.S. Hispanic Country of Origin Counts for Nation, Top 30 Metropolitan Areas."

28. Bendixen & Amandi International, "Exit Poll of Hispanic Voters in Florida."

29. Lopez and Dockterman, "U.S. Hispanic Country of Origin Counts for Nation, Top 30 Metropolitan Areas."

30. Lopez Torregrosa, "How a Surge in Puerto Rican Voters is Changing Florida Politics."

31. Ball, "Florida Sees Shift in Hispanic Vote."

32. Rayer, "Asians in Florida"; Hoeffel et al., "The Asian Population: 2010."

33. Chen, "What the Lack of Asian-Americans Says About Miami."

34. Fabrikant, "New Findings on Asian American Vote in 2012." The sample did include Asian voters in Florida.

35. Norris, Vines, and Hoeffel, "The American Indian and Alaska Native Population: 2010."

36. Covington, *The Seminoles of Florida*; Weisman, "Florida's Seminole and Miccosukee

Peoples." For good overview of American Indian politics, see Wilkins, *American Indian Politics and the American Political System.*

37. West, "A Vote for Destiny."

38. Miccosukee Tribe of Indians of Florida, "Leaders."

39. Includes those born in Puerto Rico.

Chapter 2. The Risk-Takers: Beating All Odds, Blazing the Trail for Others

Epigraph source: Shah, "Too Few Minority Politicians? You Can't Win if You Don't Run."

1. For historical overviews of black, Hispanic, and Asian electoral successes in Florida politics, cf. Jones and McCarthy, *African Americans in Florida*; Brown, *Florida's Black Public Officials, 1867–1924*; Colburn and Landers, *The African American Heritage of Florida*; Hill, "Does the Creation of Black Minority Districts Aid Republicans?"; Moreno, "Florida's Hispanic Voters"; MacManus, "The Emerging Battleground South"; MacManus, "Florida Overview"; MacManus, "Florida's Changing Metropolitan Areas"; MacManus and Stutzman, "Race/Ethnicity and Gender in Florida."

2. For excellent accounts of early African-American elected officials and struggles for equality, see Brown, *Florida's Black Public Officials, 1867–1924*; Carleton, "Negro Politics in Florida"; Colburn and Landers, *The African American Heritage of Florida*; Collins, "Past Struggles, Present Changes"; Smith, *The Civil Rights Movement in Florida and the United States*; Jones and McCarthy, *African Americans in Florida*; Klingman, *Josiah Walls*; Christopher, *Black Americans in Congress*. For Asians, see Chou and Feagin, *The Myth of the Model Minority: Asian Americans Facing Racism*. For Hispanics, see Cobas, Duany, and Feagin, *How the United States Racializes Latinos*.

3. Engstrom and McDonald, "The Election of Blacks to City Councils."

4. MacManus, *Reapportionment and Representation in Florida*; MacManus, *Mapping Florida's Political Landscape*; Hill, "Does the Creation of Majority Black Districts Aid Republicans?"

5. Bullock et al., "'Your Honor' is a Female: A Multi-Stage Electoral Analysis of Women's Successes at Security State Trial Court Judgeships."

6. National Center for State Courts. "Gender and Racial Fairness: A Resource Guide."

7. For a good historical overview of the transition from MMDs to SMDs at the congressional and state legislative levels, see Thomas F. Schaller, "Multi-Member Districts: Just a Thing of the Past?"

8. For a detailed discussion of laws and court cases driving the abandonment of MMDs, see Redistricting Task Force for the National Conference of State Legislatures, "Chapter 5: Multimember Districts."

9. Legislators elected from MMDs were elected at-large but ran for a specific seat or district. Following the reapportionment of 1971 and until 1982, Florida used a combination of multimember (MMD) and single-member (SMD) districts. Lenz and Pritchard, "Florida Legislators' Perceptions of the Change to Single-Member Districts."

10. Adams, *Latinos and Local Representation*; Walton and Smith, *American Politics and the African American Quest for Universal Freedom*; McClain and Tauber, *American Government in Black and White*.

11. Adams, *Latinos and Local Representation*, 231; Garcia and Sanchez, *Hispanics and the US Political System*. For detailed discussions of the redistricting efforts, cf. Bullock, Hoffman, and Gaddie, "Regional Variations in the Realignment of American Politics, 1944–2004"; MacManus, "Congressional Redistricting in 1992"; MacManus, *Mapping Florida's Political Landscape*; MacManus, *Reapportionment and Representation in Florida*; MacManus, "Redistricting in Florida in

2002"; MacManus, "State Legislative Redistricting in 1992"; MacManus and Gaddie, "Florida"; MacManus and Gaddie, "Reapportionment in Florida"; MacManus and Morehouse, "Race, Abortion, and Judicial Retention"; MacManus and Morehouse, "Redistricting in the Multi-Racial 21st Century"; Hill, "Does the Creation of Majority Black Districts Aid Republicans?"; Voss and Lublin, "Black Incumbents, White Districts."

12. For a discussion of this debate in Florida's 2012 redistricting, see Aubrey Jewett, "'Fair' Districts in Florida: New Congressional Seats, New Constitutional Standards, Same Old Republican Advantage?" For a discussion of how race-based gerrymandering has impacted black legislators, see King-Meadows and Schaller, *Devolution and Black State Legislators*.

13. Caress et al., "Effect of Term Limits on the Election of Minority State Legislators."

14. MacManus et al., "First Time Candidates."

15. MacManus and DePalo, "What Next? Term Limits, Gender, and New Offices Sought."

16. DePalo, *The Failure of Term Limits in Florida*; Caress et al., "Effect of Term Limits on the Election of Minority State Legislators."

17. Cf. MacManus and Quecan, "Minority Pathbreakers in Florida Politics."

18. Lublin and Brewer, "The Continuing Dominance of Traditional Gender Roles in Southern Elections"; Bullock and MacManus, "Measuring Racial Bloc Voting is Difficult for Small Jurisdictions"; Fox and Oxley, "Gender Stereotyping in State Executive Elections."

19. MacManus and Morehouse, "Race, Abortion, and Judicial Retention."

20. MacManus, "The Race to Put Women's Faces in High Places."

21. McClain and Tauber, *American Government in Black and White*, 298. For other studies of the role of the media, cf. Chaudhary, "Press Portrayals of Black Officials"; Barber and Gandy, "Press Portrayals of African American and White United States Representatives"; Hamamoto, *Monitored Peril: Asian Americans and the Politics of TV Representation*; Shah and Thornton, "Racial Ideology in U.S. Mainstream News Magazine Coverage of Black Latino Interaction, 1980–1992"; Kahn, "Does Being Male Help?"; Sylvie, "Black Mayoral Candidates and the Press"; Entman and Rojecki, *The Black Image in the White Mind*; Zilber and Niven, "Congress and the News Media"; Jeffries, "Press Coverage of Black Statewide Candidates"; Wu and Lee, "The Submissive, the Calculated, and the American Dream."

22. Banwart, Bystrom, and Robertson, "From Primary to the General Election"; Larson, "American Women and Politics and Media"; Braden, *Women Politicians in the Media*; Kahn, *The Political Consequences of Being a Woman*; Rausch, Rozell, and Wilson, "When Women Lose: A Study of Media Coverage of Two Gubernatorial Campaigns"; Major and Coleman, "The Intersection of Race and Gender in Election Coverage"; Carroll and Schreiber, "Media Coverage of Women in the 103rd Congress"; Iyengar et al., "Running as a Woman: Gender Stereotyping in Political Campaigns"; Manning-Miller, "Carol Moseley-Braun: Black Women's Political Images in the Media"; Witt, Paget, and Matthews, *Running as a Woman: Gender and Power in American Politics*. See articles in Reingold, *Legislative Women: Getting Elected, Getting Ahead*; Lawless and Fox, *It Still Takes a Candidate: Why Women Don't Run for Office*; Dunaway et al., "Traits Versus Issues: How Female Candidates Shape Coverage of Senate and Gubernatorial Races."

23. Gershon, "Media Coverage of Minority Congresswomen and Voter Evaluations."

24. Casellas and Wallace, "The Role of Race, Ethnicity, and Party on Attitudes Toward Descriptive Representation."

25. Gonzalez Juenke and Preuhs, "Irreplaceable Legislators? Rethinking Minority Representatives in the New Century"; Minta, "Gender, Race, Ethnicity, and Political Representation in the United States."

26. Adams, *Latinos and Local Representation*; Wu and Lee, "The Submissive, the Calculated, and the American Dream"; Kim, *The Racial Logic of Politics: Asian Americans and Party*

Competition; Pye, *Asian Power and Politics: The Cultural Dimensions of Authority*; Lai, *Asian American Political Action*.

27. Marshall, "Caribbean Caucus Leads to Rift in Democratic Party."

28. Brians, "Women for Women?"

29. Citrin, Green, and Sears, "White Reactions to Black Candidates"; Bullock, "Racial Crossover Voting and the Election of Black Officials."

30. Scola, *Gender, Race, and Office Holding in the United States: Representation at the Intersections*.

31. Lai et al., "Asian Pacific-American Campaigns, Elections, and Elected Officials"; Lai, "Asian Pacific Americans and the Pan-Ethnic Question"; Lai, "Voting Behavior and Political Participation"; Cain, Kiewiet, and Uhlaner, "The Acquisition of Partisanship by Latinos and Asian Americans."

32. Hero and Preuhs, *Black-Latino Relations in U.S. National Politics*; Bowler and Segura, *The Future Is Ours: Minority Politics, Political Behavior, and the Multiracial Era of American Politics*.

33. Gill, *African American Women in Congress: Forming and Transforming History*.

34. Nadia E. Brown, "Political Participation of Women of Color: An Intersectional Analysis"; Garciá Bedolla, Tate, and Wong, "Indelible Effects: The Impact of Women of Color in the U.S. Congress."

35. Jacobs et al., "Murder, Political Resources, and Women's Political Success."

36. Ross, *The Divine Nine*; Kimbrough, *Black Greek 101*; Jones, *Black Haze*; Brown, Parks, and Phillips, *African American Fraternities and Sororities: The Legacy and the Vision*.

37. See Chapter 2 on Miami in Smith and Harris, *Black Churches and Local Politics: Clergy Influence, Organizational Partnerships, and Civic Empowerment*; McDaniel. *Politics in the Pews: The Political Mobilization of Black Churches;* cf. Calhoun-Brown, "African American Churches and Political Mobilization"; Owens, *God and Government in the Ghetto*.

38. Leal, "Religion and the Political and Civic Lives of Latinos"; McDaniel, *Politics in the Pews*. For a good review of this literature, see Scola, *Gender, Race, and Office Holding in the United States*.

Chapter 3. Trailblazers: The Florida Legislature—House and Senate

1. Legislators elected from MMDs were elected at-large but ran for a specific seat or district. Following the reapportionment of 1971 and until 1982, Florida used a combination of multi-member (MMD) and single-member (SMD) districts. Allen Morris, Clerk of the House, detailed this arrangement in *The Language of Lawmaking of Florida* (1974): *Representation of the House*—All members of the House represented geographic districts which had the same number of people at the time of the 1970 federal census. The population of Florida in 1970 was 6,790,929. Divided by 120 members, this set the perfect size of a House district at 56,591 persons. The House, in apportioning itself in 1972, followed a policy of providing multi-member districts no larger than six in number for densely populated counties and single-member in rural counties. Since the U.S. Supreme Court had approved the use of multi-member districts in legislative apportionments stemming from the one-person, one-vote decision, many Floridians are represented by more than one House member. A multi-member group is based, however, upon multiples of 56,591. A five-member group, for example, would have five Representatives elected from an area which in 1970 had 282,955 people. The House embraces five six-member districts, six five-member districts, five four-member districts, three three-member districts, five two-member districts and 21 single-member districts. The range of deviation from mathematical preciseness was from +.20% (114 people) to -.10% (57 people). *Representation of the Senate*—The

Florida Senate chose in 1972 to set its size at 40 members, which was within the constitutional range of 30–40 members. This decreased the size of the 48-member Senate by eight seats prior to reapportionment. The Senate has seven three-member districts, seven two-member districts, and five single-member districts. The average populations for each Senate seat was 169,773 and the deviation in the Senate was from +.62% (1,064 people) to -.53% (899 people). In 1982, Florida abandoned MMDs in response to complaints that they were discriminatory against minorities. Republicans in the legislature joined with black legislators (both were minorities at the time) to successfully push for the switch to all SMDs. MacManus, *Reapportionment and Representation in Florida*; Skene, "Reapportionment in Florida."

2. The 1986 *Thornburg v. Gingles,* 478 U.S. 30 (1986), decision by the U.S. Supreme Court signaled to states that they should create minority-majority legislative districts where possible.

3. Morris, *The Florida Handbook 1969–1970.*

4. Key, *Southern Politics in State and Nation.*

5. *The Florida Handbook 1971–1972.*

6. Colburn, "Florida's Legacy of Misdirected Reapportionment."

7. MacManus and Colburn, "Florida Politics."

8. For detailed discussions of the redistricting efforts, cf. Bullock and Gaddie, "Variations in the Realignment of American Politics"; MacManus, "Congressional Redistricting in 1992"; MacManus, *Mapping Florida's Political Landscape*; MacManus, *Reapportionment and Representation in Florida*; MacManus, "Redistricting in Florida in 2002"; MacManus, "State Legislative Redistricting in 1992"; MacManus and Gaddie, "Florida"; MacManus and Gaddie, "Reapportionment in Florida"; MacManus and Morehouse, "Race, Abortion, and Judicial Retention"; MacManus and Morehouse, "Redistricting in the Multi-Racial 21st Century"; Hill, "Does the Creation of Majority Black Districts Aid Republicans?"; Voss and Lublin, "Black Incumbents, White Districts."

9. See Brown, *Florida's Black Public Officials 1867–1924.*

10. Gwyndolen Clarke-Reed was born in Delray Beach but spent her early life with her grandparents in New York. She finished college, began teaching, and got involved in community planning and school board politics in New York before moving back to Florida in 1985. Despite being considered an "outsider" at first, she won election to the Deerfield Beach City Council, where she served for 12 years. In 2008, when State Rep. Jack Seiler (2001–2009) left the House because of term limits, she ran for his seat and won. Since taking office, she has seen a large influx of Brazilians into Deerfield Beach, making Portuguese the second language in the area.

11. Asians have been the fastest growing in-migrant group in Florida, and the rate is largely driven by new arrivals. Griezo et al., "The Foreign-Born Population in the United States: 2010."

12. Morris and Morris, *The Florida Handbook 2013–2014*, 231.

13. Associated Press, "De la Parte New Senate President."

14. Hayes, "Louis de la Parte Used Politics to Help Others."

15. The year Rubio became Speaker (2006) marked the 10th anniversary of the Republican takeover of the Legislature. The Republicans' ascendancy to majority status in both houses "was attributed to the shift to single-member districts, which started the rise in black and Hispanic membership in the 1980s." Morris and Morris, *The Florida Handbook 2013–2014*, 234.

16. Florida House of Representatives, "Proceedings of the Republican Conference in the House Chamber."

17. Naturally, there was some disagreement about how many of these ideas became law. Rubio himself asserts that "All 100 ideas were passed by the Florida House. Fifty-seven of these ideas ultimately became law, including measures to crack down on gangs and sexual predators,

promote energy efficient buildings, appliances and vehicles, and help small businesses obtain affordable health coverage." Rubio, "Biography."

18. Inconsistency exists in family historical documents about the senior and junior suffixes in the father's and son's names. But the subject of this story used "Jr.," according to his daughter Malinda, and that is how he is referred to here.

19. Florida Department of State, "A Brief History: Territorial Period."

20. The Florida Legislature had elected Wilkinson Call to represent the state in the U.S. Senate for a third term in May 1891. In December 1891, the Senate received two sets of credentials for the same seat, Call's and those of Democrat Robert H. M. Davidson, a former member of the U.S. House of Representatives. He had been appointed by the governor when the legislature's vote was disputed as invalid because one house lacked a quorum. The Senate allowed Call to take his seat and sent the credentials of both claimants to the Committee on Privileges and Elections. In January 1892, the committee declared unanimously that Call had been properly elected, pointing out that the law governing Senate elections made no reference to a quorum of either house. Of the 100 members of the Florida Legislature, 52 had voted, 51 in favor of Call, forming a majority of the both houses combined.

21. Augustine.com, "The Cigar Makers."

22. Information about the Alligator Farm's founding and operation came from Adams and Shriver, *The St. Augustine Alligator Farm.*

23. Florida School for the Deaf and Blind, *Florida School Herald.*

24. *St. Augustine Record,* "F. Charles Usina Highway Appropriately Named."

25. Florida School for the Deaf and Blind, *Florida School Herald.*

26. City of St. Augustine, Florida, "Great Floridians 2000."

27. When the author asked the Florida legislative library for a list of Hispanic legislators, Martinez's name was missing from the list. The reason may be that when he served in the Legislature, it was common for Hispanics to self-identify as white because the only choice in the racial/ethnic category was white or black. The U.S. Census introduced the Hispanic origin term on its long-form questionnaire in 1970 and on all forms in 1980. See Demby, "On the Census."

28. Claude Kirk won an upset victory over a Democrat in 1966, becoming the first Republican Governor in Florida since Reconstruction. Bennett, "Claude Kirk."

29. *St. Petersburg Times*, "Martinez Over Spicola, Slightly."

30. Henry Cisneros was elected Mayor of San Antonio in 1975, and Federico Peña was elected Mayor of Denver in 1983.

31. *Sun-Sentinel*, "Joseph Menendez Martinez, Jr., Obituary."

32. *Fort Lauderdale News and Sun-Sentinel*, "House Candidates Have Varied Views, Backgrounds."

33. Vinciguerra, "Kirk Slate, Demo Vets Score Big."

34. Call, "Low Voter Turnout Shows Apathy."

35. *Fort Lauderdale News*, "Special Primary Tomorrow Livened by GOP Infighting."

36. *Fort Lauderdale News,* "Ex-Legislator Cries Hoax."

37. Hopkins, "Tuesday's Runoff Primaries Set Stage for General Election."

38. Hopkins, "Calhoun Wins by 21 Votes; Haddad's In."

39. Hopkins, "GOP Candidates Ooze with Vote Optimism."

40. Call, "Primaries Have Produced Strong Nominee Slates for State Legislature."

41. Hopkins, "GOP Fund Created by Party."

42. Hopkins, "Tuesday Is Voters' Day of Decision."

43. Hauser, "'Sweeping Changes' to Aid South Broward?"

44. Alvarez, "Claude R. Kirk, Jr., Former Florida Governor, Dies at 85."

45. Call, "Kirk's Gamble on Voters Paid Off."
46. Associated Press, "Joe Lang Kershaw, Legislator, Dies at 88."
47. *Miami Times*, "Joe Kershaw, Earl Carroll Win."
48. Black Archives Research Center, "The Founders: The Creation of the Black Archives."
49. *Florida Times-Union*, "Today in Florida History June 27th."
50. McKnight, "Quorum Call."
51. Shell-Weiss, *Coming to Miami: A Social History*, 219–20.
52. McKnight, "Quorum Call."
53. Associated Press, "Joe Lang Kershaw, Legislator, Dies at 88."
54. Wills, "Black Woman's Voice Makes Itself Heard."
55. Some feminist groups continue to argue that the "deadline" for ratification is not legally valid. As of this writing, nearly every session of the Florida Legislature has seen a bill introduced to ratify the ERA.
56. For more information about the A. Philip Randolph Institute, which is affiliated with the AFL-CIO, see http://apri.org/.
57. Florida Memory, "Roxcy Bolton: A Force for Equality."
58. Viglucci, "Ex-Rep. John Plummer."
59. Pinder, "The Political Papers Newsletter."
60. Ted Lyons, a prominent political activist in Florida, was appointed to a job in the U.S. Government Printing Office during the Reagan Administration. See *Baltimore Afro-American*, "National Roundup."
61. Division of Elections, "September 9, 1980 Primary Election."
62. Silva, "Rosenthal Must Wonder, What's in a Name?"
63. *Miami Herald*, "Advertisement."
64. Grimm, "Family Name Is Plummer's No. 1 Helper."
65. Viglucci, "Ex-Rep. John Plummer."
66. Gyllenhaal, "3 Incumbents Lose State House Races."
67. In Operación Pedro Pan (Operation Peter Pan), Cuban parents sent their children to the United States in fear of violence and government indoctrination. Between 1959 and 1962, some 14,000 children found home in temporary shelters or with relatives. Up to that time, it was the largest recorded exodus of unaccompanied minors in the Western Hemisphere. For more information, see http://www.pedropan.org/category/history.
68. Shell-Weiss, *Coming to Miami*.
69. Caldwell, "Husband-Wife Legislators Keep It in the Family."
70. Davenport, "Federal Judge Nixes License Plates With Cross, 'I Believe.'"
71. DNA testing has helped exonerate more than 300 people in the United States, including Wilton Dedge, who was convicted of rape on scant evidence consisting of eyewitness misidentification, hair analysis, and dog scent. See the blog of the Innocence Project, http://www.innocenceproject.org.
72. The boy had been rescued while floating on an inner tube near Fort Lauderdale, after his mother and 11 others had drowned trying to flee Cuba on a raft. See Public Broadcasting Service, "A Chronology of the Elián Gonzalez Saga."
73. For a summary of events in Colombia, see Sipress, "U.S. Reassesses Colombia Aid."
74. The Internal Revenue Code grants tax-exempt status to organizations that meet certain requirements. See http://www.irs.gov/Charities-&-Non-Profits/Charitable-Organizations.
75. Spain arranged for money and war materials to help the American colonies against the British. See http://teachinghistory.org/history-content/ask-a-historian/22894.
76. See U.S. House of Representatives, "The First Hispanic American to Serve in Congress."

77. For a timeline of Nicaraguan history, see http://web.stanford.edu/group/arts/nicaragua/discovery_eng/timeline/.

78. For a summary of ideology and domestic politics in Nicaragua from the 1960s to the mid-1980s, see http://www.brown.edu/Research/Understanding_the_Iran_Contra_Affair/n-sandinistas.php.

79. For a summary of the Bright Futures scholarship issues, see http://www.miamiherald.com/news/local/education/article1961828.html.

80. Blacks had served in the U.S. military since the Civil War, but in segregated units. After World War II, President Harry Truman issued Executive Order 9981, declaring "equality of treatment for all persons in the armed forces without regard to race, color, religion, or national origin." See http://www.trumanlibrary.org/anniversaries/desegblurb.htm for more information. Integration became a reality in the wars in Korea in the early 1950s and Vietnam in the 1960s.

81. Binder, "Gov. Lawton Chiles of Florida."

82. Hurst, *It Was Never About a Hot Dog and a Coke!*

83. Taken from Souto's newsletter as a member of the Miami-Dade County Commission, March 4, 2014, http://www.americantowns.com/fl/miami/news/commissioner-javier-d-souto-newsletter-district-10-february-28-2014-18280144. Souto has tried to keep Francisco's story alive through the Francisco Foundation, which offers scholarships to Miami-Dade College, and through the Francisco Human Rights Park adjacent to the West Dade Regional Library.

84. Bohning, "Site Change Called Fatal to Invasion."

85. For a 30-year timeline comparing significant events in the HIV/AIDS epidemic in the United States and Florida, see http://www.floridahealth.gov/diseases-and-conditions/aids/surveillance/_documents/fact-sheet/HIV-30-Years-History1.pdf.

86. For more information about the Department of Elder Affairs, see http://www.agingcarefl.org/the-department-of-elder-affairs/.

87. Bousquet, "Florida Supreme Court."

88. The term DREAMers refers to Development, Relief, and Education for Alien Minors, federal legislation that would improve immigration relief for students whose parents come to the United States illegally. See http://www.immigrationpolicy.org/issues/DREAM-Act.

89. Pudlow, "Governor Signs Undocumented Attorney Bill."

90. Mitchell, "Florida Gov. Rick Scott Signs Bill."

91. Democrat John Cortes defeated the incumbent Ricardo Rangel in 2014 to win a seat in the Florida House of Representatives.

92. Hernández, "Elias 'Rico' Piccard."

93. Radio Martí is a federally financed effort to broadcast news and programs in Spanish to Cuba. Named after a Cuban liberation hero, the broadcasts are complemented by TV broadcasting and an Internet website. See http://www.martinoticias.com/.

94. See Rubio's biography on his U.S. Senate web page at http://www.rubio.senate.gov/public/index.cfm/about?p=biography.

95. U.S. Sen. Bob Dole of Kansas ran unsuccessfully for president against incumbent Democrat Bill Clinton in 1996. See Dole's biography at http://www.biography.com/people/bob-dole-9276436.

96. For a summary of Rubio's higher education proposals in the U.S. Senate, see Rubio, "Making Higher Education Affordable Again."

97. Leary, "Marco Rubio's Meteoric Rise in Florida Politics."

98. See McKay Scholarship Program for students with disabilities, https://www.floridaschoolchoice.org/Information/McKay/.

99. It was later in the summer of 2009 that Sen. Mel Martinez decided to retire early.

100. The American Recovery and Reinvestment Act, federal legislation designed to create new jobs and spur economic activity in response to the economic crisis in 2009. See http://www.recovery.gov/arra/About/Pages/The_Act.aspx/.

101. Ojito, "The Long Voyage from Mariel Ends."

102. An S.O.S. Venezuela rally took place in Doral in February 2014 to support protesters in Venezuela standing up to President Nicolas Madura's regime, http://miami.cbslocal.com/2014/02/22/s-o-s-venezuela-rally-held-in-doral/.

103. Vicente Martinez-Ybor, a native of Spain, and his partners built a company town called Ybor City, now a National Landmark Historic District. See http://www.yborcityonline.com/upcoming-events/ybor-city-heritage.

104. Jewish immigrants also emigrated to the area. Patrick, "Immigration & Ybor City, 1886–1921."

105. The Kaiser Permanente insurance company originated during the Great Depression to serve industrial workers in California, http://share.kaiserpermanente.org/article/history-of-kaiser-permanente/.

106. At the time this interview with de la Parte took place, investigators had connected President Nixon to a 1972 break-in at Democratic Party headquarters in Washington's Watergate building. Three of the five burglars were Cuban nationals, and one purportedly had trained Cuban exiles in guerrilla activity after the Bay of Pigs invasion. Nixon would resign August 9, 1974. See Lewis, "5 Held in Plot to Bug Democrats' Office Here" and a full account in Bernstein and Woodward, 1974.

107. José Martí, a native of Havana, spent the last 14 years of his life in New York, writing for newspapers and organizing attempts to expel Spain from Cuba. He died while leading a small invading force in 1895 but it wasn't until the 1920s and 1930s that he became a martyr to the cause. http://www.loc.gov/rr/hispanic/1898/marti.html.

108. Associated Press, "De la Parte Is Senate President."

109. Catherine Real, an attorney, was interviewed by the author March 5, 2015.

110. Spiro Agnew, U.S. vice president under Richard Nixon, resigned in 1973 after a lawsuit revealed he had accepted bribes while a public official in Maryland. Clines, "Spiro T. Agnew, Point Man for Nixon."

Chapter 4. Trailblazers: State Executive Offices—Governor, Lieutenant Governor, and Cabinet

1. Candidates for Governor and Lieutenant Governor run as a team on the same ticket. Gubernatorial candidates choose their Lieutenant Governor running mates but do not have to do so until after the primary.

2. Morris, *The Florida Handbook 1973–1974*.

3. These changes, together with the Legislative Reorganization Act of 1969, which led to annual meetings of the Legislature (as opposed to the biennial meetings) and the creation of permanent legislative staffs, effectively counterbalanced the new powers of the Governor's office. Structural changes were one giant step taken to modernize Florida's government. Their importance became even more evident as the state's population continued to explode. MacManus and Colburn, "Florida Politics."

4. The mayoral position is actually a nonpartisan post. But Martinez's Democratic registration was a well-known fact, stemming from his previous experience as the president of the teacher's union.

5. Singleton had headed the Secretary of State's Division of Election under Gov. Askew and

was likely to have been appointed as Secretary of State when Smathers resigned to run. However, Askew chose Jesse McCrary, Jr., because Singleton had "refused to require non-incumbent candidates to submit disclosure statements whey they filed for the 1978 elections"—a position counter to the spirit of the Sunshine Amendment, a major policy priority of Gov. Askew. See Dyckman, *Reubin O'D. Askew*, 222.

6. On July 24, 2015, the Florida Commission on Ethics imposed a $1,000 fine on Carroll for failing to disclose all her income from the Allied Veterans of the World group on financial disclosure forms submitted in 2010 when she served in the Florida House of Representatives. Carroll had worked on public relations for the group which had claimed it was a charity. State investigators (FDLE) found no criminal connections between Carroll and Allied Veterans and passed the issue to the Ethics Commission. While Carroll had submitted an updated financial disclosure form, the Ethics Commission ruled that it did not excuse the original under-reporting error. Auslen, "Former Lt. Gov. Jennifer Carroll Admits to Ethics Violation, Pays Fine."

7. Dyckman, *Reubin O'D. Askew*, 69.

8. Wills, "She's 'Tops' in the State."

9. Morris, *The Florida Handbook 1949–1950*.

10. Morris, *The Florida Handbook 1963–1964*.

11. Range later resigned after being criticized for spending too much time back in Miami at the family's funeral home and being inattentive to problems in the Department of Community Affairs. Dyckman, *Reubin O'D. Askew*, 144.

12. *Miami Herald,* "Mr. Jesse J. McCrary, Jr.—Obituary."

13. Askew was asked what was his proudest accomplishment: "What I enjoyed the most was bringing people into their own government" appointing African Americans, Hispanics, and women to public office, "people who were systematically, intentionally" kept from voting. Klas, "Askew and Hatchett."

14. Van Gieson, "Jamerson Vows to Boost Schools."

15. The school opened in August 2003. Douglas L. Jamerson is a magnet school focused on engineering and mathematics within a specialized curriculum. It also offers Exceptional Education Programs including Voluntary Pre-K blended, Autistic (ASD), Communication Disorders (CD), Specific Learning Disabilities (SLD) and gifted services. The Midtown Campus was opened in August of 2015.

16. Nickens, "Memories of Jamerson Warm House Chamber."

17. Martinez, interview March 23, 1999.

18. Ibid.

19. Ibid.

20. Noll, "For the Students."

21. For a description of the District's structure, including basin boards, see Office of Program Policy Analysis and Government Accountability, "Sunset Memorandum."

22. Kleindienst and Hirth, "GOP's Martinez Wins Governorship."

23. Martinez, interview March 23, 1999.

24. Martinez, interview April 13, 1999.

25. Clements, *A Legacy of Leadership*.

26. A bipartisan coalition of Republicans and conservative Democrats voted for Sen. John Vogt, D-Cocoa Beach, over Jenne, the more liberal Democrat Hollywood. Vogt publically pledged to "do whatever he could to implement the policies of Republican Gov. Bob Martinez." See Hirth, "Jenne's Presidency Bid."

27. Martinez, interview April 13, 1999.

28. Rimer, "The 1990 Elections."

29. Martinez, interview March 23, 1999.
30. Guidry, "Gov. Bob Martinez's Leadership."
31. Clements, *A Legacy of Leadership*, 381.
32. Farrington, "Ex-Fla. Lieutenant Governor Jennifer Carroll Discusses Resignation."
33. Cordner, "Bipartisan Push to Get Florida's New Lt. Gov. to Have Concrete Duties, Goals."
34. Ibid.
35. López-Cantera, "Young Cubans-Americans Remain Committed to a Free Cuba."
36. Turner Tech Oral History Archive, "Oral History Interview with Athalie Range," March 22, 2002.
37. University of Florida Oral History, "Tell the Story," Interview with Athalie Range, Aug. 28, 1997, available at http://ufdc.ufl.edu/UF00005670/00001/print?options=1JJ*.
38. *South Florida CEO*, "Athalie Range, the Pioneer," October 2004.
39. Dunn, *Black Miami*.
40. Shell-Weiss, *Coming to Miami*.
41. Dunn, *Black Miami*.
42. Ibid.
43. Ibid.
44. *South Florida CEO*, "Athalie Range, the Pioneer."
45. Wills, "She's 'Tops' in the State."
46. *Miami Herald*, "Mr. Jesse J. McCrary, Jr.—Obituary."
47. Ibid.
48. Prince, "Riots, Urban, of 1967."
49. *Miami Herald*, "Mr. Jesse J. McCrary, Jr.—Obituary."
50. Kennedy, "Negro Lawyer Appointed Assistant Attorney General."
51. Vandervalk, "Negro Represents State, Wins Supreme Court Suit."
52. *Miami Herald*, "Mr. Jesse J. McCrary, Jr.—Obituary."
53. Ibid.
54. Ibid.
55. McCrary, "Dade County Bar Luncheon."
56. Moss, "Jamerson Once Again Fights for His Dream."
57. Harper, "Around the Dome, Echoes of the Past."
58. Woods, "A Brief History of St. Joseph Catholic Church in St. Petersburg, Florida."
59. Moss, "Jamerson Once Again Fights for His Dream."
60. Joy Frank, legislative affairs director for Commissioner Jamerson, interview with the author, Jan. 23, 2015.
61. Dyckman, "Jamerson Deserves Job."
62. Rado, "Commissioner Race a Study in Contrasts."
63. Dyckman, "Jamerson Deserves Job."
64. Peter Rudy Wallace, former Speaker of the Florida House of Representatives, interview with the author, Aug. 21, 2014.
65. Laurey Stryker, former Assistant Commissioner of Education under Betty Castor and Jamerson, interview with the author, Jan. 22, 2015.
66. Cathy Kelly, former official with the Florida Education Association, interview with the author, Jan. 26, 2015.
67. Rochelle, *Words with Wings: A Treasury of African-American Poetry and Art*.
68. Morgan, "Jamerson Makes His Bid Official."
69. Cathy Kelly, interview with the author, Jan. 26, 2015.
70. Louka, "Education Chief Visits Citrus."

71. Debenport, "Jubilant About Jamerson."

72. Video interview with Jamerson, conducted by Bernadette Morris, public affairs, Miami Dade Community College, Wolfson Campus, May 9, 1994, Wolfson Moving Images Archives, Item No. MDC00732.

73. Laurey Stryker, interview with the author, Jan. 22, 2015.

74. Betty Castor, former Commissioner of Education, personal interview with the author, Jan. 22, 2015.

75. Rado, "Commissioner Race a Study in Contrasts."

76. Griffin, "Chiles Names Jamerson New Secretary of Labor."

77. Caldwell, "Democrats Turn Testy in Senate Debate."

78. Cote, "A Deep Speech That Was Ever So Simple."

Chapter 5. Trailblazers: The Florida Supreme Court

1. Morris and Morris, *The Florida Handbook 2009–2010*.

2. MacManus and Morehouse, "Race, Abortion, and Judicial Retention."

3. Barnes, "Republicans Target Three Florida Supreme Court Justices." The three were Peggy Quince, Barbara Pariente, and Fred Lewis. Each easily won their retention election.

4. These groups opposed the retention of these Justices for their 2010 decision "to reject a nonbinding amendment allowing Floridians to refuse to buy mandatory health insurance"; a 2003 death penalty case in which the Court had reversed the murder conviction of a man and ordered a retrial on technical ground—a decision reversed by the U.S. Supreme Court; and general discontent with their 2000 rulings on ballot recounting related to the *Bush v Gore*, No. 00-949, case; and decisions of redistricting and property taxes. See Alvarez, "G.O.P. Aims to Remake Florida Supreme Court"; Goodman, "Conservative Activists Take Aim at Florida Justices"; Lopez, "Koch Brothers Set Sights on Florida Supreme Court Justices"; Kaczor, "Florida Supreme Court Justices Face Unusual Election Challenge."

5. Klas, "In Surprise Move, Florida GOP Opposes Supreme Court Justices' Retention in November"; Mitchell, "Three State Supreme Court Justices Easily Returned to Bench, Despite Active Opposition."

6. Dyckman, *A Most Disorderly Court*, 138.

7. Quince is the only Supreme Court Justice to be jointly appointed by two governors. At the time of the appointment, Gov. Chiles was still in office but Gov. Jeb Bush had been elected to succeed him. Chiles died before his term was up and was succeeded by Gov. Buddy MacKay-D, who served out Chiles's term before Bush took office.

8. The report is available on the Florida Courts website at http://www.flcourts.org/gen_public/family/diversity/index.shtml.

9. Supreme Court of Florida, "Administrative Order: In Re: Standing Committee on Fairness and Diversity."

10. Bousquet, "Cuban American Gets Top Post."

11. Kennedy, "Labarga First Cuban-American Chief Justice."

12. *Brown v. Board of Education* (1954), the case in which the U.S. Supreme Court ruled that segregation was unconstitutional. Among the plaintiff attorneys was Howard University graduate Thurgood Marshall, who would later be appointed to the U.S. Supreme Court. See Howard University's website commemorating the case at http://www.brownat50.org/.

13. Associated Press, "Letter Bomb Kills U.S. Appeals Judge."

14. Cantero, "What I Learned from My Fiction Writing Professor, Part I."

15. Saunders, "First Hispanic Named to Top Court."

16. For a good explanation of Florida's merit retention system for appellate-level judges and justices, see Florida Supreme Court, "Merit Retention & Mandatory Retirement of Justices of the Supreme Court."

17. The three Supreme Court Justices under attack were: Barbara Pariente, Fred Lewis, and Peggy Quince. See Allen, "Florida's New Battleground: The State Supreme Court."

18. Klas, "Former Justice Joins Pushback in Merit Retention Debate Over FSC Justices."

19. For a retrospective on the Terri Schiavo case, see Haberman, "From Private Ordeal to National Fight: The Case of Terri Schiavo."

20. *Law 360*, "Q&A With White & Case's Raoul Cantero."

21. Hurst, *It Was Never About a Hot Dog and a Coke!*

22. McFadden, "Mary Peabody, 89, Rights Activist, Dies."

23. Firestone, "The 43rd President: The Florida Supreme Court."

24. *Provenzano v. Moore*, Florida Supreme Court, no. 95,973 (corrected). http://www.floridasupremecourt.org/decisions/pre2004/ops/95973a.pdf (accessed February 17, 2015).

25. *State of Florida v. DiGuilio,* 491 So. 2d 1129 (1986), https://www.courtlistener.com/opinion/1807773/state-v-diguilio/ (accessed February 17, 2015).

26. Wagner, "*Where the Injured Fly for Justice.*"

27. Barkett is not an Hispanic but was born in Ciudad Victoria, Mexico. She became a U.S. citizen in 1958. Her family, immigrants from Syria, moved to Miami when Barkett was quite young. Barkett is Florida's first Hispanic and first Arab-American Florida Supreme Court Justice.

28. Arab American Institute, "Together We Came: Rosemary Barkett"

29. Rehnquist Center, "Biographical Information: The Honorable Rosemary Barkett."

30. *In re Guardianship of Estelle M. Browning, Florida v. Herbett*, 568 So. 2d 4 (1990), http://abstractappeal.com/schiavo/browning.txt (accessed February 2, 2015).

31. *Riley v. California*, 573 U.S. ___ (2014), http://www.law.cornell.edu/supct/pdf/13-132.pdf (accessed February 2, 2015).

32. *Griswold v. Connecticut*, 381 U.S. 479 (1965), https://supreme.justia.com/cases/federal/us/381/479/case.html (accessed February 2, 2015).

33. *Roe v. Wade*, 410 U.S. 113 (1971), https://supreme.justia.com/cases/federal/us/410/113/case.html (accessed February 2, 2015).

34. *Bowers v. Hardwick*, 478 U.S. 186 (1986), https://supreme.justia.com/cases/federal/us/478/186/case.html (accessed February 2, 2015).

35. *Lawrence v. Texas*, 539 U.S. 558 (2003), https://supreme.justia.com/cases/federal/us/539/558/ (accessed February 2, 2015).

36. *Brown v. Board of Education of Topeka*, 347 U.S. 483 (1954), https://supreme.justia.com/cases/federal/us/347/483/case.html (accessed February 2, 2015).

37. *Faragher v. Boca Raton*, 524 U.S. 775 (1998), https://supreme.justia.com/cases/federal/us/524/775/case.html (accessed February 2, 2015).

38. *Davis v. Monroe County Bd. of Ed.*, 526 U.S. 629 (1999), https://supreme.justia.com/cases/federal/us/526/629/ (accessed February 2, 2015).

39. *Shahar v. Bowers*, 836 F. Supp. 859 (N.D. Ga. 1993), http://law.justia.com/cases/federal/district-courts/FSupp/836/859/1949292/ (accessed February 2, 2015).

40. *Title VII of the Civil Rights Act of 1964*, Public Law 88-352, §2000e, *U.S. Code* 40, http://www.eeoc.gov/laws/statutes/titlevii.cfm (accessed February 2, 2015).

41. *Chandler v. Miller*, 520 U.S. 305 (1997), https://supreme.justia.com/cases/federal/us/520/305/case.html (accessed February 2, 2015).

42. Four students were killed and nine others injured when National Guard troops opened

fire at a rally protesting the Vietnam War on May 4, 1970. See National Public Radio, "Kent State Shooting Divided Campus and Country."

43. The Black Panthers, founded in 1966, originally sought to protect Black Americans from police brutality but evolved into a revolutionary political group. See Duncan, "Black Panther Party."

44. Pudlow, "A Celebration and a Challenge."

45. Citizens United, a leading conservative organization, won an important decision in 2010, when the U.S. Supreme Court ruled that the government may not ban political spending by corporations in candidate elections. In dissent, Justice John Paul Stevens called the opinion "a grave error" because it treated corporate speech the same as that of human beings. See Liptak, "Justices, 5–4, Reject Corporate Spending Limit."

46. Pudlow, "Chief Justice Peggy Ann Quince of the Supreme Court of Florida."

47. Menzel, "News Service of Florida Has: Five Questions for Jorge Labarga."

48. U.S. National Archives and Records Administration, "Declaration of Independence: The Signers' Gallery."

49. Pudlow, "Jorge Labarga: Chief Justice of the Florida Supreme Court."

50. Ibid.

51. Supreme Court of Florida, No. SC11-2568, Florida Board of Bar Examiners Re: Question as to whether undocumented immigrants are eligible for admission to the Florida Bar, March 6, 2014.

52. Menzel, "News Service of Florida Has: Five Questions for Jorge Labarga."

53. Julie Kay, "Middle Class Getting Squeezed Out of Courts."

Chapter 6. Trailblazers in Congress: U.S. House and U.S. Senate

1. For a detailed description of redistricting in 1982, see MacManus, *Reapportionment and Representation in Florida.*

2. These 10 state Senators were Corrine Brown (D-District 17), James C. "Jim" Burke (D-District 107), William A. "Bill" Clark (D-District 91), James T. "Jim" Hargrett, Jr. (D-District 63); Douglas L. "Tim" Jamerson (D-District 55), Alfred J. "Al" Lawson (D-District 63), Willie F. Logan, Jr. (D-District 108), Jefferson "Jeff" Reaves, Sr. (D-District 106), Alzo J. Reddick, Sr. (D-District 40), John Thomas (D-District 16).

3. MacManus, *Reapportionment and Representation in Florida.*

4. MacManus and Colburn, "Florida Politics."

5. MacManus, "Redistricting in Florida in 2002."

6. The Legislature did not adopt a congressional redistricting plan either during the regular session that adjourned March 14, 1992, or during a special session that adjourned April 1, 1992. A three-judge panel then held that the congressional redistricting plan adopted in 1982 violated Article I, §2 of the U.S. Constitution; the Equal Protection Clause of the 14th Amendment of the U.S. Constitution; the one-person, one-vote principle; and the Voting Rights Act of 1965. On May 29, 1992, the Court ordered the state to conduct the 1992 congressional election and subsequent congressional elections in accordance with a redistricting plan adopted by the Court. Redistricting Task Force for the National Conference of State Legislatures, "Florida Redistricting Cases: The 1990s"; also see Morris and Morris, *The Florida Handbook 2013–2014*, 267.

7. O'Connor, *Drawing the Map: Redistricting in the South.*

8. BlackPast.org, "West, Allen (1961–)."

9. Stephen Zack, a partner in the Boies, Schiller & Flexner law firm, would become the first

Hispanic president of the American Bar Association in 2010. For more information, see the firm's website at http://www.bsfllp.com/lawyers/data/0398.

10. Yanez, "Ros-Lehtinen Takes Seat Race."

11. Sheridan, "Ros-Lehtinen Brings Anti-Communist Fervor to Once Staid Committee."

12. For a good description of the direct file process, see Office of Juvenile Justice and Delinquency Protection, "Juvenile Transfer."

13. Victor Anfuso, a Democrat, was born in Sicily and immigrated to the United States in 1914. He served in Congress 1951–1953 and again 1955–1963. See http://bioguide.congress.gov/scripts/biodisplay.pl?index=A000255.

14. For more information about Rafael Díaz-Balart, see the testimony he gave before Congress May 3, 1960, http://www.latinamericanstudies.org/us-cuba/Díaz-Balart.htm.

15. See more about Ambassador Kirkpatrick in Associated Press, "Former U.N. Amb. Jeane Kirkpatrick Dies."

16. Learn more about the passage of the Civil Rights Act in Breitzer, "Civil Rights Act of 1964."

17. For more about Democratic U.S. Sen. Henry "Scoop" Jackson, see http://bioguide.congress.gov/scripts/biodisplay.pl?index=j000013.

18. U.S. Sen. George McGovern, from South Dakota, won the Democratic nomination for President but lost to incumbent Republican Richard Nixon in 1972. See http://bioguide.congress.gov/scripts/biodisplay.pl?index=m000452.

19. Cuban-born Armando Perez Roura founded Radio Mambí in the 1980s with the aim of overthrowing Castro's regime. See http://www.miaminewtimes.com/bestof/2013/award/best-spanish-language-radio-personality-3699427/.

20. After fleeing Cuba in 1959, Waldo Díaz-Balart studied art in New York before moving permanently to Europe in 1970. For more information about his life and art, see Hedgecoe, "The Man Who Knew Fidel Castro, Warhol, and Franco's Spain."

21. Mario gave his prior state legislative service as a primary reason for switching districts: "This is a natural move for me; in my years of public service at both the federal and state levels, I have had the privilege of representing most of the communities that make up Congressional District 21, including Hialeah, Westchester, Doral, Kendall, Miami Lakes, Hialeah Gardens, Medley and Palmetto Bay." See Kleefeld, "Rep. Mario Díaz-Balart Officially Switching Districts."

22. For more information about *bolita* and gambling in Florida, see the article by Klas, "Gambling's Long History in Florida."

23. For a detailed summary of the events in Judge Hastings' impeachment trial, see https://www.senate.gov/artandhistory/history/common/briefing/Impeachment_Hastings.htm.

24. In 1983, six years before his impeachment, a Miami jury unanimously found Hastings "not guilty of charges [that] he and friend William Borders conspired to take $125,000 from an FBI agent posing as a convicted racketeer in turn for the judge agreeing to cut a jail term and return $1 million in seized property." Groer, "Senate Verdict."

25. For more information about the Commission, see http://www.csce.gov.

26. Levin College of Law, "Virgil Hawkins Story."

27. U.S. House of Representatives, "Carrie P. Meek."

28. Davies, "Charm Made Carrie Meek Effective."

29. Ibid.

30. U.S. House of Representatives, "Carrie P. Meek."

31. Davies, "Charm Made Carrie Meek Effective."

32. Bethune served as president of Bethune-Cookman College, one of the few places young black men and women could go to college, from the 1920s until 1942. A civil rights activist, she

served as an advisor to President Franklin D. Roosevelt and his wife, Eleanor Roosevelt, for many years. See more at http://www.biography.com/people/mary-mcleod-bethune-9211266#synopsis.

33. Rafael Díaz-Balart described his political involvement in Cuba when Castro came into power in testimony before Congress May 3, 1960. See the testimony in full at Díaz-Balart, "Communist Threat to the United States Through the Caribbean."

34. See the newspaper's website at http://www.diariolasamericas.com.

35. See Mondale's views on Central America in a presidential debate Oct. 21, 1984, at http://www.debates.org/index.php?page=october-21-1984-debate-transcript.

36. The congressman expressed his hopes for immigration reform to Fox News Latino. See Llorente, "Mario Díaz-Balart: President Obama Only Thinks of Immigration Reform in Election Season."

37. *Daytona Beach Morning Journal*, "Carrie Meek to Replace Cherry."

38. Nielsen, "Ron Book Remains Top Dog on Florida Lobbying Scene."

39. *Sun-Sentinel*, "Pitts-Lee Case Over, Scars Remain."

40. To learn more about Sen. Turner, see Herrera, "William Turner, State Senator, Integrated Dade School Board."

41. Kennedy, "Death-Penalty Changes on Agenda for New Year."

42. Learn more about Frank Scruggs and his service to state government at http://www.bergersingerman.com/people/frank-scruggs/.

43. Daryl Jones ran for governor in 2002 and was Jim Davis's choice as lieutenant governor in 2006. See Skoloff, "Fla. Gov. Candidate Names Running Mate."

44. Hollis and Kleindienst, "Sit-in Ends—Governor Gives a Bit."

45. Padilla, "March on Tallahassee: One Florida, But Many Foes."

46. Clary, "Jeb Bush's Anti-Affirmative Action Plan Ignites Firestorm."

47. Padilla, "March on Tallahassee: One Florida, But Many Foes."

48. Huey Long (1893–1935) used his power as governor of Louisiana to expand infrastructure and social services, http://www.history.com/topics/huey-long.

49. Kam, "Florida GOP Aims to Weaken Class-Size Amendment as Final Caps Take Effect This Year."

50. U.S. House of Representatives, "Meek, Kendrick B."

51. The NATO Parliamentary Assembly was organized to strengthen relations among member democracies on both sides of the Atlantic. See http://www.nato-pa.int/Default.asp?SHORTCUT=8.

52. To learn more about the wade-in, see Wyman, "Lauderdale Marks 50th Anniversary."

53. Bender, "The Dirtiest Political Race in America."

54. Ibid.

55. President George W. Bush used the phrase in a speech to the NAACP in July 2000. For a full text, see http://www.washingtonpost.com/wp-srv/onpolitics/elections/bushtext071000.htm.

56. For a journalist's interpretation of Rachel Jeantel's testimony, see Cobb, "Rachel Jeantel on Trial."

57. CPAC is an annual political conservative conference attended by conservatives and hosted by the American Conservative Union, the largest and oldest conservative organization in the nation. See http://www.conservative.org/.

58. Klas, "Broward GOP Launches Web Site."

59. Terris and Goldmacher, "The Making of Allen West Inc." For more information about the foundation, see http://www.allenwestfoundation.org.

60. Givhan, "Hats Off for Florida Congresswoman-elect Frederica Wilson."

61. Sherman, "Congresswoman-elect Frederica Wilson Says Hat Ban Started in 1800s But Can Be Waived."

62. Sangillo, "Frederica Wilson (D)."

63. Ibid.

64. Griffith-Roberts, "Making the Grade in Life," *Southern Living*, May 1993.

65. *Huffington Post,* "Rep. Frederica Wilson."

66. *BlackPast.org*, "Wilson, Frederica (1942–)."

67. Frederica Wilson. "Biography."

68. *BlackPast.org*, "Wilson, Frederica (1942–)."

69. Clark, "Female Inmates Moved Near Families."

70. Clark, "Family Ties Aided for Female Inmates."

71. *BlackPast.org*, "Wilson, Frederica (1942–)."

72. *Answers.com*, "Frederica Wilson."

73. *Ballotpedia*, "Frederica Wilson."

74. *Huffington Post*, "Rep. Frederica Wilson."

75. Frederica Wilson, "Biography."

76. Florida Department of State Division of Elections, Election Reporting System.

77. For more information about Jorge Mas Canosa, see Rohter, "An Exile's Empire," and Rohter, "Jorge Mas Canosa."

78. Learn more about the organization at http://www.canf.org.

79. For a summary of the race, see Mazzei, Veiga, and Chang, "In GOP Pickup."

80. Sen. Clay presented two compromises, one in 1820 and another in 1850, to keep the Union together. See Public Broadcasting Service, "The Compromise of 1850."

81. "The Greatest Generation" was coined by journalist Tom Brokaw as the title of his 2005 book, which focused on the generation of Americans who had grown up in the Great Depression, fought in World War II, and went on to build the modern America.

82. Deslatte and Hafenbrack, "Florida Republican Mel Martinez Announces Resignation from the Senate." For more information about the exodus of 14,000 children from Cuba, see http://www.pedropan.org.

83. U.S. military surveillance had spotted nuclear missile sites in Cuba that were being built by the Soviet Union in October 1962. President Kennedy responded with a naval blockade of the island and a demand that the sites be dismantled. After three tense days, the Soviets agreed, in exchange for a U.S. promise not to invade Cuba. See John F. Kennedy Presidential Library and Museum, "Cuban Missile Crisis."

84. U.S. House of Representatives, "Martinez, Melquiades R. (Mel)."

85. *St. Petersburg Times*, "McCollum for GOP."

86. See Weiner, "The Worst Debate Moments Ever" for this and other examples of political debate gaffes.

87. U.S. House of Representatives, "Martinez, Melquiades R. (Mel)."

88. Ibid.

Chapter 7. Summary and Reflections: Push Factors at Work in Trailblazers' Lives

1. Brown, *Florida's Black Public Officials, 1867–1924*, 13. Also see Shoffner, "Reconstruction and Renewal, 1865–1877."

2. Mormino and Pozzetta. *The Immigrant World of Ybor City: Italians and Their Latin Neighbors in Tampa, 1885–1985*; Pérez, "Cubans in Tampa: From Exiles to Immigrants, 1892–1901."

3. Perez, "Cubans in the United States"; García, *Latino Politics in America: Community, Culture, and Interests.*

4. Woltman and Newbold, "Of Flights and Flotillas: Assimilation and Race in the Cuban Diaspora."

5. Santiago, "It's a Hot Season for Cuban-Americans."

6. Grimm, "Remapping Run Amok Fuels Hastings Return."

7. Filkins, "Hastings: People Must Talk with Us."

8. Bousquet, "Turnout Crucial for Black Candidates."

9. Due, "Despite Odds, Meek Makes History."

10. Hallifax, "1st Hispanic Takes Place on State High Court."

11. In 1962, the U.S. Supreme Court ruled in *Baker v. Carr*, 369 U.S. 186 (1962), that population equity was the appropriate measure of representational fairness. In 1964, it ruled in *Wesberry v. Sanders*, 376 U.S. 1 (1964), that the one-person, one-vote principle was to apply to both houses of the Legislature. After several unsuccessful attempts by the legislature, the courts finally stepped in and did it (MacManus, *Reapportionment and Representation in Florida*). It was not until January 15, 1968, that the U.S. Supreme Court ordered Florida's congressional districts to be realigned on the one-person, one-vote principle in the case *Swann v. Adams*, 385 U.S. 440 (1967).

12. United Press International, "Barron Likely to Run Rules Panel."

13. Ellis and Hawks, "Creating a Different Pattern: Florida's Women Legislators, 1928–1986," 80.

14. Clayton, *African Americans and the Politics of Congressional Redistricting.*

15. Branch, "Two Lay Claim to Second Latin Seat in House."

16. Ibid.

17. Grech, "Haiti Native's House Victory Makes History"; Grech, "New Legislator Credits a Lifetime of Determination."

18. The Brutus vs. Roberts-Burke race reflected tensions between African Americans and Caribbean blacks. Brutus made this remark on the campaign trail: "When the politicians are cutting the cake, we are at the bottom of the table, looking up, and when you are under the table, you get whatever falls off, the crumbs." Casimir, "Haitians Seek Office."

19. Ibid.

20. Grech, "Brutus Campaigns for a Comeback"; Grech, "Lawyer Poised to Make History"; Grech, "Pounding the Pavement."

21. Fielder, "Lopsided Latin Vote Doomed Richmond Bid."

22. *Sun-Sentinel*, "Choose Bucher in House District 86."

23. Lindley, "McCrary Choice Symbol of New Day for Minorities."

24. Dyckman, "Florida's First Governor Who Championed Black Causes."

25. Florida Supreme Court Portrait Gallery, "Justice Joseph W. Hatchett."

26. Kleindienst, "Chiles, Bush Appoint First Black Woman to Florida Supreme Court."

27. Ibid.

28. Silva, "A Bush by Any Name is Just as Good."

29. Foglesong, *Immigrant Prince: Mel Martinez and the American Dream.*

30. Kumar, "Martinez to be Face of GOP."

31. Pinzur, "GOP Hopes to Break into Black Democratic Monolith."

32. Pinzur, "Brown Overcomes Carroll to Retain 3rd District Seat"; Pinzur, "Widespread 3rd District Campaign Tough, Carroll has Set Her Standards High."

33. Prior to the 2008 presidential election, one survey found that 44% of Florida's 1.1 million Hispanic voters hail from the Dominican Republic, Colombia, Venezuela, Nicaragua, and other

Latin American countries—slightly more than the Cubans, at 40% (Woods, "Rising Hispanic Vote Shifts Focus Off Cuba").

34. Lipman, "Rep. Hastings Pressures Chiles on Education Job."

35. Nickens, "Legislator Runs for Castor's Job."

36. Valbrun, "Haitian-Americans: Their Search for Political Identity in South Florida."

37. McAndrews estimated that the Asian Americans make up only 1% of Florida's population in the early 1990s; Lee, "She's the First Asian Woman in the Florida Legislature."

38. Ibid.

39. Ibid.

40. Hilliard, "West, Allen (1961–)."

41. *Miami Herald*, "Arnett Girardeau."

42. Fielder, "Lopsided Latin Vote Doomed Richmond Bid."

43. Padilla, "Puerto Rican Politics Invade City Beautiful."

44. Hunt and Jacobson, "Hispanic Visitors Boost Bush, Urge Voter Action."

45. Pugh, "White Can Be Right."

46. Shoettler, "Black Republicans Make Inroads."

47. Merrill and West, *Using Biographical Methods in Social Research.*

48. Steward, "Florida Supreme Court Justice Leander Shaw Retires."

49. Ibid.

50. Fielder, "GOP Takes Aim at State's Top Post"; Levy, "Icon: Bob Martinez."

51. Agrawal, "Defying Harvard Law School's Verdict."

52. Kallested, "Florida A&M Proud of Political Ties."

53. See Kimbrough, "Self-Assessment, Participation, and Value of Leadership Skills" and Kimbrough, "The Impact of Membership in Black Greek-Letter Organizations" for an overview of the role of these groups in developing black leaders.

54. Cunningham, "Can African-Americans Find Their Voice in Cyberspace?"

55. Ibid.

56. Follick and Dunkelberger, "Get Used to Hearing the Name Rep. Marco Rubio."

57. Guardia, "Latino/a Fraternity/Sorority Ethnic Identity Development."

58. Chasko, "House Race: Who Knows Kendall Best?"

59. Bridges, "Kendrick Meek Begins Campaign for Mother's Seat."

60. Corral, Ovalle, and Vasquez, "Cuba Issue Propels Mario Díaz-Balart."

61. Adams and Shiver, *The St. Augustine Alligator Farm.*

62. Protection of Hispanics and other language minorities was added to the 1975 revision of the Voting Rights Act.

BIBLIOGRAPHY

Abney, Glen, and John D. Hutcheson. "Race, Representation, and Trust: Changes in Attitudes After the Election of a Black Mayor." *Public Opinion Quarterly* 45, no. 1 (1981): 91–101.

Acosta, Yesenia D., and G. Patricia de la Cruz. *The Foreign Born from Latin America and the Caribbean: 2010*, 3. Washington, D.C.: U.S. Census Bureau, 2011.

Adams, Florence. *Latinos and Local Representation: Changing Realities, Emerging Theories*. New York: Garland, 2000.

Adams, William R., and Carl Shriver. *The St. Augustine Alligator Farm: A Complete History*, rev. ed. St. Augustine, Fla.: n.p., 2005.

Agrawal, Ravi. "Defying Harvard Law School's Verdict," *Harvard Crimson* (Cambridge, Mass.), June 3, 2002. http://www.thecrimson.com/article/2002/6/3/defying-harvard-law-schools-verdict-tucked/.

Allen, Greg. "Florida's New Battleground: The State Supreme Court." *National Public Radio*, November 6, 2012. Accessed January 20, 2015. http://www.npr.org/2012/11/06/163232298/floridas-new-battleground-the-state-supreme-court.

Alvarez, Lizette. "Claude R, Kirk, Jr., Former Florida Governor, Dies at 85." *New York Times*, September 28, 2011.

———. "G.O.P. Aims to Remake Florida Supreme Court." *New York Times*, October 2, 2012.

Arab American Institute. "Together We Came: Rosemary Barkett." Published online, July 1, 2014. http://www.aaiusa.org/together-we-came-rosemary-barkett.

Asian American Legal Defense and Education Fund. "The Asian American Vote: A Report on the Multilingual Exit Poll from the 2012 Presidential Election." Published online, May 3, 2013. http://aaldef.org/AALDEF%202012%20Exit%20Poll%20Presentation.pdf.

Associated Press. "Bay of Pigs Prisoners 1962." Part of *The Big Story: Bay of Pigs*. Published online, accessed February 16, 2015. http://bigstory.ap.org/content/bay-pigs-prisoners-1962.

———. "De la Parte Is Senate President." *Sarasota Herald-Tribune* (Fla.), July 2, 1974.

———. "De la Parte New Senate President." *Daytona Beach Morning Journal* (Fla.), July 2, 1974.

———. "Former U.N. Amb. Jeane Kirkpatrick Dies." *NBC News*, December 8, 2006. http://www.nbcnews.com/id/16108507/ns/politics/t/former-un-amb-jeane-kirkpatrick-dies/#.VOPDn_msX_F.

———. "Joe Lang Kershaw, Legislator, Dies at 88." *Lakeland Ledger* (Fla.), November 11, 1999. http://news.google.com/newspapers?id=YeRNAAAAIBAJ&sjid=T_oDAAAAIBAJ&pg=5371,117130&dq=joseph+lang+kershaw+died&hl=en.

———. "Letter Bomb Kills U.S. Appeals Judge." *New York Times*, December 17, 1989. http://www.nytimes.com/1989/12/17/us/letter-bomb-kills-us-appeals-judge.html.

Audebert, Cédric. "Residential Patterns and Political Empowerment Among Jamaicans and Haitians in the U.S. Metropolis: The Role of Ethnicity in New York and South Florida." *Human Architecture: Journal of the Sociology of Self-Knowledge* 7, no. 4 (2009): Article 6.

augustine.com. "The Cigar Makers." Online visitors' guide, accessed February 12, 2015. http://augustine.com/history/old-st-augustine/pomar-cigars.php.

Auslen, Michael. "Former Lt. Gov. Jennifer Carroll Admits to Ethics Violation, Pays Fine." *Tampa Bay Times*, July 24, 2015.

Ball, Molly. "Florida Sees Shift in Hispanic Vote." *Politico*, April 15, 2011. http://www.politico.com/news/stories/0411/53227.html.

Ballotpedia. "Frederica Wilson." N.d. http://ballotpedia.org/Frederica_Wilson.

Balseiro, Jose Agustin, ed. *The Hispanic Presence in Florida: Yesterday and Today 1513–1976*. Miami, Fla.: E. A. Seemann, 1976.

Baltimore Afro-American. "National Roundup." December 12, 1981. http://news.google.com/newspapers?nid=2205&dat=19811212&id=JeZfAAAAIBAJ&sjid=RQMGAAAAIBAJ&pg=2711,3928970.

Banerjee, Neela. "Black Churches Struggle Over Their Role in Politics." *New York Times*, March 6, 2005.

Banwart, Mary Christine, Dianne G. Bystrom, and Terry Robertson. "From Primary to the General Election: A Comparative Analysis of Candidate Media Coverage in Mixed-Gender 2000 Races for Governor and U.S. Senate." *American Behavioral Scientist* 46, no. 5 (2003): 658–76.

Barber, J. T., and O. H. Gandy, Jr. "Press Portrayal of African American and White United States Representatives." *Howard Journal of Communications* 2, no. 2 (1990): 213–25.

Barnes, Robert. "Republicans Target Three Florida Supreme Court Justices." *Washington Post*, October 30, 2012.

Barreto, Matt A. *Ethnic Cues: The Role of Shared Ethnicity in Latino Political Participation*. Ann Arbor: University of Michigan Press, 2010.

Beltran, Cristina. *The Trouble with Unity: Latino Politics and the Creation of Identity*. New York: Oxford University Press, 2010.

Bender, Michael. "The Dirtiest Political Race in America." *Bloomberg Businessweek*, October 18, 2012. http://www.businessweek.com/articles/2012-10-18/the-dirtiest-political-race-in-america.

Bendixen & Amandi International. "Exit Poll of Hispanic Voters in Florida." November 8, 2012. http://bendixenandamandi.com/wp-content/uploads/2011/05/ElectionResults-ExitPoll.pdf.

Bennett, George. "Claude Kirk, 1926–2011, Remembered as Flamboyant, Game-Changing Florida Governor." *Palm Beach Post* (Fla.), September 28, 2011. http://www.palmbeachpost.com/news/news/state-regional/claude-kirk-1926-2011-remembered-as-flamboyant-gam/nLyPx/.

Berkman, Michael B., and Robert E. O'Connor. "Do Women Legislators Matter?" *American Politics Quarterly* 21, no. 1 (1993): 102–24.

Bernstein, Carl, and Bob Woodward. *All the President's Men*. New York: Simon and Schuster, 1974.

Binder, David. "Gov. Lawton Chiles of Florida, Populist and Former Senator, Dies at 68." *New York Times*, December 14, 1998. http://www.nytimes.com/1998/12/14/nyregion/gov-lawton-chiles-of-florida-populist-and-former-senator-dies-at-68.html.

Bishin, Benjamin G., and Casey A. Klofstad. "The Political Incorporation of Cuban Americans: Why Won't Little Havana Turn Blue?" *Political Research Quarterly* 65, no. 3 (2012): 586–99.

Black Archives Research Center, Florida Agricultural and Mechanical University. "The Founders: The Creation of the Black Archives." Published online, accessed February 17, 2015. http://famu.edu/index.cfm?MEBA&THEFOUNDERS.

BlackPast.org. "West, Allen (1961–)." Accessed July 2, 2014. http://www.blackpast.org/aah/west-allen-1961.

———. "Wilson, Frederica (1942–)." *Remembered & Reclaimed*. http://www.blackpast.org/aah/wilson-frederica-1942.

Bohning, Don. "Site Change Called Fatal to Invasion." *Miami Herald* (Fla.), January 5, 1997. http://www.latinamericanstudies.org/bay-of-pigs/site.htm.

Boswell, Thomas D. *Ethnic Segregation in Greater Miami, 1980–1990*. Miami, Fla.: Cuban American National Council, 1992.

Bousquet, Steve. "Cuban American Gets Top Post." *Miami Herald* (Fla.), July 1, 2014.

———. "Florida Supreme Court Says Tampa Immigrant Can't Get Law License." *Tampa Bay Times* (Fla.), March 6, 2014. http://www.tampabay.com/news/courts/florida-supreme-court-says-tampa-immigrant-cant-get-law-license/2168868.

———. "Joyner Blazes Trail in the State Senate." *Miami Herald* (Fla.), November 19, 2014. http://www.miamiherald.com/opinion/op-ed/article4013714.html.

——— "Turnout Crucial for Black Candidates." *Miami Herald* (Fla.), September 24, 1992.

Bowler, Shaun, and Gary M. Segura. *The Future is Ours: Minority Politics, Political Behavior, and the Multiracial Era of American Politics*. Los Angeles: Sage, 2012.

Braden, Maria. *Women Politicians in the Media*. Lexington: University of Kentucky Press, 1996.

Branch, Karen. "Two Lay Claim to Second Latin Seat in House." *Miami Herald* (Fla.), January 15, 1992.

Bratton, Kathleen, Kerry L. Haynie, and Beth Reingold. "Gender, Race, Ethnicity and Representation: The Changing Landscape of Legislative Diversity." In *The Book of the States 2008*, 73–79. Lexington, Ky.: Council of State Governments, 2008.

Breitzer, Susan. "Civil Rights Act of 1964." In *Encyclopedia Virginia*, edited by Virginia Foundation for the Humanities. Published online, accessed February 17, 2015. http://www.encyclopediavirginia.org/Civil_Rights_Act_of_1964.

Brewer, Sarah E., and David Lublin. "The Continuing Dominance of Traditional Gender Roles in Southern Elections." *Social Science Quarterly* 84, no. 2 (2003): 379–96.

Brians, Craig Leonard. "Women for Women? Gender and Party Bias in Voting for Female Candidates." *American Politics Research* 33, no. 3 (2005): 357–75.

Bridges, Tyler. "Kendrick Meek Begins Campaign for Mother's Seat." *Miami Herald* (Fla.), July 8, 2002.

British Broadcasting Corporation. "1962: Bay of Pigs Prisoners Fly to Freedom." Published online, accessed February 16, 2015. http://news.bbc.co.uk/onthisday/hi/dates/stories/december/24/newsid_3295000/3295045.stm.

Brown, Canter, Jr. *Florida's Black Public Officials, 1867–1924*. Tuscaloosa: University of Alabama Press, 1998.

Brown, Nadia E. "Political Participation of Women of Color: An Intersectional Analysis." *Journal of Women, Politics & Policy* 35, no. 4 (2014): 315–48.

Brown, Tamara L., Gregory S. Parks, and Clarenda M. Phillips. *African American Fraternities and Sororities: The Legacy and the Vision*. Lexington: University of Kentucky Press, 2005.

Bullard, Angela M., and Deil S. Wright. "Circumventing the Glass Ceiling: Women Executives in American State Governments." *Public Administration Review* 53, no. 3 (1993): 189–202.

Bullock, Charles S., III. "Racial Crossover Voting and the Election of Black Officials." *Journal of Politics* 46, no. 1 (1984): 238–51.

Bullock, Charles S., III, Donna R. Hoffman, and Ronald Keith Gaddie. "Regional Variations in the Realignment of American Politics, 1944–2004." *Social Science Quarterly* 87, no. 3 (2006): 494–518.

Bullock, Charles S., III, and Susan A. MacManus. "Measuring Racial Bloc Voting Is Difficult for Small Jurisdictions." *National Civic Review* 73, no. 7 (1984): 336–42.

Bullock, Charles S., III, Susan A. MacManus, Karen Padgett Owen, Corttney C. Penberthy, Ralph O. Reid, and Brian McPhee. "'Your Honor' is a Female: A Multistage Electoral Analysis of Women's Successes at Securing State Trial Court Judgeships." *Social Science Quarterly* 95, no. 5 (2014): 1322–45.

Burch, Audra D. S. "Four Haitian-Americans Hoping to Make History in Congressional Race." *Sun-Sentinel* (Fort Lauderdale, Fla.), April 29, 2010.

Burrell, Barbara. "Political Parties and Women's Organizations: Bringing Women into the Electoral Arena." In *Gender and Elections: Shaping the Future of American Politics*, edited by Susan J. Carroll and Richard L. Fox, 143–68. Cambridge: Cambridge University Press, 2006.

Button, James W. "Blacks." In *Florida's Politics and Government*, edited by Manning J. Dauer, 289–90. Gainesville: University of Florida Press, 1984.

Buzzacco-Foerster, Jenna. "Scott, Crist Running Mates Show Importance of Hispanic Vote, Miami-Dade." *Naples News* (Fla.), July 26, 2014. http://www.naplesnews.com/news/state/scott-crist-running-mates-show-importance-of-hispanic-vote-miamidade_25389324.

Cain, Bruce E., D. Roderick Kiewiet, and Carole J. Uhlaner. "The Acquisition of Partisanship by Latinos and Asian Americans." *American Journal of Political Science* 35, no. 2 (1991): 390–442.

Caldwell, Alicia. "Democrats Turn Testy in Senate Debate." *St. Petersburg Times* (Fla.), September 3, 2000.

Caldwell, Tanya. "Husband-Wife Legislators Keep It in the Family." *Sun-Sentinel* (Fort Lauderdale, Fla.), March 25, 2004.

Calhoun-Brown, Allison. "African American Churches and Political Mobilization: The Psychological Impact of Organizational Resources." *Journal of Politics* 58, no. 4 (1996): 935–53.

Call, Harvey A. "Kirk's Gamble on Voters Paid Off in GOP Strength and Leadership Approval." March 29, 1967.

———. "Low Voter Turnout Shows Apathy but Kirk Forces Record Political Gains." *Fort Lauderdale News* (Fla.), March 1, 1967.

———. "Primaries Have Produced Strong Nominee Slates for State Legislature." March 15, 1967.

Cantero, Raoul. "What I Learned from My Fiction Writing Professor, Part I." *The Record: Journal of the Appellate Practice Section*, Fall 2010. http://www.flabarappellate.org/record/APP-Sept2010.pdf.

Caress, Stanley M., Charles Elder, Richard Elling, Jean-Philippe Faletta, Shannon K. Orr, Eric Rader, Marjorie Sarbaugh-Thompson, John Strate, and Luke Thompson. "Effect of Term Limits on the Election of Minority State Legislators." *State and Local Government Review* 35, no. 3 (2003): 183–95.

Carleton, William G. "Negro Politics in Florida: Another Middle-Class Revolution in the Making." *South Atlantic Quarterly* 57 (Autumn 1958): 419–32.

Carroll, Susan. *Women as Candidates in American Politics*, 2nd ed. Bloomington: Indiana University Press, 1994.

Carroll, Susan, Debra L. Dodson, and Ruth B. Mandel. *The Impact of Women in Public Office: An Overview*. New Brunswick, N.J.: Rutgers University, 1991.

Carroll, Susan, and Richard L. Fox, eds. *Gender and Elections: Shaping the Future of American Politics*. Cambridge: Cambridge University Press, 2006.

Carroll, Susan, and Ronnee Schreiber. "Media Coverage of Women in the 103rd Congress." In *Women, Media, and Politics*, edited by Pippa Norris, 131–48. New York: Oxford University Press, 1997.

Casellas, Jason P., and David L. Leal. "Minority Representation in the US Congress." In *The*

Political Representation of Immigrants and Minorities: Voters, Parties and Parliaments in Liberal Democracies, edited by Karen Bird, Thomas Saalfeld, and Andreas M. Wüst, 183–206. London: Routledge, 2011.

Casellas, Jason P., and Sophia J. Wallace. "The Role of Race, Ethnicity, and Party on Attitudes Toward Descriptive Representation." *American Politics Research* 43, no. 1 (2015): 144–69.

Casimir, Leslie. "Haitians Seek Office: New U.S. Citizens Want Political Voice." *Miami Herald* (Fla.), May 4, 1998.

Chasko, Ana Acle. "House Race: Who Knows Kendall Best?" *Miami Herald* (Fla.), October 27, 1994.

Chaudhary, A. G. "Press Portrayal of Black Officials." *Journalism Quarterly* 57, no. 4 (1980): 636–41.

Chen, Elaine. "What the Lack of Asian-Americans Says About Miami." *WLRN.com*, July 11, 2013.

Chou, Rosalind S., and Joe R. Feagin. *The Myth of the Model Minority: Asian Americans Facing Racism*. Boulder, Colo.: Paradigm, 2008.

Christopher, Maurine. *Black Americans in Congress*. T. Y. Crowell Junior Books, 1976.

Citrin, J., D. P. Green, and D. O. Sears. "White Reactions to Black Candidates: When Does Race Matter?" *Public Opinion Quarterly* 54, no. 1 (1990): 74–96.

City of St. Augustine, Florida. "Great Floridians 2000: F. Charles Usina." Accessed July 3, 2014. http://www.staugustinegovernment.com/the-city/featured-stories-archive/2_03/great_fla_bios/charles_usina.cfm.

Clark, Lesley. "Family Ties Aided for Female Inmates." *Miami Herald* (Fla.), n.d.

———. "Female Inmates Moved Near Families." *Miami Herald* (Fla.), August 12, 1998.

Clary, Mike. "Jeb Bush's Anti-Affirmative Action Plan Ignites Firestorm." *Los Angeles Times*, March 7, 2000. http://articles.latimes.com/2000/mar/07/news/mn-10921.

Clayton, Dewey M. *African Americans and the Politics of Congressional Redistricting*. New York: Garland, 2000.

Clements, Patricia Lasche. *A Legacy of Leadership: Florida Governors and Their Inaugural Speeches*. Tallahassee, Fla: Sentry Press, 2005.

Clines, Francis X. "Spiro T. Agnew, Point Man for Nixon Who Resigned Vice Presidency, Dies at 77." *New York Times*, September 19, 1996. http://www.nytimes.com/1996/09/19/us/spiro-t-agnew-point-man-for-nixon-who-resigned-vice-presidency-dies-at-77.html.

Cobas, José A., Jorge Duany, and Joe R. Feagin, eds. *How the United States Racializes Latinos*. Boulder, Colo.: Paradigm, 2009.

Cobb, Jelani. "Rachel Jeantel on Trial." *New Yorker*, June 27, 2013. http://www.newyorker.com/news/news-desk/rachel-jeantel-on-trial.

Colburn, David R. "Florida's Legacy of Misdirected Reapportionment." *Ocala Star-Banner*, May 13, 2012. http://www.ocala.com/article/20120513/OPINION/120519920.

———. *From Yellow Dog Democrats to Red State Republicans: Florida and Its Politics since 1940*. Gainesville: University Press of Florida, 2007.

Colburn, David R., and Jane L. Landers, eds. *The African American Heritage of Florida*, Gainesville: University Press of Florida, 1995.

Colburn, David R., and Susan A. MacManus. "Foreword." In *Jigsaw Puzzle Politics in the Sunshine State*, edited by Seth C. McKee, xiii–xix. Gainesville: University Press of Florida, 2015.

Cole, Leonard A. *Blacks in Power: A Comparative Study of Black and White Elected Officials*. Princeton, N.J.: Princeton University Press, 1976.

Collins, LeRoy. "Past Struggles, Present Changes, and the Future Promise for Civil Rights in Florida and the Nation." In *The Civil Rights Movement in Florida and the United States*, edited by Charles U. Smith, 9–28. Tallahassee, Fla.: Father and Son Publishing, 1989.

Cook, Elizabeth Adell. "Voter Responses to Women Senate Candidates." In *The Year of the Woman: Myths and Realities*, edited by E. A. Cook, S. Thomas, and C. Wilcox, 217–36. Boulder, Colo.: Westview, 1994.

Cordner, Sascha. "Bipartisan to Get Florida's New Lt. Gov. to Have Concrete Duties, Goals." *WFSU*, February 7, 2014. http://news.wfsu.org/post/bipartisan-push-get-florida-s-new-lt-gov-have-concrete-duties-goals.

Corral, Oscar, David Ovalle, and Michael Vasquez. "Cuba Issue Propels Mario Diaz-Balart." *Miami Herald* (Fla.), November 6, 2002.

Cote, Neil. "Deep Speech that was Ever so Simple." *Tampa Tribune* (Fla.), January 18, 1994.

Covington, James W. *The Seminoles of Florida*. Gainesville: University Press of Florida, 1993.

Cunningham, Dayna. "Can African-Americans Find Their Voices in Cyberspace?" Interview with Henry Jenkins. *Public Broadcasting Service*, March 2, 2009. http://henryjenkins.org/2009/03/can_african-americans_find_the.html.

Darcy, R., Susan Welch, and Janet Clark. *Women, Elections, and Representation*. Lincoln: University of Nebraska Press, 1994.

Dáte, S. V. *Jeb: America's Next Bush*. New York: Jeremy P. Tarcher/Penguin, 2007.

Dauer, Manning J., ed. *Florida's Politics and Government*, Gainesville: University Press of Florida, 1980.

Davenport, Jim. "Federal Judge Nixes License Plates with Cross, 'I Believe.'" *USA Today*, November 10, 2009. http://usatoday30.usatoday.com/news/religion/2009-11-10-christian-license-plate_N.htm.

Davies, Frank. "Charm Made Carrie Meek Effective Even When Outnumbered." *Miami Herald* (Fla.), September 25, 2002. http://www.billnelson.senate.gov/newsroom/news/charm-made-carrie-meek-effective-even-when-outnumbered.

Daytona Beach Morning Journal (Fla.). "Carrie Meek to Replace Cherry." March 28, 1979. http://news.google.com/newspapers?nid=1873&dat=19790328&id=gYgfAAAAIBAJ&sjid=6tIEAAAAIBAJ&pg=1455,4860060.

Debenport, Ellen. "Jubilant About Jamerson." *St. Petersburg Times* (Fla.), April 30, 1994.

Demby, Gene. "On the Census, Who Checks 'Hispanic,' Who Checks 'White,' and Why?" Code Switch Blog, National Public Radio, June 16, 2014. http://www.npr.org/blogs/codeswitch/2014/06/16/321819185/on-the-census-who-checks-hispanic-who-checks-white-and-why.

DePalo, Kathryn A. *The Failure of Term Limits in Florida*. Gainesville: University Press of Florida, 2015.

Deslatte, Aaron, and Josh Hefenbrack. "Florida Republican Mel Martinez Announces Resignation from the Senate." *Los Angeles Times*, August 8, 2009. http://articles.latimes.com/2009/aug/08/nation/na-martinez8.

Diaz-Balart, Rafael Lincoln. "Communist Threat to the United States Through the Caribbean." Testimony before the U.S. Senate Subcommittee to Investigate the Administration of the Internal Security Act and Other Internal Security Laws, of the Committee of the Judiciary. May 3, 1960. http://www.latinamericanstudies.org/us-cuba/diaz-balart.htm.

Division of Elections, Florida Department of State. "September 9, 1980 Primary Election." Reproduced online, accessed February 17, 2015. http://election.dos.state.fl.us/elections/resultsarchive/DetailRpt.Asp?ELECTIONDATE=9/9/1980&RACE=STR&PARTY=REP&DIST=114&GRP=&DATAMODE=.

Dixon, Anthony E. *A Timeline of the African Diaspora Experience in Florida*. Tallahassee, Fla.: Archival and Historical Research Associates, 2014.

Dodson, Debra, ed. *Gender and Policymaking: Studies of Women in Office*. New Brunswick, N.J.: Rutgers University, 1991.

Dodson, Debra L., and Susan J. Carroll. *Reshaping the Agenda: Women in State Legislatures*. New Brunswick, N.J.: Rutgers University, 1991.

Dolan, Kathleen. "Gender Differences in Support for Women Candidates: Is There a Glass Ceiling in American Politics?" *Women & Politics* 17, no. 2 (1997): 27–41.

Due, Tananarive. "Despite Odds, Meek Makes History." *Miami Herald* (Fla.), January 5, 1993.

Dunaway, Johanna, Regina G. Lawrence, Melody Rose, and Christopher R. Weber. "Traits versus Issues: How Female Candidates Shape Coverage of Senate and Gubernatorial Races." *Political Research Quarterly* 66, no. 3 (2013): 715–26.

Duncan, Garrett Albert. "Black Panther Party." *Encyclopædia Britannica*. Published online, accessed February 18, 2015. http://www.britannica.com/EBchecked/topic/68134/Black-Panther-Party.

Dunn, Marvin. *Black Miami in the Twentieth Century*. Gainesville: University Press of Florida, 1997.

Dunn, Marvin, and Alex Stepick. "Blacks in Miami." In *Miami Now: Immigration, Ethnicity, and Social Change*, edited by Guillermo J. Grenier and Alex Stepick, 41–56. Gainesville: University Press of Florida, 1992.

Dyckman, Martin. "Florida's First Governor Who Championed Black Causes." *St. Petersburg Times* (Fla.), April 1, 2008.

———. "Jamerson Deserves Job." *St. Petersburg Times* (Fla.), December 16, 1993.

———. *A Most Disorderly Court: Scandal and Reform in the Florida Judiciary*. Gainesville: University Press of Florida, 2008.

———. *Reubin O'D. Askew and the Golden Age of Florida Politics*. Gainesville: University Press of Florida, 2011.

Eisinger, Peter K. "Black Employment in Municipal Jobs: The Impact of Black Political Power." *American Political Science Review* 76, no. 2 (1982): 380–92.

Ellis, Mary Carolyn, and Joanne V. Hawks. "Creating a Different Pattern: Florida's Women Legislators, 1928–1986." *Florida Historical Quarterly* 66, no. 1 (1987): 68–83.

Enciso, Carmen E. *Hispanic Americans in Congress, 1822–1995*. Washington, D.C.: U.S. Government Printing Office, 1995.

Engstrom, Richard L., and Michael D. McDonald. "The Election of Blacks to City Councils: Clarifying the Impact of Electoral Arrangements on the Seats/Population Relationship." *American Political Science Review* 75, no. 2 (1981): 344–54.

Entman, R. M., and A. Rojecki. *The Black Image in the White Mind: Media and Race in America*. Chicago: University of Chicago Press, 2000.

Ericson, David F, ed. *The Politics of Inclusion and Exclusion: Identity Politics in Twenty-First Century America*. New York: Routledge, 2011.

Espino, Rodolfo, David L. Leal, and Kenneth J. Meier, eds. *Latino Politics: Identity, Mobilization, and Representation*. Charlottesville: University of Virginia Press, 2007.

Evers, Charles. "The Black American and the Press." In *The Black Politician: His Struggle for Power*, edited by M. M. Dymally, 70–72. Belmont, Calif.: Duxbury Press, 1971.

Fabrikant, Mel. "New Findings on Asian American Vote in 2012 Show Range of Political Leanings by Ethnic Group and Geographic Location." *Paramus Post*, January 17, 2013. http://www.paramuspost.com/article.php/20130117121752163.

Farrington, Brendan. "Ex-Fla. Lieutenant Governor Jennifer Carroll Discusses Resignation." *Associated Press: Florida*, April 9, 2013.

Fernandez, Ronald. *America Beyond Black and White: How Immigrants and Fusions Are Helping Us Overcome the Racial Divide*. Ann Arbor: University of Michigan Press, 2010.

Fielder, Tom. "GOP Takes Aim at State's Top Post; Martinez Leads Pack of Hopefuls." *Miami Herald* (Fla.), August 31, 1986.

———. "Lopsided Latin Vote Doomed Richmond Bid." *Miami Herald* (Fla.), August 1989.

Filkins, Dexter. "Hastings: People Must Talk with Us." *Miami Herald* (Fla.), October 10, 1992.

Firestone, David. "The 43rd President: The Florida Supreme Court; Florida's Justices Call for Ballot-Counting Rules." *New York Times*, December 3, 2000. http://www.nytimes.com/2000/12/23/us/43rd-president-florida-supreme-court-florida-s-justices-call-for-ballot-counting.html.

Florida Bar News. "Godinez-Sampiero Finally Becomes Florida Lawyer." December 15, 2014. https://www.floridabar.org/__85256AA9005B9F25.nsf/0/3A670C910F44826185257DA8004EBAF0?OpenDocument.

Florida Department of State. "A Brief History: Territorial Period." Published online, accessed February 12, 2015. http://dos.myflorida.com/florida-facts/florida-history/a-brief-history/territorial-period/.

Florida Department of State Division of Elections. "Election Reporting System." Accessed online on March 21, 2016. https://results.elections.myflorida.com/.

Florida House of Representatives. H.R. 9077, "Caribbean Heritage Month." Adopted April 14, 2011. http://www.myfloridahouse.gov/Sections/Bills/billsdetail.aspx?BillId=46945.

———. "Proceedings of the Republican Conference in the House Chamber." September 13, 2005.

Florida Memory, Division of Library and Information Services. "Roxcy Bolton: A Force for Equality." Published online, accessed February 12, 2015. https://www.floridamemory.com/photographiccollection/photo_exhibits/roxcy/bio.php.

Florida School for the Deaf and Blind. *Florida School Herald*, LXXI, no. 2 (October 1971).

Florida Supreme Court. "Merit Retention & Mandatory Retirement of Justices of the Supreme Court." Published online, accessed January 20, 2015. http://www.floridasupremecourt.org/justices/merit.shtml.

Florida Supreme Court Portrait Gallery, "Justice Joseph W. Hatchett." Accessed July 23, 2013. http://www.floridasupremecourt.org/about/gallery/hatchett.shtml.

Florida Times-Union (Jacksonville, Fla.). "Today in Florida History June 27th." Blog post, June 27, 2011. Published online, accessed February 17, 2015. http://jacksonville.com/opinion/blog/400579/rocker419/2011-06-27/today-florida-history-june-27th.

Foglesong, Richard E. *Immigrant Prince: Mel Martinez and the American Dream*. Gainesville: University Press of Florida, 2011.

Follick, Joe, and Lloyd Dunkelberger. "Get Used to Hearing the Name Rep. Marco Rubio." *Sarasota Herald-Tribune* (Fla.), August 13, 2006.

Foner, Eric. *Freedom's Lawmakers: A Directory of Black Officeholders During Reconstruction*, rev. ed. Baton Rouge: Louisiana State University Press, 1996.

Fort Lauderdale News (Fla.). "Ex-Legislator Cries Hoax." March 1, 1967.

———. "Special Primary Tomorrow Livened by GOP Infighting." February 27, 1967.

Fort Lauderdale News and Sun-Sentinel (Fla.). "House Candidates Have Varied Views, Backgrounds." February 25, 1976.

Fossett, Mark A., and K. Jill Kiecolt. "The Relative Size of Minority Populations and White Racial Attitudes." *Social Science Quarterly* 70, no. 4 (1989): 820–35.

Fox, Richard L . "Congressional Elections: Where Are We on the Road to Gender Parity?" In *Gender and Elections: Shaping the Future of American Politics*, edited by Susan J. Carroll and Richard L. Fox, 97–116. Cambridge: Cambridge University Press, 2006.

Fox, Richard L., and Jennifer L. Lawless. "Entering the Arena? Gender and the Decision to Run for Office." *American Journal of Political Science* 48, no. 2 (2004): 264–80.

Fox, Richard L., and Zoe M. Oxley. "Gender Stereotyping in State Executive Elections: Candidate Selection and Success." *Journal of Politics* 65, no. 3 (2003): 833–50.

Garcia, F. Chris, and Gabriel R. Sanchez. *Hispanics and the U.S. Political System: Moving into the Mainstream*. New York: Pearson/Longman, 2008.

García, John A. *Latino Politics in America: Community, Culture, and Interests*. 2nd ed. Lanham, Md.: Rowman & Littlefield, 2012.

García, Maria Christina. *Havana USA: Cuban Exiles and Cuban Americans in South Florida, 1959–1994*. Oakland: University of California Press, 1997.

García Bedolla, Lisa, Katherine Tate, and Janelle Wong. "Indelible Effects: The Impact of Women of Color in the U.S. Congress." In *Women and Elective Office: Past, Present, and Future*, 3rd ed., edited by Sue Thomas and Clyde Wilcox, 235–52. New York: Oxford University Press, 2014.

Garvin, Glenn. "Anniversary Recalls Rescue by Miami Cubans." *Miami Herald* (Fla.), November 15, 2014. http://www.miamiherald.com/news/nation-world/world/americas/cuba/article3952975.html.

George, Paul S. "Colored Town: Miami's Black Community, 1896–1930." *Florida Historical Quarterly* 56, no. 4 (1978): 432–77.

Gershon, Sarah Allen. "Media Coverage of Minority Congresswomen and Voter Evaluations: Evidence from an Online Experimental Study." *Political Research Quarterly* 66, no. 3 (2013): 702–14.

Gill, LaVerne McCain. *African American Women in Congress: Forming and Transforming History*. New Brunswick, N.J.: Rutgers University Press, 1997.

Girard, Chris, Guillermo J. Grenier, and Hugh Gladwin. "Exile Politics and Republican Party Affiliation: The Case of Cuban Americans in Miami." *Social Sciences Quarterly* 93, no. 1 (2012): 42–57.

Givhan, Robin. "Hats Off for Florida Congresswoman-elect Frederica Wilson." *Washington Post*, December 2, 2010.

Gonzalez Juenke, Eric, and Robert R. Preuhs. "Irreplaceable Legislators? Rethinking Minority Representatives in the New Century." *American Journal of Political Science* 56, no. 3 (2012): 705–15.

Goodman, Josh. "Conservative Activists Take Aim at Florida Justices." *The Pew Charitable Trusts*, June 22, 2012. http://www.pewtrusts.org/en/research-and-analysis/blogs/stateline/2012/06/22/conservative-activists-take-aim-at-florida-justices.

Graphic Maps. "Caribbean." Part of *World Atlas*. Published online, accessed February 7, 2015. http://www.worldatlas.com/webimage/countrys/carib.htm.

Grech, Daniel A. "Brutus Campaigns for a Comeback." *Miami Herald* (Fla.), September 3, 2000.

———. "Haiti Native's House Victory Makes History." *Miami Herald* (Fla.), November 8, 2000.

———. "Lawyer Poised to Make History." *Miami Herald* (Fla.), October 29, 2000.

———. "New Legislator Credits a Lifetime of Determination." *Miami Herald* (Fla.), November 9, 2000.

———. "Pounding the Pavement" *Miami Herald* (Fla.), September 3, 2000.

Greenspan, Eliot, and Neil Edward Schlecht. *Frommer's Cuba*, 3rd ed. Hoboken, N.J.: Wiley, 2007.

Grenier, Guillermo J., Lisandro Pérez, and Nancy Foner. *The Legacy of Exile: Cubans in the United States*. Boston: Allyn & Bacon, 2002.

Griezo, Elizabeth M., Yesenia D. Acosta, C. Patricia de la Cruz, Christine Gambino, Thomas

Gryn, Luke J. Larsen, Edward N. Trevelyan, and Nathan P. Walters. "The Foreign-Born Population in the United States: 2010," U.S. Census Bureau: May 2012. http://www.census.gov/prod/2012pubs/acs-19.pdf.

Griffin, Michael. "Chiles Names Jamerson New Secretary of Labor." *Sun-Sentinel* (Fort Lauderdale, Fla.), December 31, 1994.

Griffith-Roberts, Carolanne, and Tim W. Jackson. "Making the Grade in Life." *Southern Living* (May 1993): n.p.

Grimm, Fred. "Family Name Is Plummer's No. 1 Helper." *Miami Herald* (Fla.), November 6, 1980.

———. "Remapping Run Amok Fuels Hastings Return." *Miami Herald* (Fla.), September 13, 1992.

Groer, Anne. "Senate Verdict Near at Alcee Hastings Impeachment Trial." *Orlando Sentinel* (Fla.), October 19, 1989.

Grose, Christian R. *Congress in Black and White: Race and Representation in Washington and at Home*. New York: Cambridge University Press, 2011.

Guardia, Juan R. "Latino/a Fraternity-Sorority Ethnic Identity Development." *Hispanic Outlook in Higher Education*, September 10, 2007.

Guidry, Joe. "Gov. Bob Martinez's Leadership Deserves Special Place in Florida's History." *Tampa Tribune* (Fla.), November 2, 2014. Accessed November 16, 2014.

Gyllenhaal, Anders. "3 Incumbents Lose State House Races; Runoffs Lie Ahead for at Least 9 Seats." *Miami Herald* (Fla.), September 8, 1962.

Haberman, Clyde. "From Private Ordeal to National Fight: The Case of Terri Schaivo." *New York Times*, April 20, 2014. http://www.nytimes.com/2014/04/21/us/from-private-ordeal-to-national-fight-the-case-of-terri-schiavo.html?_r=0.

Hajnal, Zoltan L. "White Residents, Black Incumbents, and a Declining Racial Divide." *American Political Science Review* 95, no. 3 (2001): 603–17.

Hallifax, Jackie. "1st Hispanic Takes Place on State High Court." *Orlando Sentinel* (Fla.), October 5, 2002.

Hamamoto, D. Y. *Monitored Peril: Asian Americans and the Politics of TV Representation*. Minneapolis: University of Minnesota Press, 1994.

Harper, James. "Around the Dome, Echoes of the Past." *St. Petersburg Times* (Fla.), March 29, 1998. http://faculty.usfsp.edu/jsokolov/mclin/harper.html.

Hattam, Victoria. *In the Shadow of Race: Jews, Latinos, and Immigrant Politics in the United States*. Chicago: University of Chicago Press, 2007.

Hauser, Mike. "'Sweeping Changes' to Aid South Broward?" *Fort Lauderdale News* (Fla.), March 29, 1967, South Broward edition.

Hawks, Joanne V., and Carolyn Ellis Staton. "On the Eve of Transition: Women in Southern Legislatures, 1946–1968." In *Women in Politics: Outsiders or Insiders?* 4th ed., edited by Lois Duke Whitaker, 137–47. Upper Saddle River, N.J.: Prentice Hall, 2006.

Hayes, Stephanie. "Louis de la Parte Used Politics to Help Others." *St. Petersburg Times* (Fla.), September 30, 2008.

Hedgecoe, Guy. "The Man Who Knew Fidel Castro, Warhol and Franco's Spain." *IberoSphere*, November 4, 2011. http://iberosphere.com/2011/11/spain-news-4042/4042.

Hernández, Arelis R. "Elias 'Rico' Piccard: Puerto Rican Community Activist." *Orlando Sentinel* (Fla.), November 27, 2013. http://articles.orlandosentinel.com/2013-11-27/news/os-obit-elias-rico-piccard-20131127_1_puerto-rican-social-worker-activist.

Hero, Rodney E., and Robert R. Preuhs. *Black-Latino Relations in U.S. National Politics*. New York: Cambridge University Press, 2013.

Hill, Kevin. "Does the Creation of Majority Black Districts Aid Republicans?" *Journal of Politics* 57, no. 2 (1995): 384–401.

Hilliard, Constance. "West, Allen (1961–)." *BlackPast.org*. Published online, accessed February 20, 2015. http://www.blackpast.org/aah/west-allen-1961#sthash.cmNP8frT.dpuf.

Hirth, Diane. "Jenne's Presidency Bid Appears To Be Doomed." *Sun-Sentinel* (Fort Lauderdale, Fla.), November 7, 1986.

Hoeffel, Elizabeth M., Sonya Rastogi, Myoung Ouk Kim, and Hasan Shahid. "The Asian Population: 2010." *2010 Census Briefs*. U.S. Census Bureau, March 2012. http://www.census.gov/prod/cen2010/briefs/c2010br-11.pdf.

Hollis, Mike, and Linda Kleindienst. "Sit-In Ends—Governor Gives a Bit." *Orlando Sentinel* (Fla.), January 20, 2000. http://articles.orlandosentinel.com/2000-01-20/news/0001200065_1_kendrick-meek-jeb-bush-sit-in-ends.

Hopkins, John. "Calhoun Wins by 21 Votes; Haddad's In." *Fort Lauderdale News* (Fla.), March 15, 1967.

———. "GOP Candidates Ooze with Vote Optimism." *Fort Lauderdale News* (Fla.), March 24, 1967.

———. "GOP Fund Created by Party." *Fort Lauderdale News*, March 26, 1967.

———. "Tuesday Is Voter's Day of Decision." *Fort Lauderdale News* (Fla.), March 26, 1967.

———. "Tuesday's Runoff Primaries Set Stage for General Election." *Fort Lauderdale News* (Fla.). March 12, 1967.

Huddy, Leonie, and Nayda Terkildsen. "The Consequences of Gender Stereotypes for Women Candidates at Different Levels and Types of Office." *Political Research Quarterly* 46, no. 3 (1993): 503–25.

Huffington Post. "Rep. Frederica Wilson." N.d. http://www.huffingtonpost.com/rep-frederica-wilson/.

Hunt, April, and Susan Jacobson. "Hispanic Visitors Boost Bush, Urge Voters to Action." *Orlando Sentinel* (Fla.), July 3, 2002.

Hurst, Rodney L., Sr. *It Was Never About a Hot Dog and a Coke! A Personal Account of the 1960 Sit-In Demonstrations in Jacksonville, Florida and Ax Handle Saturday*. Livermore, Calif.: WingSpan Press, 2008.

Iyengar, Shanto, Nicholas A. Valentino, Stephen Ansolabehere, and Adam F. Simon. "Running as a Woman: Gender Stereotyping in Political Campaigns." In *Women, Media, and Politics*, edited by Pippa Norris, 77–98. Oxford: Oxford University Press, 1997.

Jacobs, David, Pamela M. Paxton, Aubrey L. Jackson, and Chad A. Malone. "Murder, Political Resources, and Women's Political Success." *Social Science Research* 42, no. 2 (2013): 513–26.

Jeffries, Judson L. "Press Coverage of Black Statewide Candidates: The Case of L. Douglas Wilder of Virginia." *Journal of Black Studies* 32, no. 6 (2002): 673–97.

Jewett, Aubrey. "'Fair' Districts in Florida: New Congressional Seats, New Constitutional Standards, Same Old Republican Advantage?" In William J. Miller and Jeremy D. Walling, eds. *The Political Battle over Congressional Redistricting*, 111–35. Lanham, Md.: Lexington Books, 2013.

John F. Kennedy Presidential Library and Museum. "The Bay of Pigs." Published online, accessed February 12, 2015. http://www.jfklibrary.org/JFK/JFK-in-History/The-Bay-of-Pigs.aspx.

———. "Cuban Missile Crisis." Published online, accessed February 12, 2015. http://www.jfklibrary.org/JFK/JFK-in-History/Cuban-Missile-Crisis.aspx.

Jones, Ashby. "Efforts to Oust State Supreme Court Justices Fail." *Wall Street Journal*, November 7, 2012.

Jones, C. E., and M. L. Clemons. "A Model of Racial Crossover Voting: An Assessment of the Wilder Victory." In *Dilemmas of Black Politics*, edited by G. Persons, 128–146. New York: HarperCollins, 1993.

Jones, Maxine D. "No Longer Denied: Black Women in Florida, 1920–1950." In *The African American Heritage of Florida*, edited by David R. Colburn and Jane L. Landers, 240–74. Gainesville: University Press of Florida, 1995.

Jones, Maxine D., and Kevin M. McCarthy. *African Americans in Florida*. Sarasota, Fla.: Pineapple Press, 1993.

Jones, Ricky L. *Black Haze: Violence, Sacrifice, and Manhood in Black Greek-Letter Fraternities*. Albany: State University of New York Press, 2004.

Kaczor, Bill. "Florida Supreme Court Justices Face Unusual Election Challenge." *The Ledger* (Lakeland, Fla.), October 27, 2012. http://www.theledger.com/article/20121027/POLITICS/121029389.

Kahn, Kim F. "Does Being Male Help? An Investigation of the Effects of Candidate Gender and Campaign Coverage on Evaluations of U.S. Senate Candidates." *Journal of Politics* 54, no. 2 (1992): 497–517.

———. "The Distorted Mirror: Press Coverage of Women Candidates for Statewide Office." *Journal of Politics* 56, no. 1 (1994): 154–74.

———. *The Political Consequences of Being a Woman*. New York: Columbia University Press, 1996.

Kallested, Brent. "Florida A&M Proud of Political Ties." *Miami Herald* (Fla.), October 5, 1992.

Kam, Dara. "Florida GOP Aims to Weaken Class-Size Amendment as Final Caps Take Effect This Year." *Palm Beach Post* (Fla.), February 1, 2010. http://www.palmbeachpost.com/news/news/state-regional/florida-gop-aims-to-weaken-class-size-amendment-as/nL2tW/.

Karnig, Albert K., and Susan Welch. *Black Representation and Urban Policy*. Chicago: University of Chicago Press, 1980.

Kathlene, Lyn, Susan E. Clarke, and Barbara A. Fox. "Ways Women Politicians Are Making a Difference." In *Reshaping the Agenda: Women in State Legislatures*, edited by Debra L. Dodson and Susan J. Carroll, 31–38. New Brunswick, N.J.: Rutgers University Press, 1991.

Kay, Julie. "Middle Class Getting Squeezed Out of Courts. So What is Being Done About it?" *Daily Business Review* (Miami, Fla.), January 26, 2015. http://www.dailybusinessreview.com/id=1202716142877/Middle-Class-Getting-Squeezed-Out-of-Courts-So-What-is-Being-Done-About-it.

Kennedy, George. "Negro Lawyer Appointed Assistant Attorney General." *Miami Herald* (Fla.), April 1, 1967.

Kennedy, John. "Death-Penalty Changes on Agenda for New Year." *Orlando Sentinel* (Fla.), December 10, 1999. http://articles.orlandosentinel.com/1999-12-10/news/9912100087_1_lethal-injection-electric-chair-years-on-death.

———. "Labarga First Cuban-American Chief Justice: Immigrant Jurist Says He Will Strive to Build More Inclusive Society." *Palm Beach Post* (Fla.), July 1, 2014.

Kent, Mary Mederios. "Immigration and America's Black Population." *Population Bulletin* 62, no. 4 (December 2007).

Kerstein, Robert. *Politics and Growth in Twentieth-Century Tampa*. Gainesville: University Press of Florida, 2001.

Key, V. O., Jr., *Southern Politics in State and Nation*. New York: Alfred A. Knopf, 1949.

Kim, Thomas P. *The Racial Logic of Politics: Asian Americans and Party Competiton*. Philadelphia: Temple University Press, 2007.

Kimbrough, Walter. *Black Greek 101: The Culture, Customs, and Challenges of Black Fraternities and Sororities*. Madison, N.J.: Fairleigh Dickinson University Press, 2003.

———. "Self-Assessment, Participation, and Value of Leadership Skills, Activities, and Experiences for Black Students Relative to Their Membership in Historically Black Fraternities and Sororities." *Journal of Negro Education* 64, no. 1 (1995): 63–74.

Kimbrough, Walter, and P. Hutcheson. "The Impact of Membership in Black Greek-Letter Organizations on Black Students' Involvement in Collegiate Activities and Their Development of Leadership Skills." *Journal of Negro Education* 67, no. 2 (1998): 96–105.

King-Meadows, Tyson, and Thomas F. Schaller. *Devolution and Black State Legislators*. Albany: State University of New York Press, 2006.

Kitano, H. H. L., and R. Daniels. *Asian Americans: Emerging Minorities*, 3rd ed. Upper Saddle River, N.J.: Prentice Hall, 2001.

Klas, Mary Ellen. "Askew and Hatchett: Wit and Wisdom Before Leadership Florida." *Miami Herald* (Fla.), March 14, 2014. http://miamiherald.typepad.com/nakedpolitics/2014/03/askew-frequently-appointed-the-states-first-black-supreme-court-justice-joseph-hatchett-who-later-became-a-federal-judge.html.

———. "Broward GOP Launches Web Site to 'Save Allen West' from Redistricting Doom." *Tampa Bay Times* (Fla.), January 3, 2012. http://tampabay.com/blogs/the-buzz-florida-politics/content/broward-gop-launches-web-site-save-allen-west-redistricting-doom.

———. "Former Justice Joins Pushback in Merit Retention Debate Over FSC Justices." *Miami Herald* (Fla.), September 11, 2012. http://miamiherald.typepad.com/nakedpolitics/2012/09/three-justices-raised-more-than-1-m-and-restore-justice-has-raised-41000-villalobos-most-of-the-money-comes-from-the-s.html.

———. "Gambling's Long History in Florida." *Tampa Bay Times* (Fla.), November 24, 2009. http://www.tampabay.com/news/perspective/gamblings-long-history-in-florida/1054214.

———. "In Surprise Move, Florida GOP Opposes Supreme Court Justices' Retention in November." *Miami Herald* (Fla.), September 21, 2012.

Kleefield, Eric. "Rep. Mario Diaz-Balart Officially Switching Districts, Running for His Brother Lincoln's House Seat." *Talking Points Memo*, February 11, 2010.

Kleindienst, Linda. "Chiles, Bush Appoint First Black Woman to Florida Supreme Court," Knight Ridder/Tribune News Service, December 8, 1998.

Kleindienst, Linda, and Diane Hirth. "GOP's Martinez Wins Governorship." *Sun-Sentinel* (Fort Lauderdale, Fla.), November 5, 1986. http://articles.sun-sentinel.com/1986-11-05/news/8603080130_1_steve-pajcic-first-florida-governor-runoff.

Klingman, Peter D. *Josiah Walls: Florida's Black Congressman of Reconstruction*. Gainesville: University Press of Florida, 1976.

Kraus, Neil, and Todd Swanstrom. "Minority Mayors and the Hollow-Prize Problem." *PS: Political Science & Politics* 34, no. 1 (2001): 99–105.

Krogstad, Jens Manuel. "After Decades of GOP Support, Cubans Shifting Toward the Democratic Party." *Pew Research Fact Tank: News in the Numbers*, June 24, 2014. http://www.pewresearch.org/fact-tank/2014/06/24/after-decades-of-gop-support-cubans-shifting-toward-the-democratic-party/.

Kumar, Anita. "Martinez to be Face of GOP." *St. Petersburg Times* (Fla.), November 14, 2006.

Kunerth, Jeff, and Stephen Hudak. "Anniversary Brings Memories of Violence, Fight for Equality." *Orlando Sentinel* (Fla.), June 29, 2014.

Lai, James S. *Asian American Political Action*. Boulder, Colo.: Lynne Rienner, 2011.

———. "Asian Pacific Americans and the Pan-Ethnic Question." In *Minority Politics at the Millennium*, edited by Richard Keiser and Katherine Underwood, 203–26. New York: Garland, 2009.

———. "Voting Behavior and Political Participation." In *The Greenwood Encyclopedia of Con-*

temporary Asian American Issues. Vol. 2, edited by Edith Chen and Grace Yoo, 685–702. New York: Greenwood.

Lai, James S., Wendy K. Tam Cho, Thomas P. Kim, and Okiyoshi Takeda. "Asian Pacific-American Campaigns, Elections, and Elected Officials." *PS: Political Science & Politics* 34, no. 3 (2001): 611–17.

Larson, Stephanie Greco. "American Women and Politics in the Media: A Review Essay." *PS: Political Science & Politics* 34, no. 2 (2001): 227–30.

Law 360. "Q&A With White & Case's Raoul Cantero." September 10, 2009.

Lawless, Jennifer L. "Politics of Presence? Congresswomen and Symbolic Representation." *Political Research Quarterly* 57, no. 1 (2004): 81–99.

Lawless, Jennifer L., and Richard L. Fox. *It Still Takes a Candidate: Why Women Don't Run for Office*, rev. ed. New York: Cambridge University Press, 2010.

Lawless, Jennifer L., and Sean M. Theriault. "Women in the U.S. Congress: From Entry to Exit." In *Women in Politics: Outsiders or Insiders?* 4th ed., edited by Lois Duke Whitaker, 164–81. Upper Saddle River, N.J.: Prentice Hall, 2006.

Lawson, Steven F. *Running for Freedom: Civil Rights and Black Politics in America Since 1941*. New York: McGraw-Hill, 1991.

Leader, Shelah Gilbert. "The Policy Impact of Elected Women Officials." In *The Impact of the Electoral Process,* edited by L. Sandy Maisel and J. Cooper, 265–84. Beverly Hills, Calif: Sage, 1977.

Leal, David L. "Mexican-American and Cuban-American Public Opinion: Differences at the State Level?" In *Public Opinion in State Politics*, edited by Jeffrey Cohen, 53–78. Stanford, Calif.: Stanford University Press, 2006.

———. "Religion and the Political and Civic Lives of Latinos." In *Religion and Democracy in the United States: Danger or Opportinity?* edited by Alan Wolfe and Ira Katznelson, 308–54. Washington, D.C.: American Political Science Association, 2010.

Leary, Alex. "Marco Rubio's Meteoric Rise in Florida Politics." *Tampa Bay Times* (Fla.), November 26, 2014. http://www.tampabay.com/news/politics/elections/marco-rubios-meteoric-rise-in-florida-politics/1127114.

Lee, Elisa. "She's the First Asian Woman in the Florida Legislature," *Asian Week*, March 11, 1994.

LeMay, Michael C. *The Perennial Struggle: Race, Ethnicity, and Minority Group Relations in the United States*. Upper Saddle River, N.J.: Pearson/Prentice Hall, 2009.

Lenz, Timothy O., and Anita Pritchard. "Florida Legislators' Perceptions of the Change to Single-Member Districts." *State and Local Government Review* 23, no. 3 (1991): 134–38.

Levin College of Law, University of Florida. "Virgil Hawkins Story." Accessed September 16, 2014. http://www.law.ufl.edu/about/about-uf-law/history/virgil-hawkins-story.

Levy, Art. "Icon: Bob Martinez," *Florida Trend*, July 1, 2009.

Lewis, Alfred E. "5 Held in Plot to Bug Democrats' Office Here." *Washington Post*, June 18, 1972. http://www.washingtonpost.com/wp-srv/national/longterm/watergate/articles/061872-1.htm.

Lindley, Mary Ann. "McCrary Choice Symbol of New Day for Minorities," *Lakeland Ledger* (Fla.), July 23, 1978.

Lipman, Larry. "Rep. Hastings Pressures Chiles on Education Job." *Palm Beach Post* (West Palm Beach, Fla.), December 11, 1993.

Liptak, Adam. "Justices, 5–4, Reject Corporate Spending Limit." *New York Times*, January 21, 2010. http://www.nytimes.com/2010/01/22/us/politics/22scotus.html?pagewanted=all&_r=0.

Llorente, Elizabeth. "Mario Diaz-Balart: President Obama Only Thinks of Immigration Reform in Election Season." *Fox News Latino*, October 2, 2014. http://latino.foxnews.com/latino/

politics/2014/10/02/rep-diaz-balart-president-obama-only-thinks-immigration-in-election-season/.

Lopez, Ashley. "Koch Brothers Set Sights on Florida Supreme Court Justices." *Florida Center for Investigative Reporting*, October 1, 2012. http://fcir.org/2012/10/01/koch-brothers-set-sights-on-florida-supreme-court-justices/.

Lopez, Mark Hugo, and Daniel Dockterman. "U.S. Hispanic Country of Origin Counts for the Nation, Top 30 Metropolitan Areas." *Pew Research Hispanic Trends Project*, May 26, 2011. Accessed January 6, 2015. http://www.pewhispanic.org/2011/05/26/us-hispanic-country-of-origin-counts-for-nation-top-30-metropolitan-areas/.

Lopez, Mark Hugo, and Paul Taylor. "Latino Voters in the 2012 Election." Pew Research Hispanic Trends Project, 7 November 2012. http://www.pewhispanic.org/2012/11/07/latino-voters-in-the-2012-election/.

López-Cantera, Carlos. "Young Cuban-Americans Remain Committed to a Free Cuba." Originally printed in *Miami Herald* (Fla.), May 20, 2014, since removed. Archived at *Capitol Hill Cubans*. http://www.capitolhillcubans.com/2014/05/young-cuban-americans-remain-committed.html.

Lopez Torregrosa, Luisita. "How a Surge in Puerto Rican Voters is Changing Florida Politics." *Yahoo! News*, October 20, 2014. http://news.yahoo.com/how-a-surge-in-puerto-rican-voters-is-changing-florida-politics-150912696.html.

Louka, Loukia. "Education Chief Visits Citrus." *St. Petersburg Times* (Fla.), March 15, 1994.

Lublin, David, and Sarah E. Brewer. "The Continuing Dominance of Traditional Gender Roles in Southern Elections." *Social Science Quarterly* 84, no. 2 (2003): 379–96.

MacManus, Susan A. "Congressional Redistricting in 1992: A Decade Long Battle." In *Mapping Florida's Political Landscape*, edited by Susan A. MacManus, 117–75. Tallahassee: Florida Institute of Government, Florida State University, 2002.

———. "The Emerging Battleground South: Population Change and Changing Politics." In *Presidential Elections in the South: Putting 2008 in Political Context*, edited by Branwell D. Kapeluck, Laurence W. Moreland, and Robert P. Steed, 99–136. Boulder, Colo.: Lynne Rienner, 2010.

———. "Florida Overview: Ten Media Markets—One Powerful State." In *Florida's Politics: Ten Media Markets, One Powerful State*, edited by Kevin A. Hill, Susan A. MacManus, and Dario Moreno, 1–64. Tallahassee: John Scott Dailey Florida Institute of Government, Florida State University, 2004.

———. "Florida: The South's Premier Battleground State." *American Review of Politics* 26 (Summer 2005): 155–84.

———. "Florida's Changing Metropolitan Areas: Age, Race/Ethnic, and Gender Patterns of the 1990s Create Challenges for the New Millennium." In *On the Verge: Florida's Megacities in the New Millennium*, edited by Lance deHaven-Smith and Dena Hurst, 66–106. Tallahassee: Florida Institute of Government, Florida State University, 2000.

———, ed. *Mapping Florida's Political Landscape*. Tallahassee: Florida Institute of Government, Florida State University, 2002.

———. "Population Shifts Change a Region's Politics: The Old South Morphs into the New." In *Writing Southern Politics: Contemporary Interpretations and Future Directions*, edited by Robert P. Steed and Laurence W. Moreland, 167–88. Lexington: University of Kentucky Press, 2006.

———. "The Race to Put Women's Faces in High Places: Florida's Parties Keep Score in the Early 2000s." *Florida Political Chronicle*, 15 (Spring 2004): 19–38.

———, ed. *Reapportionment and Representation in Florida: A Historical Collection.* Tampa: Intrabay Innovation Institute, University of South Florida, 1991.

———. "Redistricting in Florida in 2002: A Different State and Legal Environment." In *Mapping Florida's Political Landscape*, edited by Susan A. MacManus, 9–53. Tallahassee: Florida Institute of Government, Florida State University, 2002.

———. "The South's Changing Demographics." In *Oxford University Handbook on Southern Politics*, edited by Charles S. Bullock III and Mark Rozell, 47–79. New York: Oxford University Press, 2012.

———. "State Legislative Redistricting in 1992: Precedent-Setting Decisions in a Diverse Florida." In *Mapping Florida's Political Landscape*, edited by Susan A. MacManus, 176–235. Tallahassee: Florida Institute of Government, Florida State University, 2002.

———. "V. O. Key Jr.'s *Southern Politics*: Demographic Changes Will Transform the Region; Inmigration and Generational Shifts Speed Up the Process." In *Unlocking V. O. Key Jr.: "Southern Politics" for the Twenty-First Century*, edited by Angie Maxwell and Todd G. Shields, 185–206. Fayetteville: University of Arkansas Press, 2011.

———. "Voter Participation and Turnout: It's A New Game." In *Gender and Elections: Shaping the Future of American Politics*, edited by Susan J. Carroll and Richard L. Fox, 43–73. Cambridge: Cambridge University Press, 2006.

———. "Women Follow Different Paths to the Florida Legislature: A Look at the Class of 2002–2004." *Florida Political Chronicle*, 16 (Spring 2005): 11–28.

MacManus, Susan A., Charles S. Bullock III, Kathryn A. DePalo, and Rachael Ivey. "First Time Candidates: How Strategic are Women Running for the State Legislature?" In *Women in Politics: Outsiders or Insiders?* 5th ed., edited by Lois Duke Whitaker, 129–42. New York: Prentice Hall, 2010.

MacManus, Susan A., Charles S. Bullock III, Karen L. Padgett, and Brittany Penberthy. "Women Winning at the Local Level: Are County and School Board Positions Becoming More Desirable and Plugging the Pipeline to Higher Office?" In *Women in Politics: Outsiders or Insiders?* 4th ed., edited by Lois Duke Whitaker, 117–36. Upper Saddle River, N.J.: Prentice Hall, 2006.

MacManus, Susan A., Joanna M. Cheshire, Tifini L. Hill, and Susan C. Schuler. "Redistricting in Florida: Loud Voices from the Grassroots." In *Jigsaw Puzzle Politics in the Sunshine State*, edited by Seth C. McKee, 126–62. Gainesville: University Press of Florida, 2015.

MacManus, Susan A., and David R. Colburn. "Florida Politics: The State Evolves into One of the Nation's Premier Political Battlegrounds." In *The History of Florida*, edited by Michael Gannon, 415–43. Gainesville: University Press of Florida, 2013.

MacManus, Susan A., and Kathryn DePalo. "What Next? Term Limits, Gender, and New Offices Sought." Presented at the annual Midwest Political Science Association meeting, Chicago, Illinois, April 11–15, 2007.

MacManus, Susan A., and Ronald Keith Gaddie. "Florida." In *Redistricting in the 1980s*, edited by Leroy Hardy, Alan Heslop, and George Blair, 51–59. Claremont, Calif: The Rose Institute of State and Local Government, 1993.

———. "Reapportionment in Florida: The Stakes Keep Getting Higher." In *Reapportionment and Representation in Florida: A Historical Collection*, edited by Susan A. MacManus, 457–88. Tampa: Intrabay Innovation Institute, University of South Florida, 1991.

MacManus, Susan A., Aubrey Jewett, Thomas R. Dye, and David J. Bonanza. *Politics in Florida*, 3rd ed. Tallahassee: Florida Institute of Government, Florida State University, 2011.

MacManus, Susan A., and Lawrence Morehouse. "Race, Abortion, and Judicial Retention: The Case of Florida Supreme Court Chief Justice Leander Shaw." In *National Political Science Re-*

view. Vol. 5, *The Changing Racial Regime*, edited by Matthew Holden, Jr., 133–51. New Brunswick, N.J.: Transaction, 1995.

———. "Redistricting in the Multi-Racial 21st Century: Changing Demographic and Socioeconomic Conditions Pose New Challenges" and update. In *Mapping Florida's Political Landscape*, edited by Susan A. MacManus, 54–86. Tallahassee: Florida Institute of Government, Florida State University, 2002.

MacManus, Susan A., and Andrew Quecan. "Minority Pathbreakers in Florida Politics." presented at the annual Midwest Political Science Association, Chicago, Illinois, April 11–15, 2007.

MacManus, Susan A., and Mary Stutzman. "Race/Ethnicity and Gender in Florida: Demographic and Socioeconomic Trends Transform the Sunshine State." In *New Voices in the Old South: How Women & Minorities Influence Southern Politics*, edited by Todd G. Shields and Shannon G. Davis, 99–145. Tallahassee: John Scott Dailey Florida Institute of Government, Florida State University, 2008.

Major, Lesa Hatley, and Renita Coleman. "The Intersection of Race and Gender in Election Coverage: What Happens When the Candidates Don't Fit the Stereotypes?" *Howard Journal of Communications* 19, no. 4 (2008): 315–33.

Maness, William H. *Dear William: The Yeast Is There*. Author, 2000.

Manning-Miller, Carmen L. "Carol Moseley-Braun: Black Women's Political Images in the Media." In *Mediated Messages and African-American Culture*, edited by Venise T. Berry and Carmen L. Manning-Miller, 117–30. Thousand Oaks, Calif.: Sage, 1996.

Marshall, Toni. "Caribbean Caucus Leads to Rift in Democratic Party." *Sun-Sentinel* (Fla.), March 29, 2003.

Martin, Elaine. "Bias or Counterbalance: Women Judges Making a Difference." In *Women in Politics: Outsiders or Insiders?* 4th ed., edited by Lois Duke Whitaker, 255–71. Upper Saddle River, N.J.: Prentice Hall, 2006.

Martin, John L., Leon F. Bouvier, and William Leonard. "Shaping Florida: The Effects of Immigration, 1970–2020." Washington, D.C.: Center for Immigration Studies, December 1995. http://cis.org/FloridaImmigrants19702020.

Martin, Mart. *The Almanac of Women and Minorities in American Politics 2002*. Boulder, Colo.: Westview, 2001.

Martinez, Bob. Interview by Julian Pleasants. Samuel Proctor Oral History Program, University of Florida, March 23, 1999. http://ufdc.ufl.edu/UF00005615/00001/2x?search=martinez.

Martinez, Mel, and Ed Breslin. *A Sense of Belonging: From Castro's Cuba to the U.S. Senate, One Man's Pursuit of the American Dream*. New York: Crown Forum, 2008.

Mazzei, Patricia, Christina Viega, and Daniel Chang. "In GOP Pickup, Miami Rep. Joe Garcia Loses to Carlos Curbelo." *Miami Herald* (Fla.), November 5, 2014. http://www.miamiherald.com/news/local/community/miami-dade/article3569095.html.

McClain, Paula. "Minority Group Influence: Agenda Setting, Formulation and Public Policy." In *Urban Violence: Agendas, Politics, and Problem Redefinition*, edited by Paula McClain, 74–75. New York: Greenwood, 1993.

McClain, Paula D., and Steven C. Tauber. *American Government in Black and White*. Boulder, Colo: Paradigm, 2010.

McCrary, Jesse J., Jr. "Dade County Bar Luncheon." Speech delivered at the Columbus Hotel, Miami, Fla., November 14, 1978. Available in FAMU Black Archives.

McDaniel, Eric L. *Politics in the Pews: The Political Mobilization of Black Churches*. Ann Arbor: University of Michigan Press, 2008.

McDermott, Monika L. "Race and Gender Cues in Low-Information Elections." *Political Research Quarterly* 51, no. 4 (1998): 895–918.

McFadden, Robert D. "Mary Peabody, 89, Rights Activist, Dies." *New York Times*, February 7, 1981. http://www.nytimes.com/1981/02/07/obituaries/mary-peabody-89-rights-activist-dies.html.

McKnight, Robert W. "The Final Nail in the 'Pork Chop Gang' Coffin." *Sunshine State News* (Fla.), July 30, 2014. http://www.sunshinestatenews.com/print/5911575.

———. "Quorum Call for Representative Joe Lang Kershaw (D., Miami)." Blog post, March 29, 2013. Published online, accessed February 17, 2015. http://blogs.tallahassee.com/community/2013/03/29/32-quorum-call-for-representative-joe-lang-kershaw-d-miami/.

McMiller, Darryl L. "Boosting Latino and Black Political Participation: The Impact of Associational and Religious Resources." *Politics & Policy* 33, no. 3 (2005): 444–68.

Meier, Kenneth J. "Representative Bureaucracy: An Empirical Analysis." *American Political Science Review* 69, no. 2 (1975): 526–43.

Menzel, Margie. "News Service of Florida Has: Five Questions for Jorge Labarga." *News Service of Florida*, January 31, 2014.

Merrill, Barbara, and Linden West. *Using Biographical Methods in Social Research*. Newbury Park, Calif.: Sage, 2009.

Merritt, Sharyne. "Sex Differences in Role Behavior and Policy Orientations of Suburban Officeholders: The Effect of Women's Employment." In *Woman and Local Politics*, edited by Debra Stewart, 115–29. Metuchen, N.J.: Scarecrow, 1980.

Mezey, Susan Gluck. "Increasing the Number of Women in Office: Does It Matter?" In *The Year of the Woman: Myths and Realities*, edited by E. A. Cook, S. Thomas, and C. Wilcox, 255–70. Boulder, Colo.: Westview, 1994.

Miami Herald (Fla.). "Advertisement: Alan Rosenthal's Problem." October 30, 1980.

———. "Arnett Girardeau: State Senate Candidate." October 1, 1982.

———. "Joe Kershaw, Earl Carroll Win." May 31, 1968.

———. "Mr. Jesse J. McCrary Jr.—Obituary." October 30, 2007.

Miccosukee Tribe of Indians of Florida. "Leaders." Miami, Fla.: Published online, 2011. Accessed February 19, 2015. http://www.miccosukee.com/tribe/.

Minta, Michael D. "Gender, Race, Ethnicity, and Political Representation in the United States." *Politics & Gender* 8, no. 4 (2012): 541–47.

Mitchell, Tia. "Florida Gov. Rick Scott Signs Bill to Give In-state Tuition to Undocumented Students." *Tampa Bay Times* (Fla.), June 9, 2014. http://www.tampabay.com/news/politics/stateroundup/florida-gov-rick-scott-signs-bill-to-give-in-state-tuition-to-undocumented/2183562.

———. "Three State Supreme Court Justices Easily Returned to Bench, Despite Active Opposition." *Tampa Bay Times* (Tampa, Fla.), November 6, 2012.

Mladenka, Kenneth R. "Blacks and Hispanics in Urban Politics." *American Political Science Review* 83, no. 1 (1989): 165–91.

Mohl, Raymond. "Miami: The Ethnic Cauldron." In *Sunbelt Cities: Politics and Growth since World War II*, edited by Richard M. Bernard and Bradley R. Rice, 58–99. Austin: University of Texas Press, 1983.

———. "On the Edge: Blacks and Hispanics in Metropolitan Miami since 1959." *Florida Historical Quarterly* 69, no. 1 (1990): 37–56.

———. "The Pattern of Race Relations in Miami since the 1920s." In *The African American Heritage of Florida*, edited by David B. Colburn and Jane L. Landers, 240–74. Gainesville: University Press of Florida, 1995.

Mohl, Raymond, and George E. Pozzetta. "Immigration and Ethnicity in Florida History." In

The History of Florida, edited by Michael Gannon, 470–96. Gainesville: University Press of Florida, 2013.

Moore, Robert C. "Religion, Race, and Differences in Political Ambition." *Politics & Gender* 1, no. 4 (2005): 577–96.

Moreno, Dario. "Cuban American Political Power: Challenges and Consequences." *Cuban Affairs* 1, no. 4 (2006): 1–23.

———. "Florida's Hispanic Voters: Growth, Immigration and Political Clout." In *Florida's Politics: Ten Media Markets, One Powerful State*, edited by Kevin A. Hill, Susan A. MacManus, and Dario Moreno, 83–100. Tallahassee: John Scott Dailey Florida Institute of Government, Florida State University, 2004.

Morgan, Lucy. "Jamerson Makes His Bid Official." *St. Petersburg Times* (Fla.), December 14, 1993.

Mormino, Gary R. *Land of Sunshine, State of Dreams: A Social History of Modern Florida* Gainesville: University Press of Florida, 2005.

Mormino, Gary R., and George E. Pozzetta. *The Immigrant World of Ybor City: Italians and Their Latin Neighbors in Tampa, 1885–1985*. Gainesville: University Press of Florida, 1998.

Morris, Allen. *The Florida Handbook 1949–1950*. Tallahassee, Fla.: Peninsular Publishing, 1949.

———. *The Florida Handbook 1963–1964*. Tallahassee, Fla.: Peninsular Publishing, 1963.

———. *The Florida Handbook 1969–1970*. Tallahassee, Fla.: Peninsular Publishing, 1969.

———. *The Florida Handbook 1971–1972*. Tallahassee, Fla.: Peninsular Publishing, 1972.

———. *The Florida Handbook 1973–1974*. Tallahassee, Fla.: Peninsular Publishing, 1973.

———. *The Language of Lawmaking in Florida*. Tallahassee, Fla.: Office of the Clerk of the House of Representatives, 1974.

Morris, Allen, and Joan Perry Morris. *The Florida Handbook 1997–1998*. Tallahassee, Fla.: Peninsular Publishing, 1997.

———. *The Florida Handbook 2009–2010*. Tallahassee, Fla.: Peninsular Publishing, 2009.

———. *The Florida Handbook 2013–2014*. The Clerk of the Florida House of Representatives. http://www.myfloridahouse.gov/contentViewer.aspx?Category=PublicGuide&File=Florida Handbook.html.

Moss, Bill. "Jamerson Once Again Fights for His Dream." *St. Petersburg Times* (Fla.), December 20, 1993.

National Center for State Courts. "Gender and Racial Fairness: Resource Guide." Published online, accessed January 31, 2015. http://www.ncsc.org/Topics/Access-and-Fairness/Gender-and-Racial-Fairness/Resource-Guide.aspx.

National Endowment for the Humanities. *Reporte Oral El Caseo de la Embajade del Peru y el Mariel Exodo Masivo de Cubanos*. ReEncuentro Cubano, 1981.

National Public Radio. "Kent State Shooting Divided Campus and Country." *Talk of the Nation*, May 3, 2010. http://www.npr.org/templates/story/story.php?storyId=126480349.

National Security Archive. "Bay of Pigs: 40 Years After, Chronology." Published online, accessed February 16, 2015. http://www2.gwu.edu/~nsarchiv/bayofpigs/chron.html.

Nickens, Tim. "Legislator Runs for Castor's Job." *Miami Herald* (Fla.), December 14, 1993.

———. "Memories of Jamerson Warm House Chamber." *St. Petersburg Times* (Fla.), April 26, 2001.

Nielsen, Allison. "Ron Book Remains Top Dog on Florida Lobbying Scene." *Sunshine State News* (Fla.), June 12, 2014. http://www.sunshinestatenews.com/story/ron-book-remains-top-dog-florida-lobbying-scene.

Noll, Jody. "For the Students: The 1968 Florida Teacher Strike." Thesis, University of South Florida, June 5, 2012. http://dspace.nelson.usf.edu/xmlui/bitstream/handle/10806/4728/Jody%20 thesis.pdf?sequence=1.

Norris, Tina, Paula L. Vinces, and Elizabeth M. Hoeffel. "The American Indian and Alaska Native Population: 2010." *2010 Census Briefs*. U.S. Census Bureau, January 2012. http://www.census.gov/prod/cen2010/briefs/c2010br-10.pdf.

O'Connor, Daniel J., III. *Drawing the Map: Redistricting in the South*. Prepared for the Southern Legislative Conference of The Council of State Governments. Atlanta, Ga.: The Council of State Governments, 2000. https://www.slcatlanta.org/Publications/IGA/DrawingTheMap.pdf.

Office of Economic and Demographic Research, The Florida Legislature. "Demographic Estimating Conference Executive Summary December 1, 2015." http://edr.state.fl.us/Content/conferences/population/demographicsummary.pdf.

Office of Juvenile Justice and Delinquency Protection. "Juvenile Transfer to Criminal Court." In *Juvenile Justice Reform Initiatives in the States, 1994–1996*. Published online, accessed February 12, 2015. http://www.ojjdp.gov/pubs/reform/ch2_j.html.

Office of Program Policy Analysis and Government Accountability, Florida Legislature. "Sunset Memorandum: Governance of Florida's Water Management Districts Options for Legislative Consideration." December 19, 2007. http://www.floridasunsetreviews.gov/UserContent/docs/File/WMD_Governance_Options.pdf.

Office of the Clerk, Florida House of Representatives. *The People of Lawmaking in Florida, 1822–2015*. Tallahassee: Published online, 2015. http://www.myfloridahouse.gov/FileStores/Web/HouseContent/Approved/ClerksOffice/ThePeopleOfLawmakingInFlorida.pdf.

Ojita, Mirta. "The Long Voyage from Mariel Ends." *New York Times*, January 16, 2005. http://www.nytimes.com/2005/01/16/weekinreview/16ojito.html?_r=0.

Olorunnipa, Toluse. "South Florida Leading National Census Trend." *Miami Herald* (Fla.), March 18, 2011.

Owens, Michael Leo. *God and Government in the Ghetto: The Politics of Church-State Collaboration in Black America*. Chicago: University of Chicago Press, 2007.

Pachon, Harry, and Louis DeSipio. "Latino Elected Officials in the 1990's." *PS: Political Science & Politics*, 25, no. 2 (1992): 212–17.

Padilla, Maria. "March on Tallahassee: One Florida, But Many Foes." *Orlando Sentinel* (Fla.), March 8, 2000. http://articles.orlandosentinel.com/2000-03-08/news/0003080155_1_president-george-bush-bush-family-kweisi.

———. "Puerto Rican Politics Invade City Beautiful." *Orlando Sentinel* (Fla.), October 2, 2002.

Parra Herrera, Jose Dante. "William Turner, State Senator, Integrated Dade School Board." *Sun-Sentinel* (Fort Lauderdale, Fla.). November 2, 2002. http://articles.sun-sentinel.com/2002-11-02/news/0211010893_1_mr-turner-overtown-school-board.

Patrick, Maureen J. "Immigration & Ybor City, 1886–1921." Published online, March 1, 2007. http://cigarcitymagazine.com/immigration-ybor-city-1886-1921/.

Pérez, Lisandro. "Cubans in the United States." *Annals of the American Academy of Political and Social Science* 487, no. 1 (1986): 126–37.

Pérez, Louis A., Jr. "Cubans in Tampa: From Exiles to Immigrants, 1893–1901." *Florida Historical Quarterly* 57, no. 2 (1978): 129–40.

Pew Forum on Religion & Public Life. "Chapter 6: Social and Political Attitudes." In *Asian Americans: A Mosaic of Faiths*. Washington, D.C.: Pew Research Center, July 19, 2012. http://www.pewforum.org/2012/07/19/asian-americans-a-mosaic-of-faiths-social-and-political-attitudes/.

Phelps, Sherelle. *Contemporary Black Biography: Profiles from the International Black Community*. Farmington Hills, Mich.: Gale Research, 1998.

Pinder, Mamie. "The Political Papers Newsletter," 14th ed. Miami, Fla.: Self-published. April 10, 2010.

Pinzur, Matthew I. "Brown Overcomes Carroll to Retain 3rd District Seat." *Florida Times-Union* (Jacksonville, Fla.), November 8, 2000.

———. "GOP Hopes to Break into Black Democratic Monolith. Republicans Say Getting their Uncensored Message Out to African-American's is the Key to Eroding Blacks' Overwhelming Support for Democrats." *Florida Times-Union* (Jacksonville, Fla.), April 25, 2001.

———. "Widespread 3rd District Campaign Tough, Carroll Has Set Her Standards High." *Florida Times-Union* (Jacksonville, Fla.), October 30, 2000.

Plutzer, Eric, and John F. Zipp. "Identity Politics, Partisanship, and Voting for Women Candidates." *Public Opinion Quarterly* 60, no. 1 (1996): 30–57.

Poggione, Sarah. "Women State Legislators: Descriptive and Substantive Representation." In *Women in Politics: Outsiders or Insiders?* 4th ed., edited by Lois Duke Whitaker, 182–99. Upper Saddle River, N.J.: Prentice Hall, 2006.

Polivka, Larry, and Jack Osterholt. "The Governor as Manager: Agency Autonomy and Accountability." *Public Budgeting & Finance* 5, no. 4 (1985): 91–104.

Porter, Bruce, and Marvin Dunn. *The Miami Riot of 1980: Crossing the Bounds*. Lexington, Mass.: D. C. Heath, 1984.

Price, Hugh Douglas. *The Negro and Southern Politics: A Chapter of Florida History*. New York: New York University Press, 1957.

Prince, Carl E. "Riots, Urban, of 1967." *Dictionary of American History*. Published online: 2003. Accessed February 16, 2015. http://www.encyclopedia.com/doc/1G2-3401803621.html.

Prindeville, Diane-Michele. "A Comparative Study of Native American and Hispanic Women in Grassroots and Electoral Politics." *Frontiers: A Journal of Women Studies* 23, no. 1 (2002): 67–89.

———. *On the Streets and in the State House*. New York: Routledge, 2004.

Public Broadcasting Service. "A Chronology of the Elián Gonzalez Saga." *Frontline: Saving Elián*. Published online, accessed February 17, 2015. http://www.pbs.org/wgbh/pages/frontline/shows/elian/etc/eliancron.html.

———. "The Compromise of 1850 and the Fugitive Slave Act." *Africans in America*. Published online, accessed February 12, 2015. http://www.pbs.org/wgbh/aia/part4/4p2951.html.

Pudlow, Jan. "A Celebration and a Challenge." *Florida Bar News*, June 1, 2004. http://www.floridabar.org/divcom/jn/jnnews01.nsf/8c9f13012b96736985256aa900624829/03361d0f36ad508e85256ea0005009de!OpenDocument.

———. "Chief Justice Peggy Ann Quince of the Supreme Court of Florida." *Florida Bar Journal* 82, no. 9 (2008): n.p.

———. "Governor Signs Undocumented Attorney Bill." *Florida Bar News*, June 1, 2014. http://www.floridabar.org/DIVCOM/JN/JNNews01.nsf/RSSFeed/52B54E465C469EE785257CDD0044AFD4.

———. "Jorge Labarga: Chief Justice of the Florida Supreme Court." *Florida Bar Journal* 88, no. 8 (2014): n.p.

Pugh, Tony. "Hastings Captures Runoff." *Miami Herald* (Fla.), October 2, 1992.

———. "Voters Vindicate Outspoken Hastings." *Miami Herald* (Fla.), October 3, 1992.

———. "White Can Be Right." *Miami Herald* (Fla.), September 20, 1992.

Pye, Lucian W. *Asian Power and Politics: The Cultural Dimensions of Authority*. Cambridge, Mass.: Belknap Press of Harvard University Press, 1985.

Rado, Diane. "Commissioner Race a Study in Contrasts." *St. Petersburg Times* (Fla.), November 1, 1994.

Rausch, John David, Jr., Mark Rozell, and Harry L. Wilson. "When Women Lose: A Study of Media Coverage of Two Gubernatorial Campaigns." *Women & Politics* 20, no. 4 (1999): 1–21.

Rayer, Stefan. "Asians in Florida." Bureau of Economic and Business Research, University of Florida, August 27, 2014. Accessed January 24, 2015. http://www.bebr.ufl.edu/articles/population-studies/asians-florida.

Redistricting Task Force for the National Conference of State Legislatures. "Chapter 5: Multimember Districts." Published online, last update, October 31, 2003. Accessed January 31, 2015. http://www.senate.leg.state.mn.us/departments/scr/redist/red2000/ch4multi.htm.

———. "Florida Redistricting Cases: the 1990s." Published online, last update, November 6, 2000. Accessed March 11, 2015. http://www.senate.leg.state.mn.us/departments/scr/redist/redsum/flsum.htm.

Reeves, K. *Voting Hopes or Fears? White Voters, Black Candidates & Racial Politics in America*. New York: Oxford University Press, 1997.

Rehnquist Center. "Biographical Information: The Honorable Rosemary Barkett." Published online, accessed February 18, 2015. http://www.rehnquistcenter.org/mediaconference/rosemary_barkett.cfm.

Reingold, Beth. *Legislative Women: Getting Elected, Getting Ahead*. Boulder, Colo.: Lynne Rienner, 2008.

———. "The Uneven Presence of Women and Minorities in America's State Legislatures—And Why It Matters." *Scholars Strategy Network*, October 2012. https://thesocietypages.org/ssn/2012/11/12/minority-representation/.

Rieff, David. *Going to Miami: Exiles, Tourists, and Refugees in the New America*. Boston: Little, Brown, 1987.

Riley, Jason L. "Why Liberals Should Stop Trying to 'Help' Black Americans." *New York Post*, June 28, 2014.

Rimer, Sara. "The 1990 Elections: Governors—Florida; Chiles Triumphs on Little Money." *New York Times*, November 7, 1990. http://www.nytimes.com/1990/11/07/us/the-1990-elections-governors-florida-chiles-triumphs-on-little-money.html.

Rivers, Larry Eugene. "Florida's African American Experience: The Twentieth Century and Beyond." In *The History of Florida*, edited by Michael Gannon, 444–69. Gainesville: University Press of Florida, 2013.

Rochelle, Belinda. *Words with Wings: A Treasury of African-American Poetry and Art*. New York: HarperCollins, 2001.

Rohter, Larry. "An Exile's Empire: A Special Report. With Voice of Cuban-Americans A Would-Be Successor to Castro." *New York Times*, May 8, 1995. http://www.nytimes.com/1995/05/08/us/exile-s-empire-special-report-with-voice-cuban-americans-would-be-successor.html.

———. "Jorge Mas Canosa, 58, Dies: Exile Who Led Movement Against Castro." *New York Times*, November 24, 1997. http://www.nytimes.com/1997/11/24/us/jorge-mas-canosa-58-dies-exile-who-led-movement-against-castro.html?pagewanted=all&src=pm.

Rose, Harold M. "Blacks and Cubans in Metropolitan Miami's Changing Economy." *Urban Geography* 10, no. 5 (1989): 464–86.

Rosenthal, Cindy Simon. *When Women Lead*. New York: Oxford University Press, 1998.

Ross, Lawrence C. *The Divine Nine: The History of African-American Fraternities and Sororities*. New York: Kensington, 2001.

Rubio, Marco. "Biography." Office of U.S. Senator Marco Rubio. Accessed March 11, 2014. http://www.rubio.senate.gov/public/index.cfm/about?p=biography.

———. "Making Higher Education Affordable Again." Remarks as prepared for delivery at Miami-Dade College, Miami, Fla., February 10, 2014. http://www.rubio.senate.gov/public/index.cfm/2014/2/rubio-proposes-ideas-for-higher-education-reform-at-miami-dade-college.

Sainsbury, Brendan, and Luke Waterson. *Lonely Planet Cuba*, 7th ed. Oakland, Calif.: Lonely Planet, 2013.

Saint-Germain, Michelle A. "Does Their Difference Make a Difference? The Impact of Women on Public Policy in the Arizona State Legislature." *Social Science Quarterly* 70, no. 4 (1989): 956–68.

Sanabonmatsu, Kira. "State Elections: Where Do Women Run? Where Do Women Win?" In *Gender and Elections: Shaping the Future of American Politics*, edited by Susan J. Carroll and Richard L. Fox, 189–214. Cambridge: Cambridge University Press, 2006.

Sangillo, Gregg. "Frederica Wilson (D)." *National Journal*, October 24, 2010.

Santiago, Fabiola. "It's a Hot Season for Cuban-Americans Pounding Pavement for Political Career." *Miami Herald* (Fla.), July 4, 1982.

Saunders, Jim. "First Hispanic Named to Top Court." *Florida Times-Union* (Jacksonville, Fla.), July 11, 2002. http://jacksonville.com/tu-online/stories/071102/met_9885611.html.

Schaller, Thomas F. "Multi-Member Districts: Just a Thing of the Past?" *Sabato's Crystal Ball*, March 21, 2013. Accessed January 31, 2015. http://www.centerforpolitics.org/crystalball/articles/multi-member-legislative-districts-just-a-thing-of-the-past/.

Schmidt, Ronald, Sr., Yvetta M. Alex-Assensoh, Andrew L. Aoki, and Rodney E. Hero. *Newcomers, Outsiders, and Insiders: Immigrant and American Racial Politics in the Early Twenty-first Century*. Ann Arbor: University of Michigan Press, 2010.

Schneider, Mike. "Martin Family Lawyer Known for Civil Rights Cases." *Associated Press*, March 30, 2012.

Schoettler, Jim. "Black Republicans Make Voter Inroads." *Florida Times-Union* (Jacksonville, Fla.), April 22, 2003.

Schweers, Jeff. "Annette Taddeo Speaks About Her Hispanic Heritage During Visit to UF." *Gainesville Sun* (Fla.), September 29, 2014.

Scola, Becki. *Gender, Race, and Office Holding in the United States: Representation at the Intersections*. New York: Routledge, 2013.

Shah, Hemant, and Michael Thornton. "Racial Ideology in U.S. Mainstream News Magazine Coverage of Black-Latino Interaction, 1980–1992." *Critical Studies in Mass Communication* 11, no. 2 (1994): 141–61.

Shah, Paru R. "Too Few Minority Politicians? You Can't Win if You Don't Run." *The Conversation*, October 31, 2014. Accessed January 30, 2015. http://theconversation.com/too-few-minority-politicians-you-cant-win-if-you-dont-run-33349.

Shell-Weiss, Melanie. *Coming to Miami: A Social History*. Gainesville: University Press of Florida, 2009.

Sheridan, Mary Beth. "Ros-Lehtinen Brings Anti-Communist Fervor to Once-Staid Committee." *Washington Post*, April 10, 2011. http://www.washingtonpost.com/world/ros-lehtinen-brings-anti-communist-fervor-to-once-staid-committee/2011/03/25/AF5AI6GD_story.html.

Sherman, Amy. "Congresswoman-elect Frederica Wilson Says Hat Ban Started in 1800s But Can Be Waived." *PolitiFact Florida*, November 19, 2010. http://www.politifact.com/florida/statements/2010/nov/19/frederica-wilson/congresswoman-elect-wilson-says-hat-ban-started-18/.

Shofner, Jerrell H. "Custom, Law, and History: The Enduring Influence of Florida's 'Black Code.'" *Florida Historical Quarterly* 55, no. 3 (1977): 277–98.

———. "Florida and Black Migration." *Florida Historical Quarterly* 57, no. 3 (1979): 267–88.

———. "Reconstruction and Renewal, 1865–1877." In *The History of Florida*, edited by Michael Gannon, 260–75. Gainesville: University Press of Florida, 2013.

Sigelman, Carol K., Lee Sigelman, Barbara J. Walkosz, and Michael Nitz. "Black Candidates, White Voters: Understanding Racial Bias in Political Perceptions." *American Journal of Political Science* 39, no. 1 (1995): 243–65.

Silva, Helga. "A Bush by Any Name is Just as Good." *Miami Herald* (Fla.), May 21, 1982.

Silva, Mark. "Rosenthal Must Wonder, What's in a Name?" *Miami Herald* (Fla.), October 16, 1980.

Sipress, Alan. "U.S. Reassesses Columbia Aid." *Washington Post*, September 10, 2001. http://www.latinamericanstudies.org/colombia/efforts.htm.

Skene, Neil. "Reapportionment in Florida." In *The Florida Handbook 2013–2014*, edited by Allen Morris, Joan Petty Morris, and the Florida House of Representatives, Office of the Clerk, 254–76. Tallahassee: Florida House of Representatives, Office of the Clerk, 2013.

Skinner, Richard, and Philip A. Klinkner. "Black, White, Brown and Cajun: The Racial Dynamics of the 2003 Louisiana Gubernatorial Election." *The Forum* 2, no. 1 (2004): n.p;.

Skoloff, Brian. "Fla. Gov. Candidate Names Running Mate." *Washington Post*, September 14, 2006. http://www.washingtonpost.com/wp-dyn/content/article/2006/09/14/AR2006091400674.html.

Smith, Charles U., ed. *The Civil Rights Movement in Florida and the United States*. Tallahassee, Fla.: Father and Son Publishing, 1989.

Smith, R. Drew, and Fredrick C. Harris, eds. *Black Churches and Local Politics: Clergy Influence, Organizational Partnerships, and Civic Empowerment*. Lanham, Md.: Rowman & Littlefield, 2005.

Smith, Stanley K. "Florida Population Growth: Past, Present and Future." Bureau of Economic and Business Research, University of Florida. Published online, June 1, 2005. http://www.bebr.ufl.edu/content/florida-population-growth-past-present-and-future.

Smooth, Wendy G. "African American Women and Electoral Politics: Journeying from the Shadows to the Spotlight." In *Gender and Elections: Shaping the Future of American Politics*, edited by Susan J. Carroll and Richard L. Fox, 117–42. Cambridge: Cambridge University Press, 2006.

Snipe, Tracy D. "The Role of African American Males in Politics and Government." *Annals of the American Academy of Political and Social Science* 569, no. 1 (2000): 10–28.

Souto, Javier D. "Commissioner Javier D. Souto Newsletter District 10—February 28, 2014." Office of Commissioner Javier D. Souto, March 4, 2014. http://www.americantowns.com/fl/miami/news/commissioner-javier-d-souto-newsletter-district-10-february-28-2014-18280144.

State of Florida Black History Month. "Black Firsts in Florida." Accessed March 20, 2016. http://www.floridablackhistory.com/leaders.cfm.

St. Augustine Record (Fla.). "F. Charles Usina Highway Appropriately Named." March 23, 1966.

Steward, Monica. "Florida Supreme Court Justice Leander Shaw Retires," *Miami Times* (Fla.), December 10, 2002.

St. Petersburg Times (Fla.). "Martinez Over Spicola, Slightly." August 31, 1974. http://news.google.com/newspapers?nid=888&dat=19740831&id=FEBSAAAAIBAJ&sjid=SnkDAAAAIBAJ&pg=3898,3442175.

———. "McCollum for GOP." August 30, 2004. http://www.sptimes.com/2004/08/30/Opinion/McCollum_for_GOP.shtml.

Sun-Sentinel (Fort Lauderdale, Fla.). "Choose Bucher in House District 86." April 21, 2000. http://articles.sun-sentinel.com/2000-04-21/news/0004200936_1_political-novice-healey-s-family-election.

———. "Joseph Menendez Martinez, Jr., Obituary." December 6, 2009.

———. "Pitts-Lee Case Over, Scars Remain." July 20, 1998. http://articles.sun-sentinel.com/1998-07-20/news/9807170338_1_pitts-and-lee-freddie-pitts-wilbert-lee.

Supreme Court of Florida, "Administrative Order: In Re: Standing Committee on Fairness and Diversity," No. AOSC08-91, December 3, 2008.

Swain, Carol. *Black Face, Black Interests: The Representation of African Americans in Congress.* Cambridge, Mass.: Harvard University Press, 1995.

———. Review of *Voting Hopes or Fears? White Voters, Black Candidates, and Racial Politics in America*, by Keith Reeves. *Journal of Politics* 61, no. 1 (1999): 223–25.

Swers, Michele L. *The Difference Women Make.* Chicago: University of Chicago Press, 2002.

Sylvie, G. "Black Mayoral Candidates and the Press: Running for Coverage." *Howard Journal of Communications* 6, no. 1-2 (1995): 89–101.

Tampa Bay Times (Fla.). "Editorial: Florida Judiciary Needs More Diversity." May 30, 2014.

———. "Editorial: Sen. Arthenia Joyner of Tampa Makes History Again." November 21, 2014. http://www.tampabay.com/opinion/editorials/editorial-sen-arthenia-joyner-of-tampa-makes-history-again/2207454.

Tauber, Steven C. "African Americans in the Contemporary Florida Legislature." In *Politics in the New South: Representation of African Americans in Contemporary Southern State Legislatures*, edited by Charles Menifield and Steven Schaeffer, 43–72. Albany: State University of New York Press, 2005.

Taylor, Paul, Mark Hugo Lopez, Jessica Martínez, and Gabriel Velasco. "When Labels Don't Fit: Hispanics and Their Views of Identity." *Pew Hispanic Trends Project.* Published online, April 4, 2012. Accessed January 23, 2015. http://www.pewhispanic.org/2012/04/04/when-labels-dont-fit-hispanics-and-their-views-of-identity.

Terris, Ben, and Shane Goldmacher. "The Making of Allen West Inc." *National Journal*, August 1, 2013. http://www.nationaljournal.com/magazine/the-making-of-allen-west-inc-20130801.

Thomas, Sue. *How Women Legislate.* New York: Oxford University Press, 1994.

———. "The Impact of Women on State Legislative Policies." *Journal of Politics* 53, no. 4 (1991): 958–76.

Thomas, Sue, and Clyde Wilcox, eds. *Women and Elective Office.* New York: Oxford University Press, 1998.

Tolleson-Rinehart, Sue. "Do Women Leaders Make a Difference: Substance, Style, and Perceptions." In *Gender and Policymaking: Studies of Women in Office*, edited by Debra L. Dodson, 149–65. New Brunswick, N.J.: Rutgers University Press, 1991.

Totenberg, Nina. "Supreme Court Justice Souter to Retire." *National Public Radio*, April 30, 2009. http://www.npr.org/templates/story/story.php?storyId=103694193.

United Press International. "Barron Likely to Run Rules Panel." *Miami Herald* (Fla.), November 10, 1982.

University of Texas at Austin. "Politics in the Pews: Researchers Explore the Role of Religion in Mobilizing African American and Latino Voters." May 5, 2008. http://news.utexas.edu/2008/05/05/politics_religion.

U.S. House of Representatives. "The First Hispanic American to Serve in Congress." *U.S. House of Representatives History, Art & Archives.* Published online, accessed February 17, 2015. http://history.house.gov/Historical-Highlights/1800-1850/The-first-Hispanic-American-to-serve-in-Congress/.

———. "Martinez, Melquiades R. (Mel)." *U.S. House of Representatives History, Art & Archives*, accessed May 2, 2014. http://history.house.gov/people/detail/15032401306.

———. "Meek, Carrie P." *U.S. House of Representatives History, Art & Archives*, accessed June 21, 2014. http://history.house.gov/people/detail?id=18110.

———. "Meek, Kendrick B." *U.S. House of Representatives History, Art & Archives*, accessed June 28, 2014. http://history.house.gov/People/Detail/18768.

U.S. National Archives and Records Administration. "Declaration of Independence: The Signer's Gallery." Published online: n.d. http://www.archives.gov/exhibits/charters/declaration_signers_gallery.html#.

Valbrun, Marjorie. "Haitian-Americans: Their Search for Political Identity in South Florida." *Alicia Patterson Foundation*, 2001. http://aliciapatterson.org/stories/haitian-americans-their-search-political-identity-south-florida.

Vandervalk, Marge. "Negro Represents State, Wins Supreme Court Suit." *Tallahassee Democrat*, July 20, 1970.

Van Gieson, John C. "Jamerson Vows to Boost Schools." *Orlando Sentinel* (Fla.), January 4, 1994.

Verdeja, Sam, and Guillermo Martinez, eds. *Cubans: An Epic Journey*. St. Louis, Mo.: Reedy Press, 2012.

Viglucci, Andres. "Ex-Rep. John Plummer, Won in Upset in '80." *Miami Times* (Fla.), September 7, 1985.

Vinciguerra, Tom. "Kirk Slate, Demo Vets Score Big." *Fort Lauderdale News* (Fla.), March 1, 1967.

Voice of America. "America's Black Churches Debate Role in Society." October 30, 2009. http://www.voanews.com/articleprintview/302987.html.

Voss, D. Stephen, and David Lublin. "Black Incumbents, White Districts: An Appraisal of the 1996 Congressional Elections." *American Politics Research* 29, no, 2 (2001): 141–82.

Wagner, Deborah Hardin, ed. *"Where the Injured Fly for Justice": Reforming Principles Which Impede the Dispensation of Justice to Minorities in Florida*. Tallahassee: Florida Supreme Court, 1990. http://www.floridasupremecourt.org/pub_info/documents/racial.pdf.

Walton, Hanes, Jr., and Robert C. Smith. *American Politics and the African American Quest for Universal Freedom*, 4th ed. New York: Pearson/Longman, 2008.

Wasniewski, Matthew A. *Women in Congress, 1917–2006*. Washington, D.C.: U.S. Government Printing Office, 2006.

Weatherford, Doris. *Women in American Politics: History and Milestones*. Washington, D.C.: CQ Press, 2012.

Weiner, Rachel. "The Worst Debate Moments Ever." *Washington Post*, November 10, 2011. http://www.washingtonpost.com/blogs/the-fix/post/the-worst-debate-moments-ever/2011/11/10/gIQATweo8M_blog.html.

Weisman, Brent R. "Florida's Seminole and Miccosukee Peoples." In *The History of Florida*, edited by Michael Gannon, 195–219. Gainesville: University Press of Florida, 2013.

Weiss, Debra Cassens. "Florida Lawmakers Pass Bill Allowing Noncitizens Who Stayed in the US Illegally to Get Law Licenses." *ABA Journal*, May 5, 2014. http://www.abajournal.com/news/article/florida_lawmakers_pass_bill_allowing_noncitizens_who_stayed_in_the_us_illeg.

West, Patsy. "A Vote for Destiny." *Seminole Tribune*, n.d. Accessed January 24, 2015. http://www.semtribe.com/SeminoleTribune/Archive/40anniversary/destinyvote.html.

Whitaker, Lois Duke. "Women and Sex Stereotypes: Cultural Reflections in the Mass Media." In *Women in Politics: Outsiders or Insiders?* 4th ed., edited by Lois Duke Whitaker, 81–95. Upper Saddle River, N.J.: Prentice Hall, 2006.

———, ed. *Women in Politics: Outsiders or Insiders?* 4th ed. Upper Saddle River, N.J.: Prentice Hall, 2006.

Whitby, Kenny J. *The Color of Representation: Congressional Behavior and Black Interests*. Ann Arbor: University of Michigan Press, 1998.

Wiatrowski, Kevin. "Joyner, Next Top Democrat in Senate, Honored in Tampa." *Tampa Tribune* (Fla.), May 7, 2014.

Wilkins, David E. *American Indian Politics and the American Political System*, 2nd ed. Lanham, Md.: Rowman & Littlefield, 2006.

Williams, Kim R. *Mark One or More: Civil Rights in Multiracial America*. Ann Arbor: University of Michigan Press, 2011.

Williams, L. F. "White/Black Perceptions of the Electability of Black Political Candidates." In *National Political Science Review*. Vol. 2, *Black Electoral Politics*, edited by Lucius J. Barker, 45–64. New Brunswick, N.J.: Transaction, 1990.

Wills, Martee. "Black Woman's Voice Makes Itself Heard." *Tallahassee Democrat* (Fla.), n.d.

———. "She's 'Tops' in the State." *Tallahassee Democrat* (Fla.), February 16, 1971. In the Florida State Archives, Tallahassee, Fla.

Wilson, Federica. "Biography." Office of Congresswoman Federica Wilson. Published online, n.d. http://wilson.house.gov/about/full-biography.

Wilson, Kenneth L., and W. Allen Martin. "Ethnic Enclaves: A Comparison of the Cuban and Black Economies in Miami." *American Journal of Sociology* 88, no. 1 (1982): 135–60.

Winsboro, Irvin D. S., ed. *Florida's Freedom Struggle: The Black Experience from Colonial Times to the New Millennium*. Cocoa, Fla.: Florida Historical Society Press, 2010.

Witt, Linda, Karen M. Paget, and Glenna Matthews. *Running as a Woman: Gender and Power in American Politics*. New York: The Free Press, 1994.

Woltman, Kelly, and K. Bruce Newbold. "Of Flights and Flotillas: Assimilation and Race in the Cuban Diaspora." *Professional Geographer* 61, no. 1 (2009): 70–86.

Woods, Casey. "Rising Hispanic Vote Shifts Focus Off Cuba." *Miami Herald* (Fla.), August 25, 2008.

Woods, Keith. "A Brief History of St. Joseph Catholic Church in St. Petersburg, Florida." Published online, accessed March 11, 2015. http://www.stjosephstpete.org/saint-joe-history.htm.

Wu, H. Denis, and Tien-Tsung Lee. "The Submissive, the Calculated, and the American Dream: Coverage of Asian American Political Candidates in the 1990s." *Howard Journal of Communications* 16, no. 3 (2005): 225–41.

Wyman, Scott. "Lauderdale Marks 50th Anniversary of Fight to Desegregate Beach." *Sun-Sentinel* (Fort Lauderdale, Fla.), July 1, 2011. http://articles.sun-sentinel.com/2011-07-01/news/fl-beach-desegregation-anniversary-20110701_1_colored-beach-wade-ins-civil-rights.

Yanez, Luisa. "Ros-Lehtinen Takes Seat Race to Succeed Pepper Tight to the End." *Sun-Sentinel* (Fla.), August 30, 1989. http://articles.sun-sentinel.com/1989-08-30/news/8902280553_1_ros-lehtinen-republican-ileana-ros-lehtinen-gerald-richman.

Zilber, J., and D. Niven. "Stereotypes in the News: Media Coverage of African-Americans in Congress." *Harvard International Journal of Press/Politics* 5, no. 1 (2000): 32–49.

INDEX

Page numbers followed by *i* or *t* indicate material in illustrations or tables.

Florida Government and Politics
Series editors, David R. Colburn and Susan A. MacManus

Florida has emerged today as a microcosm of the nation and has become a political bellwether in national elections. The impact of Florida on the presidential elections of 2000, 2004, and 2008 suggests the magnitude of the state's influence. Of the four largest states in the nation, Florida is the only one that has moved from one political column to the other in the last three national elections. These developments suggest the vital need to explore the politics of the Sunshine State in greater detail. Books in this series will explore the myriad aspects of politics, political science, public policy, history, and government in Florida.

The 57 Club: My Four Decades in Florida Politics, by Frederick B. Karl (2010)
The Political Education of Buddy MacKay, by Buddy MacKay, with Rick Edmonds (2010)
Immigrant Prince: Mel Martínez and the American Dream, by Richard E. Fogelsong (2011)
Reubin O'D. Askew and the Golden Age of Florida Politics, by Martin A. Dyckman (2011)
Red Pepper and Gorgeous George: Claude Pepper's Epic Defeat in the 1950 Democratic Primary, by James C. Clark (2011)
Inside Bush v. Gore, by Charley Wells (2013)
Conservative Hurricane: How Jeb Bush Remade Florida, Matthew T. Corrigan (2014)
The Failure of Term Limits in Florida, by Kathryn A. DePalo (2015)
Jigsaw Puzzle Politics in the Sunshine State, edited by Seth C. McKee (2015)
Making Modern Florida: How the Spirit of Reform Shaped a New State Constitution, by Mary E. Adkins (2016)
Florida's Minority Trailblazers: The Men and Women Who Changed the Face of Florida Government, by Susan A. MacManus with Barbara A. Langham, Lauren K. Gilmore, and Tyler B. Myers (2017)